D1714910

Studies in English Puritanism
from the Restoration to the Revolution,
1660—1688

Studies in English Puritanism from the Restoration to the Revolution, 1660–1688

by

C. E. WHITING

Charles Edwin

Reprints of Economic Classics
AUGUSTUS M. KELLEY PUBLISHERS
New York 1968

Published by

FRANK CASS AND COMPANY LIMITED

67 Great Russell Street, London WC1

by arrangement with The Trustees of the

Society of Promoting Christian Knowledge

Published in the United States by

Augustus M. Kelley, Publishers

New York, New York 10010

First edition   1931

New impression   1968

SBN 7146 1382 7

Library of Congress Catalog Card No. 68—56060

Printed in Great Britain

PREFATORY NOTE

THESE Studies have been made from time to time, in the course of writing a History of Restoration Puritanism, a work which has occupied the author for a number of years. This will explain certain limitations and omissions. It is hoped that these chapters form more or less a unity in giving a description of Puritan life, thought, controversy, and organisation during the period between the Restoration and the Revolution. The subject is English Puritanism, and therefore little or no reference is made either to Scottish Presbyterianism or Irish Protestantism.

The writer desires to express his thanks to the Rev. Canon S. L. Ollard, M.A., for advice and information on several points, to the Rev. F. Hope Scott, M.A., for the first note on p. 53, and to the Rev. W. K. Firminger, D.D., for the second note on p. 492. He must also thank the Rev. W. K. Lowther Clarke, D.D., for his help in seeing the book through the press, and the Church Historical Society for assistance towards its publication.

v

CONTENTS

ILLUSTRATIONS

AUTHORITIES

AGNEW, D. C. A. "Protestant Exiles from France." 3rd ed. 2 vols. Edinburgh, 1886.

AMOS, A. "The English Constitution in the Reign of King Charles II." London, 1857.

AUBREY, J. "Brief Lives, chiefly of Contemporaries," ed. by A. Clark. 2 vols. Oxford, 1898.

AYLESBURY, THOMAS EARL OF. "Memoirs." 2 vols. London, 1890.

BABINGTON, C. "Mr. Macaulay's Character of the Clergy." Cambridge, 1849.

BARCLAY, R. "The Inner Life of the Religious Societies of the Commonwealth." 2nd ed. London, 1877.

BARDSLEY, C. W. "Curiosities of Puritan Nomenclature." London, 1897.

BARNES, AMBROSE. Life. Surtees Society, No. 50.

BASTIDE, C. "The Anglo-French Entente in the Seventeenth Century." London, 1914.

BAXTER, R. "Reliquiæ Baxterianæ," ed. by M. Sylvester. London, 1696.

—— Works, ed. by W. Orme. With a Life of Baxter. 23 vols. 1830.

BELL, W. G. "The Great Fire of London." London, 1920.

BESSE, J. "Sufferings of the People called Quakers." 2 vols. London, 1753.

BIRCH, T. "Life of Tillotson." 2nd ed. London, 1753.

BOASE, C. W. "Registrum Collegii Exoniensis." Oxford Hist. Soc., 1894.

BOGUE, D., and BENNETT, J. "History of the Dissenters." 4 vols. London, 1808–1814.

BOHUN, E. Diary and Autobiography, ed. by S. W. Rix. Beccles, 1853.

BONET-MAURY, G. "Early Sources of English Unitarian Christianity," trans. by E. P. Hall. London, 1884.

BOSELEY, I. "The Independent Church of Westminster Abbey." London, 1907.

BRAILSFORD, M. B. "Quaker Women, 1650–1690." London, 1915.

BRAITHWAITE, W. C. "The Beginnings of Quakerism." London, 1912.

—— "The Second Period of Quakerism." London, 1919.

BROOK, B. "Lives of the Puritans." 3 vols. London, 1813.

BROWN, J. "The Life of John Bunyan." 3rd ed. London, 1887.

ix

BROWNE, J. "The History of Congregationalism in Norfolk and Suffolk." London, 1877.

BUNYAN, J. Works, ed. by H. Stebbing. 4 vols. London, 1859.

BURN, J. S. "History of the Foreign Protestant Refugees." London, 1846.

BURNET, G. "A History of My Own Times," Part I. 2 vols, ed. by O. Airey. Oxford, 1897.

BURRAGE, C. "Early English Dissenters." 2 vols. Cambridge, 1912.

CALAMY, E. "Abridgement of Mr. Baxter's Life and Times." 2nd ed. 2 vols. London, 1713.

—— "A Continuation of the Account of the Ministers." 2 .vols. London, 1727.

—— "Historical Account of My Own Life," ed. by J. H. Rutt. 2nd ed. 2 vols. London, 1830.

—— "A Letter to Archdeacon Eachard." London, 1718.

CARDWELL, E. "Documentary Annals of the Church of England." 2 vols. Oxford, 1839.

CASSAN, S. H. "Lives of the Bishops of Bath and Wells." 2 vols. London, 1830.

CLARENDON, EDWARD EARL OF. Life, and "Continuation of the History." Oxford, 1842.

CLARENDON, HENRY EARL OF. State Letters, 1687–1690. 2 vols. Oxford, 1763.

—— Correspondence, ed. by S. W. Singer. 2 vols. London, 1828.

CLARK, H. W. "History of English Nonconformity." 2 vols. London, 1911–1913.

CLARKSON, T. "Memoirs of the Life of William Penn." 2 vols. London, 1813.

COLLIGAN, J. H. "The Arian Movement in England." Manchester, 1913.

"Confessions of Faith of the Baptist Churches." Hanserd Knollys Soc., 1854.

CORNISH, J. "Life of Mr. Thomas Firmin." London, 1680.

COSIN, BISHOP. Correspondence, ed. by G. Ornsby. Surtees Soc., Nos. 52 and 55.

CRAMP, J. M. "Baptist History." London, 1871.

CROESE, G. "General History of the Quakers." London, 1696.

CROSBY, T. "History of the English Baptists." 4 vols. London, 1738–1740.

CROSS, F. W. "History of the Walloon and Huguenot Church at Canterbury." Huguenot Soc. of London. XV. 1898.

DALE, B. "Yorkshire Puritanism and Early Nonconformity," ed. by T. G. Crippen. Bradford, 1909.

DALE, R. W. "History of English Congregationalism." London, 1907.

DAVIDS, T. W. "Annals of Evangelical Nonconformity in Essex." London, 1863.

"Depositions from York Castle," ed. by J. Raine. Surtees Soc., No. 40.

DENSHAM, W., and OGLE, J. "Story of the Congregational Churches of Dorset." Bournemouth, 1899.

DIXON, W. H. "Life of William Penn." London, 1872.

D'ORLEANS, PÈRE. "Histoire des Révolutions d'Angleterre." 3 vols. Amsterdam, 1714.

DOUGLAS, D. "History of the Baptist Churches in the North of England." London, 1846.

D'OYLY, G. "Life of William Sancroft." 2 vols. London, 1821.

DRYSDALE, A. H. "History of the Presbyterians in England." London, 1889.

EACHARD, L. "History of England." 3 vols. London, 1718.

EDWARDS, T. "Gangræna." 1646.

ELLIS, H. Original Letters. Second Series. Vol. IV. London, 1827.

ELLIS, J. "The Ellis Correspondence," ed. by Hon. G. A. Ellis. 2 vols. London, 1829.

ELLWOOD, T. "The History of Thomas Ellwood." London, 1714.

"Essex Hall Year Book."

EVANS, B. "The Early English Baptists." 2 vols. London, 1864.

EVANS, T. S. "Life of Bishop Frampton." London, 1871.

EVELYN, J. Diary, ed. by Austin Dobson. 3 vols. London, 1906.

EWALD, A. C. "Life and Times of Algernon Sidney." 2 vols. London, 1873.

FEILING, K. "History of the Tory Party, 1660–1714." Oxford, 1924.

FERGUSON, R. S. "Early Cumberland and Westmorland Friends." Carlisle, 1871.

FLETCHER, J. "History of Independency in England." 4 vols. London, 1862.

"Foreigners Resident in England," ed. by W. D. Cooper. Camden Series, 1862.

FOUNTAINHALL, JOHN, LORD. "Chronological Notes of Scottish Affairs from 1680 to 1701," ed. by Sir W. Scott. Edinburgh, 1822.

FOWLER, T. "History of Corpus Christi College." Oxford Hist. Soc., 1893.

FOX, G. "Journal," ed. by N. Penney. 2 vols. Cambridge, 1911.

—— "The Shorter Journal," ed. by N. Penney. Cambridge, 1925.

FOXCROFT, H. C. A Supplement to Burnet's "History of My Own Time." Oxford, 1897.

FROUDE, J. A. "Bunyan." London, 1909.

GILDON, C. "The Postboy Robbed of his Mail." 2nd ed. London, 1706.

GORDON, A. "Heads of English Unitarian History." London, 1895.

—— "Unity Church, Islington." London, 1917.

—— "Freedom after Ejection." Manchester, 1917.

—— "Addresses Biographical and Historical." London, 1922.

GOUGH, J. "History of the People called Quakers." 4 vols. Dublin, 1789.

GRAHAM, J. W. "Life of William Penn." 2nd ed. London, 1918.

GRANVILLE, R. "Life of Dennis Granville." Exeter, 1902.

GRANVILLE, DEAN. Letters. Surtees Soc., Nos. 37 & 47.

GRATTON, J. "Journal of the Life of John Gratton." London, 1720. (Another ed. London, 1779.)

GRAY, A. "Debates of the House of Commons, 1667 to 1694." 10 vols. London, 1763.

GRAY, Z. "Examination of the Fourth Volume of Neal's History of the Puritans." London, 1739.

HALLEY, R. "Lancashire, its Puritanism and Nonconformity." 2nd ed. London, 1872.

HANBURY, B. "Historical Memorials Relating to the Independents." 3 vols. London, 1839–1844.

HANCOCK, T. "The Peculium." 2nd ed., ed. by W. E. Collins. London, 1907.

—— "The Act of Uniformity a Measure of Liberation." London, 1895.

HARRIS, C. "Historical and Critical Account of the Life of Charles II." 2 vols. London, 1766.

HARRIS, W. "Memoirs of Thomas Manton." London, 1725.

"Hatton Correspondence." Camden Series. 1878.

HAWKINS, R. "Life of Gilbert Latey." London, 1707.

HENRY, PHILIP. Diary and Letters, ed. by M. H. Lee. London, 1882.

HEYWOOD, OLIVER. Diaries, ed. by J. Horsfall Turner. 4 vols. Brighouse, 1882–1885.

HODGKIN, L. V. "A Quaker Saint of Cornwall." London, 1927.

HODGKIN, T. "Life of G. Fox." 3rd ed. London, 1906.

HUNT, J. "Religious Thought in England." 3 vols. London, 1870–1873.

HUNTER, J. "The Rise of the Old Dissent, exemplified in the Life of Oliver Heywood." London, 1842.

IVIMEY, J. "History of the English Baptists." 4 vols. London, 1811–1830.

JENKINSON, W. "London Churches before the Great Fire." London, 1917.

JESSOPP, A. "The Prophet of Walnut-tree Yard." In "The Coming of the Friars." London, 1899.

JOLLY, T. "Notebook of Thomas Jolly." Chetham Soc., 1895.

JONES, R. M. "Studies in Mystical Religion." London, 1909.

—— "Spiritual Reformers in the Sixteenth and Seventeenth Centuries." London, 1914.

JOSSELIN, R. "Diary." Camden Series, 1908.

KENNET, BISHOP WHITE. "Register and Chronicle." London, 1728.

—— "History of England." 2nd ed. London, 1719.

KERSHAW, S. W. "Protestants from France in their English Homes." London, 1885.

KIFFIN, W. "Remarkable Passages in the Life of William Kiffin," ed. by W. Orme. 1823.

KITCHIN, G. "Roger L'Estrange." London, 1913.

LATIMER, J. "Annals of Bristol in the Seventeenth Century." Bristol, 1900.

LEWIS, J. " History of the Rise and Progress of Anabaptism in England." London, 1738.

LIGHT, A. W. " Bunhill Fields." London, 1913.

LLOYD, W. " The Story of Protestant Dissent and English Unitarianism." London, 1899.

LUTTRELL, N. " Brief Historical Relation of State Affairs." 6 vols. Oxford, 1857.

MACKENZIE, E. " History of Newcastle." 2 vols. 1827.

MACKINTOSH, SIR J. " History of the Revolution." London, 1834.

MACLEANE, D. " History of Pembroke College." Oxford Hist. Soc., 1897.

MAGRATH, J. R. " The Flemings in Oxford." 2 vols. Oxford Hist. Soc., 1903-1913.

MARTINDALE, A. " Life of Adam Martindale." Chetham Soc., 1845.

MARVELL, A. Works. With a Life by Capt. E. Thompson. 3 vols. London, 1776.

—— Poems and Letters, ed. by H. M. Margoliouth. Oxford, 1927.

M'CRIE, T. " Annals of English Presbytery." London, 1872.

MIALL, J. G. " Congregationalism in Yorkshire." London," 1868.

MOENS, W. J. C. " The Walloon Church of Norwich." Huguenot Hist. Soc. London. I. 1887.

MUDDIMAN, J. G. " The King's Journalist." London, 1923.

MUGGLETON, L. " True Account of the Trial and Sufferings." London, 1808.

NEAL, D. " History of the Puritans," ed. by J. Toulmin. 5 vols. London, 1796. (Another ed. 4 vols., 1732-38.)

NEWCOME, H. Diary. Chetham Soc., 1849.

—— Autobiography. 2 vols. Chetham Soc., 1852.

NIGHTINGALE, B. " The Old Independent Chapel, Tockholes, Manchester." 1886.

—— " Lancashire Nonconformity." 6 vols. London, 1890-1893.

—— " The Ejected of 1662 in Cumberland and Westmorland." 2 vols. Manchester, 1911.

—— " Early Stages of the Quaker Movement in Lancashire." 1921.

NOAKE, J. " Worcestershire Sects." London, 1861.

NOBLE, M. " Memoirs of the Protectoral House of Cromwell." 2nd ed. 2 vols. Birmingham, 1787.

NORTH, R. " Lives of the Norths," ed. by A. Jessop. 3 vols. London, 1890.

NUTTER, B. " The Story of the Cambridge Baptists." Cambridge, 1912.

ORME, W. " Life of John Owen." London, 1826. (Published in Vol. I of " The Works of John Owen," ed. by T. Russell. 1826.)

OVERTON, J. H. " Life in the English Church, 1660-1714." London, 1885.

PACET, J. " The New Examen." Edinburgh and London, 1861.

PAGITT, E. " Heresiography." 6th ed. London, 1661.

PALMER, S. "The Nonconformists' Memorial." 2nd ed. 3 vols. London, 1802.

PARKER, I. "Dissenting Academies in England." Cambridge, 1914.

PARKER, S. "History of His Own Time." Trans. by T. Newlin. London, 1727.

PATRICK, S. "Autobiography." London, 1889.

PERRY, CANON G. G. "History of the Church of England." 3 vols. London, 1861–1864.

PIKE, G. H. "Ancient Meeting-Houses." London, 1870.

PLUMPTREE, E. H. "Life of Bishop Ken." 2 vols. London, 1890.

POPE, W. "The Life of Seth Ward, Bishop of Salisbury." London, 1697.

POWICKE, F. J. "Life of the Rev. Richard Baxter." London, 1924.

—— "Richard Baxter under the Cross." London, 1927.

PRIDEAUX, HUMPHREY. Letters to John Ellis. Camden Series, 1875.

REES, T. MARDY. "History of the Quakers in Wales." Caermarthen, 1925.

REES, T. "History of Protestant Nonconformity in Wales." 2nd ed. London, 1883.

"Revolution Politics." London, 1733.

ROGERS, E. "Life and Opinions of a Fifth Monarchy Man." London, 1867.

ROKEBY, T. "A Brief Memoir of Mr. Justice Rokeby," ed. by J. Raine. Surtees Soc., No. 47.

ROSS, A. "Pansebeia." London, 1683.

RUSSELL, RACHEL LADY. Letters. London, 1820.

SALMON, N. "Lives of the English Bishops." London, 1733.

SALMON, T. "Examination of Bishop Burnet's History." 2 vols. London, 1724.

—— "Critical Review of the State Trials." London, 1738.

"Savile Correspondence." Camden Series, 1858.

SEATON, A. A. "The Theory of Toleration under the Later Stuarts." Cambridge, 1911.

SECCOMBE, T. "Lives of Twelve Bad Men." 2nd ed. London, 1894.

SEFTON-JONES, M. "Old Devonshire House by Bishopsgate Street." London, 1923.

SEWELL, W. "History of the Quakers." 2 vols. London, 1722. In one volume 1725. (The last is the edition usually quoted unless the number of the volume is specifically given.)

SHAW, W. B. "The Story of Presbyterianism in Wigan." London, 1912.

SHEFFIELD, J., DUKE OF BUCKINGHAM. Works. 2 vols. London, 1723.

SIDNEY, A. "Letters of the Hon. A. Sidney to the Hon. Henry Savile." London, 1742.

SKEATS, H. S., and MIALL, J. G. "History of the Free Churches." London, 1868.

SMILES, S. "The Huguenots." London, 1867.

SMITH, JOSEPH. "Bibliotheca Anti-Quakeriana." London, 1873.

SMITH, " A Descriptive Catalogue of Friends' Books." 3 vols. London, 1867–1893.

SMITH, R. " The Theory of Religious Toleration under Charles II. and James II." Cambridge, 1911.

SMYTH, R. Obituary. Camden Series, 1849.

Staffordshire Incumbents and Parochial Records, 1530–1680. Salt Archæological Soc., 1915.

STANFORD, C. "Joseph Alleine. His Companions and Times." London, 1861.

STEPHENS, SIR J. F., " History of the Criminal Law of England." Vol. I. London, 1883.

STOUGHTON, J. " History of Religion in England." 6 vols. London, 1881.

SUMMERS, W. H. " History of the Congregational Churches in the Berkshire, South Bucks, and South Oxon Association." Newbury, 1905.

TALLACK, W. "George Fox, the Friends and the Early Baptists." London, 1868.

TATHAM, G. B. " Dr. John Walker and the Sufferings of the Clergy." Cambridge, 1911.

TAYLOR, A. "History of the English General Baptists." 2 vols. London, 1818.

TERRILL, E. (and others). " The Records of a Church of Christ meeting in Broadmead, Bristol," ed. by N. Haycroft. London, 1865.

THORESBY, R. Diary. 2 vols. London, 1830.

—— Letters of Eminent Men to Ralph Thoresby. 2 vols. London, 1832.

TOULMIN, J. " Life of the Rev. John Biddle." London, 1789.

—— " Historical View of the State of the Protestant Dissenters in England." London, 1814.

TULLOCH, JOHN. " Rational Theology in England in the Seventeenth Century." 2 vols. 2nd ed. Edinburgh, 1874.

TURNER, F. S. " The Quakers." London, 1911.

TURNER, J. H. " The Northowram Registers." Brighouse, 1881.

—— " Nonconformity in Idle." Bradford, 1876.

TURNER, J. L. " Original Records of Early Nonconformity." 3 vols. London, 1911.

URWICK, W. " Historical Sketches of Nonconformity in the County of Chester." London, 1864.

—— " Nonconformity in Hertfordshire." London, 1884.

VAUGHAN, R. A. " Hours with the Mystics." 3rd ed. 2 vols. London, 1880.

VENABLES, E. " Life of Bunyan." London, 1888.

WADDINGTON, J. " Congregational History." 4 vols. London, 1876–1880.

WALKER, J. " The Sufferings of the Clergy." London, 1714.

WHITING, J. " A Catalogue of Friends' Books." London, 1708.

—— " Persecution Exposed." 2nd ed. London, 1791.

WHITLEY, W. T. "Minutes of the General Baptist Churches of England." Vol. I. London, 1908.

—— "The Baptists of London." London," 1928.

—— "History of the British Baptists." London, 1923.

—— "The Baptists of North-West England, 1649–1913." London, 1913.

WILDE, R. Poems, ed. by J. Hunt. London, 1870.

WILKINS, W. W. "Political Ballads of the Seventeenth and Eighteenth Centuries." 2 vols. London, 1860.

WILLCOCK, J. "Life of Sir Henry Vane the Younger." London, 1913.

WILLIAMSON, G. C. "Lodowick Muggleton. A Paper read before the Sette of Odde Volumes." London, 1919.

WILLIAMSON. Letters to Sir Joseph Williamson. Camden Soc. 2 vols. 1874.

WILSON, W. "The History and Antiquities of the Dissenting Churches in London." 4 vols. London, 1808.

WOOD, A. "Athenæ Oxonienses." 2 vols. London, 1721.

—— "Life and Times." Vols. I–III. Oxford Hist. Soc., 1891–1894.

YORKSHIRE, North Riding Records. Vols. V and VI. Quarter Sessions Records, ed. by J. C. Atkinson. 1888–1889.

ABBREVIATIONS

Calamy	= Calamy: "Abridgement and Continuation." 4 vols.
C.S.P.D.	= Calendar of State Papers, Domestic, Charles II.
D.N.B.	= The Dictionary of National Biography.
E.H.R.	= *English Historical Review.*
Hist. MSS. Com.	= Historical MSS. Commission Reports.
Palmer	= S. Palmer: "Nonconformists' Memorial."
S.P.D.	= State Papers Domestic, Charles II.
State Trials	= "A Complete Collection of State Trials." 4th ed. London. 1776.

STUDIES IN ENGLISH PURITANISM

I

THE ACT OF UNIFORMITY

" THERE were a great number of men who lost their livings upon the coming of the King. Some were possessed of sequestered livings, and where the former incumbents were surviving they had to give way to those who had a right. Others had taken the Covenant, and some the Engagement, and having so far entangled themselves, were not willing to declare solemnly against their own act; others were against episcopacy and a liturgy and all forms of prayer, and refused to conform on that account; some had been too far concerned in helping to throw down the Church and abolish the Common Prayer in the late unhappy times; some were not in orders at all, and others had taken Presbyterian orders, and were not willing to take orders from a bishop." [1] When the sequestered clergy came back and claimed reinstatement they were usually restored without question, but in cases where the sequestered incumbent was dead, those who had been presented since January 1643 were confirmed in possession for the time being, provided they had not declared in favour of the late King's execution, and did not reject infant baptism. Some of these persons, however, seeing what was coming, voluntarily resigned, and in some cases the intruded minister invited the old incumbent back. The Act for Confirming and Restoring of Ministers passed by the Convention Parliament received the King's assent on September 13th, 1660, but it was not confirmed, in spite of great efforts to get the Bill passed, by the Cavalier Parliament. In some quarters there was much murmuring,[2] and some incumbents were only removed with difficulty. Thus, Clement Hatch, the intruded rector of Lydford, Devon, conformed in order to keep the living, and the extruded minister had to get an action for ejectment.[3]

There were many men holding livings during the years 1660

[1] Autobiography of Richard Kidder in Cassan's " Bishops of Bath and Wells," II. 112.
[2] " A Plea for Ministers in Sequestrations," 1660.
[3] Kennet, " Register and Chronicle," p. 784.

to 1662 who had not the slightest intention of conforming to the Anglican system. Henry Newcome at the end of 1660 was anxious to be preferred to one of the fellowships of the collegiate church of Manchester, and Sir George Booth was doing his best to obtain the appointment for him. Newcome wanted to hold the post without conforming, and he asked Booth if he thought the King would allow him to do so, making it plain at the same time that he wished this indulgence to extend to the congregation as well as to himself.[1] Baxter was in much the same case. He talked about having been ordained by a bishop. He had been made deacon by the Bishop of Worcester on St. Thomas's Day, 1638, but there is no record of his having been ordained priest, nor, for that matter, is there any record of his having been ordained a presbyter by the presbytery, though the latter is possible. By the rules of the Church of England a deacon may not celebrate the Holy Communion, yet he did so. Though he never took part in a Presbyterian ordination himself, he believed presbyterian and episcopal ordination to be equally valid. If, as seems certain, he was not in priest's orders, he was disqualified for preferment in the Church of England, and this he considered a grievance.[2] Thomas Jolly, minister of Altham, was cited on the information of a neighbouring magistrate to appear in the ecclesiastical court at Chester, where he was suspended for refusing to use the Book of Common Prayer. He was prohibited from preaching, and was silenced one week sooner than he would have been under the provisions of the Act of Uniformity.[3] In October 1661 the Bishop of Salisbury forbade the vicar of Shinfield, Bucks, to allow a man named Stanley, an Anabaptist cordwainer, to officiate in the church. Stanley refused to obey the bishop, spoke of him with contempt, and publicly praised the " good old times." The incumbent abetted him; the Prayer Book was not read in the church, and the local authorities refused to interfere, and Stanley, with the support of " sixty stout fellows " from Reading and the neighbourhood, set the bishop at defiance.[4] These were just a few cases out of many. Moreover, there were many men holding livings who had taken the Covenant, by which they had sworn to extirpate prelacy, that is to say, the government of the Church as Anglicans understood it. If, in spite of the changed circumstances, they still felt themselves bound by it, it was absurd to think that they could remain members of a Church whose constitution they had pledged themselves to overthrow.[5]

[1] Henry Newcome, " Autobiography," I. 128–132.
[2] *Times Literary Supplement*, January 22nd and 29th, February 5th and 12th, 1925.
[3] Halley, " Lancs. Puritanism and Nonconformity," p. 348.
[4] C.S.P.D., October 9th, 17th, 21st, 24th, 1661.
[5] " Seditious Preachers, Ungodly Teachers," 1709, p. 47.

Something like the Act of Uniformity was inevitable; the chaos could not go on indefinitely. The defenders of the Act, replying to the assertion that if there were no compulsion or subscription the ministers would in time come to agreement on small matters of ceremonial or doctrine, answered that they had had two years already, and were no nearer agreement.[1] The licence which had prevailed since the King's return had to be brought to an end. Comprehension, even if it had been practicable, would have been useless: the Church would only have been torn by contending parties, and would have lost all sense of its mission under the deadening influence of faction. Clarendon was inclined to moderation, because he considered it the most prudent course. He had no sympathy with the Puritan party, because of their politics, but he was acutely conscious that an immediate settlement was urgent. Until that was done controversy and disturbance and plots would continue. Any settlement almost would be better than none. Nevertheless, he did not approve of all that was in the Act of Uniformity, and he had struggled against some of its clauses, but Parliament was too strong for him.[2]

The King, mindful of what he had said at Breda, did his best to obtain some form of religious comprehension, and when he could not get that, he was anxious to modify the stringency of the Act of Uniformity. In spite of all that has been said about him, he was not a Papist[3]; the men who knew him best described him as uncertain in his religious beliefs; indeed he was thought by some to be a Deist and a follower of Hobbes.[4] In his boyhood he saw the unpopularity of the Church of England under his father and Laud. The Puritans had overthrown the Church, murdered his father, and sent him into exile. In Ireland Papist and Puritan were constantly flying at each other's throats. In Scotland the Presbyterian ministers had convinced him that Presbyterianism was " no religion for a gentleman." In France the Anglicans in exile had done little to make their church precious in his sight.[5] Anti-Romanism had been drilled into him in his youth, yet abroad he had seen a great deal in the Roman Church that attracted him. Roman Catholicism was his mother's religion, yet his father had died for Anglicanism. The Romanists had fought for his father, and had been faithful to himself after Worcester fight, while Presbyterians and Churchmen had welcomed him back. It is not surprising that he had the tolerant spirit which comes from indifference; and the true key to Charles's policy lies in the fact that he was perfectly

[1] Kennet, " Reg.," p. 737.
[2] Keith Feiling, " Hist. of the Tory Party," pp. 104–105; *idem*, " Clarendon and the Act of Uniformity," *E.H.R.*, XLIV. 289.
[3] D'Orleans, " Histoire des Révolutions," III. 381.
[4] " The Works of John Sheffield, Duke of Buckingham," II. 58.
[5] Halifax, " Character of Charles II," published 1750.

honest in his desire for a general toleration. He had no scheme
to bring in Roman Catholicism at the expense, and to the
destruction, of other forms of Christianity. The fact that he
became a Roman Catholic on his deathbed no more proves that
he was a Roman Catholic earlier in his reign than the conversion
of Newman proves Newman a Romanist in his youth. Charles
wished to show kindness to Roman Catholics because they had
showed kindness to him. He described himself, and that truly,
as an enemy to all severity in religion. He struggled long and
hard against the persecuting spirit, and at last gave up the
struggle in disgust. At Breda he had declared his belief in
religious freedom, but the charge that he violated his Declaration
is without foundation. He had merely promised that there
should be no interference with liberty of conscience till Parliament had arranged a settlement of the religious question. His
hope of a national Church which would include within its bounds
all who would consent that its chief pastors should be called
bishops was impossible to realise. He pressed Parliament to
give him some power of indulgence, but that body refused,
reminding him that his Declaration from Breda had not been a
promise to give general toleration, but " a gracious declaration
to comply with the advice of Parliament." Finally, the Act of
Uniformity was passed, containing many things which he disliked. What was he to do? Should he stand out and risk being
sent on his travels again? What advantage would that have
been to the cause of the Dissenters? Moreover, there is yet
another point to consider, which is that a promise to do his best
to get liberty of conscience for them was one thing, but to allow
those who did not accept the principles of the Church to possess
her property and offices, while preaching a hostile doctrine and
despising her rules, was another.

The greater part of the nation approved of the Act of Uniformity. They felt that till Puritanism was rendered impotent
both Church and Crown were in danger. Evelyn and Reresby
were as firm on the point as Cosin and Patrick. It was not merely
the work of the House of Lords and a set of revengeful bishops.
The Act had the approval not only of the great majority of the
clergy, but also of a greater majority of the laity. William Dell,
who had been Master of Caius College, Cambridge, and rector
of Yelden, Beds, went out in 1662. His parishioners had complained that he had allowed " one Bunyan, a tinker," to preach
in his church on Christmas Day.[1] The church-going laity
wanted the ministrations of their own clergy, and it is not
at all to be supposed that the old régime had been popular
among them.

The Act of Uniformity has been called a persecuting Act,
but the Long Parliament had been more severe to the Churchmen

[1] Hist. MSS. Com., VII. 102.

than the Churchmen were to Dissenters.   Edward VI., Elizabeth, James I., and Charles I. had been content to limit the discretion of the clergy by prescribing the forms of prayer and ceremonial. Under the Commonwealth even a psalm book was provided for the worshippers, while the Westminster Assembly had made much more rigid the limits of doctrine and discipline.   Before the over-throw of the Church the bishops had been left to enforce discipline, with some supervision from the High Commission Court.   Under the Commonwealth Parliament controlled everything, and where the Presbyterian system had been adequately established, as in London and Lancashire, the ministers and elders were set to watch one another.   The use of the Prayer Book had been forbidden even in private: the date on which the prohibition came into force was also a St. Bartholomew's Day.[1]

One thing which made the ejected ministers very sore in 1662 was that they were turned out on St. Bartholomew's Day, whereby they lost their Michaelmas tithes.   The original draft of the Act had given them till Michaelmas Day, but this had been altered during the progress of the Act through Parliament.   In the Commonwealth days the ejected royalist clergy had, at least in theory, been granted one-fifth of the revenues of their livings, though in actual fact these fifths were seldom paid.[2]   Walker stated that scarcely one in ten of the royalist clergy received the fifth in full value or without great trouble.[3]   Thus, Lever, the intruded minister of Brancepeth, refused to pay the fifth to Cosin's children.   After some trouble, he was ordered to pay both the fifth and the arrears, but there is no evidence that he ever did so.[4]   Bishop Morton of Durham sent in a humble petition for his money, £800 a year, but did not receive a penny for four years.   Bishop Morley did not receive anything from his canonry of Christ Church, Oxford, for twelve years.[5]   Sometimes all the revenues and lands belonging to a bishopric were sold and divided before the bishop could procure an enforcement of the order made in his favour.   Sometimes the arrears of former years which had been forborne by a bishop out of kindness to a tenant were seized by the Sequestrators, and an order was obtained to set aside the Parliament's general order.   This happened in the case of Bishop Hall.   Many shifts and evasions were adopted by the clergy who succeeded the sequestered incumbents.   Thus, Parliament at first had ordered the fifth to be paid to the wives and children of all sequestered persons, but those in possession refused to pay because *clergymen* had not been expressly mentioned. Parliament then renewed the order in more express terms.   The

[1] W. T. Whitley, " Baptists and St. Bartholomew's Day," *Trans. Bapt. Hist. Soc.*, I. 27.
[2] Fuller, " Church History," 1655, Bk. XI. p. 230.
[3] Walker, " Sufferings," pp. 99–100.
[4] Osmond, " Life of John Cosin," 1913, p. 145.
[5] " The Bishop of Winchester's Vindication," 1683, p. 526.

new men deducted the taxes they had to pay, and complained that their tithes were so ill paid that they themselves would starve if they paid the fifth.   If the sequestered minister had a wife and no children, or children and no wife, or only one child, they pretended his case did not come within the letter of the law, which said *wife and children*.   If he had means of his own, they said there was no need to pay him the fifth.   Some frightened the claimant with fresh charges of malignancy.   Others who had livings in the great towns disclaimed tithes, and only accepted " gifts " from their parishioners: they were then able to say that the old incumbent had no legal share in the free gratuities of the people.   When the sequestered minister sued for his fifth they took advantage of a parliamentary order which denounced as enemies of the State all persons who molested those who had been put into livings by order of Parliament.   Sometimes when the fifth was granted it was only granted " until further orders," the first payment was long delayed, and the succeeding payments were irregular and soon discontinued.   To a bachelor nothing was either allowed or intended by Parliament.   In 1654 an ordinance was issued cancelling the allowance unless the sequestered clergy-man moved away from the neighbourhood of his former benefice. By a decree of November 24th, 1655, the " outed clergy " were made incapable of earning their living by their own profession.[1] There was some ground for the bitter saying of an Anglican pamphleteer that mercy had not fled the land in 1662, but had been driven out some twenty years before.[2]   Edmund Calamy replied to Walker's statements about the fifths: " I conceive it no easy thing to make a calculation in this case.   However, he has taken notice of several that received fifths and I of several that paid them, and we need not doubt but there were many more than we were able to recover.   And at any rate it was better than the Act of Uniformity." [3]   It was not a very convincing answer.   This much may perhaps he said: under the Common-wealth the " outed ministers had at least a claim to legal redress; the House of Commons in 1662 had refused even this semblance of kindness.   A greater number had been expelled during the Civil War and under the Commonwealth, but that expulsion had been more gradual, and had been, at least ostensibly, on political or moral rather than religious grounds." [4]   They had been ejected for " viciousness of life," " errors in doctrine," " superstitious innovations " in worship, and " malignancy " against the Parliament.[5]   Bramhall declared that the greater part of those sequestered under the Commonwealth were turned out for

---

[1] " The Friendly Debate," 1670, Pt. III.
[2] " Seditious Preachers, Ungodly Teachers," 1709, p. 54.
[3] Calamy, " The Church and Dissenters compared as to Persecution," 1719.
[4] J. R. Green, " Hist. of the Eng. People," III. 362.
[5] White, " First Century of Scandalous Malignant Priests," 1643.

THE COMMONWEALTH.

From "Arbitrary Government Displayed to the Life." 2nd edition, 1683.

Facing p. 7.

Studies in English Puritanism.

prelacy, supposed Arminianism, or for interest in the civil differences.[1] Many hundreds of the clergy were turned out for loyalty. Among the accusations were preaching obedience to the King, preaching against sacrilege and rebellion, bowing at the Holy Name, being in possession of popish books, or keeping company with Papists.[2] Accusations of misconduct were listened to with eagerness. Amusements of which the Puritans disapproved were treated as evidence of bad character, and any lying story told against a loyal Anglican by an aggrieved parishioner or bitter sectary was accepted as sufficient evidence by the hostile inquisition which had been set up. Error in doctrine and superstition in worship generally meant that the incumbent believed the teaching of the Church of England, and had tried to maintain the ordinary decencies of worship. For this he had been sequestered, not by any ecclesiastical authority, but by Commissioners appointed by a Parliament composed chiefly of enemies of the Church.[3]

The Act of Uniformity was largely the result of the violent proceedings of the Puritans themselves in the day of their power. " The Anglican of the Restoration was a religious persecutor inspired by political panic, the Puritan of the Commonwealth was a persecuting social reformer inspired by religious fervour." [4] The ejection of the ministers of 1662 partook to some extent of the nature of a voluntary withdrawal. They could have kept their livings if they could have accepted the conditions. The clergy turned out under the Commonwealth went out without conditions, and under the Act of Uniformity no troops of horse were sent to see that no one gave shelter to the ejected clergy or their families. The balance of suffering, on the whole, was probably during the reign of the Presbyterian and Independent.

The main source of our information about the ejected clergy is Edmund Calamy, the grandson of the Edmund Calamy who was ejected from St. Mary Aldermanbury in 1662. In the Third Part of Baxter's Life, or rather Autobiography, a list was given of a number of the ejected ministers. Calamy the younger wrote in 1702 " An Abridgement of Mr. Baxter's History of His Life and Times, with an Account of the Ministers Ejected." In 1713 he produced a new edition in two volumes. During that time he had accumulated a great deal of information, and his list was greatly increased and many of his biographies were enlarged. Proceeding with his collection of details, he published in 1727 two additional volumes called " A Continuation of

[1] Kennet, " Reg.," p. 820.　　[2] *Idem, ibid.*, p. 763.
[3] See " A Narrative of the Proceedings of the Commissioners appointed by O. Cromwell, for ejecting Scandalous and Ignorant Ministers," 1655; " Truth Appearing," 1654; " Innocency Appearing," 1654; " A Petition for the Vindication of the Public Use of the Book of Common Prayer," 1654; " Mr. Sadler Re-examined," 1654, etc.
[4] H. Hensley Henson, " Puritanism in England," 1912, p. 282.

the Account of the Ministers Ejected." These two volumes contain entirely fresh material. In 1775 Samuel Palmer published in two volumes " The Nonconformists' Memorial." It claimed to be an abridgement of Calamy's work, with corrections, additions, and new anecdotes. In 1802 he published a new edition in three volumes. He inserted Calamy's additions in their proper places, which makes his work much easier to use. He omitted an amount of relatively unimportant matter, such as copies of testimonials respecting the ordination and induction of the ministers, some of the less important inscriptions on their tombs, together with the scandalous stories about them from Anthony à Wood and John Walker, and Calamy's refutation of these. He retained the lists of their publications, and sometimes added to them, though he frequently abridged their titles. His corrections and additions are to be treated with caution. It is not uncommon to find that Calamy was right and Palmer wrong after all, and naturally there are many of Calamy's misstatements which he was unable to correct.[1]

There was much controversy in later days on the question whether the expulsion in 1662 was greater or less than the expulsion of the Anglican clergy under the Commonwealth. There was a traditional belief that in the latter case there had been 10,000 ejections. John White, the chairman of the Parliamentary Commission for Religion, and author of " The First Century of Scandalous Malignant Priests," is credited with the boast that he and his colleagues had ejected 8000, though his actual words as quoted seem to be that 8000 " were unworthy and scandalous and deserved to be cast out." [2]   Now the total of livings in England and Wales was something over 9000.[3] Adding curacies, less in number then than to-day, lectureships and university offices, the total number of clerical posts was probably, therefore, under 11,000. When White died in 1644, the King still held half the country, and if all the clergy had been turned out in the other half, the number could not have been anything like 8000 in White's lifetime, though, of course, the sequestrations went on for years after his death. In reply to Calamy's " Account " of the sufferings of the Bartholomew men, Dr. John Walker, in 1714, published his " Sufferings of the Clergy," though the vastness of his work shows that he must have been collecting his material for years. He gave 3334 cases of ejected clergy and schoolmasters. John Withers, a Nonconformist minister of Exeter, who attacked Walker's work,[4]

[1] Calamy, "Hist. Account of My Own Life "; " Calamy as a Biographer," by Alexander Gordon, *Trans. Cong. Hist. Soc.*, August 1914, pp. 233–247.
[2] Walker, " Sufferings," Pt. I. p. 199.
[3] " The Valor Beneficiorum," 1695, says 8693; Chamberlayne's " State of Britain," 1684, 9725.
[4] J. Withers, " Remarks on Dr. Walker's Late Preface," 1715.

computed that 2399 of these were clergymen. Calamy himself replied to Walker in a tract, " The Church and Dissenters Compared as to Persecution." [1] Walker made comparison between the men ejected under the Commonwealth and at the Restoration, and said scornfully that among the latter were " not a few mechanics and fellows bred to the meanest occupations . . . troopers and others who had served in the rebel armies." [2] He has been described as " always a truthful man, and usually an angry man, hence at the mercy of story-builders." [3] In computing that about 2400 clergy (as distinct from schoolmasters) were ejected, a number much below the traditional number, he has, however, certainly understated his case: wherever full information is available large additions can be made. In Dorset and Worcester the figures can be doubled; in Leicester they can be increased by half; in Cumberland and Westmorland a number of names can be added, and the same is true for other counties. It has been estimated that it would be reasonable to add fifty per cent. to Walker's numbers, which would bring the total parochial sequestrations roughly to 3500.[4]

Baxter said that under the Commonwealth " almost all the Welsh clergy were ejected." In Lancashire—and probably the case was the same everywhere else—many who were ejected on one occasion were restored on another, or found their way into another parish. Thus, several who had been ejected for refusing the Covenant obtained vacant livings from Cromwell's Triers, especially after the Covenant had ceased to be looked upon as important.[5]

A calculation of the numbers of London clergy turned out under the late régime was published in 1661. It stated that the total of the ministers of London within the Bills of Mortality (besides St. Paul's and Westminster) turned out of their livings by sequestration and otherwise was 115, whereof above forty were Doctors of Divinity, and that most of them were plundered of their goods, and their wives and children turned out of doors. Those imprisoned in London and in ships and gaols and castles in the country numbered twenty; twenty-five had fled to avoid imprisonment; twenty-two had died in remote parts and in prison, and about forty churches had been left without a settled minister.[6]

The names given in Calamy's and Palmer's lists really fall

---

[1] 1719. [2] Walker, " Sufferings," Preface, p. xiv.
[3] Alexander Gordon, " Calamy as a Biographer," *Trans. Cong. Hist. Soc.*, August 1914, pp. 233–247.
[4] G. B. Tatham, " Dr. John Walker and the Sufferings of the Clergy," 1911, p. 132; B. Nightingale, " The Ejected of 1662 in Cumberland and Westmorland," I. 44.
[5] Halley, " Lancs. Presbyterianism and Nonconformity," pp. 345–346.
[6] " A General Bill of the Mortality of the Clergy of London . . . printed against St. Bartholomew's Day," 1661.

into three divisions. First there were those who were ousted before St. Bartholomew as holders of sequestered livings. With these may be included men who, like Baxter, were refused permission to continue their ministrations. Secondly there were the beneficed clergy and endowed schoolmasters who were deprived by the Act of Uniformity. Thirdly there were those who held no benefice at the time of the Act, who, though they had formerly held posts as lecturers and curates, were no longer allowed to officiate in any way unless they conformed. Such were Henry Newcome and Philip Henry, and there were a few persons, like Increase Mather, who had begun to preach, but as yet had received no ordination. These men Calamy and Palmer refer to as " silenced."

There are some doubtful cases which do not fall into either of these classes. Such is that of John Ray, the eminent scientist. Strictly speaking, he ought not to be on the list at all, for he never left the Church of England. Nevertheless, he could not obey the Act of Uniformity. He had never taken the Covenant, and often declared that he thought it unlawful, but he said he could not declare that it did not bind those who had taken it, for he feared it might, so he resigned his fellowship at Trinity College, Cambridge.[1] But he conformed as a layman to the Church of England, and disapproved of separation, though even after the Revolution he refused to accept clerical preferment in the Church.[2] According to Calamy, he said that he could not give his unfeigned assent and consent to the Prayer Book, particularly objecting to sponsors in baptism.[3]

It is traditional that the number of the ejected on St. Bartholomew's Day, 1662, was 2000. How far is this statement true? Archdeacon Eachard gave the total as about 2000.[4] Bishop Morley of Winchester said that this estimate included not only those who refused to conform, but also the intruders, some hundreds in number.[5] Baxter said 1800. Omitting duplicates, and counting those who conformed afterwards, Calamy's volumes give about 2465 names. Palmer gives about 2480, including 230 who conformed afterwards. But neither list is more than roughly correct. Fresh names have been discovered in most counties, and, on the other hand, doubt has been thrown on some. Dr. Alexander Gordon thought that those of the ejected who neither conformed nor resorted to other ways of living, but maintained a Nonconformist ministry, were not more than 1800.[6]

---

[1] W. Derham, " Memorials of John Ray," edited by E. Lankester, 1846, pp. 15–16.
[2] Idem, ibid., pp. 85–97; Calamy, II. 87, 111, 120.
[3] Calamy, III. 121.   [4] " Hist. of Eng.," III. 88.
[5] " The Bishop of Winchester's Vindication," 1683, p. 489.
[6] Alexander Gordon, " Calamy as a Biographer," Trans. Cong. Hist. Soc., August 1914, p. 239.

But taking for the present the number 2250 as the total of the ejected, it must be noted that Calamy did not claim that these were all turned out at Bartholomew tide. He includes all those who were turned out from the Restoration to the day the Act of Uniformity came into force. Does this really matter, if the total number is accepted as a fair estimate? It matters to this extent, that the whole of the 2000 odd did not go out as sufferers for conscience' sake. Baxter refers to hundreds who were turned out of livings that had been sequestered under the Commonwealth to make room for the old incumbents. How many these were we cannot exactly say. But 606 petitions for restoration were sent in to the House of Lords in 1660. These petitions were presented in pursuance of two orders of the House of Lords, one of June 22, 1660, for securing the tithes and other profits of sequestered livings in the hands of churchwardens or overseers of the poor of the several parishes, until the titles of sequestered clergy and of the present possessors should be determined; the other of June 23rd, giving the Clerk of Parliament power to insert in the foregoing general order the names of those who should bring in petitions to have the benefit thereof.[1] Some not only petitioned for reinstatement, but also thought that they might have the profits which had been kept from them, or that at least their arrears of fifths might be paid. We may perhaps assume that most of these petitions were successful as regards reinstatement, though not for their lost incomes. Yet some of the intruding ministers got other livings, and we cannot be certain whether the number above mentioned was increased after the Act for Restoring the Clergy was passed in September 1660, but probably it was. Certainly, in Richard Gilpin's case, the sequestered incumbent of Greystoke did not claim till 1661. In Cumberland and Westmorland not more than half a dozen appear to have waited for the Act of Uniformity.[2] Take two cases also in London. John Simpson is recorded as excluded from the lectureship in St. Botolph's, Bishopgate, but he left at the Restoration, and died in 1662. William Taylor, the incumbent of St. Stephen's, Coleman Street, was found by Calamy himself to have died in September 1661.[3]

It is impossible to get the exact numbers. No two writers seem to agree, even in their calculations of the number of names in Calamy and Palmer. Even then we should be no nearer to exactitude until we had some means of testing the accuracy of these lists in every detail. One modern writer calculated, after carefully comparing Walker and Palmer, that certainly 303 of the

---

[1] MSS. of the House of Lords, Hist. MSS. Com., 7th Report, Pt. I. pp. 104–108.
[2] Nightingale, " The Ejected of 1662 in Cumberland and Westmorland," I. 75.
[3] Kennet, " Reg.," p. 800.

ejected ministers, and possibly eighty-four others, were displaced to make way for their predecessors. He came finally to the conclusions thus set forth:

Ejected in 1660		324
Ejected in 1662		1873
Ejected at uncertain dates .	.	152
Silenced		98
	Total	2447

Of these 254 afterwards conformed.[1]

But this calculation is based on Palmer's earlier edition of 1775, and not on his later and better edition. The number of persons ejected in 1660 and at uncertain dates is probably much greater than is here suggested. The ejections began after the fall of Richard Cromwell, when some ministers at least were turned out by their parishioners to make way for the old incumbents. It seems probable, therefore, that the number turned out at St. Bartholomew is less than the number given above. Here is another estimate:

Ejected 1660 and 1661 .	.	422
Ejected at uncertain dates .	.	135
Ejected in 1662 . . .	.	1820
Silenced in 1662 .	.	115
	Total	2492

In addition there were sixty doubtful cases.[2]

Of the above total there afterwards conformed 254 or 257. Of the 1935 given as ejected or disabled by the Act of Uniformity, seventy were twice evicted, once in 1660 and again in 1662.[3] Probably in both these estimates the number of those ejected before St. Bartholomew's Day is under-stated. Walker represents 800 clergy as claiming reinstatement at the Restoration, and even then, compared with the number of those turned out under the Commonwealth the number seems surprisingly small. But an investigation which has been made in the case of twelve men who were ejected from Lancashire livings at various times before 1660 throws some light on the matter. Two recovered their benefices at the Restoration, two had previously been restored under the Commonwealth, two obtained higher preferment, apparently instead of their former livings, three had died, one had gone abroad, while of the remaining two nothing is known.[4]

[1] *Trans. Cong. Hist. Soc.*, V. 296–297.
[2] *Christian World*, August 29th, 1912.
[3] " Another Calculation of the Ejected," *Trans. Cong. Hist. Soc.*, V. 386–388.
[4] Halley, " Lancs. Puritanism," p. 346.

Allowing for those who were ejected to make way for their predecessors, it would seem that the number of those who went out for conscience' sake is very considerably less than 2000.

But the whole matter of the numbers is all the more complicated by the fact that we cannot absolutely trust Calamy's or Palmer's lists. Calamy did a monumental work of patient research, but he had not access to all the sources of information available to modern scholars. In his own time details of his work were disputed. Thus, Kennet found a good many mistakes in the names given for the diocese of Peterborough.[1] Calamy represents the ejectments in London as amounting to 293. The total number ejected or silenced in the metropolitan area was 121.[2] Additional names have been found in Essex by T. W. Davids.[3] Canon Curteis, however, declared that half Calamy's cases in that county were not true cases of ejectment. The same writer said that in Hertfordshire four-fifths of Calamy's names disappear under investigation.[4] On the other hand, Urwick has increased Calamy's numbers for that county.[5] So has Dale for Yorkshire,[6] and Dr. Nightingale for Cumberland.[7]

Another source of information has of late years been examined. By an order made by Parliament in 1661 a subsidy was demanded from the clergy of England and Wales. Of the rolls of the twenty-two English dioceses five remain (two in an incomplete condition), while of the Welsh dioceses three remain. They have been carefully examined by Professor G. Lyon Turner, as a means, where possible, of checking Calamy and Palmer, inasmuch as they tell us in a number of cases whether a man had been turned out before 1662. His results are as follows:

In thirty-one cases Calamy and Palmer are confirmed.

In fifty-nine cases they show Calamy right as to the name, but are able to give information as to the date in cases where he did not know it.

In seven cases Calamy and Palmer are right as to the name, but wrong as to the date.

In one case Calamy gives one name and Palmer another as ejected from one parish. The rolls show *both* men ejected, each from a separate parish.

In five cases names are to be added which were in neither Calamy's nor Palmer's lists.

Of the 104 cases thus mentioned, it appears that forty-five were turned out before 1662, and fifty-nine at St. Bartholomew's Day.[8]

[1] Kennet, " Reg.," p. 807.
[2] T. G. Crippen in " Victoria Hist. of London," I. 376.
[3] " Evangelical Nonconformity in Essex."
[4] G. H. Curteis, " Bampton Lectures on Dissent," 1872, p. 68, note.
[5] W. Urwick, " Nonconformity in Herts."
[6] B. Dale, " Yorkshire Puritanism and Early Nonconformity."
[7] Nightingale, " The Ejected of 1662 in Cumberland and Westmorland."
[8] " The Clerical Subsidy, 1661," *Trans. Cong. Hist. Soc.*, VII. 16–33.

The results of all this seem to be two: (1) the evidence is all in favour of the general accuracy of Calamy as regards names, but not dates; (2) that if the other dioceses were like those mentioned, the number of those ejected at the Restoration is greater, and that of those ejected at St. Bartholomew less than is usually supposed. This is borne out by a letter written by William Hooke to a late colleague in the north of England, in which reference is made to 1600 removed on St. Bartholomew's Day, and as many turned out before. The last part of this statement is doubtless an exaggeration, but it tends to bear out the general contention above.[1]

A certain number, estimated at about 250, did not at first conform, but came back to the Church later on. Thus, Richard Kidder, vicar of Stanground, in Hampshire, refused to subscribe at first, but, after a careful study of the Book of Common Prayer, conformed two years later, and became Bishop of Bath and Wells.[2] Dr. John Conant, Rector of Exeter College, Oxford, and one of the Savoy Commissioners, went out in 1662, and conformed seven years afterwards.[3] Probably among the 250 there were some who could not really be described as ejected clergy. They had been obliged to make room for the lawful incumbent on his return. They may have been quite willing to accept the new order of things, but had to find fresh work elsewhere. Thus, Samuel Grastie[4] was removed, or removed himself, from Woodchurch in Cheshire to make way for the sequestered incumbent, George Burgess, and afterwards held a living in Cumberland.[5]

Of the list of those who conformed afterwards—"the New Conformists," as they were called—it has been calculated that thirty-five were removed from a sequestered benefice by the return of their predecessors. Eighteen others were similarly removed, though there was no such reinstatement of the former incumbent; while five conformed at once, but removed to another sphere of work. With regard to others of these "New Conformists," the date of their resignation or the place which they resigned is uncertain. It follows, therefore, that out of the 250 there were certainly less than 190 who actually retired at St. Bartholomew on account of conscientious scruples.[6]

Most of the ejected were known as Presbyterians, but there were numerous Independents, and a smaller number of Baptists. The last named would have been excluded by the Presbyterians

---

[1] Stoughton, "Hist. of Religion in Eng.," III. 295, 503–504.
[2] Cassan, "Lives of the Bishops of Bath and Wells," II. 110–112.
[3] Palmer, I. 230.
[4] Calamy, III. 172.
[5] Nightingale, "The Ejected of 1662 in Cumberland and Westmorland," I. 715–717.
[6] "The New Conformists," *Trans. Cong. Hist. Soc.,* VI. 266.

themselves if they had been in power, while both Independents and Baptists would no more have submitted to a Presbyterian organisation than they would to an Episcopalian. There were others who held such opinions that if any of the chief sects had been established they could not have conformed, and most of these had no ordination of any kind whatever.

The question of ordination formed one of the greatest difficulties. Of the men thrust into livings under the Commonwealth some had Presbyterian ordination, some had none. Since the Reformation there had been stray cases of men holding office in the Church of England without being episcopally ordained; most, if not all, of them having been originally members of foreign Protestant churches. A great deal was now made of this, and it was argued that the Church was now putting a slight on the foreign churches, but Churchmen replied that there was a great difference between foreign imperfect churches, which had the misfortune, through no fault of their own, to have no bishops, and men who denied episcopacy and set up a new and schismatical method of ordination.[1] Whatever might have happened in the past in the case of individuals, the Church of England took her stand on the ancient episcopal succession, and demanded that all her clergy should be ordained in the ancient way. Those who had been ordained in the Presbyterian way refused to be reordained, as they called it, and the curious argument was put forward that the Church of England herself did not allow reordination, and as a proof of this it was pointed out that if a Roman priest joined the Church of England he was not reordained.[2] But this was to miss the point. The Church of England did not reordain the Roman priest because he was a priest already, but she insisted that the Presbyterian would have to be ordained by a bishop because he was not a priest, and, to do him justice, he did not claim to be. Clarendon tried to smooth the difficulty by saying that no such thing as reordination was required, but only conditional ordination. " If the former (ordination) is good this will be void, if the former void this will be effective." [3] This talk about a conditional form was merely a compromise to save the face of the Presbyterians. It is true that no such thing as reordination was required, even of Presbyterians. On the Catholic theory of ordination they had not been ordained at all; they had merely been set apart for a Presbyterian ministry by people who had no right to ordain. Whether the Anglican was right or wrong is not the point that concerns us here, but that position was the essence of the Anglican system.[4] The Non-

---

[1] Foxcroft, " Supplement to Burnet," p. 70.
[2] Clarendon, " Continuation," p. 1077.   [3] *Idem, ibid.*, p. 1078.
[4] Preface to the Ordinal in the Book of Common Prayer; Edward Denny, " The English Church and the Ministry of the Reformed Churches," London, 1900.

conformists' objection to receiving episcopal ordination was that what was to them reordination nullified their former ordination, and invalidated their previous ministrations.[1] This difficulty was made greater for them by at least one bishop, Hall of Chester, who insisted that if he ordained them, they should expressly renounce their previous orders.

The declaration of assent and consent, which had met with very little opposition in Parliament, was another great difficulty. The Nonconformists took pains to distinguish between assent and consent. They might consent to read the book if obliged, but they held that assent would imply that it was so good that it needed no alteration.[2] The clause was not really so stringent as that. The lawyers always interpreted the assent and consent as referring not to the book, but to the use of the book. It was never interpreted as agreement with every statement in it, and the words were altered in 1865 to make this clear.[3] The Nonconformist objections to the Prayer Book were many and varied. Henry Hickman,[4] like many others at the time, published a defence of Nonconformist principles. His work, written in answer to Durel and other Anglican writers, while professing the great loyalty of Nonconformists to the King, stated their objections to the Caroline settlement and the Book of Common Prayer. Small and great things are mixed together in this little treatise, and the subjects follow one another in somewhat haphazard fashion. The chief things complained of are the accusation of heresy against the Presbyterians, infrequency of the celebration of the Holy Communion (an unfair objection seeing that the Prayer Book ordered one on all Sundays and holy days), the excessive number of festivals, the reading of the Apocrypha, the surplice, the use of the Gloria Patri after the Psalms, bowing at the Holy Name, standing at the Gospel, altars, kneeling at communion, private celebrations of the Holy Communion, various matters in the baptismal service, the use of the sign of the cross, the setting up of crosses on church towers, infant baptism, the bad translation of the Psalms, the Ordinal, and other things.[5] This book itself is a proof, if proof were needed, that the differences between the Nonconformist and the Anglican were too many and great for a satisfactory compromise to be possible. It would be hopeless to expect assent and consent to every word in the Book of Common Prayer from people like Edward Bagshawe, who was a prisoner in Newgate for twenty-two weeks for refusing to take the oath of allegiance, in which he objected to the word " willingly." [6]

[1] Calamy, " Abridgement," p. 199.
[2] Clarendon, " Continuation," p. 1078.
[3] M. Gwatkin, " Church and State in England," 1917, pp. 353–354.
[4] Palmer, I. 245; Kennet, " Reg.," p. 750.
[5] " Apologia pro Ministris in Anglia (vulgo) Nonconformistis," 1665.
[6] Aubrey, " Brief Lives," I. 85.

The Act of Uniformity required the clergy to take the oath of canonical obedience, a phrase which many of them misinterpreted or misunderstood, and to swear obedience to the ordinary according to the canons of the Church. The word ordinary not only included the bishop of the diocese, but other ecclesiastical superiors as well, including lay chancellors. The Presbyterian, who was really very sacerdotally inclined, held that the keys of authority belonged to the clergy only [1] and looked upon lay chancellors as an abomination. But probably the greatest difficulty to the Nonconformists was the renunciation of the Solemn League and Covenant, which they had not only taken themselves, but also forced other people to take. Even those who had not taken it found a great difficulty in the way of renunciation. The King had taken it three times, and in their view this would mean that he and thousands of his subjects were now ordered to commit perjury. Probably the authorities would have been much wiser if they had let the Covenant sink into oblivion, even though there were very many people who still considered themselves pledged to everything in it, but to the Government it was still a dangerous standard of rebellion.

All things considered, it is likely that the majority of the Dissenters were of the same mind as William Bowles of York, who was buried on the eve of St. Bartholomew in 1662 : " Being asked in his last illness what of conformity he disliked, he answered, 'The whole.' " [2] Nevertheless the fundamental difference between the Churchman and the Nonconformist lay in their conception of Church government. The Bishops stood by what they believed to be the primitive and Catholic and divinely appointed system of hierarchical government. The Nonconformist did not believe that system to be primitive or Catholic or divinely appointed. The Bishops were for a reformed Catholicism, the Nonconformists were Puritan and Protestant. It was not merely a question of wrangling and possible compromise over details. The theological strife of the previous hundred and thirty years had produced two opposing parties with a different theological outlook and habit of mind ; two parties which could not possibly settle down side by side in the same communion, holding opposing systems of worship and doctrine. Both of them believed in a national Church, but each of them had very strong ideas as to what it should believe and how it should worship. The division must have come sooner or later. That is sad enough, but what is still more sad was that the division should have brought with it such bitterness and uncharitableness.

" The bishops carry themselves so high," complained Samuel Pepys ; [3] that is to say, they were uncompromising in main-

---

[1] Drysdale, " Hist. of Presbyterianism in England," p. 385.
[2] Palmer, III. 455.　　　　　　　　[3] " Diary," November 19th, 1662.

taining their principles. But it is certain that a number of them did their best to soften the severity of the Act. Archbishop Juxon even suffered a Nonconformist minister in his diocese to continue officiating one part of the day, while the orthodox incumbent performed the other service.[1] Bishop Hackett tried to win over two of the most distinguished Nonconformists in his diocese, Dr. John Bryan [2] and Dr. Obadiah Grew,[3] and allowed them to continue their ministry for a month after St. Bartholomew's Day. Bishop Sanderson of Lincoln had a list of Nonconformist ministers against whom he was urged to take proceedings. When he felt he was drawing near his death he destroyed it rather than let it fall into the hands of his successors.[4] It was he who said that " more was imposed on the ministers than he wished had been." " On the passing of the Act he sent for Mr. Matthew Sylvester, whose living was in his diocese, and treating him with great civility, earnestly pressed him not to quit his living, and patiently heard him state his difficulties, and when he found he could not obviate them to his satisfaction he lamented it." [5] Bishop Laney of Lincoln was also very tolerant. " Not I, but the law," he used to say, and to use his own expression, he would look through his fingers.[6] Bishop Piers of Bath and Wells gave permission to William Thomas of Ubleigh, or Ubley, in Somersetshire, to preach on Sunday, August 24th, but he did not.[7] Anthony Tuckney, Master of St. John's College, Cambridge, and Regius Professor of Divinity,[8] was ejected, and Dr. Peter Gunning, afterwards Bishop of Ely (1675–1684), allowed him a very considerable annuity as long as he lived.[9] Bishop White Kennet gives a long list of instances of the lenity and charity of the Bishops towards the Nonconformist ministers after their ejection, all of which he has drawn from Calamy.[10] A great many of the lower clergy also did not come behind in this respect. Stillingfleet, at his rectory of Sutton in Bedfordshire, sheltered one of the ejected ministers, and took a large house, which he converted into a school, for another, Richard Kennet, who lived there until his death in 1670.[11] William Bagshawe, " the Apostle of the Peak," was ejected from Glossop. John Sandiforth, his successor, used to attend his sermons whenever he visited Glossop in

---

[1] Perry, " Hist. of Church of Eng.," II. 369.
[2] Calamy, II. 735; IV. 850.
[3] *Idem*, II. 736; IV. 850.
[4] " The Conformists' Plea for the Nonconformists," 1681, p. 26.
[5] Calamy, " Hist. Account of My Own Life," II. 111 ; *idem*, " Continuation," II. 449.
[6] Halley, " Lancs. Puritanism," p. 351.
[7] W. Hunt, " Hist. of Diocese of Bath and Wells," 1885, p. 220; Calamy, II. 587.
[8] Calamy, II. 77; III. 114.
[9] Salmon, " Lives of the English Bishops," p. 253.
[10] Kennet, " Reg.," pp. 813–820.   [11] Calamy, II. 118.

after years.[1] Of the clergy it was noticed that the worst persecutors were those who had been bigots in the former days, and
had now conformed. None are more bitter against former
associates than converts. On the other hand, it is certain that
even in the days when persecution was at its worst, the King's
judges, as well as those of the ecclesiastical courts, were often
exceedingly lenient. Neither was it all bitterness on the Nonconformist side. With a certain amount of inconsistency, a
considerable number of nonconforming divines, though they
believed the terms for ministerial conformity impracticable, yet
made no scruple about joining in lay communion with the
Established Church. Dr. John Bryan, who founded the Presbyterian congregation in Coventry, said he had ten objections to
ministerial conformity, but was willing to practise lay conformity.
Thus, after the exercise of their ministry, the ministers attended
the parish church for divine service, and were sometimes communicated there. ˙To this may probably be traced the rise of
what was in after years known as occasional conformity.[2] For
quite a long time after the Ejection a number of the original
Nonconformist ministers refused to hold their meetings during
the time of the service at the parish church. It was long before
any of them thought of ordaining others to continue the schism;
and it was remarked by some, as a credit to the moderation of
part at least of the ejected, that many of their sons conformed,
and were useful and eminent in the Church of England.[3]

There is no doubt that some of the ejected suffered great hardships, especially at first. They went out before their September
tithes were due, and in many cases they had a difficulty in getting
their share of the year's tithes from their successors. But " there
was a great regard paid to the ejected and silenced ministers
by the patrons of the churches which their nonconformity left
vacant. Some patrons forbore to present a new clerk till they had
tried all means to persuade the former incumbent to conform
and accept a new presentation. . . . Others left them the
nomination of their successors, by which they had opportunity of
putting in their sons or kinsmen, or treating with strangers for
some allowance or other consideration to be made to them." [4]
Sometimes an attempt was made at an arrangement with the
incoming vicar. Newcome said Sir George Booth, later Lord
Delamere, having a living vacant, the rectory of Thornton-le-
Moor, from which Samuel Fisher had been ejected,[5] offered
" to give me the living, that is, to a friend of mine for me." This
seems to imply that he might nominate someone to the patron,
with whom he might make some arrangement. It was given to

[1] W. H. G. Bagshawe, " The Bagshawes of Ford," 1886, pp. 7–92.
[2] Collier, " Eccles. Hist.," 1852, VIII. 442–443.
[3] Kennet, " Reg.," p. 938.   [4] *Idem, ibid.*, p. 894.
[5] Calamy, II. 124; III. 169.

one of Delamere's chaplains, a Presbyterian named Shaw, who announced his intention of conforming, a condition being made that Shaw should sign a bond to resign it whenever Delamere asked him.   Shaw evaded the engagement, at first promising to pay Newcome £40 a year, and after considerable delay offering £20, and finally refused to sign the bond at all.   Delamere tried to make similar arrangements about the living of Ashton-under-Lyne in favour of John Harrison, ejected there, offering to put in Harrison's son Maurice, but Harrison made use of his interest on behalf of Mr. Ellison, who was probably, therefore, much of his own way of thinking.   Shaw gave out that "Delamere engaged his livings for the Nonconformists."[1]   At Tarrant Hinton, in Dorset, Timothy Sacheverell was ejected, and was requested by the patron to nominate a friend who would hold the living and pay him the profits, but he refused.   The patron, however, insisted that he should nominate his successor, which he did.[2]

When the Nonconformists saw that the law was not going to be altered, they proceeded to take what steps they could to mitigate the situation for themselves.   They made lists of all the ejected ministers in every county,[3] and collected money from kindly disposed persons for their maintenance.   For that purpose they had City and County Committees elected, and treasurers appointed to receive and distribute money to the necessitous ejected who could produce certificates of their sufferings.

Nonconformist writers complained that "the ministers were not only excluded from preferments, but cut off from all hope of a livelihood, as far as the industry and craft of their adversaries could reach.   Not so much as a poor vicarage, not a blind chapel or a school was left them: nay, though they offered (as some of them did) to preach for nothing, it must not be allowed them." "Though they were as frugal as possible, they could hardly live.   Some lived on little more than brown bread and water, many had but eight or ten pounds a year to maintain a family, so that a piece of flesh had not come to their tables in six weeks time; their allowance would scarce afford them bread and cheese.   One went to plough six days and preached on the Lord's Day."   One case frequently referred to was that of Dr. Cornelius Burgess,[4] ejected from St. Andrew's, Wells, who was reduced to beggary, a man whose income had formerly been £1000 a year.   This, however, was largely because he had expended all his money in the purchase of episcopal lands, which were

---

[1] "Newcome's Diary," I. September 14th, 1662; Halley, "Lancs. Puritanism," pp. 368–369; Calamy, II. 396; III. 562.
[2] Calamy, III. 424.
[3] "An Exact Catalogue of the Names of Several Ministers lately Ejected out of their Livings in Several Counties," 1663, gives a list of names in ten counties.
[4] Calamy, II. 586; IV. 736.

restored to their rightful owners at the Restoration.[1] In May 1673 Baxter met Bishop Gunning of Chichester, and went to his lodgings with him. Gunning said that it was not a case of conscience with the Nonconformists, but a desire to keep their reputation, and that they were as well off as the Conformists. Baxter tells us he denied this, and put the real facts before the bishop.[2] Thomas Woodcock, who had been ejected from St. Andrew's, Undershaft,[3] discussed the subject in 1681 with John Warren, who had been ejected from Hatfield Broad Oak[4] and the latter said that the ministers who went out in 1662 were generally well provided for.[5]

Many of the deprived clergy had friends and benefactors among the nobility and gentry, especially among the ladies of quality, though John Collinges protested that the amount of financial help they received from this source had been much exaggerated,[6] while Kennet hints that they depended on the countenance and protection of some of these when they refused to conform. But these sympathizers would be a comparatively small number, for most members of the upper classes were in favour of the Anglican settlement, and as a rule only the most distinguished of the ejected received such patronage. " Some invited their late ministers, who had made themselves incapable of public service, to live with them in their private families as chaplains, or tutors, or stewards, in greater ease and sufficient plenty." [7] John Howe lived for five years in Ireland as chaplain to Lord Massarene. Dr. Jacomb, ejected from St. Martin's, Ludgate, lived at the town house of the Countess of Exeter, whose chaplain he had formerly been. Flavel lived at Hudscott Hall, in Devonshire, the residence of the Rolls family. John Thornton, chaplain of Woburn Abbey, had no living to lose, but remained a Nonconformist. During the life of the first Duke of Bedford he lived at Woburn, reading mathematics with William Lord Russell, and afterwards resided there with Lady Rachel, until he lost his sight and retired into private life.[8]

About twenty obtained chaplaincies in hospitals or prisons.[9] A few were appointed to chaplaincies in factories abroad, but there was great opposition to this in several cases. Some went to Scotland, Ireland and America, and prospered there. The Dutch encouraged some to settle in Holland. Matthew Newcomen, for instance, became minister of the English Church at Leyden.[10] Many kept schools, or prepared students for the

[1] C.S.P.D., March 2nd, 1663; Neal, " Puritans," 1732–1738, IV. 403.
[2] " Rel. Baxt.," III. 104–105.
[3] Calamy, II. 44; III. 62. [4] *Idem*, II. 298; III. 460.
[5] " Camden Miscellany," XI. 89. R. Hooke, " The Nonconformist's Champion," 1682, p. 33.
[6] John Collinges, " A Reasonable Account," 1679.
[7] Kennet, " Reg.," p. 894. [8] " Letters of Lady Rachel Russell," I. 114.
[9] Kennet, " Reg.," p. 888 ff. [10] " Ultimum Vale," 1663.

universities, or took in pupils to board with them, and in spite of persecution were able to make a living. The provisions of the Act of Uniformity against schoolmasters were not effectively applied, and in the north of England in particular were rarely enforced. Segar, master of the public school at Blackburn, even retained his post without subscribing. He afterwards became a Nonconformist minister in Darwen.[1] Adam Martindale made a fair living by keeping a school. At one period he took the precaution not to take boys old enough to be examined on oath, and never allowed his maidservant to enter the room where he was teaching, lest she might be made to bring evidence against him.[2]

Some, like Henry Sampson, the ejected vicar of Framlingham,[3] took up the practice of medicine. Between thirty and forty did so. Four at least became lawyers. Others applied themselves to secular employments of greater or less importance, a number possibly turning to their original trades and occupations. Thus, William Benton, ejected from Thurnscoe, Yorkshire, became a malster, though he continued preaching, for he was once imprisoned in York Castle for doing so.[4] Tobacco-cutting is said to have become the occupation of some. Some had private means, while a few married rich wives. Those of them who had money ministered to those who had not, and they were very hospitable to their poorer brethren. Peter Ince [5] got a living as a shepherd on the estate of Mr. Grove, a wealthy man living at Birdbush, in Wiltshire, who when he discovered who his shepherd was built him a meeting-house, where he gathered a Nonconformist congregation.

In discussing how the ejected ministers gained a livelihood, neither Calamy nor White Kennet touches on the most common method—namely, as ministers of Nonconformist congregations. Baxter, indeed, said that by far the greater number forbore all public preaching, and only taught some few in private, at such hours as did not clash with the Church services. " Those that live where they can find small need of their preaching, or else have no call or opportunity, and cannot remove their dwellings, do hold no assemblies, but as other men, do content themselves to be auditors. Those that live where there are godly and peaceable ministers, who yet need help, do lead the people constantly to the parish churches, and teach them themselves at other hours, and help them from house to house: this is ordinary in the counties, and even in London, with many ministers that hold no assemblies, yea, many that were ejected out of City parish churches." [6] Then what were all the meetings

---

[1] Halley, " Lancs. Puritanism," p. 364.   [2] *Idem, ibid.*, p. 399.
[3] Calamy, " Hist. Account of My Own Life," I. 75.
[4] Horsfall Turner, " Northowram Registers."
[5] Calamy, II. 759; IV. 869.
[6] " The Nonconformists' Plea for Peace," 1679, pp. 235-240.

which were broken up by the authorities during all these years? The fact remains that the majority of Nonconformist congregations which to-day trace their descent back to the Restoration period, confess their origin to be due to the ministers who were turned out in 1662. The ministers who held meetings were usually maintained by their congregations, and it was stated that, owing to the liberality of their supporters, many of them were better off than some of the ministers of the Church.[1]

Much has been written about the loss which the Church of England suffered by ejecting so many learned men. To lose learned men is undoubtedly a great loss, but we must avoid exaggeration. All the learning and godliness did not depart on St. Bartholomew's Day; in fact there has hardly ever been a period in which the English Church could show a more brilliant galaxy of scholars than it possessed under the later Stuart sovereigns. The men who went out represented all types of intellect. Thus, of 121 men ejected in London between 1660 and 1662, forty were graduates of Oxford and Cambridge, including six Doctors of Divinity, and eight were graduates of other universities. It is not recorded that the other seventy-three had any degree at all.[2] Taking Palmer's list in " The Nonconformists' Memorial," a rough calculation shows that about 130 or 140 had been fellows, tutors, or other office-holders in the universities. Again, about 150 have a fair list of publications after their names. These 150 include many of the 130 or 140 just mentioned. Examining the lists of published works, we find, as we should find in any similar list of clerical authors during almost any period, that the majority of the books are works of piety, devotion, and controversy, sermons largely predominating. But outstanding names are few, as at all times: there are never very many men who stand head and shoulders above the crowd. In an Appendix to this chapter there is given what seems to be a fair list of the more distinguished men.

Without carping criticism, we might ask whether a fellowship at the time of the Commonwealth really meant that the holder was a first-rate scholar, or whether theological orthodoxy counted for more than mere learning. In Palmer's list of those ejected directly from Oxford and Cambridge one is struck by the comparative fewness of the learned works produced by them. Take, for instance, the case of Edmund Stanton, D.D., who was Fellow of Corpus Christi College, Oxford, and in 1648 President. He was also a member of the Westminster Assembly. All he wrote was a small " Treatise of Christian Conscience," " A Dialogue between a Minister and a Stranger," and some Latin verses at

---

[1] Salmon, " Exam. Burnet," I. 546. For a detailed statement of the after careers of the ejected see Kennet, " Reg.," pp. 889–938, and the criticisms of Kennet's list in Calamy, " Hist. Account of My Own Life," II. 547.
[2] T. G. Crippen, " Victoria Hist. of London," I. 376.

the accession of Charles II.,[1] though there seems no doubt in his particular case that he was a man of learning. Learning at both universities had undoubtedly declined. Sancroft found at Emmanuel College, Cambridge, in 1660 that there was outward conformity, but that Hebrew and Greek were out of fashion. Ten years later Dr. John North, afterwards Master of Trinity, found that the seniors were " grave and empty men," who spent most of their time in bowls and gossip. The senior common rooms in 1670 would have many members who had entered in the Parliamentary times.[2] At Oxford, Wood—a somewhat jaundiced witness, it must be admitted—spoke scornfully of the condition of the university, though he thought the people who were coming in were worse than those who were going out. He said in 1662 that it was then " an age wherein zealous concernment in studies is laughed at, and many wonder at the folly of those before the war time, that spent so much time and broke their brains in scholastic divinity and metaphysics."[3] On the other hand, Burnet, though he could hardly speak of his own knowledge, said that learning was then in a flourishing condition, that the oriental languages were much studied, the Fathers much read, and mathematics and philosophy held in great esteem.[4] However this may be, not all the learned men left the Church of England at the Restoration. Amongst those who remained behind were the men who won for Anglican scholarship in their day the epithet of *stupor mundi*. The Church had been rent and torn, but while she retained Wilkins, Sanderson, Thorndyke, Cosin, Barrow, Pearson, Jeremy Taylor, Whichcote, Cudworth, More, Sancroft, Patrick, Stillingfleet, Sparrow, Bull, Leighton, South, and others like them, she could face the future with a calm courage.

There was certainly some difficulty in finding successors to take the places of all those who went out, and there is little doubt that some incompetent persons crept in. At Coley, in Yorkshire, after Oliver Heywood's ejection, there were six ministers in twelve years, two of whom left under a cloud,[5] and a contrast has been drawn between the pious, learned and able Nonconformists who were turned out, and the numerous incompetent, irreligious and ignorant persons whom the bishops put in.[6] As for the education of the new ordinands, it must not be forgotten that for many years the universities had been in the hands of the Puritans, that the sons of Church-people would have

[1] Calamy, II. 63; III. 97; Richard Mayo, " The Life and Death of Edmund Staunton, D.D.," 1673.
[2] A. Gray, " Cambridge Univ.: An Episodical Hist.," Cambridge, 1926, p. 195.
[3] Wood, " Life and Times," I. 360, 465.
[4] Salmon, " Examination of Burnet," I. 540.
[5] Hunter, " Oliver Heywood," p. 140.
[6] Halley, " Lancs. Puritanism," pp. 392–393.

had little or no opportunity of learning Anglican theology there, and that this would distinctly reduce the number of Oxford and Cambridge candidates at first. Some of the unsatisfactory clergy, too, were probably to be found among those who simply made a profession of conformity without intending to observe it.[1] On the other hand, it was stated that the churches rendered void by Nonconformity were filled with men of learned education and good character, very different from those put in under the Commonwealth, " mean and mechanic fellows, scandalous for their ignorance." [2]

The expulsion meant more than the loss of individual members, however eminent and distinguished; " it was the close of an effort which had been going on since the Reformation to bring the Church of England into closer union with the Protestant churches of the Continent." [3] Henceforth, the Anglican Church had nothing to do with these, but firmly asserted its Reformation position as Catholic and reformed. Hitherto, the name Puritan had been loosely used to include persons within and without the national establishment who desired what they believed to be a purer doctrine and worship. Burnet says that at this time the name of Puritan was changed into that of Protestant Nonconformist.[4] Some of the people hitherto called Puritans remained in the Church, and became what was afterwards known as the Low Church party; but the majority went out. After this the word Puritan generally dropped out of use, and the people formerly called by that name are henceforth mostly to be found in the ranks of the Nonconformists. Not all, as we have seen; for the complaint of the Anglican was that so many subscribed on St. Bartholomew's Day who did not really accept the principles of Anglicanism. Sheldon wanted to keep them out. So did Ward of Salisbury and others. But under the pressure or influence of bishops like Juxon, Earle, Morley, Sanderson, Lacey, Wilkins and Reynolds, many of them remained in the Church. Henceforward the Church cannot claim to be the Church of the whole nation. In addition to the Romanists, she is faced by organised and increasing bodies of Dissenters. They call themselves Nonconformists, or nonconforming Churchmen, it is true, for they cannot quite get rid of the idea that there can only be one Church for the nation. Onward to the Revolution there will be futile attempts to heal the breach by compromise or comprehension. Finally, in 1689, the only other alternative, that of toleration, will be accepted, and all claim to membership of the Church will cease, though the members of the various sects will still call themselves Nonconformists.

[1] Stoughton, " Hist. of Religion in Eng.," III. 492.
[2] Kennet, " Reg.," p. 789.
[3] J. R. Green, " Hist. of Eng. People," III. 362.
[4] Burnet, " Own Time," I. 345.

But St. Bartholomew's Day was not the birthday of Nonconformity, as is so often claimed—Nonconformity, that is, in the modern sense. True, the *name* Nonconformist first appeared at that time, but there had been separations from the Church of England long before that; Baptists, Independents, Quakers, and many other sects had split off at various times in the century succeeding the Elizabethan settlement, and had set up for themselves. The people who went out in 1662 formed Congregationalist, Baptist, and so-called Presbyterian churches. This introduced no new factor into the situation; it was but a continuation of what had gone on on a smaller scale before. It was only the name that was new. The new separatists called themselves Nonconformists, or sometimes nonconforming Churchmen, but the Church-people called them Dissenters, and that is what they were, though they shied at the name, for they dissented from the Church's system, doctrine and worship. The real Nonconformists were the men who remained in the Church but did not conform. What the Act of Uniformity did was to accept the facts, and the date of its coming into operation merely marks the day when a new schism took effect and some old ones were recognised as permanent. Henceforth, the idea of reuniting all the sects into one national Church becomes increasingly recognised as hopeless, and Dissent is accepted as a permanent factor in the national life.

The Independents and Baptists were again what they had been before the Commonwealth—bodies separated entirely from the Anglican Church. The Quakers had been separate from their very beginning, and so had many of the numerous minor sects. But to all these has now been added a new body—the Presbyterians. The difference in their case was that they did not think at first that the schism would be permanent. They hoped for a reaction, which might lead to their comprehension in the national Church. Some had hoped that their going out would cause fresh confusions, and upset the re-established system. They thought that if they went out in great numbers Parliament would drop the test, or that their party would be able to make better terms. But once out, when they found their hope unrealised, they could not go back again.[1] Some of them were in favour of occasional attendance at the Church services. But they were for a long time only a loose federation of congregations. Looking to a future comprehension, they would not think of the present needs, and so form themselves into an efficient organisation. The ministers contented themselves with gaining a livelihood by their ministrations during the present distress. It was probably their lack of organisation and common purpose which made the Presbyterian churches so weak against the storms of unbelief and Unitarianism which beat upon them later.

[1] N. Salmon, " Lives of the English Bishops," 1733, p. 37; T. Salmon, " Examination of Burnet," I. 340.

At first some of the ministers contented themselves with what they called repetitions. It had long been their custom to repeat the outlines of their discourses, or of the discourses of other preachers, to their families and friends on Sunday evenings. After their ejectment they often conducted these repetitions on weekday evenings as well. These domestic exercises became public services. Preaching tours were arranged by them or for them. Thus, the nonconforming Churchman, as he called himself, became what other people called him, a Dissenter and a separatist.

The laity were not turned out. Those of them who were validly baptized were members of the Church by virtue of their baptism. Of course, as a result of the long period of ecclesiastical anarchy and the doctrines preached by Anabaptists and others in Anglican pulpits, there were very many people who were not baptized at all. Numbers of the laity deliberately went out; that is to say, they went and worshipped elsewhere, that was all. For years now Presbyterians, Congregationalists, Baptists and others had got possession of Anglican buildings to the exclusion of the rightful owners. These people were not turned out of the Church of England. They had left it long ago, did not profess to be members of it, depised it, and hurled at it all the epithets which Israel of old had hurled at the enemies of God. Now, as they believed, the hireling shepherds, mumbling the mass-book, or something as bad, and wearing the rags of the Scarlet Woman, had come back, so they fled from the presence of the idolater. All this can be found in scores of pamphlets of the time. Their consciences told them that they must continue to worship in their own way. Thus, the members of the Independent church at Altham, in Lancashire, declared that they intended to continue the connection, and that neither censures in the bishops' courts nor Acts of Parliament could discharge their pastor from his office.[1] If they chose, however, to follow with their favourite minister, they had no ground for complaint if they were not allowed any of the privileges of membership of the Church with which they refused to unite. That the authorities tried to suppress them was another matter.

Similarly, no one denied the ministers were members of the Church if they were baptized, and so long as they did not deliberately separate from it. Some of them had Anglican orders, and forsook the Anglican Church. But the great question for the majority of them was whether men with Presbyterian ordination were *clergy* of the Church of England. As that Church held a definite position on the subject which they could not conscientiously accept, they went out, or, as they preferred to say, were turned out. They were turned out, or went out, because they refused to accept what they considered to be re-ordination,

[1] Fletcher, " Hist. of Independency," IV. ch. iii.

and many of them were honester men than some at least who stayed in.

Many of those who conformed in 1662 or later had no real sympathy with Anglicanism; they took the oaths but did not keep them, they neglected to use the Prayer Book, and they preached against the institutions to which they had sworn submission.[1] Or if they did not go so far as that, they performed divine service in a way which showed their contempt for the Prayer Book. Many of them gabbled the service so as to get more time for long extemporary prayers in the pulpit, and for the sermon. In some places the congregation waited outside till it was time to come in for " the conceived prayer " and sermon. These extemporary prayers offered in the pulpit before the sermon in place of the Bidding Prayer became a distinctive party badge. Communicants were allowed to receive standing or sitting as they preferred, and the altar was sometimes brought down into the body of the church for them. In 1662 Archdeacon Basire said that in many churches in Northumberland there were neither Bibles, Prayer Books, surplices, fonts, altars, nor anything else necessary for the service of God. Dean Granville complained of his curate in Cornwall not using the surplice, in order to please the people. In 1675 Bishop Croft of Hereford did not think it " wise to be zealous for the surplice." In 1684 there were still churches in the diocese of Bath and Wells where there was no surplice, where the altar had no cover, or was not railed off, and where there was no chalice or no Prayer Book.[2] The members of the Puritan party in the Church refused to catechise the children on Sunday afternoons because it interfered with their sermons, and because, of course, they disliked the doctrines of the Church Catechism. Archdeacon Conant held conventicles in his house, and administered the sacrament to people sitting in their pews.[3] When Kidder became incumbent of St. Helens, London, he found members of his congregation who refused to kneel to communicate, and Henchman, Bishop of London, advised him not to drive them away.

The Bishops had special difficulties with a somewhat numerous class of men, the lecturers. They were not curates, but only preachers, and were almost independent of the ecclesiastical authorities. Many of them were Nonconformists at heart, and by their discourses did much to undermine the respect of their hearers for the rules and customs of the Church. A tract which was really a mock history of the Nonconformists' doings since St. Bartholomew's Day, and gave what pretended to be a burlesque record of the minutes of their meetings, satirised the nonconforming Churchman who did not go out as one who "complieth

[1] Overton, " Life in the Eng. Church," p. 1.
[2] Ken's Visitation Articles, 1684.
[3] C.S.P.D., 417/136, December 5th, 1681.

with the public injunctions of the Church, yet professeth they are a burden and a grief to him." [1] Some of the Anglican ministers wore no cassock, set up miserable readers in order to make the Prayer Book contemptible, and then prayed for an hour themselves, preached old sermons of Puritan preachers, " full of cant about indwelling, soul-saving, and heart supporting," they put on a countenance of Puritan gloom, set the Sabbath above holy days, and " a pure heart above the surplice," and were more full of doctrine than the inculcation of good works.   They complained about the ceremonies, christened, married and buried by the Directory, and gave communion in the same way, dispensing with kneeling even in public. [2]   Others neglected the observation of festivals, for their own convenience changed the customary hours of service, and sometimes omitted services, at least in the afternoon.   On the other hand, there were some, not puritanically minded, who put off the services that they and their congregation might go to a horse race or some other amusement. [3] Ralph Josselin was summoned to the bishop's court in 1669 for not wearing the surplice, and returned " safe."   He was recalcitrant up to 1680, in which year he noted, " Rid to court; the matter is the surplice, which I see no sin to use, and shall endeavour to live as quietly as may be, to the end of my race." [4]

When Frampton became Bishop of Gloucester in 1680 he found several " Covenanting priests and intruders," who did not use the Prayer-Book services.   One of them told him that if he did, it hindered him from praying in the pulpit as long as he desired. In one place he visited he found the congregation had never heard the Litany.   Another incumbent held a morning lecture in another church as well as his living, and never used the Prayer Book in either.   This man used to read the consecration prayer in the Communion service, and apparently communicated his parishioners, from the reading-desk, without ever communicating himself. [5]   This was not uncommon. [6]   Nicholas Billingsley, who had been ejected from Webley, in Herefordshire, [7] was in episcopal orders, and later in the reign got possession of the chapel of ease at Blakeney, in Gloucestershire, one of those episcopal chapels about which there arose so much difficulty at this period.   Here he was said to preach rhapsodies without sense or coherence, used as little as he liked of the Prayer Book, neglected holy days, and to show his contempt for the surplice, carried one during the service slung over his shoulder. [8]   Joseph

[1] " Cabala: or, an Impartial Account of the Nonconformists' Private Designs, Actings and Ways," by Sir John Birkenhead, 1663.
[2] " The Mystery and Iniquity of Nonconformity," 1664.
[3] R. Granville, " Life of Dennis Granville," p. 131.
[4] " Diary of Ralph Josselin," May 17th, 1680.
[5] T. S. Evans, " Life of Bishop Frampton," 1871, pp. 133–140.
[6] See " Parish Churches turned into Conventicles," by Richard Hart, 1683.
[7] Calamy, II. 358.
[8] T. S. Evans, " Life of Bishop Frampton," 1871, pp. 133–140.

Crabb, vicar of Netherbury, Dorsetshire, had been chaplain to a regiment under the Commonwealth, and had not received Anglican orders, unless he had done so after November 20th, 1660. He had never administered the sacraments, but he had preached against Anglicanism, and had prayed publicly that the King might not come to the throne. In consequence of all this he was ejected by the local justices from Netherbury vicarage about May 1661.[1] He afterwards conformed, and was presented to the living of Axminster, but, said Calamy, " though he was in the established Church, yet in his principles and way of preaching and praying, he so resembled the Nonconforming ministers that he was still looked upon as one of them." [2] In 1665 objection was made to Thomas Sanderson, vicar of Thengdon, Northamptonshire, on the ground that he did not read Morning and Evening Prayer, and had not subscribed the declarations.[3] Edmund Hickeringill, vicar of All Saints', Colchester, boasted of breaking the law wholesale; he had not worn a surplice, except at Communion, for several years, he did not wear a hood in summer-time because it was too hot, and he was against all vestments and all ceremonies. He insinuated that none of the clergy really conformed, and declared that the bishops were as bad; in particular he complained of the way in which the latter administered confirmation without any inquiry as to the fitness of the candidates.[4] In 1666 there was an Act before Parliament to unite the churches of Southampton into one parish, and it was stated that during the last twenty years only one parish out of the five then existing had been served by " a conformable minister." [5]

" Thus preposterous are we," wrote Dennis Granville, " in our obedience and conformity wherein we pride ourselves, to the exclusion of some honester and more sincere men than ourselves, who had given as loud an assent and consent to our Common Prayer Book as we had, had they expected to have been indulged half so far as we indulge ourselves." [6] These men were the real Nonconformists, not the Dissenters, and they were represented in the eighteenth century by the Low Church party. In that century of slackness, coldness, and inefficiency, their principles and customs spread so widely, and rooted themselves so deeply, that in the days of the Oxford Movement it came as a shock to the majority of Churchmen to be told that neglect of the plain rules of the Prayer Book was not loyalty to the Reformation settlement, and was disloyalty to the Church of England.

---

[1] C.S.P.D., 446/37.   [2] Calamy, III. 451–452. Palmer omits him.
[3] Kennet, " Reg.," p. 758.
[4] Hickeringill, " The Black Nonconformist," 1681.
[5] Hist. MSS. Com. VIII. i. MSS. House Lords, 103*b*, 134; Lords Journals, XII. 34; Commons Journals, VIII. 683.
[6] R. Granville, " Life of Dennis Granville," p. 216.

Strange scenes sometimes occurred in churches during the Commonwealth times. There was a certain John Simpson who was a lecturer at St. Botolph's, Bishopsgate Street, and was a Baptist with leanings to Antinomianism. This man got together a party in the parish, and tried to oust Zachary Crofton, the rector, and on occasion when Crofton was preaching in the pulpit Simpson would be preaching in the opposite gallery.[1] There were violent scenes in Rochester cathedral in 1656, when Richard Coppin and his followers argued hotly with their opponents amid roars of laughter and rude interruptions. Disorder was frequent in the churches, and the wildest doctrines were preached. As far as the Church of England was concerned, the Act of Uniformity brought deliverance from this kind of thing, and from the irresponsible autocracy of the Puritan minister. Under the Cromwellian system the parish minister, whether ordained or not, whether Presbyterian, Anabaptist or Fifth Monarchy man, could preach and do exactly as he liked, provided his preaching and behaviour did not savour of " popery " or " prelacy." If he satisfied the central authority at Westminster for approving public preachers, was accepted by the Triers, and was not turned out by the Ejectors, the parish had to receive him and pay for his maintenance. They had also to accept such ministrations as he chose to give them. But it was quite possible that he would confine those ministrations to those whom he called " the godly "—that is to say, certain persons of whose spiritual condition he was pleased to approve.[2] Many of the Puritan ministers arbitrarily refused baptism to the majority of their parishioners, some refused to baptize children, and many parishes never had a celebration of the Holy Communion at all. No one says that these men were not honest and conscientious. But they were not members of the Church of England. What the Commonwealth had set up was an ecclesiastical Civil Service, the servants of which had possession of the property of the Church.

Moreover, the Act of Uniformity was the work of the great majority of the nation, acting in a constitutional way through its representatives in Parliament. Both the Conformists and Nonconformists desired that the matter should be settled in that way. It was the laity, through their accredited representatives (for whether the list of voters was large or small that same Parliament did in its early days represent the feeling of the nation), who made the Act more stringent than it otherwise would have been. The Nonconformists wished the King to exercise a prerogative which he thought he possessed, and which his Parliament denied that he possessed. Because they had helped to bring the King back, the Puritans thought he ought to exercise

---

[1] Kennet, " Reg.," p. 797.
[2] T. Hancock, " The Act of Uniformity a Measure of Liberation," 1895.

an autocratic power, as Cromwell had done, to give them licence to do as they pleased.

The greatest harm which came from the Act of Uniformity was due to the way in which it was put in force. When it was finally passed, the King should have let it alone. Charles had given the malcontents to understand that between the time when the Act was passed and the " appointed day " he would try to get the operation of the Act postponed, provided that they would use the Prayer Book as much as they conscientiously could. But they did not use the Prayer Book, and he did not get what he wanted. Immediately after the Act came into force he began to talk about making use of his dispensing power. That, of course, met with great opposition, and even the Dissenters themselves, or the majority of them, feared lest such a power might be used for the advantage of the Papist. The constant hope, nevertheless, that something would be done to nullify the Act of Uniformity kept many, who had been surprised into separation, from reconsidering their decision. The persecution to which the ejected and their followers were liable, persecution which meant fines, imprisonment, and sometimes death in prison, increased the bitterness, and hardened the schism. Persecution, to be successful, if it could be successful, should be steady, ruthless, and systematic. In the whole dark history of religious persecution this has hardly ever been the case, and it certainly was not so in in England, where the laws of the Clarendon Code were only executed spasmodically, and where there were always very many sympathisers ready to shield the persecuted.

In one respect at least the Act of Uniformity was a failure. Reference has already been made to the " nonconforming conformists "—that is, men who took the oaths and made the subscriptions, and then ignored the rules of the Church. But there were some Nonconformists who remained in the Church and did not even technically conform. One of these was Henry Swift, vicar of Penistone, Yorkshire, for forty years. The chief families in the parish, the Bosvilles, Riches, and Wordsworths, were of Puritan sympathies, and so he had their support. There was some question about the right of presentation to the living, which occasioned a lapse after Swift died in 1689, which may have conduced to this irregular proceeding. At the Archbishop's visitation in 1674 he was presented for not burying the dead according to the rites of the Book of Common Prayer, for not wearing a surplice in church, for not announcing holy days, for preaching without his surplice, and for instructing the children in other catechisms than that provided by the Prayer Book.[1] Heyrick, who refused to conform,[2] was allowed to continue Warden of Manchester collegiate church. John Tilsley, vicar

[1] Hunter, " Life of Oliver Heywood," p. 156; " Yorkshire Diaries and Autobiographies," Surtees Soc., p. 157.   [2] But cf. Halley, p. 367.

of Dean, in Lancashire, was ejected by the local magistrates soon after the Restoration. Later on Bishop Wilkins permitted an arrangement by which Tilsley was to preach while the vicar read the prayers. A new vicar was appointed during the time that Tilsley thus acted as lecturer. This was Richard Hatton, who, though he was willing to conform, refused to renounce the Covenant. Nevertheless, though the induction was technically void, Bishop Pearson inducted him on the King's presentation. Tilsley was, in 1678, presented at the Assizes for nonconformity, and ejected.[1] Joseph Thompson, vicar of Sefton, Lancashire, gave way to the lawful incumbent in 1660, and afterwards acted as his curate for a time.[2] But Calamy counts him as one of the ejected Nonconformists.[3] Robert Sherborne, who was ejected from the vicarage of Cawood, was the son of Robert Sherborne, vicar of Brayton, near Selby. The father conformed and kept his living, and the son went to live with him, and assisted him without conforming, the elder reading the prayers and administering the sacraments, the younger usually preaching.[4] At Southwold, in Suffolk, there was a vicar named Sharpen, who lived at a distance, and only preached in his church once a month; but he allowed the Dissenters to use the church every Sunday, and during the week if they wished. Every fourth Sunday in the month the Anglican priest and the Independent minister both held services, the custom being that he who entered the church first officiated first. When he finished the other took his turn, most of the congregation remaining through both services. But a new incumbent was appointed in 1680, and then the Dissenters had to find a place of their own.[5] At Poole, in Dorsetshire, Thomas Thackham remained undisturbed by the Act of Uniformity till 1667. His successor, Samuel Hardy, also a Nonconformist, held the living till 1682. The parish was a royal peculiar, and outside the jurisdiction of the bishop, which explains why these vicars were able to set ecclesiastical authority at naught for so long a time. John Wesley, who had been ejected from Winterbourne Whitechurch, was minister of an Independent congregation in Poole until he died in 1670, and there is reason to believe that after his death his congregation did not fill up his place for two years, attending Hardy's services instead, though Hardy was accustomed to use just so much of the Prayer Book as he liked.[6]

There are other instances of Nonconformists holding livings. John Chandler, who had Presbyterian ordination, remained vicar

[1] Halley, " Lancs. Puritanism," p. 362; Calamy, II. 402.
[2] " Victoria Hist. of Lancaster," II. 67.
[3] Calamy, II. 411.
[4] *Idem*, II. 816.
[5] Browne, " Congregationalism in Norfolk and Suffolk," p. 434.
[6] Densham and Ogle, " Congregational Churches of Dorset," p. 182.

of Petto, in Essex. Ashurst, the incumbent of Arlsey, in Bedfordshire, who had, however, been episcopally ordained,[1] continued
to officiate, using portions of the Prayer Book, and depending on
the contributions of his flock for his maintenance. He was old,
and the living was very poor, so perhaps it was thought he was
not worth troubling about.[2]   In the diocese of Gloucester, Henry
Stubbs was allowed to keep his living, and Richard Hawes,
in the diocese of Llandaff, was allowed to preach without
subscribing.

There were in the rural deanery of Clun four well-known
Puritans, Samuel Berkeley, rector of Clungunford (1630–1672),
George Lawson of More (1657–1678), John Gough of Bucknell
(1647–1674), and John Wilcox of Mainstone (1649–1688). It is
uncertain whether they conformed, or whether powerful patrons
enabled them to retain their livings.[3]   These four are doubtful
cases, but the others mentioned above ought not to be enumerated
among the ejected. They neither went out nor were silenced.

In many large parishes where it was too far for the people in
the outlying districts and hamlets to attend the parish church,
chapels-of-ease had been built in past times for their convenience.
Some of these, especially in the counties of Lancashire and
Yorkshire, were in the hands of Nonconformists for a long time
after the Restoration. In some cases, owing perhaps to a dearth
of curates, they were unprovided for, and the Dissenters stepped
in and made use of them. In other cases Presbyterians and
others, who had been appointed curates in charge of them before
the Restoration, remained in possession without conforming,
sometimes without this laxity coming to the bishop's notice, or at
any rate without his taking any steps to interfere. In 1667, the
Nonconformists got possession of the chapel of Darwen, Lancashire, which had been supplied by the clergy of the parish
since the Restoration. By some oversight on the part of the
authorities they got a licence for it after the Declaration of
Indulgence, broke into it, and kept possession for some years.[4]
Thomas Kay, or Key, and after him Charles Segar, both Dissenters, ministered at the ancient chapel at Walmsley, near
Bolton, and the Church did not recover possession till 1706.[5]
There was a more doubtful case at Rivington. Samuel Newton,
who was ejected from the chapel, found it unoccupied, and conducted services there; and was succeeded by John Walker.[6]
But since Newton died *incumbent* of Rivington, perhaps he con-
formed.[7] John Jolly, without conforming, got possession of
Norbury chapel.[8]   He also preached occasionally at Gorton

[1] Calamy, II. 93.   [2] Kennet, " Reg.," p. 758.
[3] " Shropshire Arch. Soc.," 3rd Series, IX. 309.
[4] Nightingale, " Lancs. Nonconformity," II. 238.
[5] *Idem, ibid.*, III. 44.   [6] *Idem, ibid.*, III. 81.
[7] Halley, " Lancs. Puritanism," p. 363.
[8] See the " Notebook of Thomas Jolly."

chapel, which seems to have remained more or less in Dissenting hands till the end of the century.[1]

At Rusholme there was a chapel known as Birch chapel, which had been built by the Birch family on their estate. In 1662 Robert Birch was ejected, and became a physician. The local magnates, Squire Worsley, Colonel Thomas Birch, and Captain Oliver Edge, who paid the stipend of the minister, would not have a Conformist, and in 1672 invited Henry Finch, who had been ejected from Walton, to minister there, but the building was recovered by the Church of England at the Revolution.[2] One Harrison, it is uncertain whether his Christian name was Cuthbert or Ralph, arrived from Ireland soon after 1662, and got possession of Elswick chapel. Bishop Wilkins did nothing in the matter, though Harrison officiated at marriages there. He was licensed to it in 1672.[3] For a time after the ejection of John Walker from Newton Heath chapel, Manchester, the Nonconformists had possession. Then Lawton, a Conformist, was minister there till 1688, and the Dissenters regained it once more till the end of the century.[4] James Wood was ejected from Chowbent chapel in 1662, but seems to have ministered occasionally there before 1676. After 1688 the Dissenters had it uninterruptedly till 1723, when the Church acquired it and consecrated it.[5] Many of these chapels seem to have been unconsecrated buildings. From Hindley James Bradshaw was ejected in 1662, and no Anglican curate was appointed till 1668. In 1690 Thomas Whalley, a Dissenter, was put in as minister by one of the trustees. A lawsuit followed, which was won by the Church of England, in 1697.[6] Peter Atkinson[7] and his son, also called Peter,[8] were in such favour with the local gentry that they were able to remain at Elhill chapel long after the Act of Uniformity. Henry Welsh of Chorley ministered in his chapel till his death in 1665, and it has been suggested that the rector of the parish provided some one to read the service, and then the Nonconformist prayed and preached.[9] Thomas Gregg is spoken of as ejected from St. Helen's episcopal chapel in Lancashire in 1662; but he seems to have continued to preach there till his death in 1681. Bishop Cartwright promised to appoint a curate to the chapel, and so to put an end to this intrusion, but nothing was done, for in 1688 James Naylor was Presbyterian minister there, and the building was not recovered by the Church till 1710.[10]

[1] Nightingale, " Lancs. Nonconformity," V. 50.
[2] Halley, " Lancs. Puritanism," pp. 358–359.
[3] Idem, ibid., pp. 360–361; Nightingale, " Lancs. Nonconformity," I. 213.
[4] Nightingale, " Lancs. Nonconformity," V. 38.   [5] Idem, ibid., V. 94.
[6] " Hist. Soc. Lancs. and Cheshire," 1910, p. 67.
[7] Calamy, II. 410; III. 566.   [8] Idem, II. 417; III. 573.
[9] " Victoria Hist. of Lancaster," II. 68.
[10] Nightingale, " Lancs. Nonconformity," IV. 128; Halley, " Lancs. Puritanism," p. 361; " Cartwright's Diary," Chetham Soc., XXI. 206.

The minister of Toxteth Park episcopal chapel in 1662 was Thomas Crompton. He did not conform, but remained undisturbed. The local magnate, Lord Molyneux, was a Romanist, and held the appropriated tithes. The Dissenters held the building on a lease from him, and apparently his agents entered it in their books as a house belonging to him.[1] Timothy Smith was another Lancashire minister counted among the ejected, though he remained at Longridge chapel, near Preston in Lancashire, till his death in 1679. " It being an obscure place with a small salary, there was no striving for it," says Calamy.[2]

From Rainsford chapel, in Lancashire, Roger Baldwin was ejected, but James Bradshaw, who had been ejected from Hindley chapel, moved there, and got possession in 1672. He lived there in peace, part of the time through the forbearance of Bishop Pearson, and he kept it by a subterfuge. When his churchwardens attended a visitation they were asked, " Have you the Common Prayer read yearly in your chapel? " The usual question was thus modified for Bradshaw's benefit, and the wardens could reply in the affirmative, because he was on friendly terms with some of the neighbouring clergy, and he got some of them to come every year and read the Prayer Book service. He was not ejected till somewhere about 1700.[3] There was a second Thomas Crompton,[4] who was ejected in 1662 from Astley chapel, in the parish of Leigh, Lancashire. Calamy says that on the invitation of the congregation he returned thither, and preached, without subscription, contenting himself with reading a few of the prayers. Here there was a dispute about the right to the patronage, and it was only after long legal proceedings that the question was decided in favour of the vicar of Leigh. While the litigation was going on, Crompton kept possession, and died there.[5] John Lever, of Cockey Moor chapel, was silenced, according to Calamy, in 1662. But he was there in the following year, when articles were presented in the Chester consistory court against the wardens for " allowing Nonconformists to preach there." [6] John Angier, of Denton in Lancashire, remained in possession of the chapel there without conforming, under three bishops. He was related to some of the best families in the county, and was very popular. After his death in 1677 a Conformist was appointed.[7]

---

[1] Nightingale, " Lancs. Nonconformity," VI. 82 ; Halley, " Lancs. Puritanism," pp. 359–360.

[2] Calamy, II. 412 ; III. 567 ; Palmer, II. 367.

[3] Nightingale, " Lancs. Nonconformity," IV. 170 ; Halley, " Lancs. Puritanism," pp. 361–362 ; " Hist. Soc. Lancs. and Cheshire," 1910, p. 67.

[4] Palmer, II. 351.

[5] Halley, " Lancs. Puritanism," p. 363.

[6] Idem, ibid., pp. 363–364.

[7] " Hist. Soc. Lancs. and Cheshire," 1880–1881, p. 169 ; Nightingale, " Lancs. Nonconformity," V. 355–356.

There was an old episcopal chapel at Idle, in Yorkshire, and at the Leeds Sessions in 1689 the Nonconformists applied for a licence for it, and it was granted. But it was a consecrated building, and at the Barnsley Sessions in the same year it was taken away from them. Dissenters had used it previously, for Thomas Johnson, ejected from Sherburn, Leeds, preached there publicly for two years, beginning in 1672. He received no fees, did not live in the place, but rode over to it from his home at Painsthorpe, near Wakefield, and so apparently no notice was taken for a time.[1]

Some of the chapels, of course, were built by local landed proprietors. Thus, at Great Houghton Hall, near Darfield in Yorkshire, there was a chapel erected in 1650. After 1662 a number of Nonconformist ministers came under the protection of Sir Edward Rhodes, and after his death, of his widow. Oliver Heywood often preached at Houghton, so did Thomas Johnson mentioned above.[2] The chapel afterwards came into the hands of the Church of England.[3] At Ellenthorpe, near Boroughbridge, Lady Brooke built a small chapel in 1658, and Presbyterian ministers officiated at it.[4] Robert Dyneley, the squire of Bramhope in Wharfedale, the head of an old Yorkshire family, built a chapel there in 1649, and appointed as minister Jeremiah Crossley,[5] and he continued there under his patron's protection without conforming. Dale says, " He did not comply with the Act of Uniformity, and may therefore he reckoned among the ejected ";[6] a somewhat surprising statement. This chapel at Bramhope is said to have been one of the earliest instances of a foundation for religious purposes under a private trust deed. There were at least four others in the diocese of York: Ellenthorpe, Morley, Stannington, and Great Houghton. After a generation the Dyneley family conformed, and the chapel became episcopalian. Of the others, Ellenthorpe, Morley, and Stannington remained Nonconformist.[7] The old parochial chapelry of Charlesworth, in Glossop parish, with burial rights attached, remained in Presbyterian hands from 1662 to the reign of Anne, when it passed to the Independents.[8] Nathaniel Baxter, who was ejected from St. Michael-upon-Wyre, Lancashire, was some years afterwards invited by Mr. Pegg, proprietor of Beauchief Abbey, in Derbyshire, to preach in the unoccupied chapel there, which he did without molestation for seventeen

[1] Turner, " Nonconformity in Idle."
[2] *Idem, ibid.*; Dale, " Yorkshire Puritanism and Nonconformity," p. 90.
[3] Hunter, " Life of Oliver Heywood," pp. 163–164, implies it did not.
[4] Miall, " Congregationalism in Yorkshire," p. 264.
[5] Palmer calls him Zachariah.
[6] " Yorkshire Puritanism and Early Nonconformity," p. 46.
[7] Hunter, " Life of Oliver Heywood," pp. 163–164; Miall, " Congregationalism in Yorkshire," pp. 259, 320.
[8] J. C. Cox, " Victoria Hist. Derbyshire," II. 32.

years, Mr. Pegg paying him a salary of £16 a year.[1] John
Jones, ejected from Mellor, on the borders of Derbyshire, in 1660,
preached in the district round Hatherlow in Cheshire till his
death in 1671.   He held services in Chadkirk and other episcopal
chapels.   In 1672, or thereabouts, his son, Gamaliel Jones,
settled down in Chadkirk.   He was a pupil of Frankland, and
therefore probably not ordained in the Church of England.   He
was not turned out till 1706, when the building became episcopalian once more.[2]   At Honley, in Yorkshire, Mr. Dury, or
Drury, a Nonconformist minister, kept possession of the public
chapel.[3]   Ringway chapel, in Cheshire, originally episcopal, was
in the hands of the Nonconformists till 1720.   John Brereton
ministered there for some time.[4]   At Whitley chapel, in the same
county, John Machin did not conform, but remained until his
death in 1664.   He was followed by a Nonconformist minister
named Kynaston, and he by Ralph Ainsworth.[5]

These cases of holding office without conforming occurred
mostly in the north, particularly in Lancashire, and less so in
Yorkshire.   The chapels especially were often in out-of-the-way
places, far from the reach of informers.   Some of them were
unoccupied, and in some cases, perhaps, the patron had no wish
to make any changes as long as the ecclesiastical authorities
took no steps.   That people not in Anglican orders were ministering in them was in some cases undoubtedly known to the
authorities,[6] but they did, perhaps could do, nothing.

At North Meols, in Lancashire, James Starke remained rector
from 1640 to 1684.   He was a friend of the Nonconformists, and
seems to have been counted as one.   It has been suggested that
if he had conformed it would have been remarked upon by his
Nonconformist friends.   He certainly preached in the parish
church at Ormskirk in 1677, at the funeral of Nathaniel Heywood,
who had been ejected from that parish.[7]   The fact that he
preached the funeral sermon of a Dissenter shows his sympathies,
the fact that he preached in a parish church is of no great weight
one way or the other.   Oliver Heywood was occasionally
invited to preach by the conforming clergy.   William Tong, a
friend of Philip Henry, preached sometimes at Cockshot chapel,
in Shropshire, but the vicar of Ellesmere made complaint in
the ecclesiastical courts, and he had to cease.[8]   John Salkeld,
ejected from Worlington, in Suffolk, sometimes preached in the

---

[1] Halley, " Lancs. Puritanism," p. 387.
[2] Urwick, " Nonconformity in Cheshire," pp. 312–322.
[3] Hunter, " Life of Oliver Heywood," p. 157; Palmer, III. 438.
[4] Calamy, II. 134; Urwick, " Nonconformity in Cheshire," p. 369.
[5] *Idem, ibid.*, p. 404.
[6] " Church Discipline after the Reformation," Hist. Soc. Lancs. and Cheshire,
1912, p. 43.
[7] Calamy, II. 394; Nightingale, " Lancs. Nonconformity," VI. 8.
[8] Wilson, " Dissenting Churches in London," II. 23.

parish churches of Walsham-le-Willows and Badwell Ash. In 1670 it was discovered that Nonconformists had taken upon themselves to conduct services and to preach in All Saints', Sudbury. They read some portions of the Book of Common Prayer, and then prayed and preached in their own way. The King commanded Bishop Reynolds of Norwich to inquire into the matter, and it was found that there had been no Anglican clergyman there for six years, and that the living was very poor. The King ordered the matter to be attended to, the income increased, and a priest provided.[1] Daniel Ray, ejected from Ridgewell, Essex, took up his abode in 1673 at Burstall, in Suffolk. There, without any disturbance from the incumbent, who had another living, he preached in the parish church every other Sunday until his death in 1677.[2] In 1675 Baxter preached on ten successive Sundays in the parish churches of Rickmansworth, King's Langley, and the neighbourhood. In some places the authorities were not so complacent. Joseph Sherwood, who was ejected from St. Hilary, Cornwall, went to live at St. Ives, where he was cited for non-attendance at church. He promised to attend the next Sunday, provided there was a sermon, but said he was not going there merely to hear the clerk read prayers. Warned by a friend that there would be no minister present, he did not attend, and was cited again. He went to church the Sunday after this second citation, found only the clerk there reading prayers, and went himself into the pulpit and preached. For this the magistrates sent him to prison in Launceston gaol. Sherwood addressed the chairman of the bench with the words, " If you die by the common death of all men, God never spake by me." Palmer and Calamy gravely relate as " a strange providence " that Robinson, the chairman in question, was shortly afterwards gored to death by a bull, an event which so affected one of the other magistrates, a Mr. Godolphin, that he declared he would never persecute Dissenters again, and was as good as his word.[3] On one occasion Tillotson allowed Richard Stretton to preach in St. Lawrence, Jewry, but was rebuked for doing so by the Bishop of London.

APPENDIX TO CHAPTER I

A LIST OF THE MORE DISTINGUISHED MEN AMONG THE EJECTED

Alleine, Joseph, ejected from Taunton. Author of " An Alarm to the Unconverted," and " Theologia Philosophica." Preacher and theologian.[4]

Alleine, Richard, ejected from Batcomb, Somersetshire. Theological writer. Author of " Vindiciæ Pietatis." [5]

---

[1] C.S.P.D., June 21st and 29th, 1670; Browne, " Congregationalism in Norfolk and Suffolk," pp. 443–446.
[2] Palmer, II. 213.   [3] Calamy, III. 215; Palmer, I. 350.
[4] Palmer, III. 208.   [5] Palmer, III. 167; Wood, " Athenæ," II. 689.

Annesley, Samuel, ejected from St. Giles's, Cripplegate. Eminent Non-conformist preacher in London.[1]

Bagshawe, Edward, ejected from Amersden, Oxon. A voluminous theological writer.[2]

Bates, William, ejected from St. Dunstan's in the West. Theologian. Author of " The Harmony of the Divine Attributes," 1675.[3]

Baxter, Richard, ejected from Kidderminster. Perhaps the most volumin-ous writer of them all. He wrote over a hundred and sixty books. A complete catalogue is given at the end of Orme's Life, and in Calamy's Abridgement. His works embrace the Evidences of Religion, Doctrine, Christian Ethics, Baptism, Nonconformity, Popery, Antinomianism, Quakerism, Millenarianism, besides works on political, historical and devotional subjects.

Burgess, Cornelius, ejected from St. Andrew's, Wells. Theological writer, controversialist and preacher.[4]

Calamy, Edmund, ejected from Aldermanbury. A member of the West-minster Assembly, and one of the authors of " Smectymnuus." [5]

Calvert, James, ejected from Topcliffe, Yorkshire. Theologian and Latin scholar.[6]

Calvert, Thomas, ejected from All Hallows, York. Theologian and oriental scholar.[7]

Caryl, Joseph, ejected from St. Magnus, London. Author of an Exposi-tion of the Book of Job, originally published in eleven quarto volumes, and part-author of an English-Greek Lexicon.[8]

Cawton, Thomas, ejected from Merton College, Oxford. Oriental scholar.[9]

Clark, Samuel, ejected from St. Benet Fink. A voluminous writer on theology, history (he wrote " The Marrow of Ecclesiastical His-tory "), and geography. He also produced an English Dictionary.[10]

Clark, Samuel, ejected from Grendon, Buckinghamshire. Son of the Samuel Clark mentioned above. Author of " Annotations on the Bible " and " A Survey of the Bible." [11]

Collinges, John, ejected from St. Stephen's, Norwich. Author of many theological works.[12]

Conant, John, ejected from the Rectorship of Exeter College, Oxford. Learned scholar. " Conanti nihil difficile," wrote Humphrey Prideaux.[13]

Corbet, John, ejected from Bramshot, Hampshire. Scholar and theo-logian.[14]

Cradock, Samuel, Fellow of Emmanuel College, Cambridge, ejected also from North Cadbury, Somerset. Author of expositions and studies of Scripture.[15]

Firmin, Giles, ejected from Shalford, Essex. Theological writer and controversialist.[16]

---

[1] Palmer, I. 124; Wood, " Athenæ," II. 966.
[2] Palmer, III. 111–114.   [3] Palmer, I. 115–119.
[4] Palmer, III. 217; Wood, " Athenæ," II. 247.
[5] Palmer, I. 76–80.   [6] Palmer, III. 472.
[7] Palmer, III. 458.   [8] Palmer, I. 146–148.
[9] Palmer, I. 252; III. 130; Wood, " Athenæ," p. 583.
[10] Palmer, I. 97–102.   [11] Palmer, II. 301–303.
[12] Palmer, III. 9–11.
[13] Palmer, I. 229; Wood, " Athenæ," I. 912.
[14] Palmer, III. 259; Wood, " Athenæ," II. 673.
[15] Palmer, III. 178–181.   [16] Palmer, II. 214.

Flavel, John, ejected from St. Clement's, Dartmouth. Theological writer and preacher.[1]

Gale, Theophilus, Fellow of Magdalen College, Oxford. A voluminous writer in English and Latin. His chief fame rests on his great work, " The Court of the Gentiles," published in four volumes in 1669–1677.[2]

Gilbert, Thomas, ejected from Edgmund, Shropshire. Scholar and theologian.[3]

Gilpin, Richard, ejected from Greystoke, Cumberland. Preacher. Wrote on demonology and kindred subjects.[4]

Goodwin, John, Theologian and controversialist.[5]

Hall, Thomas, ejected from King's Norton, Worcestershire. Theological writer.[6]

Harmer, John, ejected from the Professorship of Greek at Oxford, and later from Ewhurst, Hampshire. Author of many works of classical scholarship.[7]

Heath, Richard, ejected from St. Alkmund's, Shrewsbury. One of the greatest oriental scholars of his time.[8]

Henry, Philip, ejected from Worthenbury, North Wales. Scholar and divine.[9]

Hickman, Henry, Fellow of Magdalen College, Oxford. The vindicator of the Nonconformist position.[10]

Howe, John, ejected from Great Torrington, Devon. A famous preacher and theologian.[11]

Humphrey, John, ejected from Frome, Somerset. Learned and voluminous theological writer.[12]

Jacomb, Thomas, ejected from St. Martin's, Ludgate. Fellow of Trinity College, Cambridge.[13] The catalogue of his books sold after his death, " Bibliotheca Jacombiana " (several copies in the British Museum), proves his wide range of learning.

Jellinger, Christopher, ejected from South Brent, Devon. Theological writer.[14]

Jenkyn, William, ejected from Christ Church, Newgate Street. Scholar and theologian.[15]

Manton, Thomas, ejected from St. Paul's, Covent Garden. Author of Expositions on the Epistles of St. James and St. Jude.[16]

Martindale, Adam, ejected from Rosthorne, Cheshire. Mathematician and scientist.[17]

Mather, Increase, the famous New England divine and theologian. Palmer says he was in Guernsey at the time of the Restoration, and was offered a living in England if he would sacrifice his principles.[18]

Morton, Charles, ejected from Blisland, Cornwall, and founder of the academy at Newington Green.[19]

[1] Palmer, II. 18; Wood, " Athenæ," II. 870.
[2] Palmer, I. 243–244.
[3] Palmer, I. 309; III. 145; Wood, " Athenæ," II. 916.
[4] Palmer, I. 386.   [5] Palmer, I. 196–198.
[6] Palmer, III. 412.   [7] Palmer, II. 265.
[8] Palmer, III. 153.   [9] Palmer, III. 483.
[10] Palmer, I. 245.   [11] Palmer, II. 81–91.
[12] Palmer, III. 190.
[13] Calamy, II. 45; Wood, " Athenæ," II. 800.
[14] Palmer, II. 71.   [15] Palmer, III. 109.
[16] Palmer, I. 175–179.   [17] Calamy, II. 135; III. 173.
[18] Palmer, II. 245.   [19] Palmer, I. 348.

Nesse, Christopher, ejected from Leeds. Theological writer. Wrote a Commentary on the Old Testament in four folio volumes, " Compendium of Church History," etc.[1]

Nye, Philip, ejected from St. Bartholomew's Exchange. One of the chief Independents under the Commonwealth. Theologian and controversialist.[2]

Owen, John, ejected from the Deanery of Christ Church, Oxford, in 1569. Between the years 1660 and 1688 alone he produced over thirty theological works, many of them in folio.[3]

Peto, Samuel, ejected from Sandcroft, Suffolk. Scientist and theologian.[4]

Plumstead, Augustine, Fellow of Trinity College, Cambridge. Compiled a Biblical Concordance in English, Hebrew and Greek. Was not ejected from any known preferment, but became an Independent minister.[5]

Poole, Matthew, ejected from St. Michael's, Quorn. Author of " The Nullity of the Romish Faith," 1664, " Synopsis Criticorum," in five volumes, folio, 1669–1674.[6]

Quick, John, ejected from Broxton, Devon. Author of " Synodicon in Gallia Reformata." [7]

Rule, Gilbert, ejected from Alnwick. Tutor in the University of Glasgow, Sub-Principal of King's College, Aberdeen. After the Revolution Principal of the University of Edinburgh.[8]

Seaman, Lazarus, ejected from Allhallows, Bread Street. " A learned man and left a great library.[9]

Sylvester, Matthew, ejected from Gunnerby, Lincolnshire. The editor of Baxter's " Life and Times." [10]

Tombes, John, ejected from Leominster. Theologian and controversialist.[11]

Troughton, John, Fellow of St. John's, Oxford. " The best scholar of them all, well-studied in the schoolmen." [12]

Trueman, Joseph, ejected from Cromwell, Nottinghamshire. Author of an erudite work, " The Great Propiation." [13]

Wilde, Robert, ejected from Aynho, Northamptonshire. Verse writer and wit.[14]

Wilkinson, Henry, junr., ejected from the Principalship of Magdalen Hall, Oxford. Author of many Latin works.[15]

Woodbridge, Benjamin, ejected from Newbury. Scholar and theologian.[16]

---

[1] Palmer, III. 441.
[2] Palmer, I. 96; Wood, " Athenæ," II. 502.
[3] Palmer, I. 198–208.
[4] Palmer, III. 285.   [5] Palmer, III. 297.
[6] Palmer, I. 167–169.   [7] Palmer, II. 10.
[8] Calamy, II. 514; IV. 576.   [9] Palmer, I. 80.
[10] Palmer, II. 419–421.   [11] Palmer, II. 293–296.
[12] Wood, " Athenæ," II. 686; Palmer, I. 235; III. 128.
[13] Palmer, III. 93.
[14] Palmer, III. 26–27; Wood, " Athenæ," II. 21.
[15] Palmer, I. 241–243.
[16] Palmer, I. 290; Wood, " Athenæ," II. 774.

II

PRESBYTERIANISM was a system which in doctrine was Calvinistic, and in ecclesiastical polity was more fully developed in Scotland and Geneva than in England. As far as it was ever established in this country it reached its highest point under the Commonwealth. The Westminster Assembly probably represented its high-water mark, and when the Independents came into authority under Cromwell, Presbyterianism soon lost much of its power and influence. The general outline of the system was this:—

Each parish—for it was a parochial system—was governed by the Kirk Session. Each Kirk Session deputed one or two ministers and from two to four elders to attend the meetings of the Classis, called also the Classical Presbytery, which had the rule over a group of parishes. There was a difference, however, between the English and Scottish systems. In Scotland, in all assemblies above the Kirk Session the clergy were equal in number to the laity, or even slightly preponderant. In England the laity were in the minority always. Next above the Classis came the Provincial Assembly (called in Scotland the Synod), consisting of representatives from the Classes. This Assembly only came into existence in London and Lancashire.[1] The crown of the system was to have been a National Assembly, consisting of representatives from the Provincial Assemblies. If it had ever met it would not have been like the Scottish General Assembly, a court of final ecclesiastical appeal, for Parliament had reserved that right to itself. But it never did meet.

Although Presbyterianism had been established by law under the Commonwealth, it never took firm root in England. English people objected to the ecclesiastical domination which was so manifest in the Scottish Church. The Parliamentary attempt to establish the system of classes was vain in spite of the ordinances which were issued. In Essex and London the system seems to have come into operation, but in many counties, such as Cheshire, there were no classes at all. In Cumberland, though so close to Scotland, no great effort was made to introduce them, though something of the kind was attempted in 1645–1646.[2] In Worcestershire, under Baxter's influence, and in

[1] Gordon, " Freedom after the Ejection," p. 151.
[2] Nightingale, " The Ejected of 1662," I. 106.

43

some other counties there were unions of ministers who met as advisory bodies, but possessed no jurisdiction, and even differed among themselves on the principles of Church government.   In Lancashire and Yorkshire the Presbyterians seriously tried to include the Independents in their system.[1]   In Devonshire there was a voluntary association of Nonconformist ministers consisting of seven divisions, which probably represented the seven classes into which it had originally been intended to divide the county.[2]

Baxter, who denied that he was a Presbyterian, though he preferred " presbyter " to " priest," said: " Though Presbytery took root in Scotland, yet it was but a stranger here.   Most that ever I could meet with were against the *jus divinum* of lay elders, and for the moderate primitive episcopacy, and for an accommodation of all parties in order to concord." [3]   After the Restoration, however, true Presbyterianism was practically non-existent.   Writing in 1680, Baxter said that there was no single Presbyterian congregation in London except among the tolerated Walloons.   At the Restoration the whole system of classes and synods disappeared.[4]   In Lancashire the classical assemblies held their last meetings in 1660 and adjourned, apparently intending to meet again.   The last classis met at Manchester on August 14th, 1660, and adjourned to the second Tuesday in December, but did not reassemble then or afterwards.[5]

The majority of those who retired from their livings during the two years after the Restoration are usually included under the general name of Presbyterian.   " It would be wide of the mark to suppose that they bore any resemblance to the wild sectaries and fanatics of the times.   These, in fact, were the objects of their special aversion, and stood opposed to all their ideas of clerical dignity, church order, and official authority.   In their very dress and outward deportment these two parties were antipodes.   While the one party retained the close-cropped and ungainly appearance of the Independents in the days of Cromwell, our Presbyterian clergy developed into the full periwigs and flowing luxuriance of band and habit which usually characterised persons of their station after the Restoration." [6]   But all this tended to a social exclusiveness which caused some offence to the other separated brethren.

Baxter, speaking for himself and many others who " went out," said that they would have been willing to accept " Usher's model " of episcopacy, and that they did not object to bishops

---

[1] Gordon, " Freedom after Ejection," p. 152.
[2] J. F. Chanter, " Life of Martin Blake," 1910, pp. 133–134.
[3] " Rel. Baxt.," p. 146.
[4] Baxter, " The Nonconformists' Plea for Peace," 1680; M'Crie, " Annals of English Presbytery," p. 306.
[5] Halley, " Lancs. Puritanism," pp. 338–339.
[6] M'Crie, " Annals of English Presbytery," p. 242.

as such. Neither had they any objection to the English parochial system with one clergyman in authority. Moreover, the squires and county gentry preferred that system, as it gave them more influence in local ecclesiastical matters, and the Nonconformists were most anxious to retain their support.[1] Again, the question of the King's supremacy over the Church never seems to have roused any scruples in the minds of the Presbyterians, though it did in the minds of the Independents, who were opposed to monarchical government both in Church and State. They did not even object to State establishment or State endowment, for they had been established under the Commonwealth, and in 1672 Charles II. commenced the gift to the Presbyterian ministers of Ireland known as the Regium Donum, a grant of £600 a year as a reward for their loyalty. Discontinued for a time, it was restored by William III., increased by George I., and continued till the disestablishment of the Irish Church in 1869.

What they really objected to was not even doctrine, but certain points in the service book and ceremonies. Still more they objected to a genuine episcopacy, which they scornfully styled "prelacy." They have had since 1662 an undeserved reputation as martyrs for liberty. It is true that their action was one of the causes which ultimately led to religious liberty in this country, but they themselves would have disclaimed the principle. They made a distinction between sects that were "tolerable" and those which were "intolerable." Baxter declined to accept anything in the way of liberty for Independents or Roman Catholics. The idea that every sect should be allowed to go its own way, and that they all should be content to differ was hateful. "I abhor," said Baxter, "unlimited liberty and toleration of all; and think myself able to prove the wickedness of it."[2]

The Baptists and the Quakers soon after the Restoration busied themselves with schemes of organisation whereby to link their congregations together. The Presbyterians made no attempt to maintain or revive the true Presbyterian organisation, and so in the strict sense were not Presbyterians at all. Yet they still differed from the Independents. Oliver Heywood's congregation was thus described: "It was Presbyterian, the pastor taking no authority from his people to teach and preach, but deriving it by devolution from his fathers in the ministry, at whose hands he had received ordination. Neither were there deacons appointed with co-ordinate authority with the pastor, with whom alone it remained to accept into his congregation those whom he thought proper to admit, and to regulate the times, the manner, and order of the public ministrations as seemed to himself to tend most to edification."[3] It was the power of the minister

[1] Gordon, "Freedom after Ejection," p. 153.
[2] Baxter, "Plain Scripture Proof," 1651.
[3] Hunter, "Life of Oliver Heywood," pp. 237-238.

which made Milton say that presbyter was "priest writ large."
Philip Henry explained his position thus: "I do not conform to
the liturgy, etc. as a minister to read it, that I may bear testimony
against prelacy. I do conform to the liturgy as a private person,
to hear it in public assembly, that I may bear my testimony
against Independency, looking upon both of them as by-paths,
the one on the left hand, the other on the right, and the truth
between them. . . . Three things I do not like in the Independent way: (1) that they unchurch the nation, (2) that they
pluck up the hedge of parish order, (3) that they throw the
ministry in common and allow persons to preach who are un-
ordained. In two things they are to be commended: (1) that
they keep up discipline among them, (2) that they love and
correspond with one another." [1]

Discipline was firmly exercised in all Presbyterian congregations. Strict inquiry was made into the life and conversation
of every person who wished to become a member, and he had to
satisfy the minister as to the orthodoxy of his beliefs. Once
admitted, he was obliged to attend services regularly and to be
a regular communicant. Slackness or misconduct rendered him
liable to censure, and in the last resort to excommunication.

The Presbyterians, believing, as all Calvinists believed, that
their church should be the church of the nation, found themselves separated from it in small and isolated groups. Believing
in a definite hierarchical system of ecclesiastical government,
they found it impossible to maintain that system. Having very
definite views on the power, privileges, and position of the lawful
clergy, they found themselves relegated to the position of schismatics. Perhaps what brought about the decline of Presbyterianism as much as anything else was the weakness which came
from the difference between their theory and their practice.

Why, then, was the name Presbyterian retained at all? It
was retained largely for political and historical reasons. Those
who had united under the Presbyterian system during the
Commonwealth preferred to keep their old name. They disliked being confused with the Independents, who had overthrown the King, a deed against which they themselves had
protested. The name Presbyterian implied a theory of church
government alien to Independent ideas, and the name was
adhered to, though the system which it implied was in abeyance.
In popular language, indeed, the name was loosely applied to
all those who went out between 1660 and 1662 rather than accept
the episcopal system, unless they definitely called themselves by
some other name, such as Baptist or Independent. It was the
form of religion which had loomed largest in the popular eye in
the years before the Restoration, and so it became a common
custom to speak of the bulk of the outed ministers and their

[1] "Diary of Philip Henry," p. 277.

followers as Presbyterians. Some of those commonly called Presbyterians nevertheless steadfastly refused the name—Baxter complained of the custom of calling " all the Nonconformists that were episcopal or neutral by the name of Presbyterians, even those that had declared themselves against the Presbyterian frame." [1] These last made a distinction between " episcopacy " and " prelacy." They did not object to bishops, but to " Lord Bishops." Thomas Bold of Exeter thus addressed Bishop Gauden : " Reverend Sir, for so I can and will call you, in a point of good manners, though ' Reverend Father in God ' with a ' May it please your Grace ' I decline, as a title which hath in it *aliquid Antichristi*." [2]

Nevertheless, the great distinction between the Presbyterian and the Anglican turned on the question of ordination. In the Anglican system ordination by a bishop was a *sine quâ non*. The English Presbyterians of this period asserted that ordination by the presbytery was at least equally valid. John Howe was ordained by a single presbyter, Mr. Charles Herle, at Winwick in Lancashire. " Mr. Herle he always looked upon as a primitive bishop." [3] According to Calamy, Thomas Manton before the age of twenty was ordained deacon by Bishop Joseph Hall, of Exeter (afterwards of Norwich). This is probably incorrect, for a man could not be ordained deacon in the Church of England till the age of twenty-three years.[4] Palmer [5] and Wood [6] are more likely to be correct in saying that he was admitted to deacon's orders in 1660 by Bishop Sydserf, and that he was never ordained priest. Calamy, referring to the two writers mentioned above, says : " If these writers supposed, as they seem to have done, that the Doctor, who had been a celebrated preacher for years, remained till then unordained, they were much mistaken. For he was ordained by Bishop Hall, before he was twenty, and Mr. Joseph Hill of Rotterdam was positive that he never took any other than deacon's orders, and never would submit to any other ordination. For it was his judgment that he was properly ordained to the ministerial office, and that no powers on earth had any right to divide and parcel that out at their pleasure." [7]

The Presbyterians had had a great share in the Restoration. The Cavaliers had been so depressed that they could have done very little by themselves. Monk and his two chaplains, Gumble and Price, Ashley Cooper, Annesley, and Monk's great confidant, Sir William Morrice, were all Presbyterians. During the early stages of the negotiations for the King's return, however, there had been a rapid revulsion of feeling. The Presbyterians

---

[1] " The Nonconformist's Plea for Peace," 1679.
[2] " Rhetoric Restrained," 1660.   [3] Palmer, II. 81.
[4] Gibson, " Codex," p. 848.   [5] " Nonc. Mem.," I. 175, 426.
[6] " Ath. Ox.," II. 600.   [7] Calamy, III. 60.

were strong in the Convention Parliament, but not strong enough to get their own way without the help of the Independents, and they certainly could not expect the latter to assist in any rehabilitation of Presbyterianism.[1] The Presbyterians expected that they would be rewarded for their new loyalty by some modification of the Anglican system to suit their views, and in after years they had reason to regret that they had not made this a condition of the King's return. " Had we but petitioned for presbytery at Breda, it had been, as was thought, granted; but fearing what the least delay in the King's coming over might have produced, and trusting fully to the King's goodness, we hastened him over without any provision for our own safety. At that time it was that Dr. Sheldon, now Bishop of London, and Dr. Morley did poison Mr. Sharpe, our agent, whom we trusted, who, piece by piece, in so cunning a way has trepanned us, as we have never won so much as to petition either King, Parliament or Council." [2]

Two things must be remembered. Whatever Charles might have been persuaded to promise at Breda was, as the sequel showed, subject to revision by Parliament. Parliamentary aggression on the King's prerogative in religious matters had increased during the reign of his father, and was now a matter of course. It was because people like Baillie did not realise this that they complained that Charles had broken his word. Secondly, in the enthusiasm of loyalty, which was increasing daily, the feeling was voiced on all sides that presbytery was hostile to monarchy.[3] Even under the Commonwealth someone had dared to publish a savage skit, " The Coat of Arms of Sir John Presbyter." [4] " He bears per pale indented, God's glory and his own interest, over all honour, profit, pleasure countercharged: ensigned with a helmet of ignorance, opened with confidence befitting his degree, mantled with gules and tyranny, doubled with hypocrisy over a wreath of pride and covetousness: for his crest, a sinister hand holding up a Solemn League and Covenant reversed and torn: in a scroll underneath the shield these words for his motto, *Aut hoc aut nihil.* This coat armour is dispalled with another of four pieces, signifying thereby his four matches. The first is the family of Amsterdam; she bears for her arms, in a field of toleration, three Jews' heads proper, with as many blue caps on them. The second is of the house of Geneva; she bears for her arms, in a field of separation, marginal notes on the Bible falsely quoted. The third is of the country of New England; she bears for her arms, a prick-eared

---

[1] L. F. Brown, " The Religious Factors in the Convention Parliament," *E.H.R.*, XXII. 51.
[2] Robert Baillie, " Letters," Edinburgh, 1775, II. 459.
[3] " The Grand Rebels Detected; or the Presbyter Unmasked," 1660; " Presbytery Displayed," 1663, a reprint of a pamphlet first published in 1644.
[4] 1658, reprinted 1683.

preachman, preached upon a pulpit proper, holding forth to the
people a schismatical Directory. The fourth and last is Scotland:
she bears in escutcheon the field of rebellion charged with a
stool of repentance." It was in vain that the Presbyterians
proclaimed their loyalty. On April 23rd, 1661, the day of
Charles II.'s coronation, Nathaniel Heywood preached on the
text, " Mephibosheth said unto the King : Yea, let him take all,
forasmuch as my Lord the King is come again to his own house."
One of his old parishioners reminded him of it in 1662, when
the Act of Uniformity deprived him of everything.[1]

A great number of the Presbyterians " went out " before the
Act of Uniformity. Baxter's case is one of these; he preached
his last sermon before his secession on May 22nd, 1662, in
Blackfriars.[2] Long before this he had ended his ministrations
at Kidderminster. He was in that town for a few months
during the autumn of 1661, and had preached two or three
times in the parish church, but though he offered to take the
curacy, and even to preach without a stipend, the vicar would
not allow him even to deliver a farewell sermon. During his
stay in the Midlands he was to have preached at Cleobury,
but was unable to go thither, and soldiers prevented his substitute
from preaching, the churchwarden having forbidden anyone to
preach who did not hold a licence from the bishop. Baxter,
accompanied by Thomas Baldwin,[3] went to the Bishop of
Worcester, and in the presence of the Dean reminded Morley
that he had promised him a licence, and expressed his willingness
to confine his ministrations to such people as had no preacher,
but the bishop refused permission, so he preached a farewell
sermon to a gathering of his friends at Wannerton, near Kidderminster, and then returned to London.[4] The farewell sermon
he had intended to preach at Kidderminster was published many
years afterwards.[5]

Baxter has no good word for his successors in the lectureships.
They were " scandalous men." One of them " was of the
judgment and spirit of Dr. Gunning," which hardly seems the
severe criticism which Baxter intended; another was " one of
the best parts they could get, a most scandalous person," another
but " a poor, dry man," the next " a young man, the best they
could get." Bishop Morley and the Dean of Worcester both
went to Kidderminster and preached, the first " a long invective
against me," the second " to cure them of the admiration of my
person." A month after that they " preached over the same,
persuading the people that they were Presbyterians and schis-

[1] Halley, " Lancs. Puritanism," p. 343.
[2] Powicke, " Richard Baxter," I. 215.
[3] Calamy, II. 774; IV. 893.
[4] Powicke, " Richard Baxter," I. 204–206.
[5] " Mr. Baxter's Farewell Sermon," 1683.

matical, and were led to it by their over-valuing of me. The people admired at the temerity of these men, and really thought that they were scarce well in their wits, that would go on to speak things so far from the truth of men whom they never knew, and that to their own faces." [1]

Baxter's own account of his silencing in the diocese of Worcester was first set forth in a letter to Kidderminster dated November 11th, 1661, and afterwards published.[2] He referred to the discussion at the Savoy Conference on the proposition that a book which is issued by lawful authority, and enjoins nothing but what is of itself lawful, enjoins nothing that is sinful, and said that his party had denied this proposition, and had given reasons, one of which reasons was, "that it may be unlawful by accident and therefore sinful." Thus, "suppose it never so lawful of itself to kneel in the reception of the sacrament, if it be imposed by a penalty that is incomparably beyond the proportion of the offence, that penalty is an Accident of the Command, and maketh it by Accident sinful in the Commander." He said that it was for maintaining this position that he had been forbidden to preach, although his colleagues who had supported him had not been so silenced. Bishop Morley felt himself obliged to reply. He said that as bishop he was the pastor of Kidderminster, as of the rest of his diocese, and that neither he nor his predecessors had ever committed the care of it to Baxter. The lawful incumbent had returned, a man whom Baxter admitted to be of unblameable life, but had declared to be "not of such parts as are fit to qualify him for the cure of so great a congregation," a matter which it was not for Baxter to judge. "I took care," said the bishop, "the dean should be with me when I spoke to him, foreseeing what misreport would come from a man of Mr. Baxter's principles and temper. . . . My first reason for refusing him was his preaching without a licence, a thing which he has also done in the diocese of London.[3] Secondly, I had heard him at the Savoy maintaining such a position as was destructive to legislative power in God and man. Thirdly, principles of treason and rebellion are inculcated in his books." At the Savoy he often affirmed "that the command of a most lawful act was sinful, if the act commanded might prove to anyone a sin *per accidens*. When I laid this assertion to his charge and when he denied it, it being a frequent practice of his to deny what he had before affirmed, the answers which he had delivered, written with his own hand, were produced." As for his brethren, though he had often made this assertion, they had not.

[1] "Rel. Baxt.," pp. 375–376.
[2] It was prefixed to "The Mischiefs of Self-Ignorance," 1662.
[3] This was true, but in February 1661 he obtained a general licence to officiate in the diocese of London, promising not to preach against the doctrines and ceremonies of the Church (Powicke, "Richard Baxter," I. 215).

As for the question of kneeling at the Communion, the bishop pointed out that it had been expressly ruled out of the Savoy discussions as being a matter belonging to the canons, and not to the Prayer Book. As for the question itself, the Protestants of France ordered communicants to receive the sacrament standing, the Calvinists of Holland, Scotland, and Germany sitting, the Lutherans kneeling, and all of them ordered the particular posture on the same penalty, namely, that of not receiving. The complaint of keeping men from the sacrament came ill from men who had kept whole parishes without it for years, or who rejected people who would not come to be examined by them beforehand. Yet Mr. Baxter talked about being ejected because he and his friends dared not refuse the sacrament to persons who would not kneel. Morley added attestations of the truth of his statements about the Savoy Conference from Dr. Pearson and Dr. Gunning, and a catena of seditious and rebellious passages from Baxter's " Holy Commonwealth." A heated controversy now arose. Edward Bagshawe, formerly second master of Westminster School and for a time chaplain to Lord Anglesey,[1] took the matter up and wrote " A Letter unto a Person of Honour and Quality containing some Animadversions upon the Bishop of Worcester's Letter." It was published in 1662 and signed " EdwarD BagshawE = D.E." He said he was a lover of bishops, but his general attack on episcopal power showed how little he believed in bishops as the Catholic Church understands them, since he affirmed them to be nothing more than the King's subordinates for ecclesiastical affairs, and said that the King could confer the office on laymen if he liked. Morley's claim to be sole pastor of the diocese and the sole source of clerical jurisdiction therein, could, said Bagshawe, be only maintained by arguments which would support the papal supremacy. Bagshawe also denied the necessity of episcopal ordination. Baxter was offended, and expressed a wish that Bagshawe, who was a stranger to him, had not interfered. Hearing, however, that Roger L'Estrange was preparing an answer, Bagshawe forestalled him with a " Second Part of the Animadversions, with an Answer to all that L'Estrange intends to Write." L'Estrange's pamphlet was called " A Whip for Edward Bagshawe's Schismatical Animadversions," and was followed by " A Memento to all who Love the Memory of King Charles." This was also by L'Estrange, who dedicated it to Clarendon, with such a scornful reference to his opponent that the latter complained to Clarendon about it, and thus provoked from L'Estrange an appeal to the Privy Council, entitled " Truth and Loyalty Vindicated from the Clamorous Reproaches of Edward Bagshawe."[2] Another writer, S. H., joined in the controversy

---

[1] Aubrey, " Brief Lives," I. 85; Calamy, II. 542; IV. 719.
[2] Kitchin, " Sir Roger L'Estrange," p. 83; J. B. Williams, " Newsbooks and Letters," *E.H.R.*, April 1908.

with " D. E. Defeated." The pamphlet was really a reply to the
Puritan objections to episcopacy and ceremonial. The writer
railed rather than argued, but was savagely humorous at times.
" A Vindication of my Lord Bishop of Worcester's Letter " was
directed against both Baxter and his defender. The writer
accused D. E. of not giving the bishop a single good word and
of trying to pick a quarrel with him rather than trying to answer
his letter. D. E. had found fault with the union between the
bishops and the King, but the Civil War had shown that those
who attacked one also attacked the other, and that no monarchy
could exist with presbytery. Dealing with the point in dispute,
the writer affirmed that the Bishop of Worcester was the pastor
of Kidderminster, not the sole pastor, but the chief pastor, and
that Baxter had intruded himself without authority, in addition
to preaching sedition, rebellion, and schism. The controversy
came up again many years afterwards—Baxter had frequently
tilted at Morley, and in 1683 the latter, now Bishop of Winchester,
complained that his adversary called him " a preacher of un-
truths, a slanderer of Nonconformists, a blasphemer and defier
of the Deity," and had accused him of saying what was not true
about his silencing at Kidderminster. Morley this time published
a considerable volume in his own defence.[1] Baxter called on
Clarendon shortly after Morley's first letter had appeared, and
the Chancellor rebuked him for provoking the bishop, and then,
referring to another matter, asked him, " Was it a handsome thing
of Mr. Baxter to speak to so mild a man as Dr. Earle as when he
offered you a tippet when you preached before the King to turn
away in scorn, and say, ' I'll none of your toys '? " Baxter said
he had never refused, nor had he any scruples about wearing
one. He then wrote to Earle saying that his words of refusal
had been, " It belongeth not to me, Sir," because he thought it
could only be worn by a Doctor of Divinity. Earle replied that
he did not remember his exact words, but willingly accepted his
statement and reminded him that on his refusal he had told him
that others of his persuasion had not scrupled to wear it, and
" the manner of your refusing it made me think you were not well
pleased." [2]

John Shaw was Master of the Charterhouse in Hull, and
had been made one of the King's chaplains in July 1660. In
June of the following year, at the instigation of the Bishop of
London, Secretary Nicholas wrote to the Mayor and Aldermen
of Hull ordering them to forbid him to preach in Holy Trinity
Church in that town. He went up to London and saw the King,
who promised to take care of him, but desired him to refrain

[1] " The Bishop of Winchester's Vindication of Himself from Divers False,
Scandalous, and Injurious Reflections made upon him by Mr. Richard Baxter
in several of his Writings," 1683.
[2] " Rel. Baxt.," pp. 381-383.

from preaching in the forbidden building. He went next to Sheldon and asked why he had complained of him. Sheldon said he had heard a good deal about him, and that he was believed to be no friend to episcopacy or the Prayer Book. Shaw replied that he had never said a word against either of them, though he was free to admit that he would never have done anything to bring them back. The bishop asked him if he would accept a living, but he declined and returned to Hull, where he preached to such crowds in the Charterhouse that, as he says, the other churches were empty.[1] Soldiers beset the place every Sunday, but the congregation got in one way and another, and one Sunday 300 people were taken there. The bridges were drawn up to prevent them from getting away, and about sixty had to remain all night. On June 20th, 1662, Shaw removed to Rotherham, and preached there for the next few weeks. He had no benefice, but said he would not have refused a living or any clerical work " on conscience-satisfying terms." [2]

John Humphrey, a graduate of Pembroke College, Oxford, received Presbyterian ordination and became vicar of Frome Selwood in Somersetshire. At first he was a Parliamentarian, though he never took the Covenant nor joined in association with the Presbyterians, and after Charles I.'s death he preached publicly in favour of bringing back his son. After the Restoration he published as his opinion that persons in Presbyterian orders might, in order to secure " ministerial usefulness," be re-ordained by a bishop under certain conditions, and he was himself ordained deacon and priest by the Bishop of Bath and Wells, " indenting only for some little variation in the formula, and that he should not be put upon any subscription." Almost immediately he changed his mind, declared re-ordination sacrilegious and, publicly expressing his penitence for it, he renounced his Anglican orders, and tore up his letters of orders as a deacon in the presence of the bishop's registrar. After the Act of Uniformity he similarly tore up his letters of orders as priest, also before a witness. He resigned his living in August 1662 and became a Nonconformist minister in London.[3] Later in his life he seems to have taken to calling himself a Congregationalist.

Adam Martindale had been admitted to the Presbyterian ministry, and in 1660 was vicar of Rotherstone in Cheshire. He was imprisoned soon after the Restoration for refusing to read publicly a precept sent to him by a local deputy-lieutenant forbidding unlawful assemblies, but an influential friend inter-

---

[1] The Charterhouse Chapel, destroyed in 1643, was not rebuilt till 1673, and services must have been held in a room in the building, but Holy Trinity Church held over 2000 people and St. Mary's Lowgate at least 500.
[2] Calamy, II. 823, " Yorkshire Diaries," Surtees Soc., pp. 155–156.
[3] Palmer, III. 190; Macleane, " Hist. Pemb. Coll., Oxford," pp. 248–249; Wood, " Ath. Ox.," II. 1107–1111.

ceded for him, and a number of the local gentry signed a certificate of his loyalty to the King and Government, so he was
allowed to return home on giving surety in a bond for £1000.
His attitude towards the Government is shown in a passage in
his autobiography: " About 1661, when the Act of Uniformity
was going fast on, a stop was put to it for another session, that in
the meantime a benevolence to the King might be paid, or at
least engaged for by the clergy, lest the Nonconformists should
have an excuse to pay nothing when they left their estates. This
put us in a great state what to do, for it was evident if we gave not
freely that would be taken as a just reason for turning us out,
and if we did, they would turn us out just the same."[1] He
added that he gave twenty shillings himself, not being able to
do more because he had suffered so unjustly in his estate. He
relates that he only saw the Prayer Book on August 22nd, 1662,
two days before St. Bartholomew. " If I had gone to the bishop
and consented I should have been at the mercy of the bishop
and the patron, who had someone else ready. It is true that the
bishop might have judged this a lawful impediment that the book
was not come and allowed a further time. But still that put it
out of my power into his." He says the bishop might have told
him that he ought to have procured a copy from London, which
rather suggests that he could have done so if he had wished. " And
what favour could I expect from a bishop whose violent proceedings against us were so manifest? " Then follows a sneer at the
bishop for his friendship with the patron of the living, " a gentleman of £5000 a year, an old fellow-sufferer, a Parliament man,
a J.P. and I think a D.L., and above all a huge benefactor."[2]
On the day before St. Bartholomew Martindale heard from
Newcombe that the King was going to grant an indulgence to
the Nonconformists, and would be angry with those who threw
up their posts.[3] He preached at Rotherstone on August 24th,
and says he went to church and found " a great congregation
come together, but no man to break the bread of life to their
hungry souls."[4] It seems an unreasonable complaint. He had
till that day to make up his mind. As he would not conform, the
Bishop of Chester declared the living vacant and a successor was
appointed. " One gentleman cursed me one Lord's Day in the
evening for not keeping the place from such a bungler."
Whether a " gentleman " who could " curse " a minister on a
Lord's Day evening was a trustworthy judge of the ability of the
clergy it is happily not our province to determine. But in any
case the fact was that short of giving up everything the Church
of England stood for, nothing would have satisfied Martindale
and his friends.
The real hardship which the Nonconformists suffered was not

[1] " Life of Adam Martindale," p. 162.   [2] *Ibid.*, pp. 163–165.
[3] " Diary of Henry Newcome."   [4] " Life," p. 168.

that the Act of Uniformity would not allow them to minister in a Church in which they did not believe, but that succeeding Acts of Parliament would not allow them to minster at all, and inflicted heavy punishments upon them if they attempted to do so. James Janeway became pastor of a Presbyterian congregation in Jamaica Row, Rotherhithe. On one occasion soldiers broke into the meeting-house while he was preaching and tried to pull him out of the pulpit, but the bench on which they stood gave way and in the confusion of their fall he escaped out of the place. Another time, while he was preaching in the house of a gardener, a party of troopers came to look for him, but he threw himself on the ground and his congregation covered him with cabbage leaves so that he was not seen.[1] John Quick, the learned author of the "Synodicon," was ejected from Brixton in Devonshire at St. Bartholomew, but continued ministering to his congregation there till the middle of December 1663. He was seized while preaching, and sent to prison not only for his unauthorised ministrations, but also for preaching while under sentence of excommunication, and remained in gaol till March 1664. While he was there two fresh indictments were laid against him for preaching to the prisoners.[2]

Thomas Doolittle, ejected from St. Alphege, London Wall, gathered a congregation which met in a building he had erected in Mugwell or Monkwell Street. His dwelling communicated with the meeting-house, which facilitated his escape when his services were disturbed. At one time guards were posted round the house and the magistrates ordered the pulpit to be demolished, the doors fastened up, and the King's broad arrow set upon them. The building was taken from him without compensation and used for a time as the Lord Mayor's chapel. He was sued in the courts for sums amounting to several hundred pounds, being various fines for preaching. Distresses were levied on him, and he had to change his abode several times.[2] Jeremy Marsden in 1674 claimed to have changed his residence twenty-two times, but it was partly his own fault. He was mixed up in the plot of 1663, and his chief friends were to be found in the militant party. He died in Newgate in 1684.[4]

George Hughes, Fellow of Pembroke College, Oxford, was ejected from St. Andrew's, Plymouth. In 1665 he was sent, together with his son, as a prisoner to St. Nicholas Island for holding conventicles. There he remained nine months, and suffered considerably in health. He was offered his liberty if he would give surety in £1000 (Calamy says £2000) that he would not reside within twenty miles of Plymouth. His friends found the surety for him without his knowledge, and he returned

[1] Calamy, IV. 963. [2] *Idem*, II. 247; III. 331.
[3] Wilson, "Dissenting Churches in London," III. 190–199.
[4] Calamy, II. 796; IV. 942.

to Kingsbridge, where he died in 1667.[1]   Christopher Nesse,
who was ejected from Leeds, was excommunicated four times,
and finally a writ *de excommunicato capiendo* was issued against
him, but he took refuge in London.[2]   John Norman of Bridgewater was arrested for unlicensed preaching in 1663, fined £100,
and sentenced to imprisonment till the fine was paid.   After he
had been shut up in Ilchester gaol for a year and a half, the fine
was reduced to £5 and he was set free.[3]

Joseph Alleine, the author of "An Alarm to the Unconverted,"
was arrested on May 26th, 1663.   He gave as his defence that
since St. Bartholomew's Day he had preached neither in church
nor chapel, and that he had simply ministered to his own family
and those who came to hear him.   He also was sent to Ilchester
gaol.   No officer went with him, he carried the *mittimus* himself,
and when on his arrival he found the gaoler absent, there being
no one in authority to whom to deliver the document, he took
the opportunity to preach outside till someone came.   This was
afterwards treated as an aggravation of the offence.   He was
at last shut up in the Bridewell, over the common gaol.   Five
other ministers and fifty Quakers were confined in the same
room, and a little later ten other prisoners were thrust in.
The roof was so low that they could touch the tiles as they lay
in bed, and they removed the glass from the windows and also
some of the tiles, in order to get air.   For their recreation they
were allowed to walk in a small garden which adjoined the
common prison, and were troubled there by the rattling of
chains, and the shouting and singing and blasphemies of the
prisoners.   The ministers tried to hold services in their room,
but were molested by their Quaker fellow-prisoners.   Alleine,
however, got permission from the keeper to hang a curtain round
his bed, and was even allowed to walk outside for a mile or two
every morning and evening.   Friends and sympathisers sent the
incarcerated ministers an abundance of provisions.   At the
Sessions on July 14th the grand jury did not bring in a true
bill against Alleine, so he was not called.   Nevertheless he
remained in prison, and at the August Assizes a true bill was
found on the same evidence as before.   The judge, after reading
a copy of the indictment presented at the Sessions, declared
it erroneous in every respect, fined the clerk who drew it up, and
uttered severe strictures on the justices who were responsible.
The foreman of the grand jury had already pointed out to the
judge that Alleine's counsel was a Nonconformist, and inquired
whether they should present or indict him also.   The petty jury
found the prisoner guilty and he was fined 100 marks, and

---

[1] Palmer, II. 56; Macleane, "Hist. Pemb. Coll. Oxford," p. 241; Wood,
"Ath. Ox.," II. 398–399.
[2] Calamy, II. 799.
[3] *Idem*, II. 578.

sentenced to imprisonment till the fine was paid.[1] He remained
in prison till May 20th, 1664, still continuing, in spite of the
threats of the authorities, to preach to large congregations on
Sundays, and when the chaplain was ill he took his duty for him.
On July 10th, 1665, he preached at a meeting held at a house
just outside Taunton, the meeting being ostensibly a gathering of
friends to bid him farewell, as he was going away for his health.
But it contravened the Five Mile Act, and he and many of those
present went to Ilchester gaol again in consequence. He was
released after a time, but his health was undermined. He was
an invalid for the last twelve months of his life, and died in
November 1668.[2]

Richard Steel[3] and Philip Henry[4] were in 1665 made sub-
collectors of the royal aid in their district, the object being to
make a public denial of their claim to be ministers. In September
of the same year they were imprisoned for being present at a
meeting. Steel determined to remove to London, but was
stopped on the way and searched, and some papers, including
his diary, were seized and treated as suspicious documents. The
Five Mile Act forced him at last to leave his home at Hanmere in
Flintshire, and after some wanderings he retired to London in
1667 and became minister of the Presbyterian congregation in
Armourers' Hall.[5] In 1665 a conventicle was broken up in
Chester, and though many of those present escaped, some thirty
or forty were taken hiding in cupboards and under beds, among
them Major James Jolly, an old Cromwellian officer, the father
of Thomas Jolly. This conventicle was described as consisting
not of Anabaptists, " but the first and worst stamp of sectaries."
Thomas Jolly, the son, of whom it was said that after the Restoration probably no minister in Lancashire suffered more, was
ordained "in the Presbyterian way," and was for many years
minister of Altham chapel in· the parish of Whalley. He was
ejected at St. Bartholomew, and in 1663 was accused of having
a party ready to march as soon as the projected rising began.
The Altham and Wymondhouses Church Book has an entry
under the date 1663, " Pastor was prisoner twice this year, and
used badly the first time. His persecutors died sadly." In 1667
he bought a house within five miles of Altham, in spite of the
Act. The Church Book notes, " Pastor bought Wymondhouses
and removed his goods thither. Preached at one time to two
women only." In his house there was a staircase leading from
the common sitting-room, and at the bottom of the staircase was
a door so constructed that the upper half could be made to fall

[1] The full account of the trial is in the Baxter MSS. in Dr. Williams' Library
and is printed in Stamford's " Joseph Alleine," pp. 226–245.
[2] " The Life and Death of that Excellent Minister of Christ Mr. Joseph
Alleine," 1672; Wood, " Ath. Ox.," II. 420–422.
[3] Calamy, II. 708.   [4] *Idem*, II. 698.
[5] Philip Henry, " Diary and Letters."

back on brackets and form a pulpit. As soon as an alarm was given outside the house, the upper part of the door was raised again and the preacher could escape upstairs.[1]

Thomas Horrocks was ejected from Maldon in 1662.[2] After his ejectment he continued to preach, and was thrown into the dungeon of the town prison. His wife appealed to the King and Council, and Lord Manchester and Lord Robartes intervened on his behalf and procured his *habeas corpus*. Summoned before the magistrates of Maldon, he was accused of being a heretic, schismatic, and traitor, and one of the aldermen boxed his ear, knocking his cap off. Horrocks picked it up and politely thanked the aggressor. They sent him away from the town on horseback, with a sergeant on each side of him, and Alderman Hart, who had struck him, followed him as prosecutor. At the Assizes Judge Mallet reproved the alderman and said that the prisoner looked an honest gentleman who deserved no such treatment. Hart replied that he was a pestilent fellow, and only the previous Sunday had preached through the gate of the prison to a crowd of 500 people. The judge only answered that that was a proof that he was well-beloved, and acquitted him. His persecutor then entered an action against him in the Crown Office, and he was hurried that night to Romford, which brought on a violent illness. He had to appear at three Assizes, and his life was threatened. At last, however, he was cleared, and some of the judges even stepped down from the bench and embraced him. In " Informations of Meetings in Hertfordshire," January 2nd, 1664, he was described as preacher to the Anabaptists of Hertford. They were meeting, it was reported, to the number of 500 at a time, and were boasting that the time of their liberty was drawing near, whilst he was teaching them that " they must not go back, nor be daunted with any terror, lest God spew them out of his mouth."[3] There appears to be no real evidence that he was a Baptist.

Vincent Alsop was once sent to Northampton gaol for six months for holding a conventicle, though he pleaded that he was only praying beside a sick person. It is said that he once escaped from a prosecution because the informers did not know his Christian name.[4] In 1670 Manton was arrested. He had taken the oaths of allegiance and supremacy, but refused to take the Oxford oath against endeavouring any alteration in Church and State. He was released for a few days and then committed to the Gatehouse. Lady Broughton, the keeper, treated him

---

[1] "The Note-book of Thomas Jolly," Introdn., p. xxi. The "Altham and Wymondhouses Church Book," is in the same volume. Chetham Society.
[2] Palmer, II. 206.
[3] Davids, "Evangelical Nonconformity in Essex," pp. 424–425; Calamy, III. 468.
[4] Palmer, III. 48.

kindly and gave him a large room adjoining the Gatehouse and a small room for a bedroom.   For some time no one was allowed to see him but his wife and servant.   Later his children and then a few friends to the number of twelve or fifteen were allowed in, and he preached to them twice on a Sunday and once during the week.   While he was there Lady Broughton went away from London for a time, and left instructions to the turnkey that the keys were to be taken to Dr. Manton's room every night.   We are told that he ventured out twice to visit his friend Mr. Gunston of Stoke Newington " when the town was pretty empty." [1]

Richard Stretton, who is looked upon as the founder of Mill Hill chapel, Leeds, now Unitarian, ministered from 1677 onward to a Presbyterian congregation which he gathered at Haberdashers' Hall, in Staining Lane, Wood Street, Cheapside, for which a meeting-house was afterwards built close by.   In 1683 he refused the Oxford oath of non-resistance when it was tendered to him. He appeared before the King and Council, but the King refused to believe the charges laid against him and dismissed him.   He was next proceeded against under the Five Mile Act, and was sentenced to six months imprisonment in Newgate.   Here the chaplain showed him great respect, and made use of his assistance in preparing condemned prisoners for their end, amongst them Captain Walcot, who was sentenced to death for his share in the Rye House plot.   Roger L'Estrange spoke strongly of the keeper allowing " Stretton the Jesuit " to do this. [2]

As an example of the shifts to which the ministers were often put may be mentioned the case of Richard Chantry, ejected from Welford chapel, Shropshire.   He was accustomed to dress like an agricultural labourer, and with a fork over his shoulder and a Bible in his pocket would set out for a distant conventicle. In this manner he succeeded in evading the informers for years. [3] The Nonconformists of Rivington in Lancashire met in the open air at a place called Winter Hill, where seats had been cut out of the side of the hill in a kind of amphitheatre, with a stone pulpit in the centre. [4]   John Hardacre was the owner of Rawdon Low Hall in the West Riding.   After the Indulgence was withdrawn in 1672 conventicles were held in a cave under the Buckstone Rock on this estate.   The cave was sheltered by a " lean-to " roof, and was ordinarily a cowshed.   Oliver Heywood preached there sometimes, with watchers posted on the heights above. [5]   In the early 'eighties of the seventeenth century the dissenters used to meet near Olney at a place called "The three counties point," where Northamptonshire, Bedfordshire, and Buckinghamshire all met.   If attacked from either side it was easy to pass over into the adjoining county.[1]   Adam Martindale was a good mathematician and was able to take pupils as well as keeping together a Nonconformist congregation. The Conventicle Act made it dangerous for his hearers to meet in large numbers, so he divided them up, and preached the same sermon four or five times a day.   The strain of doing so made it necessary for him to discontinue his school for a time, but the offerings of his congregation were not sufficient for a livelihood, and he had to take to teaching again.[2]

It came out in 1671 that there was a certain amount of division between the London Presbyterian ministers, the two parties being the older ministers, " The Five Mile men "—*i.e.* the men who had taken the Oxford oath not to attempt to bring about changes in Church and State—who were nicknamed the " Dons," and the younger ministers, who were known as the " Ducklings." Bates, Jacomb, and Manton belonged to the former, and Annesley, Vincent Watson, and Janeway to the latter. There were several causes of coolness between them. The Dons had more influence with the upper classes, and were rather given to lording it over the Ducklings, who on their part, not being so high in position, were proud of their influence and popularity with the middle classes. James Innes,[3] backed by Lord St. Albans, had tried to bring them together again. He held a meeting of the Dons, and then, a fortnight later, one of the Ducklings, and a joint conference was held on December 27th, 1671.[4] It had been generally agreed among them beforehand not to reveal their differences to the world, and that neither party should make any proposals to the Government, for fear of being slighted and so losing influence with all parties.[5] It is to be presumed that the conference was successful.

For nearly thirty years many of the Presbyterians retained the hope that reunion with the Church of England would be made possible by such changes as would enable them to conform, and in this hope they were encouraged by many episcopalians. Baxter sympathised with this party, and would never take part in an ordination which in his mind meant a continuance of the schism, and he defended the practice of receiving communion at the parish churches.[6] Dr. Thomas Manton was succeeded at St. Paul's, Covent Garden, by Simon Patrick, and it is said that he often was present at the church to hear his successor's

---

[1] *Baptist Quarterly*, III. 320.   [2] " Life of Adam Martindale," p. 176.
[3] Calamy, II. 147; III. 176.
[4] C.S.P.D., December 13th, 1671, 294/178.
[5] C.S.P.D., December 27th, 1671, 294/235.
[6] Baxter, " Cure of Church Divisions," 1670.

discourses.[1] Francis Chandler frequently attended the services
of the Church of England, and preached between the forenoon
and afternoon services, and in the evening, in his own house or
at other places, as he had opportunity.[2] Oliver Heywood went
to church occasionally,[3] and some of the Nonconformists for a
long time held their services out of church hours, but as it became
more and more the regular thing to baptize fresh members, to
administer the Lord's Supper to the congregation, and even to
ordain new ministers, the last links with the Anglican Church
were broken. From the beginning, however, the practice of
occasional attendance at church was frowned upon in many
quarters. An entry, dated 1683, in the books of Thomas Jolly's
congregation, reads, " Some of the (members of the) church
maintained communion with the Church of England. It was
judged a matter of offence." [4]

Stillingfleet always dated the final separation of the Presbyterians from 1673.[5] The abolition of the Indulgence came as a
great shock to the Nonconformists. The Manchester ministers,
for example, held a meeting and decided to discontinue preaching
for a time, but the feeling gradually spread that the King had
withdrawn his Declaration much against his will, and that his
sympathy, like that of many other important people, was on their
side. Moreover, they had been praised in times past for their
boldness in defence of their rights; and so one by one they began
all over the country to preach again. The year of Indulgence
had given them a breathing space and strengthened them enorm-
ously, and there was now far less likelihood that they could ever
be effectually suppressed. In 1672 Presbyterians had for the
first time since the Restoration taken part in an ordination
service. The separation was complete.

As time went on two tendencies began to show themselves in
Presbyterianism. First the old Calvinism began to weaken, and
in some quarters Arminianism raised its head. Later on orthodoxy began to give place to Unitarianism. Arminianism—the
doctrine that Christ died for all and not merely for the elect—
was anathema to the majority of Nonconformists, most of whom
still held by John Calvin. In 1672, when Baxter was preaching
at Pinners' Hall, the rumour was spread, and his friends heard
it with horror, that he was preaching Arminianism.[6] John
Howe got into trouble in the same way. In 1677, at the request
of the Hon. Robert Boyle, he published a little treatise, " The
Reconcileableness of God's Prescience of the Sins of Men with the

[1] Harris, " Memoirs of Thomas Manton"; Wilson, "Dissenting Churches
in London," III. 554.
[2] Palmer, II. 221 ; Davids, " Evang. Nonconformity in Essex," p. 449.
[3] Diary, *passim.*
[4] " Altham and Wymondhouses Church Book," printed with the Note-
book of Thomas Jolly. Chetham Soc.
[5] Calamy, " Abridgement," p. 334.   [6] *Ibid.*, p. 335.

Wisdom and Sincerity of His Counsels and Exhortations, and whatever other Means He Uses to Prevent Them." The strict predestinationists immediately attacked him. Theophilus Gale published some Animadversions in the fourth volume of his ponderous work, " The Court of the Gentiles." Howe replied in a postscript to his treatise. John Troughton, ejected from St. John's, Oxford,[1] replied both to the treatise and the postscript in " A Letter to a Friend, touching God's Prescience about Sinful Actions " (1678). Thomas Danson, ejected from Sibton, Suffolk,[2] attacked Howe in " De Causa Dei; or a Vindication of the Common Doctrine of Protestant Divines concerning Predetermination . . . from the Invidious Consequences with which it is Burthened by Mr. John Howe" (1678). Howe did not reply to either Troughton or Danson, but a tract appeared in answer to the latter, bearing the title, " Remarks on a late disingenuous Discourse written by one T. D. under the pretence ' De Causa Dei,' and of answering Mr. John Howe's Letter and Postscript of ' God's Prescience,' etc., affirming as the Protestant doctrine ' That God doth by efficacious influence universally move and determine men in all their actions, even to those that are most wicked.' By a Protestant." Calamy says Andrew Marvell wrote it, and it seems to be marked in places by Marvell's humorous style.

After 1662 the distinction between the Presbyterians and the Independents necessarily ceased to be very sharp. Amongst the Presbyterians the meetings of presbyters and elders still remained, but the congregations were separate " gathered " congregations, as much as those of the Independents, and could no longer in any sense be described as parochial. Moreover, if a congregation needed a new minister he could only be appointed by agreement with the lay elders of the congregation, which was contrary to one of their root principles, that he should be appointed by ecclesiastical and not lay authority. On the other hand, the existence of a Presbyterian element in Nonconformity led to some practices contrary to strict Independent principles, e.g. ordaining at one place a number of ministers who were to be pastors of different churches in other places. Common misfortune tended to bring the two bodies into friendlier relations, as was shown by a united Communion service held at St. Bartholomew's, Thames Street, " at the Bartholomew time." [3] The ordinary man failed to see much difference between them, and so the names were used very loosely, constantly interchanged, and, indeed, in Wales became practically synonymous.[4] In the Indulgence licences of 1672 it sometimes happens that the same

---

[1] Palmer, I. 235; Wood, " Ath. Ox.," II. 686–688.
[2] Palmer, III. 86; Wood, " Ath. Ox.," II. 1016–1018.
[3] C.S.P.D., June 1st, 1667.
[4] Rees, " Hist. of Prot. Nonconformity in Wales," p. 153.

minister is described as a Presbyterian in one place and a Congregationalist in another, or a Presbyterian is stated to have been licensed for a Congregational meeting-house. Thus John Lomax, ejected from Wooler,[1] was licensed as an Independent teacher, but the house where he preached in North Shields was licensed as a Presbyterian meeting-place. John Jolly,[2] a Congregationalist, united in 1672 with Oliver Heywood and Richard Frankland, Presbyterians, to ordain a man who might be either after that.[3]   This was one of the reasons for the ultimate decline of Presbyterianism in England: it had retained so little of its distinctive character, that hardly any reason existed which would justify any attempt to remain separate. In Lancashire to-day of the congregations which trace their history back to the " Old Dissent," only four, Tunley, Risley, Dundee, and Wharton, are Presbyterian, and these have been recovered for Presbyterianism within recent times. All the rest are now either Congregationalist or Unitarian.[4] In 1645, when the country was being organised on a Presbyterian system, the county of Norfolk was divided into fourteen classes, with a total of 104 congregations. Between 1660 and 1662 115 ministers were silenced or ejected. In 1672 forty-three Presbyterian licences were issued to persons or places within the county. In 1717–18 there were only eighteen Presbyterian congregations, and four places had Presbyterian lectures. Five of these congregations afterwards turned Unitarian. Out of thirty-nine Presbyterian congregations in Suffolk in 1672, two remain; at Ipswich and Felixstowe.[5]

As long as they believed comprehension in the national Church to be possible, the Presbyterians had some reason for remaining distinct from the Independents. The failure of the Comprehension Bill in 1689, and the passing of the Occasional Conformity Bill in 1711, put an end to these hopes. The effluxion of time removed the men who left the Church in 1662. Benjamin Flower, the ejected vicar of Cardiff, was the first pastor of a Presbyterian congregation established at Devizes (Calamy says Chippenham). When he resigned in 1710 he said he thought he was the last of the Bartholomew men alive.[6] This was not the case, however, for John Humphrey,[7] who died in 1719, at the age of ninety-seven, and Nathan Denton,[8] who had been ejected from Bolton-on-Dearne, are said to have survived him.[9]

The career of Oliver Heywood presents in epitome the history of Presbyterianism from the Restoration to the end of the seventeenth century, and illustrates most of the various phases and difficulties of the life of a Nonconformist minister of the period.

[1] Calamy, II. 510; IV. 670.   [2] Idem, II. 124.
[3] Nightingale, " Ejected of 1662," I. 28–29.   [4] Idem, ibid., p. 28.
[5] Journ. Presb. Hist. Soc., I. 58; Vict. County Hist. Suff., II. 48.
[6] Ibid., I. 99; Calamy, II. 731.
[7] Calamy, II. 615.   [8] Idem, IV. 950.
[9] Wilson, " Dissenting Churches," IV. 410, says Humphreys was the last.

He was a graduate of Trinity College, Cambridge, and received Presbyterian ordination in 1652. His first wife was the daughter of John Angier, who was ejected from Denton, in Lancashire, in 1662. His brother Nathaniel was ejected from Ormskirk, in Lancashire, and he himself from Coley, a chapelry of Halifax, in Yorkshire, in 1662. As he refused to conform he was excommunicated. Nevertheless, though he was now unable to enter the church, the churchwardens came to him in July 1664 to demand the fines due for his absence from the services. Heywood spent the greater part of the rest of his life going from place to place preaching in Lancashire, Yorkshire, Staffordshire, and Cheshire. He was pursued by soldiers on several occasions, his house was frequently searched, his meetings were broken up, and he was constantly beset with spies. In 1665, because of the Five Mile Act, he had to leave Yorkshire, and lived for a short time at Denton, but in the following year he returned and settled down at Coley. Before he went to Denton he performed what Hunter, his biographer, called " the boldest act of his illegal career," by preaching in the episcopal chapel at Shadwell, near Leeds, for Mr. Hardcastle, a Baptist, who had been minister there before the Act of Uniformity, and was in prison for continuing to preach.[1] His sermons were largely attended. At home at this time he had audiences on Sunday of from forty to sixty persons, unsuspected by his enemies. In addition, he took long circuits, preaching somewhere or other every day, frequently with " a multitude of auditors." Very often he was to be found going to someone's house " to keep a fast " for some person or purpose. Quaint things happened at times. In 1667 he preached at a private house at Rawdon, but got his preaching over quickly because the Dean of York was coming to visit his house that day. In the same year he noted in his diary, " I preached at Coley chapel in public. Mr. Hoole," the curate, " having given notice the day before that he would be absent, I took advantage of the vacancy . . . a very great assembly . . . and for the issue of it the will of the Lord be done." Similar entries occur in 1668. " April 12th, I preached at Cockey chapel upon call, they having no minister. There was a numerous congregation." " April 19th, According to call I preached publicly at Cockey chapel in the afternoon, though a Conformist preached in the morning, but was willing I should share in the work." Cockey chapel was another episcopal chapel-of-ease in Lancashire. Similarly, the same year he preached in public at Bramley chapel, and noted that " though we had industriously concealed it, there was a great assembly." His brother Nathaniel preached at the same place that year. Oliver also preached at Hunslet chapel, Leeds, to " a huge numerous congregation within doors, and without such a multitude as I have seldom seen together."

[1] Hunter, " Life of Oliver Heywood," pp. 155–156.

In 1669 he recorded, " Coley chapel being destitute, they opened the doors and rung the bell, where I preached all day without interruption." This was on July 7th. Shortly afterwards he preached at Penistone, where Mr. Swift, the incumbent, had never conformed, though he had taken the oaths required by the Five Mile Act, and there was " a mighty numerous congregation." He preached again in Coley chapel in September, also at Shaw chapel, another episcopal place of worship near Oldham in Lancashire.

Next year, however, the Second Conventicle Act came out. In spite of it Heywood preached in Coley chapel on Whitsunday. " They told me there was no preaching at the chapel, and if I durst venture, the doors should be opened. I gladly accepted the call." The service was interrupted by the churchwarden and overseer, who took the names of many of those present. The diary adds that he preached several times in the week at home, " admitting only the number of four," which savours of shutting the stable door after the horse was stolen, especially as he preached at Penistone church and a number of other places almost immediately, and a warrant was out against him for his doings at Coley. A distress was levied on his goods, and practically everything he possessed was taken to pay the fine, while several of the congregation were fined also. Severe measures were being taken with the Dissenters. He recorded how Mr. Root preached at Shadwell on August 28th of that year, Lord Saville, Mr. Copley, Mr. Hammond, and forty troopers came and carried the preacher off to York, where " he was kept close prisoner, put into the low gaol among twelve thieves, had double irons laid on him for four days and nights," and was only released on " Captain Hodgson's importunity with Mr. Copley." Heywood himself was nearly in trouble again that year, and only escaped by a trick. He was preaching in a house at Bramley, when the constable, churchwardens, and others arrived. The Nonconformists pretended they were a Christmas party of friends. The constables went away, and sat in an alehouse and wrote down all their names. He was followed by the constables to another house a few days after, but escaped, and his goods were seized again by the bailiffs early in the next year. Charles II.'s Declaration of Indulgence gave him rest and peace for a time, for he received a licence to preach at his own house at Northowram, to which he had removed, and where he now had a congregation numbering over 100, though he still carried on his ministrations in various parts of the country. For a year, at any rate, his greatest interruptions were at the hands of " an Antinomian named West, who had been a Quaker," and who disturbed one of his services near Keighley, or the incursion of a magistrate demanding to see his licence. The licences were, however, withdrawn in the following February. " I gave notice to my people that our licences were recalled, and we were to preach no more by virtue of licences, and so took leave of them." He gave as his reasons, his desire to obey the authorities, that they might be convinced that they were peaceful people, and " to take off the imputation of sedition, which God knows we are not guilty of." Parliament would meet soon, and if they were peaceable their liberty might be restored by law; the licences had been given by the King's prerogative, and this might prove a matter of dangerous consequence; lastly, he did not desire to cause his people to have the burden of paying fines laid on them. Many of his followers thought it more prudent to " withdraw into more retired meetings." For a few years he kept more or less quiet, but in 1677 the tours begin again, and in the following year he was preaching in episcopal places like Toxteth chapel, Liverpool, and Furbeck church. He noted in 1678, " Discoursed with Lord Rutherford, who visited me," " Dined with Lord Rutherford at Halifax." The reason probably why he suffered very much less than some of the other Nonconformist ministers was because he had many distinguished supporters. Lady Hoyle, Lady Rhodes, Sir Ralph Knight, and many of the county landowners were amongst his friends and hearers. Lady Hewley and Lady Wharton subscribed to his work. He preached at Shaw chapel in April 1679. The meeting was disturbed, and he was taken by the high constable before Mr. Entwistle of Ormskirk, a justice of the peace. The next day Mr. Entwistle went to Rochdale and took sureties for his appearance at the next Quarter Sessions at Manchester, at which he appeared, and the case was dismissed. Nobody could look upon him as a seditious person.

But there were bad times coming. During 1682 and 1683 he had frequent escapes from soldiers, bailiffs, and constables. At the April Sessions at Pontefract in 1682 there was great rigour shown to the Nonconformists, persons were fined for not giving in the names of conventiclers, and even constables were fined and imprisoned for laxity. In August, at Halifax, people were fined for not kneeling in church. Heywood noted in 1682 that while the Nonconformist societies in his neighbourhood had been broken and scattered, so much so that in many places they were meeting at night, " vast multitudes " were flocking to his ministrations at Northowram, where so far they had been very little disturbed. In the following year he preached at Morley to 500 people, but found Cockey chapel closed against him. He was threatened with prosecution for his book " Israel's Lamentations," in which he had made some reflections on the Government and their treatment of the Bartholomew sufferers, and was summoned to the Quarter Sessions, but heard no more about the matter,

In 1684 strict warrants were issued to the constables to suppress all seditious conventicles, and the judges at York Assizes gave special instructions to the jury on the matter. On December 29th men broke in and scattered Heywood's meeting, indicted him for a riot, and bound him over to appear on his own recognisances of £100. The Dissenters in many places at this time were panic-stricken, and Heywood noted in his diary on this occasion, " Few dare own me. My wife timorous if we have more than four." At the Wakefield Sessions in January 1685 he was indicted for a riot, rout, and unlawful assembly, and fined £50. He refused to pay, and was confined in York Castle from January 26th to December 19th.

When the Declaration for Liberty of Conscience appeared in 1687 Heywood wrote, " It begets displeasure in the men of the Church of England, contentment to some Dissenters, jealousies in others, who suspect a design therein, and however it may prove, it becomes us thankfully to accept this immunity, to improve opportunities of service, and give God the glory of all." Writing about it afterwards, he said that " ministers and people did freely accept the liberty, preached the gospel freely, had numerous assemblies, solemn ordinations, conferences, and exercises set up on week days. . . . Dissenters have gained ground and become more numerous than ever. . . . Papists and Quakers complain that no one is a gainer but Presbyterians." In 1688 he wrote again, " Though Dissenters had liberty, yet we know it was not out of love to us, but for another end, for we heard the King say he was forced to grant liberty for the present to those that his soul abhorred." However, under the liberty he built his chapel at Northowram, and the first public baptism was performed in it in 1688.

He wrote several works. Besides the one already mentioned, he published a sermon entitled " Closet Prayer a Christian Duty," in 1668. Some other sermons preached at Coley had been published in the preceding year in a single volume entitled " Heart Treasure: or an Essay tending to Fill and Furnish the Head and Heart of every Christian with a Soul-enriching Treasure of Truths, Graces, Experiences, and Comforts."

Like most diarists, Heywood was somewhat of a gossip, and tells many grievous stories of alleged drunkenness, swearing, greediness, and immorality of the Anglican clergy. He speaks of the curates at Lightcliffe as " loose tippling preachers." When Mr. Drake, the vicar of Pontefract, goes round his parish with his parishioners " beating the bounds," he scornfully speaks of them as " the priest with his gang." To the Nonconformist the preaching was the important part of worship, so we can understand why he contemptuously notes that at Halifax, Dr. Hook, the vicar, being absent, the curates preached on Sunday mornings, and in the afternoon there was " nothing but the Book of Common Prayer." He was a methodical man, and kept a record of all his journeyings and preachings. He calculated that between 1665 and 1700 he had preached over 3000 sermons, and travelled over 31,000 miles. Where did the money come from for all this, to say nothing of his own maintenance? His income was derived from three sources: regular quarterly contributions of the congregation, gifts at funerals, baptisms, and other such ministrations, and allowances from sympathisers like Lady Hewley, Lady Wharton, and others, who were not members of his flock. During the latter years of his life he lived peaceably at Northowram, ministering to his congregation. He died in 1700.[1]

Down to the reign of George I. the Presbyterian body retained in their midst a number of the wealthy middle classes. But in Church government they were Presbyterians only in name, and a great change came over them in doctrine. There was a vigorous reaction against Calvinism, and at the same time Arian heterodoxy with regard to the Person of Christ was spreading among them, which accounts for the fact that in the eighteenth century many of the congregations became definitely enrolled as Unitarian. From the date of the Salters' Hall Conference in 1719 the Presbyterians became so rapidly Unitarian that it has been asserted that the Presbyterian congregations founded at the period of the Ejection did not maintain their existence more than fifty years. The Independents and Baptists were also affected by rationalism, but the few congregations which became Unitarian soon died out. These bodies found it comparatively easy to get rid of unorthodox members. But with the Presbyterians the government by lay elders prevented the congregation from asserting its will—in fact, it usually assented to the dictation of the minister and elders. In some cases, therefore, the whole congregation simply left in a body.[2] The revival of Presbyterianism in after years in England was due to an influx from Scotland,[3] where, although crushed between 1660 and 1689, it had speedily revived, and was again flourishing and vigorous.

THE INDEPENDENTS

The first Congregationalist church in this country is generally considered to have been established at Norwich by Richard Brown, somewhere about 1580. He, however, returned to Anglicanism, and in 1591 became rector of Thorpe Achurch, a living which he held for forty years. The leadership of his separated congregation passed to Henry Barrow, who established a different form of government. He was executed in 1593, and

[1] J. Hunter, " The Rise of the Old Dissent," 1842; O. Heywood, " Diary," Ed. by J. Horsfall Turner, 4 vols., 1882–1885.
[2] Barclay, " Inner Life," p. 589.
[3] Nightingale, " Lancs. Nonconformity," VI. 83.

his flock, now under Francis Johnson, retired to Holland. In 1616 Henry Jacob, who with William Bradshaw had preached Congregational principles in England as early as 1604 or 1605, established an Independent congregation in London.[1] In early Congregationalism various types of church government soon made themselves manifest:

The Brownists looked upon the church as a theocracy. Christ is the absolute King, and He rules by His Spirit acting in the individual members. All members were equal, and though a man might hold office, that office gave him no special power. Everything was settled by the majority of the votes of the members.

The Barrowists were ruled by a select body consisting of the ministers and elders. The pastor was elected by this board. Barrowism was for a long time the prevailing type of Congregationalism, but differences arose and thus there appeared several other forms.

The Johnsonians, who followed Francis Johnson, have been called the High Church Barrowists. After the congregation had elected the elders, they had no further power. The board of elders was absolute, and the congregation had simply to obey.[2]

The Ainsworthians have been called the Low Church Barrowists. Francis Johnson and Henry Ainsworth were pastors of an Independent congregation in Amsterdam, but Ainsworth separated from Johnson, and established another church, which took its name from him. Under him the power of the board of elders was reduced; its decisions could only be enforced after the whole body of the brethren had agreed to them.[3]

The Robinsonians, or Broad Church Barrowists, were less exclusive than the others. Their organisation was similar to that of the Ainsworthians, but they held that it was lawful to recognise the reality, though not the regularity, of churches differently organised, and to hold a carefully guarded communion with them.[4] In addition to the above, there was a sect called the *Wilkinsonians*. Wilkinson, their founder, thought that he and his followers were truly Apostles, and refused communion with those who denied their claim.[5]

The name Independent seems to have been first used by Henry Jacob in 1609[6] as an appellation for his particular group, but gradually the distinction between the various divisions mentioned above became less and less marked, and they all became known generically as Independents or Congregationalists, with the single exception of the Brownists, who still maintained their separate

[1] Burrage, " Early English Dissenters," I. 34.
[2] *Idem, ibid.*, I. 97.   [3] *Idem, ibid.*, I. 166–167.
[4] Dexter, " Congregationalism of the Last Three Hundred Years," p. 695.
[5] Ross, " Pansebeia," pp. 402–437.
[6] Drysdale, " Hist. of Presbyterianism in England," p. 5 note.

identity, and were recognised as a separate sect by other people. Edwards, Ross, Pagett, and all the heresiographers of the seventeenth century distinguished between them.   Brownist, however, was a nickname, and as such was disliked by those who bore it. A description of their worship was given in a tract published in 1677, " Ancient Truth Revived, or a True State of the Ancient Suffering Church of Christ, commonly but falsely called Brownists, living in London and other Places in this Nation." According to this account, in each Brownist congregation there was both a pastor and a teacher.   When they met together for worship the pastor read a portion of Scripture, with such exposition and doctrinal instruction as the time should permit, and next the teacher preached, and gave an exhortation intended to stir up the conscience of his hearers.   As well as that, the male members of the congregation " exercised their gifts in prophesying, according to the ability given them by God, by two or three at the most."   An Anglican writer said that the six principal tenets of the Independent Brownists were: (1) that national churches ceased with the Jewish Church; (2) that prelacy is antichristian; (3) that particular congregations are by Christ's institution to stand independent; (4) that ecclesiastical government is to be popular and not ministerial; (5) that Christ demands that the church shall be spiritual and composed of real saints, and (6) that the form of the particular church is decided by the mutual covenant of the members.   From all this they deduced that the parish churches of England were no true churches, and that Christians should separate from them, and if possible pull them down.[1]   The doctrines officially held by the Independents were agreed upon and set forth by a synod which met in the Savoy in 1658.[2]

The names Independent and Congregationalist have frequently been used as interchangeable terms, and for the last two hundred years the churches which described themselves as Independent have generally preserved the traditions of Congregationalist self-government.   But during the time of the Commonwealth many Congregationalists objected to being called Independents, and there were Independents who were not Congregationalist. The Independents were agreed on the one point that every separate congregation should be free from all external ecclesiastical control, and that the State should have no power in ecclesiastical matters, or at any rate that its right of interference should be so limited as to give the church the greatest possible freedom. The Congregationalists agreed as to the independence of every separate congregation, but, in addition, had a very definite theory on the manner in which such a separate Christian church

---

[1] Lamb, " A Fresh Suit against Independency," 1677.
[2] " A Declaration of the Faith and Order owned and practised in the Congregation Churches in England," 1659.

ought to be authorised.[1] This is the distinction made by a learned Congregationalist, but it seems too clear-cut for the seventeenth century. The truth is that the name Independent was often used as loosely as the name Presbyterian, and often at that date covered Congregationalists and members of some of the other sects.[2]

During the Commonwealth the old endowed parochial system had been retained, but the minister was concerned only with his own congregation, and could not be interfered with by any authority, ecclesiastical or civil, as long as his principles and practices gave no offence to the Government. So he took his stipend and inculcated what principles he chose. Sometimes he called himself a Congregationalist or Independent, and taught his people accordingly. The whole system was, to all intents and purposes, Congregationalism. But where the minister had hankerings after bishops or Presbyterian classes, some of his flock might exercise the liberty granted to everybody but the Anglican and Roman Catholic, and form a separate congregation of their own. After the Restoration such bodies were as far as possible suppressed, and their ministers had either to conform or go out. As far as the Congregationalists were concerned, the ministers lost what official position and endowed income they might have held, but on their own principles they had no right to regret this.

The chief actual differences between the Presbyterians and the Independents, during the period under review, were based almost entirely on the respective positions of their ministers. Among the Presbyterians the minister was responsible for the admission of new members and for the exercise of discipline. Among the Independents these things were settled by the votes of the congregation. The greatest difference between them was in the matter of ordination. While the Presbyterian minister was ordained by the laying on of hands, and was placed over a congregation by other ministers, the Independents considered that the ministerial office was essentially derived from the call and election of a particular church, and so they were not so particular about the imposition of the hands of the presbytery as the necessary method of ordination.[3] In theory each congregation by its divine right elected and appointed its own minister, but there seems reason to believe that in practice this was frequently a mere matter of arrangement between himself and the church officials. Henry Newcome, preaching John Jolly's funeral sermon at Gorton in 1682, gave much offence, though quite unintentionally, to some Independents present, by his remarks on church membership.[4] But the Presbyterian

[1] Dale, " Hist. of Eng. Congregationalism," pp. 375–376.
[2] Nightingale, " Ejected of 1662." I. 14.
[3] Stoughton, " Hist. of Rel. in Eng.," IV. 166–168.
[4] " Autobiog. of Henry Newcome," January 28th, 1682.

appointment by the ministry tended at times to become a similar matter of arrangement with church officers too, and thus this particular distinction between the two bodies tended to become less clear.

The Presbyterians had had a share in the Restoration, and might therefore hope for some consideration in return. The Independents had done nothing, and could expect little. Comprehension was out of the question, even if it had been consistent with their principles. Some of them, of whom Stephen Nye was one, hoped that the King would be able to grant them toleration, but the hope was vain. They had too many enemies. They had trampled down King, Church, and presbytery alike, and the common view was expressed at a later date by a writer who said that the spirit of Independency had been a spirit of envy, strife, schism, and sedition, a spirit which had offered violence to all obligations sacred and civil, which had trodden moral principles in the dirt in order to save itself, and had been a protecting shadow to Anabaptists, Seekers, Ranters, and Quakers.[1] The Independents consequently suffered like their fellows in the other sects. One of the most distinguished of them was Daniel Burgess, who was educated at Winchester School and Magdalen College, Oxford. From 1667 to 1674 he was in Ireland, whither he had been invited by the Earl of Orrery, who set up a school at Charleville and appointed him head master. In 1674 he returned to England and preached in Marlborough and the neighbourhood. Arrested on one occasion for preaching, he was committed to the common gaol at Marlborough, where he had nothing to lie down upon, and was forced to continue walking about till the following day, when his friends put a bed in through the window. After some time he was released on bail, but his imprisonment and his prosecution at the Assizes cost him a considerable sum.[2] John Humphrey, who called himself a Congregationalist in later life, spent some time in the Gatehouse prison, and his pamphlet " The Sacramental Test " was ordered by Parliament to be burnt by the common hangman.[3]

John Laxley, who was educated at St. John's College, Cambridge, became a captain in the Parliamentary army, and in 1647 took forcible possession of the living of Kibworth in Leicestershire by entering the church with a party of soldiers. He is reported to have constantly preached and prayed against the Stuarts, and to have joined with other ministers in a petition that the King might be brought to trial. He is also said to have turned the font out of the church and converted it into a horse-trough. At the Restoration he and his wife and family were turned out

---

[1] Lamb, " Fresh Suit against Independency," 1677.
[2] Calamy, II. 760; IV. 872; Wilson, " Dissenting Churches in London," III. 496.
[3] Calamy, II. 615; Wood, " Ath. Ox.," II. 1107.

with great violence, so much so that his wife became blind from her injuries, and he himself was arraigned for high treason for saying in the pulpit that he thought hell had broken loose.[1]

Philip Nye, ejected from St. Bartholomew's, behind the Exchange, had been a stout opponent of the King. When Monk brought his army to London, Nye and John Owen consulted with Whitelocke and St. John about raising troops to drive him out, and offered to raise £100,000 for the purpose. At the Restoration it was seriously debated in Council whether Nye, together with Goodwin and Hugh Peters, should be excepted from the Bill of Indemnity, but at last it was decided that if he accepted any civil, military, or ecclesiastical office he should stand as if he had been totally excepted. After this he had to keep very quiet, but he ministered to Nonconformist congregations from time to time and was one of those who opened meeting-houses after the Great Fire.[2] John Wesley, the grandfather of the great John Wesley, was ejected from Winterbourne Whitchurch in Dorsetshire. Soon after the Restoration, Gilbert Ironside, Bishop of Bristol, hearing that Wesley refused to use the Prayer Book, sent for him and inquired into his views and his orders. He treated Wesley with great kindness and consideration, and sent him away promising to do him all the kindness he could, but " the bishop was more civil to him than he to the bishop." [3] Early in 1661 information was laid against Wesley " for diabolically railing against the late King and his posterity and praising Cromwell." [4] Early in 1662 he was imprisoned at Blandford and bound over to appear at the Assizes. He continued in his living till August 17th, when he preached a farewell sermon and removed to Melcombe Regis, but the Corporation made an order against his settlement there, and his landlady was fined £20 for taking him into her house, and he himself five shillings a week as long as he remained there. Finally he settled down at Preston, a few miles from Melcombe Regis, but had to leave for a time when the Five Mile Act came out. As he continued preaching, he was several times in prison, once at Poole for six months, once at Dorchester for three months, and on several other occasions. When he died the vicar of Preston would not allow him to be buried in the church. His death, it is said, led to the death of his father, Bartholomew Wesley, who had been ejected from Charmouth in the same county.[5]

The Congregational meeting-house at Stepney, built in 1674, had a trap-door at the top of the gallery stairs, which led to a concealed suite of rooms over the ceiling. Here, if necessary,

[1] Wilson, " Dissenting Churches in London "; Calamy, II. 422; IV. 586.
[2] Calamy, II. 29; III. 28; Wilson, " Dissenting Churches in London," III. 71–77.
[3] Kennet, " Reg.," 919; C.S.P.D., February 5th, 1661.
[4] C.S.P.D., February 5th, 1661, 30/22.
[5] Calamy, III, 429, 437–451.

they could meet in concealment and listen to the exhortations of Meade, their minister.[1] The Dissenters at Andover met in a dell four miles from the town, or in a private house at night, where they barred all doors and windows, and even put the candle out to prevent a gleam of light attracting informers.[2]

There was some attempt made in 1669 to bring about union between the Presbyterians and Independents, for the strengthening of the common interest. Baxter first proposed it to Owen. But Baxter " seemed invariably to have forgot that union will never be effected by disputing for it; and that chiding, which he called plain dealing, was very unlikely to bring it about." [3] Owen, in his " Catechism," had made two considerable concessions—namely, that the people have not the power of the keys, and that they do not give the power of the keys, or the power implied in their office, to their pastors. So Baxter proposed that they should first settle what were the essentials of religion and communion, and on that basis establish the means of union, and that nothing should be made public till they had come to some agreement. He suggested that each of them should draw up a scheme, but Owen said that Baxter had better draw one up first, and Baxter drew up an " abundance of theses " on the matters necessary for concord. Owen said there were too many, and Baxter produced an abridged list. The latter was very anxious in the matter, and when Owen retained them a few weeks for consideration, went to see Owen again and again. Owen described Baxter's scheme as " the fairest offer and likeliest means that he ever saw," but on January 25th, 1669, wrote a letter in which he stated his objections, the chief being that too many things were set down for discussion, seeing that this was only a preparatory attempt. He also thought that some of the wording, intended as a safeguard against future divisions, might be taken as reflecting on some things that had been done in the past, and that the question of the power of the civil magistrates in ecclesiastical matters might very well be left out at this stage. He objected that though Baxter's scheme kept the Baptists out, there was a loophole whereby the Socinians might creep in. Baxter's version of what happened next is as follows: " I so much feared that it would come to nothing, that I ventured to tell him what a difficulty I feared it would be to him to go openly and fully according to his own judgment, when the reputation of former actions and present interest in many that would censure him, if he went not after their narrowed judgment, did lie in his way, and that I feared these temptations more than his ability and judgment." He also sent a reply to Owen's objections. After that they visited each

[1] Fletcher, " Hist. of Independency," IV. c. III.
[2] J. S. Pearsall, " Rise of Congregationalism at Andover," 1844, p. 94.
[3] Orme, " Life of Owen," p. 236.

other, and Owen said he had received Baxter's " chiding letter," and perceived that his genuine desire to bring the matter to a successful issue was suspected, but Baxter should see that he meant what he said. Baxter waited on him time after time in vain, and after about fifteen months desired him to return the papers, which he did with the words, " I am still a well-wisher to these mathematics." This was the issue of Baxter's third attempt at union with the Independents.[1]

Jealousy and hostility between the Presbyterians and Independents manifested themselves from time to time, but on several occasions the leaders devised schemes for working in concert. In 1669 a lecture at Hackney was shared between three Presbyterians, Dr. Bates, Thomas Watson, and Peter Sterry, and four Independents, Nye, Owen, George Griffith, and Thomas Brooks.[2] In 1672 a number of London merchants and tradesmen established a Tuesday morning lecture at Pinners' Hall, and a fund was raised to pay each preacher twenty shillings for each sermon. Manton, Owen, Bates, Baxter, Collins, and Jenkyn were among the early preachers, who were carefully selected from both parties. Baxter's very first sermon raised controversy, and he soon retired from the scheme. " When I had preached there but four sermons, I found the Independents so quarrelsome with what I said that all the city did ring of their backbiting and false accusations." [3] The strife-makers were rebuked by Manton and also by Baxter, who issued a broadside, " An Appeal to the Light." On February 10th, 1677, Sir William Coventry, the Secretary, wrote to Sir Thomas Davis, Lord Mayor of London, saying that the King had been informed that a lecture or conventicle had been established at Pinners' Hall. The Lord Mayor was to take all legal methods to suppress it and to report what had been done in the matter.[4] This Pinners' Hall lecture, however, went on till 1694, but later disagreements between the Independents and the Presbyterians led to the establishment of a rival lecture at Salters' Hall. In 1678 some of the leading Nonconformists united to establish an evening lecture in a room belonging to a coffee-house in Exchange Alley, and among the preachers were Theophilus Dorrington, James Lambert, Thomas Goodwin, and John Shower.

A violent onslaught was made on the Independent system by an Anglican writer in a book published in 1677, entitled " A Fresh Suit against Independency,"' which set forth the Independent tenets and practices as they appeared to a Church of England man. Since they accepted nothing for which they

---

[1] The other two were in the days of the Commonwealth, " Rel. Baxt.," III. 61–69; Kennet, " Hist. of Eng.," III. 300–301.
[2] Gordon, " Freedom after Ejection," p. 154.
[3] " Rel. Baxt.," III. 103.
[4] C.S.P.D., February 10th, 1677; " Precedents," I. f. 188.

could not find a plain command in Holy Scripture, many of them had ceased to baptize infants, and had turned Anabaptists, or had joined some other sect. Their doctrines unchurched all Christendom but themselves, and made Christ a King without a Kingdom. The foreign Protestants utterly disliked their system, and had protested against their teachings. They had few learned men amongst them, because they held that with the pouring out of God's Spirit there was no need for human learning. They protested against forms of prayer, and let the worship of God be corrupted by ignorant men, whose errors and private animosities found vent even in their prayers. What good order could there be in their churches under popular government, when ignorant people chose their own pastors, when ministers preached what they would, when women and boys preached, and when un-ordained men even took upon themselves to administer the sacraments? According to their view, only the saints could be members of the church, but had they never heard of the Church of Sardis? What evidence was there of Christ giving power to ministers to judge the holiness of persons who wished to join them? It might be the duty of the church to turn scandalous members *out*, but that was quite another thing. All Christians had a covenant with God, but that was quite a different thing from a separate and peculiar covenant of the members of one congregation, and neither could a minister be ordained simply to be the minister of a single congregation.

The best known and probably the most important of the Independent ministers of this period was Dr. John Owen, who had been Dean of Christ Church, Oxford, and Vice-Chancellor of the University under the Commonwealth. The latter office he resigned in 1657, and he was turned out of the deanery shortly after Richard Cromwell became Protector, probably because he was mixed up in a plot against him.[1] He was opposed to the Restoration, and with Nye and Whitelocke consulted how an army could be raised to overthrow Monk. When the King came back he was not in possession of any ecclesiastical office, and so cannot fairly be counted among the ejected, and as he preached constantly to the Independents till the time of his death, he can hardly be spoken of as silenced, except so far as he was not allowed to preach in the Anglican churches. Clarendon treated him with great kindness and respect, and urged him, if he could not see his way to conform, to employ his time and abilities in theological writing, instead of violating the law and endangering the public peace by keeping conventicles. Owen gave him his word that he would be obedient, but soon afterwards was found preaching to a congregation of thirty or forty in his house at Stadham, after which Clarendon lost all confidence in him.[2]

---

[1] "Rel. Baxt.," p. 101. A full account of this is given in Guizot's "History of the Protectorate of Richard Cromwell."

[2] Grey, "Impartial Examination of Neal's Fourth Volume," pp. 394–399.

In 1661 there was published a small duodecimo volume,
" Fiat Lux, or a General Conduct to a Right Understanding
betwixt Papist and Protestant, Presbyterian and Independent,
by J. V. C., a friend to men of all religions." The author was a
Franciscan, John Vincent Cane, and " a person of honour " gave
Owen a copy of the work, with a request that he should write
a reply. His answer, which appeared in the following year, was
called " Animadversions on Fiat Lux, By a Protestant." A short
reply came from the friar in the form of an Epistle to the author,
whom he evidently suspected of being one of the more violent
of the democratic party of the Commonwealth, though he could
not guess his name. In 1664 Owen wrote " A Vindication of
Animadversions on Fiat Lux," in which he dealt not merely with
Cane's arguments, but with the whole Roman question. The
episcopal press licensers made some difficulty about the publication of the book, because the author always spoke of " Peter "
and not " St. Peter," and had further tried to prove that the
Apostle was never in Rome. It is said, however, that Sir H.
Nicholas, the Secretary of State, personally appealed to the Bishop
of London to permit it to be licensed. Clarendon was much
struck by the book, sent Sir Bulstrode Whitelocke to arrange an interview with Owen, and promised him high preferment if he would
conform.[1] He seems to have had two offers also from abroad.
The First Congregational Church of Boston invited him to preside
over it on the death of John Norton in 1663, but he was prevented
from accepting by particular orders from the King himself.[2]
He was also offered a little later a professorship of divinity in
one of the Dutch universities. After the Fire, the laws against
Nonconformity being somewhat relaxed, Owen, with some of
the other Dissenting leaders, ministered in the " tabernacles "
which were set up.

Baxter, who disliked Owen, said that hitherto he had refrained
from such public ministration, as if he had been more ashamed
or afraid of suffering than his brethren. A great many of the
Parliamentary officers and some people of rank and wealth
attended his services. He was very busy with literary work
during these years, and published in 1668 his " Exposition of
Psalm CXXX," and the first volume of his " Commentary on the
Epistle to the Hebrews." This work contained a good deal of
matter directed against the Socinians. The fourth and last
volume of it appeared in 1684. He also entered into the controversy over Samuel Parker's " Ecclesiastical Polity," by
publishing " Truth and Innocence Vindicated in a Survey of a
Discourse of Ecclesiastical Polity " in 1669. With the profits on
his books, a small legacy from a friend, Martin Owen, a wealthy
London brewer, a wealthy second marriage, and some landed
property which he possessed, he was in a much better financial

[1] Orme, " Life of Owen," p. 229.
[2] Wilson, " Dissenting Churches in London," I. 271.

position than many other Nonconformists. At one time, while living in Kensington, he even kept his coach. When the Second Conventicle Act came out in 1670, Owen issued a pamphlet, " The State of the Kingdom with respect to the present Bill against Conventicles," and laid it before the House of Lords. He was furiously attacked by George Vernon, a Gloucestershire incumbent, who wrote " A Letter to a Friend concerning some of Dr. Owen's Principles and Practices." This pamphlet of nearly eighty pages was full of abuse of Owen, who was described as " the prince, the oracle, and the metropolitan of Independency," " the Ahithophel of Oliver Cromwell, a blasphemous and perjured person, and a libeller of authority after the restoration of Charles II.," and the State was urged to take vengeance on such a miscreant. Owen replied in " A Letter to Sir Thomas Overbury," a member of his congregation. In 1671 there was some suggestion of Owen going to Harvard. In that year the college was in difficulties, and the magistrates and ministers of Massachusetts Bay addressed a letter to the Independents in England, asking for assistance for it, for a President, and for a supply of students for it from England. A reply signed by Owen and twelve Independent ministers in London was despatched early in the following year, saying they were doing what they could, and recommending as President Dr. Hoare, a graduate of Harvard, who was then proceeding to New England.[1]

After the Declaration of Indulgence was issued, the London Dissenters wished to express their gratitude to the King, and an address was drawn up by Jenkyn and Dr. Lazarus Seaman, but was thought too eulogistic. Baxter states that they could not agree about what they should say, and they finally decided to send a deputation, who should express their thanks verbally and in a guarded manner, and that this was done, the deputation being introduced to the King by Arlington. This is not accurate. An address was drawn up by Owen, agreed to by the ministers, and presented to Charles.[2]

In 1672 Joseph Caryl, who had held an Independent meeting at Leadenhall Street, died. It was proposed that as Owen's congregation was near the two should unite. This was done in 1673, and they worshipped henceforth in Bury Street, St. Mary Axe. It was a great addition to Owen's congregation of thirty-six, for there were now 170 members. It was probably one of the most aristocratic of the London Nonconformist congregations, for, amongst others, it was attended by the Countess of Anglesey, Sir Thomas Overbury, Sir John Hartopp, Lady Tompson, and Lady Vere Wilkinson, besides distinguished Cromwellian officers like " Lord " Charles Fleetwood, Major-General Des-

---

[1] Eachard gives the date of the offer as 1673, " Hist. of Eng., " III. 541.
[2] " Rel. Baxt.," III. 99; *Gentleman's Magazine*, XXXI. 253; Orme, " Life of Owen," p. 277.

borough, the brother-in-law of Cromwell, and Major-General Berry. Mrs. Bendish, Oliver's granddaughter, was also a member. Among the assistant ministers there was for a short time Robert Ferguson, the plotter. When in 1674 Owen was at Tunbridge Wells for his health, James, Duke of York, who was also there, sent for him several times, and conversed with him about the Nonconformists. When he returned to London the King sent for him, and had a long interview, in which he told him that he might always have access to the royal presence, expressed his belief in freedom of worship, and gave him a thousand guineas to distribute among the distressed Nonconformists. This became known, and a great clamour was raised that the Dissenters were being bribed to serve the popish interest. Burnet says that Stillingfleet told him that the Court had hired the Dissenters to be silent, and that the greater of them were so, and were very compliant.[1] Owen and his friends indignantly denied this.

Owen's next literary fray was with Sherlock, who in 1674 wrote a " Discourse concerning the Knowledge of Jesus Christ, and our Union and Communion with Him," in which he criticised a work of Owen's published in 1657, " On Communion with God." Owen replied with " A Vindication of some passages in a Discourse concerning Communion with God, from the exceptions of William Sherlock, Rector of St. George's, Botolph Lane." In Owen's view Sherlock had denied the doctrines of the Imputed Righteousness and Justification by Faith. A number of works appeared from the Press on Owen's side, written by Robert Ferguson,[2] Edward Polhill,[3] Vincent Alsop,[4] Henry Hickman,[5] Samuel Rolle,[6] and Thomas Danson, the ejected minister of Sibton.[7] Sherlock replied in 1675 to Owen and Ferguson, and made no reference to the other controversialists. On Sherlock's side, Thomas Hotchkiss, rector of Staunton, wrote " A Discourse concerning the Imputation of Christ's Righteousness " (1675).

Another controversy began a little later. In 1674 Owen wrote a work on the Holy Spirit. In 1678 William Clagett, one of the King's chaplains, wrote " A Discourse concerning the Operation of the Holy Spirit," in which he criticised Owen, and drew from John Humphrey, in his " Peaceable Disquisitions,"

---

[1] Burnet, " Own Times," I. 555.
[2] " The Interest of Reason in Religion," 1675.
[3] " An Answer to the Discourse of Mr. William Sherlock."
[4] " Antisozzo; or, Sherlocismus Enervatus."
[5] " Speculum Sherlockianum; or, a Looking-glass in which the Admirers of Mr. Sherlock may Behold their Man," 1674.
[6] " Prodromus; or, the Character of Mr. Sherlock's Book," 1674, and " Justification Justified."
[7] " A Friendly Debate between Satan and Sherlock " and " A Defence of the Friendly Debate."

some strictures on Clagett's lack of courtesy.   Clagett, in a second
volume, replied to Humphrey, and continued this onslaught on
Owen's book, and was about to publish a third volume, but the
manuscript was destroyed in a burning house.

In 1683 Owen was suspected of being involved in the Rye
House plot, with several other ministers.   He died in August
of that year, and was given a great funeral.   It was said that
the carriages of sixty-seven noblemen and gentlemen, besides
the numerous mourning coaches and a long procession of people
on horseback, followed him to the grave.   This does not
necessarily mean that all the " noblemen and gentlemen " were
Dissenters.   He was a well-known man, and held a high position
at Oxford, had moved in good circles, was able and learned,
and held in personal respect by many who had no sympathy
with his Nonconformity.   His fame as a scholar had been widespread, and it is said that learned Protestants from abroad
frequently came to visit him.[1]   He was the author of a great
number of theological, doctrinal, devotional, and controversial
works.

The English Independents were, more than any other sect
except the Quakers, in favour of toleration all round, and some
of the most able advocates of that policy were to be found in their
ranks.   Some of them even saw no reason why Roman Catholics
should not be allowed to worship in their own way.[2]   When
it was heard in England that their brethren, the Independents
in the New England States, were persecuting the Baptists and
Quakers there, the London Independents, led by Owen, wrote to
expostulate with them in 1669.   When James II. issued the
Declaration of Indulgence he was supported by Lobb the Independent, Alsop the Presbyterian, and Penn the Quaker, and
these three wrote pamphlets in favour of toleration which gave
much offence to many of their dissenting brethren.   Stephen
Lobb was devoted to King James, and in after years was known
as " the Jacobite Independent."   He used all his influence in
favour of toleration and urged the abolition of the Test Act,
yet he was also one of the people who advised the King to prosecute
the seven bishops.[3]

Their tolerant spirit, however, did not lead the Independents
in the direction of occasional conformity.   At Owen's death in
1683 a manuscript of his became known in which he had set
forth twelve arguments against his brethren joining in worship
" which was not of divine origin," by which he meant, amongst
other things, the worship of the Church of England.   " The

[1] Orme, "Life of Owen," p. 357; Wood, "Ath. Ox.," II. 737-748;
Palmer, I. 198; III. 131.
[2] Orme, "Life of Baxter," p. 299; Fletcher, "Hist. of Independency," IV.
c. III.
[3] Wilson, "Dissenting Churches in London," III. 438-443.

disputatious but zealous Baxter " [1] wrote a reply entitled " A Defence of Catholic Communion," in which he accused Owen of forty-two errors. [2]

There was some talk in the years preceding the Revolution about uniting for common action in disciplinary matters. [3] In 1688 a scheme for agreement between the Nonconformists was put forward, but when the Congregationalists began to debate on the proposed articles of union, it was suggested to them that such a proceeding would not be looked on with favour by the Court, and so the matter was dropped. [4] In that year the Congregationalists published " A Declaration of the Faith and Order Owned and Practised in the Congregational Churches in England, agreed upon by the Elders and Messengers," [5] apparently with no idea that the division between them and the other sects could be anything but permanent. Nevertheless, measures of co-operation in regard to finance were begun in London in 1689, and in 1690 the " Managers of the Common Fund of the Presbyterians and Independents of London " sent inquiries throughout the country for statistics and information about the ejected ministers still surviving, the number of existing and defunct congregations, possible new fields of labour, numbers of candidates for the ministry, and so on. This " Happy Union," however, though concerned merely with statistics and finance, was soon found to be unworkable. [6]

A list was drawn up in 1690 of 759 Independent and Presbyterian ministers in England and Wales. Of these 218 were described as being without any competent means of support, and 133 as not having congregations, 380 were men who had been turned out at the Restoration, and all but seventeen of them were still more or less in active service. The return is not complete, however, for several counties. [7]

[1] Skeats and Mialls, " History of the Free Churches of England," 1892, p. 49.
[2] Orme, " Life of Owen."
[3] Gordon, " Freedom after Ejection," p. 154.
[4] Kennet, " Hist. of Eng.," III. 490.
[5] London, 1688.
[6] Gordon, " Freedom after Ejection," p. 167; " Heads of Agreement assented to by the United Ministers in and about London, formerly called Presbyterian and Congregationalist," 1691.
[7] Gordon, " Freedom after Ejection," pp. 174–177.

III

THE English Baptists may be said to date from 1608, in which year John Smyth and other Puritan refugees fled from England to Holland. The earlier Anabaptists in England, whom we hear of in the early half of the sixteenth century, were foreigners, and were soon driven out or silenced by persecution. The name Anabaptist was in that century frequently used in a general way to denote any separatist of strangely unorthodox or fanatical opinions, but there were no Anabaptist English congregations in the strict sense, *i.e.* separatists who rebaptized the converts to their ways of thinking, before 1612. The name Baptist does not seem to have been applied to these before 1641. They were sometimes called Catabaptists, because they were opposed to infant baptism.[1]

In 1609 Smyth baptized himself, either by aspersion or affusion, and then baptized his congregation. Hence he became known as the Se-Baptist, though he was not the first person to deserve the name in England.[2] In 1612, Smyth being now dead, many of his followers united with the Dutch Anabaptists, known as the Waterlander Mennonites, with whom Smyth had had negotiations with a view to union. Thomas Helwys, one of Smyth's flock, however, had differed from Smyth on the question of this union, and with seven or eight followers seceded from them, and returned to London in 1612. He and his followers were opposed to Calvinism, and called themselves Free Willers. This group came to be known as the General Baptists, and in due course were organised under the title of " The General Assembly of the General Baptist Churches in England." They were called General Baptists because they believed that Christ died for all; that salvation was intended for men in general, not for particular persons. Owing to their Arminian leanings, they were never in fellowship with the great body of the Baptists. They were organised into local associations before 1651, and from 1653 onwards they have had a General Assembly, which exists to-day and possesses a long and complete series of records. In 1661 they claimed to have 20,000 members.[3] From 1642 onwards at

[1] Burrage, " Early Hist. of Dissenters," I. 26, 41.
[2] *Idem, ibid.*, I. 32, 223–224, 237.
[3] Whitley, " Minutes Gen. Assembly," I. xxvi.; *Trans. Bapt. Hist. Soc.*, I. 114.

least they maintained the principle of immersion, and it became as important in their view as their other cardinal doctrines of Believers' Baptism and General Redemption.[1] Most of the Baptist ministers came from the lower ranks of society [2] and their flocks as a rule were poor. That was why their London meeting-places were mostly in obscure places in the suburbs: they could not, like the more wealthy sects, hire expensive halls.[3] The General Baptists depended chiefly on a travelling ministry and lay preachers. Samuel Fisher, John Gosnold, Dr. William Russell, and Matthew Caffin were university men, but Fisher became a Quaker, Gosnold and Russell, though holding General Baptist views, did not belong to the Assembly, and Caffin did not take a degree. The last-named was born at Horsham of yeoman stock, had adopted the principles of " believers' baptism," and had in consequence been expelled from Oxford. He returned to his native place and taught General Baptist doctrines in the neighbourhood till his death in 1714.[4] Of the other leaders of this section of the Baptists, Richard Adams of Mountsorrel, Leicestershire, was described as " gent," and George Catheral of Ivinghoe as " of good estate ": the rest were yeomen, shop-keepers, and artisans.[5]

September 12th, 1633, was the date of the commencement of the Particular Baptists, so called because they held the Calvinist doctrine of Particular Redemption. On that day the first congregation, under a Mr. Spilsbury, formally separated from an Independent congregation which met in Blackfriars,[6] established a meeting at Wapping, and later built a meeting-house in Broad Street, near Coal Harbour.[7] A second group seceded from the same Independent congregation in 1638, and a third in 1639, the last group of seceders establishing themselves in Crutched Friars.[8] In 1644 seven congregations of Particular Baptists issued a joint Confession of Faith. After 1649 the Baptists increased rapidly, and it is believed that at the end of the Commonwealth period there were 115 General Baptist congregations in England and 131 Particular Baptist.[9]

The Particular Baptists were especially fortunate in their leaders, Kiffin, Hanserd Knollys, Gifford, Keach, and others, and during the Restoration period drew their converts from a higher grade of society than did the General Baptists.[10] William Kiffin was a wealthy London merchant, who became minister

---

[1] Whitley, " Minutes Gen. Assembly," I. xiv.
[2] *Idem*, " Hist. Brit. Baptists," p. 153.
[3] *Idem*, " Baptists of London," p. 13.
[4] *Idem*, " Minutes Gen. Assembly," I. xxi.
[5] *Idem, ibid.*, I. xlii–xliii.   [6] Cramp, " Bapt. Hist.," p. 264.
[7] *Trans. Bapt. Hist. Soc.*, I. 180.
[8] Crossby, " Hist. Eng. Baptists," III. 41; Lewis, " Rise and Progress of Anabaptism," pp. 91–92.
[9] *Trans. Bapt. Hist. Soc.*, II. 236.   [10] Barclay's " Inner Life," 596.

of the congregation which, after some wanderings, finally settled down in Devonshire Square. Hanserd Knollys had been ordained by the Bishop of Peterborough, and had held the living of Humberstone in Leicestershire. In 1636 he left the Church of England, and two years later, being in danger of the attentions of the High Commission Court, went to New England. He returned to England in 1641, became master of the free school at St. Mary Axe, and when the war broke out joined the Parliamentary army. Later he opened a Baptist meeting-house in Great St. Helen Street.[1] Benjamin Keach, one of the best known of the Baptist leaders, was a tailor living at Winslow in Buckinghamshire. Born in 1640, he seems to have been a precocious youth, for we are told that, " beginning to suspect the validity of infant baptism, which he himself received, he was baptized by immersion in the fifteenth year of his age," and at eighteen he was called to the ministry of the General Baptists.[2] One of the scholarly men in this section of the Baptist movement was Nehemiah Cox, who was minister of the congregation in Petty France from 1675 to 1688, as well as in practice as a physician. He was originally a cordwainer at Bedford and a member of Bunyan's church there, and it is related of him that on one occasion, being on trial for Nonconformity at the Bedford Assizes, he pleaded first in Greek and then in Hebrew, arguing that it was but fair that he should plead in what language he pleased.[3] Cox's colleague for many years was William Collins, who was said to have studied in England, France, and Italy. The Particular Baptists had in their ranks a number of university men.

In the sixteenth century Baptists who kept the seventh day of the week instead of Sunday were quite common in Germany. Early in the seventeenth century they made their appearance in England, but do not appear to have organised their congregations till the time of the Commonwealth. During the next fifty years Sabbatarian churches were established in England, of which three were in London, while there were others at Ingham in Norfolk, Colchester, Wallingford, and other places. Eleven in all are known as existing at this period.[4] As early as 1618 John Traske was writing and preaching Sabbatarianism, and it is held that the Old Mill Yard church which still exists in London, and meets in Canonbury every Saturday, grew out of his labours, though John James, who was executed in 1661, is generally regarded as the pastor who gathered them together at a date which is uncertain, owing to the destruction of the records in time past by fire.[5] The Sabbatarian views of these people were

[1] J. Culross, " Hanserd Knollys," 1895.
[2] Wilson, " Dissenting Churches in London," IV. 243.
[3] *Idem, ibid.*, II. 185–187.   [4] Whitley, " Hist. Brit. Baptists," p. 86.
[5] Cathcart, " Bap. Encycl.," 1883, Art. " Seventh-day Baptists."

much disliked by their fellow-Dissenters, and Dr. William Russell wrote in 1663 " No Seventh-Day Sabbath Commanded by Jesus Christ in the New Testament." Most of the original churches in England, however, have died out, or changed their opinions with regard to the Sabbath,[1] but the movement developed and continued in America. The sect was originally known as the Sabbatarian Baptists, but the name was changed to Seventh-Day Baptists in 1818.[2] The practice of observing the seventh day was not confined to them, it was found also in the other sections of the Baptist movement.[3]

Old Mill Yard church claims as one of its early pastors Dr. Peter Chamberlain,[4] a learned physician who was educated at Emmanuel College, Cambridge, Heidelberg, and Padua, at which last university he graduated M.D. He also incorporated at Oxford, and was a Fellow of the College of Physicians. He was Physician-in-Ordinary to James I. and Anne of Denmark, and later to Charles I. and Henrietta Maria. In 1651 he joined the Sabbatarian Baptists, and became a minister of the sect. Nevertheless at the Restoration he regained his old position as physician to the King. For years he lived in Coleman Street, and we hear of the church " that walked with Dr. Peter Chamberlain." He was subjected to a good deal of annoyance, and on one occasion wrote in strong terms to Sancroft protesting against being called a Jew, but he never suffered the trials which other Nonconformist ministers endured. Probably his position at Court covered him with the King's protection. In his latter days he lived at Woodham Mortimer Hall, in Essex, where he carried on a correspondence with the Archbishop of Canterbury, urging measures to reconcile and reunite all Christians. He died in 1683, and his tomb is still to be seen in the church of Woodham Mortimer.[5]

In Northumberland the Mercers' Company maintained a lectureship at Hexham Abbey, and through their instrumentality Thomas Tilham or Tillam was appointed lecturer. He was of foreign extraction, born of Jewish parents, or, according to another story, had been a Jewish proselyte,[6] and was later a Roman Catholic. Finally he became a Baptist, and was instrumental in gathering a Baptist congregation at Hexham, of which an offshoot was founded at Muggleswick in the neighbouring county of Durham. Tillam held Sabbatarian views, and in 1659 was attacked by William Foulkes, afterwards ejected from All Saints', Sudbury, in " The Jewish Sabbath Antiquated, and

[1] *Trans. Bapt. Hist. Soc.*, I. 114–116.
[2] Schaff-Herzog, " Rel. Encycl.," III., Art. " Seventh-day Baptists."
[3] Whitley, " Hist. Brit. Baptists," p. 102.
[4] Cathcart, " Bapt. Encycl.," Art. " Seventh-day Baptists."
[5] *Trans. Bapt. Hist. Soc.*, II. 1–30, 112–113. Dr. Whitley speaks of him as a General Baptist, " Hist. Brit. Baptists," p. 102.
[6] C.S.P.D., September 1st, 1661.

the Lord's Day Instituted by Divine Authority ; an Answer to T. Tillam." [1] In 1660 Tillam was suspected of disloyalty to the Government and was sent to prison, and while there an intercepted letter of his was sent to Secretary Nicholas.[2] After his release he went to Holland for a time.

Generally speaking, there were four types of Baptists: Strict and Particular, Open and Particular, Seventh-Day and Particular, and General.[3] The Strict Baptists, like Kiffin and Thomas Plant, would not hold church communion with any but baptized believers and churches constituted as such, but there . were certain Baptist congregations who allowed " open " or " mixed " communion. They held Calvinistic beliefs, but differed from the Particular Baptists in denying the absolute necessity of baptism. Tombes was prominent among these, but they were few in number. Bunyan's congregation at Bedford belonged to this section.

John Tombes was one of the most learned Baptist teachers. Educated at Magdalen Hall, Oxford, where he took the degree of Bachelor of Divinity, and was tutor to John Wilkins, afterwards Bishop of Chester, he was eminent both as a classical and a Hebrew scholar, and was for a time Master of the Temple. During the Commonwealth times he carried on a controversy with Baxter on the subject of baptism,[4] and on one occasion at least they debated face to face in the presence of a large number of their respective followers. " The victory, as usual, was claimed by both sides ; but some of the learned, who were far from approving his cause, yielded the advantage, both of learning and argument, to Mr. Tombes." [5] Soon after the Restoration he resigned the living of Leominster, and went to live at Salisbury, where he married a rich widow, and where he occasionally, at least, attended the services of the Church of England. As far as is known, he never worshipped with the Baptists in Salisbury. He had never, indeed, adopted the whole Baptist system, though he maintained the chief Baptist doctrines after he gave up his living. About 1664 he issued a challenge at Oxford to maintain those doctrines against all comers, but he was a doughty controversialist, and no one came forward to oppose him. Bishops Sanderson and Barlow of Lincoln had a high opinion of him, and he was on visiting terms with Ward, Bishop of Salisbury. He was a strong advocate of occasional communion with the Church of England, wherein he differed greatly from some of the Baptists, who had doubts about the lawfulness of listening to preachers who, in their opinion, had not been baptized. He was also a strong

---

[1] David's " Evang. Nonconformity in Essex," p. 374.
[2] C.S.P.D., 4/18, June 13th, 1660.
[3] *Bapt. Quarterly*, IV. 287.
[4] Tombes was then incumbent of Bewdley.
[5] R. Nelson, " Life of Bishop Bull," 1827, p. 251.

Calvinist. Aubrey described him as " a little man, neat limbed, a little quick searching eye, sad, grey." [1]

The Baptists numbered amongst themselves some of the best-known men of the Commonwealth period. They were especially strong in the army. Packer, Deane, Desborough, Overton, Gough, Lilburn, Harrison, Axtell, and Hutchinson were all Baptists. So were Marsden, Danvers, Walcot, Rumbold, Holmes, Gladman, and many other of those old army officers whose names are connected with the plots of the time. [2] In Monk's army in Scotland at least two regiments—his own foot regiment and Talbot's regiment—were officered entirely by Baptists, and before he began his march to England he had to cashier and arrest all these and supply their places by others. [3] Bunyan joined the Baptists in 1653, though not perhaps entirely in sympathy with the generality of them in every respect. Milton doctrinally was very much in agreement with them, though in his " De Doctrina Christiana " he said, " I adhere to the Holy Scripture alone. I follow no other heresy or sect." It has been said, however, with regard to certain chapters in that work, that they " would almost bear reprinting as modern Baptist tracts." On the other hand, the portion of the work which deals with the Divinity of Christ is sufficient to explain why he never sought membership with the Baptists. His third wife, Elizabeth Minshull, after she was widowed, returned to Nantwich, from which she had originally come, joined the Baptist congregation there, and remained a member of it until her death in 1727. [4]

In England the name Anabaptist was frequently applied to the Baptists by their opponents, though there was no real connection, historical or theological, between them and the continental Anabaptists. The Baptists themselves hotly refused the name; " Baptist, falsely called Anabaptist," is a phrase frequently met with in their writings. They held no communion with the genuine Anabaptists, and were opposed to some of their strange views, such as that Christ did not take flesh of the Virgin Mary. The Dutch Anabaptists, too, objected to the taking of oaths, and to service as magistrates or as soldiers; most of the English Baptists objected to none of these things. [5] The confusion in the popular mind was partly due to the fact that they were believed guilty of extravagances such as were seen amongst the Quakers, Fifth Monarchy men, and Ranters, which extravagances called up hazy recollections of what had been heard of the doings of the Anabaptists of Münster. The accusation of Anabaptism partly

---

[1] Crosby, " Hist. Eng. Baptists," III.; Aubrey, " Brief Lives," II. 258–260; Wood, " Athenæ," pp. 556–559; Calamy, III. 521.

[2] *Trans. Bapt. Hist. Soc.*, I. 148–155; Whitley, " Hist. Brit. Baptists," pp. 73–81, 148.

[3] Muddiman, " The King's Journalist," pp. 73–74.

[4] Whitley, " Hist. Brit. Baptists," pp. 369–372. [5] *Idem, ibid.*, pp. 46–47.

arose from the doctrines and practices of the Baptists.   They
" would admit no members to their churches, but in personal
profession of repentance and faith, on which profession the
parties were baptized.   All their subsequent arrangements were
founded on these pre-requisites." [1]   The Churchman said, " You
are Anabaptists.   You are baptizing people who have been
baptized before.   That is sacrilege.   A man can only be baptized
once."   "No," said the Baptist.   "Your infant baptism, or rather
sprinkling, is no baptism, and therefore they have not been
baptized before."   So strict were they that the General and
Particular Baptists did not accept one another's baptism.   Those
who seceded from one to the other had to be baptized again
" because," they said, " you were baptized into a wrong faith,
and so into another gospel."

There were from the first many points of contact between the
Baptists and the Quakers.   One influence, which may be
traced to the continental Baptist movement, and which was very
strong among both Quakers and Baptists, more especially the
General Baptists, was the distrust of human learning.[2]   The
doctrine of the Inner Light affected both.   George Fox himself,
through his uncle Pickering, learned something from the Anabaptists, and a " shattered " Baptist community at Mansfield had
a great influence upon him in the early days.   Many Quakers
were drawn from what Fox called " shattered " Baptist communities.[3]   John Gratton, who from a dislike to the Anglican
services had already tried Presbyterianism and Muggletonianism,
settled down at Monyash in Derbyshire in 1668, and found a
body of Baptists there.   He was " almost persuaded to be dipped,
for otherwise there was no admittance," but he could not agree
with their doctrine of baptism, and he complained that he saw
no improvement in the lives of those who had been baptized.[4]
The connection between the Baptists and the Quakers was commented on in a hostile pamphlet " The Fanatic History: or, an
Exact Relation and Account of the Old Anabaptists and New
Quakers," which appeared in July 1660.   Nevertheless, as in the
case of Gratton, the two systems seemed to have a mutual repul-
sion, and there was a strong feeling of hostility, especially
between the Quakers and General Baptists, which lasted down
to the beginning of the eighteenth century.[5]

[1] Cramp, " Bapt. Hist.," p. 198.   [2] Barclay, " Inner Life," p. 503.
[3] Nutter, " Story of the Cambridge Baptists," pp. 38–39.
[4] " The Journal of John Gratton," 1720.
[5] Whitley, " Hist. Brit. Baptists," p. 851 ; Matthew Caffin's " Faith in God's
Promises the Saints' Best Weapon," 1660, attacks the Quakers.   William
Luddington, a Baptist who had turned Quaker, wrote in 1674 an examination
of the charges made against his new associates in " The Twelve Pagan Principles held by the Quakers Seriously Considered."   Dr. William Russell, the
minister at High Hall, replied with " Quakerism is Paganism by W. L.'s
Confession," and dedicated it to William Penn.

The death of Charles I. was thought by some to clear the way for the coming of the Kingdom of Christ, and this was one of the reasons which made the Millennarian leaders oppose the movement to crown Oliver Cromwell King. As time went on and the end of the world was still postponed, their zeal for a liberal interpretation of the Scriptures turned them from the prophets to the Law. The Traskites tried to revive the Jewish Law, but a much more general movement contented itself with reviving the Jewish Sabbath. This was why Millennarianism and Sabbatarianism were combined in certain Baptists and others.[1] A considerable section of the Baptists held Fifth Monarchist views, but these views were not always combined with Sabbatarianism. Thus Hanserd Knollys, though he never became a Sabbatarian, was spoken of as a Fifth Monarchist. It is true that he believed in the coming of Christ's Kingdom on earth, but he did not believe in trying to establish it by force. His opinion on these matters was set forth in "The Parable of the Kingdon of Heaven Expounded " (1674) and " The World that Now Is, and That which is to Come " (1681), in which he testified that the Fifth Monarchy, the Kingdom of Christ and His saints on earth, would begin when Christ returned from heaven.[2] John Canne and Vasasour Powell held Fifth Monarchist views; the former, indeed, seems to have severed his connection with the Baptists to throw in his lot entirely with the Fifth Monarchist sect. The turbulent character of the latter movement, and its ramifications among the Baptists, led people to connect the Baptist movement with the equally turbulent Anabaptists of the sixteenth century. John Tombes, in protest against violence, attacked the Fifth Monarchy men in a tract published in 1664 entitled " Saints no Smiters : or, Smiting Civil Power not the Work of Saints."

In 1650 Spilsbury, Kiffin, and fourteen other Baptist leaders issued a manifesto entitled, " Heart Bleedings for Professors' Abominations: or, a faithful general Epistle, Presented to all who have known the way of Truth, forewarning them to flee security and careless walking under the Profession of the same; discovering some of Satan's Wiles, whereby also wanton persons and their ungodly ways are disclaimed." In this they disavowed the Antinomian errors and practices of the Ranters and other extremists, who in the public mind were confused with the Baptists, and denied any connection with them, or belief in their errors.[3]

But some of the Baptists seem to have held very strange views. In " The Veil Turned Aside," written by a Particular Baptist of Ashford in Kent, it was stated that most of the Baptists in Kent and Sussex denied the doctrines of the Trinity and Christ's

[1] Whitley, " Hist. Brit. Baptists," p. 86.
[2] Culross, " Hanserd Knollys," pp. 96–99.
[3] " Confessions of Faith," Hanserd Knollys Soc., 1854, pp. 293–310.

satisfaction, disbelieved God's omnipresence, and affirmed that God is in the shape of a man, and that the soul sleeps with the body in the grave. Blackwood, a Particular Baptist, made the extraordinary statement " that God's decreeing sin, being a way to manifest the glory of His justice, is a good thing: that God works about sin by removing the impediments that hindered men from sinning, and setting before them objects whereby He knows their corruptions will be enticed, and that His tendering means to all is no otherwise than the shining of the sun upon the blind." [1]   There seems to have been a decided tendency among some of the Baptists to stray along the paths of heterodoxy, and a hostile witness declared: " Of the multitude of Anabaptists [he means Baptists] that I have known, I cannot mind one that stopped there: they are Separatists, Arminians, Antinomians, Socinians, Libertines, Seekers, Familists." [2]

In 1660 there was printed and published " A Brief Confession or Declaration of Faith, set forth by many of us, who are (falsely) called Ana-Baptists, to inform all men (in these days of scandal and reproach) of our innocent Belief and Practice: for which we are not only resolved to suffer Persecution to the loss of our Goods, but also Life itself, rather than to decline the same." It was signed by " certain Elders, Deacons and Brethren, met at London, in the first month, called March 1660, in the behalf of themselves, and many others unto whom they belong, in London, and in several Counties of the Nation, who are of the same Faith with us." Forty signatures were appended, including that of Francis Smith, the Baptist bookseller, who printed and published the document. A subsequent edition said that it had been presented to King Charles II., and stated that it was " owned and approved by more than 20,000." The Assembly of the General Baptists, which met in 1663, reaffirmed this document.[3]

Their beliefs are set forth in this Confession under twenty-five heads. There are articles dealing with belief in God, the Fall of Man, Christ, the Holy Spirit, Justification by Faith, Predestination and Election, the Christian life, the Resurrection and the Judgment. Others deal with Holy Scripture as the rule of life, elders and pastors and the life they should lead according to the rules of Scripture, and the return of Christ and the rule of the saints, when " the oppressor shall be broken in pieces." The fourth article says that God desires that all men should come to the knowledge of the truth and be saved. The fifth deals with ordination. From among persons qualified by the gift of God's Spirit, some should be chosen and set apart for the ministry by

---

[1] Lewis, " Brief Hist. of Anabaptism in Eng.," pp. 91–92.
[2] Thomas Long, " No Protestant but the Dissenters' Plot," 1682.
[3] Ivimey, " Hist. Eng. Baptists," I. 278, where it is dated wrongly; Whitley, " Minutes Gen. Assembly," I. 10; Cramp, " Bapt. Hist.," p. 285.

fasting, prayer, and the laying on of hands. Such as do not repent, believe, and be baptized, but are only brought up in the schools of human learning, to the attaining of human arts, and variety of languages, with many vain curiosities of speech, seeking rather the gain of large revenues than the gain of souls to God, such we deny (as ministers). The tenth declared that children dying in infancy are not subject to eternal death. The eleventh says that the way to gather churches is to preach and baptize, " that is, in English, to dip." They deny " that scriptureless thing of sprinkling of infants, falsely called baptism." The twelfth inculcates the laying on of hands after baptism as a means of conferring the promise of the Holy Spirit. The seventeenth and eighteenth assert respectively that the church should reject heretics, and that it is possible for true believers to fall away. Two deal with finance. The sixteenth denies the lawfulness of tithes or forced contributions. Ministers should be maintained by the voluntary offerings of the brethren. This voluntary system is, by the nineteenth, to be the method by which poor members of the congregation shall be assisted, and the care of this work is to be in the hands of the deacons, who shall perform it freely and voluntarily. The last two articles maintain the right of liberty of conscience and freedom in religion and worship. There must be magistrates, but if the civil power orders in matters of religion things which we cannot obey, we must obey God rather than man. At the end they add a solemn protest against some scandalous accusations which were being bandied about London against them. " We do utterly, and from our very hearts, in the Lord's fear, declare against all those wicked and devilish reports and reproaches, falsely cast upon us, as though some of us (in and about the City of London) had lately gotten knives, hooked knives and the like, and great store of arms . . . intending to cut the throats of such as were contrary minded to us in matters of religion, and that many such knives and arms, for the carrying on of some secret design, hath been found in our houses by search." The inventors of such stories were liars, and the Baptists prayed that the Lord would not lay it to their charge.[1]

Since the Reformation the Protestant sects, dissatisfied with the Creeds, had acquired the habit of drawing up long doctrinal statements dealing with controverted questions. On the other hand some of the General Baptists were averse to the issuing of long Confessions of Faith, and thought it sufficient to demand acceptance of a brief scriptural formula as the basis of communion. For this they chose the " principles of the doctrine of Christ " as given in Hebrews vi. 1–2: (1) Repentance, (2) Faith, (3) Baptism, (4) the Laying on of Hands, (5) the Resurrection from the Dead, and (6) Eternal Judgment. Five of the General Baptist congregations in London united in maintaining these Six

---

[1] " Confessions of Faith," Hanserd Knollys Soc., pp. 107–120.

Principles: the congregations at Dockhead or Shad Thames (it was called by both names), White's Alley, Glasshouse Yard, the Park at Horsleydown and Goodman's Fields. In 1668 there was a schism in White's Alley; a number of the members, having doubts on the question of the lawfulness of the laying on of hands, were excluded from the congregation, and under Richard Allen set up a new congregation in Turners' Hall, Philpot Lane.[1] The General Assembly of the General Baptists had, therefore, two concurrent symbols, the Confession of 1660 and the Six Principles.[2]

This anxiety to obey the rules of Scripture led to three customs which were held by certain of the Baptists, though they never became compulsory, nor were they by any means universally adopted. These were: (1) the apostolic commandment to abstain from eating blood (Acts xv. 29); (2) the washing of each other's feet (John xiii. 14), only practised in a few congregations; and (3) the anointing of the sick (James v. 14, 15), the last with a strictly remedial and not sacramental purpose.[3]

All sections of the Baptists, as the word implies, were distinguished from the other sects by certain doctrines and practices connected with the sacrament of baptism. In particular they were, to use a common term of the period, Antipædobaptists— that is, they were opposed to the baptism of infants, and, secondly, they insisted on immersion.

Three methods of baptizing are found in use among Christians: immersion, affusion—that is, pouring water on the head of the candidate for baptism—and aspersion, or sprinkling. All the Baptists stood out stoutly for immersion as the only lawful means, saying that baptism by any other method was no baptism at all. But since the practice of immersion had fallen completely out of use, the difficulty arose as to how it could be revived. Could a man baptize if he had not been baptized himself? The story formerly accepted was that Richard Blunt went to Holland in 1640 or 1641 and was there immersed by John Batten, of the sect of the Collegiants or Rynsburgers of Holland. Then, returning to London, he baptized Mr. Samuel Blacklock, a teacher of one of the London congregations, and these two baptized the rest of their church. The details of this story are now disputed, though it seems correct that the English Particular Baptists restored immersion in or about 1641. It would seem that no satisfactory immersion could be procured abroad, but the foreign Anabaptists advised their English friends to imitate their example and " authorize " someone to baptize for them. Later on, after this had been done, some of them began to doubt the validity of their baptism, and became Seekers or Quakers.

[1] Wilson, " Dissenting Churches in London," I. 135.
[2] Whitley, " Minutes Gen. Assembly," I. xix.
[3] *Idem, ibid.,* I. xxi.

Francis Bampfield wrote in 1681 "שֵׁם אַחֵר, A Name, an After-one ; or, "Ονομα καινὸν, A Name, a New One." In this tract he discussed the history of the practice of immersion in England, and surmised that either the first administrator baptized himself, or that he and another baptized one another. He explained that, led by the Spirit of God, he entered the river at Salisbury, and " received his being baptized as by the hand of Christ Himself, in the face of the heavens, and so passed under water and baptized another." There was also much discussion and debate about the method of immersion.[1] In consequence of their insistence on this practice, the early Baptists were all baptized in rivers, and it was long before their meeting-houses were all supplied with convenient baptistries. The first to be so provided is believed to be that one which was built on Horsley-down in 1657.[2]

The Baptists differed from the Congregationalists in their conception of the organisation of the church. They did not believe that each local congregation was separated from and independent of all others. But while the General Baptists laid most stress on uniting all the congregations in one annual assembly, the Particular Baptists were more careful to unite all the churches in some convenient area in one Association. The Aylesbury Confession of 1678, a Particular Baptist document, makes a distinction between the church and the individual congregation. There follows thereby a distinction between the various divinely instituted offices, Messengers or Bishops, chosen by the whole church, and Pastors or Elders, elected by their particular congregations, but ordained by the Bishop, and possessing their own very distinct function.

Thomas Grantham, who had been a General Baptist pastor in Lincolnshire since 1656 and is said to have been largely responsible for the Confession of Faith of 1660, asserted the view, adopted, in principle at any rate, by the General Baptists, that the Church of Jerusalem was the mother church of all, and that all churches are bound to follow her in the observation of all things which Christ commanded.[3] That church, as he read the Scriptures, had a threefold order of ministry : First there were the Messengers or Apostles, who, like Judas, Silas, Barnabas, and others, were commissioned for a special missionary journey. Gradually, however, such persons began to have the oversight of a definite group of churches, organising new ones, guiding those already formed, and using diligence to withstand false apostles. Grantham, himself a messenger, held that messengers had jurisdiction

---

[1] "The Restoration of Immersion by the English Anabaptists and Baptists," by Champlin Burrage, *Amer. Journ. of Theology*, XVI. No. 1, January 1912.
[2] Whitley, "Baptists of London," p. 16.
[3] Grantham, "Hear the Church," 1687; Wood, "Athenæ," II. 779.

only in those churches which appointed them, or which they planted, and he denied to them the sole right of conferring ordination. Moreover, in his view, the local church which appointed a messenger had power of discipline over him. It was not a matter of Divine ordering, but merely a matter of practical utility that one messenger should not encroach on another's sphere of jurisdiction. Generally speaking, the Baptist messenger was attached to a group of churches, but the exact relation of these officers to the church at large varied somewhat in the case of Particular and General Baptists. Amongst the General Baptists, indeed, there was some opposition to the appointment of messengers, but Grantham maintained that they were set for the defence of the Gospel against false teachers, and to strengthen particular pastors against usurpers, or such as despised the ministers of Christ.[1] There were not many messengers; among the General Baptists only seven were appointed between 1660 and 1691.

Secondly, there were the Elders, more generally known as Pastors, who were responsible for the oversight of the individual congregation. The local churches usually elected their own officials. Those who had the gift of preaching might be elected ministers, with the duty of ministering the Word but not the Sacraments. From the ministers and deacons the elders were usually elected, each congregation having one or more. The elder, as a rule, retained office for life, though he could be deposed by the Church for misconduct. The local church had the right of exercising discipline over its own officials, and Grantham thought that the messengers had disciplinary powers over the officers of all the churches in his charge. The elder's authority, on the other hand, was limited to his own congregation.[2]

Last came the Deacons, whose duty it was to take care of the poor and to distribute such alms as were entrusted to the church.[3]

Great stress was laid on voluntary service. Some of the ministers were unpaid, and the elders often maintained themselves by secular occupations. In the Berkhampstead Church Book there is, under the date of 1679, a denunciation of "a set maintenance for preaching," but in 1687 systematic collections began to be made for the travelling expenses of messengers. Again, the Baptists, while setting apart a definite ministry, did not deny the presence of spiritual gifts in persons not so set apart, who might yet be of service to the congregation: hence we find lay preachers among them and even women preachers.

[1] Grantham, "Christianismus Primitivus," 1678, Bk. IV., pp. 152-170; Whitley, "Minutes Gen. Assembly," I. xxvii-xxviii.
[2] Whitley, "Minutes Gen. Assembly," I. xxxii-xxxiv; idem, "Hist. Brit. Baptists," p. 87; Grantham, "Christianismus Primitivus."
[3] Grantham, "Hear the Church," 1688.

Ordination was conferred by the laying on of hands, with fasting and prayer. The local congregation chose its own elder, but usually invited the nearest messenger, or, failing him, the elders of other churches, to ordain him. Spiritual qualifications in the candidate were insisted upon, but among the General Baptists, except in the case of an enlightened few of the more learned ministers, like Francis Bampfield, mere learning was despised.[1] The latter part of the fifth article of the Confession of 1660 is a grossly unfair caricature of the Anglican view of ordination, but for a very long time, like the Quakers, the Baptists were stout in their assertion that human learning could not make a minister.[2] No one ever asserted that it could, but it could make him more efficient, as they began to realise later on.

The two larger sections of the Baptists both agreed that great questions should be settled by General Assemblies of messengers, elders, and brethren. The General Baptist General Assembly, though prevented by persecution from meeting regularly, met several times during the Restoration period, as in 1672, when the Declaration of Indulgence gave a breathing space, and in 1678, when the Popish Plot turned everyone's attention to the Papists. From 1686 onwards, of course, there was no further difficulty. The Particular Baptists did not call a General Assembly at all till 1689. The two parties differed about the powers of such an Assembly. Grantham held that "though we ought to consider with great respect what is concluded by a General Council of Christ's true ministers, yet may we lawfully doubt of what they deliver, unless they confirm it by the Word of the Lord."[3] This in effect denied them coercive jurisdiction. The Particular Baptists, on the other hand, declared that "General Councils or Assemblies . . . make but one church, and have lawful right . . . to act in the name of Christ, it being of divine authority." Such a Council had " superintendency " over churches " within its own limits or jurisdiction " and might hear appeals in cases of injustice, heresy, or schism.[4]

There was a congregation of General Baptists in Paul's Alley on the south side of the Barbican, dating from the period of the civil wars, and under the ministry of John Gosnold. He was said to have gathered a congregation of nearly 3000, but people seem to have had the haziest idea of numbers in the seventeenth century, and it is very doubtful whether a room would have been found which would hold a third of that number. A story is told of this Baptist meeting that it was very often attended by six or seven clergymen in their gowns, who sat in a convenient

[1] Bampfield's " Plan for an Educated Ministry," *Trans. Bapt. Hist. Soc.*, III. 8–17.
[2] Jones, " Studies in Mystical Religion," p. 423.
[3] Grantham, " Christianismus Primitivus."
[4] " Aylesbury Confession."

place under a large gallery, " where they were seen by few." Discipline was strict here. If any member of the congregation absented himself on Sunday, he was visited during the week, the cause of his absence inquired, and if his excuse was not considered satisfactory he was admonished. Refractory behaviour and unbecoming conduct were visited with censure, and in the last resort with excommunication.[1]

Strict discipline seems to have been the rule throughout all the Baptist communities. The Fenstanton Baptists had a rule that persons who wilfully absented themselves from Sunday worship should be looked upon as offenders, and dealt with accordingly. If unavoidably prevented from attendance they were required, whenever possible, to give notice to the congregation beforehand. Several members were at different times excommunicated for marrying irreligious persons, or such as were not members of the congregation. John Blows, a preacher, was called to account for being absent on a day of fasting and prayer and attending a football match instead, and it was decided that he should not be suffered to preach until he showed true repentance. The congregation at Warboys excommunicated Mary Poulter for neglect of attendance at worship, and for pride and vanity; and John Christmas for unkindness to his wife, though he was forgiven on changing his life and expressing regret. Mary Drage came under censure for lying, Thomas Bass for lying and swearing, and Ellen Burgess for slandering her relatives.[2]

Kiffin's Particular Baptist congregation in London in 1666 excommunicated a young man who, in order to marry a young woman his social superior, had falsely represented himself as the possessor of a considerable sum of money.[3] A distrust of the law courts led all the Nonconformists to settle disputes as much as possible among themselves, but " the Baptists especially went far beyond the limits of such arbitration, and ordered among their members almost every description of temporal affairs," as well as spiritual.[4] On April 21st, 1671, Richard Nelson, a member of Bunyan's congregation at Bedford, was excommunicated for " being openly bishoped after the antichristian guise of the Church of England." [5]

During the Restoration period a controversy arose among the Baptists on the subject of singing hymns during worship, a practice which many Baptists considered unlawful.[6] The Presbyterians and Independents were accustomed to sing the metrical version of the Psalms, but the Quakers did not sing as a

---

[1] Wilson, " Dissenting Churches in London," III. 229–230.
[2] Cramp, " Bapt. Hist.," pp. 337–338.
[3] Pike, " Ancient Meeting-Houses," p. 37.
[4] Barclay, " Inner Life," p. 486.
[5] " The Church Book of the Bunyan Meeting," with Introdn. by G. B. Harrison, London 1928, p. 44.
[6] Skeats and Miall, " Hist. Free Churches," p. 92.

rule, and some of the Baptists agreed with them.[1] When Kiffin
opened his meeting-house in Devonshire Square his congregation
made it a custom to sing psalms. Benjamin Keach was the great
advocate of singing in worship. "Though he had very great
success in this controversy, yet it brought upon him much trouble
and ill-will. When he was convinced that singing the praises of
God was a holy ordinance of Jesus Christ, he laboured earnestly
and with a great deal of prudence and caution to convince the
people thereof; and first obtained their consent to the practice
of it at the conclusion of the sacrament in the Lord's Supper,
and had but two of the church who opposed him therein." This
practice was continued for six years, and then they agreed to do
the same on public thanksgiving days. This lasted for fourteen
years, after which it was decided to sing every Sunday, " except
about five or six persons who dissented therefrom; and if I am
not mistaken, this was the first church that thus practised this
holy ordinance." Nevertheless, for the sake of the few who
disagreed, out of a church of some hundreds, it was arranged that
the singing should only take place when the prayer was finished
after the sermon, so that those who disapproved might leave
the building. The malcontents, however, left altogether " and
founded another church upon the same principles, *singing only
excepted*." [2] Keach's great innovation, of course, lay in the hymns
as distinct from the psalms, but he won his way, and books of
hymns for communion, hymns for baptism, and general hymns,
came successively into use, especially in London.[3]

The Baptists did not cover the whole of England, but were
particularly strong in certain counties. They were generally
found in the greatest numbers in the country districts, though
there were about a dozen Baptist churches in London.
In 1669, 109 congregations of General Baptists were reported
to the Archbishop, and in 1672 licences were issued to ninety-
eight General Baptist congregations.[4] Ivimey stated that 107
Particular Baptist congregations were founded in different parts
of the kingdom before the beginning of the eighteenth century,[5]
but there were other congregations not mentioned in either list.
Scattered Baptists were, of course, found in many places. About
three-fourths of the counties of England had at least one congregation. Kent had the greatest number of congregations,
between forty and fifty at least. Leicestershire and Lincolnshire
came next, each with between thirty and forty. Buckingham-

[1] Ivimey, " Hist. Eng. Baptists," I. 520.
[2] Crosby, " Hist. Eng. Baptists," II. 373–375 ; Keach, " The Breach Repaired
in God's Worship; or Singing of Psalms, Hymns and Spiritual Songs proved
to be an Holy Ordinance of Jesus Christ, with an Answer to Mr. Isaac Marlow's
Discourse against Singing," 1691.
[3] Whitley, " The Baptists of London," p. 22.
[4] *Idem*, " Minutes Gen. Assembly," I. lvi–lxvi.
[5] Ivimey, " Hist. Eng. Baptists," I. 523.

shire had at least twenty-eight congregations, Cambridge, Sussex, Warwick, and Nottinghamshire each had ten or more. On the other hand, there were large portions of country which were barely touched, especially the northern, western, and south-western groups of English counties. In Wales they were chiefly confined to the north, where at the Restoration there were about thirty ministers and a large number of churches.[1] The Particular and General Baptists generally occupied different territory. Norfolk and Suffolk were strongholds of the Particular Baptists.

The troubles of the Baptists began before the King's return. A great part of the nation looked upon them as dangerous fanatics.[2] In May 1660 we find the London Baptists appealing for protection because already one of their meeting-places had been attacked by a mob, and the Lord Mayor was instructed to see that they were duly protected as long as they behaved peaceably and gave no trouble to the authorities.[3] But many of them soon came into conflict with the civil authorities on other grounds. There was a strong party among them, who like the Quakers, felt conscientious scruples about taking oaths. The return of the King meant that the oaths of allegiance and supremacy would be demanded of them. Some of their leaders—Tombes, Denne, Ives and others—held that such a demand came within the rights of the lawful authorities, and that therefore the oaths might be taken, but many, like Vavasour Powell, held the contrary opinion. Powell has been called by his admirers " the Whitfield of Wales." [4] Both his father and mother were people of good family, and lived at Knocklas in Radnorshire,[5] and he himself is said to have been at Jesus College, Oxford, though there is some doubt on the point. He certainly took no degree, and Simon Patrick spoke scornfully of his " kitchen Latin." [6] Neal says that he scrupled to receive Presbyterian ordination,[7] while Wood tells a story that he was not ordained at all, but got hold of the letters of orders of an old minister, erased the name, put in his own, was indicted at the Radnor Sessions for forging these papers and for sedition, and narrowly escaped the gallows.[8] Eachard called him " a bold, dangerous, and persistent man, a pragmatical enemy to monarchy and episcopacy." [9] He had

[1] Stoughton, " Hist. Rel. in Eng.," III. 284.
[2] " The Old Anabaptists' Grand Plot Discovered: with their Covenant League and Articles: and the Manner how they had conspired together to seize upon divers Cities and burn stately Towns in several Counties, as also to have shaken off all higher powers, to have pulled down Magistrates and churches, to pay no more Tithes or Taxes, but to have seized upon all Ministers' Estates, Church-lands and Livings," London 1660.
[3] " Victoria County Hist., London," I. 337.
[4] Cramp, " Bapt. Hist.," p. 362.   [5] Aubrey, " Brief Lives," II. 171.
[6] " Friendly Debate," 1668.   [7] Neal, " Puritans," IV. 448.
[8] Wood, " Athenæ," II. p. 475.   [9] Eachard, " Hist. Eng.," III. 264.

protested against Cromwell's usurpation, and at the latter end of 1654 he was at the head of some armed forces which quelled a Royalist outbreak at Salisbury, and he showed great activity in putting down similar troubles in Wales. In 1656 he left the Independents and became a Baptist. On April 28th, 1660, before the King's return, he was taken from his house and imprisoned in Shrewsbury gaol for nine weeks, but was set free with many others who had been imprisoned at the same time, their liberation being by order of the King. He returned home, and began to preach once more, but in July he was arrested again, and imprisoned by Sir Matthew Price, High Sheriff of Montgomery, and it would seem that some accusation of treason was made against him. Among the MSS. at Powys Castle is a certificate that on August 14th, 1660, at the town of Poole, in the county of Montgomery, he confessed that in 1648 Colonel John Jones, Colonel John Parton, Colonel George Twistleton, and Colonel Nutton brought him a petition to Parliament asking that the King might be brought to trial and death, and at the importunity and encouragement of these officers he had signed it, and he admitted that it had been signed at Wrexham and Denbigh. He had further stated that Colonel John Parton had been knighted by Charles II. for his services therein.[1]

Apparently further evidence was not forthcoming, for the charge seems to have broken down at the Quarter Sessions, but the oaths of allegiance and supremacy were tendered to him, and as he refused to take them, he was kept prisoner. Shortly afterwards he was sent to London, brought before the King and Council, and committed to the Fleet prison, where he remained for two years. During twelve months of this time he was so closely confined that he was not allowed to leave his chamber. This, and the offensive smell of a dunghill under his window, undermined his health, and he never completely recovered. In 1662 he was removed to Southsea Castle, and was there confined for five years.[2] In the earlier part of his imprisonment he wrote a little work with the pleasant title, " The Bird in the Cage Chirping four Distinct Notes," of which a second edition appeared in 1661.

On July 26th, 1660, a petition was presented to the King by Thomas Grantham and Joseph Wright, pastor of the church at Westby, on behalf of sundry honest and well-disposed Baptists, setting forth the sufferings that had been inflicted upon their congregations in Lincolnshire. At the same time they presented a copy of the Confession of Faith which had been drawn up in

[1] *Trans. Powysland Club*, XXI. 346.
[2] Stoughton, " Hist. Rel. Eng.," III. 283–284; Wood, " Ath. Ox.," II. 473–478; R. Williams, " Life of Vavasour Powell," *Trans. Powysland Club*, XV. 231–223; Cramp, " Bapt. Hist.," pp. 362–364; Whitley, " Hist. Brit. Baptists," pp. 105–106.

March. The petitioners complained that they had been abused
in the streets, and in their houses, threatened with hanging if they
were heard praying in family worship, and disturbed at their
prayers by beating on their doors and by the sounding of horns.
They had been stoned on their way to meetings, the windows of
their meeting-houses had been broken, and some of their members
imprisoned. Many of them had been indicted at the Sessions,
and were to be fined £20 each " for not coming to hear such men
as they provide us, of whose principles and practices we could
give a most sad and doleful, and yet a most true relation." The
petition was signed by thirty-five persons on behalf of the others.
The King replied " that it was not his mind that any of his good
subjects, who lived peaceably, should suffer any trouble on
account of their opinions in point of religion, and that he had
declared the same in several declarations." In the presence
of the deputation he sent a Member of Parliament to the Lord
Chancellor and Secretary to see what could be done in the
matter.[1] On the same day was presented to the King " An
Apology of some called Anabaptists, in and about the City of
London, on behalf of themselves and others of the same judgment
with them." It was a general protestation of their law-abiding
character, except in cases where their conscience forbade them to
obey.

By the Act for Restoring Sequestered Ministers every minister,
unless an Anabaptist,[2] who had been turned out of his living
during the troublous times, was to be restored to his living before
December 25th, 1660, and the incumbent in possession was to
vacate it peaceably. A good deal of disturbance, however,
occurred in connection with this in various parts of the country.
In Gloucestershire, for instance, some of the Cavalier party rode
about armed with swords and pistols, and ransacked the houses
of the intruded ministers. At Rencombe in that county a
Mr. Broad had been ejected as a malignant, and a Mr. Warren
had been put in his place. Broad now returned with a noisy
company of followers, shut Warren with his wife and family in
an upper room, and so distressed them by making a noise night
and day with hautboys, that Warren died in the place.[3]

William Kiffin found himself in great danger towards the end
of the year 1660. A letter had been addressed from Taunton to
Nathaniel Crabb, silk-thrower, of Gravel Lane, London, saying
that now the Princess of Orange was dead thousands of saints
were ready to put a great design into execution, if Kiffin, according to his promise, would send them ammunition, "for that they
believed the promise that one of them should chase a thousand."

[1] Crosby, " Hist. Eng. Baptists," II. 21–22; Ivimey, " Hist. Eng. Baptists,"
I. 278; Cramp, " Bapt. Hist.," p. 287; Jessey, " Lord's Loud Call," p. 15.
[2] Crosby, II. 93–94.
[3] Idem, " Hist. Eng. Baptists," II. 29.

Kiffin was seized one Saturday at midnight and put into the guard-house at Whitehall. Next evening he was examined before Monk and other members of the Privy Council, and on the following day was examined again by Lord Chief Justice Foster. As he was being taken under guard to Serjeants' Inn for this last examination, the coach passed through a crowd of people, some of whom were shouting for vengeance upon traitors. Kiffin's defence was that the letter was dated from Taunton three days before the Princess died, and that between the time of her death on Monday night, December 24th, and his arrest on Saturday night it would have been impossible for a letter to have been written from London and an answer received from Taunton. Kiffin, together with Griffin and Henry Jessey, who had also been mentioned in the letter, were discharged.[1]

Immediately after Venner's insurrection in January 1661, many of the Baptists were arrested. In London alone some 400 were taken, and on their refusal to take the oaths were committed to Newgate, the Wood Street Counter, and other prisons. The King's proclamation issued on January 10th specially mentioned the Anabaptists and Quakers as concerned in the trouble. A number of tracts and pamphlets made the accusation: one, with a fine confusion, referring to "the hideous uproar by those kinds of Anabaptistical Quakers that called themselves Fifth Monarchy men."[2] Among the Anabaptists there was a congregation whom the followers of Venner called "the (private mark) rebaptized brethren," and it has been suggested that they wore something which would only be recognised by the initiated.[3] Both Baptists and Quakers were increasing in numbers, and it was known that Millennarian views were not confined to Venner's people, nor was his the only sect given to binding kings in chains. This was why Hanserd Knollys, among others, was arrested. He was sent to Newgate, where he remained for eighteen weeks, being released at last as an act of grace at the King's Coronation.[4]

The royal proclamation had forbidden Anabaptists and other sectaries to meet together for worship. The Baptists presented a number of addresses and apologies to the King. In one they said, " We cannot imagine why bloody tenets and tragical actions should reflect upon those of our persuasion, the persons not being of our belief or practice about baptism; but to the best of our information they were all, except one, assertors of infant baptism,

[1] " Passages in the Life of William Kiffin," pp. 18–32; Evans, " Early Eng. Baptists," II. 264–266.
[2] " An Advertisement as touching the Fanatics' late Conspiracy," 1661. See also " A Judgment and Condemnation of the Fifth Monarchy Men, their late Insurrection," 1661, and " The Traitors Unveiled in a Brief and True Account of that Horrid and Bloody Design intended by those Rebellious People known by the Name of Anabaptists and Fifth Monarchy," 1661.
[3] C. Burrage, E.H.R., October 1910.
[4] Culross, " Hanserd Knollys," p. 82.

and never had communion with us in our assemblies." [1]   They complained that to be called an Anabaptist was commonly looked upon as a sufficient reason for being treated as a criminal. They did not deny that in Germany some reputed Anabaptists had been accused of dreadful beliefs and practices destructive of all government and human society, but there were Anabaptists in Germany and Holland who rejected the opinions and actions of the men of Münster.   The Baptists had no foreknowledge of Venner's outbreak, nor share in it, and were ready to hazard their lives against the insurgents.   This petition was signed by some thirty ministers and chief members of the Particular Baptist congregations, and among them, Kiffin, Denne, Gosnold, and Francis Smith.   To this address they added a copy of the petition and address of the London Anabaptists, which had been presented to the King in the previous July. [2]

" The Humble Petition and Representation of the Sufferings of several Peaceable and Innocent Subjects, called by the Name of Anabaptists, Inhabitants in the County of Kent, and Prisoners in the Gaol of Maidstone, for the Testimony of a good Conscience," dated January 25th, 1661, was presented to the King about that time.   It was signed by four of the prisoners on behalf of the rest, and set forth the troubles not only of the Maidstone prisoners, but also of their brethren in the county. Amongst other things, they complained that their houses had been broken into at dead of night without the authority of the King or any of his officials, their goods and cattle seized, and themselves made prisoners.   They set forth that the civil authority cannot lawfully force men's consciences, because this would mean that the Sultan of Turkey would then have the right to make all his subjects Mohammedans, and the King of Spain to make all his people Papists.   The Apostles refused to obey orders which were contrary to the commandments of God, and although the New Testament enjoins obedience to the civil powers, this cannot mean in religious matters, because in the Apostles' days the Empire was pagan.   Lastly, the teaching of Christianity is entirely opposed to persecution, because we are bidden to do to all men as they should do to us. [3]

On January 30th another petition, signed by twenty-six Baptist leaders, was presented to the King, and was shortly afterwards published under the title, " The Humble Representation of Several Societies Commonly called by the Name Anabaptists."

[1] Venner had declared that if he succeeded the Baptists should know that infant baptism was of Christ.   Crosby, II. 65.

[2] The Humble Petition of some commonly called Anabaptists. . . with an Apology formerly presented to the King's Most Excellent Majesty. Crosby, "Hist. Eng. Baptists," II. 35; "Confessions of Faith," Hanserd Knollys Soc., pp. 345–352.

[3] Cramp, "Bapt. Hist.," p. 285.

The petitioners disclaimed all connection with Venner's rising, on account of which many of them had been suspected and punished. They complained that their adversaries, when they had no other charge to lay against them, tendered oaths to them, in spite of the fact that Christ had forbidden all swearing, and then, when they refused to swear, threw them into prison. In order to show their obedience to authority, they had held no meetings since the Fifth Monarchy rising. In a postscript they added, " Let none judge or think amiss that we do not give the King those titles that are commonly given unto him; for it is not out of any disrespect to his person; being not willing to deny him anything that is given him of God. And for those words *thee, thou* and *thine*, we find in Scriptures to be given to the greatest and best of men that were in authority, as also to God Himself, and to our Lord Jesus Christ." [1]

In February a petition from divers persons commonly called Anabaptists, and others commonly meeting to worship God at Theobalds, was presented to the King. They disclaimed sympathy with Venner, declared that they accepted the new régime, and asked permission to worship in peace. Among the signatures were those of Spencer, Dyke, Rumbold, Packer, and Desborough.[2]

" The Second Humble Address of those that are called Anabaptists in the County of Lincoln " against persecution was dated February 6th, 1661, but had been presented to the King three weeks before. The signatories confessed that there had been cause for severity, since the King's clemency had been so abused, but they prayed that the innocent might not suffer for the guilty.[3] They concluded by saying : " But to avoid prolixity, O King, be pleased to know, that your poor subjects dare not refuse their innocent meetings, wherein their work is sincerely to worship God, and pray for Your Majesty and for all men as in duty they are bound, seeing the authority by which they are dehorted from the neglect of their assemblies (Heb. x. 25) is greater than any whereby Your Majesty can enjoin the neglect thereof. And therefore, though it cost us the loss of all that we have and are, as to things of an outward consideration, yet dare we not shrink from so great a loss. Yet are we resolved, in the strength of God, not to rebel against any of Your Majesty's commands, but in case we cannot conscionably act, we humbly purpose and heartily pray for strength to suffer patiently and joyfully." [4] Thomas Grantham was one of the signatories. Shortly afterwards he was taken at a meeting in Boston in Lincolnshire and imprisoned for fifteen months. Stories were spread that he was

---

[1] " Confessions of Faith," Hanserd Knollys Soc., pp. 357–360.
[2] Theobalds and Colonel Packer, *Trans. Bapt. Hist. Soc.*, IV. 58–63.
[3] " Confessions of Faith," Hanserd Knollys Soc., pp. 353–356.
[4] *Ibid.*, p. 355.

a Jesuit, so he published a summary of a controversy which he had had with a Roman Catholic, under the title of " The Baptist against the Papist." [1]

On February 23rd the same group presented a third address to the King, declaring their loyalty, and promising to keep the peace and to defend the King's person and government. The King replied that he was satisfied that they were peaceable men and good subjects, and that he would take care to preserve them. [2]

Another appeal addressed to the King, Parliament, and people of England and published in March of the same year, bore the title " Sion's Groans for her Distressed." It was a protest against persecution, and against the right of the civil magistrates to impose anything in the worship and service of God, the writers maintaining that liberty ought to be granted to all who did not disturb the peace of the State. [3] It was signed by Thomas Monk, Joseph Wright, George Hammond, William Jeffrey, Francis Stanley, William Reynolds, and Francis Smith. Wright was a prisoner for twenty years in Maidstone gaol for his beliefs. Hammond was pastor of a Baptist congregation at Biddenden in Kent. Jeffrey lived at Bradbourne in Kent, and his brother and he were energetic labourers for the Baptist cause in that county. [4] Monk was a Buckinghamshire farmer, while Reynolds and Stanley were Baptist workers in Lincolnshire and Nottinghamshire respectively. [5] Francis Smith presumably was the London bookseller.

Another Declaration which appeared in 1661, probably early in the year, was " A Declaration of a Small Society of Baptized Believers, undergoing the name of Free Willers, about the City of London." The signatories explained that they had recently seen a Declaration dated the 12th of last December, and signed by some persons " of the Particular judgment," in which some others of another persuasion had joined. They wished to make it clear that they did not agree with certain statements therein, and for themselves they declared that: (1) they were not opposed to magistracy; (2) they had no wish to destroy the ministry of the Established Church, though differing from it in some matters; (3) they did not countenance the irregular practices of the Quakers; (4) they were not desirous of toleration " of all miscarriage in things ecclesiastical and civil, under pretence of liberty of conscience "; (5) neither did they desire to murder and destroy those who differed from them in religion, and though

---

[1] Crosby, " Eng. Baptists," II. 149–151.
[2] Kennet, " Reg.," p. 383.
[3] " Sion's Groans for her Distressed, or, Sober Endeavours to prevent Innocent Blood. . . . Proving it the undoubted right of Christian Liberty under different Persuasions in Matters Spiritual, to have equal Protection as to their Civil Peace," 1661.
[4] Neal, " Puritans," IV. 490.
[5] Cramp, " Bapt. Hist.," p. 288,

THE LIVING CHRISTIAN AND THE DYING CHRISTIAN.
From Francis Smith's "Symptoms of Growth and Decay in Godliness." 1673.

Facing p. 104.

they could not in conscience take oaths, they were willing to suffer the penalties for not doing so. " And we further declare, as in the presence of God, Who is the searcher of all hearts, that as it hath been some of our great trouble for a long time to see some of these that are in the same faith and order with us so acting : so it is now become even an overwhelming burden upon our souls to see them running such a precipitant course, by which actings of theirs the mouths almost of all men are opened against them, and that truth they profess most ignominously branded and reproached."

The persons who signed the Declaration of December 12th had called the Independents and the Presbyterians " Christian friends." A certain Mr. William Alleyne had lately put out a book called " A Retractation to Separation," in which he had asserted that Episcopalians, Independents, and Presbyterians were all true and visible members of the Church of Christ. The three signatories of the present Declaration could not accept this position, and announced that one of their members was writing " The Retractator's Work Scanned : or, the Conceptions and Supposals of Mr. William Alleyne regulated by Scripture Record." For themselves, they owned all men friends as far as they owned God, Christ, and the truth, " but to own the best of men to be members of that body of which Christ is the Head, and to have communion with them, either to make them our mouth in prayer to God for us, or God's mouth in speaking forth His truths to us, or in breaking of bread at the table of the Lord, we cannot own them in the least."

The reason for the fewness of their own numbers was because the faithful were minished from among the children of men. The Scripture foretold that it would be so, for it was written, " The good man is perished out of the earth and there is none upright amongst men." The document was signed by Henry Adis, Richard Pilgrim, and William Cox on behalf of themselves and those that walked with them.[1]

Henry Adis was an upholsterer by trade and lived near Covent Garden. In 1660 and 1661 he wrote three tracts, in each of which the author's name was given as " Henry Adis, a Baptized Believer, undergoing the name of a Free Willer, and also most ignominiously by the Tongue of Infamy, called a Fanatic, or a Madman." The first in 1660 was, " A Fanatic's Mite cast into the King's Treasury. Being a sermon printed *to* the King, because not preached *before* the King." The second was in 1661, and was entitled " A Fanatic's Testimony against Swearing "; the third was in March 1662, " A Fanatic's Letter sent out of the Dungeon of the Gatehouse Prison," and was addressed " to all his brethren in the three nations at liberty : and also in the several

---

[1] Crosby, " Hist. Eng. Bapt.," II. 19–26; App. V. pp. 90–110; Neal, " Puritans," IV. 467.

gaols and dungeons therein." Adis could not conscientiously take an oath, and had gone to prison rather than swear allegiance to the King. Tombes, Ives, Brabourne, Denne, Hubberthorne, and others had joined in a pamphlet controversy on the subject of the lawfulness of taking oaths. " A Fanatic's Testimony " was a reply to the first four of these. Tombes published in October 1660 " Serious Considerations of the Oath of the King's Supremacy," and about six months later he published a " Supplement " to it.

Dr. John Griffith, the minister of the General Baptist congregation in Dunning's Alley, Bishopsgate Street, published in 1661 " A Complaint of the Oppressed against the Oppressors: or the unjust and Arbitrary Proceedings of some Soldiers and Justices against some sober, godly Persons in and near London, who now lie in stinking Gaols for the Testimony of a good Conscience, with some Reasons why they cannot swear Allegiance to obtain their Liberty." Shortly after publishing this he was sent to Newgate himself, and remained there seventeen months.

On November 12th, 1660, John Bunyan had intended to preach at Lower Samsell, near Harlington, and Francis Wingate, J.P., of Harlington House, was instructed to issue a warrant for his arrest, on the ground that a seditious meeting was in view. Wingate seems to have expected a meeting of the Fifth Monarchy men. A strong watch was set round the house, and Bunyan was arrested just as the meeting was beginning. Ordered to find sureties that he would abstain from unlawful meetings, he refused, was sent to Bedford gaol under the Act of 35 Eliz., and was tried at the Bedford Quarter Sessions in January 1661. The chairman was Sir John Keeling, who had no love for Puritans, and had suffered at their hands in the past, and the indictment ran that John Bunyan had " devilishly and perniciously abstained from coming to church to hear divine service," and was " a common upholder of several unlawful meetings and conventicles, to the great disturbance and distraction of the good subjects of this Kingdom." The prisoner refused to plead either guilty or not guilty, and till he pleaded one way or the other the case could not proceed. He admitted, however, that he did not go to church, and argued that we are told to pray with the spirit and not with the Prayer Book. Finally Keeling found a way out of the deadlock: Bracton had laid it down that if a prisoner persisted in a lengthy answer and would not utter either formula, it should be taken as a confession. So Bunyan was sentenced to three months' imprisonment. This seems to have been quite irregular, for he had not pleaded directly to the indictment, no witnesses had been heard against him, and the trial had consisted of little more than an altercation between him and the bench.[1] By the Elizabethan statute he was now bound to appear before the April Quarter

[1] Froude, " Life of Bunyan," ed. 1909, p. 78.

Sessions, and either promise to conform or else take an oath to abjure the realm. If he did neither of these things he was liable to suffer death and forfeiture of goods as a felon. The King's coronation, however, was fixed for April 23rd, and Charles issued a pardon to all prisoners for any offences short of felony, provided they would sue it out under the Great Seal within a year. Cobb, the Clerk of the Peace, endeavoured to persuade Bunyan to do this, but without success; in fact Bunyan seems to have thought him a false friend trying to entrap him, which appears an utterly unjust suspicion. A good deal was done for Bunyan by other people: his wife went up to London to make interest for him, and presented a petition to the House of Lords, and the High Sheriff of Bedfordshire did what he could.[1]

The House of Lords referred the matter to the judges at the next Assize, so in August 1661 Bunyan was brought before Judges Twisden and Sir Matthew Hale. They seem to have considered his conviction legal, held that he could not be tried again, and recommended him to apply for his pardon under the Great Seal. They listened patiently to his wife, and told her he must stop preaching, for if he should be caught again, he would be in still greater danger. Hale told her that her husband might either sue for his pardon or obtain a writ of error, the latter course being simpler and cheaper. They seem to have been very kind to her, but inasmuch as they could not release him at once without conditions, she thought them cruel, and as he would give no promise, he remained a prisoner. To keep him in mild confinement was really straining the law in his favour, for, as the law stood, he was liable either to be banished or executed in April 1662. He petitioned to be tried again, and thought he was hardly treated when this was refused. There were three prisons in Bedford, two large buildings used by the county and the town of Bedford respectively, and a small lock-up, fourteen feet square, standing on a bridge over the river. The last is the traditional place of his incarceration, but as he had sometimes fifty or sixty fellow-prisoners, to whom he often preached, he must have been in one of the others for the greater part of the time.[2]

Information was laid in September 1661 that Hanserd Knollys, together with Henry Jessey and John Simpson, had been preaching at Great All-hallows on a fast day, and that they preached there on Mondays and Thursdays. The informant also said that when on a previous Sunday a brief had been read in the church the King's name had been muttered, and the names of the archbishops and bishops omitted. Knollys escaped to Holland,

---

[1] Froude, " Life of Bunyan," p. 78.
[2] Whitley, " Bunyan's Imprisonments," *Trans. Bapt. Hist. Soc.*, VI. 1–24; Froude, " Life of Bunyan," p. 80; Brown, " Life of Bunyan," pp. 160–162.

and, it was rumoured, was plotting there with others who had escaped from Newgate.   He remained abroad till 1664.[1]

One of the oldest Seventh-Day Baptist congregations was accustomed to meet in Bullstake Alley.   On Saturday, October 19th, 1661, a congregation of about forty of them were holding a service in their meeting-house when they were interrupted by a justice of the peace, named Chard, and a head-borough named Wood.   The preacher, John James, a Whitechapel silk-weaver, who held some of the views of the Fifth Monarchists, was ordered to come down from the pulpit, and as he refused he was dragged down.   The members of the congregation were despatched in groups of seven to Sir John Robinson, Lieutenant of the Tower, and three other justices of the peace, who were then sitting at the Half-Moon tavern.   There the oath of allegiance was tendered them, and on their refusal to take it, they were sent, both men and women, to Newgate.   The justices then went to the meeting-house, and Sir John Robinson read to those members of the congregation who had not yet been removed a paper which stated some of the doctrines alleged to have been preached there.   This paper had been communicated to the authorities by an informer, one Tipler, a journeyman pipe-maker, who stated therein that he had overheard seditious doctrines proclaimed in the conventicle while engaged at his daily business. This Tipler was a worthless person, and no magistrate would have acted on his sole testimony, had not another neighbour corroborated his statements.   The members of the congregation, however, denied ever having heard anything of the sort.

James was next brought before the Lieutenant of the Tower. He confessed to having been cautioned by the magistrates previously, and admitted that he held some Fifth Monarchy doctrines.   One curious accusation brought against him was that it was commonly said that he had a lodger who annoyed the neighbourhood by practising on a war trumpet, but that it was really James preparing for the next insurrection.   The magistrates committed him to gaol at Newgate.   On November 14th he was brought up for trial at Westminster Hall before Chief Justice Foster and three other judges, on the charge of compassing and imagining the death of the King, endeavouring to levy war against him, and endeavouring a change of government. Under the first head he was accused of having preached: (1) that the King was a bloody traitor, a bloodsucker, and a bloodthirsty man, and that his nobles were the same: (2) that the King and his nobles had shed the blood of the saints at Charing Cross, and the blood of the Covenanters in Scotland : (3) that the King was brought in to this end, to fill up the measure of his iniquity, and that the cup of his iniquity had been filled more in the last year than in many years previously : (4) that he (the

[1] Culross, " Hanserd Knollys," pp. 82–83.

preacher) did bemoan that they had not improved their opportunity when they had the power in their hands, but that it would not be long before they had power again, and then they would improve it better; for hitherto they had not fought the Lord's battles thoroughly : (5) that the death and destruction of the King drew very near.

Tipler swore that he was in the yard of the meeting-house and heard James say this. Osborne said he was in the meeting and heard it. Another witness said he heard it in Tipler's house, and went out into the yard, but could not swear to the speaker. A fourth had heard of it, came to the place and found him preaching still, and arrested him. James denied using the words, and brought witnesses who stated that Osborne had said he was compelled to give evidence, and did not know what he swore.

James put in, as defence, besides his general denial, that he had never served against the King or his father, but had always declared against Cromwell's usurpation, and had suffered for doing so. The jury found him guilty. Brought to the bar and asked why sentence of death should not be passed, he said he wished to leave two or three scriptures with them, and quoted Jeremiah xxvi. 14-15 and Psalm cxvi. 15, and reminded the court that " he that toucheth the Lord's people toucheth the apple of His eye," and that Christ was " King of England, Scotland and Ireland, and of all the kingdoms of this world." He was then sentenced to be hanged, drawn and quartered. It was related that his wife appealed to the King, but Charles spoke of him as a rogue, and said, " He shall be hanged; yea, he shall be hanged," [1] a story which does not seem to ring true. James was treated with excessive severity, but there is little doubt that his preaching had bordered very closely on sedition. [2] The execution took place on November 26th. Before his death James appears to have preached a sermon to a small company of his friends in Newgate, in the course of which he denounced Cromwell and other earthly rulers. [3] The officials at Newgate during his last days stole his clothes, extorted sums of money from him, even the hangman threatening him with torture if he did not pay £20, a sum which he successively reduced to £10 and then to £5. The sheriff and hangman, however, suffered him to die before the cutting down and other horrors. His limbs were exposed on the city gates, and his head was set up on a pole in Whitechapel. [4]

[1] Crosby, " Hist. Eng. Baptists," II. 17.
[2] Whitley, " Brit. Baptists," 110.
[3] Crosby, II. 165-172; Stoughton, " Hist. Rel. Eng.," II. 280-283; " State Trials," II. 470-478; " The Speech and Declaration of John James, a Weaver, in the Pressyard at Newgate, on Sunday last to the Fifth Monarchists," 1661; " A Narration of the Apprehending, Commitment and Execution of John James, who suffered at Tyburn, November 26th, 1661."
[4] Pike's " Ancient Meeting-Houses," pp. 191-200.

The " Act for the Safety and Preservation of His Majesty's person and government against treasonable and seditious practices," which was the first passed by the Cavalier Parliament, was the one under which James suffered. It extended the former law of treason, and allowed evidence of " printing, writing, preaching, or malicious and advised speaking." Serjeant Glynne, on behalf of the Crown, therefore, was able to argue that it was sufficient " to prove the words substantially," and the Attorney-General said that James's words according to the new Act constituted treason, the principle being that *Mens rea facit reum*.[1]

On November 17th, 1661, the Baptist prisoners at Dover petitioned the King and the Duke of York about the treatment they had received at the hand of the mayor and justices of that town.[2] The Dover congregation seems to have been particularly steadfast, in spite of all the efforts of the authorities to break the meetings up or suppress them. Towards the end of 1661 Newgate prison was almost filled with Baptists. Out of 355 prisoners in that one prison, 289 were said to be Baptists, among them being Samuel Fisher, Thomas Parrott, Richard Pilgrim, John Griffith, and Jonathan Jennings.[3]

At the end of 1661 or the beginning of 1662 Kiffin was accused of hiring two men to kill the King. He was arrested by order of the Duke of Buckingham, who told him, according to Kiffin's own story, that if he would confess the truth, no harm should come to him. From his prison in the Gatehouse he sent a letter to the Chancellor; Lady Ranelagh carried it there for him, and Clarendon laid the letter before the King and Council. The Secretaries knew of no charge against him, and he was immediately set free. Next day he called on Clarendon to thank him, and was told that Buckingham had only arrived to bring the charge before the Council after the order for his deliverance had been decided on, but that now he must surrender himself. Kiffin went off to Whitehall to see the King, and finding that he was not in, returned to the City and procured two prominent citizens to go bail for him. Once more he went to Whitehall, where, after waiting for an hour, a message came to him from the King that he might go home. One of the pages had already told Kiffin that the King was angry with him, and he therefore set down his release to the credit of Clarendon, who, he thought, must have interceded for him. The whole affair is an example of the casual way in which affairs of State were conducted.[4]

Some time after that, Kiffin was sent for and examined by Sir Richard Browne, as there were stories going about of his being

---

[1] Amos, " Constitution under Charles II," p. 29.
[2] Crosby, " Hist. Eng. Baptists," II. 151–160.
[3] *Trans. Bapt. Hist. Soc.*, I. 150.
[4] " Remarkable Passages in the Life of William Kiffin," pp. 41–43.

mixed up in plots. A little later Sir Thomas Player, with a party of soldiers, searched his house. But this was the last time he lay under suspicion of treason, though he had a good many troubles about attending Baptist meetings.[1] On one occasion he was taken at a meeting, prosecuted, and fined £40. Finding some errors in the proceedings and at the trial, he prosecuted the informers, but it cost him £30 to get his £40 back.[2] " My Lord Arlington hath told me," he says, that though, " in every list of disaffected persons brought him, who ought to be secured, my name was always amongst them, yet the King would never believe anything against me: my Lord Chancellor being very much my friend." [3]

During 1662 the Baptist meeting-houses in London were subject not only to the interference of the authorities, but to mob violence as well. The one in Brick Lane near Whitechapel was raided six times: the soldiers smashed the pulpit to pieces, and on July 27th a multitude of butchers out of Whitechapel, together with the bailiff's followers and a number of boys, smashed the forms, windows, and doors. Another of their meeting-places was in Glovers' Hall, at the entrance to Beech Lane, which led out of Beech Street into White Cross Street.[4] The building was not visible from the street, and was approached by a narrow passage.[5] The soldiers came there on May 25th, with swords drawn, treated the worshippers with violence, and carried two to Newgate, where they were kept till the Quarter Sessions five weeks later. The same treatment was meted out to this congregation on June 1st, 8th, and 15th, on which last occasion the soldiers were so violent that some of them actually broke their muskets in knocking the pulpit to pieces. On August 3rd the Baptist prisoners in Newgate gaol met for worship. The thieves, housebreakers, pickpockets, and highwaymen imprisoned there came with violence into the room, threw the Bible on the floor, drew their knives, and attacked the party, but they defended themselves. The same thing happened the same day to the Baptist prisoners in the White Lion, Southwark.[6] At the end of December 1662 it was reported that many Anabaptists and others, taken at unlawful meetings, were in the Gatehouse, and that the King was willing to release them if they would take the oaths.[7]

The number of Anabaptists ejected on St. Bartholomew's Day 1662 was small, because few of them were beneficed in the Church. The reason that some parishes had Baptist incumbents at all was

[1] " Remarkable Passages in the Life of William Kiffin," pp. 43–45.
[2] Ibid., p. 50.   [3] Ibid., p. 46.
[4] " Behold, a Cry! or, a True Relation of the Inhuman and Violent Outrages . . . practised upon many of the Lord's People," 1662.
[5] Wilson, " Dissenting Churches," III. 217–218.
[6] " Behold, a Cry," 1662.
[7] C.S.P.D., December 28th, 1662.

that three Baptist ministers, John Tombes, Henry Jessey, and Daniel Dyke,[1] were Triers, and therefore the Commissioners had agreed to recognise the Baptists as brethren, and not to disqualify them because of their views.[2] Joseph Ivimey[3] compiled a list of ejected Baptists to which Stoughton added seventeen names.[4] Some names on this list had only a very doubtful connection with the Baptist movement, and some no connection at all. Francis Bampfield was one of the ejected, but he did not become a Baptist for some time after that. There were Baptist chaplains in the army, but not many of them, and they of course disappeared at the Restoration. Some Baptist incumbents were turned out by the Presbyterians in 1659 or at some date between that and St. Bartholomew. Dr. Whitley calculated that twenty-eight Baptists held livings under the Commonwealth and five more were chaplains, and perhaps another eleven might have to be added to the total,[5] but in a later work he has expressed his conclusion that not more than thirty Baptists drew a salary from the establishment.[6]

Persecution raged round Aylesbury in 1663. So many Nonconformists were imprisoned that the county gaol was full and two large houses were taken for the further accommodation of prisoners. Ten men, among them Stephen Dagnall, a pastor, and Thomas Monk, and two women (one of them a widow with six children), all Baptists, who had been taken at a meeting in or near Aylesbury, and legally convicted three months before, were brought up at the Quarter Sessions. The Justices applied the statute of 35 Eliz., and ordered them either to conform to the Church of England and take the oaths of allegiance and supremacy, or else to abjure the realm for life. If they did neither, then sentence of death would be passed on them, and they were given all the afternoon to decide. As they then said they could neither conform nor abjure, sentence of death was passed on them, and as they were now convicted felons, the officers seized all their goods. Such was the terror amongst the Nonconformists of the neighbourhood that they all shut up their shops. Brandon, a shoemaker, one of the men convicted, was persuaded by his wife to recant and did so, but it preyed upon his mind, and he went back to gaol of his own accord. Monk's son applied to Kiffin, who interviewed Clarendon and besought him to lay the matter before the King.[7] The King expressed his surprise that such a thing could be possible, and inquired if the law really so stood, and being informed that it was so, he despatched an

---

[1] Calamy, III. 532.
[2] Neal, " Puritans," IV. 103; Cramp, " Bapt. Hist.," p. 280.
[3] " Hist. Eng. Baptists," I. 328–329.
[4] Stoughton, " Hist. Rel. in Eng.," III. 295.
[5] " Baptists and Bartholomew's Day," *Trans. Bapt. Hist. Soc.*, I. 24–37.
[6] Whitley, " Hist. Brit. Baptists, p. 160.
[7] Mackintosh, " Hist. of Revolution," p. 172.

instant reprieve. The twelve Baptists remained in prison till the next Assizes, when the judge brought them the King's pardon, and they were set free.[1] This put an end to the worst of the violence in that district.

Thomas Tillam, together with Christopher Pooley, a Norfolk Baptist, had returned to England in the summer of 1661, accompanied by one Love, who was reported as an Independent, and preacher to a congregation of the exiles residing in Holland.[1] These three gave out that they had been in the Palatinate to settle a hundred families there.[2] Tillam was engaged in the plots in England during the next two or three years, but in 1664 he led a party of his co-religionists to found a settlement in Germany, and a letter from Rotterdam at the end of that year reported that the abominable practices of Tillam and his companions had brought reproach on the English people there.[3] He may have had some connection with the continental Anabaptists. On November 18th, 1666, Colonel Birch, an old Parliamentarian, allowed two wandering ministers from Germany, probably Anabaptists, to preach in Birch Hall in Lancashire. They continued their exhortations from 9 a.m., speaking fluent English, denouncing all manner of woe upon England and recommending people to take refuge in Germany. One of the hymns they sang, " Hark, how the trumpet sounds," was calculated to give great offence to the supporters of Church and King.[4] Whether these people were connected with Tillam in any way, we cannot say, but Tillam's vagaries, coupled with the Conventicle Act, brought the Hexham Baptist congregation to a very low ebb.[5]

Down to 1664, persecution, as far as the Baptists were concerned, seems to have been sporadic and spasmodic and, except in certain instances, not very severe. Old laws, like the Conventicle Act of 1593, were occasionally put in force, as in the case of John Bunyan, but the application of 35 Eliz. to the Baptists at Aylesbury gave great surprise. The General Baptists were able, even in 1663, to hold an Assembly which ratified the Confession of Faith of 1660.[6] Among the Baptists, however, there were men, some of them officers of the old army, who were constantly engaged in plotting against the Government. It is true that for one plotter there were hundreds who disavowed him, but as long as plots went on, and as long as there was reason to fear that meeting-houses might be centres of sedition, the authorities had to exercise all the repressive powers at their disposal. A modern

[1] Crosby, " Hist. Eng. Baptists," II. 180–185.
[2] C.S.P.D., September 1st, 1661.
[3] Ibid., December 3rd, 1664.
[4] Hunter, " Life of Oliver Heywood," p. 188.
[5] Douglas, " Bapt. Churches N. England," pp. 98–99.
[6] Whitley," Minutes Gen. Assembly," I. 22 ; T. Richards, " Wales under the Indulgence," Bapt. Quart., IV. 280.

Baptist writer has said that though the King and Sheldon have often been blamed for the Acts against Dissenters yet what they did was in self-defence, and that great provocation was given to the Government by a powerful, and militant section of the Baptists.[1] The widespread plot discovered in 1663, which caused the authorities very great alarm, provided one of the reasons for the passing of the Conventicle Act of 1664.

It was not so much the Act itself as the methods by which it was often enforced, which ultimately caused a revulsion of feeling. Thus in 1664 Benjamin Keach was arrested at a meeting at Winslow. The troopers who captured him tied him up, threw him in the road, and but for the intervention of an officer would, it is said, have trampled him to death. He was then thrown across a horse's back and carried to gaol, where he suffered great hardships until the time of his release.[2] It is probable that the soldiers were only trying to frighten their prisoner, and did not really intend to murder him, but no excuse can be made for what happened in Brecknockshire in 1664, when the body of a Baptist woman who had died, was exhumed and buried at the cross roads like a suicide.[3] An equally disgraceful scene occurred at Croft in Lincolnshire in 1666. Robert Shalder, a Baptist who had been imprisoned for his beliefs, died shortly after he was set free and was buried in the churchyard. Some of the villagers took the man's body out of the grave, drew it on a sledge to the gate of his own house, and left it there. Some verses entitled " The Dead Man's Complaint " were at a later date placed on the grave, designed, said Crosby, " to check the envy of the spiritual court who thus disgraced the dead." [4] The spiritual court had been responsible for his imprisonment, but certainly could not be held responsible for the conduct of the rough villagers. A Baptist captain, who was an official at Chatham Dockyard, and nevertheless preached openly in a meeting-house, sent a formal notice to the Admiralty somewhere about 1667 that if the enforcement of the Conventicle Act were prolonged he would refuse to work there any longer.[5]

Keach published in 1664 " The Child's Instructor: or, a New and Easy Primer." It contained, amongst other things, instructions in religion, of a somewhat polemic kind, attacking infant baptism, defending lay preaching, advocating Millennarian doctrines, and making particularly obnoxious references to the Anglican clergy. A copy fell into the hands of a local justice of the peace, named Stafford, who, with a constable, raided Keach's house, seized all the copies of the work, and bound the writer over to the Assizes in £100 for himself and two other

---

[1] " Militant Baptists, 1660–1672," *Trans. Bapt. Hist. Soc.*, I. 155.
[2] Wilson, " Hist. Dissenting Churches in London," IV. 244.
[3] T. Richards, " Wales under the Indulgence," *Bapt. Quart.*, IV. 280.
[4] Crosby, " Eng. Baptists," II. 239–240.   [5] C.S.P.D., 239/243.

sureties of £50 each. Keach appeared before Chief Justice
Hyde at the Aylesbury Assizes on October 8th and 9th, 1664, on
a charge of " maliciously writing and publishing a book " containing " damnable positions contrary to the Book of Common
Prayer." He was fined £20, sent to prison for a fortnight,
ordered to stand in the pillory for two hours at Aylesbury and
two hours at Winslow, at which latter place his book was to be
publicly burned before his face, and then to remain in prison
until he found bail for his good behaviour and for his appearance
at the next Assizes, there to renounce his doctrines and make
public submission.[1] It is not quite clear under what law he
was punished. It might have been under the Licensing Act,
13 & 14 Car. II., c. 35, s. 2, which forbade the publication of a
book asserting doctrine contrary to the Christian faith or to the
doctrine and discipline of the Church of England. If it was
treated as a libel indictable at Common Law, and not, as at
most, an ecclesiastical offence, the case was an unheard-of
extension of the Criminal Law.[2] The trial, however, seems to
show that it was held that the publication of heretical doctrines
was punishable in the Common Law courts, though this never
has been admitted since 1689.[3] Keach duly suffered his punishment and spent his time in the pillory preaching and arguing.
All copies of his book appear to have been destroyed at the time,
but he afterwards reproduced the work as nearly as possible from
memory, though with a slightly different title. For this he was
fined £20 in 1668.[4]

A General Assembly of the General Baptists met in 1668,
probably the first since 1663. It discussed the decrees of the
Assembly of 1656 with regard to marriage with persons who were
not Baptists, and issued them in an enlarged form on May 4th.
It was decreed that marriage with an unbeliever was sin. If the
offending couple, after repentance, continued to live together as
man and wife that was a continuance in sin. " We will not say
it is fornication, neither shall he who does such a thing say it is
not." But it was to be called " the sin of marrying out of the
church," and persons guilty of it ought to be excommunicated.
They realised, however, that they could hardly demand that
such persons should separate from each other, and therefore they
proposed " to accept such repentance as the reality may not be
questioned by any circumstance attending." It was felt that
the matter ought to be brought up again, and this was done from
time to time, but the former decisions were reasserted. The
decisions of 1668 were embodied in the minutes of 1704.[5]

[1] Cramp, " Bapt. Hist.," p. 295.
[2] Stephen, " Hist. Crim. Law," I. 375–376.
[3] Salmon, " Critical Review. State Trials," p. 299.
[4] Evans, " Early English Baptists," p. 307; Cramp, " Bapt. Hist.,"
pp. 296–298; " State Trials," II. 549–554.
[5] Whitley, " Minutes Gen. Assembly," I. 23–24.

The Second Conventicle Act made it impossible to hold General Assemblies and difficult to hold ordinary meetings. Hanserd Knollys was apprehended in May 1670 at a meeting in George Yard and sent to the Counter in Bishopsgate. For some years past he had been ministering to a Baptist congregation, first in Finsbury Fields, and then at Broken Wharf, Thames Street, and earning his living as a merchant trading with Holland. In prison he held services twice a week, with the prisoners for a congregation, but his imprisonment was not for long, and he was released at the next Sessions.[1]   Vavasour Powell, who had been released in 1667, had been imprisoned in Cardiff gaol in 1668 for preaching, and in 1669 was removed to the Fleet prison. He also preached frequently in the prison, and many people were allowed in to hear him. He died in gaol in October 1670, and was buried in Bunhill Fields, a great concourse of Dissenters attending his funeral. Part of his epitaph ran:—

> " Christ him released, and now he's joined among
> The martyred souls, with whom he cries, How long? " [2]

On May 29th, 1670, the Baptists of Lewes were discovered by two informers in the act of holding a meeting in a house about a mile from the town. The minister was fined £20, and forty members of the congregation were fined five shillings each. As the minister was poor, his fine was imposed on five members of the congregation, and the various sums were enforced by distress. Walter Brett, a grocer, was fined £6 for the minister and five shillings for himself. The constables seized two barrels of sugar, which he claimed to have cost him £15. Thomas Barnard and his brother were fined £11 10s. between them. Six cows were seized, worth in all £27. Richard White, a brazier, was fined £3 15s. Articles were taken from him worth upwards of £10. In levying the sums of five shillings the same system of excessive distraint was pursued; a horse was taken from a butcher, and the sheets from the bed of a mason, and his wife's underclothing.[3] An attempt at Bedford to enforce fines ordered by the Conventicle Act led to riots, and soldiers had to be quartered there. The prisons everywhere were crowded, and numbers of Nonconformists fled to Holland or America. Meetings were not held at all or held in fear and trembling. John Gratton saw the elders and ministers at Monyash thrusting each other forward to do the preaching, and each refusing his house for the meeting for fear of the fine of £20. " I left these formalists." [4]

---

[1] Culross, " Hanserd Knollys," pp. 92–93; Wilson, " Dissenting Churches in London," II. 566–568.

[2] R. Williams, " Life of Vavasour Powell," *Trans. Powysland Club*, XV. 213; " The Life and Death of Mr. Vavasour Powell " (supposed to have been written by Edmund Bagshawe), 1671.

[3] Ivimey, " Hist. Eng. Baptists," I. 366–377.

[4] " Journal of the Life of John Gratton."

It has been estimated that in 1672 there were about 420 Baptist preachers in England, scattered about the country. Many Baptists, like the Quakers, however, refused to apply for licences under the Declaration of Indulgence of 1672, because they believed that to ask for dispensation from the penal laws would be to admit their justice, and also to admit that the King could override Parliament. Many of them had served as officers in the army to prevent this very thing. No licences were asked for by Baptists in the four northern counties, though it is known that there were Baptist congregations at Muggleswick in Durham, and also in Newcastle.[1] The Lincolnshire Baptists sent Grantham and another messenger to express their thanks to the King. While doing so, they pointed out to him that his Indulgence came far short of the liberty which Christians had a right to expect, and urged him to give complete liberty to all.[2] It would seem that outside London some ninety-eight licences were issued to General Baptists.[3] In London application was made for a licence for three City Halls, the Leathersellers', Lorimers' and Pinners', for the last-named three applications being sent in, but all were refused. A licence, however, was granted for Curriers' Hall, though there was strong opposition to such buildings being used in this way.[4] A number of Baptists would be set free from prison by the King's pardon, issued in September. One of the prisoners who had reason to rejoice at the Declaration of Indulgence was John Bunyan, for thereby he gained his liberty after twelve years. His imprisonment nevertheless had only been intermittent, and he had been allowed a great deal of liberty. He says himself that in 1661 and 1662 he took every opportunity which came to him of visiting the people of God, exhorting them to continue steadfast in the faith of Christ, and to have nothing to do with the Prayer Book.[5] He went to London once during his imprisonment, and frequently went out preaching. It was owing to this persistence in preaching that at the Spring Assizes of 1662 his imprisonment was made more rigorous. He seems to have been set free for a short time in 1666. Possibly someone had interceded for him, or perhaps it was because of the plague being in Bedford that year. But in a very short time he was arrested at a meeting, and sent back to gaol. His name frequently appears, however, in the Bedford Church Book, as being present at meetings, or as being commissioned to deal with backsliding brethren. He was at a church meeting on October 9th, 1668. He was sent on visits in November 1668, and September and

---

[1] " Baptist Licences of 1672," *Trans. Bapt. Hist. Soc.*, I. 156–177.
[2] Taylor, " Hist. Gen. Baptists," I. 207.
[3] Whitley, " Minutes Gen. Assembly," I. lvi–lxvi.
[4] " Baptist Meetings in City of London," *Trans. Bapt. Hist. Soc.*, V. 74–82.
[5] Compare his tract, " I will pray with the Spirit," in which he attacks the Prayer Book as " taken out of the popish mass-book."

November 1669, and attended meetings in January and April 1670.[1]

In 1670 he is found going in and out of the prison, staying the night at times with his family, and preaching in the woods outside the town.   In 1671 he became a pastor of the Baptist congregation there, and the question was actually raised at the time whether he was eligible for the office, being a prisoner.   It was during this imprisonment that he wrote " Grace Abounding," and the first part of the "Pilgrim's Progress."   The reason why so much sympathy has been expended on Bunyan, in comparison with other Nonconformists who suffered very much worse things, is probably that his name is the most familiar of them all, and while everyone has heard about his imprisonment, comparatively few have heard, except in general terms, of the trials of the others.   " When he came abroad he found his temporal affairs were gone to wreck. . . . But yet he was not destitute of friends, who had all along supported him with necessaries, and had been very good to his family : so that by their assistance, getting things a little about him again, he resolved, as much as possible, to decline worldly business, and give himself up wholly to the service of God." [2]

Bunyan's licence under the Declaration of Indulgence of 1672 described him as " of the persuasion commonly called Congregational," though he is generally counted as a Baptist.   He disliked all party names, and thought they came from " hell and Babylon," and in " The Heavenly Footman," which was published after his death, he warned his readers against associating too much with the Anabaptists, " though I go under that name myself."   As for his congregation at Bedford, it is doubtful whether it was strictly Baptist in the ordinary sense.   He held that the question of " water-baptism," as he called it, could not be made a condition of communion, and steadfastly refused to commend a member of his flock to any congregation where baptism, as the Baptists understood it, i.e. by immersion, was made such a condition.[3]   Not that he disbelieved in baptism, for he had his son Joseph baptized in St. Cuthbert's, Bedford, on November 16th, 1672,[4] but both he and his congregation looked upon baptism as an external matter, non-essential to salvation, and desired that " saints " should be admitted to Christian fellowship without being asked whether they had been baptized or not.   To explain and defend his principles, and perhaps thereby to obtain his release, he published in the early part of 1672 " A Confession of my Faith and Reason of my Practice."

---

[1] Whitley, " Bunyan's Imprisonments," *Trans. Bapt. Hist. Soc.*, VI. 1–24; " A Relation of the Imprisonment of Mr. John Bunyan," 1765.
[2] Quoted in Froude, " Life of Bunyan," pp. 86–87.
[3] Stoughton, " Hist. Rel. in Eng.," III. 267.
[4] Brown, " Life of Bunyan," pp. 237–238.

Kiffin and Danvers violently attacked this book, especially the latter portion, in which he set forth his views on baptism and church membership. In 1673 Bunyan published his " Differences in Judgment about Water Baptism no bar to Communion," in which he pleaded that his opponents should bear patiently with brethren who could not see the necessity for baptism. He followed this up with " Peaceable Principles and True: or a Brief Answer to Mr. D'Anvers' and Mr. Paul's Books. . . . Wherein their Scriptureless Notions are Overthrown and my Peaceable Principles still Maintained."

During the year 1672 Bunyan carried on a controversy with Edmund Fowler, rector of Northill, and in later days Bishop of Gloucester. Fowler, the son of Richard Fowler, a Presbyterian who was ejected at the Restoration,[1] was a member of the Latitudinarian party, and in 1670 published " The Principles and Practices of Certain Moderate Divines of the Church of England." In the following year he followed up this defence of Latitudinarian doctrine with another work, " The Design of Christianity," in which he seemed to reduce the Christian religion to a mere system of morals, and to undermine the cardinal doctrine of Protestantism, justification by faith. Bunyan, who was in prison in Bedford, wrote in 1672 a violent and unfair attack on Fowler, " The Defence of the Doctrine of Justification by Faith," in which he called his adversary " a pretended minister of the Word," who had " vilely exposed to public view the rottenness of his heart, on principles diametrically opposite to the simplicity of the gospel of Christ." A fierce answer was printed in the September of that year. It was called " Dirt Wiped Off: or, a manifest Discovery of the Gross Ignorance, Erroneousness, and most Unchristian and Wicked Spirit of one John Bunyan, Lay-Preacher in Bedford." It was professedly written on Fowler's behalf by a friend of his, and it has been suggested that it was written by Fowler's curate, perhaps with Fowler's help. Whoever he was, the writer described Bunyan as " a wretched scribbler, a most foul-mouthed calumniator," and " so very dirty a creature " that he " disdained to dirty his fingers with him," and desired to know whether " the letting such firebrands and most impudent and malicious schismatics go unpunished " did not tend to the subversion of all government.[2] After the Declaration of Indulgence was recalled Bunyan was again imprisoned for preaching, but was released in less than six months, owing to the efforts of Dr. John Owen and Bishop Barlow of Lincoln, who recommended him to apply to the Lord Chancellor for release. He was again imprisoned " more in form than in reality," for a short period in 1675.[3]

[1] Calamy, II. 330.
[2] Brown, " Life of Bunyan," pp. 233–235; Tulloch, " Rational Theology in England," II. 437–439; " Dirt Wiped Off," 1672.
[3] Froude, " Bunyan," p. 82. The Life of John Bunyan, 1692.

A pamphlet, bearing the title " Mr. Baxter Baptized in
Blood," was published in 1673 and licensed for publication by
Samuel Parker. It related how Mr. Josiah Baxter, a godly
minister in New England, had been murdered by four Baptists in
Boston, because he had worsted the Baptist leaders there in a
disputation. Amidst " the howlings, groans, and screechings "
of his relatives, lying bound and helpless near him, he was stripped,
whipped, disembowelled, and finally flayed alive. The pamphlet
purported to be written and published by his brother, Benjamin
Baxter, then living in Fenchurch Street, London. Names,
speeches, place, and details were all exactly specified. Kiffin
brought the pamphlet before the Privy Council, who inquired into
the matter, and found there was no truth whatever in it. The
master of a ship, and a merchant, who sailed from Boston twenty
days after the affair was said to have taken place, made sworn
affidavit that nothing of the kind had happened, and that there
had been no such person in Boston as Mr. Josiah Baxter. Further
evidence showed that no such person as Benjamin Baxter lived
in Fenchurch Street, nor had lived there within the witnesses'
memory. Parker, who was rebuked by the Council for licensing
it, admitted his mistake, and publicly affirmed his belief that it
was false. Andrew Marvell even hinted that Parker had written
it himself, that men might think the Baptists like the Münster
Anabaptists.[1]

In 1673 Hanserd Knollys petitioned the King about some
property from which he considered himself unjustly excluded.
The circumstances are instructive as showing the difficulties which
arose about Government property which got into Puritan hands
during the Interregnum. About 1650 he had bought from the
Honourable Artillery Company the old Armoury House in the
Artillery Ground in Spitalfields. The Company had only a
doubtful claim to the building, which had been granted to their
use by an Order in Council of the time of James I., and the
ground was the King's, but Knollys paid them £300 for the
building, and spent another £460 in turning it into a dwelling-
house and school-house. The question of his right to it arose at
the Restoration, and the Lord Treasurer Southampton, in consideration of his poverty, as he claimed to have spent his all upon
it, directed that the lease should be given him. Colonel Legge,
the Lieutenant of Ordnance, had ignored this, seized the
property, evicted Knollys, and kept possession until his death,
when it passed to his successor, David Waters. Knollys now
petitioned the King for either £750 as compensation, or a lease
for ninety years. The petition was handed over to Lord Keeper
Finch, who submitted a report the following June to the effect

---

[1] Neal, IV. 477; Stoughton, " Hist. Rel. Eng.," III. 323; " Letters to Sir
J. Williamson," Camden Series I. 28; Marvell, " The Rehearsal Transprosed," ed. 1674, Pt. II. p. 100.

that a lease was impracticable, because the place was needed for Government purposes, the house had been granted to Waters with reversion to George Legge after him, and had become annexed to the Ordnance Office. To save the petitioner from ruin, inasmuch as he had spent so much on the property, and had had to borrow money, and was now old and poor, Finch recommended that he should be reimbursed.[1]

About 1673 there was a great controversy among the Baptists about the rite of laying on of hands on the newly baptized, which was considered by some of them an apostolic ordinance. Some of those who objected to the practice issued a tract called " A Search after Schism," which dealt severely with those who upheld it. John Griffith replied to it in " The Searcher after Schism Searched," whilst Thomas Grantham wrote ' A Sigh for Peace: or, the Cause of Division Discovered," a stout defence of the ordinance, in which he declared that he could not join in communion with those who opposed it. This was answered by Jeremy Ives, one of the London ministers, and a public debate, in which Grantham and Ives were the chief speakers, and in which Ives was said to have been worsted, was held in London.[2]

Jeremy or Jeremiah Ives was for thirty or forty years minister of the Baptist congregation which met in Old Jewry. He was a man who appeared to love controversy, and held debates with his fellow-Baptist, Grantham, with the Quakers, who were said never to have forgiven him, and, on the subject of baptism, with Benjamin Woodbridge, a Presbyterian minister of Newbury. The story is told that so famed were his powers as a disputant that King Charles on one occasion summoned him to debate with a Roman Catholic priest, that Ives appeared in clerical dress, and that the priest's surprise when he found who his opponent was gave the King infinite merriment.[3]

The unlawfulness of infant baptism was one of the cardinal principles of the Baptists, and there were many books written about it and many controversies. One of these specially centred round the name of Henry Danvers, who was a minister of a Particular Baptist congregation at the Chequer in the neighbourhood of Aldgate.[4] He had been a colonel in the Parliamentary army and Governor of Stafford under the Commonwealth, held Millennarian doctrines, and had been imprisoned in the Tower, from which he was released in 1671.[5] In 1674 he wrote a great work, a thousand pages long, entitled " A Treatise on Baptism," in which he attacked infant baptism. The book showed a con-

[1] C.S.P.D., December 21st, 1673; June 22nd, 1674, 338/84.
[2] Neal, " Hist. Puritans," IV. 627; Crosby, " Hist. Eng. Baptists," II. 277–278; Taylor, " Hist. Eng. Gen. Baptists," I. 206.
[3] Wilson, " Dissenting Churches in London," II. 444–445.
[4] Whitley, " Baptists of London," p. 113.
[5] Wilson, " Dissenting Churches in London," I. 393–396; Crosby, " Eng. Baptists," III. 97.

siderable amount of erudition, and many answers to it were written.   Macaulay says of Danvers that he drew on himself the censure of the most respectable Puritans by attempting to palliate the crimes of Mathias and John of Leyden.   It is true that a Puritan, Obadiah Wills of Devizes, attacked him and tried to saddle the English Baptists with the crimes of the German Ana-baptists,[1] and that Baxter had written a preface to Wills's work, but it is not true that Danvers tried to palliate the evil doings of 1535.   What he had done was to express doubt whether they had ever been committed.   Blenman, for whom Baxter also wrote a preface, also attacked Danvers.   Tombes wrote a defence of Baptist doctrines [2] and W. A. (probably the Rev. William Assheton) set forth once more the arguments for the Church against Dissent, but dealt more particularly with the question of infant baptism.[3]   Baxter, coming out as a principal in the fray, confuted, at any rate to his own satisfaction, Tombes' arguments, and " the strange forgeries of Mr. Danvers " and his " many calumnies against myself and writings," and set forth " a catalogue of fifty-six new commandments and doctrines, which he and the sectaries who join with him in these calumnies own." [4]   He returned to the charge again in 1676 with another reply to Danvers and Tombes in " Richard Baxter's Review of the State of Christian Infants."   Among others who took part in the controversy about baptism were Hanserd Knollys and Kiffin, who defended Danvers against Wills, Flavel,[5] and Ben-jamin Keach.   The last named had settled in London and had, in 1668, under the influence of Hanserd Knollys, seceded from the General to the Particular Baptists.[6]

In 1676 Danvers published an attack on the ordinance of the laying on of hands in a supplement to a revised edition of the " Treatise on Baptism."   Keach and Grantham both replied to him, and Grantham annexed to his reply " A Treatise of the Successors of the Apostles," in which he maintained the divine authority of the office of messenger.

The religious divisions of the time brought strife into families, and malice and uncharitableness amongst neighbours.   Agnes Beaumont of Edworth in Bedfordshire, greatly against the will of her father, joined John Bunyan's congregation in 1672, and on one occasion, in February 1674, having no other way of getting to a distant meeting, rode pillion behind Bunyan himself.   Her father locked her out and refused to let her in until she promised

---

[1] " Infant Baptism Asserted and Vindicated, in Answer to a Treatise of Baptism, by Mr. H. D'Anvers, with a censure of his Essay to Palliate The Horrid Actings of the Anabaptists in Germany," 1674.
[2] " A Just Reply to the Books of Mr. Wills and Mr. Blenman (with Mr. Baxter's injurious Preface) for Infant Baptism," 1675.
[3] " A Serious and Friendly Address to the Nonconformists. Beginning with the Anabaptists," 1675.   [4] Baxter, " Proofs of Infant Church Membership," 1675.
[5] Calamy, II. 220.   [6] Whitley, " The Baptists of London," p. 68.

to go to meetings no more. Two nights after this he died suddenly, and the story was spread that she had poisoned him at Bunyan's instigation. The coroner's jury affirmed her innocence, but her brother-in-law contested her inheritance of her father's property, and she had to buy off his hostility with a large sum of money. The poison story still went round, and when, in 1675, there was a fire in the place, she was accused of that. Yet she seems to have been a thoroughly good woman.[1] A rather different case was that of Anne Wentworth. She had been a Baptist, but had left that sect, and suffered much at the hands of her former associates in consequence. She had also been ill-treated by her husband, and had left him. She published a vindication of herself, in which she announced her willingness to return to him on condition that she should not be interfered with in her worship. Apparently she claimed a prophetic spirit, and she related how on the fifth day of the tenth month 1677 the Lord had awakened her in the night and made her sing unto Him a triumphant victorious song over her enemies. She appealed to the congregations of Anabaptists and their pastors, and asked if it was right of them to defame a neighbour in alehouses and coffee-houses; and she complained that she had been so defamed and abused for the past twenty-four years, and had been proclaimed a heathen by the church. Let them prove her guilty of the things of which they accused her before the next New Year's Day, or trouble should come upon them from the Lord, and she would be able to rejoice when they had cause to mourn.[2]

A great debate was held at Triplow in Cambridgeshire in 1676, between the Quakers and the Baptists. The disputants were Samuel Cater, who had been an associate of James Nayler, and two Baptists, Francis Holcroft and Joseph Oddy. Cater maintained that every man is enlightened by Christ, a doctrine which Holcroft described as "cursed idolatry." The debate seems to have degenerated into mere railing. Cater said that Holcroft was "in knowledge more brutish than a beast." Oddy said Holcroft was doing a great work amongst a "generation of vipers." The latter maintained the Calvinist doctrine that some infants were damned before they were born, to which Cater made the pertinent reply that our Lord said, "Of such is the Kingdom of Heaven." Finally, Holcroft "shook the dust off his feet," and Oddy and he "hastened away with railing words."[3] The two Baptists, Francis Holcroft, ejected from Clare College,

[1] "The Narrative of Agnes Beaumont," ed. by G. B. Harrison, 1929.
[2] "A True Account of Anne Wentworth's being cruelly, unjustly and unchristianly dealt with by Anabaptists," 1676; "A Vindication of Anne Wentworth, leading to the better Preparing of all People for her larger Testimony, which is making ready for the Public View," 1677–1678.
[3] Nutter, "Story of the Cambridge Baptists."

and Joseph Oddy, ejected from a fellowship at Trinity, both suffered imprisonment for their faith. Holcroft spent from 1663 to 1672 in Cambridge gaol, but during that time the gaoler, who was a secret sympathiser, allowed him to go out at night to preach in neighbouring villages. Oddy preached to large congregations at Willingham and sometimes in the fields, and endured five years' imprisonment for it. They both obtained licences in 1672, but Holcroft was imprisoned again after a time, and was sent from Cambridge to the Fleet prison in London, where crowds flocked to hear him preach. Tillotson, who was a great friend of his in Cambridge, was very kind to him.[1]

All the sects were eager controversialists. In 1678 it was reported to Sir Joseph Williamson that at Deal a Presbyterian minister had preached against the Baptists, and that one of the leaders of the latter party, meeting two Presbyterian ministers, had argued with them in a shop and later in the street. The informant, who said that the Presbyterian got the worst of it, professed great anxiety about the harm that might be done by this " impudent prating in the streets." [2]

The Assembly of the pastors and elders of the London and other Particular Baptist congregations met in London in 1677, probably in consequence of a letter which had been sent out in October 1675, requesting them to meet in the next year to take into consideration a plan to provide a standing orderly ministry in the church. This meeting adopted a revision of the Westminster Confession, in which revision Pastor Collins, a Particular Baptist, had taken a chief part, though possibly with some further revision by Kiffin and the other elders. It was issued as " A Confession of Faith by the Elders and Brethren of many Congregations of Christians, Baptized upon Profession of their Faith, in London and the Country." As far as its Calvinism is concerned, it follows closely the wording of the Westminster Confession, but on the questions of baptism, the ministry, and church government, the views of the Baptists are clearly set forth, while in an appendix infant baptism is considered and its lawfulness denied. The Confession was printed in 1677. A second edition appeared in 1688, and in 1689 the London Particular Baptists convened a General Assembly, which endorsed and re-issued it.[3]

Possibly the example of the London Particular Baptists in issuing their Confession may have inspired the General Baptists. A Confession of Faith was adopted in 1678 at a meeting of the Baptists of Oxfordshire, Buckinghamshire, Herts, and Bedford-

[1] Calamy, II. 86, 88; III. 122; Nutter, "Story of the Cambridge Baptists."
[2] C.S.P.D., September 25th, 1678, 406/166.
[3] Crosby, " Hist. Eng. Baptists," II. 312–344; Whitley, " Minutes Gen. Assembly," I. p. xix; Cramp, " Bapt. Hist.," p. 314; " Confessions of Faith," Hanserd Knollys Soc., pp. 169–246; Whitley, " Baptists of London," p. 46.

shire, held at Aylesbury. It was, in part at any rate, directed against the Christological teachings of Matthew Caffin, consisted of fifty articles, and was believed to have been drawn up by Thomas Monk of Aylesbury, the Messenger. In the following year it was published with the signatures attached of fifty-four " Messengers, Elders and Brethren," under the title of " An Orthodox Creed : or, a Protestant Confession of Faith, being an Essay to unite and Confirm all true Protestants in the fundamental Articles of the Christian Religion, against the Errors and Heresies of the Church of Rome." [1] Thomas Collier also published a Confession of Faith, which had some acceptance for a time in the west of England. [2]

In 1678 Grantham published his great book " Christianismus Primitivus," a complete exposition and defence of Baptist theology. He incorporated in this work the " Brief Confession or Declaration of Faith," set forth in the Twenty-five Articles in 1660 and ratified by the General Assembly in 1663. Before inserting it in his book Grantham had subjected it to severe revision. He made some verbal alterations, improved the grammar here and there, and made some small excisions and additions. The revised version was at a later date approved by the Assembly. [3]

The last years of Charles II. were difficult years for the Nonconformists. One of the sufferers was Francis Bampfield, one of the Sabbatarian leaders. He came of a good family in Devonshire, was a prebendary of Exeter, and held the living of Sherborne. He had been a zealous royalist, and is said to have continued the use of the Prayer Book longer than any clergyman in Devonshire. Under the influence of Baxter he had changed his views, and as he could not take the oath of allegiance, he had resigned his preferments in 1662. From 1663 to 1672 he was imprisoned in Dorchester gaol for conventicling, and during that time became a Baptist. Liberated in 1672, he baptized himself in the Avon, began to preach again, and spent eighteen weeks of that year in prison at Salisbury. In the following year he founded a church of Sabbatarian Baptists, at first in his own house in London, and then at Pinners' Hall. He converted to his own way of thinking his brother Thomas Bampfield, who had formerly been Recorder of Exeter and Speaker of Richard Cromwell's Parliament. [4]

On Saturday, February 17th, 1683, while Francis was holding a service, he was disturbed by an armed party, and when the leader announced that he had a warrant from the Lord Mayor

[1] Whitley, " Minutes Gen. Assembly," I. xix; " Confessions of Faith," Hanserd Knollys Soc., pp. 121–168.
[2] Whitley, " Brit. Baptists," p. 129.
[3] Whitley, " Minutes Gen. Assembly," pp. xviii and 10.
[4] Trans. Bapt. Hist. Soc., III. 8–17.

to stop the service, Bampfield replied that he had a warrant from " Christ, the Lord Maximus," to go on. He was fined £10, but went back to his own house and preached there. The next Saturday he was arrested again. The Recorder ordered the oaths to be tendered him, but he refused; as he put it himself, he kept on his gloves and did not put his hand on the Bible, so he was sent to Newgate.[1]   In October, as he still refused the oaths, he and several others were sentenced to imprisonment for life, and forfeiture of all their goods, and he died in the following February from sickness brought on by the vile condition of Newgate prison.[2]

John Griffith was tried at the Old Bailey before Chief Justice Saunders and three other judges at the same time as Francis Bampfield. He also refused to take the oath of allegiance, and explained that he could not do so because of the words " heirs and successors according to law," which might bind him to allegiance to a Papist, and because he could not promise conformity to the Church of England. He also was sent to Newgate. Among his fellow-prisoners there were two other Baptists, Lawrence Wise [3] and Hercules Collins, and the Baptist congregations made collections for their support.[4]

James Jones of Southwark kept a coffee-house which more than once was under suspicion of being a centre of disaffection. He was also a merchant tailor (in an affidavit made before Judge Charlton he called himself such) and pastor of a large Baptist congregation. On November 16th, 1682, he was cited before the ecclesiastical court at Doctors' Commons, on information laid by the churchwardens of his parish, St. Bartholomew, behind the Exchange, for not attending church and not receiving the sacrament. His defence was that the information of the churchwardens was uncertain; they had only declared that " they could not remember that he had been at church." He asked for a copy of the information, which was refused, and also demanded to see the authority of the court. The last request, of course, was absurd, but he looked upon the court's refusal of it as a grievance. Finally he was found contumacious and excommunicated. On February 7th, 1683, he demanded a copy of the excommunication and all other proceedings of the ecclesiastical court. Next he put in an affidavit before a judge that he had been unable to procure these. He got them at last, but at the end of term a writ of *de excommunicato capiendo* was issued

[1] Francis Bampfield, " The Lord's Free Prisoner," 1683.
[2] " A Just Appeal from the Lower Courts on Earth to the Highest Court in Heaven," 1683; Wood, " Athenæ," II. 755–756; Calamy, II. 258; III. 411; Pike, " Ancient Meeting Houses," pp. 162–168.
[3] Calamy, III. 546.
[4] The Case of Mr. John Griffith, Minister of the Gospel, and now, Prisoner in Newgate, 1683; Wilson, " Dissenting Churches," II. 176–179; " Counsel for the Living occasioned from the Dead," by Hercules Collins, 1684.

against him, so he sued out a prohibition both at the King's
Bench and at Common Pleas. In a published account of the
proceedings he set forth, for the benefit of his fellow-Dissenters,
the ways in which the writ *de excommunicato capiendo* could be sued
out. He had not discovered anything fresh, for Bunyan had
probably obtained his freedom by the same method in 1677, but
many people did not know this method of escape.[1]

Dr. Benjamin Calamy, rector of St. Lawrence, Jewry, and
chaplain to the King, printed and published a sermon entitled
" A Scrupulous Conscience," in which he challenged the Nonconformists to set forth a defence of their position. The challenge
was answered by Thomas Delaune, a native of Ireland, who had
been brought up as a Roman Catholic, and turned Protestant,
and had been obliged to leave Ireland in consequence of the
hatred aroused by his zeal for his new faith. He had settled in
London, and kept a school there, and was on terms of friendship
with the leading Baptists. He is counted by some as a Baptist,
and seems to have taken later to the printing trade. His answer
to Calamy bore the title of " A Plea for the Nonconformists."
Defoe, who wrote a commendatory preface to the seventeenth
edition, in 1733, spoke of it enthusiastically: " Never author
left behind him a more finished piece, and I believe the dispute
is entirely ended. If any man ask what we can say, why the
Dissenters differ from the Church of England, and what they can
plead for it, I can recommend no better reply that this. Let
them answer, in short, Thomas Delaune, and desire the querist
to read the book."[2] But before the work was finished at the
printers it was seized by a King's messenger in December 1683,
and the author was sent to the Wood Street Counter, " where he
had a hard bench for his bed and two bricks for his pillows."
Thence he was sent to Newgate, and placed at first amongst the
felons, though his situation was relieved after a time. He wrote
to Calamy and asked for his help, reminding him that he had
written the book at his invitation. He described his prison
quarters as perfectly resembling " that horrid place which you
describe when you mention hell," and said he " would fain be
convinced by something more like divinity than Newgate."
Calamy, however, appears to have done nothing, and in another
letter Delaune reproached him for not visiting him in prison.
His trial came on before Judge Jeffreys at the Old Bailey, in
January 1684, when he was indicted for a " false, seditious, and
scandalous libel against the King and the Book of Common
Prayer." He was sentenced to a fine of a hundred marks, to
remain in prison till it was paid, to find good security for his

---

[1] " The Admonisher Admonished: in a Modest and Impartial Narrative
of the Proceedings of the Ecclesiastical Court against James Jones, Citizen of
London," 1683; Whitley, " Brit. Baptists," p. 147.
[2] Defoe, *in loc. cit.*

good behaviour for a year afterwards, and to have his books publicly burnt before the Royal Exchange. By his imprisonment he lost his livelihood, and was unable to maintain his wife and children, having no means but such contributions as were made by friends who came to visit him. His wife and children died in prison, and last of all, after fifteen months' confinement, he himself died there. "It was very hard that such a man, such a Christian, such a scholar, and on such an occasion, should starve in a dungeon: and that the whole body of Dissenters in England, whose cause he died for defending, should not raise him £66 13*s*. 4*d*. to save his life."[1]   Evans suggested that Delaune had forbidden his friends to pay the fine, and Dr. Stoughton that Delaune courted martyrdom.[2]

Towards the end of the reign of Charles II. William Kiffin was in trouble several times. In 1682 he was prosecuted on account of fifteen meetings which he had attended, the total fines amounting to £300. But he was able to procure able counsel, who found errors in the record, and was discharged.[3] He was in danger, too, of being involved in the Rye House plot, with which he denied all complicity. He asserted that he was a stranger to Monmouth and Russell, and had never been in their company. His son-in-law, Joseph Hayes, was tried for his life in 1684 for treasonably sending money to Sir Thomas Armstrong, who had fled to Holland. Kiffin's story is that a bill of exchange was remitted to Armstrong, which was pretended to have been sent to him by Hayes, who narrowly escaped hanging. While all this was going on, a packet of letters was left at his house by someone unknown, one of the letters addressed to Judge Jeffreys, and another to himself. The latter was full of treason, and so he sent it to Jeffreys, because he saw it was intended as a trap. One of Jeffreys' clerks told Kiffin's servant that he thought he knew the hand, which confirmed Kiffin's suspicion of a trick. The storm blew over, but he says it was ruin to his son-in-law and his wife.[4]

Kiffin owed his safety, no doubt, in large measure to the fact that he had friends in high quarters. He was a merchant of high repute and great wealth. Earlier in the reign the Hamburg Company had obtained from the King a monopoly of the trade in woollen goods with Hamburg and Germany. An inquiry had been held into the matter, and Kiffin had given evidence before the House of Commons. Several members of the King's Council had a high opinion of his ability. A story is told that on one occasion Charles II. tried to borrow £40,000 from him, and that

[1] Defoe, *in loc. cit.*
[2] Evans, "Early Brit. Baptists"; Stoughton, "Hist. of Rel. in Eng.," IV. 71; Neal, "Puritans," IV. 608–609; Cramp, "Bapt. Hist.," 317–320; "Narrative of the Trial and Sufferings of Thomas Delaune," 1684.
[3] "Remarkable Passages in the Life of William Kiffin," p. 51.
[4] *Ibid.*, pp. 52–53.

he apologised for not having so much, but made him a present of £10,000. Whether this be true or not, he had much interest with the King, and sometimes appealed to him successfully on behalf of his Nonconformist brethren.[1] In 1685 his two grand-sons, the Hewlings, were executed for taking part in Monmouth's rebellion.

Not all were strong enough to hold firm during the worst persecutions. In 1684 died an ex-Baptist, John Child. This man was well-to-do, had some ability, and for a time was a Baptist preacher in Buckinghamshire. A little before the last persecution of Dissenters he moved to London, and the per-secution being very severe, he not only conformed, but wrote a book attacking the Nonconformists, especially the Baptists, entitled " A Second Argument, for a more Full and Firm Union amongst all Good Protestants." Then his conscience troubled him, and he began to believe that he was eternally lost for his apostacy, and on October 13th, 1684, he hanged himself.[2]

In 1685 died John Fownes, a minister of the Baptist congrega-tion in Bristol, a man who may reasonably be considered as one of the Baptist martyrs. Educated at Shrewsbury School and Cambridge, he had held the living of High Wycombe in Bucking-hamshire, but became a Baptist, and resigned before the Restora-tion, though Calamy and Palmer count him among the " ejected and silenced ministers." For a time he ministered to the Independent congregation at Pinners' Hall in London, but in 1678 became pastor of the Baptist congregation at Broadmead, Bristol. In 1683, owing to the persecution, meetings were held in the woods, and on March 25th a conventicle gathered in Kingswood. A body of horse and foot surrounded the place, and though Fownes was not actually taken at the meeting, but was seen coming from that direction, he was arrested and sent to Gloucester gaol " for refusing the Corporation oath and riding within five miles of a corporation." The Dissenters argued that he was not liable under the Five Mile Act, as he had resigned before the King's return. At his trial witnesses were brought to swear a riot against him, to which he replied that " he and his horse could not be guilty of a riot without company," an argu-ment which pleased the jury, the foreman referring to it when they acquitted the prisoner. In spite of his acquittal he was sent back to prison. He was offered his release if he would give his bond for his good behaviour and find sureties, but as preaching would be a breach of such a bond, he refused to give it. He appealed to the Assizes, but two of the local justices warned Judge Levinz that if he were released he would draw all the country after him. He was in very poor health, and his imprisonment had added

[1] Wilson, " Dissenting Churches in London," I. 422.
[2] " The Mischief of Persecution, Exemplified by a True Narrative of the Life and Deplorable End of Mr. John Child," 1688.

greatly to his sufferings. Levinz ordered him to be set free on bail, which was provided, but the local authorities kept him prisoner on a legal quibble. The end of the story is told in the "Broadmead Records": "On the 29th of November, 1685, our pastor, Brother Fownes, died in Gloucester gaol, having been kept there for two years and about nine months, a prisoner unjustly and maliciously, for the testimony of Jesus and the preaching of the gospel. He was a man of great learning, of a sound judgment, an able preacher, having great knowledge in divinity, law, physic, etc.; a bold and patient sufferer for the Lord Jesus and the Gospel he preached."[1]

The sufferings of the Dissenters, however, were soon to come to an end. In the year 1686 persecution ceased, and the Baptists, as well as the members of the other sects, could henceforth meet openly.

In 1685 the members of "the church of Christ meeting in Sheffield in Yorkshire . . . who are in the faith and practice of those six principles specified in Heb. vi. 1–2," gave a certificate of commendation to a poor woman of their congregation named Jane Newman. She was taking a journey to London, and a note added to the certificate states that she received 9s. 6d. from Mr. Kiffin's meeting-house. The Sheffield people were General Baptists, while Mr. Kiffin's people were of the Particular denomination, but theological differences did not prevent friendly communications or manifestations of Christian charity.[2] Doubtless, too, persecution had brought all the sections closer together.

When James II. issued his first Declaration of Indulgence the Baptists were the first to send up addresses of thanks to the King.[3] Kiffin, however, did his best to prevent the Nonconformists from thus expressing their gratitude, and said that a few, and they "generally of the meaner sort," did so. Ivimey remarked of this that he did not know what Kiffin meant by the meaner sort, when Dr. Cox, William Collins, Thomas Plant, Benjamin Dennis, and others signed declarations.[4] Another Baptist who did a great deal to keep the Dissenters from accepting the Indulgence was Joseph Stennett, the son of Edward Stennett, the Sabbatarian minister. He wrote verses against the Declaration, and these verses were printed, and copies distributed at Nonconformist meetings.

Edward Stennett was minister of the Pinners' Hall Sabbatarians from 1686 to 1689. He was a physician as well as a preacher. After the Restoration he lived at Wallingford, and occupied some rooms in the Castle, which was then standing. Among the privileges of the Castle was one that only a Lord Chief

---

[1] "Broadmead Records"; Palmer, "Nonc. Mem.," I. 309; Calamy, III. 144.
[2] *Trans. Bapt. Hist. Soc.*, VII. 19–21.
[3] Crosby, "Hist. Eng. Baptists," III. 198.
[4] Ivimey, "Hist. Eng. Baptists," I. 471.

Justice could issue a warrant for search therein. Stennett took advantage of this to hold a conventicle there. When he became pastor of the Pinners' Hall congregation he still lived at Wallingford, and only visited London to conduct his services.[1] The Pinners' Hall Sabbatarians were Calvinists, while those at the Mill Yard were Arminians.

Bunyan, "following the examples of others, did lay hold of this liberty, as an acceptable thing in itself . . . yet, in all this, he moved with caution and a holy fear, earnestly praying for averting the impending judgments." He and his people built a meeting-house in Bedford. He was against the regulation of the corporations, "and when a great man in those days, coming to Bedford upon some such errand, sent for him, as it is supposed to give him a place of public trust, he would by no means come at him, but sent his excuse." [2]

Bunyan died in 1688 in London. In his latter years he had become a very popular preacher there. Charles Doe, his biographer and early disciple, said that just before his death, if a day's notice was given, when he was going to preach, more persons came than the meeting-house would hold. Twelve hundred came once to a lecture on a week-day at seven o'clock in the morning. On August 19th he went to preach at Mr. Gamman's meeting-house near Whitechapel, but was taken ill at the house of John Strudwick, deacon of the meeting, in Red Cross Street. He preached, but it was for the last time, "for he died at the house of Mr. Straddocks, a grocer, at the Star, on Snowhill. in the parish of St. Sepulchre, London, on the 12th of August, 1688, and in the sixtieth year of his age." He had had many enemies in his early days, but now he could count on many distinguished friends; Sir John Shorter, Lord Mayor of London in 1688, was one of them, but he had them in higher quarters still. He had probably won over Charles II. To his "Discourse on Antichrist" he had written a preface in which he ascribed the best intentions to the King, and urged his co-religionists to be patient if things did not go as fast as they desired. Speaking of kings, he said, "'Tis a wonder they go as fast as they do, since the concerns of whole kingdoms lie upon their shoulders, and there are so many Sanballats and Tobiases to flatter them and misinform them. . . . Pray for the long life of the King. Pray that God would give judgment and wisdom to the King. Pray that God would discern all plots and conspiracies against his person and government." He was never interfered with after that, either by Charles or James.[3]

---

[1] Pike, "Ancient Meeting Houses," pp. 171–172.

[2] "Life of Mr. John Bunyan," 1692.

[3] Froude, "Bunyan," p. 87; see also for Bunyan the "Account of the Life of Mr. John Bunyan," published in 1692 and prefixed to what is called the third part of "The Pilgrim's Progress." It is commonly known as "The Continuation." Ivimey said it was written by an episcopalian.

In 1688 six General Baptist Churches formed an Association on the basis of the " Brief Confession " which had been drawn up in 1660,[1] but the General Baptists as a whole gradually drifted towards Unitarianism and declined in numbers. The contempt for learning, largely due to ministers who had little or none themselves, the exclusion of Scripture from their meetings, and the heterodoxy of their leaders, were conducive to the spread of Arian and Unitarian tenets among them.[2]   Caffin, for instance, though not actually adopting Unitarianism, was responsible for a good deal of doubt and discussion about the doctrine of the Trinity.   They had no strong centre in London; their congregations there generally had closer connections with provincial congregations than with those in the metropolis.[3]   Owing to their system of associated but independent congregations with a travelling instead of a settled ministry, they were never welded into a compact and energetic society.   They had no outstanding vigorous personality who could organise them, a great deal of their energy was wasted on petty disputes,[4] they were thoroughly disorganised by persecution, and lastly, there was a good deal of drift from the General Baptists, who did not believe in Calvinism, to the Particular Baptists, who did.[5]

[1] J. Hay Colligan, " The Arian Movement in England," p. 16.
[2] Barclay, " Inner Life," p. 596.
[3] Whitley, " Baptists of London," p. 68.
[4] Barclay, " Inner Life," p. 595.
[5] Whitley, " Minutes Gen. Assembly," I. xix.

IV

THE HISTORY OF THE QUAKERS

THE Quakers at the time of the Restoration were a large, un organised, and somewhat nebulous body of people who accepted the teaching of George Fox and his friends. Fox had derived his doctrines from some of the earlier Protestants in Germany, whose teachings, through the Mennonites of Holland, had come to the Baptists, the Seekers, and others in England; Winstanley and the Diggers, for example, had held the doctrines of the " Inner Light," the " New Law of Righteousness," and the " Law of Freedom." One writer of the period, indeed, declared the Quakers to be Winstanley's disciples,[1] but they had a far closer connection with the Seekers.

The Quaker doctrines were all short and simple. They believed in the Inward Light that shines in every man's soul, in the voice of the Word of God within them, and the inward communion with God which Christian men enjoy if they are really Christian. Reverence, love, and obedience are due to God and His revealed Word. In outward life they should observe their duty to their fellow-men, and should be merciful, liberal, and compassionate. Over the members of their own communion they should exercise a loving care and watchfulness, especially in religious concerns. Their lives should be characterised by moderation and temperance; in the management of their business they should be mild and moderate; in outward deportment they should be grave, in speech slow and guarded, and they should preserve a serious countenance and avoid frivolity.[2] As for their ecclesiastical position, they believed that all the churches had become corrupt in doctrine, discipline, worship, life, and manners, and a new church was being raised up by the influence and in the power of the Spirit of God.[3]

There was a vein of mysticism in the Quaker theology, and they owed a good deal to Jacob Behmen, especially the doctrine of the inward seed, a supernatural gift from God, distinct from conscience, reason, or any relics of natural goodness. Fox might easily have become a theosophic mystic like the Behmenites or Philadelphians. One of his early entries in his " Journal,"

---

[1] " Christianity no Enthusiasm," 1678, by Thomas Comber.
[2] Croese, " Gen. Hist. Quakers," pp. 30–31.   [3] Ibid., p. 25.

written when he was about twenty-four years of age, shows this plainly: " Now was I come up in spirit, through the flaming sword, into the paradise of God. All things were new; and all the creation gave another smell unto me than before, beyond what words can utter. I knew nothing but pureness and innocency and righteousness, being renewed up into the image of God by Christ Jesus: so that I say I was come up to the state of Adam which he was in before he fell. The creation was opened to me: and it was showed me how all things had their names given them, according to their nature and virtue. And I was at a stand in my mind whether I should practise physic for the good of mankind, seeing the nature and virtues of the creatures were so opened me by the Lord. But I was immediately taken up in spirit to see into another or more steadfast state than Adam's in innocency, even into a state in Christ Jesus that should never fall. And the Lord showed me that such as were faithful to Him in the power and light of Christ, should come up into the state in which Adam was before he fell; in which the admirable works of the creation, and the virtues thereof may be known, through the openings of that divine word of wisdom and power by which they were made. Great things did the Lord lead me into, and wonderful depths were opened unto me, beyond what can by words be declared: but as people come into subjection to the Spirit of God, and grow upon the image and power of the Almighty, they may receive the word of wisdom that opens all things, and come to know the hidden unity in the Eternal Being."[1] Other writers quoted and adopted Jacob Boehme's prophecies,[2] but the Quakers believed that all their visions and revelations came direct from God. They resented any suggestion of occult practices, and they also refused to be numbered amongst the Quietists or Molinists, or any of the mystic sects.[3]

" There was a quaking and trembling from the Lord, and so they called us Quakers."[4] " The Quakers fall into trances, swell, quake, tremble, yell and roar, and after the fit is over they fall threatening judgments against sinners and ministers."[5] The name was given them in 1650 in contempt, " for when they are about contemplating sacred things, that same very moment that the spirit overtakes 'em, through the commotion of their minds and the agitation of their bodies, they presently fall a-trembling, throwing themselves on the ground, oft-times frothing at the mouth and screeching with a horrible noise, . . . disturbances of the body occasioned by the resistance of the sinful stubborn flesh : which, when they have overcome, and are returned to themselves

---

[1] Fox, " Journal."
[2] F. Ellington, " Christian Information concerning these Last Times," 1664.
[3] Croese, " Gen. Hist. Quakers," pp. 91–93.
[4] F. Ellington, " Christian Information concerning these Last Times," 1664.
[5] T. Underhill, " Hell Broke Loose," 1660.

again and begun to be sensible of the illuminations and comforts of the Spirit, then they are transported into raptures of joy, which occasion these quaking and ecstatical motions of body and mind."[1] " They sometimes move themselves, or are moved so far as issues in a great trembling of the body with some or all. This often does fall out by resistance to Satan. On one occasion I was told they all trembled so that the place was shaken as with an earthquake." [2]

The Friends were naturally opposed to the priestly claims of the ministry of the Church of England. " We do not believe," said John Audland, " that priests are ministers sent from God, and we believe that we ought not to maintain them, and that their doctrine is not of Christ, and we cannot join in worship with their people, because we believe they have no health in them." [3] The Quakers held that the Church had been in darkness since the time of the Apostles, but that a new ministry had now appeared, possessing the inward light. The false ministers preached for hire, and had their authority in letters-patent from a bishop or some other man. They sprinkled infants on the face instead of ministering the baptism of the Spirit; they called bread and wine the Lord's Supper instead of giving the people the bread of life; and both in England and America they persecuted the faithful. The Quakers were the people of the Lord; all the rest were false ministers.[4] Only one set of people would be saved, those who were not ministers of national churches.[5] They refused to pay tithes, partly because they refused to support an ecclesiastical system in which they had no belief, but still more because they considered that tithes belonged to the Law and not to the Gospel. Thomas Stordy, of Moor-house, in Cumberland, set free an impropriation because he felt he had no right to such payments.[6] Francis Howgill, a West-morland Quaker, in 1665 published " The Great Case of Tithes," attacking the system, and John Audland wrote " A Letter to a Priest concerning Tithes." [7] A person who refused to pay tithes might be sentenced to excommunication in the ecclesiastical courts, and it was not till 1696 that power was given to any two justices to recover by distraint the amount of tithe due.

The Quaker was forbidden by his religion to take any oath in any circumstances whatever. On August 17th, 1664, Dr. Alan Smallwood preached a sermon in Carlisle cathedral maintaining that our Saviour did not forbid the solemn oaths

[1] Croese, " Gen. Hist. Quakers," pp. 5–7.
[2] Ibid., Pt. II. 53.
[3] " The Ministry of the Righteous Revived," 1689.
[4] J. Aynhoe, " A Short Description of the True Ministry and the False," 1672.
[5] F. Ellington, " Christian Information concerning these Last Times," 1664.
[6] Ferguson, " Early Cumberland and Westmorland Friends," pp. 109–110.
[7] " The Memory of the Righteous Revived," 1689.

required by law. Some years afterwards Gerald Benson published a reply to " Allan Smallwood D.D. as he styles himself," and asserted that the words " Swear not at all " should be taken in the most literal sense. He further declared that he had received this neither " of man nor from man," an assumption of inspiration and superior authority which made further argument impossible.[1] Another work on the same subject, published in 1675, was prefaced by a letter signed by thirteen prominent Quakers and addressed to the King and Council. The writers complained of the cruel treatment meted out to their brethren because of their inability to take the oaths, which put them at the mercy of unscrupulous men who were willing to swear anything for their own advantage.[2]

The Society of Friends strictly forbade fighting and warfare. Their adherence to this principle was illustrated in the case of Thomas Lurting, who went to sea at the age of fourteen, fought under Blake, and at the time of his conversion to Quakerism was boatswain's mate on the *Bristol* frigate. After the Restoration he was several times pressed for the navy, but he refused to do anything on board, or to eat the King's rations. Once, after he had eaten nothing for five days, he was put ashore. On another occasion the ship of which he was mate was captured by Algerine pirates. This time he so far forgot his principles as to lead the English sailors against their captors, but when the ship was recovered, instead of selling the Algerines for slaves, as was the custom in such cases, he put them ashore in safety on their own coast.[3]

The Quaker was often unfairly judged by what seemed mere eccentricities. He insisted on the use of the words " thee " and " thou " when addressing an individual, and he refused to doff his hat to any man, mere trifles of everyday life which he invested with a religious significance. Yet they were symbols of his exact truthfulness and of his meticulous care for little things in God's service, wherein, indeed, nothing is little or unimportant. Richard Farnsworth wrote in defence of the Quaker use of " thee " and " thou "[4] and Fox, Stubbs, and Furley published " A Battledore for Teachers and Professors to Learn Singular and Plural," in which from the usage of the thirty-five languages they tried to show that all languages had different pronouns of the second person singular and plural, and that therefore it was not absurd or unmannerly to use the second

[1] Benson, " A True Testimony concerning Oaths and Swearing," 1669.
[2] " A Treatise of Oaths, containing several Weighty Reasons why the People called Quakers refuse to Swear," 1675. It was answered by " The Anti-Quaker, or a Compendious Answer to a Tedious Pamphlet entitled ' A Treatise of Oaths.' By Misorcus," 1676.
[3] " The Fighting Sailor turned Peaceable Christian," *Lancs. and Chesh. Hist. Soc.*, XXXVII. 21.
[4] R. Farnsworth, " The Pure Language of the Spirit of Truth," 1655.

person singular to an individual. The book was divided into
thirty-five parts, each dealing with a separate language, and the
title-page of each part was generally outlined in the shape of a
horn book. On account of the different characters used, it is
said that several printers were needed.[1] The book was really
written by John Stubbs " of the Bishopric " (*i.e.* of Durham)
and Benjamin Furley of Colchester. Fox only knew his own
language, but he signed every page, and so gave his authority
to it.[2] It was not lawful for Quakers " to kneel or prostrate
themselves to any man, or to bow the body, or to uncover the
head to them." [3] Englishmen at that period wore their hats
all day long, even in church, where, as a rule, they only removed
them at the Sacred Name. The custom of doffing the hat as a
mark of respect for another person was French, and reminiscent
therefore to the Puritan of a popish and ungodly race. So the
Quakers sturdily refused to remove their hats except for God only.
Again, it was the will of their founder that plainness and simplicity should be marked characteristics of his followers, therefore
they must eschew all worldly vanities. Their clothes were to be
simple and without decoration. Instead of the fashionable
gorgeous headgear, the men were to wear just a plain broad-
brimmed hat, without so much as a button or loop.[4] Thoresby
noted in his diary, " I had this day a serious admonition from
old Mrs. Sykes, a noted Quaker and notable good woman, about
the vanity of foolish ornaments and ribbons." [5] The general
rule was in favour of sober colours,[6] but for all that, the Friends
refused to conform to the heathen custom of wearing black for
mourning. Quaker ladies, moreover, did not always confine
themselves to sad-coloured garments, for George Fox bought a
scarlet gown for his wife, and the Misses Fell had stockings of
sky-blue and sea-green, red petticoats and blue aprons.[7] A
defence of the special features of the Quaker system was written
by William Penn in a work which bore the title (modified in
subsequent editions), " No Cross, no Crown: or, Several
Sober Reasons against Hat Worship, Titular Respect, You to a
Single Person, with the Apparel and Recreations of the Times,
in Defence of the poor, despised Quakers, against the Practice
and Objections of their Adversaries."

[1] A. W. Tuer, " A History of the Horn Book," 1896, II. 228.
[2] Croese, " Gen. Hist. Quakers," p. 165.
[3] R. Barclay, " Apology for the True Christian Divinity," 1676.
[4] *Archæologia*, XXIV. 188.
[5] Thoresby, " Diary," April 8th, 1681. London, 1830.
[6] John Pendarves, " Endeavours for Reformation of Apparel: or, Some Reasons rendered for Saints forbearing to put upon their Garments such Trimmings and Ornaments as are altogether Superfluous and apparently Useless," 1656.
[7] Turner, " The Quakers," p. 101 ; Croese, " Gen. Hist. Quakers," pp. 182–183; " The Household Account Book of Sarah Fell," Ed. by N. Penney, Cambridge, 1920, p. 293.

The Quaker, of course, was very severe on the subject of amusements, like all the rest of the Puritans. The theatre in particular was anathema to him, not without very good reason. When an anonymous opponent spoke of the " antic tricks " of the Friends at their silent meetings, he laid himself open to a retort and got it: " And as for antic tricks, if the devil had not blinded thee, and such as thou art, thou mightest have made those ungodly meetings at play-houses the subject of thy information, and not the innocent pious meetings of the people called Quakers. For is it not obvious what impudency, antic whorish tricks and postures appear upon stages, at play-houses, in and about the cities of London and Westminster, to draw out the minds of people into vanity and a whorish spirit, as women without the appearance of modesty or sobriety in their behaviour, and men decked in women's apparel, to be examples of whorish postures? Besides the many vain shows and sights to affect and gratify the vain, wanton eyes, minds, and spirits of youth, to draw them into impudency and debauchery, such abominations as is a re-proach to the profession of Christianity, and a shame to the nation." [1]   It was remarked that Nell Gwyn, although with her gift of mimicry she could imitate anybody for the amusement of the Court, could never give anything but a forced and affected imitation of a Quaker. [2]

The Restoration theatre was bad enough, and deserved all the scathing things that the Puritans said about it, but all amusements came under the Quaker lash, even things which seem to us inno-cent country customs. Thus, Stephen Crisp wrote " A Word in Due Season; or some Harvest Meditations, with a Warning from the Lord God to all the People in England, to leave off their Wicked and Foolish Customs in the Harvest, before the Anger of the Lord be kindled against them, and there be no Remedy." Among the abominations rebuked in this tract were inordinate feasting and drinking, that abominable custom of shouting in the fields corrupt and vain harvest songs, singing some of the Psalms, " in your wicked manner of doubling and vain repetitions," and " that wicked and abominable custom of making lords and ladies amongst you in the harvest field." [3]

In 1660 the Society of Friends had not quite outgrown its early eccentricities. It was constantly at strife with the other religious sects, and on the whole was more antipathetic to the Dissenters than to the Church. The interference with other people's worship, a practice in reality alien to the Quaker spirit, died away. The Quakers were mellowing. They referred to themselves as the only " people of God " much less frequently,

---

[1] " The Popish Informer Reprehended," 1670, p. 14.
[2] Croese, " Gen. Hist. Quakers," p. 96.
[3] " Account of the Christian Experiences . . . of Stephen Crisp," 1694, pp. 147–153.

and they were less ready to hurl epithets like " priest of Baal " at Anglican and Dissenter alike.[1]

But the Friends did more than conquer themselves: they conquered the nation. Hated, despised, and persecuted, they stood firm without wavering against all the powers of the State, civil, military, and ecclesiastical. They resisted not at all, and they reviled very little, but they meekly and unflinchingly endured, and to their endurance more than to anything else was due the ultimate triumph of the cause of religious liberty. They were from first to last the genuine protagonists of liberty of conscience: whilst other sects demanded it for themselves, they claimed it for all. Not only did they claim it, but when they had the opportunity, as in Pennsylvania, they put it in practice. Their attitude is set forth in a tract of 1661 entitled " For the King and both Houses of Parliament," and signed by six Quaker leaders. They asked that there should be no more persecution for religion, " no compelling about worship." " We desire to have (who pay their taxes and assessments) as much liberty as stage-players, and mountebanks, and ballad-singers, who meet together in hundreds to the dishonour of God, and likewise all other plays, which we do not hear are called tumultuous meetings as ours are." " Let all writs and indictments, sub-poenas, and warrants have no more put in them than the things that are truly charged." They asked, further, that all laws might be collected in a short volume, that all might know them. " Let every man be free to speak his opinion in religion. The Lord made use of common people, fishermen and tent-makers, and these had not been at universities and schools of learning to train them up. And if He make use of the same to-day be not offended." All Christendom had professed the Scripture which tells us to honour all men, but they had only shown honour with hat or lip or foot, while they had hurt, murdered, and killed one another, and even their princes. The Quakers themselves had been persecuted, and twenty had died in consequence, and yet they had not been guilty of plots or insurrections or tumults against the King, the nation, or individuals. " Now therefore our desire is that we may have our liberty."

Because of their belief in the inward light given by God to the soul, the operation of the Holy Spirit and none other, the Quakers were opposed to all compulsion in religion. The magistrate might drive a man to outward conformity, but he could only make him a discontented hypocrite. Penn set forth the case for toleration in a book published in 1671, " The Great Case of Liberty of Conscience once more Briefly Debated and Defended." Briefly, the argument was this. All impositions, restraints, or persecution in religious matters are a direct invasion

[1] " Quakerism and the Church of England," *Church Quarterly Review*, XXX. 352.

of God's prerogative, for the government of conscience belongs to God, and cannot be delegated to another, because no other can be infallible. Christ's kingdom is a spiritual kingdom; worship at the command of the magistrate is not the spiritual worship which God requires, and only leads to condemnation, therefore compulsion is the overthrow of Christ's religion. Persecution and compulsion and restraint are all contrary to the teaching of Scripture, are destructive of reason, and overthrow man's natural right of liberty. They are contrary to the root idea of government, which is based on justice; moreover, temporal penalties are necessarily disproportionate to purely intellectual faults. Again, the end of government is peace, whereas persecution is the opposite of peace; moreover, it is absolutely useless, for it will neither make good subjects nor good Christians. In 1675 Penn wrote " England's Present Interest Discovered," in which he showed that toleration was good for commerce and trade, and made the entirely unfounded statement that if a country were to offer religious liberty to the Dissenters, more than a million would emigrate, and he affirmed that the greatness and prosperity of Holland were due to the fact that religious toleration was practised there. Repelling the often-repeated charge of disloyalty urged against Dissenters, he said that " a man may be a very good Englishman, but a very in-different churchman." The Presbyterians and the Anglicans from time to time discussed possible terms of reunion or com-prehension, but Penn vigorously opposed this, on the ground that if the two bodies united it would lead to the vigorous sup-pression of all other Dissenters.[1]

The Quakers began to suffer at the hands of the King's friends early in 1660; in February they endured rough usage at their meeting-place in the Palace Yard, Westminster. Some time before this Monk's army and the army in Ireland had been purged of members of the society, which goes to show that up to this time some Quakers at least had not been averse to a military career, and Monk's men in particular exhibited a strong feeling against them. On March 9th, however, Monk issued an order by which the disturbance of peaceable Quaker meetings was forbidden, " they doing nothing prejudicial to the Parliament or Common-wealth of England." [2] But little notice was taken of the order, and matters became worse rather than better.

James Nayler, the Wakefield Quaker, who had been hailed as the Messiah by a number of half-crazy women at Bristol, and had

[1] See also " Liberty of Conscience Asserted," by Crook, Fisher, Howgill and Hubberthorne, 1661 ; " Christian Religious Meetings allowed by the Liturgy," by R. Farnsworth, 1661 ; " Persecution Inconsistent with Christianity, Humane Society and the Honour of Princes," by Hubberthorne, Fisher, and Howgill, 1670; " Christian Liberty, as it was Soberly Desired in a Letter to Certain Foreign States," 1674.

[2] Braithwaite, " Beginnings of Quakerism," p. 471.

suffered imprisonment on a charge of blasphemy in consequence, sent a letter of good advice to Charles five days after the latter's return.[1] It was the first of many such epistles which he was to receive from Quaker sources. There was published that summer " A Visitation of Love unto the King," inscribed to " Charles Stuart, who is proclaimed King, and to all you that are called by the name of royal party and Cavaliers, and who have suffered for your cause and for your principles," and issued " in the name of the people called Quakers."

George Fox the younger, who was in prison, wrote " A Noble Salutation and Faithful Greeting unto thee, Charles Stuart, proclaimed King of England." In this he used that freedom which he and many others of his people used, even to the King's face, and which must have given a severe shock to obsequious courtiers.[2] He bade the King remember that he was appointed by God, and that he must not trust in the fickleness of the people who had fawned on one ruler after another. The " Salutation " was presented to the King by Richard Hubberthorne, who with George Fox the elder had been admitted to the royal presence on June 4th. Charles said to Hubberthorne in the presence of some of the courtiers, " Well, of this you may be assured, that you shall none of you suffer for your opinions or religion, so long as you live peaceably, and you have the word of a King for it : and I have also given forth a declaration to the same purpose, that none shall wrong you or abuse you." [3]

In a letter to the King which George Fox the elder wrote from Lancaster prison that year, the writer said, " Thou camest not into this nation by sword, nor by victory of war, but by the power of the Lord : now if thou dost not live in it thou wilt not prosper." He bade Charles put a stop to persecution and persecutors, because God overthrows such. " And if thou dost bear the sword in vain, and let drunkenness, oaths, plays, May games (with fiddles, drums, trumpets to play at them), with such-like abominations and vanities, be encouraged, or go unpunished, as setting up of maypoles, with the image of the crown on top of them, etc., the nations will quickly turn like Sodom and Gomorrah, and be as bad as the old world, who grieved the Lord till He overthrew them ; and so will He you, if these things be not suddenly prevented. . . . So hear and consider, and do good in thy time, whilst thou hast power." [4] Edward Burrough also set forth the claims of the Quakers to good treatment : " We are clear from the guilt of all the King's sufferings. We have not cast out others and taken their places of great benefices, neither have we

---

[1] M. Brailsford, " A Quaker from Cromwell's Army," London, 1927.
[2] " The Popish Informer Reprehended," 1670, p. 10.
[3] " An Account of Several Things that passed between His Sacred Majesty and Richard Hubberthorne," 1660; Gough, " Hist. Quakers," I. 440.
[4] Sewell, " Hist. Quakers," p. 243.

made war with carnal weapons against any. . . . Neither have
we broken oaths and engagements, nor promised freedom and
deliverance, and for self-ends and earthly riches betrayed." He
urged that the people who persecuted the King persecuted the
Quakers also ; not that he wanted a common league of vengeance ;
on the contrary, he pleaded for forgiveness all round.[1]   Other
Quaker leaders had interviews with the King soon after his return,
and endeavoured to assure him that they neither did nor taught
anything which would injure the well-being of the State.   In
November some of them made a proffer that to avoid all jealousies,
and to preserve the peace, six of their number in each county,
God-fearing and sufficient men, should undertake that their
meetings should be kept free from all connection with plots.[2]
Another paper, of the same date, was " A Declaration of the
Quakers of England." Their consciences not allowing them to
swear, and therefore rendering them liable to misunderstanding
and persecution, they affirmed in this document that they
acknowledged Charles II. as their rightful magistrate, and
promised to render him due obedience, and not to conspire
against him, but if anything were required of them contrary
to their conscience, they would rather suffer than sin by resistance.[3]   Dr. Gauden, Bishop of Exeter, the only bishop who in
the early days lifted up his voice on their behalf, declared in the
House of Lords that they were " the innocentest of all the sects." [4]
and if some consideration had been shown for them the Quakers
might all have been as royalist as William Penn.[5]   The King,
if he had had his way, would probably have given them full
toleration.   In 1660, at the request of some of the leaders, and
in particular of Margaret Fell, 700 Quakers who had been
imprisoned under the Protectorate were set free by his order.[6]

In the latter part of 1660 some Quakers were admitted to the
bar of the House of Lords, where they submitted their reasons
why they could not attend the services of the Church of England,
pay tithes, or take oaths, and they had a not unfriendly reception.
At a meeting of the Council on November 23rd a Committee was
appointed to consider the various papers and addresses which
had been sent in by the Friends, and to prepare a proclamation
or declaration thereon.   This Committee was to discover where
any members of the sect were imprisoned, for what cause they
had been committed, how long they had been in confinement,
and what should be done with regard to setting them free.[7]
Sewell says that orders were drawn up for permitting the Quakers

[1] Sewell, " Hist. Quakers," p. 240.
[2] C.S.P.D., November 23rd, 1660, 21/98.
[3] *Ibid.*, 21/99.
[4] " Episkopos Aposkopos : the Bishop Busied beside the Business," by
Samuel Fisher, 1662.
[5] Hodgkin, " George Fox," p. 176.
[6] Sewell, " Hist. Quakers," p. 251.   [7] Kennet, " Reg.," p. 313.

the free exercise of their worship, and that only the signing and sealing remained to be done when the Fifth Monarchists made insurrection.

The eccentric, and even outrageous, behaviour of some of the extremists among the Quakers led people to think them all alike. There is reason to suspect that they were sometimes blamed for the wild actions and beliefs of people like the Ranters, and that there was a popular tendency to call every eccentric religionist a Quaker, and thus the Friends often got the blame for doing things which were entirely opposed to their tenets. Many of them were imprisoned in various parts of the country in consequence of Venner's outbreak, for it was thought that if they were not actually Venner's accomplices they had the same feelings of disloyalty. Margaret Fell went twice to the King and told him that, though innocent, several thousand Quakers were in prison. An address was also presented to Charles on February 16th, 1661, on behalf of about 400 Quakers in prison in London, and above 1000 in the country besides.[1] Fox, who had been arrested but set at liberty by the intervention of powerful friends, put forth " A Declaration from the Harmless and Innocent People of God, called Quakers, against all Sedition, Plotters and Fighters in the World." The document was signed by Fox and eleven others, and presented to the King and Council.[2] It was confiscated in the press, but another was drawn up, printed, and circulated. Twenty years later it was reprinted. Some quotations from it still form part of the official " Book of Christian Practice " issued by the London Yearly Meeting.[3] Probably in consequence of Fox's " Declaration," the King issued an Order in Council that the Lord Mayor should release all the Quakers who were prisoners within the limits of the City of London, except the leaders and preachers among them, provided they engaged to be obedient in the future. The Lord Mayor, however, asked for further directions, and was told that he was not to release those who refused the oaths of allegiance and supremacy, but all those who had been taken up merely on suspicion were to be set free.[4]

On May 11th, 1661, as an act of amnesty in connection with the coronation, the King issued a proclamation ordering all Quaker prisoners to be set free without individually suing out their pardons. No fees or dues were to be demanded at their liberation, except the usual charges for food, lodging, and necessaries supplied by the gaolers. The proclamation expressed a hope that they would show loyalty and obedience thereafter, and warned them that this act of grace was no promise of in-

[1] Neal, " Puritans," IV. 7.
[2] C.S.P.D., January 21st, 1661, 28/103.
[3] E. Brockbank, " Richard Hubberthorne," 1929, p. 110.
[4] Kennet, " Reg.," pp. 364-371.

demnity for future misbehaviour.[1] Five days after this a Committee of the Commons was appointed to prepare a Bill to prevent
the ill consequences to the Government arising from the refusal
of Quakers, Anabaptists, and other persons to take the oaths.[2]

The Quakers had petitioned the House of Lords for special
treatment in respect of their peculiar difficulties, and a Committee had been appointed to consider the matter. This Committee rejected their request to be allowed to substitute " Yea "
or " Nay " for the requisite oaths, and proposed that " a promissory oath should be tendered to the Quakers, such a one as no
good subject ought to refuse." Their petition not to be compelled
to take off their hats in the King's courts and other places was
rejected, as was also their request to be excused the payment of
tithes. Two other demands in their petition—that their private
meetings should be treated as coming to church, and that they
might not be compelled to observe feasts and fasts—were referred
by the Committee to the House. The House, however, replied
by ordering the Attorney-General to prepare a proclamation for
suppressing the Quakers, and reducing them to obedience to the
laws of the kingdom.[3] The authorities looked on the refusal
to take the oaths of allegiance and supremacy as traitorous,
while refusal to take the requisite oath in a law court rendered
a witness's testimony worthless. Sir John Maynard told the
Governor of Windsor Castle in January 1661 that so many persons
had been committed at the last Sessions at Croydon for refusing to
take the oaths, that the bench was puzzled, and did not know
what to do. Some said they would not swear at all, some that
they would not take a promissory oath; others declared that, as
the King had taken no oath to preserve the laws, they would
take none to obey him.[4] These last were obviously not Quakers,
but more probably fanatical Commonwealth men, but the
refusal of the oaths was going on all over the country, and the
Government was seriously alarmed.

The Bill against Quakers and others was read in the Commons
for the first time on June 17th, and for the second time on June
29th. A petition was presented against it, and Edward Burrough,
Richard Hubberthorne, George Whitehead, and Edward Pyott
were heard at the bar of the House on July 19th. Hubberthorne
pleaded that their meetings were open and would never be used
for plots; but Burrough probably did his cause no good by saying
that they would meet in any case. Some of the members were
favourably disposed,[5] but after the withdrawal of the deputation
the Bill was read again for the third time that same day.[6] It was

---

[1] Kennet, " Reg.," p. 448; C.S.P.D., 35/47.   [2] Kennet, " Reg.," p. 448.
[3] " Lords Journals," XI. March 31st and June 6th, 1661.
[4] C.S.P.D., January 19th, 1661.
[5] George Whitehead, " Christian Progress," p. 262.
[6] " Commons Journals," VIII.

sent up to the House of Lords, but did not get through before the session ended; in fact it did not receive the royal assent till May 2nd, 1662.

The "Act for preventing mischief and dangers that may arise by certain persons called Quakers and others refusing to take lawful oaths "[1] provided that for the following offences: (a) refusing to take an oath duly and lawfully tendered, (b) persuading another person to refuse, (c) maintaining, by printing, writing, or otherwise, the unlawfulness of such oaths, or (d) the assembling of five or more Quakers over the age of sixteen for unauthorised religious worship, the penalty for the first offence should be a fine of £5, and for the second £10, to be levied by distress if necessary. Failing payment or distress, the penalty for the first offence should be three months imprisonment with hard labour, and for the second six months. For the third offence the convicted person should either abjure the realm or be transported to the plantations. Conviction should follow (a) the verdict of a jury, (b) the accused person's own confession, or (c) notorious evidence of the fact. If, however, even after conviction, the offender took the necessary oaths and gave security against attendance at meetings, he should be discharged from all penalties.[2]

In actual practice the punishments the Quakers endured were not confined to those provided by this Act. Frequently the Act was ignored in the courts, and the oaths of allegiance and supremacy were tendered in order to make the accused liable to a *præmunire*. It also became a common custom in the courts, when some charge against a prisoner could not be proved, to catch him out by tendering him the oaths. One of the most dreaded punishments was transportation to the colonies, which meant little less than slavery to a master for a term not exceeding seven years. The person sentenced might redeem himself from transportation by paying £100, but Croese said that he had never heard of any person who paid it. One of the worst features of the system was that a man might be transported to one colony and his wife to another.[3] For many ecclesiastical offences a Quaker was liable to excommunication. He was permitted, if he wished, to show cause why he should not be excommunicated, but that generally meant expensive legal fees, which the Quaker objected to paying. Indeed, Friends were often excommunicated for refusing on principle to pay quite small sums.[4] Once excommunicated, the next thing was the issue of the dreaded writ *de excommunicato capiendo*, on which the unfortunate man was thrown into gaol for an indefinite period. At the opening of the Assizes at Bala in 1677, Judge Walcot tendered the oaths of allegiance and supremacy to some Quakers, told them that

---

[1] 13 and 14 Car. II. c. 1.   [2] Sewell, " Hist. Quakers," 1722, I. 551.
[3] Croese, " Gen. Hist. Quakers," II. 2.   [4] *Ibid.*, II. 19–21.

to refuse the oaths was high treason, and threatened at the next Assizes to proceed against such offenders under the Statute *de heretico comburendo*, which had been obsolete for years and years. Thomas Lloyd of Dolobran, one of the leading Welsh Quakers, went up to London to take legal advice, and interviewed a number of members of Parliament, with the result that the Statute was repealed that year, and Walcot received a reprimand from the Government.[1]

On February 8th, 1663, ten Quakers sent a paper to the magistrates of the county of Montgomery, reminding them of the King's Declaration of December 26th, 1662, in which he had renewed his assurance and confirmation of his promises at Breda. " We understand," they said, " by these words that it is his fatherly care to publish this his declaration to stop and prevent all other acting according to former Acts made against liberty of tender consciences." They hoped that the magistrates would be as favourable to them as the King and Chief Magistrate, and they pointed out that if they did continue to persecute, it was without any order from the King.[2]

On August 22nd, 1662, in honour of the arrival of Catherine of Braganza, there was another general release of Quakers by proclamation.[3] The King frequently also gave heed to appeals and petitions from individuals and groups of prisoners, and gave them their liberty.[4] He was, perhaps, more friendly disposed towards them than to any other sectaries, but they were so bitterly disliked that it was only occasionally that he could do anything for them.

A few Friends made matters worse for the rest. In November 1662 a number of them, including Billing and Hill, were summoned before the Council, who were willing to release them if they would sign a paper promising not to make war nor to plot against the King. This they refused to do, on the ground that the Friends were a free people. The Friends, as a body, were. very displeased, because most of them would have been perfectly willing to sign such a document, and thereby many of their troubles would have been avoided.[5] They always resented the accusation that they were disloyal and rebellious.[6]

In the early years of the reign the Quakers suffered severely. In 1660 over 500 Yorkshire Quakers were in various prisons in that county, and some of them died in prison. For a meeting on November 30th, at the house of William Gradell in Scar-

---

[1] T. Mardy Rees, " Hist. Quakers in Wales," pp. 149–150.
[2] Rees, " Protestant Nonconformity in Wales," 1883, pp. 156–157.
[3] Kennet, " Reg.," p. 746; C.S.P.D., August 22nd, 1662.
[4] C.S.P.D., January 13th, 1663; February 25th, 1665, etc.
[5] *Ibid.*, November 25th, 1662.
[6] Edward Pigott, " The Quakers Vindicated from the Calumnies of those that Falsely Accuse them as if they denied Magistrates and disowned Government," 1667.

borough, twenty persons present were fined sums amounting in all to £770.[1] Thomas Ellwood was taken into custody at Oxford for refusing the oaths of allegiance and supremacy, but was set free by the influence of his father, who was a landed proprietor at Crowell, in Oxfordshire.[2]   George Fox, the younger, whose home was at Charsfield, in Suffolk, was a prisoner in the Gatehouse that same year. Joseph Coale, one of the original Berkshire Quakers, was taken at a meeting at Exeter in 1661, and imprisoned for three months for refusing to take the oaths. He and his fellow Quaker prisoners were given liberty to walk in the Castle yard for an hour or two every day, and they suffered at such times at the hands of the youth of the town, who hurled stones at them, and epithets, of which " Quaking toad " was one of the mildest. Among Coale's epistles is one to the school-masters of Exeter, urging them to teach and rule their children in the fear of the Lord.[3]

When a general discharge was made in 1661, the Quakers met persecution as soon as they were set free. The Accounts of the Parish Constable at Pannal, near Harrogate, for 1662, contain entries of expenses for carrying twenty-eight Quakers before Sir William Ingleby, for the soldiers' charges who acted as escort, for his own expenses in journeying to Ripley for their examination, and for his carrying six Quakers to York later in the year.[4] Thomas Stordy of Moorhouse in Cumberland, who refused to take the oath of allegiance, but said he would be more obedient than any who swore, was condemned " by John Lowther, a man in authority in that county," to have all his goods confiscated and to be imprisoned. He remained in gaol from 1662 until 1684, and died there.[5]   On Wednesday, June 22nd, 1662, Richard Hubberthorne, of Yelland in Lancashire, and others were holding a meeting at the Bull and Mouth, a large building near Aldersgate, used as a Quaker meeting-house, when Sir Richard Browne with a party of soldiers burst in, and the Quakers were cruelly beaten with swords and clubs, both men and women. One man was knocked down four times, and the bystanders cried shame on the outrage. Burrough, Hubber-thorne, and others were brought before Sir Richard Browne, as magistrate, and he, because Hubberthorne kept his hat on, seized him by the head and bent him nearly double. Remanded to Newgate, they were brought up at the next sessions, and sent back to gaol. In Newgate the prisoners were put into the condemned hole, and into the chapel, both crowded and filthy; Whitehead and Hubberthorne sharing a pallet in the

---

[1] J. S. Fletcher, " Yorkshiremen of the Restoration," 1921, p. 205.
[2] " The History of Thomas Ellwood."
[3] " Some Account of the Life of Joseph Coale," 1706.
[4] For this reference the author is indebted to Mr. W. J. Kaye, M.A., F.S.A.
[5] Croese, " Gen. Hist. Quakers," pp. 170–171.

hole. Hubberthorne, a young man of thirty-four, died there in August, and at the inquest the jury found a verdict of " death from natural causes." Burrough died there seven months later.[1] In the November of that year the soldiers broke up another meeting at the Bull and Mouth, and carried off forty-two persons to the Old Bridewell, in Fleet Street. Ellwood, who had recently become Milton's secretary, was seized outside the prison, and thrust in with the rest. Some of the prisoners were beaten on the bare back with holly sticks, full of knots, which tore the flesh and gave great pain. Those only who had money could obtain food in the prison, but the Friends had organised a system of relief for all poor Quaker prisoners. Carried to the Sessions at the Old Bailey in December, the cause of their committal was not stated, but the oath of allegiance was tendered to them. Ellwood pleaded that the words of the statute required him to say that he took the oath " freely and without constraint," and that, being a prisoner, he was under constraint, and ought to be set free before he could take it. Being pressed, however, he admitted that he could not take it even if he were free. With the rest he was imprisoned in Newgate, which was so packed with prisoners, Nonconformists and others, that they had to stretch hammocks " three storeys high." Worse than that, " when we came first to Newgate there lay in a little by-place, like a closet, near the room where we were lodged, the quartered bodies of three men who had been executed some days before." These were Phillips, Tong, and Gibb, who had been executed for treason on December 22nd. The crowded state of the prison brought on much sickness, and one of the prisoners died, and the coroner's jury brought in a verdict that he died from sickness brought on by overcrowding. Sir William Turner, one of the sheriffs, had some of the Quaker prisoners removed to Bridewell. The porter at Bridewell took their word that they would not try to escape, and allowed them to go thither by themselves, only stipulating that they must arrive there before bed-time; so they walked there two or three abreast. At Bridewell they were allowed a good deal of liberty, some even being permitted to go home in the evening, provided they returned next morning. This, Ellwood naïvely says, was a great convenience to those engaged in trade. On one occasion Ellwood was allowed to go to Newgate to visit Burrough and the other Quakers there. At the next Sessions at the Old Bailey, the Quakers were discharged.[2]

In 1663 several Quakers met in the house of Rupert Smyth at Worcester, not to preach, but to advise together about four children whose father had died and left them without provision. Some soldiers rushed in, arrested twenty-four of them, and put them in prison among notorious offenders. After some weeks,

---

[1] Besse, " Sufferings."   [2] " History of Thomas Ellwood."

Smyth and some of the others were brought before the magistrates, but refused to take the oaths or remove their hats, and were remanded to prison for disobedience to the King and disrespect to his representatives. Smyth was further adjudged to be out of the King's protection, and to have all his goods confiscated. After this the rest of them were brought up, and because of their meeting, and because they refused to take the oaths, they were sentenced to imprisonment, in spite of the fact that the witnesses disagreed.[1] In November of the same year a party of men, presumably armed and in the Government service, went to the Quaker burial-place at Marlborough and laid it waste.[2] John Audland, a Westmorland man, was a prisoner in Banbury for over a year, and died there of an affection of the lungs in 1663,[3] and Humphrey Smith died in Winchester gaol in the same year.[4] Mrs. Loveday Hambly, a widow living at Tregangeeves, near St. Austell, was one of the most prominent Quaker workers and sufferers in the west of England.   In 1660 she was sent to Launceston gaol for having conventicles in her house. In 1662 she was imprisoned at Bodmin for not paying tithes. In 1663 cattle to the value of £35 were seized in distraint for about £6 worth of tithe, and in 1664, for the same reason, she was once again imprisoned at Bodmin.[5] John Whitehead of York was imprisoned in Aylesbury gaol in 1661, and later on in the year at Lincoln. He was tried at the Caistor Quarter Sessions in February, 1662. There was trouble about his hat, but finally they took it off for him, and he was sentenced to imprisonment for conventicling, for refusing to give an account of his abode, and for declining the oaths, which, however, do not seem to have been tendered to him. He was set at liberty shortly afterwards, but was again arrested in July, and committed to Lincoln gaol. His trial did not take place till the Louth Quarter Sessions were held in October. Whitehead and John Cleasby refused to take the oaths, and were sentenced to a fine of £5, or three months imprisonment. In January 1663, at the next Quarter Sessions, the justices ordered them to be released and the fine remitted if they would take the oaths, but the prisoners replied that they had already suffered the penalty of the law by being kept so long in prison. At the March Assizes Whitehead was brought up again, but his case was not heard, though the other three prisoners were released; but at the Louth Quarter Sessions in April he was at last discharged. In the latter part of 1664 he was in prison at Spalding for a time.[6]

[1] Croese, " Gen. Hist. Quakers," pp. 173–175.
[2] Hist. MSS. Com. III. 93.
[3] " The Memory of the Righteous Revived," 1689.
[4] " A Collection of the Several Writings and Faithful Testimonies of Humphrey Smith," 1683.
[5] L. V. Hodgkin, " A Quaker Saint of Cornwall," 1927.
[6] " The Gospel Labours of John Whitehead," 1704.

In April 1664 two Quakers, Thomas Davenport and John Brown, prisoners in Lancaster Castle, were brought up at the Assizes. Davenport was an old and feeble man, with an ailing wife and a sick daughter, and was very poor and in debt. Brown had fought for the King in England and Ireland, and had been severely wounded. They had been taken into custody at Swarthmore, and at the Sessions had been remanded to the Assizes, because they could not take the oaths. They had already been seventeen weeks in prison, but Judge Twisden sent them back to gaol.[1] Joseph Coale was seized in a house in Reading in 1664, and taken before Sir William Armourer, who, on his refusal to take the oaths, sent him to Reading gaol. He died in prison there in 1670, aged thirty-four years, his health broken down by his long captivity.[2] Francis Howgill, one of the early Quaker leaders, was sentenced to a *præmunire* at Appleby Assizes in 1664, and remained in prison till his death in 1669.[3]

After the Conventicle Act was passed it was put in force against the Quakers with the greatest severity. Their custom of remaining in silence till one of them was moved to speak made a difficulty for those who had to punish them. Orlando Bridgeman told the jury at Hertford, " You are not to expect a plain punctual evidence against them for anything they said or did at their meeting; for they may speak to one another, though not with or by articulate sound, but by a cast of the eye, or a motion of the head or foot, or a gesture of the body. So that if you find or believe in your hearts that they were in the meeting under colour of religion in their way, though they sat still only and looked upon each other, it was an unlawful meeting."

How their conduct appeared to their enemies is shown in the following words of Bishop Parker: " The Quakers only were obstinate; for they scarce accounted any act so religious as to resist human authority. Therefore they met the oftener because they were forbid, nor could they by any force be drawn away from one another till a merry fellow hit upon this stratagem. He proclaimed in the King's name that it should not be lawful for anyone to depart without his leave; and he had scarce done this when they all went away, that it may not be said that they obeyed any man." [4]

Some of the authorities did their best to suppress Quakerism. The Lord Chancellor and Bennet told Sir Philip Musgrave what difficulties they had with the Quakers throughout the country, and how they desired to take the quickest possible means to suppress them by imprisonment and transportation. Musgrave

[1] Nightingale, " Early Stages of the Quaker Movement in Lancashire," p. 115.
[2] " Some Account of the Life of Joseph Coale," 1706.
[3] Ferguson, " Early Cumberland and Westmorland Friends," pp. 23-27.
[4] Parker, " Own Times," p. 88.

was anxious to find out by what means they could be sent abroad.[1] Some of the justices adopted the practice of only committing them for a few days for the first and second offences, in order to be able more speedily to sentence them to transportation for the third.[2] One of the people who had suffered under the first Conventicle Act was Sir John Vaughan, afterwards third Earl of Carberry, who was imprisoned for attending Quaker meetings. He was not a Quaker, but always had kindly feelings towards them.[3] The Bull and Mouth meeting-house was raided after the Conventicle Act, the preacher, William Warwick, imprisoned, and the books were seized.[4] The Act did not come into force till July 1st; but on August 12th and 13th Henry Feast and eight other Quakers were indicted at the Hertford Assizes for the third offence under it. The witnesses all said that they saw them assembled, but did not see them do or hear them say anything, and the grand jury returned a verdict of *Ignoramus*. It was then that Judge Bridgeman gave them the advice related above, and a true bill was finally returned. Ultimately one of the prisoners was found not guilty, but the rest were sentenced to transportation to Barbados or Jamaica. At the following Hertford Quarter Sessions seven persons were charged with being at a meeting, but five of them refused to plead, and remained silent. They too were transported, and in October twenty-one more were punished in the same way.[5] A petition was sent to the justices at Salisbury at the beginning of 1665 from five Quakers who had been imprisoned there since June, 1663.[6]

The Quakers suffered heavily during the Plague year. They even had their own dead-cart,[7] and Tillotson told Sancroft in September that they had buried in their own burying-ground as many as a thousand a week for some time past.[8] Their burial-ground was close to Bunhill Fields, but most of it is now covered by a school and the Memorial Buildings. In spite of Tillotson's statement, the total number of Quaker deaths registered in London was 1717, though probably, in spite of their well-known care in registration, there were some who died in prison whose names were lost.[9] Fifty-two Quakers, however, are known to have died in Newgate during the Plague, several of whom were women. Fifty-five were imprisoned in July and August in a ship, the *Black Eagle*, lying below Greenwich in

---

[1] Hist. MSS. Com., Lonsdale MSS., p. 93.
[2] Gough, " Hist. Quakers," II. 116–117.
[3] Braithwaite, " Second Period," p. 73.
[4] Kitchin, " Roger L'Estrange," p. 123.
[5] " Victoria County Hist. Hertford," IV. 358.
[6] Hist. MSS. Com., Various Collections, I. 148.
[7] Defoe, " Journal of the Plague Year."
[8] Ellis, " Original Letters," IV. cccxv.
[9] W. G. Bell, " The Great Plague," London, 1924, p. 181.

Bugby's Hole. During the seven weeks she lay there half the prisoners died.[1] Alexander Parker, George Whitehead, and Gilbert Latey worked nobly among the sufferers of all denominations in London during this year.[2]

It was remarked that the first death from plague within the city was in Bearbinder Lane, at a house near that of Edward Brush, the first Quaker to be transported to the Plantations under the Conventicle Act.[3] This was looked upon as the hand of God. Numbers of people, the Quakers among them, had proclaimed the Plague as God's judgment upon a wicked land for its persecution of the Lord's people. Charles was at first half inclined to believe it, but he inquired whether any Quakers had died, and when he found that the sickness had been as rife amongst them as among other people, seemed comforted by the thought that it could not then be looked upon as an act of divine vengeance.[4]

Ellwood, who had become tutor to Isaac Pennington's children, was soon in trouble again. In 1665 the body of Edward Perrot, a Quaker, was being carried through the streets of Amersham to the burial-ground when Ambrose Bennet, one of the local justices, came up with constables and the rabble and attacked the bearers with his sword, so that they let the coffin fall and had to leave it in the middle of the street. Ten of the party, of whom Elwood was one, were committed to Aylesbury gaol. Even then the widow was not allowed to have the body, but it lay in the street all night, and was finally buried by the authorities in the unconsecrated part of the churchyard. In Aylesbury gaol the prisoners were treated with great harshness by the authorities, who shut them up with the common felons and demanded unjust fees, which they refused to pay. At the Assizes Judge Morton reviled them, and then sent them back to the local justices, who fined them and sent them to prison for a month. Again in 1666 Ellwood was taken at a meeting, and sent to High Wycombe gaol, where he remained for three months.[5]

The Middlesex County Records show 904 convictions between July 24th, 1664, and December 31st, 1665. Of these 859 convictions were certainly for attending Quaker meetings. In connection with the London meeting-places at Mile End, Spitalfields, Clerkenwell, the Bull and Mouth, and Horsleydown there were 2100 imprisonments within twelve months.[6] Not till 1667 did the persecution under the Act slacken. All the sects had weakened under the trial except the Friends. The Presbyterians

[1] Braithwaite, " Second Period," pp. 46–48.
[2] R. Hawkins, " Life of Gilbert Latey," 1707, pp. 63–64; G. Whitehead, " Christian Progress," 1725.
[3] Whitehead, " Christian Progress," p. 300.
[4] Fox, " Journal," ed. Penney, Editor's note.
[5] " Hist. of Thomas Ellwood."
[6] Braithwaite, " Second Period," pp. 41–42.

and some others when they met for worship did so under the pretence of a common meal, with pipes, bread, cheese, and cold meat on the table, so that if the officers or informers came they might be ready to begin eating. The Quakers looked upon this trick with scorn. Some of the Baptists, of whom there were many who considered oaths unlawful, had yielded and taken them when pressed in court. The Independents had no objection to oaths in themselves, but they did not wish to take the oath of allegiance, because of their dislike to the Government. But they had to take it when it was tendered them. The Quakers, on the other hand, would not swear even to save their goods in a civil court. The persecution under the Conventicle Act ceased in London by 1668. The Quakers had won the fight, but they had incurred the animosity of the other sects, who said the persecution would never have been so severe if it had not been for them.[1]

One of the first divisions which appeared in Quakerism was due to John Perrot. Somewhere about 1660 John Love and he felt themselves moved by the Spirit to go to Rome to convert the Pope. Love died in the dungeons of the Inquisition, and Perrot was put in a madhouse, from which he was released by some high influence either in England or Rome, though Ellwood says it was by the influence of the Quakers. His somewhat unbalanced temperament was either temporarily or permanently affected, for on his release he wrote an epistle to England in which he signed himself, in somewhat papal fashion, " John," and exhorted his Quaker brethren to read his " Life " at their meetings. When he got back to England he began to advocate the view that the hat should not be removed from the head during prayer, unless the wearer were specially moved by the Spirit so to do. He seems to have had a considerable following, chiefly in London and the south, and one of his chief supporters was Robert Rich, who had been an associate of James Nayler. Ellwood adopted Perrot's view, and wrote in defence of it, but repented and confessed his error in 1666. He relates how he silenced one of Perrot's followers in Dorsetshire by telling him that he himself had been led astray, but had seen his mistake.[2] The Quakers, finding they could not persuade Perrot, at last renounced him, and he is said to have taken to wearing gay apparel and a sword, and to have visited America, where he badly misbehaved. Finally he procured a Government post, and became a severe exactor of oaths. He died in 1665, but his influence lasted. Fox was obliged to hold large meetings to bring about peace. One of these meetings was held in London in 1666, and lasted for many days, much time being taken up in reading recantations of Perrot's errors written by Friends at a distance. Some of the Quakers, like Pennington, had been greatly influenced by Perrot,

[1] Fox, " Journal," 1666; Sewell, " Hist. Quakers," 457.
[2] " Hist. of Thomas Ellwood."

and some had even thought that he was to be the medium of a new revelation. The movement can hardly be called a schism; Quakerism was not yet sufficiently an organised unity for that, but it represented a widespread feeling against Fox's leadership. It even spread to America, but Jane Stokes, one of the chief exponents of the new doctrines there, recanted in due course.[1]

In 1668 two London Presbyterians belonging to the congregation of Thomas Vincent [2] had attended a Quaker meeting and been converted. Vincent therefore preached violently against the Quakers and their doctrines, which he denounced as damnable, and thereupon Penn and Whitehead challenged him to a public debate. Vincent agreed, and the two Quakers went to his meeting-house, which was packed with his supporters, including three other Presbyterian ministers, Thomas Dawson, Thomas Doolittle, and William Maddox. The Quakers began to explain their tenets, but Vincent insisted that he should ask them questions, and inquired first whether they owned one Godhead in three distinct and separate Persons. Whitehead affirmed that the theological terms used by Vincent were unscriptural and not deducible from the texts he quoted, and demanded that his opponent should explain his meaning, for " God did not use to wrap His truths in heathenish metaphysics, but deliver them in plain language." There was a great deal of indecorous behaviour, and the Presbyterians hissed and laughed, and called Penn and Whitehead Jesuits, and other opprobrious names. The meeting lasted till midnight, and was ended by a prayer from Vincent in which he called them blasphemers. When it was over some remained behind, and the Quakers took the opportunity of defending themselves, and asked for another debate, which was refused.[3] Penn went home, and shortly afterwards produced his work " The Sandy Foundation Shaken," in which he showed heterodoxy on the doctrine of the Trinity, largely through his dislike for theological and metaphysical subtleties. Vincent called on the Government to deal with the writer for denying the Christian truth. The book had been issued without a licence, but Penn approached Arlington and explained that it was his fault, and not that of the printer, who had already been imprisoned for it. Penn was sent to the Tower in December.[4] A difficulty arose about this. Sir John Robinson, the Lieutenant of the Tower, refused to take him in without a proper warrant from the King and Council, and a warrant was issued, therefore, first by the King and Arlington, and then later, as Robinson was still unsettled, by seven members more.

[1] Braithwaite, " Second Period," pp. 35–40; Sewell, " Hist. Quakers," pp. 282–283; Graham, " Life of Penn," pp. 91–93; " Hist. of Thomas Ellwood."
[2] Palmer, I. 155–156.
[3] Neal, " Puritans," IV. 510–511; Gough, " Quakers," II. 226–228.
[4] Clarkson, " Life of Penn," 1813; C.S.P.D., Entry Book 30, f. 93.

The charge had been changed from unlicensed printing to that of blasphemy, and it was said that the King ordered the Bishop of London to proceed against Penn in his consistory court for blasphemous heresy; but the fact that the bishop did not do so rather tells against the story. Arlington is said to have pushed the matter as far as possible, from personal animosity to Admiral Penn.[1] Several clergy, Stillingfleet among them, were sent to discuss the disputed doctrines with the prisoner,[2] and under Stillingfleet's advice Penn wrote " Innocency with her Open Face," in which he expressed more orthodox views.[3] During this imprisonment he wrote one of his best-known works, " No Cross, No Crown,"[4] in which he urged constancy under trial, defended the Quaker teachings, and attacked the evils of the age. In July 1669 he wrote to Arlington a letter in which he expounded the reasons for religious liberty, and asked his help to obtain his freedom. Whether Arlington had forgiven his father and intervened, or whether it was by the influence of the Duke of York, to whom Admiral Penn had appealed, he was set free at once.[5] In fact the story of Arlington's animosity is rather discounted by a letter written to Arlington by Penn on June 9th, in which he says, " As thy candid promises of assistance are strongly encouraging, I make no apology for troubling thee with the enclosed," viz. a statement that it was not true that he denied the deity of the Son and Holy Ghost.[6]

The Quakers did all in their power to mitigate the sufferings of their fellow-religionists by personal appeals to the King. One of those who did so had a personal claim on Charles. When the King, escaping after Worcester fight, reached Brighton, or Brighthelmstone as it was then called, a fisherman named Nicholas Tattersall undertook to convey him to France. On arrival at the French coast, Richard Carver, the mate of the boat, carried the King ashore on his shoulders. At the Restoration Tattersall received an annuity of £100 a year for this service. Carver, who had become a Quaker, went to see the King in 1670, and when he was questioned on the subject of a reward, he said he wanted no reward except that Charles should set some of the Quakers free who had suffered for their faith, and he presented the King with a list of 110 Friends who had been in prison over six years. Charles promised to release six of them, but said if he let them all go, they would all be in prison again within a month. Carver paid another visit to the King a little time after, accompanied by another Quaker, Thomas Moore. The King promised to do more for him, but desired him to " wait a month or two longer." Carver made no more applications, but Moore

[1] Graham, " Life of Penn," 1918, pp. 42–44; *Archæologia*, XXXV. 72–90.
[2] C.S.P.D., Entry Book 30, f. 96.
[3] Graham, " Life of Penn," pp. 44–45.   [4] 1669.
[5] Airey, " William Penn," *Encycl. Brit.*, 9th ed.   [6] C.S.P.D., 261/130.

did so on many occasions, and one of the most energetic Friends in this respect was George Whitehead.

Before the second Conventicle Act was passed the Quakers issued a paper in which it was stated that since the King came in 8000 Quakers had been imprisoned, of whom 173 had died of confinement and hard usage, 138 had been banished, and 600 were at that moment in prison.[1] It had no effect on Parliament. Under the Act the Quakers were again the greatest sufferers, for the word " conventicle " was interpreted to include visits to the sick, meetings to raise money for the poor, funerals, and even the gathering of a few friends in a house.[2] Appeals were, as a rule, ineffectual. But in the very year in which the Act was passed, Henshaw, Bishop of Peterborough, who had issued orders to all his officials to see to its enforcement, said publicly in the " steeple-house " at Rothwell, " Against all fanatics it hath done its business except the Quakers; but when Parliament sits again, a stronger law will be made, not only to take away their lands and goods, but also to sell them for bondslaves." [3]

In 1670 the King issued an Order in Council signed by the Archbishop of Canterbury and thirteen others, to pull down the Quaker meeting-houses at Ratcliffe and Horsleydown. Peel meeting-house was ransacked, and the doors and windows were destroyed. If they met in the streets the Quakers were driven away by soldiers and beaten with the butt ends of muskets.[4] Loveday Hambly had distresses levied upon her again in 1670 and 1671. Some of the goods seized belonged to her nephew, and he got an order of restitution for them, which, however, was never carried out.[5]

An informer named John Poulter was sent out by Dr. Mews, the Vice-Chancellor of Oxford, and tried to insinuate himself among the Quakers of Buckinghamshire, but they had been warned, because he had given his secret away while he was drunk; so he then turned to the Baptists. But he could not let the Quakers alone, and together with another informer named Lacey he laid information against the Quaker conventicle held at Jordans, the house of William Russell at Chalfont St. Giles. But Poulter's character was so bad that he had to leave the neighbourhood, and Richard Aris took his place. Lacey and he accused Thomas Zachary and his wife of being present at a conventicle at Jordans, although they had been in London at the

---

[1] " A Short Relation of the Sad Sufferings and Cruel Havoc and Spoil inflicted on the Persons and Estates of the People of God in scorn called Quakers, for meeting together to worship God in Spirit and in Truth," 1670.
[2] Neal, " Puritans," IV. 409.   [3] Gough, " Hist. Quakers," II. 303.
[4] " The Cry of Innocent Blood, sounding to the Ears of each Member of Parliament: Being a Short Relation of the Barbarous Cruelties inflicted lately upon the Peaceable People of God called Quakers at . . . Horsleydown . . . also some Plain-Dealing with the Persecuting Rulers," 1670.
[5] L. V. Hodgkin, " A Quaker Saint of Cornwall," London, 1927.

time. Zachary was fined £30 by a local justice, and though he appealed to the Quarter Sessions he got no redress; instead, indeed, he was sent to the Buckinghamshire county gaol. Thomas Ellwood, at the next Sessions, brought witnesses to prove that the man and his wife had not been at the meeting, but though the fact was proved and the jury found them not guilty, Zachary only recovered £10. At the next Sessions following this Ellwood put in an indictment against Aris and Lacey for perjury, and retained counsel to prosecute the indictment. But the bench allowed the two accused to stand bail for each other, and it was not till the Sessions after that that a verdict was obtained against them. Aris fled, and Lacey, who lay in hiding for a time, went to Zachary, who was still in gaol (because the magistrates had tendered him the oaths of allegiance and supremacy), and begged his forgiveness. At Zachary's request Ellwood agreed to suspend execution as long as Lacey refrained from informing. This brought the practice to an end in this county for a time.[1]

The Quakers refused to employ tricks and shifts, and so brought the brunt of the persecution on themselves, and the other sects, especially the Baptists, could not help looking upon them as their champions. Fox was brought up in 1670 before the Lord Mayor of London, who tried to persuade him to confine his meetings to small numbers of people. Fox, however, argued that the Act did not apply to Quaker meetings, because it was directed against seditious conventicles, and theirs were not seditious, and because it was directed against worship " not according to the liturgy," whereas, since the liturgy claimed to accord with Scripture, the Quaker practice of reading and speaking Scripture was really in accord with the liturgy. So the Quakers went on holding their meetings, though the Baptists and some of the others stopped theirs for a time.[2] If anything, the Friends became bolder. At Bristol that year they met more openly than before, and they had made a habit of returning from their assemblies in bodies of six or ten, " as if they intended to outface the law." [3]

One Quaker meeting obtained for itself a place in English constitutional history. On Saturday, June 11th, 1670, the doors of the meeting-house in Gracechurch Street were nailed up and padlocked by the Surveyor-General and one of the sheriffs, by order of the King and Council. Next day the Quakers held their meeting outside in the court. A constable and some soldiers came, but the crowd was so great that they could not make their way through. Just as the meeting was breaking up the sheriff came, made proclamation commanding them to disperse, and carried away four persons to the Counter.

[1] " Hist. of Thomas Ellwood."
[2] Fox, " Journal "; Sewell, " Hist. Quakers," pp. 477–479.
[3] C.S.P.D., May 14th, 1670.

A fortnight afterwards a clergyman of the Church of England attended by order of the Lord Mayor, read the Anglican service, and preached a sermon, in which he exhorted his hearers to the exercise of Christian love and charity, though it was remarked that some of the soldiers who guarded him insulted some of the Friends unrebuked.   There was a large attendance of people, and when the priest had finished George Whitehead rose up and preached, setting forth how contrary to Christianity was all this persecution.   He was after a time pulled down and carried to the Lord Mayor, who issued a warrant to commit him to the Counter, which was then in the Gatehouse in Bishopsgate, and he was also fined £40.[1]

On August 14th, the meeting-house having been closed, and the soldiers preventing any persons from entering, Penn and Meade, the latter a merchant tailor of Fenchurch Street and a new convert to Quakerism,[2] held a meeting outside in the street, at which meeting it was estimated that some 300 persons were present.   The two preachers were arrested, and were brought up for trial on September 3rd.   The charge was that they did *vi et armis* unlawfully and tumultuously assemble together and congregate to the disturbance of the peace, that Penn preached by agreement with, and by the abetment of Meade, by reason whereof a great concourse and tumult of people did a long time remain and continue, in contempt of the King and his law, to the great disturbance of his peace, to the terror of many of his lieges and to the ill-example of others.   All this, of course, was mere legal verbiage; but they were being tried under the Common Law, and not under the Conventicle Act.   The imperfect account of the trial as it comes down to us was written by the prisoners themselves.   Consequently, it represents them as having the best of it against the judges and opposing counsel all the time.   " I cannot help thinking," says Sir James Fitz-James Stephen, " that a good many of their retorts were recollections of what they ought to have said." [3]   One of the jury was a man named Bushell.   Sir J. Robinson, Lieutenant of the Tower, objected against him that he had not kissed the book, and therefore had him sworn again.   Penn says this was done on purpose, because his conscience was tender in the matter of reiterated oaths, and it was hoped to get rid of him from the jury.[4]   Penn had some knowledge of law, and argued with the Court, and both Meade and he quoted Coke and the statutes freely.   The jury disagreed, Bushell was one of those who refused to bring in a verdict of unlawful assembly against the prisoners, and though he denied it, was accused of having thrust

---

[1] Besse, " Sufferings."
[2] Fox, " Journal," ed. by N. Penney, Editor's note.
[3] " Hist. Crim. Law of Eng.," I. 374.
[4] " The People's Ancient and Just Liberties Asserted," 1670.

himself on the jury as an abettor of faction. After a time Thomas Vere, the foreman, reported as their verdict that they found Penn " guilty of speaking or preaching to an assembly met together in Gracious Street," and that Meade was not guilty. They were then locked up without food, drink, or fire, with a threat that they should so remain till they brought in a satisfactory verdict. Penn warned the jury that if they brought in another verdict they would be perjured, and added, " You are Englishmen. Mind your privileges. Give not away your right." To which Bushell made answer, " Nor will we ever do it." Next morning the jury, after being locked up all night, returned the same verdict as before. After another day and night's imprisonment they returned a verdict of " Not guilty " against both prisoners. The Recorder then fined the jurymen forty marks each, and sentenced them to imprisonment until their fines were paid.[1] Penn thought he was now free, but there had been an altercation at the beginning of the trial about the prisoners wearing their hats in court. They were both fined for this and sent to Newgate for contempt. Penn requested his family not to pay the fine for him, but it was paid anonymously, and he was set free in time to be at his father's deathbed on September 16th.

Bushell and his companions were kept in prison for a few days, but ultimately obtained a writ of *habeas corpus*. The return to the writ stated that they were imprisoned for contempt of court in acquitting the two prisoners " contra legem hujus regni Angliæ, et contra plenum (*sic*) et manifestum (*sic*) evidentiam, et contra directionem Curiæ in materia legis." Their case was elaborately argued in the Court of Common Pleas, where a majority of the judges (ten out of twelve) decided that they had been wrongfully imprisoned, that it lies with the jury alone to judge the facts and to believe the evidence or not, and that the court can do no more than endeavour to guide the jury aright. The opinion of the court was delivered by Lord Chief Justice Vaughan, and accordingly the prisoners were discharged without being made to pay the fines imposed.[2] The old system of upsetting a verdict was a re-trial before a jury of attaint. But at this period judges frequently treated a verdict contrary to what they thought the facts of the case as misconduct on the part of the jurors, and fined them for contempt. This practice was finally declared illegal by Vaughan's judgment in this case, which was the last case in which any attempt was made to question the absolute right of the jury to give such a verdict as they think right.[3] In the Sessions House, which to-day stands on the site of the Old Bailey, there is a memorial tablet commemorating

[1] " The People's Ancient and Just Liberties Asserted."
[2] *Ibid.*, Part II. 1670. [3] Stephen, " Hist. Crim. Law," I. 375.

this trial of Penn and Meade and the courage of the jury in refusing to give a verdict against them.

The usual pamphlet war followed this trial. Thomas Rudyard, a Quaker lawyer, brought out in two parts " The People's Ancient and Just Liberties Asserted in the Trial of William Penn and William Meade." A certain " S. S." replied to this. Penn did not know who he was, but it has been suggested that it was Samuel Starling, Lord Mayor of London, and a great persecutor.[1] Penn wrote a vigorous reply, " Truth Rescued from Imposture; or, a Brief Reply to a mere Rhapsody of Lies, Folly, and Slander "[2] in which he declared himself " a professed enemy of oppression." Thomas Rudyard had written a book on the rights of juries, in which he criticised the methods by which Acts against Dissenters were enforced. Moreover, he had been very zealous in defending them in the courts. A warrant was issued against him, his house searched by soldiers, and he was carried off to Newgate on the charge of stirring up people to disobey the law, and aiding and abetting such as met in unlawful conventicles. On June 7th, 1670, he was brought before the magistrates and ordered to give security in £2000 for his good behaviour. As he refused, Sir Samuel Starling and Sir John Robinson, the Lieutenant of the Tower, committed him to gaol. He appealed, and the Court of Common Pleas found that he had been unjustly imprisoned, and he was set at liberty.

On June 29th a new indictment was framed against him, that on May 30th, when Samuel Allingbridge, a London stationer, was prosecuted for seditious words, Rudyard, in order to hinder the course of law, " did unlawfully, secretly, and subtilly by force of arms, etc.," carry away the bill of indictment. He pleaded not guilty. It was pointed out that Allingbridge had been acquitted at the same sessions at which his indictment had miscarried. The indictment against Rudyard not having been drawn to the case, Sir Samuel Starling ordered another to be drawn up which contained the substance of the former, and added " that the said Thomas Rudyard, the said 30th of May, coming to Nicholas Grove, said to him that the bill against Samuel Allingbridge was lost, and that Grove should attend next Saturday, and that Thomas Rudyard unlawfully and craftily did say to Nicholas Grove these words, viz: ' I will come to you some time this week, and we will go and drink a pint of wine with Mr. Tanner, and so make an end of the business,' in contempt of the King and his laws, to the hindrance of justice, etc." Thus the charge against Rudyard had been changed during the trial. Rudyard gave security to appear at the next sessions, but the Lord Mayor, in addition, demanded that he should give his own recognizances for his good behaviour. As the Judges had recently given their opinion against the law-

[1] Graham, " Life of Penn," p. 60.   [2] 1670.

fulness of this demand in such circumstances, Rudyard refused, and was committed to Newgate till the next Sessions. In September he was, with others, tried for contempt of court by wearing his hat. Afterwards he was committed to Newgate for being at a Quaker meeting, was fined £100 for several trespasses and contempts, and ordered to be imprisoned till the money was paid. A full account of this affair is given in the Second Part of " The People's Ancient and Just Liberties Asserted," which has an appendix in the form of a dialogue between a student of the laws and liberties of England and a citizen of London, the argument setting forth " that a jury of twelve men are the only proper judges of their neighbour's actions, and may by the established laws of England give a verdict of such facts according to their consciences, without incurring fine and imprisonment."

On January 17th, 1671, at the Richmond, Yorkshire, Quarter Sessions, the justices made the following order: " Forasmuch as the petty constables within this Riding are put to great charge in and about the levying of such sums of money as are forfeited by the Quakers for their being at unlawful conventicles, according to an Act of Parliament in that case lately made. . . . Ordered, that the respective constables shall be reimbursed such moneys as they shall disburse, and for the trouble they shall be put to in or about the putting the said Act in execution, out of such penalties as shall be by them respectively levied, according to the discretion of the justices before whom such Quakers are or shall be convicted." [1] At Thirsk Quarter Sessions, October 3rd, 1671, it was ordered that John Ford, late constable of Whitby, should give account to Sir William Caley or Sir James Pennyman of the money received by him on the conviction of Quakers. On April 16th of the following year the constable was presented for false accounts and embezzling some of the money he had received from the Quakers.[2]

In 1671 George Walkinson, of Scotton, in the county of York, bequeathed two legacies, one of £200 to the Quakers of Yorkshire, and another of £20 to those of Scotton. The bequest was not made to any Friends as individuals, but to the society. This was contrary to the law, as tending to encourage unlawful meetings, and the Government seized the money, and on June 16th made a special grant of it to John, Lord Freschville [3] who had just retired [4] from his post of Governor of York and commander of the garrison.

William Penn was imprisoned again in 1671 for being present at a Quaker meeting. The justices, Sir John Robinson, Sir Samuel Starling and others, proposed to try him, not under the Conventicle Act, but under the Five Mile Act. But the latter

[1] " North Riding Records. Quarter Sessions Records," VI. 153.
[2] Ibid., VI. 164, 169.
[3] C.S.P.D., Entry Book 21, f. 94, and 34, f. 104.   [4] May 13th, 1671.

Act did not apply to him, since he was not a minister, so they tendered him the oaths of allegiance and supremacy instead.[1] The system of distraint for fines was a great hardship to the Quakers, for the goods distrained were often valued at an absurdly low rate and sold at ridiculously cheap prices. A man named May in the same year got possession in this way of 130 sheep belonging to Dr. Thomas Lower, a Cornish Quaker, though his victim recorded that he was not enriched thereby, notwithstanding all his ill-gotten increase; " all is consumed and wasted and it proved as a canker upon all the rest of his goods, and a curse entered with it." [2]   On Christmas Day, 1671, the Mayor of Weymouth, finding several Quakers' shops open, caused the constables to throw the goods out into the streets, and then to close the windows.[3]

In Nottinghamshire the informers invented a special trick against the Quakers. They attended Quaker meetings, and recognising them, the Quakers would sit in silence. Then one of the informers would get up and begin to speak, whereupon the others would jump up and arrest the Quakers, and seize their goods. They did not content themselves with seizing what would cover the fines; they took everything they could lay their hands on, sometimes removing goods by the wagon-load.[4]

The Quakers asked for no licences under the Declaration of Indulgence. But a petition drawn up by George Whitehead and others was sent to the King in Council, urging that, since the King had decreed the suspension of the penal laws, the Quakers in prison might be released.[5] A list was put in at the same time of 114 Friends under sentence of *præmunire*, most of whom had been in prison from seven to ten years, sixty more in prison under sentence of banishment, thirty under sentence of excommunication, and over 100 for unpaid fines.[6]

The case of the Quakers was considered in Council, and orders were issued to the sheriffs to make returns to the Lord Keeper of all Quakers who were at that time in gaol. The Lord Keeper reported that:

(1) All those sentenced to transportation or to a *præmunire* could not legally be discharged except by a pardon under the Great Seal.

(2) All those in prison under writs of *excommunicato capiendo* ought not to be discharged without consideration of the cause for which the writ was issued, because in cases of

---

[1] Graham, " Life of Penn."
[2] " A Record of the Sufferings of the Quakers in Cornwall," ed. by N. Penney, 1928, p. 90.
[3] C.S.P.D., 294/224.   [4] Croese, " Gen. Hist. Quakers," p. 69.
[5] The Calendar of State Papers dates this " June ? " but the Order in Council doing what they asked was issued in May.
[6] C.S.P.D., 311/114.

tithes and other private interests the other party should first be satisfied.

(3) All those in prison for debt, or upon any process in the courts at Westminster, ought not to be discharged till it was known for what cause the process was issued, or till the debt was discharged.

(4) Those in prison for not paying fines ought not to be discharged without paying their fines or receiving a pardon.

(5) All others might be discharged.

On May 8th the King issued an Order in Council declaring that he would pardon all Quakers now in prison for any offence relating to himself, and not to the prejudice of any other person; and ordering lists of the names of such prisoners to be sent to the Attorney-General. By virtue of this order there was drawn up a list of 480 names of Quakers and others, to be included in the general pardon.[1] On June 12th a general warrant was issued for a grant-of pardon to all Quakers in gaol for all offences and contempts, absence from church, attendance at conventicles, refusal of oaths, and such-like offences.[2] On September 3rd the King issued a general pardon under the Great Seal. Four hundred and seventy-one names were included in it, and the King ordered that it should pass as one document, and that no fees were to be paid for it. Then the Quaker leaders travelled about the country, going from prison to prison and setting their brethren free. The persons specified in the pardon were not all Quakers; some, of whom John Bunyan was one, were members of other sects, whose friends, in some cases at the personal advice of George Whitehead, had petitioned for release at the same time.[3]

The Quakers had fought the battle of liberty, and the victory was largely due to them, and on this account they seem to have attracted a good many converts from the other sects. The ministers of the other denominations were annoyed, and the result was an outburst of controversial literature. Henry Hedworth the Unitarian wrote a tract, " Controversy Ended "; Penn replied with " A Winding Sheet for ' Controversy Ended.' " Hedworth also wrote " The Spirit of the Quakers Tried, according to that Discovery made by George Fox in his Book ' The Great Mystery of the Great Whore.' " This was in 1672, and he was answered by Penn in " The Spirit of Truth Vindicated." John Faldo, an Independent preacher near Barnet, and formerly a chaplain in the Commonwealth army,[4] finding some of his congregation going over to the Quakers, published a tract, " Quakerism no Christianity, Clearly Proved out of the Writings of their Chief Leaders. With a Key for the Understanding their Sense of their many Usurped and Unintelligible Words

---

[1] C.S.P.D., 307/166.   [2] C.S.P.D., Entry Book 34, f. 171.
[3] Braithwaite, *Second Period*, pp. 82–85.   [4] Calamy, II. 838.

and Phrases, to most Readers." It was largely occupied with an examination of the first 'part of Penn's " Spirit of Truth Vindicated." Twenty-one divines, among them Manton and Baxter, wrote a preface to the second edition of Faldo's tract. Penn's reply to Faldo was entitled " Quakerism a new Nickname for Old Christianity." This provoked a rejoinder in 1673, " A Vindication of ' Quakerism no Christianity' against the very Vain Attempts of W. Penn, in his Pretended Answer, with some Remarkable Passages out of the Quakers' Church Registry, wherein their Near Approach to Popery and their Bold Blasphemy is Abundantly Manifest." Penn, nothing daunted, wrote " The Invalidity of J. Faldo's Vindication of his Book called ' Quakerism no Christianity ' ' "; and he dealt with Baxter and the rest in " A Just Rebuke to One and Twenty Divines." Whitehead and he also published " The Christian Quaker and his Divine Testimony Stated and Vindicated by Scripture, Reason and Authority," the second part of which dealt particularly with the Baptists. The controversy closed with " Twenty-one Divines, whose Names are hereunder affixed, cleared of the unjust Criminations of W. Penn in his pretended ' Just Rebuke ' for their Epistle to a Book entitled ' Quakerism no Christianity,' "

In 1673 the " hat controversy " was revived by an anonymous pamphlet, " The Spirit of the Hat: or, the Government of the Quakers." It was obviously written by one of Perrot's school, and the authorship has been ascribed to William Mucklow, who lived at Mortlake, and who had suffered for Quakerism, but had in 1671 "gone out," that is, apostatized, probably over the questions raised by Perrot. Penn replied to this tract with " The Spirit of Alexander the Coppersmith, lately Revived and now Justly Rebuked." His adversary next produced " Tyranny and Hypocrisy Detected: or A Further Discovery of Tyrannical Government, Popish Principles, and Vile Practices of the now Leading Quakers," but Penn ended the wrangle with a pamphlet of 130 pages, " Judas and the Jews combined against Christ and His Followers."

In 1674 Fox was tried and imprisoned at Worcester, and he tells how " the Earl of Salisbury's son " came to his aid and took a copy of the errors which were in the indictment. Fox also had a statement of his case drawn up, and his wife took it to the King, who told her that he could do nothing, and sent her to Lord Chancellor Finch, who said that the King could do nothing except by a pardon. This, however, Fox would not receive, as to accept a pardon would be an admission of ill-doing. A petition on his behalf was presented by the Quakers, and the King ordered his release, on security to appear within a convenient time or when called for.[1]   Finch at last granted a writ of *habeas corpus* to bring the case before the King's Bench, where the indict-

[1] C.S.P.D., August 11th, 1674.

ment was quashed on the ground of errors in it, and Lord Chief Justice Hale ordered Fox to be set at liberty.[1]

The Quakers and the Baptists frequently fell foul of each other, especially on the subject of the sacraments, in which the Quakers did not believe at all. John Gratton, for instance, endeavoured to show that no man had a commission from Christ to baptize with water, since St. John the Baptist's race was run, and his ministry fulfilled.[2] In 1668 three Baptists, William Burnet, Matthew Caffin, and Jeremy Ives, attacked George Whitehead on the question of the Resurrection and the taking up of Christ's body into heaven. The irrepressible Solomon Eccles challenged the Baptists to prove who were the true worshippers of Christ, by first fasting for seven days without food or drink, and then abstaining from sleep for the same period.[3] Penn, when he was released from prison in 1669, challenged Ives to a public disputation, which took place at High Wycombe, where, according to the Quaker version of the affair, Penn easily routed his antagonist.[4] Luke Howard, who had originally been a Baptist, but had turned Quaker since the Restoration, published in 1672 "A Looking-glass for Baptists," which provoked a reply from Richard Hobbs, "The Quaker's Looking-glass Looked Upon."[5] In the same year a Baptist signing himself "H. G." the initials of Henry Grigg, published a tract, "Light from the Sun of Righteousness," which purported to be a letter from a man in England to his sister in Barbados, "but more especially for the good of poor, weak, wavering Christians to help and recover them out of the snare of Satan." The writer warned his sister against the "evil and soul-undoing" principles of the Quakers, and discussed the sacraments and the doctrine of the inward light. In "The Babylonish Baptist" George Whitehead attacked the contradictions in Grigg's pamphlet, and showed great misunderstanding of his opponent's position and meaning. Grigg replied with "The Baptist not Babylonish : or, the Quaker's Tongue no Slander," in which he accused Whitehead of "malice, ignorance and insolence."

In 1673 George Fox had many controversies in London, "where the Baptists and Socinians and old apostates were very rude, and had given forth many books against us."[6] Thomas Hicks, a Baptist minister, was one of these controversialists, and had published "A Dialogue between a Christian and a Quaker," in which all kinds of false and foolish statements were put into the Quaker's mouth. George Whitehead made a fierce assault on the Baptists in 1672 in "The Dipper Plunged: or Thomas

[1] Fox, "Journal"; Sewell, "Hist. Quakers," pp. 500–504.
[2] "Journal of John Gratton," 1779, p. 83.
[3] Sewell, "Hist. Quakers," p. 470.
[4] Airey, "William Penn," Encycl. Brit., 9th ed.
[5] Lewis, "Brief Hist. Anabaptism in Eng.," 1738.   [6] Fox, "Journal."

Hicks' feigned Dialogue between a Christian and a Quaker proved an Unchristian Forgery, consisting of Self-Contradictions and Abuses against the Truth and People called Quakers, wherein Thomas Hicks has Seconded, though in Envy Exceeded, his brother Henry Grigg in his Babylonish Pamphlet styled, ' Light from the Sun of Righteousness.' " The tract by Penn and Whitehead, entitled " The Christian Quaker and his Divine Testimony Stated and Vindicated from the Scripture, Reason and Authority," was partly concerned with the controversy with Faldo and partly with the Baptists. Hicks published a " Continuation of the Dialogue," his " dialogues or rather diabologues " as Ellwood scornfully called them, and Penn returned to the charge with " Reason against Railing and Truth against Fiction: in which Thomas Hicks' Disingenuity is Represented, his Profaneness is Rebuked, his Perjuries are Detected, his Cavils are Confounded, and Thomas Hicks is Proved to be no Christian by Several Short Arguments, raised from his ungodly Way of Procedure aganst us." [1] In a " Further Continuation " Hicks claimed to have shown the Quakers condemned out of their own mouth. The last contribution was called " The Counterfeit Christian Detected, against the Vile Forgeries, Gross Perversions, Black Slanders, Plain Contradictions and Scurrilous Language of T. Hicks, an Anabaptist Preacher, by a Lover of Truth and Peace." This was by William Penn, and probably appeared early in 1674.

In this last Penn had appealed to the Baptists for justice against Hicks' misstatements, and that there should be no pretence that they were ignorant of this appeal, copies were given away outside some of the Baptist meeting houses. A meeting of leading Baptists, " to take cognizance of Thomas Hicks' proceedings against the people called Quakers," was held in the Barbican meeting house on August 28th, 1674. More trouble arose about this. The Quaker story is that the Baptists contrived to fix the meeting for a day on which Penn and Whitehead, the Quaker champions, were away from town, and could not be brought back at such short notice.[2] The Baptist story is that they invited Penn and Whitehead to be present, but hearing that they were away, they sent to John Osgood, another Quaker, to tell him that he or any other Friends would be welcome, and that as it was only a question of facts which they had to deal with in the case of Hicks, they conceived they might proceed to hear his defence. Further, it was reported that Penn was not far from London after the invitation was sent to him. Others said that he was at home the day before.[3] Whatever happened, no Quaker was present at the meeting, which was presided over by Kiffin, who read the Quakers' appeal, and said

[1] 1673.   [2] Graham, " Life of Penn," p. 87.
[3] Crosby, " Hist. Eng. Baptists," II. 296.

their business was to decide whether Hicks was guilty of false accusations against the Quakers. Hicks made a long speech, in which he endeavoured to prove from the writings of the Quakers themselves that they were guilty of twelve errors of doctrine In fairness it must be said that he sometimes misunderstood his authorities, and sometimes quoted passages apart from their context. His attack on their matters of practice was largely directed against their methods of controversy. As regards doctrine, we may add that none of the disputants was a trained theologian, and as to the methods of controversy both sides were fairly abusive.

A full report of the meeting was published in 1674, under the title of " The Quakers' Appeal Answered." Nineteen leading Baptists signed the statement in the report that the quotations which Hicks made from the Quakers' books were authentic. Hicks being thus exonerated, the Quakers were very angry, and demanded another meeting. In a printed broadside, published in September, called " William Penn's Just Complaint," Penn offered to meet Hicks " with the Bible in one hand and his Dialogue in the other." Thomas Rudyard published " The Barbican Cheat Detected," in which he accused the Baptists of trickery in giving the Quakers only eight days notice of the meeting, and criticised their report of it.[1]

Although at first they refused, and said that no man ought to be tried twice, the Baptists at last gave way to the Quakers' clamour, and agreed to a second meeting at the Barbican on October 9th. About twenty Quakers appeared, of whom Penn was one, and he told Fox that there were 6000 persons present, an impossible number. The disputants on the Quaker side were Whitehead, Keith, Penn, and Crisp, and on the Baptist side Kiffin, Hicks, Ives, Thomas Plant, and " Robert Ferguson, a Presbyterian." The Quakers behaved in a disorderly manner, so as to displease the whole auditory.[2] This was the Baptist account; the Quaker version was that their opponents, " by clamour and insults, diverted the complainants from prosecuting their charge against Hicks, and carried their point so far as to prevent its being heard, though frequent attempts were made to read it." [3] Both accounts show that it was a very disorderly meeting, with a great deal of hooting, interruption, and rude laughter. Ellwood began the meeting by reading his charges against Hicks, who then rose to make his defence. His first point was that the Quakers denied the deity of Christ, and he made specific charges against individuals of heresy in that respect. Then they all got out of their depth and wrangled at

---

[1] The prefatory remarks to this pamphlet were dated August 26th, two days before the meeting, but that may be a printer's error.
[2] Crosby, " Hist. Eng. Baptists," II. 306.
[3] Gough, " Hist. Quakers," II. 368–371.

cross purposes. Owing to the crowded state of the room, much damage was done to the building, the doors were broken, the seats torn out of their places, and the building itself creaked alarmingly.[1] The meeting broke up when it grew dark, without having come to a decision, the Baptists still asserting the Quakers were not Christians.[2]

As the Baptists refused to hold another meeting at the Barbican, the Quakers decided to have one at their own meeting-house in Wheeler Street, Spitalfields, on October 16th. A gallery was reserved for the Baptists, and Ives, Plant, and several others were there. Hicks refused to appear, and said that the Quakers were the appellants, and had no right to be judges, but the Quakers scandalously affirmed that he was in a neighbouring ale-house all the time. There was a great noise again, and the Quakers laid it to the charge of the Baptists. The Baptists wanted to take up the general accusation that the Quakers were not Christians, and the Quakers wished to prove that Hicks had falsely accused the Friends. In fact, the whole debate, until nearly the end, was what they should debate about. The Baptists said that Ives " so managed the Quakers, that they were obliged to break up without any further proceedings in the matter." [3] George Whitehead said at the conclusion of the meeting. " I have been concerned with many disputes and controversies about religion, and with divers sorts of people, but never met with such unfair dealing, clamorous work, and hideous noise in disputes from any people as from these men."[4]

Ellwood issued a broadside entitled " A Fresh Pursuit," in which he reiterated the charges against Hicks and his friends, and offered, if they would give a fair public meeting to their adversaries, to substantiate them all. Ellwood always bore a grudge against Ives after this time.[5] Thomas Plant wrote " A Contest for Christianity, or, a Faithful Relation of Two Late Meetings." Ellwood answered in a lengthy pamphlet, " Forgery no Christianity," in which he accused Plant of giving a false and partial account, and also attacked Ives, who had written a postscript to " A Contest." Rudyard and Hicks also entered on a wordy warfare. In reply to the former's " Barbican Cheat Detected," Hicks wrote " A Reply to Thomas Rudyard's Folly and Impertinency," and Rudyard countered this with " An Answer to a Scandalous Paper of T. Hicks." In this he repeated the charge that Hicks was in an ale-house while the last meeting

[1] " A Brief Account of the Most Material Passages . . . at the Barbican Meeting," 1674.
[2] Sewell, " Hist. Quakers," pp. 507–509; Graham, " Life of Penn," pp. 87–89.
[3] Crosby, " Hist. Eng. Baptists," II. 308.
[4] " A Narrative of the Second Meeting between the People called Quakers and Baptists," 1674.
[5] See his epitaph on Ives in " The History of Thomas Ellwood," pp. 313–316.

was being held, and once more discussed whether a Quaker could be a Christian. Hicks also wrote " The Quaker Condemned out of his own Mouth." An anonymous Baptist writer published " The Quaker's Quibbles," in which he drew a comparison between the Friends and the Muggletonians. This roused George Whitehead, who answered him in " The Quaker's Plainness detecting Fallacy," in which he declared the comparison unjust and absurd; and attacking another Baptist tract, " The Quaker's Appeal Answered," he said that the " forger's compurgators," by whom he meant Hicks's defenders, had by their " injustice, partiality and false glosses . . . given the chief occasion of these late contests." He argued about the soul, the Person of Christ, the Scriptures, and the light within, and dealt with " a slanderous accusation of T. Hicks against the Quakers." It seems that Whitehead had heard of a minister playing bowls, and said such conduct was unworthy of his profession, whereupon Hicks had accused him of slandering the brethren. This was the " slanderous accusation of T. Hicks." Whitehead also attacked Ives in " A Serious Search in Jeremy Ives's Questions to the Quakers," in which he declared Ives to be manifestly no Christian, as shown by his own, " observations, reviling, and ostentation." George Keith wrote a vindication of himself against Hicks and Kiffin.[1]

All these pamphlets were issued in the latter part of 1674. It was a fierce strife, and in the end both sides felt assured of victory. " The Lord's power came over all, and all their lying, wicked, scandalous books were answered," said Fox,[2] and the Quakers claimed that many Baptists were disgusted and came over to them.[3] Their rivals, however, said that as a result of the dispute the Quakers were so chastened that they could only denounce curses and judgments. There was a story told of a Quaker prophet who denounced a Baptist minister, and threatened him with leprosy, but the curse fell on himself and his family, who all became lepers, and were only healed at the intercession of the Baptist and his congregation. This and other similar stories were published in " A True and Impartial Narrative of the Eminent Hand of God that Befell a Quaker and his Family." Rudyard promptly issued " The Anabaptists' Lying Wonders," in answer to which there appeared " The Quaker's Subterfuge; or, Evasion Overturned."[4] Whether these wonders happened or not, many people believed they did. The strife between the two contending sects raged for years, not only in in England, but even in Barbados.[5]

Baxter had a great dislike for the Quakers, whom he described

---

[1] " George Keith's Vindication from the Forgeries and Abuses of T. Hicks and W. Kiffin," 1674.
[2] Fox, " Journal."   [3] Sewell, " Hist. Quakers," p. 504.
[4] Crosby, " Hist. Eng. Baptists," II. 310–312.
[5] Whitley, " Brit. Baptists," p. 128.

as " but the Ranters turned from horrid profaneness and blasphemy to a life of extreme austerity on the other side." Writing in 1664, he said, " Many Franciscan friars and other Papists have been proved to be disguised speakers in their assemblies and to be among them : and it's very like are the very soul of all these horrible delusions, but of late one William Penn is become their leader and would reform the sect, and set up a kind of ministry among them," [1] As a matter of fact, Penn did not become a minister of the Quakers till 1668. Baxter gave them credit for relieving " the sober people " in the days of persecution by their constancy in suffering, but complained that " the poor deluded souls would sometimes meet only to sit still in silence." [2] He disliked lay preachers of any sect, and objected to the Quaker preachers as incompetent, and poured scorn on their discourses as " a pitiful, raw and ignorant, affectionate manner of expression and loudness of preacher's voice." [3]

In 1675 he was living at Rickmansworth, and finding that, through the influence of Penn, the neighbourhood abounded in Quakers, " was desirous of that the poor people should once hear what was to be said for their recovery." The result was a debate between himself and Penn, lasting for seven hours. Two rooms were filled with people, among them one lord, two knights, and four ministers of the Church of England. The subjects discussed were the ministry, the true church, and the inner light. Penn once apparently lost his temper, and called Baxter a devil, and the latter said complacently, " The success gave me cause to believe that it was not labour lost." A second debate followed, and perhaps a third.[4]

As time went on a marked divergence appeared between two sections of Quakerism. Some Friends, believing their religion to be that which more than any other satisfied the needs of the age, spent their money lavishly, laboured abundantly, and toiled to gather others into the fold. Whatever gifts they possessed, whether learning, influence, or eloquence, they used for the society. A mere collection of individuals, they felt, was incapable of the most effective missionary work : the whole system must be tightened up ; there must be order and government. Other members felt that this was contrary to the spirit of Quakerism : " Not by might, nor by power, but by My Spirit, saith the Lord of Hosts." God worked, they believed, by the influence of the Spirit within, by heavenly illumination, not through the development of a theological system or the organisation of a sect. They objected to the autocracy of Fox, they distrusted the learning of Barclay, and they were, above all, suspicious of Penn. A courtier, a scholar, and an aristocrat,

---

[1] " Rel. Baxt.," p. 77.   [2] *Ibid.*, p. 438.
[3] Baxter, " Cure of Church Divisions," 1670.
[4] Graham, " Life of Penn," p. 94; " Rel. Baxt.," II. 174.

with his insistence on law and rights, he was just the type of man to lead the society down the old bad road which the other sects had followed. This attitude of mind was expressed by William Burrell [1] and John Crook, who deplored the lack of realisation among the brethren of the all-importance of the inward light, so that they were glorying in the abilities of men, and not depending on the Spirit of Truth. [2]

It was this spirit which underlay the Wilkinson–Story revolt, this question of principle. John Wilkinson and John Story, two North of England Quakers, against whose personal character not even the most hostile critic has ever breathed a word, felt that the spiritual life of the society was in grave danger. Fox seemed to be becoming a pope, and the Yearly Meeting which he had set up a kind of supreme court. Quakers of the old school, they maintained that there could be no discipline in matters of belief. Against the view that a Christian church ought to disown its members for a breach of its fundamental articles, they held that if such articles were against the light of Christ in the individual conscience, then to demand submission to them was a breach of liberty. They objected to the rule which forbade Quakers to pay tithes, because it was a rule; they said it should be left to a man's conscience whether he paid them or not; they disliked the establishment of the Monthly and Quarterly Meetings for Women, as giving women more power than they had the ability to use, and they defended the practice of fleeing in time of persecution, [3] probably because the custom not to flee had hardened into an unwritten law; not quite though, for there had been some few instances of weakness. At Looe, in Cornwall, the Friends had met on the sands, and at Preston Patrick in the woods, so as to be able to say that they had not met in a building, which the Act forbade them to do. [4] There were many minor details also to which Wilkinson and Story objected, such as Fox's rules about marriages, the composition of the Monthly and Quarterly Meetings, the entry of " papers of condemnation " in the church books, and the practice of groaning and singing at meetings while someone else was praying. [5] They were really testifying against the crushing of individual liberty of conscience by a system of majority rule, [6] but if they had got their way about fleeing in time of persecution, it would have been a great set-back for the cause of religious liberty in England, for the Quakers hitherto had been in the forefront of the battle.

[1] " A Testimony against Hypocrites and Deceivers," 1676.
[2] John Crook, " An Epistle to all that Profess the Light of Jesus Christ within to be their Guide," 1678.
[3] *Journal Friends Hist. Soc.*, I. 57–61; X. 182.
[4] Braithwaite, " Second Period," p. 375.
[5] *Ibid.*, pp. 297–298; Barclay, " Inner Life," pp. 442–443.
[6] Hodgkin, " George Fox," p. 249.

At a Quarterly Meeting in April 1675 the malcontents made a proposal that only delegates should be allowed to take part in the business, and that others who attended, if they had anything to say, should say it and go. The meeting rejected this, and an opposition meeting was set up in the following month. An attempt at reunion was made at a great meeting at Sedbergh in 1676, but it was unsuccessful, and a good deal of personal feeling between the leaders of both parties was imported into the contest. There were three abortive meetings at Bristol in 1677, and until 1682 the controversy went on at most of the meetings throughout the kingdom. William Rogers, a wealthy merchant of Bristol, wrote a book in defence of the malcontent leaders, "The Christian Quaker distinguished from the Apostate and Innovator," a large work in five parts. Robert Barclay, on the other side wrote, "The Anarchy of the Ranters," and there seems, it is true, some ground for thinking that Wilkinson and Story and their followers had something in common with the Ranters and Seekers.[1] Ellwood, in 1682, wrote "An Antidote against the Infection of William Rogers's Book, miscalled 'The Christian Quaker.'" Rogers, in 1685, published some verses, "A Second Scourge for George Whitehead," and Ellwood, who could write better verses, responded with "Rogero-Mastix." Rogers and Ellwood held a great debate at one of the Yearly Meetings, and, according to Ellwood, after a hot discussion Rogers retired beaten. Throughout the strife the great mass of the Quakers remained faithful to Fox and his discipline, but the others continued their separate meetings till after Fox's death. Story died in 1681, and his life was written by some of his friends, under the title, "The Memory of that Servant of God, John Story, Revived." This was in 1683, and Thomas Camm, of the orthodox party, replied with "The Line of Truth," in which he set out "to detect the hypocrisy and deceit of Story's friends in applauding him." [2]   Rogers got possession of the meeting-house at Bristol in 1681, and the books belonging to it, and in Reading in 1685 the separatists at that place turned the others out into the street. Much the same thing was done in other places, but this alienated a good deal of sympathy from the dissentients, while another consequence was that in some places the records were lost.

Wilkinson never returned to the Quakers, and his schism died out early in the eighteenth century. A number of his followers returned, however, to the fold, and some of them brought back the principles of the Ranters and Seekers, with which principles some of the moderate Quakers who had not gone out with the seceders were already infected. The result was that Quakerism

---

[1] Hodgkin, "George Fox," p. 249.
[2] Braithwaite, "Second Period," pp. 299–323; Turner, "The Quakers," pp. 161–162; "The History of Thomas Ellwood."

became strongly marked by " the quietism of the Seekers, who denied all orders and officers, and the ultra-democratic views of pantheistic Ranters, who levelled all distinctions of office."[1] Stephen Crisp, as early as 1681, specified some of the subjects which were even then being discussed in Quaker circles—the mortality of the soul, the sleep of the soul, the future punishment of devils, the view that hell exists only here on earth in the conscience, and the theory that future punishment will not be eternal.[2] This heterodoxy weakened Quakerism considerably. Whatever the opinions of the founders of Quakerism had been, they were at heart sound on the fundamentals of Christianity.[3]

About 1675 the Quakers presented an address to the King and Parliament, showing that many of the Acts under which they suffered were made against popish recusants. They explained once more why they could not take the oaths, and quoted passages of Scripture against swearing. Because of this they suffered imprisonment, some of them for as long as ten or twelve years, and some had died in prison. Any person who bore malice against a Quaker could get him thrown into prison by getting some one in authority to tender him the oaths. They pleaded their honourable behaviour for fifteen years past, and begged that no penalties might be inflicted on them for obeying their consciences.[4] The petition was signed on behalf of the Quakers by James Park, John Grove, and Ellis Hookes, and was afterwards printed.

In 1675 the persecution, which had slackened somewhat, began to blaze up again. The old cry of " 1641 and the Church in danger " was raised, and Danby exerted himself to put the Clarendon Code in force again. But times were changing, and many people who had no sympathy with Dissenters of any sort were slow to prosecute them. The Court party, throughout 1676, urged the enforcement of the law, but as the fear of popery increased, the fear of the rule of the saints decreased, and after that year there were few prosecutions under the second Conventicle Act for some time, though the zeal of individuals occasionally put some of the other laws in motion.

On March 16th, 1678, there was a great debate in the House of Commons on the question, brought up by Sir Thomas Lee, of Quakers being convicted under the statutes against popish recusants. The judges had been directed by the Lord Chancellor to put the laws in execution against recusants, and the Quakers had been prosecuted under those laws, and their estates

---

[1] Barclay, " Inner Life," pp. 462–473; Braithwaite, " Second Period," pp. 469–481.
[2] S. Crisp, " A Faithful Warning and Exhortation to Friends to beware of Seducing Spirits," 1681.
[3] Wilkinson, " Storyism in Wiltshire," *Journal Friends Hist. Soc.*, XVI. 143–146; Ferguson, " Early Cumberland and Westmorland Friends," pp. 64–65.
[4] C.S.P.D., 370/41.

had been confiscated.   They had appealed, and it was considered hard that they should suffer under statutes which had been made before they were heard of.   Winnington, the Solicitor-General, said that the laws against popery were never intended to fall on the Quakers, nor was it ever conceived that they should come under Queen Elizabeth's statute against recusancy.   Sir Edward Dering thought something should be done, but he feared giving a chance whereby the Papists might escape, and considered that it would be better the Quakers should suffer than that; after all, they refused to pay their dues, and kept men out of their own.   Secretary Coventry pointed out that notwithstanding the rigours that were complained of, conventicles were as frequent as ever.   Indulgence given to people who denied the sacraments was punishment to those who believed in them.   The Quakers appeared to hold themselves absolved from all bonds of government.   Sir Humphrey Winch called the attention of the House to the fact that the penalties to which the Quakers were subject under the anti-papal laws sometimes amounted to more than their whole revenue.   Sir John Birkenhead wished to know why any distinction should be made.   The Quakers were led by the Jesuits, and called themselves Protestants, while refusing to protest against the Pope.   Colonel Titus thought it strange that those who acknowledged the Pope and those who did not should both be punished, and asked whether it was prudent to treat Protestant recusants, who believed the Pope to be Antichrist, in such a way as to unite in a common cause the Presbyterian, the Quaker, the Anabaptist, and the Independent. Sir Thomas Meres protested against taking away all the power of the anti-popery laws because Quakers were affected thereby. Waller pointed out that a Papist was not punished without conviction, and he might traverse the indictment.   If convicted, he forfeited two-thirds of his estate.   The Quaker might be tried by a single justice of the peace, mulcted of more than he was worth, and the laws against him extended to death itself.   No reason could satisfy the Quakers, but they were " the best at suffering that ever people were."   Severity, however, only brought them sympathy, and for that reason they had increased in numbers. Colonel Birch wished that if a Committee were appointed to consider the matter, it should be instructed to make a difference between Papists and Quakers and *other* Protestant Dissenters. Sir Charles Wheeler objected to the word " other " as implying that the Quakers were Protestants.   Secretary Williamson thought they could neither be considered as Roman nor Protestant recusants; they were so abominable that they were not Christians, their doctrines being inconsistent with the fundamentals of Christianity.

A Committee was appointed to inquire how far the Quakers and other Dissenters suffered from the laws against popery.[1]

[1] Grav. " Debates," V. 250–255.

When it met instances were produced of the different treatment meted out to Papists and Friends in various parts of the country. The Quakers put in a written statement on the matter, to which they said the whole body of their members would subscribe.[1] Penn gave evidence, and dared, what few other men of the time would have dared, to denounce the attempt to force the consciences of Papists by penal laws. He also asked that Quakers might be allowed to affirm instead of taking oaths. The Committee recommended relief, but Parliament was prorogued before anything was done.[2]

William Penn was very busy in politics during 1679. When Algernon Sidney sought election for Guildford, he went to support him. He tried to make a speech, but the Recorder refused to allow him, and was anxious to make him take the oaths. When his candidate was rejected, Penn proposed to get a legal opinion on the subject, visited the Whig leaders, and was active in getting up a petition.[3] He wrote " England's Great Interest in the Choice of a New Parliament," in which he urged a full inquiry into the Popish Plot, pleaded for ease to Protestant Dissenters, begged his readers to consider how the Quakers had suffered for years past, and advised that sincere Protestants, not concealed Papists, should be elected. Penn also wrote this year, " An Address to Protestants upon the Present Conjuncture," and " One Project for the Good of England, that is, Our Civil Union is our Civil Safety." In the latter, after pointing out that Protestants did not owe allegiance to a foreign power, as the Romanists did, and that it was to the advantage of both Churchmen and Dissenters that the Pope should have no dominion in England, he urged that Churchmen could not injure Dissenters without undermining liberty. He therefore proposed that everyone in England on a certain day should be compelled to make a public disavowal of the chief Roman Catholic doctrines, and of the Pope's claim to be able to depose sovereigns and absolve subjects from their allegiance. He was careful to say, however, that while he would keep Romanists out of public affairs, he would not have them punished for their beliefs. He suggested Ash Wednesday as a suitable day for the public disavowal, because on that day the Pope cursed all Protestants.

In April 1679 both Houses of Parliament were busy about the Popish Plot and with expedients for the suppression of popery. There was a great debate in the Lords about distinguishing between Nonconformists and Roman Catholics. The Quakers offered to sign a declaration of their obedience and of their opinions, and volunteered that if any Papist should be found among them, it should be treated as felony.[4] The House of

---

[1] Marvell, " Letters to the Corporation of Hull," March 23rd, 1678.
[2] Clarkson, " Life of Penn," I. 227–228.
[3] Ewald, " Life of Sidney," II. 53–63; Clarkson, " Life of Penn," I. 249–252. [4] Hist. MSS. Com., Ormonde MSS., V. 56–67.

Commons was concerning itself with the same subject, and was anxious that Papists might not shelter themselves under other names. " This difficulty," said Algernon Sidney, " is chiefly occasioned by the Quakers, who for more than one reason are thought least to deserve much to be cared for." [1]

In the autumn there was another general election, and Sidney was a candidate for Bramber. There Penn's influence was strong, and he worked hard for his friend again, but again without success. This electioneering on Penn's part caused much searching of heart amongst many of the Quakers. The Meeting for Sufferings on February 20th, 1679, instructed Thomas Zachary to write him about it, though in March they gave their approval to a letter which he had drawn up for the Friends to send to their members of Parliament asking them to redress the grievances of Dissenters. But as regards actual electioneering, the leaders, though their sympathies were Whig, urged their followers to vote for sober and moderate men, and warned them to be careful of giving offence. This excursion of Penn's into politics did them a great deal of harm. The Conventicle Act was enforced with rigour in many places because the Quakers and others had taken the opposition side at the elections. [2]   At Court it was said that if Penn or Whitehead had not taken up this political attitude, the persecution might have ceased. Sir Leoline Jenkins, the Secretary, told a Quaker, Richard Davies, that he himself was not against the Friends; but they voted for men who opposed the King's interests. [3]

In November and December 1680 there again appeared a disposition on the part of Parliament to make a distinction between Papists and Protestant Dissenters. A document, " The Case of the People called Quakers," was presented to the King and Parliament, which once more set forth their plea, and closed with a summary which estimated the known cases of suffering already endured as 10,778. [4]   The Commons appointed a Committee to inquire into the troubles of the Quakers under the penal laws. Penn, Whitehead, and Meade attended, and amongst other things were asked if they considered themselves Protestant Dissenters. Sir Christopher Musgrave said that the prisons were filled with them, many had been excommunicated, and it was a shame and scandal that they should be so used. There were several Bills before Parliament at this time for the relief of the Dissenters. The Quakers induced the Committee of the Commons to introduce a clause permitting them to make a declaration of fidelity instead of taking the oaths, and

[1] Algernon Sidney, " Letters to Henry Savile," April 28th, 1679.
[2] Whiting, " Persecution Exposed."
[3] " Life of Richard Davies," 1710, p. 184; Braithwaite, " Second Period," pp. 95, 112; Clarkson, " Life of Penn."
[4] Whiting, " Persecution Exposed," pp. 69–70.

Alderman Love and Colonel Birch carried a proposal, which, as Whitehead indignantly told them, would have given relief to the Presbyterians and Independents while leaving the Quakers exposed to persecution. None of the Bills, however, became law.[1]

Towards the end of 1681 the Quakers tried to force the hand of the Government in the matter of the tests. All over the country they were signing in great numbers the written declaration contained in the Act of 30 Car. II. for disabling Papists from sitting in Parliament, and they declared that their purpose was to manifest that they were not popish recusants, in the hope that they might not suffer under the laws against such. Ninety-four took the test " at Widow Harrison's before Sir Daniel and William Fleming " of Rydal.[2] Herbert Aubrey, a Hertford-shire justice, wrote to Sir Leoline Jenkins saying that in that county the Quakers were daily urging people to take the test, and to get certificates of having done so. The Lord Chief Baron of the Exchequer and the justices of the peace in Norfolk and Suffolk had allowed these affirmations to be made in their presence, and he himself had accepted several of these certified affirmations, but was not certain of his legal power to do so. The Secretary informed him that the matter was being considered by the Privy Council,[3] but nothing further seems to have been done.

Throughout the years 1682 and 1683 persecution raged fiercely, especially in London and Bristol. In the latter year there were 700 Quakers in prison in England at one time, and the Rye House plot, of course, made matters worse for all. By the end of 1682 nearly all the meeetings of the other Protestant Dissenters had been suppressed, except for a few who met secretly at night; but the Quakers still stood firm. John Whitehead of York was arrested in May 1682 on suspicion of being a Jesuit, and for conventicling. At the Assizes he refused the oaths, but proffered a declaration in almost the same words. This, of course, could not legally be accepted, and he remained in prison certainly for the greater part of 1683.[4] William Penn, perhaps fortunately for himself, went to Pennsylvania with 100 emigrants in 1682, to found his new colony, and remained there for two years. In Pennsylvania the Quakers would be in contact with the brethren of their own religion, and might look forward to material prosperity as a reward of industry; but they did not flee there to escape persecution; that would have been contrary to one of their chief principles. Thomas Ellwood published in 1683 " A Caution to Constables and other Inferior Officers concerned

[1] Gough, " Hist. Quakers," II. 507–511.
[2] Hist. MSS. Com., Fleming MSS. at Rydal, No. 2453.
[3] C.S.P.D., Nov. 9th, 1681, 417/88, 124; Entry Book 62, p. 357.
[4] " The Gospel Labours of John Whitehead," 1704.

in the Execution of the Conventicle Act: with some Observations Thereon." The work was brought before the notice of the King and Council, and Ellwood himself was charged before the magistrates with publishing a seditious book. He affirmed his innocence, and refused to give bail, but was released on his promise to appear when called upon.[1]

There was a strong Quaker colony in Norwich, which had been founded during the Commonwealth by Whitehead and Pennington. In March 1679 their first meeting-house was opened in Goat Lane, and meetings were held regularly, with occasional disturbances, until 1681, when a fierce persecution broke out. In the following year they were forcibly kept out of their meeting-house. Undismayed, they held their meetings in the streets, and numbers of them were arrested from time to time, until, towards the end of the year, nearly all the men, to the number of eighty, were in Norwich gaol, where they conducted the business meetings of the society, while the women and girls continued to hold meetings outside.[2]

In March 1683 Whitehead and Latey presented before the Council a paper setting forth the case of the Norwich Quakers, but were hindered from reading it on the ground that it was not in proper form as a petition. They complained of this treatment to the Lord Privy Seal, but were told that notwithstanding what had happened, the King had recommended the judges to inquire into the condition of the prisoners and the usage they were receiving. After this they had two interviews with the King himself. Whitehead gave an account of the second interview, which was at Hampton Court. "As we drew nearer we saw it was the King, and not being willing to go abruptly into his presence, to open our case to him without his leave, at a little distance I called to the King, desiring him to favour us a few words, which he presently granting, one of the gentlemen who knew us came to us, and gently took off our hats, and hung them on the pales of a fence before the court, and then we went to the King who was ready to hear us." The King discussed with them the question of hats, and their use of thee and thou and yea and nay, and pointed out that many Quakers took oaths rather than lose their vote at elections. Whitehead replied that such persons had left the society. He said further to the King, " We desire nothing to be done to the prejudice or dishonour of the King, nor to join with or promote any interest against the King. The Lord knows our hearts. We have not any design or desire for the subversion or change of the government. Nor can we reasonably be supposed to have any such design, seeing we were deep sufferers in Cromwell's time, as I myself was." The King gave them a favourable answer, promising them that

[1] " History of Thomas Ellwood."
[2] Platt, " The Quakers in Norwich," Norwich, 1926.

the case of the Norwich Quakers should be brought before the Council. At the summer Assizes they were all set free.[1]

On August 8th, 1683, the Quakers presented to the King and the Duke of York an address in which they declared themselves " clear in the sight of God, angels, and men from all hellish plots and traitorous conspiracies, and from all murderous designs against the King, his brother, or any person on earth whatsoever." It was presented by George Whitehead and others, and bore over 1000 signatures; but the persecution continued in spite of the kindly reception the petition received from the King.[2]

In 1685, by order of the Government, the Quaker meeting-house in Southwark was wrecked. It had been utterly demolished in 1670, the task of demolition having been expressly committed to Christopher Wren, who was then Surveyor-General of His Majesty's Works.[3] This time the walls of the building were left, but the wreckers tore down the wainscot, broke the benches, carted away the doors and casements, and did great damage to the grounds on which the building stood by pulling down the palings and cutting down the trees.[4] On March 1st, 1685, the Friends published another official account of the sufferings of their people. The last had been issued in 1680, and they now said that since then seventy-eight more had died through the persecution, and they gave " the total number of sufferings, imprisonments, and prosecutions since 1660 " as 12,316.[5] In the same month Whitehead, Latey, and Alexander Parker presented a petition to the new King. They complained that many of their friends had been convicted unsummoned and unheard in their own defence. Many had been fined £20 a month, or had had two-thirds of their estates confiscated. Merciless informers spoiled the goods of others, and treated them with open violence. To some not a bed was left, to others no cattle, corn, or tools. A list was appended showing that in the various counties of England 1460 Quakers were in gaol. Whitehead reminded the King that Charles II., after his coronation, had issued a proclamation discharging the Quakers from prison, and also that when he issued the Declaration of Indulgence in 1672 he also put forth letters of pardon under the Great Seal. James replied that he too intended to issue a general pardon in connection with his coronation. It had been delayed lest some persons connected with the late plot should get the advantage of it, and so be free to sit in Parliament, which would be dangerous; but he still intended that the Quaker prisoners should be discharged. " And for the Declaration you speak of in 1672, I was the cause of drawing up that Declaration, and I never gave my consent to the making

[1] Besse, " Sufferings."   [2] Sewell, " Hist. Quakers," 563.
[3] Neal, " Puritans," IV. 501.   [4] Besse, " Sufferings."
[5] " To the Bishops and Clergy of England and Wales, the State of Cruel Persecution . . . inflicted on the People called Quakers," 1685.

of it void. It was the Presbyterians who caused it to be made
void in Parliament." Whitehead urged that it was possible to
defend the Church of England and yet grant indulgence to
tender consciences, and the King replied that he quite agreed.
The Quakers also complained about the informers, and James
said he would see what measures could be taken to stop them.[1]

Not long after this another petition was presented to the
King and both Houses of Parliament, stating their grievances in
much the same way. Three hundred and twenty had died in
prison since 1660. Sometimes the goods representing fines for
eleven months together were seized at once, a proceeding which
was to the profit of the informers, who got a third of the fines.
Appeals were expensive, especially in consideration of the treble
costs against an unsuccessful appellant, yet no costs or restorations
were granted against informers who made unjust or unsuccessful prosecutions. The petitioners then proceeded to a rather neat
argument. Only a third of the fines went to the King, so that
he could only remit that proportion, and not the other two-
thirds which went to the informers and the poor, and the
petitioners naïvely inquired if it were not against his prerogative
thus to restrain his sovereign clemency.[2]

When James came to the throne Penn became a person of
great influence at Court, and of this many people were glad to
avail themselves. Admiral Penn on his deathbed had recommended his son to the care of James, Duke of York, and a
curious attachment seems to have grown up between the two,
considering how profoundly they differed in religion. But there
was a common bond between them in that they both honestly
believed in liberty of conscience. To assume, as is so often done,
that the profession of desire for liberty of conscience for all was
just a trick on the part of James to get Romanism established, is
contrary to all the facts of his life. Whether, if he had succeeded
in establishing the Roman Church as the Church of the land, the
ecclesiastical authorities would have allowed liberty of conscience is another thing. They probably would not have done
so. But the same would have been the case with the Independents if James had sought to establish them. Also, whether
James set about it in the wisest way is another matter. But the
fact remains that James did more for liberty of conscience than
was done by the boasted Toleration Act, and lost his crown
because he wanted to do then what the English people would not
do till 1829, and because their bigotry insisted on a policy to
which we owe half our troubles in Ireland to this very day. To
the ordinary man James may have been a fool to his own interest
in holding to his principles till he lost his throne, but if he had
been a hypocrite as well, shrewd men like Penn and Whitehead

[1] Besse, " Sufferings "; Whitehead, " Christian Progress," pp. 575–579.
[2] Besse, " Sufferings."

would soon have found him out. Before his coronation James told Penn that " he desired not that peaceable men should be disturbed for their religion." Penn took up his residence at Holland House, so as to be near the King, and when he wanted to return to America James would not let him go. By his influence some 1200 or 1300 Quakers were released from prison in 1686, and there was no more wholesale imprisonment after this. His efforts were not solely on behalf of the Friends. He obtained a pardon for John Locke, who had been banished in 1683, but Locke refused the pardon and remained abroad. Charlewood Lawton, who was in trouble over Monmouth's rebellion, and Aaron Smith and Trenchard, who had been concerned in the Rye House plot, obtained their pardons through Penn. By his influence Lawton and Trenchard obtained an interview with the King, who allowed the former to talk quite freely to him against the dispensing power.[1]

Only a few Quakers were out with Monmouth. Some members of the Society published a disavowal of any connection with him, and a " testimony against all plots, conspiracies, and rebellions," and said, " We conspire with no man, no sect, no sort of people, against the King, his peace, and his government." To a charge made by Roger L'Estrange in " The Observator " that Monmouth's Declaration had been printed by a Quaker printer, they replied, " We know nothing thereof, neither of the Quaker chosen, nor the chooser of him, nor of the Declaration itself, except by report."[2] George Hussey and Thomas Paul, both of Frome, and both Quakers, were executed for taking part in the rising.[3] The Quarterly Meeting books of Somersetshire have some entries about " members concerned in the late war."[4] The Taunton Monthly Meeting dealt with John Hellier and Francis Scott, who had given scandal by joining in the insurrection contrary to the principles of the Society. This Francis Scott was the husband of John Whiting's sister-in-law,[5] and in 1692 he expressed to the meeting his repentance for his conduct. Lord Macaulay makes William Penn act a shameful part in connection with the transactions at the close of the rebellion. He accuses him of wringing a heavy ransom from the friends of the Taunton girls who presented the flag and Bible to Monmouth, and of attending the executions of Alderman Cornish and Elizabeth Gaunt as a mere vulgar spectator of bloodshed, and he includes him among " the heartless and venial sycophants of Whitehall " who thought Kiffin might be bought over to the King's party by an alderman's gown and a grant of money.

[1] Graham, " Life of Penn," pp. 176–177; Croese, " Gen. Hist. Quakers," II. 105.
[2] " The Christian Principle and Peaceable Conversation of the People of God called Quakers," 1685.
[3] Locke, " Western Rebellion," p. 7.
[4] *Journal Friends Hist. Soc.*, XV. 41.   [5] *Ibid.*, XII. 36.

Macaulay has been accused of religious animus in making these charges,[1] but it is enough to say that Macaulay's history is Whig in outlook, and every friend of James was long a suspect in Whig eyes. The charges have all been abundantly disproved,[2] and need not be further referred to here.

On March 15th, 1686, moved by the various appeals which had come to him from the Quakers, the King issued a royal mandate in which he expressed his desire that the Friends should receive the full benefits of the general pardon which had been issued, and that all Quakers in prison should be discharged. He directed the Attorney-General to enter a *noli prosequi* against all processes against them, and no more such processes were to be issued from the Exchequer.[3] The prisoners met with some difficulty from the clerks and other officials in respect of fees demanded for the legal steps of their release. These appeared to them exorbitant, but after some haggling on both sides a composition was arrived at, and the matter satisfactorily settled.[4] But they still refused to pay tithes, and many of them continued to suffer on this head, and others were imprisoned this year for unlawful assembly; but most of them were discharged from time to time by the Attorney-General's order.

In 1686, mindful of his promise to the Quakers, James II. granted a commission to Richard Graham, Principal of Clifford's Inn, and to Philip Burton, both solicitors to the King, to inquire into the doings of the informers. The Commissioners authorised George Whitehead to issue summonses to those informers against whom the Quakers had complained, and to the Quakers who suffered at their hands, with instructions to both sides to bring their witnesses. The first sitting of the Commission was on June 4th in Clifford's Inn. The weather was hot and the room crowded. Some forty-three of the informers had been notified, and had brought a lawyer to defend them. Whitehead collected and fairly stated the cases of about fifty Quakers, and began with those in which the informers had sworn falsely as to the facts, and those in which excessive distress had been levied with violence. After the sitting, the case having gone badly against them, the informers tried to get Whitehead and the other leaders of their opponents imprisoned, so that the proceedings might fall; but they were unsuccessful in this, owing to their inability to find witnesses to appear against them. At the conclusion of the second and last sitting, on June 14th, the Quakers had not got through half their case, but the Commissioners thought they had heard enough evidence for their purpose. They showed

---

[1] Graham, "Life of Penn," p. 313.
[2] Hepworth Dixon, "Life of Penn"; Graham, "Life of Penn"; Paget, "New Examen," 1861.
[3] Besse, "Sufferings"; Whitehead, "Christian Progress."
[4] Gough, "Hist. Quakers," III. 177–178.

Whitehead their draft report, which he thought very deficient, for instead of dealing with matters of fact regarding the conduct of the informers, it presented proposals to limit the prosecution of Quakers to the less ruinous of the penal laws. Whitehead pointed out to them that it was not their business to dictate to the King on such matters, they only had to report on facts, but one of the Commissioners informed him that they were in a great difficulty, inasmuch as they had received a message from a great person, or persons, in the Church, urgently requesting them to do nothing which might weaken the power of the informers, as they were of great service to the Church. Whitehead pleaded for justice to be done in regard to matters of actual misconduct, and prevailed so far as to get the report amended. As, however, the Commission seemed unable to make any suggestion to the King about what should be done to the informers, the Quakers sent a paper on the subject to the Lord Chancellor, showing no vindictiveness, but merely petitioning for a number of alterations in the law and procedure.[1] The King, in August, referred the report and the case of the Quakers to the Lord Chancellor, with directions to correct their irregular proceedings of some of the justices and informers. Orders were issued to the justices to put a stop to the depredations committed by these men, who now suddenly found themselves discountenanced in the local courts. Other Dissenters now plucked up heart to prosecute some of them, and such revelations came out that some of them had to flee the country, while others were reduced to poverty by the actions taken against them.[2]

It was high time that something was done to put down this obnoxious class of people. Some of them were of the scum of the earth, and their depredations must have been enormous. William Thornaby, the son of an innkeeper at Richmond, in the period lasting from the beginning of May 1670 to the middle of June 1671, laid information of seventy-eight Quaker meetings alone. The amount of the fines levied in connection with these meetings was a few shillings short of £2000, and many of the goods taken in distress were sold to him at much below their true value.[3] The Lord Mayor of London was sitting in a Court of Aldermen in 1670, when an informer made his appearance with such a number of accusations against one person that the fines would have amounted to £500. The Lord Mayor, however, in disgust, broke up the court and refused to do anything.[4]

In 1687 the King, probably because of the revelations of the

[1] Whitehead, " Christian Progress," pp. 593–609; " Life of Gilbert Latey," pp. 118–120.

[2] Gough, " Hist. Quakers," III. 170–177.

[3] For examples of the reckless way in which distresses had been levied see instances from the Preston Quarter Sessions records in Nightingale, " Early Stages of the Quaker Movement in Lancashire "; Besse, " Sufferings."

[4] Neal, " Puritans," IV. 501.

previous year, appointed another Commission to inquire what money had been raised, and what goods had been seized, under the laws relating to religion since September 1677, and to make a return of the names of all persons who had seized such goods or received such money. It was known that a great deal of the money had been embezzled. The Dissenters, however, showed themselves unwilling to appear against the informers, and it was reported that assurances had been given by the leading clergy and laity that if they did not appear, no such methods should be allowed in the future.[1]

When James II. issued his first Declaration of Indulgence, the Quakers of London presented, on May 19th, 1687, an address of thanks, in which they said, " Though we entertain this act of mercy with all the acknowledgments of a persecuted and grateful people, yet we must needs say it doth the less surprise us, since it is what some of us have known to be the declared principles of the King, as well long before, as since he came to the throne of his ancestors." [2]   Penn and others presented it, and it is probable that Penn drew it up.[3]   One Sunday in July he preached twice to a congregation estimated at about 3000, and lauded the King and his action.[4]   James gave orders that certain Quakers who had been put into public offices should not be molested for not taking the oaths.   The King also interfered in another way.   In some places, of which Leeds was one, goods which had been seized from the Quakers were still lying unsold, and he commanded that they should be returned to their owners.   He gave a neat reply to a Quaker who stood in his presence with his hat on.   James took his own hat off and put it under his arm, which the other seeing said, " The King needs not keep his hat off for me "; to which the King replied. " You do not know the custom here, for that requires that but one hat must be on here."   In the following year a number of Quakers living in Norwich petitioned the King that they might be made freemen of the city without taking the required oaths and he gave instructions to the Attorney-General in accordance with the petition,[5] but the Corporation refused to admit them, and petitioned the King not to insist.   As there is no further record of the affair, they were probably not admitted.[6]   In 1688 there was a great deal of discussion in Quaker circles about taking part in elections, and about Quakers becoming justices of the peace and holding civic offices, and George Fox fought hard against the introduction of any political matters into meetings at all.

[1] Gough, " Hist. Quakers," III. 186–187.
[2] Paget, " New Examen," pp. 128–130.
[3] " Revolution Politics," III. 16.
[4] " The Petty–Southwell Correspondence," ed. Marquis of Lansdowne, 1928, p. 280.
[5] Sewell, " Hist. Quakers," pp. 586–589.
[6] Platt, " The Quakers of Norwich," 1926, p. 13.

In 1688 the Quakers at their Yearly Meeting approved another address to be presented to James, in which, while thanking him for his second Declaration, they requested that no one might suffer for non-payment of tithes, or for not taking oaths, and expresssed a hope that the Parliament which was to meet in November would establish complete liberty.[1] Penn, who did not care much for the issuing of the Declaration by the King's prerogative alone, very strongly opposed the order that it should be read in the churches. When the birth of the Prince of Wales took place he advised the King to celebrate the event by releasing the seven bishops, and by pardoning the Whigs and others who were exiles in Holland. But the Church of England had thoroughly disappointed and angered the King, and in the circumstances his naturally obstinate character made him refuse.[2]

Macaulay says the Quakers looked coldly on Penn, and treated him badly because he was a friend of the King and Court. He also paints in a very bad light Penn's interference in the affairs of Magdalen College, Oxford, though Penn certainly was endeavouring to serve the cause of peace. The records of the Friends discount considerably the suggestion that he was unpopular in Quaker circles,[3] but there is no doubt that he was looked upon with very unfriendly eyes in other quarters because of his support of the King's Declaration of Indulgence. It was even reported of him that he was a Papist, and had been educated at the Jesuit College at S. Omer, and even Tillotson believed it, though he afterwards accepted Penn's disavowal.[4] The real fact was that he had been educated under Amyrault at the Protestant Academy at Saumur, and the story probably arose from a confusion of names. A London newsletter dated January 13th, 1683, reported that he had recently died in Pennsylvania, and that before his death he had declared himself a Papist.[5] In December, when James fled, Penn was arrested and brought before the Council, and only liberated on bail of £6000. It was said that Aaron Smith, for whom he had obtained a pardon, made as much mischief for him as he could. In February 1689, hearing that another warrant was out for his arrest, Penn wrote to elicit the sympathies of Lord Shrewsbury, but when he appeared before the Council again, in spite of his known sympathy for James, no treasonable practices could be proved against him, and he was discharged.

By a special provision of the Toleration Act, the Quakers were excused from taking the oaths required of other Dissenters, and were allowed to make a solemn declaration instead. Henceforward they might worship in their own way.

[1] Sewell, " Hist. Quakers," p. 588; Paget, " New Examen," p. 285.
[2] Graham, " Life of Penn," p. 185.
[3] Idem, ibid., pp. 303–307; Sewell, " Hist. Quakers," p. 593.
[4] Airey, " William Penn," Encycl. Brit., 9th ed.
[5] Hist. MSS. Com., Egmont MSS., II. 126.

V

QUAKER LIFE AND ORGANISATION

FOR more than twenty years the Quakers endured a storm of persecution such as no other religious body endured throughout that period. The general dislike for them was shown in other ways. Thus, in 1664 William Strange of Dunstable left by will ten pounds for the poor of the parish, with the proviso that none of it was to be given to " Quakers and common beggars." [1] Their disuse of the sacraments and the ancient ministry, and their refusal to pay tithes, of course, alienated the Anglicans. [2] The Presbyterians were very bitter against the Friends. When the Quaker movement began, the Presbyterians were in possession of most of the churches, so that when George Fox, in his early days, went into the steeple-houses and was offended at what he heard there, it was not by Anglican doctrines that he was disturbed, but by the rampant Calvinism, the long dry sermons, and the tedious prayers. When the Restoration came, the Quakers were no longer seeking for truth, but their doctrines were settled. The Anglican squires and parsons persecuted them, but they had comparatively little controversy with them. One of the chief reproaches the Friends hurled at their opponents was the number of times some of them had changed their position in order to keep their benefices. " Dr. Witty "—*i.e.* Robert Witte, M.D.—a celebrated physician, " said I ought to have sworn allegiance to the King. . . . He was a great Presbyterian, and I asked him whether he had not sworn against the King and the House of Lords. And now had he not sworn for the King, and what was his swearing good for? " [3] Sewell said, writing of the year 1660, that when the Presbyterians temporised and joined with the Episcopalians to keep their benefices, many of their hearers left them and joined the Quakers. [4] The Society of Friends had much in common with some of the early Baptists, and particularly with the General Baptists, but the Quaker rejection of baptism was an effective barrier between them. [5] Many of the Quakers would not grant the name of

[1] *Journal Friends Hist. Soc.*, I. 109.
[2] " Jesuitico-Quakerism Examined," 1680.
[3] Fox, " Journal," 1665; Louise Creighton, " Life and Letters of Thomas Hodgkin," 1917, p. 189.
[4] Sewell, " Hist. Quakers," p. 253.
[5] Tallack, " George Fox, the Friends, and the Early Baptists," 1868.

Christian to the other denominations. They themselves alone were the Church of Christ. " All you churches and sects by what name soever you are called, you are the seed of the Great Whore." [1] Some of the early Quakers spoke frequently of non-members of the Society as heathen.[2] George Fox spoke of the heathen as better than those people who called themselves Christians and yet said they would not have known of the existence of God or Christ unless the Scriptures had declared it to them. His argument was that the heathen and the patriarchs knew that there was a God, though they had not the Scriptures. The Quakers, of course, knew by the inward light.[3] One of William Penn's publications was entitled " Truth Exalted, in a Short but Sure Testimony, against all those Faiths and Worships that have been Formed and Followed in the Darkness of Apostasy, and for that Glorious Light which is now Risen and Shines Forth in the Life and Doctrines of the Despised Quakers." [4] On the other hand, Baxter, who thought their doctrine of the inner light a blasphemous assumption of personal inspiration by the Almighty,[5] found it difficult to believe that they were Christians at all, and Thomas Hicks, the Baptist, wrote " A Dialogue between a Christian and a Quaker." One pamphleteer, to their great indignation, traced their origin to David George, and John of Leyden and the early Anabaptists. Some people thought them mad, and one writer accused them of magic, and said that devils appeared at their meetings.[6] Ralph Josselin complained about the increase of their numbers, and said, " I do not question the downfall of that sect under the feet of Christ and His saints." [7]

All this accounts, perhaps, in some measure, for the persecutions the Quakers suffered when the sectarians got the upper hand. " In New England, a set of fiery zealots, who through impatience under sufferings from the bishops in Old England, had fled from thence, being invested with power, and placed at the helm of government, exceeded all others in their cruelty towards this people." [8] A petition was presented to Charles by Burrough and other Friends on behalf of the Quakers who were being persecuted in the English Plantations, and the King issued a *mandamus* forbidding them to be put to death in New England. Nevertheless, they still suffered many barbarities there, as well as in Barbados, Nevis, the Bermudas, Antigua, and Jamaica. The whole story is a sad commentary on Puritan appeals for liberty of conscience in England. It was, however,

---

[1] E. Burrough, " The Memorable Works," 1672, p. 416.
[2] Hancock, " The Peculium."
[3] G. Fox, " The Heathen Divinity set upon the Heads of all called Christians," 1671.   [4] 1688.
[5] " Rel. Baxt.," p. 77.   [6] " The Fanatic History," 1660, p. 224.
[7] " Diary of Ralph Josselin," Dec. 15th, 1674.   [8] Besse, " Sufferings."

not merely their teaching which made trouble for the Friends in some of the colonies: it was their actions. Fox, Penn, and the other leaders were zealous for the evangelisation of the slaves, and in 1676 the Assembly of Barbados passed " An Act to prevent the People called Quakers from bringing Negroes to their Meetings." [1]

The Quakers in Reading gaol in 1664, appealing for deliverance, explained that they could not join the Church because of the pride, swearing, and cruelty therein.[2] In 1670, Edward Bourne, a Quaker physician, fixed to the door of the steeplehouse (*i.e.* the cathedral) at Worcester, a paper denouncing those who loved the chief places in the assembles and salutations in the markets as " Antichrist's ministers and false prophets who sought their gain from every quarter." He suffered three days imprisonment for this. Bourne was the author of " An Answer to Dr. Good (so-called) his ' Dialogue against those called Quakers,' wherein he hath Forged the Quaker and Confuted Himself." This was published at Worcester in 1675. Dr. Thomas Good, Master of Balliol College, Oxford, had published in 1674 " Firmianus and Dubitantius: or, Certain Dialogues concerning Atheism, Infidelity and Popery."

Herbert Thorndyke, prebendary of Westminster, said that the Quakers were no more Christians than the Gnostics or Manichaeans or Mohammedans, and thought they should all be sent into banishment.[3] Whitehead and another Quaker wrote in reply, " The Popish Informer Reprehended for his False Information against the Quakers' Meetings." [4] An Episcopal clergyman in Lincolnshire wrote in 1675, " A Friendly Conference between a Minister and a Parishioner of his Inclining to Quakerism," and attacked " the absurd opinions of that sect." He was answered in the following year by Thomas Ellwood, who in " Truth Prevailing and Detecting Error " affirmed that the clergyman had not given a true representation of Quaker doctrines, and concluded with an attack on tithes. Two answers appeared in 1677. The clergyman published " A Vindication of ' The Friendly Conference ' from the Exceptions of Thomas Ellwood," while Thomas Comber, vicar of Westerham, in Kent, wrote " The Right of Tithes Asserted and Proved

---

[1] *Encycl. Brit.*, 9th ed. Art. " Quakers "; Francis Howgill, " The Popish Inquisition Newly Erected in New England," *see* " The Dawnings of the Gospel Day," 1670; John Whiting, " Truth and Innocency Defended. . . . in Answer to Cotton Mather," 1702; George Bishop, " New England Judged. . . . A Relation of the Sufferings of the Quakers in New England from . . . 1656 to 1660. . . . A Further Relation of the Cruel and Bloody Sufferings of the Quakers in New England continued to 1665," 1703.

[2] C.S.P.D., July 22nd, 1664.

[3] H. Thorndyke, " A Discourse of the Forbearance, or the Penalties, which a Due Reformation Requires."

[4] 1670.

from Divine Institution, Primitive Practice, Voluntary Donations, and Positive Laws." Next year Ellwood replied to them both in his " Foundation of Tithes Shaken," while Comber answered Ellwood in a pamphlet, " Christianity no Enthusiasm," in which he criticised the inspiration and revelation claimed by the Quakers, and said that other sects made exactly the same claims. He attacked, as a denial of their baptism, the way in which they mentioned their own names: " called of the world John Whitehead," " one whom the world calls James Nayler," " one who is known to the world by the name of James Parnell."

John Alexander, a minister at Leith, received a copy of some seventeen queries, sent " for one, or all the ministers in Scotland to answer." Here are some of the queries: " Whether or not grammar or logic, and the many tongues and languages which began in Babylon is an infallible rule to make a minister of Christ? And whether or not Elisha the ploughman, Amos the herdsman, Peter and John the fishermen, who could hardly read a letter, with many others who were not bred up in these things, logic and grammar and the many languages, if they could not be ministers of Christ Jesus? Yea or Nay. Whether or not your singing of David's psalms, his prayers, prophecies, fastings, reproaches, weepings, mournings, lamentations, and complaints how he was mocked, have any warrant in Scripture? And you bring all these together in metre without distinction. Have ye not done this yourselves? Or did the Apostles it to the saints in the primitive times? Or have ye the same spirit the Apostles had? Or a larger measure of it than the Apostles had, by which ye have turned these into metre since the Apostles' days? And what was the psalms, hymns, and spiritual songs they sang in the primitive times? Answer these things by plain Scripture. Whether or not Christ and the Apostles gave forth a command that they should keep the Sabbath Day? Let us see where it is written in the Scriptures. But the first day of the week the saints did meet together. This is Scripture. But let us see the Scripture for a Sabbath Day in the New Testament, which speaks for a rest for the people of God. But is this a day? Yea or Nay. Whether is there any Scripture, or command in all the New Testament for the sprinkling of infants? Let us see Scripture, without adding or diminishing from it, that ye do not bring the plagues upon you for it: for the plagues are added to them that adds: for we do expect plain Scripture from you for this, without any shuffling meanings, or consequences; or else never pretend Scripture rule more; but acknowledge that it hath been your meanings and consequences that have been your rule."

Alexander did not answer plain Yea or Nay. He wrote a book of over 200 pages, entitled " Jesuitico-Quakerism Examined, or, a Confutation of the Blasphemous and Unreasonable Principles of the Quakers, with a Vindication of the Church of God in Britain from their Malicious Clamour and Slanderous Aspersions." [1] The Bishop of Edinburgh's licenser wrote a prefatory note, in which he described the work as a "vindication of those solid articles of our faith, ignorantly and unreasonably invaded by that heretical fry of Quakers," and he judged that it would "prove a very useful book." The Quakers thought differently, and G. K. (George Keith) wrote in reply, "Truth's Defence, or, the Pretended Examination of John Alexander of Leith of the Principles of those (called Quakers) Falsely Termed by him Jesuitico-Quakerism, Re-examined and Confuted." It was published in 1682, and covered the whole ground of the controversy, though the accusations of popery were very slightly dealt with.

Probably the commonest accusation against the Quakers was that they were Papists in disguise. William Brownsword, vicar of Kendal from 1659 to 1672, a Presbyterian who conformed in 1660, ingeniously endeavoured to prove that the doctrines of the Friends were derived from Roman Catholic writers.[2] At the time of the Restoration the Roman Catholic party at Court frequently said that the Quakers were the best of all the sects, and this was immediately seized upon by their enemies as a proof of a secret understanding.[3] Baxter, who believed that the Jesuits were surreptitious members of the sects,[4] saw a connection with popery in the Quaker denial of the sufficiency of Scripture and their assertion of the need of a judge of controversy superior to Scripture. In 1661 the Romanists volunteered a discussion with the Quakers, and though some of the Quaker leaders disliked the idea, a meeting was held, but nothing of course came of it. The Earl of Derby proved, to his own satisfaction, that "Quaking is the offspring of Popery." [5] Broadsheets such as "The Quakers and Papists Paralleled " [6] were taken as expositions of the truth. William Prynne wrote a tract, "The Quaker Unmasked, and Clearly Detected to be but the Spawn of Romish Frogs, Jesuits, and Franciscan Friars, sent from Rome to Seduce the Intoxicated, Giddy-pated English Nation." A treatise entitled "Foxes and Firebrands," published anonymously,[7] said that there was a Jesuit who lurked and taught among the Quakers for twenty years together. It was another version of the story that the Jesuits had taken twenty years to create the sect in order to injure the Church of

---

[1] London, 1680.   [2] Brownsword, " The Quaker Jesuit," 1660.
[3] Sewell, " Hist. Quakers," p. 281.
[4] Baxter, " Key for Catholics," 1659.
[5] Charles Earl of Derby, " Truth Triumphant, in a Dialogue between a Papist and a Quaker," 1669.
[6] London, 1674; " A Humble Apology for Nonconformists," 1669, p. 103.
[7] Part I, 1680, by Dr. J. Nalson; Part II, 1682; Part III, 1689, by Robert Ware.

England. The Quakers said that no statements could be more false and foolish. Barclay was accused in 1688 of being a Jesuit and of having intrigued with Father Petre, to whom he had never spoken.[1]

The Quakers had a defender in Titus Oates, who wrote a letter in 1679 recommending that William Dewsbury should be discharged from prison, and declaring that he was no Jesuit. He enclosed a certificate from some persons who had known Dewsbury for more than twenty years, and said, " I look upon it to be more discretion not to meddle with any Protestant Dissenters in this day; but bend our forces against the common enemy of the Protestant religion, the Papist, and endeavour to win by arguments those that are Dissenters from us. . . . For I know the Jesuits and the Quakers, and there is such a vast difference in points of religion, that it is as possible to reconcile light and darkness as to reconcile them; though they may appear different from us, yet I think they are no murderers, as the Papists have been and are." [2]

The Quakers carried on several literary controversies with the Romanists, and some wrote violently against the Church of Rome, as, for instance, Josiah Cole, who in 1667 wrote " The Whore Unveiled, or the Mystery of the Deceit of the Church of Rome Revealed." Samuel Fisher said, " The Quakers are of the Catholic Church, if thou wilt know, as thou dost, what Catholic is, and so are not the Papists, that are of no church but that of Rome. The Church of Rome is but a particular church, as that of England or another national one, but the Catholic Church is general and universal . . . a church that had its being from Abel unto this day." [3]

There was one instance of friendliness between a Roman Catholic priest and the Quakers. When Katherine Evans and Sarah Chivers fell into the hands of the Inquisition in Malta, Gilbert Latey, the Court tailor who turned Quaker, went to Lord D'Aubigny, the Lord Almoner to the Queen Mother, since he had some influence in Malta, " and notwithstanding the way of the Lord was evilly spoken of, and His people were looked upon by man as speckled birds, and went as with their lives in their hands, the power of God was wrought on this Lord Obaney (sic), although he was a priest in orders, that he was very kind and free to Gilbert, and reasoned with him like Felix with Paul. . . . Coming another time to wait upon him, he bid Gilbert follow him, which doing, he went into the Queen's chapel, where Gilbert, seeing the people on their knees, and

---

[1] Barclay, " Vindication," written 1689.
[2] " Faithful Testimony of William Dewsbury," 1691, p. 343. For the accusation of Popery against the Quakers, see also " The Snake in the Grass," 1698, p. 187.
[3] Samuel Fisher, " The Testimony of Truth," 1679.

the candles lighted on the altar, made a halt, and asked the Lord Obaney what he meant by bidding him come in there. ' For,' said he, ' thou knowest I can bow to nothing.' Upon which he answered, ' Follow me, and nobody shall hurt you nor meddle with you.' Upon which Gilbert followed him through the chapel to a room behind the altar, where was another of the Queen's priests, and there being some lesser altars, the Lord Obaney said to Gilbert, ' You never yet saw me in my priestly habit, and now you shall.' And whilst he was making ready, the power of the Lord worked so much on Gilbert, that he stepped up on a place they called a private altar, and the word of the Lord came to him to preach truth unto them." This, however, did not cause the strained relations which might have been expected, for when the two women reached England in 1661 after their release, Latey brought them to D'Aubigny to thank him, and the latter said to them, " Good women, for what service or kindness I have done you, all that I shall desire of you is, that when you pray to God, you will remember me in your prayers." And so they parted.[1]

In the early days of the movement there were ebullitions of fanatical and eccentric conduct, but the number of such cases can easily be exaggerated. One Sunday in the summer of 1659 a Quakeress got into the pulpit of St. Mary Aldermanbury, and sat there sewing, making it impossible for the preacher to occupy his usual place.[2] Henry Newcome had a similar experience. " August 26th, 1660 (Sabbath), as I was preaching in the forenoon, a poor woman came into the church in sack-cloth and ashes and stood with hair about her ears, before the pulpit, all the sermon time. They said it was Judge Fell's wife. It is a mercy, I said then, these wild beasts that now a little amaze us, have not before this time overrun us." [3] Some entered the conventicles, found fault with the discourses and the prayers, and spoke openly and loudly against them,[4] the proceedings often terminating in an unseemly wrangle. There were some who, saturated with the writings of the prophets of the Old Testament, and stirred by passages such as Isaiah xx. 2–3, felt it a call to go naked and barefoot, proclaiming woe on some city which seemed especially sunk in wickedness.[5] One " walked naked through Skipton declaring the truth, and another was divinely moved to go naked through several years to market places, and to the houses of gentlemen and clergymen," for which he suffered " hooting, pelting, coach-whipping, and horse-whipping." [6] Some women also went naked as a sign. Fox says that many did so.[7]

[1] " Life of Gilbert Latey," pp. 50–56.
[2] Thomas Underhill, " Hell Broke Loose," 1660.
[3] Henry Newcome, " Autobiog.," p. 126.
[4] Croese, " Gen. Hist. Quakers," p. 26.   [5] C.S.P.D., January 12th, 1661.
[6] Other examples are given in " Hell Broke Loose," 1660.
[7] Fox, " Journal," sub 1664.

Perhaps the best known of these eccentrics was Solomon Eccles, or Eagle, who had been a musician, but on becoming a Quaker had destroyed his instruments. In 1663, at the time of Bartholomew Fair, he passed through Smithfield with only a cloth round his waist, bearing a pan of fire and brimstone on his head, and calling on people to repent and remember Sodom. One Thomas Taunton accompanied him, carrying his clothes. For this they were both sent to prison. It was probably the same man whom Pepys saw in Westminster Hall in July 1667, in a similar lack of attire, crying, " Repent! repent! " [1] In 1669 Eccles went into a Roman Catholic chapel in Galway during Mass, naked to the waist, with a chafing dish of coals and burning brimstone upon his head, crying out, " Woe to these idolatrous worshippers! God hath sent me this day to warn you and to show what will be your portion except you repent! " [2] About 1680 Eccles repeated a challenge he had made before to the members of the other sects. He would prove the claims of the Quakers by abstaining from food and sleep longer than any champion they could produce. His offer was accepted in February 1681 by John Pennyman, an ex-Quaker, but there seems no evidence to show that the contest took place.[3]

Some of the Quakers entered the churches and interrupted the services and the preachers. Thomas Slinger, vicar of Helmsley, Yorkshire, was conducting a funeral on April 29th, 1665, when he was assaulted by a party of Quakers, who tore his surplice and Prayer Book.[4] A Quaker woman entered Windermere church during service on Christmas Day, 1666, and annoyed the congregation by her behaviour, " standing in the midst of the church, where with loud, strange, inarticulate noises," she drowned the voice of the preacher, and in the time of prayers " she spoke aloud and delivered herself in a great impetuous rabble of slanderous language," and called the clergyman " covetous, and a greedy deceiver of the people." In the churchyard afterwards she abused both the clergyman and some of the parishioners.[5] On October 1st, 1678, a conventicle of nearly 100 Quakers was held at Windermere, close to the parish church, and they prayed and preached so loudly as to disturb the congregation. A justice had the Quaker preacher arrested, but another began at once. The preachers were fined £20 each. The next day eight preachers and fifty others were convicted, and warrants issued for levying the fines.[6] They pestered

---

[1] Pepys, " Diary," July 29th, 1667.
[2] Sewell, " Quakers," p. 470.
[3] " The Quaker's Challenge Answered, By a Stripling of the Lamb's Army," 1681.
[4] " Depositions in York Castle," pp. 128–129.
[5] Magrath, " The Flemings in Oxford," I. 164–165.
[6] C.S.P.D., 406/220.

the clergy and the justices of the peace with letters,[1] and they wrote letters to the King with a simplicity and directness which must have surprised him.

George Fox the younger thus addressed the King in 1661: " O King, he who is King of Kings sees and observes all thy actions in the midst of darkness, and seeing that they proceed from thence, even thy most hidden counsels can by no means escape the sight of God, so that there remain no lurking places for thy specious and pretended words, and therefore hath he freely observed all thy wiles and treacheries, laid for those who did no hurt, and hath also manifested them unto all men, and that at the very time when thou didst make those great and fictitious promises, and only didst play the hypocrite; wherefore thou hast angered God, when at the time thou didst promise liberty unto us, thou didst then suffer that outrage to be done us, and the imprisonment of so many men for the testimony of a good conscience. . . . And I have had it often in my thoughts both before and after thy restoration to the kingdom, when I had considered the fast and established idolatry of this land, that it had been better for thee that thou hadst never come hither, because I find it has been to thy ruin; and I have often prayed to God that thou wouldst become of that mind as to depart again out of the kingdom, that while thou hast life left thee and space to repent, thou mayest repent of thine iniquities. Do not, O King, suffer any one to flatter thee; God will not be mocked, what any man shall sow, that shall he also reap; consider with thyself, how thy brother, the Duke of Gloucester, was so suddenly and unexpectedly cut off, who might have survived after thy death; and do not imagine that thou canst be preserved by men, when God sets upon thee; and God's will shall stand, that his kingdom may extend over all. . . . These things that I write are true, and I would have thee to know that I write these things both godlily and lovingly; as for my own part, though I suffer many miseries from without, yet I have that inward peace with God, that exceeds all earthly crowns." It is said that when the King read it, the Duke of York told him that the man ought to be hanged, but that the King replied that it would be better that they themselves took heed to amending their lives and manners.[2]

William Dewsbury in 1661 wrote an " Address to the King," beginning, " Oh, King, hear the word of the Lord God, which came unto me about the sixth hour in the morning of the twentieth day of the third month, 1661. Thus saith the Lord through his servant." Among other things, he bade him " put away all sports, plays, pastimes, drunkenness, uncleanness." Let him not persecute the faithful, " who are haled to and fro as sheep that are slaying all the day long in tumults, afflictions,

[1] " The Fanatic History," 1660, p. 224.
[2] Croese, " Gen. Hist. Quakers," 1696, pp. 163–165.

stonings, stripes, prisons, and death." He complained that there had been set up proud, covetous men that knew not God, to be teachers in the land, who drew people into idolatry, worshipping they knew not what. At the time of writing Dewsbury was a prisoner in York gaol, but before he could send the letter to the King by " a private and safe hand," he was set at liberty with others of his brethren by the King's proclamation " which we own as an act of justice." [1] " W. C.," a Quaker, wrote to the King on June 18th, 1663, and told him that the greatness of his sins, and the profaneness of the Court, city, and country cried for vengeance. He begged that Parliament might be dissolved, the Council made purely Protestant, and that four peaceable prelates, four Presbyterians, and four Independents, might be summoned to settle the question of church government. He further exhorted him to live chastely with his Queen and to silence lying spirits.[2]

Charles Bailey, or Bayly, a prisoner in Newgate, Bristol, wrote to the King on September 4th, of the same year, threatened him with " the whirlwind of the Lord," exhorted him to avoid rioting and excess, chambering and wantonness, urged him to repentance and warned him against flatterers.[3] He was sent to the Tower for seditious practices early in 1664 and was still in prison, petitioning for release, in 1667. Probably in May of that year he wrote from the Tower " a few words of good counsel and advice unto the King of England from the King of Heaven." Let him restore liberty of conscience, and there would be no more plottings. Those who persuaded him to the contrary were his enemies. Let him beware of exasperating factions about differences in lesser matters of religion.[4] Ellington wrote a warning message of destruction " given to thee, O King Charles " and all others.[5] Peter Acklom, a Quaker prisoner in Hull, appealed to Charles, addressing his letter " to the King of Great Britain, whom the Lord hath set upon the throne of his father's kingdom, to rule the nations in righteousness, justice, and mercy." [6]

When James II. came to the throne some of the Quakers are said to have addressed him as follows : " We condole with thee in the death of our friend Charles. We are glad thou art come to be our ruler. We hear thou art a dissenter from the Church of England and so are we. We hope thou wilt allow us the liberty thou takest thyself, and so farewell." [7]

[1] " Faithful Testimony of William Dewsbury," 1691, pp. 186–191.
[2] C.S.P.D., June 18th, 1663.   [3] C.S.P.D., September 4th, 1663.
[4] C.S.P.D., January 21st, 1664, 91/10 May, 1667, 202/82.
[5] " Christian Information Concerning these Last Times," by F. Ellington, 1664.   [6] C.S.P.D., March 29th, 1664.
[7] " Lord Preston's Letter Book," Hist. MSS. Com. VII. Pt. I, p. 379. A somewhat different version is given in Gough, " Hist. Quakers," III. 160. But Gough, although the letter is given also by Eachard and Hume, thought it fictitious.

Not only did the Quakers write letters to the Kings of England, they sent them to other sovereigns as well. Perrot, in 1661, published a letter " To the Prince of Venice and all his Nobles " ; Fox wrote to the Emperor, the King of France, the King of Spain, and even the Pope, and his boldness in rebuking the Pope roused the anger of some of the Romanists at Court. Some at least of the letters were translated into Latin. In 1679 Fox, who had previously published a set of queries for the Pope and his followers, had them translated into Latin by Sewell, and sent them with a covering note to Innocent XI. Several times Fox addressed remonstrances to John Sobieski, King of Poland, about the persecution of Quakers in that country, and of these letters one which was sent in 1677 was translated into German. William Penn wrote to the same sovereign somewhere about 1680. In 1684 Fox wrote to the Duke of Holstein, and he is also said to have written to the Jews at Amsterdam, " the rulers of lesser Africa," and the Sultan of Turkey.

In 1678 Barclay wrote a Latin epistle to all the ambassadors and plenipotentiaries at Nymwegen, exhorting them to put forth their best endeavours for the peace and safety of Christians. He sent to each of them copies of his " Apology for the True Christian Divinity," one for himself and one for the sovereign he represented. Fox wrote them an epistle at the same time. Barclay sent his theological " Theses " to the doctors, professors, and students of theology, both Popish and Protestant, throughout Europe, desiring them to examine them and return their answers.[1] Early in 1682 the Emperor of Morocco sent a special ambassador to Charles II and the Quakers seized upon the chance of trying to convert him. They obtained an interview with him on February 11th, but it was said that the ambassador, after listening gravely to them, told them that though their religion might make them good men in this world, it would never take them to a better.

The Quakers claimed that by the power of the Spirit within them they wrought miracles. In 1649 George Fox, then twenty-five years old, began to work miracles of healing. In that year he cured a woman who had lost her reason : as he explained it, he cast a devil out of her.[2] In 1683 he healed James Claypole of the stone by laying his hands on him.[3] Numerous other instances of cures effected by Fox and others have been recounted. In 1683 he was speaking in Gracechurch Street, in the yard outside the meeting-house, when a constable interrupted him. Fox told him to be patient, but after a little while the man insisted on his discontinuing his speech, and took him into the

---

[1] Croese, " Gen. Hist. Quakers," pp. 89–91 ; Sewell, " Hist. Quakers," *passim.*

[2] Croese, " Gen. Hist. Quakers," pp. 27–28.

[3] " The Short Journal of George Fox," ed. by N. Penney, p. 78.

meeting-house. Another Quaker immediately rose up and
addressed the crowd. The constable showed no roughness or
rudeness, but merely took Fox by the hand. About seven
weeks afterwards they heard that the man had been ill practically
ever since, so ill that he could hardly walk about his bedroom,
and had suffered in addition from an acute pain in his shoulder
and arm. It was suggested to him that this might have been
caused by pushing about among the crowd, but he said he
hated having to interfere with the meetings, and had been
struck at the heart before he laid a hand on Fox.[1] This is one
of many examples of miraculous judgments which fell upon
their persecutors.[2]

The early Quakers also claimed the gift of prophecy. Thomas
Ibbitt of Huntingdonshire went about London a few days before
the Great Fire denouncing that a judgment of fire would come
down upon the city. When the fire broke out, he stood in
Cheapside in front of the flames, spreading out his arms to stay
them, and if he had not been pulled away would have been
burnt to death.[3] Four years before the fire another Quaker,
Thomas Bugg by name, had passed through the streets of
London preaching that unless the people repented, the Lord
would destroy the city like Nineveh. When these things came
to pass the Quakers found in them a proof of the inspiration of
their prophets. Edward Burrough and George Fox the younger
were eminent prophets. In the latter's " Collected Writings "
his prophecies are brought forward as a witness of the divine
origin of the Quaker doctrines. George Fox the elder also saw
prophetic visions: " As I was walking in my chamber with my
eye to the Lord, I saw the Angel of the Lord with a glittering
drawn sword southward, and as though the court had been all
of fire; and not long after the wars began in Holland, and the
sickness began, and the Lord's sword was drawn." [4] The prophecies and revelations were not always true. In 1673 Henry
Winder, a man who lived near Penruddock in Cumberland, was
accused by two Quakeresses of murdering his new-born child.
After being annoyed in this way for a year, Winder set the case
down for hearing at the Carlisle Assizes in August 1674. But
in the meantime the three Quakeresses (a third had joined the
others) appealed to a justice named Huddleston, and to the
sheriff of the county, and Winder also besought Huddleston to
inquire into the case. The women declared that the child was
buried at a certain spot on Hutton John Common. Margaret
Bradley drew with her staff a circle of about ten yards in circumference, and said that she had received a revelation from
Jesus Christ that the child was there. But when the digging
began the ground was so hard that the spectators sarcastically

[1] " Short Journal," p. 81.   [2] Fox, *ibid.*, pp. 79–80.
[3] Sewell, " Hist. Quakers," pp. 446–447.   [4] Fox, " Journal," 1664.

advised the diggers to try a softer place. Winder got £200 damages in an action for defamation of character. Some of the recorded visions, too, are not very convincing. A Quaker called Serle, a weaver, in the year 1662, saw these words written in legible characters round a kettle, " Woe to England, for poisoning of Charles II, Cardinal, I understand *Moloch*. Twenty nations with him. England's misery cometh." Some of the neighbours also saw this mysterious writing, which remained for an hour and then vanished.[1]

With all their peculiarities, the Quaker leaders were men of wonderful missionary enthusiasm and zeal. George Fox, in the course of his travels, visited nearly every county in England and Wales. He was in Scotland in 1657, Ireland in 1669, the West Indies and the American colonies from 1671 to 1673, Holland in 1677, and again in 1684. He was imprisoned eight times; his last imprisonment, which began in 1675, lasing fourteen months. John Whiting travelled all over England. Stephen Crisp, a Colchester man, during the space of thirty-five years, journeyed incessantly in England, Scotland, Holland, Germany, and the Low Countries.[2] John Camm, one of the Westmorland Quakers, who had been sent forth to the ministry by George Fox, was a delicate man who could not walk upstairs without help, and towards the end of his life could not walk half a mile at a time; yet he travelled on horseback all over England, preaching and winning converts.[3] It was said of Roger Haydock by his brother, " From his going abroad till his death was twenty-four and a half years, in which, notwithstanding imprisonment, sickness, and weakness of body and family, he travelled by sea and land 32,727 miles, and ministered in 2609 meetings or churches." [4] It is almost invidious to single out names. In their enthusiasm some of them hoped to convert the Pope and the Sultan. During the first thirty years of the society Quaker writings were translated into several European languages. The Friends often went very long distances to attend their meetings. At the Quarter Sessions at Helmsley, in Yorkshire, on July 12th, 1664, twenty-three Quakers were tried for being present at a conventicle at the house of John Dickinson of Burnistoun. They had come from Scarborough, Whitby, and ten other places.[5]

There were, of course, secessions from the Society of Friends from time to time. The " hat controversy " brought about the " disowning " of Perrot, and the Wilkinson–Story controversy caused the departure of many besides the two leaders. John

---

[1] Croese, " Gen. Hist. Quakers," Pt. II. 30.
[2] " A Memorable Account of the Christian Experiences of Stephen Crisp," 1694.
[3] " The Memory of the Righteous Revived," 1689.
[4] Fox, " Journal," ed. by N. Penney, Note.
[5] " North Riding Records. Quarter Sessions Records," VI. 79.

Pennyman left the Quakers in 1670, as a protest against what he considered undue influence with the liberty of prophesying. Nathaniel Smith, a Cheshire man who had been a Quaker for fourteen years, dedicated the story of his recantation to Lord Delamere.[1] Francis Bugg, a wool merchant and clothier, quarrelled with some of the Suffolk Friends, and about 1680 left the society. Henceforward he was a fierce opponent, and wrote about twenty books against Quakerism, armed with an inside knowledge and with a familiarity with its weak points. George Keith, a scholarly man, a student of theology and philosophy, had been a leader amongst the Quakers, had written a number of works in defence of their doctrines,[2] and had been prosecuted in 1683 for teaching school without a licence. The Friends "disowned" him in 1692, and after heading a Quaker schism for a time, he joined the Church of England, and was ordained, after which he wrote vigorously on behalf of his new opinions, and was attacked with equal vigour.[3]

At least one episcopally ordained clergyman was a member of the Society of Friends for a time. John Coughen, who though of English parentage was born in Holland, was ordained by Bishop Reynolds of Norwich, but in May 1663 announced his conversion to Quakerism and became a Quaker preacher. Returning to Holland, he fell under the influence of Edward Richardson, who was the minister of the English church at Haarlem, and he abandoned Quakerism and took up the study of medicine.[4]

John Whiting reckoned seven great persecutions of Quakers during the Restoration period. The first was in 1660, the second in 1662, the third from 1664 to 1667, the fourth in 1670, the fifth from 1675 to 1680, the sixth from 1682 to 1685, and the seventh in the early part of the reign of James II. They suffered more than any other sect under the Conventicle Acts. They alone did not give way to the storm, in fact it was said that they gave the informers so much to do that they had less leisure to attend to the meetings of the other sectaries. The records at the Friends' House, however, seem to show that the amount of suffering, even among the Quakers, under the Clarendon Code, has been greatly over-estimated. While the persecution was at its height, they engaged in foreign missions and subscribed largely to various local causes, which they could not have done if the fines and confiscations had been so overwhelming as is commonly said. Again, special privileges were

[1] "The Quakers' Spiritual Court Proclaimed: a Narrative of Two Trials at the Peel in St. John's Street," 1669.
[2] *E.g.* "The Universal Free Grace of the Gospel Asserted," 1671; "The Benefit, Advantage, and Glory of Silent Meetings," 1678.
[3] *E.g.* "The Portraiture of Mr. George Keith the Quaker in opposition to Mr. George Keith the Parson," 1700.
[4] *Journal Friends Hist. Soc.*, XIX. 22–24.

often allowed to imprisoned Quakers, and they might have had more had they been willing to pay for them.[1] They carried on the business of the society in gaol, they frequently went out of gaol to transact it, or to attend to their own private affairs. In 1662 the Quaker prisoners confined in the friary at Ilchester actually kept a school there, attended by some seventy children. The vicar of the parish tried to stop it, but the Quakers declined to give up the work as long as the children came. After a time, however, the three Friends who were most responsible, John Anderton, Matthew Perrin, and Henry Lavor, were put into the common gaol by day, and only allowed to go to the friary at night, so the school came to an end.[2] There is a certificate extant, dated 1683, that notice of an intended marriage had been published among the Quaker prisoners in Newgate and Bridewell, and that no impediment had been alleged.[3] Some of the magistrates did their best to obviate the worst severities. The Quakers were liable to punishment under many Acts of Parliament, and a great number of magistrates took advantage of this to sentence them to the lighter penalties. The King, too, interfered on their behalf again and again. The Act 35 Elizabeth, with its sentence of death or abjuration of the realm, was the worst of the Acts, for since the Quaker could not take an oath, nothing remained for him but the death sentence, but judges who were otherwise hostile to the Quakers discouraged prosecution under this statute. Here is an example. William Alexander, of Needham in Suffolk, was, with some other men, indicted as a Quaker under this Act. When called on to plead guilty or not guilty, he hesitated, and the judge said, " Why don't you plead ? " Alexander replied, " What wouldst thou advise us to plead ? " " If you ask my advice," answered the judge, " you shall have it, and I'll advise you to plead not guilty." They therefore pleaded accordingly. The judge then told the prosecutors that now they must prove these men neither to have been at their own parish church, nor at any other church or chapel, else they were not within the Act. Alexander and his friends were consequently discharged.[4] The King's judges, as distinct from the justices of the peace, did their best for them, but not all the justices were cruel. When an infirm woman of over eighty was brought before the justices at Fen Stanton, Huntingdonshire, in 1683, and the ecclesiastical authorities pressed for her imprisonment as contumacious, the magistrate refused, saying, " She is fitter for her grave than to be brought hither." Sometimes the officers had compassion, as in a case in Leicestershire, in 1670, when those sent to levy a

[1] Dudley, " Nonconformity under the Clarendon Code," *American Hist. Rev.*, October 1912.
[2] *Journal Friends Hist. Soc.*, VIII. 18–19.   [3] *Ibid.*, II. 15.
[4] Gough, " Gen. Hist. Quakers," I. 461.

distress on a poor family made a false return to the warrant, declaring on oath that they had taken everything. As time went on sympathy for the persecuted increased. People refused to buy goods which had been seized, and Besse mentions one case in Cheshire where some confiscated cheese had been distributed to the poor, and more than half of it was returned.[1] In 1674 there was a distraint on John Gratton's house at Monyash, in Derbyshire. The goods were proclaimed at the market cross, but no one would buy. The constable reported this at the next sessions, and one of the justices told him to take them into Yorkshire and sell them there, but Sir Henry Every, the presiding justice, would not permit it, saying that " he loved honest Friends and was much against proud priests." He also said that the Earl of Devonshire and his lady had asked him to befriend Gratton; and he protected him several times after this.[2] Sometimes, too, the persecuted parties had friends among the jurymen. There was a complaint at Dover in 1665 that the grand jury, mostly composed of fanatics, refused to find a true bill against the Quakers.[3]

The Quakers kept accurate records of the sufferings of their members at the hands of the persecutors. Joseph Besse compiled a great history, in which he collected under the various counties a mass of names and dates and details.[4] Written in two large folio volumes it was a plain statement of facts, without exaggeration and with singularly little bitterness. The Friends did their best to mitigate the troubles of their co-religionists, and also rendered charitable assistance to many of the sufferers belonging to the other sects, in spite of the abuse they often received from them.

The life of John Whiting might be taken as an example of the difficulties and dangers to which the profession of Quakerism was liable. He was one of the lesser leaders of the movement, and for the chief facts of his life we are indebted to his autobiography, which he published in 1715, under the title of " Persecution Exposed, in some Memoirs relating to the Sufferings of John Whiting." He was born, of good yeoman stock, at Nailsea in Somersetshire, in 1656. His parents were Quakers, but his father died when he was only two years old. In 1660 his mother was sent to Ilchester prison with over 200 other Quakers, and remained there some months, during which time the grandfather had charge of her little children. John, a serious and precocious boy, yet perhaps not more precocious than many other children of this time, developed a strong enthusiasm for Quakerism at an early age. " I was taken off at about twelve years old from all my vain sports and pastimes, for having been on a time with

---

[1] Besse, " Sufferings."   [2] " Journal of John Gratton," p. 114.
[3] C.S.P.D., October 15th, 1665.
[4] Besse, " Sufferings of the Quakers," 2 vols., 1753.

other boys at play, when I came home at night I was so exceedingly troubled and condemned in myself for my vanity, that I
made a covenant with the Lord that if he would forgive me for
Christ's sake, I would never go to such vain pastimes again."
Early he learned the evil of taking off his hat to people. The
use of the " plain language " was a great difficulty to him, but
he found no peace till he " took up the cross in that respect."
He tells us also that God discovered to him in his boyhood the
evil of " hireling priests," with their " erroneous ways and
worships." There is a strong resemblance, though no direct
connection, between this autobiography and that other story
of the travail of a soul, John Bunyan's " Grace Abounding."
Whiting tells us how, in 1673, he went through " deep inward
exercises, under the work of truth in myself, and ate my bread
with fear and trembling, but had my spiritual support and
comfort also." His sister Mary, with whom he lived, was
" raised in a testimony and went travelling." Together they
went preaching in Buckinghamshire and in London, after which
she travelled north while he returned home for the winter.
Next year, at her desire, he left Nailsea, and passing by Northampton, " when it lay in ashes," Leicester, and Nottingham, he
at length arrived at Norton in the county of Durham, where
his sister died in May.[1] In 1678, for refusing to pay tithes,
Whiting, with another Quaker named Sharp, was brought before
John Bayley, Chancellor of the diocese of Bath and Wells, " a
proud imperious man," who held his court " in an angle of the
cathedral," and ordered their hats to be removed. Sharp
objected that he was an old man and might take cold, to which
the chancellor replied that it wouldn't matter if his head were
off as well. " Then he asked me why I did not pay ' Mr.
Ancketyll ' as he called him, his tithes " and " gave me very
abusive language (being a very haughty, passionate, as well as
envious man) ill-becoming his place." Whiting was formally
admonished and dismissed for a week, but Sharp was sent to
prison at Ilchester. He had made matters worse at the trial
because, hearing the organ and the choristers while the case
was going on, he accused his judges of idolatry. Whiting
appeared again the next week, and on his appearance demanded
a copy of the accusation. Asked if he would answer it on oath,
he refused, though threatened with excommunication. At length
a copy was given him, and the proctor demanded a fee of ten
groats for it, which Whiting refused, on the ground that every
man had a right to have a copy of the charge made against
him. " He asked me whether I thought they could write for
nothing. I told him he that set them to work must pay them :
he said I might take it, but must pay for all at last. I told him
when I paid for the rest I would pay for that, and so we parted."

[1] " Early Piety Exemplified in the Life and Death of Mary Whiting," 1680.

In his autobiography Whiting translates the Latin copy of the libel with comments. The titles of the chancellor are popish and unscriptural. Ancketyll, the rector of Nailsea, ought not to be called " Mr.," because we must call no man our master. There are no titles like " parish church," " diocese of Bath and Wells," or names of months, such as January, February, in Scripture. The libel stated that tithes were " of the Common Law and statutes of the realm." " But not," says Whiting, " by the Gospel or Law of God, and all laws contrary to that are *ipso facto* null and void, says doctor and student." [1] Again, he says that custom is no good ground for a minister of the Church to follow, " for the customs of the people and nations are commonly vain, Jer. x. 3." The libel stated that the predecessors of the present clergy had been in peaceable possession of the tithes. " In the late turn of times, doth not this justify the late usurpation, when the Church of England men were turned out and others put in their places, except they turned with the times, as many of them did? " It was not true, as the libel stated, that the rector took tithes during his incumbency, because several Quakers refused to pay. The only real answer Whiting makes to any statement in the charge is a denial of the accuracy of the assessment. His statement is that they assessed his corn at £3340 (which must be a mistake) " when all the corn I had was worth but about £10 and the tithes about £1." As he still refused to pay, he was excommunicated.

In 1679 he was arrested on a writ *de excommunicato capiendo*, and taken to prison at Ilchester. After that, he never returned again to his father's house " to inhabit there." At Ilchester he found a number of other Quakers, one of whom, John Sage, had been there since 1666, and was now over eighty years of age. There were so many prisoners there that as well as in the common gaol some were kept in the old nunnery close by, and some in the old friary at the other end of the town. Whiting at first was imprisoned in the nunnery, but used to attend Quaker meetings in the friary. In the following year he removed to the friary, and there great meetings were held, other Friends attending from a distance. He was at liberty " to walk in the fields to read and meditate for some hours together." He carried on a controversy with a Presbyterian of the town, named Singer, a controversy resulting later in the publication of his book, " A Threefold Apology for the People of God, called Quakers." In 1680 the Duke of Monmouth rode through Ilchester in the course of his progress through the west. " We stood in the friary gate as he rode through the town. Taking notice of so many Quakers together with their hats on, he

[1] This may bear reference to a small law book " Doctor and Student," written by Christopher Saint-Germain, and published about 1530. There was an edition in English published in 1623.

stopped and put off his hat to us. We did not say anything, for fear of undermining his popularity, as a watch was kept on him." In September of that year the Quarterly Meeting was to be held at Ilchester, but a justice of the peace arrived with a troop of soldiers to stop it. The visiting Quakers had gone to an inn kept by one Robert Abbott, and on the information of a rival innkeeper they were found there, and Abbott lost in fines and fees the sum of £60, which, however, the Quakers paid for him. The jealous innkeeper, Giles Bate, came to misfortune and died poor, but not before he had done despite to the Quakers, because in 1681 he was made gaoler of Ilchester, and put Whiting in the common gaol, in a " dark nasty hole called Doctors' Commons, where they used to put the condemned men," and where the prisoner lay on straw on a damp earthen floor. However, this did not last long. In this same year he went to a friend's house at Walton on Pollen Hill for the night, and next day to the burial of a young man at Street. There he met two of his fellow-prisoners, and they returned to prison together. Apparently as his imprisonment was likely to be protracted, he made over his house at Nailsea, in which a relative was acting as caretaker, to the Friends for a meeting-house. Next year he went to Nailsea, and then on to Bristol, where he had the misfortune to meet his keeper, and he had to promise him to remain away only a night or two. After this successful trip, he seems to have remained quiet for a time, apparently satisfied with large Quaker meetings at the gaol, these being held as often as three times a week. But in 1683 he took another holiday, and went love-making. The lady was Sarah Hurd, of Long Sutton, daughter of one of his fellow-prisoners, and she in due time accepted his proposal of marriage, though the wedding did not take place for some time. She herself was imprisoned the next year. But after a short period of close confinement they went off together, rode to Yeovil, Bath, Bristol, and Nailsea; then went back to Bristol for the fair, and returned to imprisonment. Ambrose Rigg, a Quaker who was imprisoned in Horsham gaol from 1662 to 1672, was actually married in prison to Mary Luxford, a fellow-prisoner. In 1685 Whiting was summoned to the Assizes at Taunton, " I being at my own house at Nailsea, newly come home (as I did sometimes, as I could have liberty to see how things were), had a message sent me the day before the Assizes began." He walked the thirty miles to Taunton, and arrived in time. Fourteen Quakers were discharged, but he was not one of them; so he returned to Ilchester, but got another holiday after a time to go to the Quarterly Meeting at Grenton, after which he went to visit Sarah Hurd at Long Sutton. James was now on the throne, and the keepers, thinking that the Quaker prisoners would soon be discharged, grew careless; so we find Whiting travelling about a good deal.

He had intended to be married this summer, but Monmouth's invasion occurred, and owing to the troubles which came in consequence, the wedding was postponed for another year. Monmouth's friends had tried in vain to get the Quaker prisoners in Ilchester to join the Duke. The result was that some of the Duke's friends found themselves prisoners too, but the Quakers " went in and out as at other times." Sarah Hurd's brother-in-law, a man named Scott, went to Taunton to sell horses to Monmouth, and was persuaded to join him. Whiting, accompanied by Mrs. Scott, went to fetch him back, and Mrs. Scott appealed to the Duke personally " not to take it amiss if her husband went home, for it was contrary to our persuasion to appear in arms," and Monmouth gave his consent. Whiting stayed at Long Sutton until after the battle of Sedgemoor, and then went back to Ilchester, thinking prison the safest place. The keepers began to be very severe, shut the prisoners in close confinement, and demanded heavy fees. When Whiting refused he was put in irons, had to lie on the floor, and was even threatened with the common gaol, where the small-pox had broken out. But after thirteen weeks of hardship, he received his old easy imprisonment again. Finally, James put out his general proclamation of general pardon, and on " the thirtieth day of the month called March," 1686 (he cannot quite get free from the pagan names of the months), he was discharged, after six years and nine months of imprisonment. In May 1686 he was married, and settled down for a time at Long Sutton. He lived till 1722.

The story of John Whiting's life shows how in some cases the worst sufferings to which the Quakers were liable might be mitigated. Their imprisonment cannot always have been very rigorous. But there is another and much darker side of the picture. The roll of Quaker sufferers during this period of less than thirty years is so large that a few examples must suffice.

Isaac Pennington the younger, between 1662 and his death in 1679, underwent six imprisonments. In 1662 he endured seventeen weeks, in 1664 seventeen or eighteen weeks, in 1665 four weeks, again in 1665 and 1666 nine months, and from the latter part of 1666 to the early part of 1668 he was incarcerated for about a year and a half. All these imprisonments were in Aylesbury gaol. His last and greatest imprisonment was in the years 1670 and 1671, when he was in Reading gaol for a year and three-quarters. Visiting some Quakers imprisoned in that place, he was himself seized, carried before Sir William Armourer, and returned to the gaol as a prisoner. In a period of ten years and a half he spent four and three-quarter years as a captive.[1] William Dewsbury was a prisoner in York Castle in 1661. Later in the year he was in Newgate, where he certainly

[1] Whiting, " Persecution Exposed."

remained till April 1662. At the end of the year he was in
York Castle again, and remained there for some months. He
was in Warwick gaol during 1663, 1664, and 1665. Writing in
December, 1686, he related that he had then been prisoner in
Warwick for nineteen years, during four of which he had been
close prisoner, and his health had been impaired thereby. He
died in Warwick in 1688.[1] Even in Oliver's days William
Moxon, of Murdon in Wiltshire, was sued for tithes, by William
Gunn, the vicar of the parish, and an excessive distress was
levied on him in consequence. Gunn seems to have pursued
Moxon with an unrelenting hostility. In 1661 he got him
imprisoned for two years. After that let Moxon tell his own
tale. " He sued me in the Exchequer, in Chancery, at Common
Law, and in the bishop's court. He outlawed me. He excommunicated me. He took me up seven times with bailiffs and
apparitors. He caused me to be brought four times to this
Fisherton Anger prison, and once he carried me to London.
First and last and in all I have been a prisoner on his account
about two-and-twenty years, and only for conscience' sake. And
notwithstanding my imprisonment, since that time he had an
execution against me, contrary to their law. And he being
lately dead [Moxon was writing in 1684] hath left me a prisoner,
and hath taken no care at all for my releasement." However,
he was released soon after this, but in 1687 a distress was again
laid on him for the non-payment of tithes.[2]

It was not merely the enforcement of severe laws from which
the Quakers suffered: it was the savage methods by which
they were enforced. Men's tools were taken away under a
distraint when there were other goods which might have been
seized, the object being to deprive them of their means of livelihood. Judge Keeling caused the goods of several poor people
in Bedfordshire to be taken away from them, and then threatened
the neighbours who relieved their distress. The soldiers sent to
disperse meetings pricked the worshippers with their swords,
beat them with clubs, rode them down, rolled them in the mud,
and threw them into any pond which happened to be near.
At Reading Assizes in 1661 a Quaker complained of three of
his cows having been stolen and found in possession of the thief.
Being a Quaker, he could not swear, so his neighbours swore
for him; but the judge at once put the oath of allegiance to
him, and, on his refusal to take it, sent him to gaol. Women
with their children at their breasts were sent to filthy holes
called prisons, and there was more than one case of women,
about to become mothers, being frightened into premature birth,
or even to death, by the brutalities of those who attacked the
meetings. William Williams, a Cambridgeshire Quaker, a poor

[1] " The Faithful Testimony of William Dewsbury," 1689.
[2] Besse, " Sufferings."

man with a large family of small children, was sent to prison in 1662. His wife appealed to a brutal justice, who told her " to fry her children for steaks, and eat them, if she wanted food." " He died not long after in much trouble and horror of mind," said Besse. In the same county one man suffered distress of goods to the value of £2 10s. for not paying a tithe of twopence, while another, for not going to church, had sixty beasts taken from him, to the value of £183. Cradles were taken from under children, and bed-clothes from the sick. Sympathising neighbours, whether Churchpeople or not, were fined for refusing to help in the seizure of the goods. William Hall of Congleton, Cheshire, had a mare seized under a distress. After a time the mare came home of her own accord. Hall went with two neighbours to report to the magistrate where she was, and was promptly arraigned at the Assizes for stealing the animal. However, a jury acquitted him. The justices themselves were some-times as violent as the rough soldiers in breaking up meetings. Some of them went to break up a meeting at Newton, in Cheshire, where they found a man leading the congregation in prayer. One justice, a man named Needham, proceeded to beat those present with his cane, till his companions intervened. There was a miserable dungeon in Chester, a mere hole in the rock, in which on occasion Quakers from North Wales were incarcerated, and where existence must have been torture.[1] Some Quakers were imprisoned for unlawful cohabitation because they had been married after the Quaker form. Sometimes the clergy demanded wedding fees of Quakers who had not been married in church. Thomas Mounce, of Liskeard, was sent to gaol for not appearing in the archdeacon's court as defendant in a tithe suit. After two years' imprisonment Judge Archer decreed his commitment illegal. He then fined him £5 for not taking off his hat in court, and on non-payment of the fine ordered him back to prison. The clergy brought many suits against the Quakers for tithes. For this they had legal justification, but there was no justification for some of them personally assaulting the recalcitrant tithe payer. There was a meeting at Eyam, in Derbyshire, in 1661, at which a woman was found praying. The constables and soldiers dragged her out and nearly tore the clothes from her back. Some other women were dragged out by the hair, and others by the feet with their heads dragging on the ground. Constables rifled prisoners' pockets, and took their coats from them. The gaolers did their part also. In 1660 the keeper of Durham gaol demanded 22s. 6d. a week from each Quaker prisoner for beds, and as this was not paid, he threw twenty of them into a small, stinking dungeon where they could not all lie down at once, and thirteen into another, where they all remained for five days. Henry Jackson was

---

[1] T. Mardy Rees, " Hist. Quakers in Wales," p. 60.

shut up with others in Warwick gaol in a noisome room, and
was charged threepence for a quart of water.   The food brought
to the prisoners by Friends was taken from them, and even the
people outside, hearing of it, threw bread over the wall to
them.[1]   The Quakers presented to the justices of Durham at
Quarter Sessions in 1682 a memorial of their sufferings in that
county.   They told how two informers went to a woman's
house at Raby.   She had some friends there having a meal
with her.   She invited the two men to share her meal, which
they did, and then went away and swore a conventicle against
her.   From a poor old woman who subsisted on the charity of
her friends they took away most of the clothing she possessed.
A Gateshead justice called Headley with his own hands stripped
a Quaker, and ordered an officer to whip him through the
streets.   In Cirencester the officers breaking up a meeting even
took the staff out of a blind man's hand, and beat him with it.
In Gloucester, in 1670, an old woman was thrown downstairs,
her shoulder dislocated, and her injuries were so serious that
she died soon after; and a jury had the wickedness to bring in
a verdict of " Death by the visitation of God."   In the same
city, in 1677, an old man named Peace was dragged into the
street, lifted up by his girdle, and then hurled to the ground.
In Hampshire, a Quaker having been sent to prison, the informers
visited his house in his absence, beat and terrified his wife and
children till they fled, and then plundered the place, carrying
away his goods in carts and on their backs.   Not only did they
do this, but they burned a quantity of timber, and ruined and
destroyed an orchard which he had planted.

Two Quakers were taken at a meeting in Hereford in 1661,
and sent to prison.   After some time they were taken out of
their beds at midnight by command of a certain Captain Brunton,
who took them to the guard, caused them to be tied neck and
heels, and then ordered lighted matches to be tied between the
fingers of one of them, the excuse being to make them confess
knowledge of a plot.   Next day they were taken before the
mayor, who tendered them the oaths, and then sent them to
prison, where they were kept with irons on their legs for five
months.   One place of imprisonment to which the Quakers
were assigned in Hereford was so filthy and noisome that a
visitor told one of the turnkeys that it was not a place to put a
dog in, to which he replied, " No, nor yet to put a devil in."
Nicholas Ridley, a Quaker, interceded with Sir Richard Browne,
the Lord Mayor of London, for mercy on his wife, who was
lying sick in Bridewell.   All the comfort he got was to be told
that if she died he could get another wife the sooner, and he
was sent to prison in Newgate for asking.   On October 10th,
1664, Hannah Trigg was brought before the Sessions in London

[1] C.S.P.D., September 3rd, 1666.

and sentenced to transportation. A certificate was put in that she was under sixteen years of age, but the justices said this was untrue. The poor girl died in Newgate of the plague, and was buried with great indignities in a felon's grave. In 1665 a woman over sixty, and an old man, were sent to Bridewell, and ordered to be whipped. There must have been some curious scenes in courts at times. At the September Sessions in 1670, in London, thirteen Quakers appeared on a charge of unlawful meetings. As they did not take their hats off, the gaolers and marshals did it for them. The Lord Mayor rebuked them for doing so, and ordered them to put them on again for them. Then the clerk ordered the prisoners to take them off themselves, which they refused to do. Then the Recorder ordered the officers to take their hats off for them a second time, and fined some of the prisoners twenty marks and others twenty nobles for disrespect to the Court.

One favourite trick of the persecutors was to smear the faces of their prisoners with filth. Filth was their portion, for all the prisons were filthy. This was bad enough, but the way in which men and women were herded together was worse, and when simple, decent people had in addition to endure the companionship of the vilest refuse of humanity, their mental sufferings must have been almost unendurable. The Quakers constantly complained to the authorities. Appeals, petitions, account of sufferings were continually drawn up and sent to all whom they might concern, from the King downwards. Sometimes they were sent to prison for this, as at Norwich in 1670, when their petition was described as " scandalous expressions against Mr. Mayor, and Mr. Steward and the Court of Aldermen." In 1674 Sarah Reynolds of Stourbridge, a poor widow with five children, was committed to Worcester gaol for not paying ninepence, which had been demanded from her " towards the repair of the steeple house." Others were sent to prison in 1681 for refusing to pay a rate for the repair of St. Nicholas's church. Prosecuted in the ecclesiastical court, they appeared before Bishop Fleetwood, who was angry with them for keeping their hats on. Afterwards they wrote to him explaining their principles in this respect, and telling him that the King had shown no anger when they had not taken off their hats to him.[1] Informers sometimes swore that people were at conventicles when they were not. On June 27th, 1681, some informers swore that Henry Hayden and his wife were at a Quaker meeting at Worcester, though they had been at church, and had even received the sacrament that day. Others had been brought up at the Assizes at the same time, but the untrustworthiness of the informers' evidence led to the grand jury refusing to find a true bill against them. Nevertheless, the justices at the Sessions,

[1] Noake, " Worcestershire Sects," p. 254.

on these men's evidence, made an order for a distress against eight persons, and under it pewter, goods in houses and shops, malt, a mare, and other things to the value of £68 11s. were seized.[1]

A truly scandalous thing happened in Norfolk in the year 1676. The wife of Francis Larder, a Quaker, died. Orders had been issued to seize the bed from under her, but she died before this could be done. The parish priest and his clerk, not having received the burial fees, persuaded some people to take the coffin out of the grave some days after the funeral. In doing so it broke. They then tied it up, carried it into the market-place at Fakenham, and set it down before another Quaker's door. In Norwich, on one occasion, when a Quaker was charged with treasonable language, the testimony of an idiot was accepted against him. The Nonconformists were powerful in that city, and combined to make trouble for the Friends.[2] In 1670 Nathaniel Price of Farnefield, Nottinghamshire, a poor fatherless boy, whom his friends in charity had apprenticed, was taken at a meeting, and having nothing else to discharge his fine, the officers took away his coat and breeches, four halfpence, his knife, sheath, and scissors. A blind man of Burford, in Oxfordshire, was sent to prison in 1663 for not attending church, and remained in gaol for eight and a half years. At Ilchester John Anderton and Richard Lincoln were put in iron fetters for several days and nights, and led through the town by day by the common hangman. In 1683 soldiers went to the house of a Quaker at White Lackington, Somerset, while the owner was in prison, and remained there carousing till the evening of the next day. They carried away a rick of hay and two hogsheads of cider, besides one which they drank on the spot. At Haverhill, Suffolk, in 1670, the Quakers, being kept out of their meeting-house, assembled in the streets and the local authorities employed two men with halberds to drive them up and down, which they did, frequently striking them and threatening to kill them. At Horsleydown, in 1663, a party of soldiers came to a meeting, and as they entered, fired their muskets, and then carried many away to prison. Soldiers, sometimes of the King's Regiment and sometimes of Monk's Regiment, appeared again at many successive meetings. They knocked some down with their muskets, and cut others over the head and face with their swords; some charged their muskets with powder, held the muzzles close to women and fired them off, burning their clothes and scorching them; some even broke their own swords and staves by the violence of the blows they laid on without distinction of age or sex. There was a complaint made by the Quakers in Reading gaol in 1664 that the magis-

[1] Noake, " Worcestershire Sects," p. 259.
[2] Platt, " The Quakers in Norwich," Norwich, 1926.

trates, in breaking up a meeting, pricked the women with an instrument like a pack needle.[1] Fellow-prisoners joined in the baiting and tormenting of the Quakers sometimes, and, amongst a crowd of felons, they occasionally went in danger of their lives. In the same way the mob could easily be stirred up against those who were not in prison when there was a chance of looting a Quaker's shop.

In 1662 Major Wilde, with a party of soldiers, conveyed a man over sixty years of age, and in bad health, from Evesham to Worcester. They drove him on foot before their horses, and when he could not keep up he was dragged along. The major himself rode him down with his horse, and threatened to pistol him. At last they set him on a horse, which they whipped up hill and down dale, his appeals for mercy only meeting with derision. He died soon after his arrival in Worcester. In 1665 Richard Seller, a Quaker fisherman, was pressed for the navy. As he refused, he was hoisted on board a ketch with a tackle and kicked. When the ketch arrived at the Nore he was hauled on board the *Royal Prince* in the same way through a gun-port. He was then beaten by the boatswain, and then by the captain, and hung up by the wrists to the mizzen shrouds. The yeomen beat him again and again. The admiral ordered him to be put in irons and kept without food or drink. He remained like this for twelve days, and was then sentenced to death by a court-martial; but when it came to the time of the execution the admiral set him free. He made himself very useful on board in looking after the sick and in other ways, though he steadfastly refused to fight, and at length received a certificate of discharge.

Four Manx Friends, William and Mary Callow, and Evan and Jane Christian, were turned out of the Isle of Man in 1665, and their property was confiscated, and for four years they were driven backwards and forwards between that island, England, Ireland and Scotland, now in prison, now driven out in such haste that they had no time to take their children, appealing repeatedly and in vain to this, that, and the other authority.[2] At one time orders were issued to transport William Callow to Virginia, and he was actually carried on board ship for that purpose, but the sailors refused to weigh anchor, saying that they had never heard of a ship which carried Quakers against their will which ever prospered. In 1664 some other Quakers had been sentenced to transportation to the West Indies, and the gaoler had made arrangements with the master of a ship to carry them there. When the latter learnt from the Quakers that they were being sent against their will, he said he only carried free men. After several refusals, and after putting them ashore once, he at last took them on board. Finding his

[1] C.S.P.D., July 9th, 1664.   [2] C.S.P.D., 239/56.

ship delayed by contrary winds, he put them ashore again, and gave them a certificate stating that he had done so.[1] They went and reported the matter to the Council, who directed the Sheriff of Hertfordshire to keep them in prison till a ship could be found for them. This was never done, and they remained in prison for seven years, and were at last released by order of the King. Not long afterwards three Quakers were put ashore from the ship *Mary Fortune* of Bristol, with a certificate from the master and seven of his crew stating that they refused to take them. The certificate further said that there was a law in Barbados that whoever brought persons to the island against their will was liable to heavy penalties, and must take them back at his own expense.[2] Finally, an embargo was laid on all merchant ships in the port of London, and orders were given that no ship should be allowed to go down the river without a pass from the admiral, which was refused in the case of ships going to the West Indies unless they promised to carry Quakers. Some few, indeed, were sent abroad, but of those sentenced to banishment, some died in prison or on board ship, some renounced their Quakerism, and some were redeemed by relatives who were not Quakers. It has been calculated that 230 Quakers were sentenced to transportation under the first Conventicle Act, but no case is known of the penalty having been awarded to any member of the other sects. Of the Quakers only about twenty were actually sent abroad, and nine of them did well in their new surroundings; but as a general rule those who received this sentence remained in prison till 1672.[3] This punishment was not prescribed by the second Conventicle Act. Reading the story of the persecutions, it is difficult not to feel some sympathy with Sewell, who said, " Many of the persecutors, both justices, informers and others, came to a miserable end : some by sudden or unnatural death, others by lingering sickness or distemper, or by foul and stinking diseases taken out of this life; whilst some, who by spoil had scraped much together, fell to great poverty and beggary." [4]

Among the things for which the Quakers were punished at various times and places were disturbing the clergy during service, calling the clergy opprobious names, such as "dumb dogs," " hirelings," " false prophets," " deceivers," refusing to pay tithes, rates, or levies for the militia, refusing to take the oaths, keeping their places of business open on holy days, such as Sundays and Christmas Day, using their own burial-grounds, refusing to take off their hats in the law courts or in church, meeting in conventicles, not attending church, not being married in church, and not sending their children to school. In Wales

[1] C.S.P.D., November 19th, 1664.   [2] C.S.P.D., January 7th, 1665.
[3] Braithwaite, " Second Period," p. 50.
[4] Sewell, " Hist. Quakers," p. 511 ; Besse, " Sufferings," *passim.*

several were punished under a misconstruction of the Vagrancy Acts by being whipped and then given a pass. One man was prosecuted for travelling on the Lord's Day, because he had walked from his home to the place of meeting.[1]

Despite this persecution the spirit of the Quakers was unbroken: to all the efforts of the authorities they opposed the sheer dead weight of meekness and obstinacy. Driven out of their meeting-houses, they met in the streets outside, however bad the weather might be, and even in the depth of winter. Soldiers came and pushed and kicked and cuffed them up the street, and as soon as the soldiers ceased to drive, they began again to hold their meeting. If the meeting-house was pulled down, they met in the ruins. Fined by the magistrates, they refused to pay. Sentenced to gaol, they went without resistance.

In 1661, at the March Assizes held at Chard in Somerset, some 200 of them appeared for trial. They had walked from Ilchester gaol, twelve miles away, attended by a single keeper. In April of the same year John Scarfe and Thomas Salthouse were given their liberty from Ilchester gaol, but the court required sureties of them before they went home, one to Lancashire, and the other to Westmorland, that they would not return to Somersetshire for three years. This they refused, and so were sent back to prison. Even the children stood firm. In 1662 two boys, aged thirteen and sixteen respectively, were sent to Bridewell. Their arms were put in the stocks, which so pinched them that their wrists were badly swollen. The keeper could not make them work, and they refused all food except such as they were able to buy with their own money. They continually protested their innocence, and even wrote, during their imprisonment, an epistle to the Quaker children, urging them to stand faithful in their testimony against the unrighteous.

In 1663 the soldiers turned the Friends out of their meeting-house at Colchester, and in addition broke the seats and the windows. They met in the streets, and were attacked by a troop of horse. One of the sufferers, when a trooper was beating him with his sword and the blade fell out of the hilt, meekly picked it up and gave it to him again. On another occasion the Colchester Quakers were so beaten with clubs and carbines that the spectators were moved to tears of pity. The soldiers were even allowed to beat them with clubs into which they had put iron spikes, and one old woman was wounded in twelve places with one of these weapons. This kind of thing went on for nearly six months. In 1664 Colonel Walter Slingsby broke up a Quaker meeting in the Isle of Wight, and sent some of those present to prison. He reported, in a tone of exasperation, that Priscilla Morley, one of the prisoners, being ill at the time,

---

[1] Croese, " Gen. Hist. Quakers," II. 19; T. Mardy Rees, " Hist. Quakers in Wales," pp. 61, 64.

died in prison rather than pay half a crown.[1]   In August 1671 there was a Quaker meeting at Parkfield in Suffolk.   Eleven men were arrested, and refused to give their names.   Sir Thomas Meadows, a local justice, issued a warrant to the constable to bring these people before him, but when the warrant was shown to them they refused to move, pointing out that the document said " bring."   The constable at last procured a cart, and he and his assistants lifted them into it bodily.   They remained perfectly helpless, stretched out at the bottom of the cart, so that he had to put one in on the top of the other, and when the cart reached its destination, they refused to get out, so the carter unfastened the harness, threw up the shafts, and toppled them all out together in a heap.   Having thus insisted on the strict letter of the warrant, they gave their names, and were dismissed till they should be sent for.[2]

Quakers annoyed orthodox people by refusing to close their places of business on Christmas Day.   When loyalists shut their shops on January 30th, the anniversary of the death of Charles I., and on May 29th, the day of Charles II.'s return, the Quakers kept theirs open.   The Mayor of Rochester complained to Williamson in 1676 that he had endeavoured to get January 30th observed with decorum in the town, and that Samuel Fox, a tailor, refused to close his shop.   The mayor, with some of the aldermen and councillors, went to him personally, and as he then refused, they ordered the constables to shut it, but he reopened as soon as they had gone.[3]   At Plymouth, on April 7th, 1677, the Quakers were turned out of their meeting-house, and until September 29th met in the streets.   Then a new mayor was appointed, and they returned to their meeting-house, only to be turned out again.   " They assembled in the open street three times a week, enduring the extremity of cold and inclemency of weather all the winter, abused by the rabble and scum of the people, and sometimes by the officers and soldiers of the garrison, who threw squibs of fire and hot burning coals on them, pushing them up and down the street, and bedaubing them with filth, all which and much more they endured with unwearied patience for the space of more than twelve months." [4]

The Quakers were quite able at times to puzzle their adversaries.   At Yarmouth, in November 1667, a Friend was standing on a block addressing about 150 people, when a constable came to arrest him.   The Quaker said, " If thou hast any authority, show it me, and I will with patience go with thee, but if thou canst not show me any, I shall not stir."   The constable, not sure apparently how far his authority extended, went to consult the bailiffs, but when he came back he found the meeting over and the Quaker gone.[5]   They were capable of making shrewd

---

[1] C.S.P.D., Dec. 10th, 1664.   [2] C.S.P.D., 292/27.   [3] C.S.P.D., 378/165.
[4] Besse, " Sufferings."   [5] C.S.P.D., November 4th, 1667, 222/50.

answers to dangerous questions. On one occasion at Norwich a Quaker was asked in court whether he thought the King was a heretic, and he replied that if the King lived in the light of Christ he could not condemn him, but if he did not, then God condemned him, and he could not justify him.[1] Gilbert Latey, though he gave up his business as a Court tailor and became a Quaker, did not lose his business instincts. There was a house in Wheeler Street, held in his name but used as a meeting-house. When the Government set about demolishing such buildings in 1670, he put in a needy member of the society as his tenant, so that the house became in the eyes of the law an inhabited dwelling, even though meetings might be held in it. This plan saved the building, so the Quakers did the same with some of their other meeting-houses.[2]

The following dialogue took place at the Worcester Assizes in July 1662. Robert Smith was indicted for refusing to take the oath of allegiance. He stood with his hat on. The judge inquired, " What is the reason you appear thus contemptuously before the court with your hat on? " Smith replied, " My hat is my own. I came truly by it, and it is not in contempt I wear it." " But," said the judge, " by it you contemn the authority and law of this kingdom." To which the prisoner answered, " Where is that law that forbids a man to wear his own hat? Instance it." " It is a custom in England to show their subjection to authority by putting off their hats," said the judge. " It is a custom in England for men to wear or come before courts with their coats or cloaks, and I am here without either, and is not one as much a contempt as the other? " Smith replied. So he was fined £5, and the gaoler ordered to remove his hat for him, The trial then proceeded. He was sentenced to a *præmunire*, remained in prison ten years, and all his property was confiscated. In the later years of the persecution the Quakers adopted the practice of coming to trial armed with law-books, and arguing from them.

Sir Richard Browne, Lord Mayor of London,[3] had been a Major-General under Cromwell, but after the Restoration became a most violent and brutal persecutor. A Quaker prisoner who had once been a soldier under him on one occasion rebuked him, and threw up some of his old misdeeds against him. The other prisoners did not approve of this, but signified that though the facts might be true, a magistrate upon the bench ought to be treated with due respect and honour.[4] One severe rebuke, however, was made publicly by a number of them. In 1664 Samuel Sandys, of Roger Ground near Hawkshead, was carried to his burial after dying in prison. The Quakers affixed to his

[1] Platt, " The Quakers in Norwich," 1926.
[2] Braithwaite, " Second Period," p. 77.
[3] In 1660–61. [4] Sewell, " Hist. Quakers," p. 342.

coffin an inscription, " This was a prisoner for the Lord Jesus Christ, and for the testimony of the truth of God as it is in Jesus hath he offered up his life for a witness thereof, and for an example and encouragement to all that shall be in the truth, and a warning to them that persecute the truth, that make widows and fatherless children, that they may consider the dreadful Judgment Day, and everlasting sentence from Christ in that day, which saith ' Go into everlasting punishment ' to them that did not visit Christ in prison, and what will become of them that cast into prison where He is manifest in His members? " In December 1663 Thomas Speed wrote from Newgate prison in Bristol to the mayor of that city a letter commencing, " The God of heaven is not well pleased with thee, because thy ways are not found right in His sight." It was a touching and manly letter in many ways, and yet was hardly calculated to make an unsympathetic magistrate feel more kindly disposed towards the prisoner. Most of the Quaker leaders suffered imprisonment at some time or other, some of them repeatedly, and many of their writings are addressed from some gaol or other. George Fox the younger sent " Two General Epistles " from the Gatehouse prison in 1660. William Bayly of Poole wrote in Hertford prison, in 1663, " A Grievous Lamentation over thee, O England, for Persecuting and Oppressing the Children of the Most High." John Camm wrote a " Testimony " from Appleby gaol. John Whitehead, while in Aylesbury gaol in 1661, wrote his " Small Treatise . . . of those Things I have Heard of the Father." In Lincoln gaol in 1662 he wrote a tract, " For the Vineyard of the Lord of Hosts," and about the same time, in conjunction with Martin Mason, " An Expostulation with the Bishops of England." King Charles II. did what he could for the Quakers on many occasions. When, in 1661, William Leddra, a Cornish Quaker, was hanged at Boston,[1] he forbade any more hangings of the kind. When Edward Burrough was committed to Newgate in 1662, the King sent a special order to the Sheriffs of London to release him and others, but they managed somehow to evade the order, and Burrough died there.[2] In a raid by the soldiers at the " Bull and Mouth " a man named John Trowel was killed. The coroner's jury returned no verdict because, though there was evidence that he was beaten and knocked down, the confusion had been so great that no definite person could be accused. If a verdict had been returned that he had been killed, but no particular person charged, then the city would have been liable to a heavy fine for conniving at murder in broad daylight in a public place. A Quaker reported the matter to the King, who said to him, " I assure you it was not by my advice that any of your friends should be slain. You must tell the magistrates of

[1] New England.   [2] Sewell, " Hist. Quakers," pp. 363-364.

the city of it, and prosecute the law against them." [1] In 1666 Charles issued an order for the release of George Fox, which ran: "The King being certainly informed that George Fox was a man principled against all plotting and fighting, and had been ready at all times to discover plots rather than make any . . . therefore his pleasure was that he should be discharged from his imprisonment." This was not the only time that Fox was set free by the King's order, and many other Quakers had reason to be thankful to Charles for the same interference on their behalf. In March 1665, Margaret Fell, who had already been in prison fourteen months,[2] was sentenced to the penalties of *præmunire*. In June 1668 she returned to her home at Swarthmoor, after four and a half years' incarceration, though the *præmunire* still hung over her head and she was liable to reimprisonment at any moment. The King, however, seems to have interfered to prevent the confiscation of her property. Her son, George, who in a petition to the King had spoken of his father as "a grand malignant," petitioned Charles again in 1665 "for the estate of his mother, forfeited for life, because she had run herself into a *præmunire* for embracing the fanatic opinions of the Quakers." [3] Margaret Fell married George Fox in 1669. She was again imprisoned in the next year, but released by discharge from the King in 1671.[4] Daniel Fleming of Rydal, who had been one of the most active of the magistrates in trying to make the Westmorland Quakers conform, and had used all his influence to stiffen the King's judges to severe courses with them,[5] was very annoyed at the discharge of Mrs. Fell in 1668 "from her easy imprisonment," as he called it. He wrote strongly to Williamson about it, complaining that leniency of this kind was a great discouragement to the King's servants when they tried to enforce the law.[6]

It is estimated that during the Commonwealth 3170 Quakers suffered for their religion. The majority of the first preachers died in prison. Twenty Quakers died in London gaols in 1662, twenty-five in 1664, fifty-two in 1665, and, in addition, seven others had their health broken and died as a result. The relation of the sufferings of the Friends fills in Besse's work over 1400 closely printed folio pages, and with all that writer's care, his lists are incomplete. According to Mr. Braithwaite, the indexes of that great work contain 12,406 names. Mr. Joseph J. Green, another Quaker historian, calculated, however, that 20,721 names were to be found in Besse. But some of the names occur more than once, and the list includes the sufferers under the Common-

---

[1] Sewell, "Hist. Quakers," pp. 335–336.
[2] "The Examination and Trial of Margaret Fell," 1664.
[3] Gaythorpe, "Swarthmoor Meeting House," *Trans. Cumb. and Westm. Antiq. Soc.*, 1906.
[4] Hodgkin, "George Fox," pp. 217–218.
[5] C.S.P.D., February 19th, 1664.   [6] C.S.P.D., August 21st, 1668.

wealth as well as during the Restoration period. Many, of course, suffered several times in both periods. Both writers, however, agree that a fair estimate of the number of persons who suffered in one way or another during the reigns of Charles II. and James II. would be considerably over 15,000. When we come to the actual deaths from persecution, it is easier to make a fairly correct estimate. Besse gave a list of 366 names, including those who died under the Commonwealth. The number of deaths given in the records at the Friends' House is much the same. Mr. Braithwaite estimated that 320 died during the years after the Restoration, but thought that this number might be raised to 450 at least. Mr. Green also estimated the number of deaths at 450. If it is remembered that on one occasion it was calculated that 4200 Quakers were in gaol, it does not seem that these writers have exaggerated in any degree. From a careful examination of the records of the society it appears that the value of the property of Quakers seized or destroyed down to 1688 must have been more than a million sterling.[1] A mere array of statistics, however, would give a very insufficient idea of what the Quakers really suffered. Their careful records, written in the simplest language, and bearing the stamp of truth in every line, give a vivid picture of all that they endured. That which they had to bear was not merely the enforcement of the law (apart from the question whether the law, as it was enacted, was right or wrong), it was the misuse of the law, it was the way the law was used to cloak wicked and abominable cruelty. It was not simply the question of one church trying to compel people by force to accept certain beliefs and practices, though it is perfectly true that this was the case; but much more than this, it was that men of no religion were seizing the opportunity thus afforded to lie and slander and rob and oppress, and to fill their pockets with ill-gotten gains. Such horror and disgust were at last aroused that the wiser people began to see in religious persecution a noxious tree, in whose branches lodged every unclean and hateful bird.

Till 1668 the Society of Friends consisted of a number of independent congregations, having friendly relations with each other, and brought into contact by the travelling ministers. Membership was open to all approved persons, though children were not considered as members.[2] But there was an inner and an outer membership. The outer membership consisted of those persons who held the Quaker beliefs, but there was a strict inner membership of those in whose hands was also the power of exercising discipline. It was possible to attend the meetings for worship without being a member of either kind.

---

[1] Braithwaite, " Second Period," pp. 114–115; *Encycl. Brit.*, 9th ed., Art. " Quakers."
[2] Barclay, " Inner Life," p. 39.

Discipline was very strict. Full members might be expelled from church meetings for improper conduct. If their conduct had been very bad, they might be publicly " testified against," and their name and offence entered in a book. On showing repentance they were restored, but first had to sign the entry of their condemnation in the book. Outer members also might be " testified against " in the same way.[1]

The whole Quaker organisation developed out of this system of meetings, new meetings for different purposes being arranged as the need for them showed itself. Thus, in 1665 the Friends, always remarkable for their charity, found the maintenance of so many newly-made widows and orphans a great strain. Hitherto the duty of raising money for the support of the poor had been in the hands of the men. So they asked " the most grave and solid women of their church " to assist them. The London meetings of the women for this purpose gave rise in time to the Women's Monthly Meetings in other parts of England. Fox took up the development and organisation of these in 1671.[2] So with the travelling ministers. In the early days it was quite simple for the ministers to meet together and arrange the preaching in the various centres among themselves. Hence, there grew up the " Morning " or " Ministers' Meeting," which met early on Sunday mornings, and after 1673 on Monday mornings, to settle the preaching arrangements.[3] The " Second Day's Morning Meeting " had also the duty of supervising books.

During the years 1666 to 1668 George Fox travelled about the country arranging and organising the whole system of meetings, and from that time onward the full and complete system of meetings was in working. Fox had a great gift for organisation, but doubtless something was due to the ability of Penn, Barclay, and other leaders. Above the ordinary Church Meeting for business and discipline, comes the Monthly Meeting, representing several churches. This has its due relation to the Quarterly Meeting, representing a still larger association, and above all comes the Yearly Meeting. Dr. Hodgkin compared the Yearly Meeting to Convocation, the Quarterly Meeting to the synod of a county, and the Monthly Meeting to the " vestry " (" ruridecanal council " would have been better) of a cluster of parishes.[4] The system has continued to the present day, although the names of some of the meetings do not now very accurately represent the periods at which they are held. There was never any clear-cut difference between the business of Monthly and Quarterly Meetings. The former dealt more par-

[1] Barclay, " Inner Life," pp. 360–364.
[2] Braithwaite, " Second Period," p. 273.
[3] Barclay, " Inner Life," pp. 380–381.
[4] Hodgkin, " George Fox," p. 206; Barclay, " Inner Life," p. 393.

ticularly with local business, some of which, however, had to be reported to the Quarterly Meeting. It also concerned itself with bad behaviour (to be married by a priest in a " steeple-house," or to pay tithes or church rates was very bad behaviour), relief of sufferings, cases of which had to be reported to the higher meetings, education, burial-grounds, the provision of registers, transference of members from one place to another, and so on. If an offender was not amenable to the rebukes of the Monthly Meeting he was reported to the Quarterly Meeting as having " departed from the truth," which meant that he had ceased to be a member.[1]   Records of proceedings at meetings were carefully kept, a clerk being elected for the purpose.

At first the Yearly Meetings were local and the Quarterly Meetings were linked up with these. But Fox decided on a great central Yearly Meeting in London. The business to be done at it was to come from the Quarterly Meetings, unless something of pressing necessity arose after the latter were over. The great Yearly Meeting would be attended by delegates from the Quarterly Meetings and by the travelling ministers, other members of the society not being restrained from attendance. The first of these meetings was held in February 1669, and it met with such boldness and openness that it attracted a good deal of outside attention. It was discontinued from 1673 to 1678, from which year onwards it has had an unbroken existence.[2] The Yearly Meeting had in some respects a connection, in idea at least, with the Annual Meeting of Ministers. Fox set this up permanently in 1668. There had not been one of these meetings since 1661.[3]

In 1672 it was decided to establish a central body of representatives to meet every Whitsuntide in London, " to advise about the managing of the public affairs of Friends throughout the nation." But whereas at the Yearly Meeting any Friend could be present, in addition to delegates and ministers, at this meeting only the representatives and ministers might attend, unless special permission were given. Another central body was established in 1676, and called the Meeting for Sufferings.[4] Its duty was to collect and keep records of the sufferings of Friends, and to do what was possible for their relief. It might make use of the law in a straightforward manner if redress could be obtained that way; but it was not to do anything that savoured of legal chicanery. There was to be a full meeting of this body before each law term began. In the intervals a weekly meeting was to be held of London members, reinforced

---

[1] Braithwaite, " Second Period," pp. 258–259.
[2] Barclay, " Inner Life," pp. 394–395; Braithwaite, " Second Period," p. 277.
[3] Braithwaite, " Second Period," p. 255.
[4] *Journal Friends Hist. Soc.*, XXI. 2–4.

by any country members who wished to come. The London
members of the committee were called on for this service during
one term in four. The country members were composed of
representatives of each county, chosen by the Quarterly Meetings
and were to be prepared to go up to London when required.
This Meeting for Sufferings still exists. It meets on the first
Friday of every month, and is now the general executive body
of the Society of Friends,[1] a sort of standing committee to
direct affairs during the interval between the Annual Meetings.[2]

In 1679 the Yearly Meeting directed that the expenses of
Friends who had to wait on the King or the courts should be
paid out of the general collection from the counties, and that
such expenditure should be in the control of the Meeting for
Sufferings. This control in the course of time extended to all
expenditure.[3] Voluntary contributions were raised for the support of the travelling ministers and their families; their travelling
expenses were frequently paid, and, as much of their journeying
was on horseback, the local meetings often had to provide
fodder and bedding for the preacher's horse. This system of
maintenance was one of the grievances of Wilkinson, Story, and
Rogers, who spoke of the ministers thus maintained as Fox's
hirelings.[4] The Quakers have always been liberal in their
charities. The York Quarterly Meeting in 1677 raised a large
sum of money for the poor Friends who were in prison, not to
be bestowed as a gift, but to enable them to work for their
living. They were taught to cut corks and pick oakum; the
material being provided, wages paid to the prisoners, the corks
and oakum sold, and the whole thing put on a business foundation.[5] In March 1683 the York Quarterly Meeting sent £30 to
the poor Quaker sufferers in Bristol. On May 8th, 1688, the
Quakers of Bristol, in spite of all they had gone through in
recent years, raised among themselves, by a collection at the
door of their meeting-house, the sum of £21 2s. 2d. for the
poor French Protestant refugees in that city.

The popular idea of a Quaker meeting is that of a number of
people sitting in silence, waiting for the Spirit to move some
one to speak. In reality, silence is the exception and not the
rule, though the practice of keeping silence increased somewhat
during the persecutions, inasmuch as juries sometimes acquitted
Quakers of holding a conventicle on the ground that no one
was speaking. There was infrequent reading of the Scriptures,
not from any lack of reverence for them; but because the
Church service was read from a book, some Quakers, apt to go
to the opposite extreme, would read nothing.[6] Swarthmoor

[1] Braithwaite, " Second Period," pp. 281–285; Neal, " Puritans," IV.
510–511; Croese, " Gen. Hist. Quakers," Pt. II. 97–104.
[2] T. Mardy Rees, " Hist. Quakers in Wales," p. 213.
[3] Braithwaite, " Second Period," p. 285.   [4] Idem, ibid., pp. 360, 366.
[5] Journal Friends Hist. Soc., X. 189.   [6] Barclay, " Inner Life," pp. 401–

meeting-house, which George Fox built in 1688 for the Friends there, still has the Bible which he presented, and which was orginally chained to the reading-desk.[1] The Quakers opposed all forms and ceremonies in worship, and yet were attacked by Perrot because they retained a single rule about taking off their hats at the time of prayer. He argued that there was no reason why a man should not keep his hat on, or take his shoes off, or fall on his face, if he felt disposed; in fact, the only way to avoid a charge of ceremonialism was to have no rules at all. No man, said William Salt, should act outwardly further than he saw inwardly. There should not be fixed times, or even places, for worship. You should worship when you liked, where you liked, and how you liked, or, rather, as the light within guided you.[2] Others desired the abolition of Church offices, and preached complete Quietism, " waiting in stillness and quietness, not out of words only, but also out of thoughts and imaginations." [3] This attitude towards worship was part of the objection to the ministry which Fox had set up.[4] Penn said that if you have a church, you must have a government and pastors,[5] but his opponents replied that the Spirit of God was the only governor and pastor, moving in individuals as He willed.[6] It followed from Quaker principles that Sunday could not be regarded as a day of obligation, but that all days were equally holy. Sunday was merely a convenient day for meeting together, but in the great cities they assembled for worship several days a week.[7] On the same grounds they kept no special holy days or festivals, and caused much ill-feeling by opening their shops on Good Friday.

The Yearly Meeting in 1675 sent out an epistle " concerning sighing, groaning, and singing in church," in which it was decreed that these practices were not to be discouraged except when indulged in immoderately. Fox allowed singing in meetings, but it does not seem to have been common, and the practice was one of the things objected to by Wilkinson and Story. The general feeling, however, seems to have been that there was no objection to rhyming or metrical hymns, provided that they were sung by people who were in the grace of God.[8]

The Friends did not, like many members of the other sects, go to the churches of the Establishment to be married. Weddings

[1] Hodgkin, " George Fox," p. 73.
[2] Salt, " Some Breathings of Life from a Naked Heart," 1663; Barclay, " Inner Life," p. 433.
[3] " A Real Demonstration of the True Order in the Spirit of God," 1663.
[4] " The Spirit of the Hat," 1673, believed to have been written by William Mucklow.
[5] W. Penn, " Alexander the Coppersmith," 1673.
[6] Barclay, " Inner Life," pp. 431–438.
[7] Croese, " Gen. Hist. Quakers," p. 56.
[8] Barclay, " Inner Life," pp. 452, 461–462.

took place in their own meetings, without any formalities or ceremonies, the bride and bridegroom simply pledging their troth in the presence of witnesses, who signed the certificate of marriage. The form of words at present in use among the Friends is taken, with a few alterations, from the Commonwealth Directory of Public Worship.[1] After 1668 a certificate was put in that the proposals of marriage had been laid before both the Men's and Women's Meetings, the Monthly and Quarterly Meetings, and that no impediment had been alleged. The clergy occasionally made trouble about this, because they lost their wedding fees, and sometimes Quakers were delated by officious persons on a charge of unlawful cohabitation because they had not been married according to the rites and ceremonies of the Church. A vain attempt was made in a case at the Nottingham Assizes in 1661 to prove Quaker marriages unlawful; but the judge held that it was the consent of the parties which constituted the marriage.[2] In 1682 Sir Matthew Hale gave an important decision on the subject. A Quaker was sued for some pre-nuptial debts contracted by his wife, and his counsel put forward the argument that he was not liable as the marriage was null, not having been solemnised according to the rites of the Church of England; but Hale strongly reprehended this defence, which, if it had been allowed, would have made the issue illegitimate and incapable of succession.[3]

The Quakers were very strict in their discipline with regard to marriages. At Worcester, Robert and Susan Knight were made to sign a confession of repentance for " being joined together in marriage by a national priest " before they were readmitted as members. James Stafford, of the same congregation, confessed to " taking a wife out of the world, not convinced of the truth, and in being married by a priest, and at a time when my child was dead in my house, and in seeking a wife sooner than a year after the decease of my former one." There is an entry in the books of the same congregation: " Ordered, that George Fox's paper concerning marrying within a year be copied out of a book called ' The Mirror of Justices,' in which those who marry within a year after their wife or husband's death are declared fit to be punished by corporal punishment in divers manners."[4] There was some discussion at the time of the Wilkinson–Story controversy as to whether the legal position of Quaker marriages might not be safeguarded by some civil procedure; but this was rejected as a concession to weakness and worldliness.[5]

---

[1] Barclay, "Inner Life," p. 407.   [2] Sewell, "Hist. Quakers," p. 283.
[3] Burnet, "Life of Sir Matthew Hale," 1682; Roger North, "Life of Francis, Lord Guildford."
[4] Noake, "Worcestershire Sects," pp. 253–254, 263.
[5] Clarke, "Hist. Nonconformity," II. 135; Barclay, "Inner Life," p. 442–443.

The Quakers registered and recorded everything. Sir Philip Musgrave complained in 1663 that they kept copies of proceedings against them by the justices of the peace, in order to be ready against the time when they could call the justices to account.[1] By a minute of the " fifteenth of the seventh month," 1673, they ordered that " two of a sort of all books written by Friends be collected and kept together . . . and one of every sort written against the truth," and they further directed that Penn and Whitehead should attend to the matter. Thus arose the great library of Quaker and anti-Quaker literature now at the Friends' House. John Whiting published, in 1708, " A Catalogue of Friends' Books," in which he recorded the names of over 2600 publications which had been issued from the press since the foundation of Quakerism. The names of the authors were given in alphabetical order, and all works of which the date was known were given under the authors' names. These works varied in size from single sheets (Whiting gave the number of pages even to a fraction) to large folios; but very few ran to more than three or four pages, and most of them were of quarto size. The list is, of course, incomplete, and, curiously enough, Whiting omitted one of his own books. A rough calculation shows that from the Restoration to the Revolution some 1600 of these works had come from Quaker pens, and the number might be added to considerably if we could include some of the books of which Whiting did not know the date. Moreover, he gave a list of books written originally in High and Low Dutch which had not been translated when he wrote, and some fifty-five of these were written between 1660 and 1689. The spread of Quakerism on the continent is shown by the fact that many of the English works had already been translated into Latin, French, and Dutch.

In England the licensing laws were a great hindrance, because of the penalties attached, and the printers who did most of the Quaker work were frequently sent to prison. During the years between 1662 and 1680, and between 1685 and 1688 the Quaker writings were generally printed without a printer's name. But writers and distributors were also liable to penalties, and a number of Quakers suffered under this head, because Sir Roger L'Estrange's spies were everywhere.[2] One question which still requires to be answered is how the Quakers, who had no connection with the Stationers' Company, managed to print as many books as they did during the period, especially as they had to print so many secretly, and the Government did everything in its power to prevent them. The history of their secret press has yet to be discovered.[3]

It is impossible to read any of the Quaker writings without

---

[1] C.S.P.D., March 2nd, 1663.   [2] Barclay, " Inner Life," pp. 418–419.
[3] Arber, " The Term Catalogues," 1903–1906, I. xii. xiii.

being struck with the simple and straightforward way in which they said what they had to say. They attempted no tricks of style, they practised no rhetoric, they indulged in no exaggeration, they told a plain tale in the language of plain men. In theological controversy, it is true, they frequently became abusive, but men of much better education than most of the Quakers had received were equally violent in denunciation and equally offensive in the use of brutal epithets. But when the Quaker was telling a Quaker story, he sometimes rivalled John Bunyan himself in the simplicity and power with which he spoke; the reason being that both derived their literary style from the same source, the English Bible. Even the titles of Quaker books sometimes have an artlessness and pathos that the reader finds most arresting. Take, for example, this passage from " A Memorable Account of the Christian Experiences, Gospel Labours, Travels, and Sufferings of that Ancient Servant of Christ, Stephen Crisp." [1] " So I went to Heidelberg to the prince of that land, and had a good opportunity with him, and laid before him the danger of his proceeding on a persecution. He heard me with a great deal of friendliness and discoursed things at large with me, and in several things promised it should be better, as it did also after come to pass. So having finished that service in Germany I returned, and being come into the Low Country again I went to Groningen, where divers had believed in the Name of Jesus the Light of the World, whom when I had visited in the power of God and strengthened in the faith, I left and returned through Friesland to Amsterdam, where by reason of my now speaking in their language, meetings grew exceeding great and many strangers came flocking in, and a great openness I found in the country." [2] Or take the oft-quoted passage in which George Fox described his last interview with the Lord Protector: " And after this I met him riding into Hampton Court Park, and before I came at him he was riding in the head of his Life Guard, and I saw and felt a waft of death go forth against him, and he looked like a dead man, and when I had spoken to him of the sufferings of Friends, and warned him as I was moved to speak to him, he bid me come to his house, and so I went to Kingston, and the next day went up to Hampton Court, and then he was very sick, and Harvey told me, which was one of his men that waited on him, that the doctors were not willing I should come in to speak with him; and so I passed away, and never saw him no more." [3]

Like the early Baptists, many of the Quakers had a distrust of human learning as a qualification for the ministry; they even thought the possession of it a hindrance. George Fox opposed the establishment of Oliver's college at Durham.[4] Barclay, him-

[1] 1694.   [2] Pp. 29–30.
[3] Fox, " Diary," 1658.   [4] " Journal," I. 190.

self a learned man, said that the illiterate men whom God had raised up to be ministers of the Gospel were able, by the certain evidence of the Spirit within themselves, to correct the errors of the translators of the Scriptures.[1]   But men of the higher ranks, like William Penn, Isaac Pennington, and Robert Barclay himself, and university men like Samuel Fisher, could not really despise education.   Moreover, their frequent theological disputes tended to the increase of theological knowledge, so the contempt for human learning soon passed away, and we hear of the establishment of Quaker schools, and of a demand for lexicons of Hebrew and Greek.[2]

Samuel Fisher was a graduate of Trinity College, Oxford, and had been vicar of Lydd in Kent, but he resigned the living, became a Baptist minister, and published a treatise, " Baby Baptism mere Babism."   In 1655 he turned Quaker.   After the Restoration he endured four and a half years of prison life, of which two years were spent in the White Lion prison at Southwark.   He died in 1665.   His greatest literary work was " Rusticus ad Academicos," a defence of Quakerism in which he showed a sound knowledge of the canon and the textual criticism of the Scriptures.   The style, however, was involved, fanciful and sesquipedalian.   Thus, when John Owen committed himself to the statement that the variant readings in the original texts of the Scriptures were of divine origin, and intended to encourage the study of the Bible, Fisher replied, " Whence came this whiffle and whimsy within the circumference of thy figmentitious fancy? "[3]   The most learned Quaker of the seventeenth century, and the best exponent of Quaker theology, was Robert Barclay.   He was born in 1648, had some of the best blood of Scotland in his veins, was educated abroad, and afterwards travelled on the continent for the Quaker cause.   His numerous writings were collected in a large folio, called " Truth Triumphant," which was published in 1692.   His most important work was " An Apology for the True Christian Divinity, as the same is Held Forth and Preached by the People called in Scorn Quakers," published in 1676, and dedicated to King Charles II. In this work he set forth in fifteen propositions the fundamentals of Quaker doctrine, and replied to the various objections which had already been made to them.   It was in this book that the doctrine of the inner light, though held and believed from the beginning of Quakerism, was first systematically formulated. Barclay was a widely read scholar, and he cited a great number of authors, ancient and modern, in confirmation of the doctrines he expounded.   The exposition is clear and systematic, the style generally simple, and it is usually impossible to mistake the meaning.   The " Apology " was hardly so original as has been

---

[1] Barclay, " Apology."   [2] Barclay, " Inner Life," pp. 502–504.
[3] Neal, " Puritans," IV. 421–422; " Camb. Hist. Eng. Lit.," VIII. 111.

supposed, for it owed much to the Westminster Confession and the Shorter Catechism, the order of his fifteen propositions manifestly following the order of the questions in the latter.[1] The most comprehensive of Barclay's works, it was written in Latin, and soon translated into English and Dutch, and before the end of the century eleven editions were printed in England, three in Ireland, and six in America. The writer of the preface to the " Apology " in the folio edition of the collected works apologised for the scholarly method and style of the book, " for we make that sort of learning no part of our divine science. But that was not to show himself; but out of his tenderness to scholars, and as far as the simplicity and purity of the truth would permit, in condescension to their education and way of teaching of those points herein handled." The Quakers fully realised the value of the work to their cause, and collections were made at the meetings to raise funds for a large edition of 8000 copies for free distribution. Nevertheless, it had not the effect that might have been expected, for though a few scholars on the continent wrote Latin answers to it, it met with very few attacks, and outside Quaker circles seems to have fallen rather flat.[2]

The Friends from the beginning made great use of the ministry of women, and many of them were as active in preaching as the men. Margaret Fell published a tract in 1666, entitled " Women's Speaking Justified, Proved and Allowed of by the Scriptures, all such as Speak by the Spirit and Power of the Lord Jesus, and how Women were the First that Preached the Tidings of the Resurrection of Jesus, and were sent by Christ's own Command, before He ascended to the Father. John xx. 17." A postscript begins : " And you, dark priests, that are so mad against women's speaking, and it's so grievous to you, did not God say to Abraham, ' Let it not be grievous to thy sight because of the lad, and because of thy bondwoman ? In all that Sarah hath said to thee, hearken to her voice ' ? (Mark here.) The husband must learn of the woman, and Abraham did so, and this was concerning the things of God." Elizabeth Hooton, " an ancient woman," was a pertinacious missionary. She went to Whitehall, and testified in sackcloth and ashes, she waylaid the King and presented him with petitions, and wrote letters to him. She endured cruel sufferings at the hands of the

---

[1] T. Hodgkin, " George Fox," 3rd ed., 1906, p. 6.

[2] Turner, " Quakers," p. 200; Barclay, " Truth Triumphant." Barclay followed it up in 1679 with " A Vindication of his Apology for the Christian Divinity professed by the People called Quakers; in Reply to the Exceptions made against it by one John Brown, in his Book called, ' Quakerism the Pathway to Paganism.' " Dr., afterwards Dean, Hicks, preached a sermon before the University of Oxford on June 11th, 1680, which was afterwards published under the title, " The Spirit of Enthusiasm Exorcised," and was in great measure a reply to these writings of Barclay.

New England Puritans, returned to England to continue her
" gospel work," and set off in 1671, with Fox and others, to
the West Indies, and died and was buried in Jamaica.[1] For
her agitation for prison reform in the days when prisons were
dens of filth, fever, and iniquity, she has been called " a sixteenth-
century Elizabeth Fry." Mary Fisher, a servant girl from Pontefract, was imprisoned in York Castle, whipped in Cambridge,
and imprisoned in Boston, New England. A party of six
Quakers, including John Perrot, set out in 1657 to convert the
Sultan of Turkey. Mary Fisher was the only one of them who
arrived at their destination, and the Sultan, who probably
looked upon her as one of " the afflicted of Allah," listened to
her, treated her kindly, and even with respect, and sent her
home.[2] She afterwards married William Bayly, a Quaker sea
captain, and settled down. Katherine Evans, a farmer's wife
whose home was at Englishbatch, near Bath, suffered imprisonment for her missionary efforts in England, Scotland, and Ireland,
and with a companion, Sarah Chivers, a Wiltshire woman, was
three and a half years in a prison of the Inquisition at Malta.[3]
Barbara Blaugdon, a governess, went as a missionary to Ireland.
Loveday Hambly, Margaret Fell, Guilielma Penn, and many
others, put their purses and their energies constantly at the
service of the cause. Others were active with their pens.
Theophila Townshend of Cirencester, wrote " An Epistle of
Love to Friends in the Women's Meeting in London." [4] Elizabeth Bathurst was the writer of " Truth's Vindication: or a
Gentle Stroke to Wipe Off the Foul Aspersions, False Accusations, and Misrepresentations cast upon the Quakers." [5] Dorcas
Dole published in 1685 a small tract, " A Salutation of my
Endeared Love to the Faithful in all Places " written while " a
prisoner in Newgate for the Testimony of Jesus," and urging
her fellow-sufferers to patience and endurance. In the last fifty
years of the seventeenth century over eighty women writers
were active on behalf of Quakerism.[6] Only two women during
the same period seem to have written against Quakerism. One
of these was Jane Turner of Newcastle-on-Tyne, who, in 1653,
wrote a little book entitled " Choice Experiences "; the other
was Eleanor James, the wife of a London printer. She published, in 1687, " A Defence of the Church of England, in a
Short Answer to the Canting Address, with a Word or Two
concerning a Quaker's Good Advice." [7]

[1] Sewell, " Hist. Quakers," I. 618–620.   [2] *Idem, ibid.*, I. 472–474.
[3] " A Short Relation of the Cruel Sufferings of Katherine Evans and Sarah
Chivers," 1662.
[4] 1680.   [5] 1683.
[6] Their names are to be found in Joseph Smith's " Catalogue of Friends'
Books," 1857.
[7] *Journal Friends Hist. Soc.*, X. 93–95; Joseph Smith, " Bibliotheca Anti-
Quakeriana," 1873, pp. 249–250.

There were Quaker ladies in high circles.   Anne, Viscountess
Conway became a Quakeress, and Quaker meetings were held
in her chamber, to which she was usually confined through ill
health.   She corresponded with the leading Friends, and Henry
More, who had been tutor to herself and her brother, was
greatly concerned at her conversion.   He issued pamphlets
against the Quakers, wrote letters to William Penn on the
subject of the sacraments, and had an interview with Fox; but
in conversing with the latter " he felt himself as it were turned
into brass, so much did the spirit, crookedness, or perverseness
of that person move and offend his mind." [1]   Lady Conway
was also interested in the mystical and the occult, and Baron
van Helmont, the son of the distinguished chemist, having
similar interests, lived in her house, and regularly attended
Quaker meetings. [2]   She has been called " an hysterical invalid." [3]
An invalid she certainly was, but after her death in 1679 a
collection of Latin philosophical treatises was published in
Amsterdam, the first of which was a translation of a work by
Lady Conway, " a certain English countess learned beyond her
sex." [4]

The Quakers had also an eminent patroness abroad, the
Princess Elizabeth, the sister of Prince Rupert.   She had been a
pupil of Descartes, and had also come under the influence of
Jean Labadie, who taught a kind of mysticism something like
Quakerism, but with a mingling of Anabaptist doctrines.   Elizabeth spent her later life as Abbess of Herford in north-east
Westphalia.   The convent had long been secularised, but its
possessions gave her an income and a little territorial jurisdiction,
as well as the title of Princess and Prelatess of the Holy Roman
Empire.   George Fox's stepdaughter, Mrs. Keith, together with
a Dutch Quakeress and Robert Barclay, visited her, and she
became very friendly with Barclay, and kept up a correspondence
with him afterwards, signing herself " your affectionate friend,
Elizabeth."   She and Barclay had great arguments; perhaps
he was bolder, inasmuch as he too had Stuart blood in his veins,
and was her third cousin.   He even dared to rebuke her for
making use of the services of an ordained minister, " concurring
to keep up that which God is pulling down," but she was not
convinced.   Though she never became a Quakeress she showed
her sympathy with the Quaker sufferers in England by inducing
her brother Rupert and her mother's friend, Lord Craven, to
intercede for them.   Fox, Barclay, Penn, and Keith, while on a
tour amongst the German Friends, visited her twice in the year

[1] Richard Ward, " Life of Henry More," 1710, p. 197.
[2] Tulloch, " Rational Theology in England in the Seventeenth Century,"
II. 325–329.
[3] " D.N.B."
[4] *Journal Friends Hist. Soc.*, VII. 7–17.

1677, and she seems to have corresponded with the leading Quakers until her death in 1680.[1]

Another royal lady of the House of Stuart actually became a Quakeress. This was Jane Stuart, born in Paris in 1654, the natural daughter of James Duke of York by a mother whose name is unknown. Jane came to England in 1660, and appears to have been for a time under the care of her father's first wife, Anne Hyde. The Duke, before he became a Catholic, had been known, at least once, to attend a Quaker meeting; Quakers frequently visited him, and Penn was on terms of intimate friendship with him. After a time Jane was sent to Germany, where she spent some part of her girlhood. In all probability she would visit the Princess Elizabeth, and at her little court would again come in contact with Quaker doctrines and Quaker missionaries. When she actually became a Quakeress is unknown, but there is a story that after her return to England she was once imprisoned for her religion, though the story that Ellwood was her fellow-prisoner must be wrong, because she was only twelve years old at the time of his last imprisonment, and, indeed, her name does not appear in the list of sufferers in the Quaker cause. She married a Quaker after the Quaker form, but on the way from the meeting-house the horses took fright, and the bridegroom was killed.

In 1688, when James fled from England, Jane went away secretly, travelled about the country for some time, and in 1689 settled down at Wisbech, where she got work as a reaper. Then she bought a spinning-wheel and made a living by spinning flax and wool, which she sold in the market-place. At Wisbech she remained till her death, a constant attendant at Quaker meetings. Her refined speech, and the fact that she was once caught reading a Greek Testament, made people suspect that she was more than she seemed. After the Revolution some search was made for her, the Whigs being anxious to get evidence from her that James's infant son was really supposititious. The Duke of Argyle, who was sent to seek for her, traced her to Wisbech, but she recognised his arms upon his coach and went into hiding until he had departed. Only once did she leave her life-long retreat, and that was at the time of "the Fifteen," when she heard that the Pretender had landed at Peterhead, hired a chaise, and travelled to Scotland to see her brother. She died in 1742, and traditions of her lingered long after her death—how her cellar was filled with birds, which she loved and tended, how kind she was to children, how she was buried in the Friends' burying-ground, at her own request, under a rowan tree which she had planted there. Her grave is still

[1] E. Godfrey, "A Sister of Prince Rupert," 1909, Ch. XVI.; Graham, "Life of Penn," pp. 109–112; Masson, "Milton," V. 595; Hodgkin, "George Fox," pp. 256–259.

marked with her name and age and the date of her death, and there is an entry in the Friends' burial register, " Supposed to be descended from James 2nd, and she lived in a cellar in the Old Market, Wisbech." It was not till long after her death that her full story was discovered. Charles Stuart, her grandfather, gave his life for the Church of England, James Stuart, her father, gave his crown for the Church of Rome, and Jane Stuart for her religion gave up for fifty-four years almost everything that men hold most dear.[1]

The great centre of Quakerism until two or three years ago was in Devonshire House, Bishopsgate.[2] The origin of their settlement there came about in this way. The Great Fire having destroyed the Quaker meeting-house at the " Bull and Mouth " in Aldersgate, the Friends decided to become the tenants of a portion of Devonshire House. This was a large house, built at very great cost in the sixteenth century by one Jasper Fisher, and known for a long time as Fisher's Folly. Its later name was derived from the fact that it had become the property of the Earl and Countess of Devonshire. The house was now untenanted, though in the hands of the lessees, and at first the Quakers sub-leased a portion of the building from the last, at a rental of £70 a year. As soon as they entered into possession in 1666, the authorities seized it, locked it up, and marked it with a Government broad arrow to denote that it was now Government property. Nothing daunted, however, the Quakers removed the lock, took possession once more, and continued their meetings, with much less interference than they had suffered in their other places of worship. About the same time the Baptists occupied another portion of the house, and a Baptist congregation continued there, or at least on the same site, till 1870, when they moved away to Stoke Newington.

Lord Devonshire ultimately sold the buildings and site to a number of speculators, and a great part of the house was pulled down. One of these speculators was Dr. Nicholas Barebone, the son of Praisegod Barebone, and from him, though the " Bull and Mouth " was now rebuilt, the Friends bought a site on which in 1678 they erected a meeting-house, practically on the site of what was till a year or two ago " The Old Meeting-House." Mindful of the development of their society and its organisation, they made also provision for committee rooms, and a dwelling-place for distressed members of the sect.[3]

Swarthmoor, near Ulverston, became another of the important centres of seventeenth-century Quakerism. Here Fox converted

---

[1] Brailsford, " Quaker Women," 1915, pp. 304–323; " A Stuart among the Quakers? " *Journal Friends Hist. Soc.*, X. 263–268; Graham, " Life of Penn," p. 112.

[2] It is now at Friends' House, Euston Road.

[3] M. Sefton Jones, " Old Devonshire House by Bishopsgate," London, 1923.

Margaret Fell, the wife of Judge Fell, the Judge of Assize for the Chester and North Wales circuit, and Chancellor, in 1655, of the Duchy of Lancaster.   Fell never became a Quaker himself, perhaps on account of his official position, but he allowed the meetings to be held in his house.   Here, in 1656, the first General Meeting was held.   Margaret Fell, *née* Margaret Askew, and great-granddaughter of Anne Askew, lost her first husband before the Restoration, and married Fox in 1669.   At Swarthmoor George Fox built a little meeting-house, still standing and bearing the inscription E. DONO. G. Fox. 1688.   It has been modernised, but has the gallery characteristic of so many seventeenth-century meeting-houses.   One of the Swarthmoor servants, Thomas Salthouse, became a Quaker preacher.   William Caton, secretary to Margaret Fell and tutor to her family, described as probably the best educated and most refined minister of the first generation of Quakers, preached Quakerism not only in England, but also in France and Holland before his death in 1665.[1]

[1] Hodgkin, " George Fox," p. 73.

VI

THE MINOR SECTS

ONE of the most striking features of the Commonwealth period was the luxuriant growth of new religious sects. Yet in 1672 all the licences under the Declaration of Indulgence, as far as they specified the denomination of the recipient, were granted to Presbyterians, Independents, or Baptists, with one single exception, that of an Antinomian. Nevertheless, Cominges, the French Ambassador, calculated that there were sixty different religious bodies in England in 1666,[1] while Roger L'Estrange, in 1681, seemed to think there were 170 of them.[2] Baxter mentions several, and frequent references are found to others.

Thomas Underhill, writing in 1660, said that the Anabaptists, Familists, and Grindletonians shrouded themselves at first under the names of Independents and Separatists,[3] and since sectarian appellations were so loosely used that in 1672 a man could be called a Congregationalist in one licence and a Baptist in another, it was possible that when in doubt the officials gave to these sects the generic name of Independents. It may be, also, that, like the Quakers, many of them kept quiet and did not apply for a licence. Probably some of the licences in which no particular denomination is mentioned may have been granted to some of these congregations. None of the names appears in Sheldon's census, but it may be that when the parochial clergy came across congregations reported to have eccentric views they confused them with the Quakers. It seems quite clear, nevertheless, that some of these minor sects existed right through the Restoration period, and were in existence at its close. Not only so, but a few new and short-lived religious bodies actually came into existence during those years. No one of the existing lists, however, is complete, nor do all the lists give the same names. Neither do all the various names represent sects in the modern sense of independent, organised, ecclesiastical systems. Seventeenth-century writers often spoke of a sect where we should speak of a party or a school of thought. Pelagians, Arminians, Arians, Antinomians, Millennarians, and Latitudinarians were

---

[1] " Relation de l'Angleterre en l'année 1666," quoted in W. G. Bell's " The Great Fire of London," 1920, p. 304.
[2] *Observator*, July 13th, 1681.
[3] Underhill, " Hell Broke Loose," 1660.

severally to be found in more than one of the various churches. Sceptics have little claim to be a religious denomination, while the Anti-Scripturians of the seventeenth century had equally little claim to the title of Christian.

THE FIFTH MONARCHY MEN

In all ages of the Church, Millennarianism—the doctrine of the reign of Christ and His saints on earth for a thousand years—has had a great attraction for certain types of religious minds, and has had special strength in times of turmoil and commotion. In recent years the walls of our towns have been placarded with announcements that " Millions now living will never die," while those whose memories go back to the Victorian era can remember the sensation caused at different times by the prophecies of Baxter and Cumming. Millennarianism was very common in the seventeenth century, especially during the period of the Puritan Revolution. The upholders of it derived their ideas chiefly from the books of Daniel and Revelations. Four great monarchies had existed on the earth—Assyria, Persia, Greece and Rome. The Old Testament prophesied a fifth— the Kingdom of Christ. This they believed would be established immediately. The veil would be taken from the eyes of the Mohammedans, the Jews would be called into the Christian kingdom, Rome would fall, and the Roman Empire come to an end. The devil would be chained, and the saints would begin to possess the earth and all the wealth amassed by the wicked. Then Christ would sit in judgment, the wicked would be cast into hell, Christ would reign over a world-wide temporal kingdom for a thousand years, and the saints would reign with Him.[1]

The heresiographers distinguished the Millennarians or Chiliasts from the Fifth Monarchy men. Tenison similarly divided the " sensual Millennarians " from the Fifth Monarchists.[2] There were men like Henry Mede and Henry More, who believed that in God's good time there would be a millennial reign of Christ. Edward Bagshawe held this view, and protested that this doctrine had been looked upon with prejudice because some people who had preached it had really tried to establish their own reign.[3] Then there were men who were constantly wrestling with the problems of Daniel and the Revelations, trying to discover signs of fulfilment according to schemes of their own. Some of them believed themselves inspired with the spirit of prophecy. Thus, George Foster claimed that God the Father had spoken to him as he lay in a trance for twenty-two

---

[1] " The Postboy," II. 426.
[2] " A Discourse concerning a Guide in Matters of Faith," 1683.
[3] " The Doctrine of the Kingdom and Personal Reign of Christ," 1669.

hours, and his name was changed in a vision to Jacob Israel Foster. He saw that the Jews would return to their own city, and the Lord would reign among His saints on Mount Zion. Heaven, or the third and highest dispensation, must be about Jerusalem. An expedition was to be sent to the Holy Land, which for the credit of England must be led by an Englishman. When they arrived at Jerusalem they were to die, but they would soon rise up again and die no more. The time of restitution would be in the year A.D. 7000, after which there would be no hell nor devils left.[1] Thirdly, there were men whose theological views with regard to the Second Coming were coupled with republican principles; who believed that the prophecies would be brought to fulfilment by the efforts of the true believers. It was written that under Christ's banner the saints should be victorious, in battle one of them should chase ten, and ten a thousand, and they were prepared to spread their doctrines by the sword. Many of them believed and hoped that Oliver's reign would prove to be the commencement of the millennial dawn. It was in this hope that some of them supported him, and it was in their disappointment at finding these hopes unfulfilled that they rose in rebellion in 1657. Even the extremists did not all belong to the sect of the Fifth Monarchists, for some of them were Baptists, but they all held that the world must be prepared for the Second Advent by putting all power in Church and State in the hands of the godly.

In 1642 John Archer published "The Personal Reign of Christ upon Earth," and about this time there was a meeting-house of Fifth Monarchy men in Blackfriars.[2] John Rogers, son of Nehemiah Rogers, prebendary of Ely and rector of St. Botolph's, Bishopsgate, became one of the chief upholders of the militant movement. He was born in 1627, was ordained to the Presbyterian ministry in 1647, but renounced Presbyterianism and joined the Independents in the following year. Sent by the Council of State to Ireland in 1651, Christ Church cathedral, Dublin, was given him for his ministry. Here he found Colonel Hewson, the Governor of Dublin, amongst his congregation, and he also served under Hewson in the field against the Irish rebels. But Rogers did not get on well in Ireland. Thomas Patient, the head of the Baptist congregation at Waterford, protested against Rogers's views on infant baptism, and stirred up a schism in his congregation, and he returned to England in the spring of 1652. In England he quarrelled with Serjeant Maynard, who had been counsel against him in a suit brought against him for non-residence in his parish of Purleigh. He had another quarrel, with Zachary Crofton, then Presbyterian minister of Garlick Hythe. Rogers had established a lecture on

[1] "Christianity no Enthusiasm," 1678, p. 93.
[2] Champlain Burrage, E.H.R., Oct. 1910.

Friday evenings at the church of St. Thomas the Apostle, in London, and Crofton published a pamphlet against him, entitled " A Taste of the Doctrine of Thomas Apostle's." Rogers had by this time become one of the leaders and ministers of Fifth Monarchism. Many of the army officers—Harrison, Overton, Alured, Okey, Rich, Danvers, and others—belonged to the party. Some of the Baptists, especially those who leaned towards German Anabaptism, held Fifth Monarchist views. John Tillinghast, minister of Trunch in Norfolk, gave up his living to proclaim the new doctrines. In 1654 he published " Knowledge of the Times: or, A Resolution of the Question, How Long it shall be unto the End of Wonders," and the year after, " Generation Work: or a Brief and Seasonable Word offered to the View and Consideration of the Saints and People of God in this Generation, with a Key to Unlock the Mystical Numbers of Daniel and the Revelations." It was a very militant creed, and many of the Independent officers accepted it. The saints had drawn the sword, and had overthrown the King, and the lords and the bishops. There still remained presbytery, lawyers, and the Rump. When they had pulled down these last remnants of Antichrist they would carry the holy war against all the enemies of Christ throughout the world. In 1653 Rogers published " Ohel or Bethshemesh, a Tabernacle for the Sun," a defence of the Independent system against the Presbyterian, and an exposition of his views on church discipline. He set forth the strong resemblances, as he saw them, between Presbyterianism and papistry, and he replied to Zachary Crofton's attack, which he called " that frothy, nameless pamphlet of a lying libeller and scandalous Philocompos, that is much cried up by that party for his voluble tongue." Crofton accepted the challenge cheerfully, and immediately [1] published " Bethshemesh Clouded : or, Some Animadversions on the Rabbinical Talmud of Rabbi John Rogers of Thomas Apostle's, London: called his Tabernacle for the Sun, his Irenicum Evangelicum, or his Idea of Church Discipline. In which you have his Spirit in some Measure Refuted, by Zachary Crofton, Minister of the Word." He attacked his rival's book very completely; the size, price, frontispiece, and title-page all came under the lash. He accused him of pride and insolence in Ireland, and of pluralism in England, and said that his anger against Maynard arose from the fact that though he held the livings of Purleigh in Essex and St. Thomas the Apostle in London, he had tried hard to get St. Martin's-in-the-Fields, and Maynard had prevented him.

Rogers's next book was called " Sagrir : or, Doomsday Drawing Nigh with Thunder and Lightning to Lawyers," and was published in October 1653. It attacked the clergy, and their tithes, and the whole parochial system. Lawyers were compared to

[1] 1653.

the locusts out of the bottomless pit,[1] and their end was prophesied as coming to pass shortly.   The four beasts of Revelation were interpreted as the four great monarchies, the ten horns [2] as the ten European kingdoms which arose out of the ruins of the Roman Empire, the last of the four; while the little horn [3] was ingeniously explained as William the Conqueror and his successors, whose line was finally cut off for ever by the abolition of monarchy in England in 1649.   The Fifth Monarchy was now appearing; by 1660 it would have extended as far as Rome; by 1666 it would be visible in all the world, and would redeem men from the bondage both of Church and State.

Many of the Fifth Monarchists were violently opposed to the Protectorship of Cromwell, while those who favoured it at first gradually changed their minds.   Vavasour Powell, the Baptist, Feake, and Rogers all preached against him.   Rogers published in 1654 " Mene, Tekel, Perez; or, A Little Appearance of the Handwriting (In a Glance of Light) against the Powers and Apostates of the Times.   By a Letter Written to, and Lamenting over, Oliver, Lord Cromwell."   Feake, Rogers, and John Simpson were imprisoned, but Simpson gave in his submission to the new régime.   Tillinghast said, with some exaggeration, that in Oliver's time the prisons were full of Fifth Monarchy men.[4] He himself had dated his " Signs of the Times," his " eight last sermons " dealing with the Fifth Kingdom, from " the Watchtower in Windsor Castle " in 1656.   There was some reason for it, for they were continually plotting against the Government. In prison at Lambeth Rogers wrote " Prison Morning Beams," but this was destroyed or lost, all but the " Introduction," which he incorporated in another work, " Jegar-Sahadutha: or a Heart Appeal," a history of his sufferings at Windsor, whither he had been removed by the Council in 1655.   Feake was there too, and they had access to each other, and preached and prayed so much that Rogers was sent to the Isle of Wight, where he complained that his gaoler treated both himself and his wife with great brutality.   He was released in January 1657, but had only been at liberty twelve months when he was imprisoned once more, with Harrison and many others, for complicity in the first Fifth Monarchy rising organised by Thomas Venner in April 1657.   A number of persons belonging to Venner's congregation in Swan Alley were also imprisoned.   This time Rogers was only in prison for three months.   John Canne, who had been Episcopalian, Brownist, and Baptist, but was now a Fifth Monarchist, published in 1657 " The Time of the End," to which Feake and Rogers each wrote a preface.   On April 1st, 1658, Canne and eight others were arrested and imprisoned for holding a meeting in Coleman Street.   Canne himself was in gaol

[1] Rev. ix. 3.   [2] Dan. vii. 7.   [3] Dan. vii. 8.
[4] Hunt, " Religious Thought in England," I. 244.

for three weeks, but Wentworth Day was fined £500 and sentenced to twelve months imprisonment, and John Clarke 200 marks and six months.[1]

After the fall of Richard Cromwell the Rump Parliament was restored by the army, and supported by the Fifth Monarchy men, who looked to Sir Henry Vane as their political leader. Rogers was a chaplain in the army which put down Booth's rising, and perhaps as a reward was made a lecturer at Shrewsbury, and allowed to have St. Julian's Church for his ministrations, though it is doubtful whether he ever went there.[2]

Then came the Restoration, followed by Venner's second insurrection at the beginning of 1661. The Government had received intelligence of the designs of the Swan Alley conventiclers, and had arrested most of the ringleaders, including Cornet Day, Quartermaster-General Courtney, Colonel Overton, and Major Allen; but they had not seized the turbulent wine-cooper who was the most dangerous of them all. When the insurgents sallied out of Coleman Street on the night of that fatal Sunday in January, they marched first to Rogers's old church of St. Thomas the Apostle.[3] London was kept in commotion for several days, twenty soldiers and citizens were killed, and Venner and a dozen of his followers were executed. Courtney was kept in the Gatehouse for six months, and finally released on giving security of £1000 to go abroad within fifteen days and not return.[4] But the members of the sect were a source of trouble to the authorities for a long time to come. They joined with the Presbyterians in encouraging people to oppose the use of the Prayer Book in the London churches.[5] Rogers, however, retired to Holland. In early life he had studied medicine at Cambridge, and he took the degree of M.D. at the University of Utrecht in October 1662. He then returned to England, and took up his quarters in Bermondsey, practised physic, and held meetings in his house. In 1664 he took the M.D. *ad eundem* at Oxford.[6] During the Plague year he was advertising specifics of his own devising, but it is to be feared they were not as successful as he expected, for nothing is heard of him afterwards.[7] Canne went to Amsterdam in 1664, and died there in 1667.

A little before the time of Venner's rising there were various prophetic papers published, one of which contained a prophecy of marvellous things which were to come to pass before 1670. In this paper was a story that the Viceroy of Aleppo had sent a letter to the Jews of Jerusalem to let them know that two aged

[1] J. R. Boyle, " The Memoirs of Master John Shaw," Hull, 1882, pp. 199–215.
[2] E. Rogers, " Life and Opinions of a Fifth Monarchy Man," London, 1867.
[3] *Idem, ibid.*, p. 327.   [4] *Idem, ibid.*, p. 328.
[5] C.S.P.D., 32/97, March, 1661.
[6] Wood, " Fasti," II. 159; " Ath.," II. 594.
[7] E. Rogers, " Life and Opinions of a Fifth Monarchy Man," p. 330.

men, who claimed to be a thousand years old, had arrived in his city, preaching repentance, and prophesying wars throughout the world in 1661. Asia should burn like fire, Europe should be destroyed, rivers would be turned into blood, and there would be earthquakes in divers places. The number of believers in Christ would be found to be very few, but a Great One should arise shortly, and the Judgment Day would come to pass in 1670. Pepys, however, wrote on November 25th, 1662: " Some of the fanatics do say that the end of the world is at hand, and that next Tuesday is the day." [1] One of the prophetical works was entitled " Romae Ruina Finalis, Anno Dom. 1666; or, A Treatise wherein is Clearly Demonstrated that the Pope is Antichrist, and that Babylon the City, or Rome, shall be Utterly Destroyed and Laid in Ashes in the Year 1666. And that the Turk shall shortly afterwards be Destroyed by Fire from Heaven: presently after which will be the Second Coming of Christ and General Resurrection." [2] Another bore the title, " Joyful News for all Christendom." It was published in 1661, and prophesied the total destruction of the Turks in 1662.

George Fox heard that the Fifth Monarchy men expected the Second Advent in 1666, so in 1661 he was " moved to give forth a paper to them." They thought that Christ was coming to set up His kingdom, and then they thought they were to kill the Great Whore, " but I told them the Whore was alive in them," and " their looking was like unto the Pharisees' ' Lo here,' ' Lo there,' but Christ was come." Christ said His kingdom was not of this world, and therefore His servants did not fight, " And therefore all ye Fifth Monarchy men that be fighters with carnal weapons; ye are none of Christ's servants but beasts and whores." [3]

Towards the end of 1661 the Government was informed that the teachers of the sect were preaching busily in Yorkshire, Durham, Devonshire, and Yarmouth, and that their chief teachers were Palmer, Helmes, Blecher, and Feake. In London their chief centre was in Limehouse, where they were accustomed to meet in the house of a wealthy brewer named Andrews, while Venner's son-in-law, Medley, was their treasurer.[4] Christopher Feake had been a minister of the Establishment, then had joined the Baptists, and finally became one of the most eminent exponents of Fifth Monarchism. At St. Peter's, Cornhill, in All Saints', Hereford, and at Blackfriars he preached his doctrines, and thundered against Cromwell. In 1653 he was sent to prison, where he remained for several years, but was preaching again in the City of London in 1658.[5] Towards the

[1] " Diary." [2] Hunt, " Religious Thought in England," I. 245.
[3] Fox, " Journal," 1661. [4] C.S.P.D., November 28th, 1661.
[5] Brook, " Lives of the Puritans," III. 308–311.

end of 1663 warrants were out for his apprehension on a charge of sedition, but he had retired to Dorking. Early in January, while he was preaching at a conventicle there, the constables broke down the door and arrested him. He admitted that he did not attend church, and said that he could give no allegiance to the Government. He was taken to London by a guard of soldiers, for there were people there who had threatened to kill him on account of Venner's insurrection.[1]

In spite of the failure of their prophecies, many of this sect remained undiscouraged, and their number even increased. At a meeting of Presbyterian ministers in London in 1664, great complaints were made of the falling away of many of their leading supporters to the Fifth Monarchists. One of the Millennarians, a man named Talbot, was actually keeping a diary, in which he recorded the evil doings of the judges and others against the day of reckoning which would surely come.[2] But they had the same difficulty about their meetings as the other sects had. Two of their number, Vernon and Glasse, were holding a conventicle in Cannon Street in March 1664 when they were raided by the authorities. Glasse and Vernon, described as Major Vernon, and some of the others got away. They heard from Captain Cox, one of the officers who broke up their meeting, that they had been betrayed by some of those present, so they issued a notice to their followers that Vernon and Glasse and others would hold meetings near Bishopsgate, but the place would not be communicated till an hour before the time.[3]   In the following year an informer told Lord Arlington that the leader of the sect in London was Helmes, who had succeeded " that fanatic prophet Feake." [4]   This was Camshaw Helmes, who had been ejected from Winchcomb in Gloucestershire, but some time before the Bartholomew Act.[5] Early in 1666 it was reported to the Government that the Fifth Monarchy men were busily conspiring again, and were holding meetings in retired places in Epping Forest and Enfield Chase, and in London; and that Hugh Courtney and Walter Thimbleton had been seen lurking about.[6] The sect had a meeting-house at Oldbury, in Worcestershire. In 1667 a troop of horse under Major Wild went from Stourbridge to Oldbury, and found a large congregation listening to a preacher, who was addressing them from an outdoor pulpit. Seeing the cavalry coming, he warned his hearers, threw off his gown and periwig, and disappeared. There was some fighting when the soldiers tried to disperse the assembly, and some prisoners were taken, but were

[1] C.S.P.D., December 31st, 1663; January 2nd and 5th, 1664.
[2] C.S.P.D., June 2nd; October 27th, 1664.
[3] C.S.P.D., 449/33.   [4] C.S.P.D., May 3rd, 1665.
[5] Palmer, II. 256.
[6] Rogers, " Life and Opinions of a Fifth Monarchy Man," pp. 328–329.

bound over to the next Sessions. The proceedings at the service had taken the form of psalm-singing, after which the preacher offered a prayer, and then discoursed on the words " Thy kingdom come," which he expounded as referring to the millennial kingdom on earth, which was quite different from the eternal kingdom of glory.[1] There was no doubt that this was a Fifth Monarchist conventicle, but the evidence is not always clear. In March 1668 a conventicle held in Blue Anchor Alley, in Old Street, London, was described as a meeting of this sect, and the preacher as a Fifth Monarchy man from Herefordshire. But it was reported that on the following Sunday the Fifth Monarchy preacher Vavasour Powell was to preach at one of the five houses in the Alley. Now Vavasour Powell was a Baptist. Still, in this instance the spy so far recognised this as to speak at the same time of " Commonwealth fighting Baptists seasoned with Fifth Monarchy principles." [2]

Very little is heard of these people during the later years of Charles II. A meeting of them was reported in June 1678 at Brooking Wharf in London, the preacher, Mayhew, speaking from the text 2 Cor. xiii, 14.[3] Mayhew was probably the man ejected from Roydon in Suffolk,[4] but nothing is known of him. There was a pamphlet published in 1688 which bore the title, " A Modest Enquiry into the Meaning of the Revelations in a Letter to all such as Wait for the Kingdom of Christ. By a Lover of the Second Coming of our Lord Jesus, and of the Blessed Millennium." It was an interpretation of the book of Revelations from the Fifth Monarchy point of view, and violently anti-Roman. Though the sect died out, its principles were upheld by members of other religious bodies, even the Church of England. John Mason, rector of Water Stratford, in the county of Buckinghamshire, announced to his congregation that he was Elias, that two witnesses had been given him to bear out his testimony, that Christ had appeared to him and told him that he would not die before the Second Advent, and that the Millennium would begin in that parish. There were some tumultuous happenings there as the time he foretold drew near.[5] He gathered a collection of people together waiting for the end of the world. They lived in a barn, but their leader died, and the assembly broke up.[6] In " The Midnight Cry," a sermon on the parable of the Ten Virgins, which reached a fourth edition in 1692, he proclaimed the speedy coming of the Lord. In 1700 the Millennarians were expecting the Advent in another five years.

---

[1] " Victoria County History, Worcestershire," II. 75.
[2] C.S.P.D., 237/140.   [3] C.S.P.D., 404/217.
[4] Palmer, III. 285.
[5] Hunt, " Rel. Thought in Eng.," I. 243.
[6] Salmon, " Lives of the English Bishops," 1733, p. 259.

THE MUGGLETONIANS

The Muggletonians took their name from Lodowick Muggleton, who was one of their two founders. They have borne other names, such as " Believers in the Third Record," and " Believers in the Commission of the Spirit "; but the name which has stuck to them is that of Muggletonians. The popular idea of these people is due to the vivid but inaccurate description of Macaulay, who says that " A mad tailor, named Ludovick Muggleton wandered from pothouse to pothouse, tippling ale, and denouncing eternal torments against all those who refused to believe on his testimony that the Supreme Being was only six feet high, and that the sun was just four miles from the earth." [1]   The facts are as follow. Lodowick (not Ludovick) Muggleton was born in 1609 in Walnut Tree Yard, now called New Street, in Bishopsgate Without, where his father, John Muggleton, had some repute as a smith, farrier, and horse-doctor, or as we should say, veterinary surgeon. A tract issued during his lifetime says that the parents came from Chippen-ham,[2] but the truth seems to be that their original home was at Wilbarston, in Northamptonshire, near Market Harborough, where the name still survives. Lodowick was the youngest of John Muggleton's three children—two sons and a daughter—by his first wife, and was baptized at St. Botolph's, Bishopsgate. The mother died in 1612, the father afterwards married again, and young Lodowick was for some years boarded out in the country. At the age of fifteen or sixteen he returned to London, and was apprenticed to John Quick, a tailor who lived in Walnut Tree Yard. When his apprenticeship was finished he became a journeyman in the shop of one Richardson, a clothier and pawnbroker in Houndsditch. Here he fell in love with his master's daughter, and Mrs. Richardson promised him a hundred pounds to set him up in business as a pawnbroker on his marriage. He had for some time being undergoing various religious experiences. Though he had been baptized in the Church of England, he is said in the course of his career to have tried successively the Presbyterians, Independents, Anabaptists, and Quakers.[3] While with the Richardsons he came in contact with his cousins, William and John Reeve. These were the sons of a decayed Wiltshire gentleman who had once been Clerk to the Deputy of Ireland. They had both been appren-uced to the tailoring trade, and William Reeve and Muggleton had worked side by side. The Reeves were strong Puritans, and were horrified that their cousin was going to set up as a pawnbroking usurer. In 1631 Muggleton went to work for

[1] Macaulay, " Hist.," I. 164.
[2] " A Modest Account of the Wicked Life of that Grand Impostor Lodowick Muggleton," 1676.
[3] " A Modest Account."

LODOWICKE MUGGLETON.
THE LORD'S LAST HIGH PRIEST UNDER JOHN REEVE IN THE
COMMISSION OF THE SPIRIT:

From "Divine Songs of the Muggletonians." 1829.

Facing p. 242.

John Reeve, who was in business for himself in St. Thomas
Apostle Street, in the city, and under the influence of his cousin,
Lodowick became filled with the fear of hell-fire if he carried
out his intention, so the wedding never took place.

The next few years seem to have been a time of religious
stress and conflict for Muggleton. He tried the various Puritan
preachers, was troubled with doubts and agitated by visions of
devils and everlasting fire. About 1635 he married his first
wife, Sarah, who bore him two daughters, who survived their
parents. Sarah Muggleton only lived three or four years, and
in 1642 he married again. His second wife, Mary, died in
1648, leaving a third daughter, who died young.

About 1650 Muggleton came under the influence of two of
the Ranter leaders, John Robins, who declared himself to be
God Almighty, and Thomas Tannye, who claimed to be God's
high priest sent to gather together the Jews. Probably about
this time also Muggleton came under the influence of the theology
of Jacob Boehme: his writings show clear signs of Boehme's
mysticism and phraseology. Lodowick and his cousin John
Reeve now began to see visions and hear voices, though at first
Reeve was the follower and Muggleton the leader. These visions
went on during the greater part of the year 1651, and among
the divine messages received was one to the effect that Muggleton's daughter Sarah, at that time quite a child, was established
to be a prophetess and teacher to all the women of London.
Muggleton and Reeve were now joined by Thomas Turner, and
they united in denouncing Tannye as a false prophet. He was
allowed a month to repent, and as he failed to do this, they
sentenced him to eternal damnation. Shortly after this Tannye
was drowned at sea, an event which greatly favoured the claims
the prophets were now putting forth. They also denounced
Robins, who is said to have written a letter of recantation
shortly afterwards. However this may be, he was still claiming
to be God Almighty in 1657,[1] and Muggleton ultimately declared
him to be Antichrist. In 1652 Reeve, who now appeared as
the leader, published "A Transcendant Spiritual Treatise," in
which he set forth their claims. By personal communication
" by voice of words from Jesus Christ," he had been appointed
to be the messenger of the new dispensation, and Muggleton
was to be his " mouth," as Aaron was to Moses. They were to
be the two witnesses mentioned in the eleventh chapter of the
Revelations. They had received their doctrines " from the holy
spirit of the man Jesus, the only true God unto all his elect."
They were the forerunners of the visible appearing of the distinct
personal God in power and great glory in the clouds of heaven.
They were to seal the elect and the reprobate in their foreheads
in preparation for the final judgment of the world.

[1] " The Ranters' Creed," 1657.

The prophets, then, had received the right of blessing and cursing, and could slay unbelievers and sentence them to eternal damnation. Muggleton cursed a man named Penson, who retaliated by smiting the prophet on the head, for which sin he died within a fortnight. Many of the Ranters were cursed. Several instances occurred in which the person who had received the sentence died, or went out of his mind, or came to ruin. Some of the rank and file assumed to themselves, without authority, the right of blessing and cursing. One of them, a man called Cooper, solemnly cursed fifteen men at once because they scoffed. Alarmed at his own presumption, and having been struck with sickness, perhaps in consequence of the alarm, he sent for Muggleton and told him what he had done. The prophet forgave him, but he was convinced in his own mind that the fifteen were all doomed. Reeve was threatened by the Government that if he were not less lavish with his curses a warrant would be issued against him. He replied with more threats of damnation against the authorities. So the two prophets were brought before the Lord Mayor, and on refusing to give bail, were imprisoned in Newgate on September 15th, 1653, one of the great days in the Muggletonian calendar. So unpopular were the two men that they were in danger of being hanged by their fellow-prisoners. They next wrote a letter sentencing both the Lord Mayor and Recorder to damnation. When their trial took place they were sentenced to imprisonment in Bridewell, where they remained seven months.

In 1656 Reeve and Muggleton put forth an exposition of their doctrines in " The Divine Looking-glass," a work which described itself as " An Epistle written by inspiration from the fiery glorious Spirit of Jesus Christ, that immortal Jew and spiritual Lion of the tribe of Judah, who alone is the Lord Protector of heavens, earth, angels, and men. Unto Oliver Cromwell, that mortal Jew and natural lion of the same tribe according to the flesh, who is styled Lord Protector of England, Scotland and Ireland, through the secret decree of this most high and mighty God. And to his, and the Commonwealth's most eminent Council and head officers in martial affairs within his dominions, as the forerunner of the sudden dreadful appearing of this impartial Judge of quick and dead, with His elect angels, to make an everlasting separation between the persons of tender-hearted Israelites and bowelless Canaanites." In an epistle prefixed to this book Muggleton stated that " God spake these words unto John Reeve: ' I have given thee understanding of My mind, in the Scriptures above all men in the world ' . . . that is, more spiritual knowledge of the Scriptures than all the men in the world." Reeve, whose health had been undermined by his imprisonment a few years previously, died at Maidstone in 1658. He did not ascend to heaven in a cloud in the presence of his enemies, but this did not shake Muggleton's faith in his commission, and he gave out that a double portion of the Spirit now rested on himself.

Laurence Claxton, who had been a Ranting preacher and held a benefice under the Cromwellian establishment, resigned his living in 1658, joined the Muggletonians, and wrote four books in defence of his new principles, chiefly against the Quakers.[1] He began to have exalted notions of his own importance, and in 1660 produced a fifth work called "The Lost Sheep Found," in which he claimed to be "commissioned," and to be the equal of Reeve, and said that Muggleton was only Reeve's mouthpiece. Muggleton replied that Reeve was like Elijah, and he himself was as Elisha, therefore Claxton could only be as Gehazi, dependent on his master's will and pleasure. He forbade Claxton to write any more on the subject of the commission, and attributed his fall from truth to his wife, Frances Claxton, who had been cursed by Reeve. Claxton, having been blessed, could not be cursed, but his maintenance allowance from the Muggletonians was withdrawn, and after being some time in opposition, he recanted and was received back.[2] He died in Ludgate prison as a debtor in the year 1667, or thereabouts, though his debts seem to have been due to other people's dishonesty and not his own.[3] There was only one more case of rebellion against the prophet's authority during the rest of his life-time. In 1662 Muggleton published "A True Interpretation of the Eleventh Chapter of the Revelation of St. John . . . whereby is unfolded and plainly declared the whole covenant of God concerning Himself, the devil and all mankind, from the foundation of the world to all eternity, never before revealed by any of the sons of men until now." In 1663 he visited Nottingham at the invitation and expense of a joint society of Behmenists and Quakers. In that year he published "A Stream from the Tree of Life: or, the Third Record Vindicated: being the Copies of several Letters and Epistles wrote by the two last Witnesses of Jesus Christ: wherein Truth rides Triumphant, and Imagination is Confounded." While he was travelling in the north he was arrested at Chesterfield on the instance of John Cooper, the vicar, and was imprisoned in Derby gaol for nine days. While there he had an interview with Gervase Bennett, the magistrate who had given the nickname of Quakers to the Society of Friends. There seems to

---

[1] "The Right Devil Discovered," 1659; "The Quakers' Downfall," 1659; "A Paradisical Dialogue between Faith and Reason," 1660; "A Wonder of Wonders," 1660. John Harwood, a Yorkshireman, replied to the second of these in "The Lying Prophet Discovered and Reproved," 1659.

[2] Muggleton said he was four years in opposition, but came back in 1661, but he either stated the period or the date wrongly.

[3] A. Gordon, "Ancient and Modern Muggletonians," Trans. Liverpool Lit. and Phil. Soc., 1870; Muggleton, "Acts of the Witnesses," 1699, pp. 80-82.

have been almost a public disputation in the gaol, held in the presence of other magistrates, the gaoler, and the sheriff's attendants. The only thing the two disputants agreed on, however, was the mortality of the soul.[1] Soon after his return home Muggleton married his third wife, Mary, who survived him. In 1665 he published " A True Interpretation of all the Chief Texts and Mysterious Sayings and Visions opened of the whole Book of the Revelations of St. John." This was a volume of 240 pages. His next work (apart from his controversial writings against the Quakers mentioned elsewhere) was a little pamphlet against witchcraft, which appeared in 1669, with the title " A True Interpretation of the Witch of Endor." He tried to explain what a familiar spirit really was, and argued that it was impossible to raise the spirit without the body. The following year he was in trouble again. His books were seized by the authorities of London, who declared them blasphemous and ordered them to be destroyed. He himself escaped capture, but had to go into hiding for a time.

The works of Muggleton and Reeve contain the names of forty-six persons who were assured individually, either by word or by letter, of their eternal blessedness, and 103 who were similarly assured of their eternal misery. The former list begins with the names of Muggleton's daughters, Sarah and Elizabeth, together with a boy whose name is not given, who were all three blessed by Reeve in 1652, and ends with the name of Sarah Delmaine, to whose zeal is due the collection of the writings of the two prophets. Of the other list, nearly half consists of Quakers' names.[2]

In fact the Quakers seem to have been one of Muggleton's pet aversions. They were all damned, because they were of the race of the serpent's seed and of the family of Cain, for Cain was the devil's bastard, begotten of Eve in Paradise. After the two prophets were released from prison in 1654 they held a disputation with Fox and some of his followers at Eastcheap. Muggleton claimed that this discussion was a serious check to the progress of Quakerism. Henceforth there were frequent controversies between the two parties. Muggleton solemnly cursed Fox and four of his followers, one of whom was Richard Farnsworth. This did not make for amenity or agreement. Altogether, at different times, Muggleton doomed more than fifty Quakers to everlasting perdition.[3] The titles of some of their works will be almost sufficient to give an account of the paper warfare which went on for over ten years. In 1663 Muggleton published " The Neck of the Quakers Broken, or

[1] Williamson, " Lodowick Muggleton," in " Ye sette of Odd Volumes."
[2] Alex. Gordon, " The Origin of the Muggletonians," *Trans. Liverpool Lit. and Phil. Soc.*, 1869.
[3] Turner, " The Quakers," p. 183.

Cut in Sunder by the Two-edged Sword of the Spirit which is put into my Mouth, First in a Letter to Edward Bourne [in reply to one by the latter], Secondly in answer to a Letter [the text of which is given] to [or rather " by "] S. Hooton and W. S. Thirdly in a Letter to R. Farnsworth, Quaker, [in reply to a letter of which the text is given], Fourthly in answer to a printed pamphlet of the said R. Farnsworth, entitled ' Truth Ascended.' Amsterdam [really London] 1663." In the following year Muggleton wrote " A Letter sent to Thomas Taylor, Quaker, in the Year 1664. In Answer to many Blasphemous Sayings of his in several Pieces of Paper, and in the Margent of a Book." This was published in London in 1665. Isaac Pennington, the younger of that name, next appeared on the scene with " Observations on some Passages of L. M. in his Interpretations of the Eleventh Chapter of Revelations. As also in some Passages in that Book of his Styled ' The Neck of the Quakers Broken ' and in his ' Letter to Thomas Taylor.' " George Fox also came into the fray with " Something in Answer to Muggleton's Book, which he calls ' The Quaker's Neck Broken.' "

At last Muggleton replied. His answer bore the following title: " A Looking-glass for George Fox, the Quaker, and other Quakers, wherein they may see themselves to be right Devils. . . . Wherein is set forth the Ignorance and Blindness of the Quaker Doctrine of Christ within them, and that they cannot nor do they understand the Meaning of the Scripture, neither have the Gift of the true Interpretation of the Scripture, as will appear in the Pages following." [1] There are thirty-six chapters in this book. The first is " Of a Catalogue of Damned Quakers," and makes the following pronouncement: " Reeve and I damned you, Edward Burrough and Francis Howgill, fourteen years ago. The following are now pronounced damned; Fox, Burrough, Howgill, Edward Bourne, William Smith, Samuel Hooton, Richard Farnsworth, Thomas Taylor, John Perrot, Richard Whitpane, John Harwood, Richard Hubberthorne, Fox the younger, and that great lubbardly fellow spoken of in ' The Quaker's Neck Broken.' " Muggleton also replied to Pennington, but not till 1669, when he issued from the press " An Answer to Isaac Pennington Esq., his Book entitled ' Observations on Some Passages of L. M's Interpretations of the Eleventh Chapter of Revelations,' also some passages of that book of his entitled ' The Neck of the Quakers' Broken ' and in his ' Letter to Thomas Taylor.' "

William Penn was the next protagonist of the Quakers. Some years previously he had gone to Ireland to manage his father's estates. There he probably met some of the Muggletonian converts in Cork. Certainly he came under the influence there

---

[1] 1668.

of Richard Farnsworth, one of the Quakers who had been cursed in 1654. Penn became a Quaker himself, and returned to England in 1668. Josiah Cole, a prominent Friend, had been solemnly damned by Muggleton, and had died a few days later. Really he had been in very bad health for some time, but the Muggletonians interpreted it as a proof of the prophet's claims, and some of the Quakers were alarmed. To reassure his followers, Penn wrote in 1672 " The New Witnesses Proved Old Heretics, a letter to Ludovic Muggleton, an Accuser of the Brethren, False Prophet, and Impostor (though otherwise an Adversary of Little Moment)." He sentenced Muggleton to the bottomless pit, and challenged him and his " six-foot God," and " all the host of Luciferian spirits." The prophet promptly pronounced sentence of eternal damnation on Penn, and further replied in the following year with " The Answer to William Penn, Quaker, his book entitled ' The New Witnesses Proved Old Heretics.' Wherein he is proved to be an ignorant spatter-brained Quaker, who knows no more what the true God is, nor His secret Decrees, than one of his Coach-horses does, nor so much, for the Ox knoweth his Owner, and the Ass his Master's Crib, but Penn doth not know his Maker, as is manifest by the Scripture, which may inform the Reader, if he mind the Interpretation of the Scripture in the Discourse following." Another work which appeared in this strife was by " Thomas Thompson " (a pseudonym) ; " The Quakers' Quibbles set forth. . . . Also the pretended Prophet and last Witness L. Muggleton and the Quakers compared, etc." This book appeared in 1674, and belaboured both parties to the contest.

John Gratton, the Quaker, while he was a seeker after truth, heard of Muggleton and Reeve, was at first attracted by their teachings, bought, as he says, eight shillings worth of their books, and " was like to be deceived." But he was soon disillusioned, " for they that were of that opinion, and carried away to believe the false prophet Muggleton (for Reeve was dead), had no worship at all : and when we met together (those few that were) at one widow Carter's, we were not for either waiting upon God, or for any other exercise at all of either preaching, praying, or reading Holy Scriptures : no, we had no more to do, but to believe Muggleton and be saved : so we spent some time in discourse, and then parted." " I found that Muggleton's spirit took more delight to curse than to bless. Then I wrote a letter to him, and made twelve or fourteen objections against his doctrine, and sent it to him to London. To which he sent me a letter and referred me to his books, but did not answer any of the objections ; but told me he judged I wrote in ignorance and inquiringly, and therefore forbore to curse me till further trial. But I left him, and sat down satisfied that he was a false prophet." [1] In 1671 Gratton converted a

---

[1] " Journal of John Gratton," 1779, pp. 33–34.

woman, a Baptist, to Quakerism. Her husband, a Muggletonian, wrote to Muggleton to ask him to curse Gratton, which the prophet did by letter.[1] The Quaker gives a most amusing account of an interview with Muggleton in 1674, when Barclay, Livingstone, Hague, and he visited him at his house in London. Muggleton came in and asked if either of them was Gratton. Barclay replied, " Art thou a prophet and needest thou to ask? " Muggleton said, " You are a Scotchman, and I will have nothing to do with you, for I was lately cheated by a Scotchman." Gratton says that he asked Muggleton how he came by his authority. Had he seen anything or heard any voice? He answered " No." (But certainly Muggleton had claimed this before.) Gratton also inquired if he had power to bless a man after he had cursed him, or *vice versa*. He said he had not. He then cursed several of them, " and when he had done, he was so pleased, that he said it did him more good than if a man had given him forty shillings. Upon which I asked him what he thought of me and what would become of me. He answered . . . saying several times, ' If you be careful it will be well with you in the end.' " Then Gratton said, " Oh, what a false prophet art thou! " and then told him his name. Muggleton was " sadly confounded." In connection with this interview Livingstone reported that he himself had been cursed by a Muggletonian woman at Chesterfield, and that the prophet there and then confirmed the curse.[2]

Muggleton said of the Quakers that at the first they used to fall into witchcraft fits, " supposing it was the Spirit of Christ that moved you to foam at the mouth, and sigh, and groan and howl," [3] but he added that these manifestations had of late become rare or ceased altogether, and this he put down to the terror of his curses.

In 1675 Deborah Burnet, widow of John Burnet, one of his earliest disciples, died and left Muggleton as her executor. He was forced to bring a lawsuit in respect of some houses which had belonged to her in the Postern. This necessitated his attendance in the Court of Arches (in which all cases relating to wills were then tried), but as soon as he appeared he was arrested and imprisoned on a charge of blasphemy. During his imprisonment there was another revolt against his authority. Walter Buchanan and three others accused him of teaching which was false in itself and contrary to the doctrine of Reeve. Muggleton replied by letter from the prison. Buchanan and another were damned, and the other two excommunicated. Only one was ever allowed to return to the fold.[4]

After much delay Muggleton was tried at the Old Bailey on

[1] " Journal of John Gratton," 1779, p. 83.
[2] *Ibid.*, pp. 100–102.   [3] " A Looking-glass," p. 36.
[4] Gordon, " Ancient and Modern Muggletonians," *Trans. Liverpool Lit. and Phil. Soc.*, 1870; Williamson, " Lodowick Muggleton"; Jessop, " The Prophet of Walnut Tree Yard."

January 17th, 1677. The judges were Atkins, who was inclined to be lenient, and Sir Richard Rainsford, C.J., who was the reverse.[1] It was not easy to bring home the accusation of blasphemy; Muggleton had published nothing since 1673, so he came within the scope of the Act of Indemnity of 1674. However, a copy of his work " The Neck of the Quakers Broken " was produced, with the imprint " Amsterdam, 1663." It was shown that the place stated was false, as the book had really been printed in London. It was then assumed that the date was also false, that it was really printed in 1676, and had been antedated to get the protection of the Act of Indemnity. This was untrue, and the Quaker answers to the book might have been brought forward in evidence if Lodowick had had his wits about him. But Muggleton, " following the example of Christ," disappointed his followers by remaining silent during the trial. His counsel, whom he called " a deceitful knave and fearful fool," declared himself ashamed to plead on behalf of such a blasphemous cause, and contented himself with urging merely a technical point with respect to the date of the publication of some of the books which had been seized in Muggleton's house, but this was overruled by the court. The jury found the prisoner guilty of writing and publishing " a malicious, scandalous, blasphemous, seditious, and heretical book." Jeffreys, as Common Serjeant of the City of London, had to act as the mouthpiece of the court and deliver the sentence. He regretted, he said, that the court had no punishment to fit the crime, but Muggleton should have an " easy, easy, easy punishment." This kind of talk was not peculiar to Jeffreys in the courts of the seventeenth century. The sentence was that he should stand in the pillory from 11 a.m. to 1 p.m. on three different days at the Exchange, Temple Bar, and Smithfield respectively, and *without the usual protection to his head*. His books were to be burnt before his face by the common hangman, and he was to be fined £500 or, in default, to go to prison. He could not pay, and so was sent to Newgate, where he remained for six months. He was sixty-eight years of age, and his life among the felons there must have been terribly hard. He was released on July 19th, 1677 (which is consequently another of the sacred days of the sect), on payment of £100, which was contributed by his friends, and finding two securities for life.[2] It was a severe punishment, and

---

[1] Muggleton afterwards published an account of the trial in a pamphlet, " A True Narrative of the Proceedings at the Sessions House in the Old Bailey, 17th January, 167⅞, giving a full account of the Trial and Sentence of Lodowick Muggleton for Blasphemous Words and Books," London, 167⅞. Another copy has the extended title, " News from the Sessions House in the Old Bailey, being a True Account, etc.," and is dated 1676. There is also an account of the trial in the " Acts of the Witnesses of the Spirit."

[2] Irving, " Life of Jeffreys," pp. 34–39; " A True Account of the Trial and Sufferings of Lodowick Muggleton, left by our Friend Powell," London, 1808.

the crowd at the pillory, who nearly killed him with their missiles, made it worse. It may have been some comfort to him to know that many of the witnesses died shortly afterwards. In one case his wife, Mary, pronounced sentence, and the victim died within six weeks. But there seems no doubt that the punishment cowed Muggleton, who is said never to have passed a sentence of damnation afterwards. After this he seems to have lived a fairly quiet life. In 1680 he published " Letters to R. Pierce concerning the Holy Ghost," and two years later " A Discourse between T. Reeve and R. Leader . . . recited by L. M., etc." This was an account of a discussion on the nature of God in 1653 between Leader and the prophets. The book called " The Acts of the Witnesses of the Spirit " was written by Muggleton in his old age, and was published in 1699, two years after his death. Its full title will give the scope of its contents: " The Acts of the Witnesses of the Spirit, in Five Parts, by Lodowick Muggleton, one of the Two Witnesses, and the Prophets of the only high, immortal, glorious God, Christ Jesus: left by him to be published after his Death, that after Ages may see some of the Acts of the Two Witnesses of the Spirit, as well as their Writings and their Doctrine now in this Last Age. As they have read some of the wonderful Acts of Moses and the Prophets, and the Acts of the Apostles, so there will be some remarkable Acts of the Witnesses of the Spirit left upon Record, of their Births, Parentage, Revelations, Disputes, Troubles, Trials by Jury, Imprisonment, and Punishment they underwent for declaring the Lord Jesus to be the only God, which Declaration of theirs accords with the Prophecy of Isaiah, chap. IX, verse 6th. ' For unto us etc.' " It was described as " edited by T. T.," i.e. Thomas Tomkinson, one of Muggleton's disciples.

Muggletonianism spread. There were followers of the prophet in south Ireland early in the reign of Charles II. Reeve's work, " The Transcendant Spiritual Treatise," was translated into German for the benefit of continental converts about 1666. Not that Muggleton travelled about as an apostle. He maintained himself by tailoring for a great part of his life, though no doubt his books brought him in some money. He did not go out of his way to preach his doctrines. If people went to him he answered questions.[1] When his friends wrote to him about their private affairs he gave advice, very often good advice, expressed in homely fashion, as can be seen from the large number of his letters still extant. He was not a well-educated man, but he had a native shrewdness, and as he advanced in life his followers respected him more and more as a seer, and received his oracular responses with awe. His portrait in the National Portrait Gallery shows that he had light brown hair, and gives the impression that he was tall. Muggleton died at

[1] " John Gratton's Journal," pp. 100–102.

his house in the Postern in 1697. Some 250 of his disciples
followed him to his grave in the Bethlehem new churchyard,
where Reeve also had been buried. Liverpool Street station
covers the site, and both the churchyard and the tombs of the
prophets have long since disappeared.[1]

Muggleton's view of his own position as a prophet was as
follows: No man could come to the assurance of the favour of
God but in believing that God gave this power unto John
Reeve and himself. He had power given him over all other
gods and infinite spirits whatever. He had the keys of heaven
and hell, and none could get into heaven except he opened the
gates. He had power to remit the sins of those who received
his doctrine, and to retain and bind their sins upon the consciences of those who refused or despised it. In doctrine, knowledge, judgment, and power he was above all men, either prophets
or apostles, since the beginning of the world, or that should be
hereafter whilst the world should endure. There was no true
minister or ambassador of God in the world except himself, and
there should be no other till the world's end. God, external to
himself, had spoken to him in audible words in the hearing of
the ear. No person condemned by him could make any appeal
to God, because God was not in the world at all. God had
given him the power to condemn, " and in this regard I am
alone and only judge what shall become of men and women
after death; neither shall those who are damned by me see any
other god or judge but me." [2]

The doctrine of the Two Witnesses was set forth in Muggleton's
work, " A True Interpretation of the Eleventh Chapter of the
Revelation," published in 1662. The two witnesses were
Muggleton and Reeve. They were to prophecy for 1260 days,
beginning in February 1651. Fire proceeded out of them—
that is to say, they had power to curse to all eternity, and to
shut the heaven of men's hearts that it rained not, by which
was meant that after the sentence of eternal death was passed
there could be no motion of the Spirit of God in the heart of man.
When they had finished their testimony, the Beast (by which
was meant the spirit of reason in the Lord Mayor, aldermen,
and jury) out of the bottomless pit (or the abyss of their imagination) should kill them, which meant they would have killed
them if their law could have done it. Their dead bodies, by
which was signified the letter of the Scripture, should be seen
in the streets of the city, that is, the hearts of men, for three and
a half days. This really meant 1350 years, for during that
period the letter of Scripture lay dead. The people who dwell
on the earth[3] rejoice over the letter of the Scriptures, the spirit
and life of them having been put to death.

[1] Jessop, " The Prophet of Walnut Tree Yard "; Williamson, " Lodowick
Muggleton."
[2] Sewell, " Hist. Quakers," p. 387.   [3] Rev. xi. 10.

The spirit of life entering into the dead bodies [1] signifies that the Commission of the Spirit entered into the letter of the Law and Gospel, and by a true interpretation the dead letter stands upon its feet and thereby kills the spirit of reason with death eternal. Muggleton seemed at a loss to explain the twelfth verse, which describes how the two witnesses ascended to heaven in a cloud.[2] Muggleton was the last revealer of the Scriptures. If men did not believe in his commission, they might launch into all those pleasures which others, less knowing, call vices.

The other principal doctrines set forth by Muggleton were these:

(1) The substance of earth and water was eternally in the presence of God. Darkness, death, and hell lay secretly hidden in the earth. The word " create " could not possibly mean make out of nothing. Dead matter must be eternal, for it could never proceed from the mouth of Him who is the Life and Light.[3]

(2) There is no Trinity. The Christian Trinity was described by Muggleton as a " three-headed monster, and the work of Antichrist."

(3) There is one God. " He hath a body of His own, as man hath a body of his own: only God's body is spiritual and heavenly, clear as crystal, brighter than the sun, swifter than thought, yet a body." This body is like a man's both in compass and substance. Muggleton developed this thesis after his discussion in 1653 with Richard Leader, a New England merchant, who had come back to England disgusted with the narrowness of American Puritanism, and made some advances to the prophets. Muggleton identified body with person, and thought God could not be a person without a body.

(4) There is no devil, except what is in us, for the devil died in Eve and filled her with all wickedness, which we receive from her. He had incarnated himself in the virgin womb of Eve as Christ in Mary. The only devil now is human reason. This is the Beast of Revelations, and must not be consulted at all.

(5) The Muggletonian doctrine of the Incarnation was expressed in this way: God is a spiritual man, and in time His spiritual body brought forth a natural body. Christ's soul is the Godhead. Elijah was Christ's protector when He became a child, and filled Christ with revelations when He was on earth, and

[1] Rev. xi. 11.
[2] See " A True Interpretation," by Lodowick Muggleton, 1662, and " The Principles of the Muggletonians Considered—A True Representation of the Absurd and Mischievous Principles of the Sect," 1694.
[3] Hunt, " Religious Thought in England," I. 243.

spoke the words at Christ's baptism, " Thou art my beloved Son." In other words, God left the government of heaven to Elijah, and came down on earth in human form as God the Son, and suffered and died on the cross.

(6) The soul sleeps or dies with the body, and will be raised with it. Angels' and men's souls alike, therefore, are mortal. Reeve wrote in 1658, just before he died, " Joyful News from Heaven; or, the Soul's Mortality Proved." In this he showed quite clearly that what he meant by mortality was the doctrine of the sleep of the soul. But angels differ from men in that they are the only beings of pure reason.

(7) There is a heaven of infinite light and bliss a short distance away beyond the stars. There is no hell at present, but after the last judgment, when the stars are extinguished, there will be one on earth.

(8) The doctrine of man is the doctrine of the two seeds: the seed of Cain, the devil's descendants, and the seed of righteous Abel. When the sons of God mingled with the daughters of men, there was produced a hybrid race. All men to-day are hybrids, but as each has more of one seed than the other, so are his chances of salvation. Reason is the diabolic nature in man, faith the divine nature. The spirit eats and drinks within us, and is a natural fire of reason. It also dies, yet in such a way that those who are good men here will be united into one spirit and body with God at last. Salvation, therefore, is the effect of the spiritual principle in man, and has nothing to do with creeds.

(9) The Scriptures contradict astronomy, and astronomy, being based on human reason, is wrong. The sun goes round the earth, and is very little larger than it appears.

(10) Prayer is a sign of weakness. God has set the world going and given every man a conscience, and so does not interfere any more. This was Muggleton's view. Reeve held that God did exercise oversight with regard to human actions. On occasions He has made revelations. The first time was to Moses and the prophets, the second time to Christ and the Apostles, and the last to Muggleton and Reeve. He will not interfere any more with the world. So there are no set days or forms of worship. There should be no prayer and no preaching. Therefore, the nearest approach to worship amongst the Muggletonians is the meeting at which the works of Muggleton and

Reeve are read. When the prophet was alive he expounded the Scriptures at their meetings and answered questions. But Muggleton did not mind if they chose to sing hymns. It could not do good, but if it pleased them, he was willing to let them do it.

(11) The greatest sin of all, which is really the sin against the Holy Ghost, the unforgivable sin, is to disbelieve the two prophets. In such cases the prophet has the right to declare the unbeliever eternally lost.

(12) It is not lawful to bear arms or to take an oath. Muggleton himself several times paid the fine for not accepting certain municipal offices when called on. Some of the Muggletonians denied the lawfulness of magistrates. But Muggleton held that while the law and magistrates were there we must obey them and pay the taxes.

(13) Morality is useful for producing goodness, just as light was produced by darkness, but that is all that can be said for it.[1]

Among the early followers and converts were Richard Leader, Jeremiah Mount, Captain Clark, Captain Stacey, John Saddington, and Thomas Tomkinson. Saddington was a Leicestershire man, who was engaged in the sugar trade in London, and stood manfully at Muggleton's side when his authority was questioned. He wrote " A Perspective Glass for Saints and Sinners " and " The Articles of True Faith depending upon the Commission of the Spirit." Thomas Tomkinson had been converted by Claxton's writings, and although for some years after his conversion he occasionally attended the services of the Establishment, he gathered together a small group of some twenty converts in north-east Staffordshire. Later on he went to London, where he became prominent among the brethren, and in 1695 published a work entitled " Muggletonian Principles Prevailing." [2] It is believed that he wrote the dedicatory epistle, addressed " to all true Christian people," prefixed to the " Acts of the Witnesses of the Spirit." A Muggletonian named Powell was sentenced to imprisonment for six months in 1682 for blasphemy, and was only released on recognizances.[3] This Powell left behind him " A True Account of the Trial and Sufferings of Lodowick Muggleton," which was published in

---

[1] " The Postboy," II. 425; Gordon, " Origin of the Muggletonians," *Trans. Liverpool Lit. and Phil. Soc.*, 1869; Williamson, " Lodowick Muggleton," in " Ye sette of Odd Volumes," 1919.

[2] A. Gordon, " Ancient and Modern Muggletonians," *Trans. Liverpool Lit. and Phil. Soc.*, 1870.

[3] Newsletter, " Admiralty Greenwich Hospital," II. 60, November 8th, 1682.

1808. " Our friend Powell, who witnessed his trial and all his sufferings . . . gives a more full and particular account of the whole proceedings than the Prophet left on record." The returns of 1676 noted the existence of a body of thirty Muggletonians at Ashford in Kent. On August 18th, 1693, Titus Oates married Margaret Wells, living in Bread Street, London, a Muggletonian and the widow of a Muggletonian.[1]

The sect has lasted right down to the present day, and the books of Muggleton and Reeve and later teachers found a reading public well into the nineteenth century. " A Book of Letters or Spiritual Epistles," being copies of 168 letters written by the two prophets, and collected by Alexander Delmaine, was reissued, with a supplement containing twenty-three more letters, in 1755. " The Works of John Reeve and Lodowick Muggleton, the two last Prophets of the Only True God, our Lord Jesus Christ " were published in three volumes in 1832.

In 1829 Joseph and Isaac Frost selected " from the oldest manuscripts " and published in a volume of over 600 pages, " The Divine Songs of the Muggletonians." The book contained 228 songs, many of them prefaced by the title of a popular tune. Thus, the first, written by John Peat, was to be sung to the tune of " De'il take the wars." It began

> " In sixteen hundred fifty and one,
> This morning God did freedom proclaim,
> Christ did declare himself God alone
> Unto his Ambassador, John Reeve by name;
> Lodowick Muggleton was also included,
> Wisdom to the elect to make known,
> Showing how reason is utterly excluded
> From the eternal Jehovah's throne."

No. 13, by William Wood, painter, was made to welcome the Prophet Muggleton into Braintree, Essex:

> " You, great Sir, we greet in love,
> The object vipers would destroy,
> Since your company in Braintree
> Now once more the saints enjoy;
> By a power that divine is
> Makes our water sweet as wine is."

The same writer wrote No. 20:

> " And out of their mouths proceeds spiritual fire
> To burn up all those that against them conspire:
> With the sword of the Spirit, divine truth to defend,
> And to cut them all down that with truth do contend;
> They have also the keys of heaven and hell,
> No champion like these in this region doth dwell."

---

[1] Seccombe, " Lives of Twelve Bad Men," p. 149.

No. 41 refers to John Robins, the Ranter:

> " Witness John Robins, that mighty prince of devils:
> Who with lying signs appeared,
> Which poor deluded souls received,
> To their ruin here, and hereafter:
> But his power did bow down
> To Reeve the great; and Muggleton."

No. 98 deals with the day of the Prophet's trial, when

> " . . . Balaam Jeffreys was left the court's sentence to pass,
> Which he did with a voice that did bray like an ass."

Before No. 148 is a note: " These verses were made by John Ladd, and sung before the prophet Muggleton, on the 19th day of July, 1681, old style, being kept as a day of jubilee for his happy deliverance out of prison ":

> " And you, great Sir, who bonds for truth
> So lately did retain:
> Rejoice with us, at being set
> At liberty again;
> With dangers and such perils we
> Poor mortals are oppressed;
> But death at last will set us free
> With an eternal rest."

No. 169, written by John Peat, describes the Last Judgment:

> " The fate of the cloth in the end most disgraceful,
> They who with kings and with rulers could dine,
> Will, by their own clan be found out deceitful,
> The bishops will then lodge with devils and swine,
> Instead of a silk gown to clothe the false rubbish,
> Or bottle of claret to please his proud heart,
> Or fine high cock'd mitre, to make him look bobbish,
> The waters of death will new torments impart."

The believers in the Third Commission were to be found in Somersetshire and Derbyshire in mid-Victorian times. Usually they had no fixed meeting-place, but assembled in private houses and inns, generally in some place where their books could conveniently be stored. At their meetings they read the Scriptures, which can only make wise to salvation those who have received the light of the Spirit to understand the mind of God, the writings of Muggleton and Reeve, and in modern times " The Book of Enoch " and " The Testament of the Twelve Patriarchs." There is a Muggletonian hymn-book, entitled " Christian Hymns and Spiritual Songs for those who follow the Third Commission," but these hymns express thanksgiving only. There are no fixed times of meeting, but February 16th, which commemorates the founding of the sect, is called " The Great Holiday," and July 30th, the day on which Muggle-

ton was released from prison, is known as " The Little Holiday."
In 1869 the London members of the sect bought the house,
7, New Street, Bishopsgate Without, which stands on the site of
Muggleton's birth-place in Walnut Tree Yard.   There they kept
the founder's portrait, death-mask, and manuscripts, and there,
at any rate till recently, a little group, consisting chiefly of
descendants of the earlier members, for no attempt is made to
gain converts, met to carry on the traditions.   There are still
members of this communion in Derbyshire, and they used to
hold a yearly meeting at the Drury Lowe Arms, Denby, near
Heanor.[1]

UNITARIANISM

The word Unitarian was at first a vague term, and in England
in the seventeenth century the name scarcely denoted a sect at
all.   Curiously enough, the term Trinitarian was first applied
to those who attacked the orthodox doctrine of the Trinity,
but Servetus applied the word to the holders of that doctrine as
a term of reproach.[2]   The first beginnings of Unitarianism were
in Italy; then it passed to Switzerland, Poland, and other
countries to which the Reformation had penetrated.   In 1550
the first Unitarian party made its appearance in the Strangers'
Church in London.   The movement was fostered abroad by
Ochino, Acontius, the Sozzini and others.   Pagitt and Ross
speak of a sect of Anti-Trinitarians called the Polonian, or Polish
Arians, which sprang up in Poland about 1593.[3]   There was a
small sect in England in the early part of the seventeenth century,
known as the Legatine Arians, or, as they were sometimes
called before 1620, the Scattered Flock.   Their first teachers in
England were the three brothers Legate.   Thomas Legate was
imprisoned in Newgate as an Arian heretic, and died there in
1607.   Bartholomew Legate, his brother, was tried on a charge
of Arianism and other heresies before the consistory court of the
diocese of London, sentenced to death, and burned at the stake
at Smithfield in March 1612, while about a month later Edward
Wightman was burnt at Lichfield for the same offence of heresy.[4]
Anti-Trinitarian opinions were found in the first Baptist church
founded in London in 1613 by Thomas Helwys, and during the
reign of Charles I. there were persons in England whose orthodoxy
on the question of the Nature and Incarnation of the Son of

[1] Braithwaite, " Second Period of Quakerism," p. 372; Reynolds, " English Sects," London, 1921, p. 116.   For a list of books dealing with Muggleton
and Muggletonianism see Smith, " Bibliotheca Antiquakeriana," 1873, pp.
301–333, 376–377.
[2] J. Hay Colligan, " The Arian Movement in England," p. 2.
[3] Pagitt, " Heresiography," p. 159.
[4] " A Relation of Several Heresies," 1646; " A True Relation of the . . .
Condemnation and Burning of Bartholomew Leggatt and Edward Wightman
. . . their most blasphemous and false opinions," 2nd ed., 1692.

God was at least doubtful.[1] Anti-Trinitarians were to be found
in various sects. Thomas Collier (1634–1691), a Particular
Baptist, is said to have denied the Trinity, so did the Lemarists
and so did Lodowick Muggleton.[2]

In 1651 John Fry was turned out of Parliament for Sabellianism.[3] On December 22nd, 1661, died Thomas Lushington,
a follower of Socinus (the Latinised form of Sozzino), who had
translated and published various Socinian writings, and who
had held a prebendal stall in Salisbury, and the rectory of
Burnham Westgate in Norfolk, though at the time of the Rebellion he had given them up.[4] In 1668 William Penn was sent
to the Tower for seven months for his " Sandy Foundations
Shaken," which was at least Sabellian in tendency. In this
book he attacked " those so generally believed and applauded
doctrines of one God subsisting in three distinct and separate
Persons." But when Penn and his friends discovered that they
were being taken for pupils of Socinus and Biddle they were
alarmed, and Penn himself published in 1669 " Innocency with
her Open Face," in which he drew more closely towards the
orthodox doctrine. Robert Barclay, in his " Apology for the
True Christian Divinity " in 1676, put forth a doctrine which
was tinged with Sabellianism, like that of Penn, but there was
henceforth a clear breach between the Quakers and the Unitarians, and the latter taunted the Friends with having quickly
changed their opinions.

Ephraim Pagitt wrote in 1645 that both Socinians and Arians
were to be found in England. The distinction between the two
at this time was not always clear, but, generally speaking, the
Arian believed in the divinity of Christ but not the deity, while
the Socinian did not really accept either. These two strains
more or less united to form the later Unitarianism, but as far as
Arianism was concerned there was sympathy rather than agreement with the Unitarians. Christopher Sand, the younger, in
his " Bibliotheca Antitrinitariorum," published posthumously in
1684 in Amsterdam, though he insisted on the unity and denied
the Trinity, held the Arian doctrine of a divine and pre-existent
Christ. John Milton, though in his later years he belonged to
no sect at all, was definitely Anti-Trinitarian. His religious
views, in their more or less final form, he set down in his treatise,
" De Doctrina Christiana." This was probably written after
the Restoration, and had been entrusted to Skinner, who had
intended to publish it. Government officers apparently had
seized it at some time or other, and it was only discovered in
the State Paper Office in 1823. As in " Paradise Lost " and

[1] J. Hay Colligan, " The Arian Movement in England," pp. 7, 8.
[2] A Gordon, " Heads of Unitarian History," p. 19.
[3] J. Hay Colligan, " The Arian Movement in England," p. 10.
[4] Wood, " Ath. Ox.," II. 71–72.

" Paradise Regained," only more so, the doctrine of the Son
set forth is distinctly Arian, in its denial that the Son is
co-equal and co-eternal with the Father. All the attributes of
Godhead belong to the Father alone, but the Son was begotten
by the will of the Father, who bestowed upon Him a portion of
the Divine Nature. The Holy Spirit was later in time than the
Son, is inferior to the Son, and a creature of the Almighty,
whose minister He is. Like Biddle, Milton treated the Holy
Spirit, not as a power or an influence, but as a kind of
semi-divine being, greater than the angels.[1]

Of the Anti-Trinitarian lines of thought which converged to
form Unitarianism, the doctrine of the Socinians had the greatest
influence. These held the general views held also by the Latitudinarians, e.g. that there is no rule but Scripture, no guide
but reason, and that salvation may be gained in all churches
simply by keeping the commandments of God in imitation of
Christ. Latitudinarianism, with its indefinite liberalism and its
minimising spirit, tended to lead through Non-Trinitarianism to
Anti-Trinitarianism, and so to Unitarianism. Abraham Wood-
head, the Roman Catholic controversialist, asked how Protestants
could insist that their religion was founded on the Bible only
and at the same time make use of words like consubstantial.[2]
Some writers saw a connection between Arminianism and
Socinianism. The two strains certainly met in Thomas Firmin,
who was influenced by John Goodwin in one direction, and by
Biddle in the other.[3] In 1699, indeed, the Bishop of Worcester
treated the two as identical, but the connection between them
lies rather in a habit of mind. They were both revolts, one
against the domination of Calvinism, the other against the
domination of Catholic orthodoxy. The Socinians of the seventeenth century, who were much nearer Socinus in their
Christology than those of the eighteenth century,[4] insisted on
the unity of the Godhead, and denied that Christ was the
pre-existent Son of God. They held that He satisfied by His
death the justice of God, and then became Lord and King.
This was really a form of Adoptionism, but they were willing to
invoke Christ as God, which Biddle and his sect refused to do.[5]

The name Unitarian did not actually appear in England till
after the middle of the seventeenth century. It had first been
given, about 1638, to the members of the Church founded by
Francis David in Transylvania. The Polish Socinians disliked
the name, but it became applied to them all the same. It was

---

[1] Dowden, " Puritan and Anglican," 1923; Macaulay, " Essay on Milton."
[2] " The Protestant's Plea for a Socinian," 1686. Tenison replied in 1687
with " The Difference between the Protestant and Socinian Methods."
[3] J. Hay Colligan, " The Arian Movement in England," pp. 16–17.
[4] Idem, ibid., p. 152.
[5] Bonet-Maury, " Early Sources of English Unitarian History," ch. x.

probably first used in England by Henry Hedworth in 1673, not so much as the name of a sect, but as a word covering very varying schools of thought which differed in their Christology and only agreed in accepting the supremacy of the Father.[1] Like Socinian, Unitarian was frequently used as a term of opprobrium.

The principal founder of Unitarianism in England was John Biddle, who was born in 1616. He was educated at Magdalen College, Oxford, of which he was a Master of Arts, and is said to have been a good Latin scholar as well as a devout and earnest man. In 1641 he became the master of the grammar school in the parish of St. Mary-le-Crypt, Gloucester, where the studies of his leisure moments led him to adopt Socinian views. In 1644 his doctrines had been called in question, and he had been imprisoned. In 1645 he published his " Twelve Arguments against the Deity of the Holy Ghost," for which he was committed to prison in the December of that year, though he was almost immediately set at liberty, on giving a bond to surrender himself when called upon by the Committee of Parliament. Usher had a conference with him in June 1646, but of course failed to persuade him. An appeal to Sir Henry Vane was unsuccessful, and he appeared before the Committee of the House of Commons. He was sentenced to be imprisoned, and his book by special order of Parliament was burnt by the common hangman.[2] In 1648, while in prison, he printed " A Confession of Faith concerning the Trinity according to Scripture." On May 2nd, 1648, an ordinance for the punishment of blasphemies was introduced into the House of Commons, and Biddle and Paul Best, one of his friends and disciples, were in great danger, inasmuch as the ordinance had been specially directed against Biddle and his teachings, and some of the orthodox party were clamouring for his execution. Though the ordinance was never passed, Biddle remained in prison till 1651.[3] Thomas Firmin, then a young apprentice in London, petitioned Cromwell for Biddle's release, but Cromwell replied, " You curlpate boy, you! Do you think I'll show favour to a man that denies his Saviour and disturbs the Government? "[4]

At Biddle's instigation, at least, the Racovian Catechism was published in 1651, a Latin catechism which had been begun by Socinus and completed by some of his followers in 1605. This new edition was also burnt by the common hangman in 1652, in which year Biddle either translated or caused it to be translated into English, shortly afterwards sending forth from the

[1] *Trans. Unitarian Hist. Soc.*, II. iv. 138 ff.
[2] " God's Glory Vindicated and Blasphemy Confuted in Answer to Biddle's Twelve Arguments," 1647.
[3] Walter Lloyd, " The Story of Protestant Dissent and English Unitarianism," pp. 165–166.
[4] Kennet, " Reg.," p. 761.

press a translation of the life of Socinus.[1] In 1653 appeared
" The Apostolical and True Opinion concerning the Holy
Trinity, Revived and Asserted; partly by Twelve Arguments
Levied against the Traditional and False Opinion about the
Godhead of the Holy Spirit: Partly by a Confession of Faith
Touching the three Persons. Both which, having been formerly
set forth in those years which the respective Titles bear, are now
so altered, so augmented, what with Explications of the Scriptures,
what with Reasons, what finally with Testimonies of the Fathers
and of others, together with Observations thereupon, that they
may justly seem new." [2] It was really a collection of Biddle's
writings in one volume, with a prefatory letter to Sir Henry
Vane. In the Confession of Faith he insisted on the unity of
God. He acknowledged the divinity of Jesus Christ, not as a
distinct person, but as united to " the only person of the infinite
Almighty Essence." He was not eternal God, but a man
approved and exalted to be Lord and Christ, and so was the
chief Son, the spiritual heavenly Lord and King set over the
Church. Biddle also denied the personality of the Holy Spirit:
the Holy Ghost was merely the " gift of God." A reply was
published in 1654, and bore the title " The Divinity of the
Trinity Cleared. By Wiping Off the False Glosses put upon
several places of Scripture by Mr. John Biddle, in his Book
entitled ' The Apostolical and True Opinion touching the Holy
Trinity, etc.' Written by a very Learned Man, lately deceased."
The writer was John Brayne. In 1653 Biddle had opened a
conventicle in London, which technically might be called Independent, but which, because of the Anti-Trinitarianism taught
in it, was closed by the authorities in 1654.

   In 1654 Biddle published his " Twofold Catechism "—the one
simply called a Scripture Catechism, the other a brief Scripture
Catechism for Children. For this he was ordered to appear
before Parliament, was again sent to prison, and his Catechism
burned by the common hangman by order of Parliament. Dr.
John Owen was commanded by the Council of State to write a
refutation, and in 1655 he published his " Vindiciæ Evangelicæ,"
a volume of 700 pages, in reply to the Catechisms, which Owen
said had been sold not only in England, but also overseas. On
the dissolution of Parliament Biddle had been set free, but in
1655 he was again sent to Newgate under the ordinance of
1648, a thoroughly illegal proceeding. Oliver was anxious to
avoid sentence of death being passed on him, and sent him to
the Scilly Islands for three years, and gave him £25 a year out
of his own pocket. He returned to London some time before
the Restoration, and resumed his meetings, though he held

---

[1] A. Gordon, " Heads of Unitarian History," pp. 18–19.
[2] The separate title-page of " A Confession of Faith Touching the Holy
Trinity, According to the Scripture," is dated 1648.

them more or less privately. On June 1st, 1662, he was taken from his lodgings, where he and his friends had met for worship, and was carried before Major-General Sir Richard Browne, who refused bail, and Biddle was thrown into a dungeon. The Recorder, however, released the prisoners on their giving security to appear at the next Sessions. When they appeared Biddle was sentenced to a fine of £100, and each of his hearers £20, and to be imprisoned till the fines were paid. The sheriffs were willing to release Biddle from a great part of the penalty, and would have accepted £10, which he would have paid, but Sir Richard Browne insisted on the full sum. In five weeks he was taken with some disease owing to the noisomeness of the place in which he was confined. Application was made to Browne to let him be removed, but he refused. Meynell, one of the sheriffs, however, gave permission, but it was too late to save him, and he died two days after his liberation, on September 22nd, 1662, in his forty-seventh year, and was buried in Moor-fields.[1] He was described as a man of " sharp and quick judg-ment, and a prodigious memory, wonderfully versed in the Scriptures, and could not only repeat all St. Paul's Epistles in English, but also in the Greek tongue, which made him a ready disputant." Those who knew him said he was sober in dis-course, with nothing of impiety or scurrility in him, and exceedingly devout.[2]

Probably the treatment Biddle received drove him further and further from orthodoxy. He said that Christ was truly God, by being truly, really, and properly united to the only Person of the Infinite and Almighty Essence. The Trinity he explained as God the Father, the man Jesus Christ, and the Holy Spirit, the gift of God through Jesus Christ. In his catechism he even went so far as to attribute to God a bodily and visible shape, with human affections and passions.[3]

Among the early Unitarian preachers contemporary with Biddle was John Cooper, who had succeeded him in the master-ship of the school at Gloucester. He was later ejected from Cheltenham.[4] He became the minister of a Unitarian con-gregation at Cheltenham, which he served for twenty years, from 1662 to 1682. John Knowles, a London disciple of Biddle, an Independent, preached Anti-Trinitarianism in Chester in 1650, " the earliest known course of avowed Anti-Trinitarianism in an English pulpit," [5] i.e. if we do not count the Strangers' Church sermons in 1550. He died in 1668. Another was Paul

[1] Wood, " Athenæ," II. 299–306; " Joannis Bidelli Vita," 1682, said to have been written by John Farrington of the Inner Temple; Toulmin, " Life of Biddle."
[2] Kennet, " Reg.," pp. 760–761.
[3] Stoughton, " Hist. Rel. Eng.," III. 335–336.
[4] Palmer, II. 232.
[5] Gordon, " Heads of Unit. Hist.," p. 18.

Best, Biddle's companion in tribulation, who died in 1657. Most interesting of all, perhaps, was Nathaniel Stuckey, who translated Biddle's " Two-fold Catechism " into Latin, and published with it a short piece of his own on the death of Christ. He died of the plague in 1665 at the age of sixteen.[1] Paul Hobson taught that God was never at enmity with man, but man with God; that Christ did not reconcile God to man, but man to God, and did not purchase love, life, and salvation, but was sent to manifest them. Like Biddle, he was a Socinian.[2] Nevertheless, for many years after the death of Biddle there was no really important Anti-Trinitarian teacher in England.

One of the leading supporters of Unitarianism was Thomas Firmin, a wealthy and benevolent silk merchant of French descent, who had a business in Lombard Street, and was a friend of Biddle. After the death of Biddle, Firmin attended some of the churches of the Establishment, and was intimate with some of the leading Anglicans of the Latitudinarian school, such as Whichcote, Provost of King's College, Cambridge; Worthington, Master of Jesus College, Cambridge; Fowler, and Tillotson. The friendship between Firmin and Tillotson was so close that the latter, when Dean of Canterbury, left it to Firmin to find supplies for his London lectureship when he had to leave town.[3] Some of the Latitudinarians were at heart in sympathy with Unitarian views. Firmin, like others of the early Unitarians, thought it would be better to leaven the old churches rather than found new ones. Moreover, the Anglican Church was not very exacting, and only demanded from the laity a belief in the Apostles' Creed. The sects were much more inquisitive, but we find Firmin on particular terms of friendship with Penn and other Quakers.

In 1662 a letter was sent by the Unitarian congregations in Poland to friends in England, asking for charitable contributions. They had been persecuted, and many of them driven out of the country by the Jesuits. Firmin collected some help from private persons, and even induced several of the parochial clergy to have collections in their churches for this object.[4] Henry Hedworth gave him much assistance in this work.[5] Three years later appeared a translation of a work, " De Uno Deo Patre," by Johann Krell, a Polish Unitarian. This English translation was published, at Firmin's expense, under the title, " The Two Books of John Crellius Francus touching One God the Father, etc." The publisher was Richard Moon, who at his house, " The Seven Stars," had for twenty years past printed nearly

[1] Bonet-Maury, " Early Sources of English Unitarianism," ch. x; Duae Catecheses.
[2] T. Long, " No Protestant but the Dissenters' Plot," 1682.
[3] Gordon, " Heads of Unit. Hist.," p. 24.
[4] Kennet, " Reg.," p. 761.
[5] J. Hay Colligan, " The Arian Movement in England," p. 6.

all the translations of Socinian treatises which had appeared in England. Bonet-Maury suggests that Firmin may have had something to do with the translation, but Dr. Gordon calls him " a comparatively illiterate man."

The Polish Unitarians kept up a close connection with their English sympathisers. Christopher Krell, the second son of the Johann above mentioned, was pastor of a Polish Unitarian congregation at Freidrichsberg in Silesia, and twice visited England, once in 1666, and again in 1668. His son Samuel and one of his daughters were sent to England to be educated, and lived with the mother of the precocious Nathaniel Stuckey, who published in 1664 the Latin version of the Longer and Shorter Unitarian Catechisms. Samuel, after completing his education at Amsterdam, became pastor of a congregation at Koenigswald, near Frankfort on the Oder, but kept up a correspondence with, and occasionally visited, his friends in England, Tillotson and Sir Isaac Newton. In 1680, when subscriptions were raised in England for the persecuted French Protestants, Firmin subscribed liberally, and was treasurer of the fund, and he also busied himself with relief for the exiled Polish Calvinists. His hands were already fairly full with schemes of practical philanthropy in England, but in works of this kind he was untiring.

When Thomas Gouge, ejected from St. Sepulchre's, London, in 1662, took up the work of distributing Bibles and religious books amongst the people of Wales, Firmin supported the scheme heartily. Gouge, according to Calamy, had given up his living " on some dissatisfaction about the terms of conformity," but had refrained from setting up a conventicle of his own.[1] Amongst the books he caused to be translated and distributed were the Church Catechism and the Book of Common Prayer. Firmin supplied the money, and gained the sympathetic interest of Tillotson and Whichcote. Dr. Alexander Gordon has described this as " the first public platform of united religious and educational work in which Anglicans and Nonconformists found it possible to co-operate." [2] In 1689 Firmin had something to do with the publication of " The Naked Gospel," written in defence of ecclesiastical comprehension by Dr. Arthur Bury, an Anglican clergyman of Latitudinarian views.

Firmin had learnt his heterodoxy in the first place from Biddle, and was a Socinian like Biddle, Milton, and others. They had held that the Father was the only true God, who ruled the world by delegated agents, called the Son and Holy Ghost, who might be looked upon merely as inferior deities delegated by the one God. But he came under the influence of Stephen Nye, the Anglican rector of Little Hormead, Hert-

[1] Palmer, I. 185.
[2] A. Gordon, " Addresses, Biographical and Historical," p. 105.

fordshire, and grandson of Philip Nye, the great stalwart of the Independents. Under his influence Firmin drew towards Sabellianism. Father, Son, and Holy Ghost were manifestations of the one God, and Jesus Christ could still be called God, inasmuch as in Him the Godhead had been pre-eminently manifested to mankind.[1]

In 1682 an Epistle with some tracts annexed was presented, through the agency of M. de Verze, to Ahmet ben Ahmet, the ambassador to England from the Sultan of Morocco. The work claimed to be written by " two philosophers " of " that sect of Christians that are called Unitarians," and assumed the common ground that the ambassador, like the writers, was a Unitarian in denying any distinction or plurality of persons in the Godhead. The use of the word Unitarian for the name of a sect was new. The document presented to the ambassador was not actually published till 1708.[2] " A Brief History of the Unitarians, called also Socinians," published in 1687, was written by Stephen Nye, though published anonymously, apparently at the request of Firmin.[3] In this work the word Unitarian was used broadly to include all who asserted the unity of the Godhead, as opposed to the Trinitarians, and it included both Socinians and Arians, and those who, like Firmin, held that the doctrine of the Trinity prevented the entrance of the Jew and the Mohammedan into the Christian fold. The " Brief History " took the form of four " Letters " addressed to a friend, the friend being Firmin, and there was appended a letter " by a person of excellent learning," believed to be Henry Hedworth; and an opponent, replying to the work some four years later, accused it of containing little history but much abuse of divers authors.[4] He pointed out that the Unitarians allowed Arians to be Christians, because they agreed with them that the Father only is God. The difference between them lay in the fact that the Arians allowed pre-existence to the Son, and said that He created the world, which the Socinians denied, saying, like the writer of the " Brief History," that He was a man, a prophet, a messenger, a creature, but not divine.[5]

Another Unitarian work appeared in 1688. The author was Sir Peter Pett, and the title was " The Happy Future State of England." But Unitarianism did not flourish in England as a sect. All sects alike detested it. John Owen had replied to

[1] Cornish, " Life of Mr. Thomas Firmin "; Gordon, " Addresses, Biog. and Hist.," p. 107.
[2] A. Gordon, " Addresses, Biog. and Hist.," p. 113; *idem*, " Heads of Unit. Hist.," pp. 22–24; Tenison MSS., Lambeth, p. 673.
[3] *Trans. Unit. Hist. Soc.*, Vol. I. Pt. I, Art., " Work in the Field of Unitarian History."
[4] " An Answer to the Brief History of the Unitarians," by William Basset, rector of St. Swithin's, London. London, 1693.
[5] " Answer to the Brief History."

Biddle's " Catechism " in his " Vindiciæ Evangelicæ." John
Tombes, similarly, in 1669 had published " Emmanuel, or
God-Man, a Treatise wherein the Doctrine of the first Nicene
and Chalcedon Councils . . . is asserted against the lately
vented Socinian Doctrine." And there were others. Only one
of the 2000 ejected had, as far as is known, adopted Unitarian
views. This was William Manning, one of the ejected of Suffolk,
who had collected an Independent congregation at Peasenhall,
and who was said to have been made a Socinian by reading
Sherlock's " Vindication of the Trinity," which was published
in 1690.

Soon after the Revolution there appeared three volumes of
Socinian tracts, of which the first volume contained chiefly
reprints of Biddle's writings, and the second at least four tracts
written by Nye. In 1694 Nye wrote " Considerations on the
Explications of the Trinity addressed to H. H.," *i.e.* Henry
Hedworth. Firmin seems to have been financially responsible
for Nye's work, and in 1697, the year of his death, there was
distributed at his expense another tract by Nye, in which the
name Unitarian was disclaimed. The writer admitted a similarity of critical method in dealing with the Scriptures between
the Unitarians and Socinians, and affirmed boldly that for a
Christian a creed of one article only was necessary—that Jesus
was the Messiah.

Heterodoxy had long been prevalent in high quarters in the
Church of England, while the Presbyterians and other sects
became largely permeated by Unitarianism, so much so that in
1697 a deputation of Dissenting ministers besought William III.
to forbid the printing of Socinian books.[1] There was no need,
therefore, to set up separate Unitarian congregations, and no
such attempt was made till 1773, even if the terms of the
Toleration Act had not made it exceedingly difficult to do so.
The Act excluded any Nonconformist who preached or wrote
against the Trinity, though till 1698 no statute dealt with
Anglicans who did this.

THE ANTINOMIANS

The Antinomian sect was founded by John Agricola in 1536,[2]
but the person who was chiefly responsible for the introduction
of its doctrines into England was Dr. Tobias Crisp, who died in
1642 or 1643. He had a considerable following, both among
the clergy and the laity. Antinomian teachings were rampant
in the army, at least during the first Civil War. " The books
of Dr. Crisp, Paul Hobson, John Saltmarsh, Cradock and
abundance such like, were the writings most applauded; and
he was thought no spiritual Christian but a legalist, that savoured

[1] J. Hay Colligan, " The Arian Movement in England," p. 45.
[2] Ross, " Pansebeia," p. 406.

not of Antinomianism, but was sugared with the title of free grace." [1] Sir Charles Firth thinks it must soon have been expelled from the army,[2] but in 1648 Samuel Rutherford, Professor of Divinity in the University of St. Andrews, published "A Survey of the Spiritual Antichrist, opening the Secrets of Familism and Antinomianism in the Antichristian Doctrine of John Saltmarsh and William Dell, the present Preachers of the Army now in England, and of Robert Town, Toh. Crisp, H. Denne, Eaton and others." Saltmarsh was minister of Brastead, in Kent, and, next to Crisp, the chief leader of the party. "Free Grace; or, the Flowings of Christ's Blood freely for Sinners" was one of his books; "Sparkles of Glory" was another.

"Patrons of free vice under the mask of free grace," [3] "breaking the two tables in order to prevent popery," [4] the Antinomians rejected the moral law, because they said it was useless under the Gospel.[5] If Christ has paid the whole debt, there is nothing owing. God has made a covenant of grace absolutely, and has tied man by no conditions. "Free" grace means that man is passive even in receiving the gifts of God. Christ, therefore, is ours without faith, though it is by believing that we know He is ours. The child of grace never doubts after he is once assured of salvation. "Believe and obey"; where God works, obedience follows.

Good works do not further, nor bad works hinder, salvation. God does not chasten men for sin, for if he is in a state of grace, whatever he does is not sin. Murder, adultery, drunkenness, and such-like are sins in the wicked, but not in the children of grace. However much believers do such things, God loves them. No man should be troubled in his conscience for any sin, and no Christian should be exhorted to perform the duties of Christianity. A hypocrite may have all the graces that were in Adam before his fall, and yet be without Christ. Christ is the only subject of all graces, and no Christian believes or works any good. Only Christ can do that. He died, intercedes, and saves, so there is no need to take care what we do. It is a sin to ask God's pardon, for that would be doubting Him. He is only angry that man should fear Him. He is not angry because of sins, because He is not as we are, and therefore sees no sin: neither does He love any man for his holiness, for sanctification is no evidence of a man's justification.[6]

---

[1] "Rel. Baxt.," p. 43.
[2] Firth, "Cromwell's Army," 1901, p. 346.
[3] Calamy, Sermon before the Lords. Christmas Day, 1644; Kennet, "Reg.," p. 730.
[4] Pettitt, "Visions of Reformation," 1683, p. 93.
[5] "A Discourse of Toleration," 1660.
[6] Ross, "Pansebeia," p. 406; "The Postboy," pp. 238–239; Hunt, "Religious Thought in England," I. 249–253.

With the Antinomians the witness of the Spirit was merely immediate and without reference to sanctification. All doctrines and revelations must be tried by Christ rather than by the Word. A Christian was not to pray except when the Spirit moved him: all other askings or seekings of God were but the askings of creatures as creatures. The Scriptures were only to be understood as the Spirit revealed them. The commands of Scripture were not a law to Christians, the real law was the law written in their hearts. The Holy Ghost took the place of the natural faculties of the soul, and so controlled all internal and external acts.[1]

Against these people and their teachings Baxter wrote his first book, " Aphorisms of Justification." On more than one occasion he accused the Independents of holding Antinomian views. In a sermon which he preached at Pinners' Hall in 1675 he caused considerable offence by not only making this charge, but using language which seemed to reflect on the personal character of some of their ministers. A paper controversy followed. Baxter issued a sheet called " An Appeal to the Light," which was answered by " Animadversions on a Sheet of Mr. Baxter's, entitled ' An Appeal to the Light ' for the Further Caution of his Credulous Readers." The author showed that Baxter had made unfounded charges, and ought not to have ranked Owen, Tully, and Bagshawe with Saltmarsh and Robson. Baxter replied in 1676 with " A Treatise of Justifying Righteousness," in which he dealt chiefly with the Antinomians, and quoted in his own support a large number of writers. He must have been rather surprised to find himself entangled in this controversy, for in 1664 he had written that the sect had so suddenly died out that members of it were rarely to be found, and little to be heard of.[2]

In 1690 Tobias Crisp's works were republished by his son Samuel. To this edition was prefixed a curious document signed by twelve of the leading Nonconformist ministers, stating that the discourses as published were really Dr. Crisp's. They gave them no commendation, but merely stated their belief that such was the case.[3] Evidently there were still people to whom these works would appeal: indeed, there were such in the early part of the eighteenth century. Baxter, in 1690, issued his " Scripture Gospel Defended," a work which he had written thirteen years

[1] Comber, " Christianity no Enthusiasm," 1678, p. 90; Rutherford, " Survey of the Spiritual Antichrist," 1648, pp. 173–175.
[2] F. J. Powicke, " Bulletin, John Ryland's Library," V. 460. They were mentioned as still existing in Long's " No Protestant but the Dissenters' Plot," 1682, and Tenison's " A Discourse concerning a Guide in Matters of Faith," 1683.
[3] Orme, " Life of Baxter," pp. 671–673; " Christ Alone Exalted, being the Complete Works of Tobias Crisp, with Prefaces by Samuel Crisp and R. Lancaster," London, 1690; Powicke, " Life of Baxter," 1924, pp. 237–245.

before, but now brought into the controversy aroused by Samuel Crisp's filial action. Thomas Beverley replied with his " Conciliatory Judgment concerning Dr. Crisp's Sermons and Mr. Baxter's Dissatisfactions " in 1690.

Thomas Jolly seems to have had some experience of the Antinomians. He noted in 1672 that a certain Charles Riley, who intended to hear an Antinomian minister named Parr on the following Sunday, dreamt that Jolly was going to preach on that day on Rom. x. 16. ("I not having preached on that subject before, nor he knowing my purpose any other ways.") He therefore went to hear Jolly instead, and finding his dream come true, " it issued in a saving change upon him." [1] Jolly also noted that " a popular Antinomian preacher named Hartley was discovered and driven out of the country in 1674 for scandalous practices, and that one of Hartley's followers was convicted and condemned to be burnt for assisting in the murder of her husband." [2]

THE LIBERTINES

Most contemporary writers treat the Libertines as separate from the Antinomians, though they are both traced to the same founder, John Agricola,[3] who is said to have begun to promulgate his teaching in 1535. It is difficult to distinguish their doctrines from those of the Antinomians, but the sects split off from each other so easily that the two may be different. The Libertines believed that the Law was not given to Christian men, for it pertained to the wicked and not to the godly, and therefore the Ten Commandments need not be taught in church to the regenerate, since such persons, being led by the Spirit, do their duty willingly. It was sufficient for a wicked man to believe, and not doubt his salvation, and he would be saved: good works could not help salvation, nor evil works hinder. The rule of the Law was not a rule of life, and therefore a Christian man could not be known by his life.

THE SEEKERS

" They damned all for apostates." [4]   In these words an anonymous writer described a large but unorganised body of people who described themselves as Seekers, or Waiters, or Expecters.

[1] " The Note-book of Thomas Jolly," p. 9; " The Altham and Wymondhouses Church Book."
[2] " The Note-book of Thomas Jolly," p. 14.
[3] Edwards, " Gangræna," 1646; " A Relation of Several Heresies," 1646; Samuel Rutherford, " Survey of the Spiritual Antichrist," 1648; Underhill, " Hell Broke Loose, or the History of the Quakers both Old and New," 1660; Long, " No Protestant but the Dissenters' Plot," 1682; Pettitt, " Visions of the Reformation," 1683, pp. 90–91.
[4] " A Discourse of Toleration in Answer to a Discourse of the Religion of England," 1660.

John Goodwin said they were " a generation who thought they did God service by overlooking all that is written, and looking for something higher, more mysterious and more sacred." [1] They were not, strictly speaking, a sect, for they had neither church, ministry, nor ordinances. A recent writer has found their origin in the Legatine Arians, [2] and Baxter, of course, found a Jesuit influence behind them; [3] but no one knows exactly when they first arose, and no founder's name is connected with them; like the Ranters, they represented similar tendencies of thought which affected people in various parts of the country. [4] There were men who claimed that God revealed His mind and will to His servants in reference to their salvation, without scriptures, or ministers, or ordinances, but by revelations and visions. They were common in the army from about 1645 onwards. Some, both officers and men, declared they had received such revelations and visions, and that they had the gift of prophecy. They held the most varied views. A lieutenant denied the Trinity, and said it was only a Trinity of offices, that Christ's presence in heaven could not be proved by Scripture, and that the resurrection of the dead was very doubtful. Boggis regretted that he knew so much of the Bible, as it was only paper. Clarkson said he would not have people live upon black and white (by which he meant printed books), and said that they themselves could reveal God. Mrs. Attaway was one of their women preachers. [5] These people have been spoken of as Seekers, or Religious Sceptics, but Edwards distinguished the Seekers and Waiters from the Sceptics and Questionists. But the Seekers questioned most things. They held that the Scriptures were uncertain, that the ministry of the existing churches was null and without authority, that the worship and ordinances of their day were vain, and that miracles would be necessary to re-establish faith. The true church was in the wilderness, the true worship, the true ministry, the true Scriptures, and the true ordinances had all been lost, and they were now groping and seeking for these. [6] A contemporary writer divided them into the following classes:

(1) The most moderate declared they were seeking a true church and ministry. Such a church and ministry existed, but they were at a loss to know what they were. Some, however, believed that they were not

---

[1] Goodwin, " Catabaptism," 1655.
[2] Burrage, " Early English Dissenters," I. 31.
[3] " Key for Catholics," 1659.
[4] Rufus M. Jones, " Studies in Mystical Religion," p. 452.
[5] Edwards, " Gangræna "; Comber, " Christianity no Enthusiasm," 1678, p. 89.
[6] " Rel. Baxt.," p. 76.

yet in existence, but that God would send new
apostles to establish them.

(2) Others were seeking whether there existed any " organised political church," *i.e.* one with a settled polity,
which could be considered as the true one, and
whether it would have any ordinances or ministry.

(3) A third group denied the possibility of any " political "
church, ministry, or ordinances in this world.

(4) Another group agreed with the last, but held that they
had to seek for the " universal church." As for the
Scriptures, many of them maintained that we have
no certainty of their truth or authority.

(5) Others believed in the existence of a true church, but
believed themselves to be above all ordinances.

(6) Lastly, there were those who held that the whole company of believers should have outgrown such things
as Scriptures, ministry, or ordinances.[1]

The Seeker movement gradually died out. Ross omitted them
from his edition of the " Pansebeia " published in 1683, but
other people mention them about the same time, and a little
later.[2] Some of the more moderate of them joined the Quakers,
though it cannot be shown, as some have asserted, that Quakerism
was simply a natural development of Seeker doctrine. Some
became Ranters, and the tendency to fanaticism which was so
often manifest in the Seekers made the transition easy.

The Ranters

The Ranters were the wildest of all the sects of the period,
and no one had a good word to say for them. Pagitt was
inclined to class them with the Atheists. The central idea of
their teaching was that God is essentially in every creature.
One Spirit pervades the universe, and that Spirit is revealed in
a measure in all that exists. Thus, Pantheism was the basis of
what religious philosophy they had. They recognised nothing
divine but this Spirit within them—that is to say, they set up as
their guide the light of nature, to which they gave the name of
the indwelling Spirit, or, as they sometimes called it, " Christ
in man." They disbelieved in the Scriptures, in ministry, and
in ordinances. There was, therefore, no authority external to
themselves: they were " led by the Spirit," and needed no
other guide. The Christ of the Gospel story was only a figure

[1] " The Great Plot for Restoring Popery," London, 1663; Kennet, " Reg.,"
p. 396.
[2] Long, " No Protestant but the Dissenters' Plot," 1682; Pettitt, " Visions
of Reformation," 1683, where Sceptics are distinguished from Seekers; Tenison,
" Discourse concerning a Guide in Matters of Faith," 1683; " The Muses'
Farewell to Popery and Slavery," 1690, p. 27.

or type of the new dispensation that was now come.[1] Hence, though some of them doubtless were honest and sincere men, the Ranters were largely characterised by Antinomian libertinism. Possibly the name Libertines given in some of the lists of sects refers either to these or to the Antinomians. God, they held, regarded not the outward actions, He only looked upon the heart; the heart being right, outward actions mattered not at all.

The Ranters were not an organised body, nor did they agree among themselves. "The Ranters' Bible," a tract published in 1650, divided them into the following sects:

(1) The Familists of Love. These are better considered in connection with Familism.
(2) Shelomethites. Among these to swear and blaspheme was a badge of honour. Some of them were found near Uxbridge, where over thirty of them had been arrested. Baxter referred to the same thing. " I have myself letters from Abingdon, where among both soldiers and people this contagion did then prevail, full of horrid oaths, and curses and blasphemy, not fit to be repeated by the tongue and pen of man, and this all uttered as the effect of knowledge and a part of religion, and a fanatic strain, and fathered on the Spirit of God." [2]
(3) Clements. These believed in repentance after death.
(4) Athians. These held the doctrine of the sleep of the soul. There were some of them at King's Lynn.
(5) Nicolaitanes. These lived in promiscuous immorality. They did not believe in marriage, and were plunderers and robbers.
(6) Marcionites. These believed that there were two Gods, one the author of good and the other of evil, and it was their practice to drink healths to the devil.
(7) Seleucian Donatists. These denied the authority of the Bible, and made a practice of burning Bibles. They refused all authority and discipline, and also practised immorality.

The tract referred to is quite short, but bears a portentous title: " The Ranters' Bible: or, Seven Several Religions by them held and maintained, with full Particulars of their strange Sects and Societies: their new Places of Meetings, both in City and Country: their Manner of Life and Conversation, their blasphemous Opinions of our Lord and Saviour Jesus Christ,

[1] Rufus M. Jones, " Studies in Mystical Religion," p. 469; " Christianity No Enthusiasm," p. 92.
[2] " Rel. Baxt.," p. 77.

and their burning of His Blessed Word and sacred Scriptures:
the names of their new Gods and worshipping of the Sun and
three black Clouds, with their Manner of their idolising them.
North, West, East and South: their drinking of healths to the
Devil and disposing of Places in Hell, their blasphemous Creed
and Litany: their savage Opinion to lie with any Man's Wife,
either in Houses, Fields, or Streets, in the Presence of Hundreds
of People: their Declaration in Kent: the apprehending of
Thirty of them near Uxbridge with their Trials and Examina-
tions, and the routing and dispersing the rest of their fellow
Ranters near Lynn in Norfolk: a strange Voice, from Heaven,
speaking to one Mr. Roulston, a London Ranter, upon his
going from Whitechapel to meet some of his Fellow Citizens at
Hackney, and the great things that happened thereupon, to the
Admiration of the Reader: the coming in of Seven Hundred
since the second of this instant December, their Recantation,
Oath, and Protestation. And Mr. Roulston's Letter to his late
fellow Ranters, with his Advice and Proposals, to be published
in all Cities and Market Towns throughout England and Wales.
Published by Mr. Gilbert Roulston, a late Fellow Ranter."

One of the wildest of the sect was Abiezer Coppe, whose
followers were known as " Ranters, or High Attainers." At
first this man was a zealous Anabaptist, but he claimed to have
fallen into a trance, which continued three or four days, during
which he went down to hell, and had revelations which he
published in a book entitled " A Fiery Flying Roll: A Word
from the Lord to all the Great Ones of the Earth, whom this
may Concern: Being the last Warning Piece at the Dreadful
Day of Judgment." In it he said that as the King, the lords,
and the bishops had had their turn, so the surviving great ones
who opposed the Eternal God, who is universal love, would
also be overthrown. It was a book full of curious ravings.
Coppe attacked Christian duties, a godly life, and what he
called " plaguey holiness," and confessed that it did him more
good to run on men, and tear them by the hair, and curse like
a devil, and make them swear by God, than to join in the practice
of the aforesaid " plaguey holiness." [1] Parliament ordered the
book to be burnt by the common hangman, and the author
was confined in Newgate. There he wrote a retraction, prefaced
by an apology to Parliament and the Council. It was printed
in 1651, with the title " Coppe's Return to the Ways of Truth,
in a Zealous and Sincere Protestation against Several Errors,
and in a Sincere and Zealous Testimony to Several Truths; or,
Truth Asserted against and Triumphing over Error; and the
Wings of the Fiery Flying Roll Clipped, etc. By Abiezer Coppe,
the (supposed) Author of the Flying Roll." It was an extraordinary production, written in short simple sentences, and in it

[1] Long, " No Protestant but the Dissenters' Plot," 1682.

he recanted the following errors: that there is no sin and no God, that man the mere creature is very God, that God is in man, or in the creature and nowhere else, that cursing and swearing, adultery, and fornication are not sins, and that a community of wives is lawful. He also denied, quite untruthfully, the authorship of " The Roll."

John Tickell,[1] the minister of Abingdon, after Coppe's release held a debate with him in Burford church, and evidently had his doubts of the sincerity of the recantation. So, towards the end of the year, he published an attack on Ranterism, Familism, and Coppe, entitled " The Bottomless Pit Smoking in Familism. As may appear by a Short Discourse on Gal. i. 9, together with some brief notes on Abiezer Coppe's Recantation Sermon as 'twere, preached at Burford, September 23rd, 1651." Incidentally he mentioned the Act which Parliament had passed against the Ranters, and said it had done good.

Some of these men were undoubtedly mentally deranged. John Robins and Joshua Garment, with some of their followers, were brought before Thomas Hubert, one of the Middlesex justices, in 1657. They told him that Robins was God Almighty, and that Garment was his prophet. In the presence of the magistrate Garment and the women prisoners threw themselves at Robins' feet and lay there prostrate, while the " prophet," clasping his master's legs, cried " Deliver us, Deliver us! " Robins stamped on the floor, clapped his hands, and said " Arise, and be hanged," whereupon the whole party arose from the ground saying " Arise for ever." [2] The story seems almost incredible, till we remember James Nayler, the Quaker, parading the streets of Bristol as the Messiah, with women shouting Hosannah before him. Robins and his party were sent to Clerkenwell prison, though Bedlam would seem to have been a better place. Amongst his prophecies he had foretold that his wife, Joan, was about to bring forth the Messiah.

Joseph Salmon and Jacob Bauthumley, or, as the name would now be spelt, Bothamley, were two prominent Ranters. George Fox came across Salmon in company with a band of Ranters in the gaol at Coventry, and says that Salmon afterwards wrote a book of recantation, and so they were all set at liberty. Bauthumley wrote a tract, " The Light and Dark Sides of God: or, a Plain Brief Discourse of his Light Side (God, Heaven and Earth), the Dark Side (Devil, Sin and Hell): Also of the Resurrection and Scripture." This was published in London in 1650. Another work ascribed to him is " A Brief Historical Relation of the most Material Passages and Persecutions of the Church of Christ . . . collected out of the Acts and Monuments of the Church written by Mr. Fox . . . by J. B." This was printed in 1676.

---

[1] Wood, " Athenæ," II. 499, 914.   [2] " The Ranters' Creed," 1657.

Thomas Underhill said of the Ranters that they made it the very essence of their religion to swear the most foul-mouthed oaths by multitudes, and openly blasphemed the God of heaven, and they met and danced and roared together and committed filthiness without shame. They went into frenzies, and lay with their bodies swollen, acted strangely, and fell into raptures and blasphemings. Cromwell's Act against Blasphemy was witness to the truth of this.[1]

In his early days Bunyan read some of the books of the Ranters, but was unable at first to make up his mind about them. One of his friends " turned a most devilish Ranter, and gave himself up to all manner of filthiness, especially uncleanness, and would also deny that there was a God, angel, or spirit: and would laugh at all exhortations to sobriety. When I laboured to rebuke his wickedness he would laugh the more, and pretend that he had gone through all religions and could never light on the right till now." Bunyan met some other people, hitherto strict in religion, who had been carried away by the Ranters. " These would also talk with me of their ways and condemn me as legal and dark; pretending that they only had attained to perfection that could do what they would and not sin." [2]

If only half the things told of the Ranters are true, they must have exhibited an extraordinary phenomenon of religious degeneration. At their worst their gatherings must have been disgraceful orgies, at their best they were meetings where the so-called worshippers smoked and shouted. Doctrinally, their contemporaries saw in their teachings a revival of ancient Gnosticism.[3] It is not likely that any educated people were found among them, though Dudley North accused Lord Chief Justice Scroggs of having been a Ranter.[4] In opposition to Ranting views on marriage and morals, some people went to the opposite extreme. " A Looking-glass for the Ranters," a tract published in 1653, is an exposition of the blessedness of virginity, and asserts that carnal marriage for the procreation of children is not of Divine institution.

Their vagaries and extravagances were not, in a sense, so surprising as they seem, when we consider the spirit of the times. The King had been put to death, and the Church overthrown. Ecclesiastically every man said and thought and did whatever was good in his own eyes, and could be as ostentatious about it as he liked withal. The only people who had to keep their beliefs and practices as quiet as possible were the

---

[1] " Hell Broke Loose, or a History of the Quakers, both Old and New," by Thomas Underhill, 1660.

[2] John Bunyan, " Grace Abounding."

[3] " The Ranters' Religion," 1650, contained a copy of some blasphemous verses said to have been found on one of them.

[4] North, " Life of Sir Francis North."

Anglicans and Romanists. With the restoration of order and settled authority, the more extravagant ebullitions gradually died down. Many Ranters, no doubt, ultimately found a spiritual home among the greater sects, especially the Quakers. But the sect continued to exist. Pagitt mentions them in 1661, and we have a few references to them in Fox's " Journal." [1]

Samuel Butler gave a sarcastic portrait of the Ranter. " He believes all religion consists in looseness, and that sin and vice is the only duty of man. . . . He is loth that iniquity and vice should be thrown away as long as there may be good use for it, for if that which is wickedly gotten may be disposed to pious uses, why should not wickedness itself as well? He believes himself shot-free against all the attempts of the devil, the world and the flesh, and therefore is not afraid to attack them in their own quarters, and encounter them at their own weapons. . . . A saint that is strong in grace may boldly engage himself in those great sins and iniquities that would easily damn a weak brother, and yet come off never the worse. . . . He is but a hypocrite turned the wrong side outward, for as the one wears his vices within and the other without, so when they are counterchanged the Ranter becomes a hypocrite and the hypocrite an able Ranter. . . . He is a monster produced by the madness of this latter age." [2]

Ranters were still in existence in the reign of Queen Anne. Gildon says they despised the ordinances and duties of religion. They said that Moses, Christ, and Mohammed were all impostors, and they spoke of the Bible ironically as the " divine legacy." They still practised a community of women, and drank, danced, and sang obscene songs at their meetings. They disowned the authority of magistrates, and to them Christian liberty was nothing but liberty to sin. [3]

THE SALMONISTS

Joseph Salmon, the Ranter, was the author of " Heights in Depths, and Depths in Heights: or, Truth, no less secretly than sweetly, speaking out of its Glory," which was published in 1651. During the Commonwealth, after preaching at various places in Kent, he set up a course of preaching in Rochester cathedral every Sunday. Like many others of that time, he professed to see visions. His sermons were very full of allegory—in fact he forced an allegorical sense on the plainest historical passages of Scripture, and he is said to have preached a sort of

[1] See also references to them in Chamberlain, " Present State of England," 1674; Pettitt, " Visions of Reformation," 1683, pp. 90, 91; Tenison, " Discourse concerning a Guide in Matters of Faith," 1683.
[2] Butler, " Characters "; H. Morley, " Character Writings of the Seventeenth Century," 1891, pp. 403–404.
[3] " The Postboy," p. 429; " The Routing of the Ranters," 1650; " The Ranters Ranting," 1650.

Ranting Familism. In 1655 his flock seemed to be falling off, and he was preaching only once a Sunday, so he went abroad, and some of his followers brought Richard Coppin to take his place.[1] Nothing further was heard of Salmon, but a sect of Salmonists was spoken of as still existing in 1706. One of the essentials of their system was the holding of conferences, at which they proposed and answered difficulties. They were so zealous for liberty of conscience that they would admit no one to their meetings till he had abjured all persecuting principles, and denied the right of magistrates to interfere with any man in the practice of his religion. As the seventeenth century drew towards a close they seem to have approached gradually the doctrines of Quakerism, and those of Molinos, the Spanish Quietist " that was put in the Inquisition lately at Rome for his new doctrine." [2]

The Coppinists

Richard Coppin, who succeeded Salmon at Rochester, had a wandering religious career. He was brought up in the Church of England, turned Presbyterian in 1646, then became an Independent, and then a Baptist. Finally, he says, he received an inward experience and commission to preach, " not from Oxford or Cambridge, or the schools of Antichrist," but " given by Christ at Sion House in heaven." [3] His first publication came out in 1649, under the title of " Divine Teachings," and had a preface " wherein is something of the Mystery of Alpha and Omega, with a prophetical hint," this preface being written by Abiezer Coppe. This is the mystery of Alpha and Omega as set forth by that divine:—

The A or Alpha is triangular. In this the Trinity is seen by the immortal only; the figure only, and perhaps scarcely that, is seen by the mortal eye. A, or Trinity, is the effluence or outspreading of divinity, or outgoing of God into all things. The figure is thus:

A.   FATHER   Alpha

$$\text{SON} \quad \text{God} \quad \text{SPIRIT}$$

Aleph or Alpha in its circularity makes up the Omega, which is in figure thus:

ω or O,

which is the eye or globe of eternity, wherein the end meets the beginning, and all is swallowed up into unity, and thus is Alpha

[1] Rosewell, " The Serpent's Subtlety Discovered," 1656.
[2] " The Postboy," II. 431.
[3] " Truth's Testimony," by R. Coppin, 1655.

and Omega, the beginning and the end.   At the end of this introduction or preamble Coppe wrote:

My [1] heart, my blood, my life, is Thine
It pleases me that [2] Thou art mine.
I'll [3] curse Thy flesh, and [4] swear Th'art fine,
For [5] ever Thine I mean to be,
As [6] I am that I am, within A. C.

[1] Script. est.   [2] Cant. ii.   John xvii.   [3] Neh. iii.
[4] Ezek. xvi.   [5] Mal. iii.   Heb. xiii.   [6] Script. est.

Post Script

Before God, this is one of the songs, O Zion.
Before holy man (whose holiness stinks above ground)
It's at least whimsey, if not blasphemy,
But wisdom is justified of her children.

Turning from the preface to the work itself, in three separate sections Coppin set forth his views.   God is the original.   They who know Him, know the original, and He only can make Himself known.   The wisdom of man is folly, but as every age grows near its end, which is God, the manifestation of truth appears more glorious.   The Spirit, which is infallible, infinite, and perfect, is the interpreter of Scripture.   The spiritual man knows all things, which spiritual man is Emmanuel or Christ in us.   God is in every one, though all know not a like manifestation of Him.   The Scriptures and ourselves are the grave, wherein the glorious God lies buried, and through His resurrection in us we come to have a right knowledge of ourselves and them.   The highest wisdom of man cannot reveal the mind of God to us without the Spirit.   The life of a saint is the life of God, which is all, and contains all, and cannot expect help from anything but itself.   The saints are one with Christ both in sufferings and glory.   Christ is the eye by which we see all truth, and God dwells in us as in Christ.   The indwelling God in us extinguishes all lights by which we formerly walked, and takes away all formal, outward, shadowy, and imperfect things.   Antichrist in man opposes Emmanuel or God in us.   The subjects of election and reprobation are not persons, but the good and evil in man.   Salvation and life eternal are completed in union, and in the return from the fountain into the fountain of life again.   The rising from the grave is a rising to newness of life.   To be in Christ is resurrection to the soul when it discovers that Christ and the saints make up one glorious body, and so discovers their union with God by the resurrection of Christ in them.   The Resurrection Day is simply the heightening of the saints' joy and sinners' torment.   When we are fleshly Christ is buried in us, but when the trumpet sounds—that is, when God calls from above—then Christ comes forth, and we are changed into a new nature.   There is no rising again of this earthly body, which is nothing. God's love is to the creature, His hate is to that which is in the creature, and is revealed against all evil. The wrath of God is the lake of fire in which evil shall be burnt. God is in hell as well as in heaven. The great love of God is shown in wrath and judgment, pouring out the one and executing the other, not upon us, but on sin in us, to its destruction and our salvation. Hence we are saved as by fire. The flesh of man is the seat of sin, and nothing but earth, and is the habitation of the devil; the old man, which is sin, is the sinner; the new man sinneth not. The design of God in leaving man to himself was to manifest His own power and to show the creature's weakness. The vision of God stays sin, and when Christ is revealed in His saints, the devil is chained up. The title-page says that this work manifests " some sparks of the glory that shines and dwells in Richard Coppin."

In " Man's Righteousness Examined," an exposition of the second chapter of St. Peter's second Epistle, published in 1652, Coppin said that man's holiness and righteousness were good as to men, but as to God, evil and abominable. All sin is forgiven, and Christ has made a full end of it. Not to believe that is damnation. Though we deny Christ He cannot deny us. False teachers for gain may buy and sell the Gospel, but their judgment tarrieth not.

It was not to be expected that such teachings would pass without comment. John Osborne, minister of Bampton-in-the-Bush, debated publicly with Coppin in 1651, and attacked him in a pamphlet, " The World to Come; or, The Mystery of the Resurrection Opened," in which he made a vigorous attack on his various heresies as set forth in " Divine Teachings." At Worcester Assizes in 1652 Coppin was tried on a charge of blasphemy, laid against him by some ministers in Worcestershire. Specifically, he was charged with saying:

(1) That there were evil angels, meaning the ministers, who told people of damnation, and that such ought not to be heard or believed.
(2) That all men would be saved.
(3) That those who accepted his teachings were in heaven.
(4) That God was as much in them as in Christ.
(5) That the Day of Judgment had begun a hundred and sixty years previously.
(6) That there was no general Day of Judgment.
(7) That there was no heaven but in man.
(8) That hell only existed for those who thought there was such a thing.

Baron Wilde found him not liable under the Blasphemy Acts, but bound him over to the next Assizes. When he appeared six months afterwards, he was remanded to the Oxford Assizes. He appeared there in March 1653, but the jury disagreed, and he was bound over to the next Oxford Assizes; but all attempts to produce sufficient evidence failed, and he was discharged. In July 1654 he was tried on much the same charges at the Gloucester Assizes.[1] In consequence of these troubles he came to be an advocate of toleration in religion. In 1653 he published a sermon which he had preached in Somerset House on May 1st, " Saul Smitten for not Smiting Amalek," in which he prophesied the end of the supporters of the Rump and the Church of Rome. He urged that no man should be forced to any form or method of worship, because all forms would cease and come to nothing when God should be pleased to enable men to see the emptiness of such things. In the following year he published a Christmas sermon, which he had preached at St. Giles's, Cripplegate, under the title of " A Man-Child Born, or God Manifest in the Flesh," in which he had allegorised the whole story of the Incarnation in this wise. Christ is God manifest in the flesh. His being born of the Virgin Mary was but a sign : His being born in us is the substance. God, the Father of Jesus, is our father and husband ; we are his spouse, and the mother of Jesus. Christ, or the man-child born in us, is both governor and government. To own any other is a sin and a work of the devil. He is the Wonderful Counsellor without whom we cannot defend our-selves in the Lord's cause against our enemies. The Mighty God is both Father and Son, the only power ever dwelling, ruling, and manifesting itself in us through the whole creation. Christ is the holy seed, sown and brought forth in us. As there is a day on which it is said that Christ in the flesh was born of the Virgin Mary, so there is also a day, or year of jubilee, in which Christ in the spirit is to be born in every one of us.

In 1655 Coppin went to take charge of Salmon's flock in Rochester cathedral. He preached twice every Sunday, and great numbers came to hear him. The other ministers of the neighbourhood accused him of blasphemy. " I heard him preach," says one of them, " that Christ the Redeemer was a sinner in respect of His human nature . . . and that neither Job nor St. Paul did speak of the resurrection of the body." [2] Certain ministers began to preach in the cathedral every week, refuting the errors which Coppin preached on Sundays, and challenges were hurled forth by both parties. On four different days in December 1656 the cathedral rang with the clamours of debate, as various ministers came to argue with him. Accord-ing to his opponents, he never stood his ground, but delivered " wild, impertinent discourses," and on the last day of the four " his carriage was wild." Both sides wrote their own account

---

[1] " Truth's Testimony," by R. Coppin, 1655.
[2] Rosewell, " The Serpent's Subtlety Discovered," 1656.

of the affair. Coppin entered the cathedral on the first day, December 3rd, accompanied by his followers, went up into the pulpit, and began with prayer, " though it is known he does not believe in prayer and only condescends to it for the infirmity of others." [1]   The mayor and Captain Smith, who commanded the guard, then asked the people to be quiet, and to allow the debate to be conducted in peace.   Rosewell complained that he had been given to understand that the debate was to have been managed by the mayor and magistrates and army officers, and that he was to have spoken first.   He said his conscience would not let him join in Coppin's prayer, so he would offer prayer himself before the proceedings went further.   Then they argued Rosewell's statement that Coppin was a perverter of Scripture, a blasphemer of Christ, and a " venter " of damnable heresy. Coppin said all kinds of wild things.   In the course of his argument that Christ was in every man, he committed himself to the utterance that as for the goats on the left hand at the Judgment, Christ was an accursed goat.   Members of the audience joined in the dispute in spite of the mayor's warning.   The following Sunday, Daniel French, minister of Stroud, took up the argument.   Before Coppin could commence the Sunday morning sermon, French said that he had heard Coppin say strange things on the previous Sunday.   Coppin replied that truth was always strange to those who were strangers to it. French said he wished to speak to the people after Coppin had finished his sermon, but Coppin answered him that the sermon would be so long that there would be very little time.   However, when he had finished, a debate commenced and went on for some time.   On Tuesday, December 11th, Coppin and Rosewell wrangled again, and there was a great deal of unseemly laughter, which Captain Smith vainly tried to suppress.   Both of the disputants got well out of their depth.   Rosewell contradicted himself, and there was a roar of laughter, which, however, he said was directed at Coppin.   He told his opponent to rub his brazen face and go on, and when Coppin accused him of being at a loss for an answer, he said he could fetch an oyster wife from Billingsgate to answer him.   Coppin made more heretical statements, such as that Christ offered for His own sins as well as for the sins of the world, and that the Trinity only meant three different manifestations of the Godhead.   French and others joined in the wrangle.

Two days later the argument was renewed.   It was begun by William Sambrook, and carried on by Rosewell and Coppin. Accusations of disloyalty to the Government were freely made. Coppin said Rosewell opposed religious freedom as granted by the Instrument of Government, which allowed the unfettered practice of religion except in the case of popery, prelacy, and

[1] Rosewell, " The Serpent's Subtlety Discovered."

seditious and licentious practices, the last a delightful touch. After a violent dispute the Presbyterian ministers went away, and Coppin offered to meet the Anabaptists next, and asked them to name a day. The authorities, however, turned him out of the cathedral; but he preached standing on a tombstone in the churchyard. Meanwhile, the ministers had laid twenty-five articles of accusation against him on grounds of heresy and blasphemy, and he was thrown into Maidstone gaol.[1] The Restoration at least delivered the cathedrals and churches from these scenes. Coppin, while in prison, wrote " Crux Christi, and Judgment Executed," [2] in which he prophesied the near approach of the time when God's wisdom would be manifested throughout the world. His last book, which appeared in 1659, was called " Michael Opposing the Dragon." It was a reply to an attack made on him by Edward Garland, who had written an " Answer " to Coppin's pamphlet, " A Blow at the Serpent," and was a continuation of the arguments which had been begun in Rochester cathedral. Nothing more is heard of him afterwards. But his followers, who must have been few in number, seem to have kept together, for the sect of the Coppinists is heard of as late as 1706. Their doctrines were then said to be the following. They denied the resurrection of the body, taking as their authority the text, " Flesh and blood shall not inherit the Kingdom of God." There is no eternal hell. The punishment of sin is temporary. Sin will suffer hereafter in a body, but not in the body of the wickedest man (whatever that may mean). The devil and hell will be destroyed at the last, and all will be absorbed in the Deity, just as all flowed from the Deity in the beginning, and so God will be all in all. They had peculiar views on prayer. Since St. Matthew's version of the Lord's Prayer differs from St. Luke's, it must have been spoken extempore by our Lord, and cannot be an invariable or absolute form of words for all conditions. It does not suit all conditions, inasmuch as it does not mention all, e.g. the King and the saints departed. As a sect they were said to boast of their logic, and to be exceedingly fond of disputation.[3] Coppin's works were being republished and sold as late as 1764, and in that year a Nonconformist minister found it worth while to preach a sermon refuting them.[4]

THE FAMILY OF LOVE

" The Ranters' Bible " referred to in a section of the Ranters under the title of " Familists of Love," and said they were the

---

[1] W. Rosewell, " The Serpent's Subtlety Discovered," 1656; R. Coppin, " A Blow at the Serpent: or, a Gentle Answer from Maidstone Prison," 1656.
[2] 1657. [3] " The Postboy," II. 428–429.
[4] " The Sadducee Detected and Refuted. In Remarks on the Works of Richard Coppin," by James Relly. London, 1764.

followers of a German who had propagated their opinions in Holland some forty years previously. The writer accused these people of wearing no clothes at their meetings, and of dancing and promiscuous immorality thereat, and said that they believed neither in God, devil, heaven nor hell, but they worshipped the sun and practised a community of goods and women. Fuller associated the Ranters and the Familists.[1] Ross described the Familists as making open profession of immorality, and practising community of women.[2] Elsewhere it was related that the Ranters believed themselves incapable of sinning, imagined themselves in Adam's state as he was in Paradise, and divested themselves of clothing at their meetings.[3]

Now there was a sect called the Adamites, which appeared from time to time in ecclesiastical history, and which is said to have sprung from the Carpocratians and Prodicians. It was revived in Flanders in the early part of the twelfth century, and reappeared in Bohemia in the fifteenth century under a certain Picard, who taught his sect to go naked and to call him Adam, and said they were the real freemen, while all who wore clothes were slaves.[4] It was also found about the same time in Poland. Ross, writing in 1653, said that in recent years there had been some people called Adamites in Amsterdam; that they prayed in a state of nudity, and that they called their meetings paradise, but he did not actually say that they were also found in England.[5] Pagitt spoke of them as though they existed in this country.[6] The Adamites were mentioned in 1683 as professing to be disciples of Adam in his first innocency.[7] Lord Halifax referred to them as a still-existing sect,[8] while Henry More spoke of them as looking on it as a piece of perfection to go naked.[9] The heresiographers, however, generally distinguished between the Adamites and the Family of Love.[10] Perhaps the people classed under the head of Familists of Love in 1650—that is to say, the Ranter Familists—or some of them, were the people elsewhere called Adamites.

The real Familists, or Family of Love, were often confounded in earlier days with the Anabaptists, though the latter strongly objected to the identification.[11] As a matter of fact, the Familists

---

[1] " Church History."   [2] " Pansebeia," pp. 387–389.
[3] " An Account of the Life and Acts of Mr. John Bunyan," 1692, p. 22.
[4] " A Relation of Several Heresies," 1646.
[5] Hook, " Church Dictionary," ed. 1864; Ross, " Pansebeia," p. 406.
[6] Pagitt, " Heresiography," 1661.   [7] Pettitt, " Visions of Reformation."
[8] " The Anatomy of an Equivalent," 1688.
[9] More, " Divine Dialogues," ed. 1713, p. 189.
[10] Underhill, " Hell Broke Loose," 1660; Pagitt, " Heresiography," 1661; Chamberlayne, " Present State of England," 8th ed., 1674; Roger L'Estrange, " A Further Discovery of the Plot," 1680; Pettitt, " Visions of Reformation," 1683, pp. 90–91.
[11] " A Discovery of the Abominable Delusions of those who call themselves the Family of Love," 1622.

had something of an Anabaptist origin. Their founder, David Joris, or George, who was born at Delft in 1501, joined the Anabaptists in 1534, but soon left them to found a sect of his own. He was a mystic, and he taught that Moses was the prophet of hope, and Christ the prophet of faith. He claimed to be the true David who should restore the kingdom, and the true Messiah who would never die, or if he did, would rise again. He himself was the prophet of love, and he would raise the tabernacle of God, not by suffering, but by meekness.

His successor, Heinrich Niklaes, of Amsterdam, who was born about 1502, maintained the same things, but declared himself to be the restorer of the world and the prophet sent by God. He wrote an epistle to the daughters of the Earl of Warwick in the time of Edward VI, dissuading them from Bible reading and the hearing of sermons, and his epistle was answered by Henry Ainsworth.[1] After the death of Nicholas, Tobias, " a Fellow-Elder in the Household of Love," wrote " Mirabilia Opera Dei," in which he described certain wonderful works of God which happened to Henry Nicholas even from his youth, and how the God of heaven had united Himself with him, or, as it was expressed, " the power of the Highest came upon his Godded man and did instruct and speak to him," and raised up His gracious word on him, and how He had chosen and sent him to be a minister of His gracious word. Christopher Viret, or Vittel, a joiner, introduced the sect into England about 1560, and by 1578 the members had become so numerous in this country that the Privy Council tried to suppress them. On October 3rd, 1580, Queen Elizabeth issued a proclamation ordering the clergy to give all assistance to the bishops in their efforts to this end. Search was to be made for Familist books, and all persons in possession of them after this would be imprisoned, and the books burned. The Familists were described in the proclamation as a dangerous sect, because it was one of their principles to deny their membership if it would be to their advantage to do so.[2]

Henry Nicholas believed that he had been made one with the Deity, and that he and his followers had been called to found a society for the establishment of a new era, the reign of the spirit of love, and their duty was to teach men to love one another. They were careful to avoid forming a sect, and conformed to the established religion of the place where they were, without believing in it. They allegorised all the statements of the New Testament: the Crucifixion of Christ was the crucifying of the old man, the Resurrection was a rising to newness of life, the Last Judgment was the establishment in the natural man of the

[1] Underhill, " Hell Broke Loose," 1660.
[2] Hunt, " Religious Thought in England," I. 234-235; " Christianity No Enthusiasm," 1678, pp. 85-86.

life of righteousness and equity, the seven devils of Mary Magdalene were the seven deadly sins.[1] Tomkins, a chaplain to the Bishop of London, said of them, " They have a fancy that Christ was not any one person, but a quality, whereof many are partakers; that to be raised is nothing else but to be regenerated or endued with the said quality, and the separation of them which have it, and them which have it not, is Judgment.[2]

Their doctrines may be thus summed up :

There is no other Christ but holiness, and no other Antichrist but sin. Adam was all that God was, and God all that Adam was. The Family of Love had attained the perfection of Adam which he had before the Fall.

There is no resurrection of the flesh. The resurrection is a rising from sin and wickedness. The dead shall rise and live in Henry Nicholas, and in the illuminated elders everlastingly. Henry Nicholas is raised from the dead ; the judgment is already come, and he is the judge.

There have been eight great lights of the world. Christ was the seventh, Henry Nicholas the last and greatest. There was never truth published since the Apostles' time till Henry Nicholas preached. He can no more sin than Moses or Christ. He is the true prophet of God sent to blow the last trump of doctrine which shall be published on the earth.

There is none other deity belonging unto God but such as men are partakers of in this life. Christ is not God. He is not one man, but an estate and condition of men, common to so many as have received the doctrine of Henry Nicholas.

In Henry Nicholas dwelleth all perfection, holiness, and knowledge, and the illuminated elders also are deified in this life and cannot sin.

The Law may be fulfilled in this life.

Heaven and hell are present in this world, and there is none other.

Angels are born of women.

It is not lawful to say " God save anything," for all things are ruled by nature and not directed by God.

It is not lawful to bury the dead or to give alms to such as are not of their profession, and wives who are not of their belief may be rejected. All men not of their congregation, or who have revolted from them, are dead.

Every day in the week should be a Sabbath.

It is lawful to do whatsoever the higher powers command to be done, though it is against the commandment of God.

The bearing of weapons is forbidden. But to prevent members from becoming marked men they may carry staves.

The service now used in the churches is naught.

[1] Hunt, " Religious Thought in England," I. 236–237.
[2] Tomkins, " Modest Pleas for Comprehension," 1675, p. 155.

No man should be put to death for his opinions.

A man is admitted publicly by the bishop or elder, after election by the brethren, if he admits the doctrine of the community of goods.

No man can be baptized till he attains the age of thirty years.

Their name, " The Family of Love," has seemed to many persons more suggestive of earthly than heavenly love, but there is nothing in their writings at all suggestive of those practices which have been charged against the Adamites or Familist Ranters. Several writers complained, indeed, that they kept their teaching so secret that it was difficult to find them out. " They will profess to agree in all things with the Church of England, or the Church of Rome, or anything else." [1] None but those who were inclined to join them was allowed to see their books, and it was one of their rules to deny their doctrines to outsiders. " They have certain sleights among themselves to answer any question that may be demanded of them. They decree all men to be infants under the age of thirty, so if they be asked whether their infants may be baptized they say ' Yea,' meaning thereby he is an infant until he attains to thirty years." [2] One of their rules was that they ought to keep silence among themselves, that the liberty which they had in the Lord might not be espied of others, and their practice, when asked a question, was to wait a great while, and then say " Surely " or " So." [3]

In the Lambeth Palace Library is a manuscript copy of a Familist hymn-book, translated into English from a Dutch edition of the hymns of Henry Nicholas. It was probably compiled before the end of the sixteenth century, but was never printed and published, for reasons of secrecy.[4] Several of the works of Nicholas were, however, translated and printed in England about the middle of the seventeenth century, among them the " Introduction to the Holy Understanding of the Glass of Righteousness: wherein are uttered many Notable Admonitions and Exhortations to the Good Life: also sundry Discreet Warnings to beware of Destruction and of Wrong Conceiving." This was published in 1649, and the same year Giles Calvert, the Dissenting bookseller, issued " Revelatio Dei: the Revelation of God and His Great Prophecy, which God now (in the last day) hath showed unto His Elect, set forth by H.N." " The Prophecy of the Spirit of Love set forth by H.N." was also issued in 1649 by the same publisher. Calvert published other Familist tracts in 1656: " An Apology for the Service of Love,"

[1] Pagitt, " Heresiography," p. 116.

[2] " The Displaying of an Horrible Sect of Gross and Wicked Heretics naming themselves the Family of Love," by John Rogers, 1578.

[3] Ross, " Pansebeia," pp. 404–405; Pagitt, " Heresiography," pp. 105–106; Berens, " The Digger Movement," 1906, pp. 15–18.

[4] Burrage, " Early English Dissenters," pp. 209-214.

288   STUDIES IN ENGLISH PURITANISM

"A Brief Rehearsal of the Good-willing in England, which are
named the Family of Love," and "The First Exhortation of Henry
Nicholas to his Children and to the Family of Love."

In 1687 a deputation of members of the Family of Love
presented an Address to James II. The King asked them about
themselves. "They told him their custom was to read the
Scriptures and to preach, but did not give him any further
account, only said that for the rest they were a sort of refined
Quakers, but their number was very small, not consisting, as
they said, of above three score in all, and these chiefly belonging
to the Isle of Ely." [1] This evidently refers to the number of
members of that particular congregation, for Samuel Rutherford,
referring to their statement in the above address that they were
few in number, said, "They were pestering twelve counties of
England." [2]

Various sects of Familists are heard of, such as Hethering-
tonians, and Grindletonians, of whom more later. There were
also said to be Familists known as the Castalian Order, Familists
of the Mountains, Familists of the Valleys, Familists of the
Scattered Flock, and Familists of Cap's Order; but whether
these were found in England we are not told. [3]

The Familists were believed to be still in existence in 1706.
Charles Gildon distinguished them from the Adamites. Referring to the latter, he said that there were divers forms of these,
but all private, and that children were not admitted to their
meetings because Adam and Eve were perfect man and woman.
But he repeated the stories of immorality at meetings, and of a
community of women, in his section on the true Familists. He
described the charity of the latter to their poorer members, and
said that jealousy was unknown among them. They held that
the joys of the blessed are only here in love, since after death
the soul, which is the emanation from the deity, returns into it
again, and is lost in the eternal ocean of being. The greatest
sin of all is want of faith, which alone produces damnation—
that is, unhappiness here. "Wicked men do the hardest of
God's works, and so the devil is God's most faithful servant to
perform His will, as we see in the Book of Job." They held
also that Scripture is for novices, not for strong Christians. [4]

[1] Evelyn, "Diary," June 16th, 1687.
[2] Braithwaite, "Beginnings of Quakerism," p. 24.
[3] Ross, "Pansebeia," p. 365; Pagitt, "Heresiography," pp. 115–116.
[4] "The Postboy," 1706, pp. 427–428; see also "A Brief Discovery of the
Blasphemous Doctrine of Familism. First conceived and brought forth into
the World by one Henry Nicholas of the Low Countries of Germany about an
Hundred Years ago: and now very boldly taught by one Mr. Randall, and
sundry others in and about the City of London, whom Multitudes of People
follow, and which Doctrine many embrace," London, 1645; "A Description
of the Sect called the Family of Love," 1641, which describes how Mrs. Susannah Snow of Pirford, near Chertsey, was led away by them, and at length
went mad, but was delivered by a miracle from God.

The Etheringtonians or Hetheringtonians

The Etheringtonians were the followers of one John Etherington or Hetherington, a box-maker by trade, who began to preach his peculiar views in 1623. For some of his doctrines he had been tried in 1626, and had suffered three years' imprisonment. He had a violent enemy in Dr. Stephen Denison, vicar of St. Katherine Cree, who preached against him in his church, and published the sermon under the title of " The White Wolf." Denison, his curate, Henry Rowborough, and a number of laymen, presented him to the Archbishop, and brought articles against him in the High Commission Court. Pagitt said that he recanted at St. Paul's Cross, but Etherington affirmed that he had only denied what he had never preached. Denison accused him of being a Familist, and said that he could not be believed because he would, as a member of the sect, deny in public what he believed in private. Etherington hotly denied that he was a Familist, and said that a book which he had written against Anabaptism was a proof of his statement. He brought charges of immorality against his opponent, to whose Calvinistic doctrines he objected, and who, he complained, had found fault with him for saying that repentance goes before remission of sins.

Etherington was accused of being an unlawful teacher of conventicles, and of expounding the Scriptures in a way contrary to the teaching of the Church of England, of abusing the clergy, and of enticing many persons from their parish churches to become schismatics. He said that, although he had been for thirty years a student of the Scriptures, he had never been a teacher, except so far as one Christian can help another. As for conventicles, he said that Cæsar might command places for public worship, but he could not forbid private worship in any place. He denied that the Church of England was a true church, said that ordination did not make a true minister, and that baptism and Holy Communion conferred no grace. He held peculiar views on the Sabbath, and it is not very clear what he did believe on this subject, because some of his statements are conflicting. He said that since the Apostles' time the Sabbath was of no force, and that every day is a Sabbath, as well as the Lord's Day, or Sunday. What he seemed to hold was that it is good to keep the Sabbath, but that no man is bound to do so. Another peculiarity of his was a belief that the books of Esdras are, and ought to be, esteemed part of the canonical Scriptures. Pagitt said he added these peculiarities to the general Familist doctrines. His disciples maintained that they could not err in giving deliberate sentences on points of divinity. In any case, it is hardly likely that this sect held together long, though it seems to have been in evidence at the Restoration.[1]

THE GRINDLETONIANS

Roger Brierley, curate of Grindleton chapel, near Colne in Yorkshire, taught Familist doctrines with some approaches to Quakerism.[2] His sermons, or rather notes of them, were published in Edinburgh in 1670, and in London in 1677, under the title, " A Bundle of Soul Convincing, Directing and Comforting Truths: clearly deduced from divers select Texts of Holy Scripture, and practically improven, both for Conviction and Consolation." In a prefatory " Epistle to the Reader " an unknown admirer gave an account of the origin of what he called Grindletonism. When Brierley preached " none, either in their Gentilish nature, nor in their self on-taken Jewish righteousness, nor in any formal way either to Law or Gospel, could stand their ground, if they dealt truly with themselves, but they fell convicted under his message." His preaching was the demonstration of the Holy Ghost to the broken heart of man of the unchangeable love, against which sin, death, and Satan cannot prevail; God's unchangeable love, able to cast out of the conscience and heart of man all fear and torment. His ministry drew men from all round about to hear him, and great contentions were stirred up, and he was suspected of heresy. In order to brand his followers as sectaries they called them Grindletonians, after the name of the place. They brought accusations against him in the High Commission Court, and he was in prison at York for a time. Fifty articles were exhibited against him, but not one was proved at the trial. After a sermon preached by him at the cathedral he was dismissed, and received permission from Archbishop Toby Matthew to exercise his ministry as before. He died at Burnley in Lancashire. This, of course, was the statement of a violent partisan, who also said that their opponents could not find one sect " to parallel them to." [3] People certainly connected the Grindletonians with the Familists.

According to Pagitt the doctrines of the Grindletonians were as follows:

Scripture is but for novices.

The Sabbath is to be held as a lecture day.

To pray for the pardon of sin after a man is assured of God's love is to offer Christ again.

[1] " The Defence of John Etherington against Stephen Denison and his Witnesses," 1641; " The Deeds of Dr. Denison a little more Manifested," 1642; Pagitt, " Heresiography," pp. 108–109; " Christianity No Enthusiasm," 1678, p. 26.
[2] Braithwaite, " Beginnings of Quakerism," p. 24.
[3] " A Bundle," etc., 1677.

Their spirit is not to be tried by the Scriptures, but the Scriptures by their spirit.

When God dwells in a man He fills the soul, and lust can no more exist there.

There is no more need for ordinances, or for preaching against the sins of the wicked.[1]

Underhill said they were akin to the Family of Love, and that there were many of them in the Yorkshire villages in the time of Elizabeth and James I. Baxter said of them, " I had an old godly friend that lived near them and went once among them, and they breathed on him, so as to give him the Holy Ghost, and his family for three days after perceived him as a man of another spirit, as half in an ecstasy, but coming to himself he came near them no more." [2]

THE SWEET SINGERS OF ISRAEL

The Swarthmore Papers, under the date 1659, refer to a sect called the Singers, who were bitter enemies of the Quakers.[3] Gildon refers to a sect called the Sweet Singers of Israel. These were much like the Ranters. They met in alehouses and ate, drank, and smoked while others sang the praises of God and His saints. They held that eating and drinking and society were blessed of God, and that they themselves were sinless, because all sin is forgiven to those who put their faith in the death of our Lord. The blessed will be employed in singing praises in the New Jerusalem, therefore the best preparation for death consists in singing, eating, drinking, and making merry.[4] Williamson received information in June 1678 of a meeting of Sweet Singers in Moorfields, where Mr. Cockin was one of the leaders. This may be the same body referred to by the same informer, R. Stephens, on June 3rd of that year, as " a sort of Muggletonians " in Moorfields, only the preacher's or leader's name is given as Handson. He said they expounded the Scriptures according to their pleasure. Sometimes they sang " Divines' songs," and then turned to drinking, for the place was a kind of alehouse.[5] They are mentioned in " The Muses' Farewell to Popery and Slavery," 1690, and in 1733 by Salmon.[6]

There was also a sect called the Sweet Singers in Scotland, but there they were known also as Gibbites, from their leader, John Gibb, a sailor of huge stature, and a " great professor."

[1] Pagitt, pp. 114, 116; " Christianity No Enthusiasm," 1678, p. 5; Denison, " The White Wolf," p. 39.

[2] Baxter, " Treatise of the Sin against the Holy Ghost," p. 149.

[3] See also " Advice to the Men of Shaftesbury," 1681, which speaks of them as in England during the Commonwealth.

[4] " The Postboy," pp. 427-428; " Christianity No Enthusiasm," 1678, p. 100.

[5] C.S.P.D., 404/88, 253.

[6] " Lives of the English Bishops," 1733, p. 173.

They were first heard of in Scotland at Borrowstones, about
1680. They had napkins dyed in the blood of Stewart and
Potter, the Covenanting martyrs, and these they waved wildly
during their devotions, calling loudly on God at the same time
for vengeance on the murderers. Three of them were executed
in Edinburgh on May 11th, 1681, for disowning the King and
saying it was lawful to kill him and his judges. The Duke of
York offered them a pardon on the scaffold if they would only
say " God save the King," but they refused.[1]

The Scotch Sweet Singers renounced the Bible as printed,
and the preachers and doctrines of all other sects. To this they
added: " We renounce and decline all authority throughout
the world, and all that are in authority, and all their acts and
edicts, from the tyrant Charles Stuart, to, etc. We renounce
the names of the months, as January, February, March, April,
May, June, July, August, September, October, November,
December; Sunday, Monday, Tuesday, Wednesday, Thursday,
Friday, Saturday, Martinmas, Holy-days, for there is none holy
but the Sabbath-day, Lammas-day, Whitsunday, Candlemas,
Beltan; cross stones and images, fairs named by saints, and all
the remnants of popery, Yule or Christmas, old wives' fables
and by-words, as Palm-Sunday, Carlin-Sunday, the 29th May,
being dedicate by this generation to profanity, Pasch-Sunday,
Hallow-even, Hogmany Night, Valentine's Even, no marrying
in the month they call May, the innumerable reliques of popery,
atheism and sorcery, and New-year's day, and Hansel-Monday,
dirges and lykewakes, Valentine's fair, chapels and chaplains;
likewise Sabbath-day's feastings, blyth-meats, banquetings, revel-
lings, piping, sportings, dancing, laughing, singing profane and
lustful songs and ballads, table lawings, monk lands, friars'
lands, black-friars' lands, kirk and kirk-yards, and market-crosses,
font-stones, images, registers of lands and houses, register bonds,
discharges, and all their law works, inhibitions, hornings, letters
of adjudications, ships passes, profanity, and unchaste thoughts,
words, and actions, formality and indifferency, story-books and
ballads, romances and pamphlets, comedy-books, cards and dice,
and such like, we disown all of them, and burn them the sixth
day of the week, being the 27th day of the fifth month, 1681,
at the Canongate Tolbooth Ironhouse." [2]

They refused all Covenants and declarations, and adhered to
no preachers save their own leaders, Meiklejohn, Gibb, and
David Jamieson. Bands of them went about singing Psalms
lxxiv., lxxix., lxxx., lxxxiii. and cxxxvii., which they considered
appropriate to the times. Gibb proclaimed that he, with the

[1] Fountainhall, " Chronological Notes of Scottish Affairs," ed. 1822,
pp. 10–12.
[2] Woodrow, " Hist. Church Scotland," II. App. p. 80. Edinb. 1722,
quoted in Scott's note to Fountainhall, " Chronological Notes," p. 12.

Holy Ghost, would right all evil done to the martyred Covenanters by destroying all human inventions. He was called by
his disciples, mostly hysterical women who had left their homes
and husbands, King Solomon, and they believed him to be the
second Solomon, who would build them into a perfect spiritual
temple in himself. From time to time they fell at his feet and
worshipped him. The members of the sect lived an ascetic life,
their diet being bread and water, keeping long fasts, and wandering about the fields weeping. They gave reverence to no man
for conscience' sake. They insisted on what they called " the
pure text of the Bible," and burnt all Bibles that came in their
way, because they had human additions, such as metrical psalms,
pictures, divisions into chapters and verses, or even printers'
ends. In their conversation and preaching they were guilty of
the wildest blasphemies, and Cargill, the Covenanting leader
who went to visit them on the Pentland Hills, where they had
collected together, left them possessed with the conviction that
Gibb was an incarnate devil. The dragoons rounded up a
great number of them, and they were imprisoned in the Canongate Tolbooth; but James Duke of York set them free on bail
in August 1681, on condition that they should give up their
disloyalty. They behaved exactly as before, and Gibb, Jamieson,
and two of the women were imprisoned again. In gaol they
disturbed the devotions of the other prisoners by their wild
cries, and a Cameronian named Jackson rose up and beat Gibb
severely, but in vain, for after that he used to sit behind the door
howling till the prayers were finished. The two men were
banished to America, where it was said Gibb caused much awe
to the Indians by his intercourse with the devil.[1] He was
certainly mad. His followers seem to have continued for some
time longer, for the Covenanters solemnly denounced the sect
in October 1686.[2] This was a very different sect from the
English Sweet Singers of Israel.

THE GORTINIANS

The Gortinians were the followers of Samuel Gorton, who
was banished out of New England about the year 1646. They
taught that those who were not of their way were Antichrists,
idolaters, and false teachers, that the rise of their sect was the
appearance of the Messenger of the Covenant and Christ's
coming to His temple, and that whatever the saints declared in
matters of religion must be the voice of the Son of God. Gorton
denied the Trinity and the Incarnation. There was not one

[1] " God's Justice Exemplified," p. 62, quoted by Scott in his note to Fountainhall.
[2] J. K. Hewison, " The Covenanters," 1913, II. 340–343, 493; C. S. Terry,
" Hist. Scot.," 1920, pp. 453–454; Andrew Lang, " Hist. Scot.," 1900–1907,
III. 359.

individual Christ who took our humanity, and consequently Christ did not die upon the cross. What was meant by Christ's death and suffering was nothing else than the dying and suffering of the saints. Similarly, there was no resurrection in the orthodox sense. Christ revealed His will by no voice other than the voice of the spirit in the saints. Since the spirit thus spoke, all preachers who prepared their sermons were nothing but " idol shepherds of Rome." All oaths were unlawful. Gorton set forth all this in his " Simplicity's Defence against seven-headed Policy." [1] In a sermon preached in Coleman Street about the year 1647 Gorton affirmed that everything which had an end was a carnal ordinance, and came from the devil, and he gave as instances—baptism, lords, chaplains, ruling elders, and so on.[2] Whether this obscure sect lasted until the Restoration is at least doubtful.

THE VANISTS

Closely allied with the Seekers (Burnet actually calls them Seekers) were the people known as Vanists, the followers of Sir Henry Vane the younger. Baxter says that Vane's religious views were expressed in such obscurity that it was difficult to say what his opinions really were.[3] Burnet says much the same, and remarks of his prayers and sermons at the meetings of his followers that they were of " so peculiar a darkness, that though I have sometimes taken pains to see if I could find out his meaning in his words, yet I never could reach it." [4] The fact was that he was a mystic who had been influenced by the writings of Boehme. He believed therefore, that God manifested Himself directly to the soul of man, and man learned spiritual things by the direct illumination of God. His largest and most important theological work was " The Retired Man's Meditations; or, the Mystery and Power of Godliness." This was published in 1655. In parts it is so obscure as to be almost unintelligible, full of allegorical interpretation of Scripture and of mysticism of the cloudiest kind. Burnet learned from Vane's friends that he was inclined to accept Origen's notion of a universal salvation not only for sinners, but also for the fallen angels, and that he held the pre-existence of the soul.[4] The work above mentioned showed Millennarian tendencies as well. One distinction he made in this book laid him open to contemporary criticism, viz. the distinction between the natural conscience, the source of ordinary right and obligation, the legal conscience, the source of the ordinances and dogmas of religion, and the evangelical conscience, which is found at the stage when

---

[1] Rutherford, " Survey of the Spiritual Antichrist," 1648. N. Morton, " New England's Memorial," 1669.
[2] Underhill, " Hell Broke Loose," 1660, pp. 12–13.
[3] " Rel. Baxt.," p. 75.   [4] Burnet, " Own Times," I. 285.

the human spirit attains to hold intercourse, " high, intuitive, and comprehensive," with the divine. As a consequence of his mystical views of the relation between the human soul and God, he denied the need of clergy or ecclesiastical organisation or discipline, and he asserted a principle of universal toleration.[1] In 1661 he wrote " An Epistle to the Mystical Body of Christ on Earth." Here again his mystical attitude to religion is manifest. The Kingdom of God is within man, hidden and concealed from the world. " Those that are in the kingdom, and in whom the power of it is, are fitted to fly with the church into the wilderness, and to continue in such a solitary, dispersed, desolate condition, till God call them out of it. They have wells and springs opened to them in the wilderness, whence they draw the waters of salvation, without being in bondage to the life of sense." [2]

Vane, when at Belleau, his home in Lincolnshire, was accustomed to gather a congregation together and preach to them. He did the same also in London. " The Great Plot for Restoring Popery,[3] which referred to the Vanists as among the sects " spawned by the Jesuits," a statement with which Baxter agreed,[4] said that Mrs. Hutchinson and Mrs. Dyer were the prophetesses of his sect in New England.[5] But if Vane had many followers, it is not very likely that they held together as a separate religious body long after his death.

THE BEHMENISTS

Mysticism characterised much of seventeenth-century religion irrespective of sect. It influenced the Quakers, the Vanists, the Philadelphians, and others outside the Church of England, and was not to be without its effect even amongst Anglicans. We hear of the existence in England of the Weigelians, Paracelsians, and Behmenists, all holding the same views as the Vanists, " but they think meet to take another name." [6] and Rutherford mentioned Schwenkfeldians as among the Puritan mystical sects.[7] But they were all much the same, and may be classed under the general head of Behmenists, the English name for the followers of Jacob Boehme, the German mystic, who was born in 1575, and died in 1624. Underhill spoke of him as " the German Paracelsian prophet." [8] He wrote many books, and these, especially in the Commonwealth times, were translated into English,

[1] Willcock, " Life of Vane," pp. 253–259; Wood, " Ath. Ox." II. 291.
[2] R. M. Jones, " Spiritual Reformers in the Sixteenth and Seventeenth Centuries," pp. 271–279.
[3] London, 1663.
[4] " Key for Catholics," p. 318.
[5] Kennet, " Reg.," p. 396.
[6] " The Great Plot for Restoring Popery," 1663.
[7] S. Rutherford, " Survey of the Spiritual Antichrist," 1648.
[8] " Hell Broke Loose," 1660.

and had great influence in this country. In his writings, based, as he believed, on trances, visions, and revelations, he set forth the uselessness of human reason in spiritual matters and the vanity of sacraments and ecclesiastical organisation, and asserted that salvation comes only from the indwelling presence of Christ in the soul. He thought that all his theological system came from within, and he only accepted the Scriptures as far as they agreed with his views. When a passage conflicted with his doctrines, he would say something of this sort: " It is evident that the dear man Moses did not write this." He owed much, however, to preceding mystical writers, Schwenkfeld, Weigel, and Paracelsus. Weigel taught him the value of waiting in passivity for the coming of the Divine Word, and said that if God dwells in a man, that man is in paradise, and that man, as body, soul, and spirit, belongs to three worlds, terrestrial, astral, and celestial. Paracelsus laid stress on the power of faith to penetrate the mysteries of nature, and said that real knowledge comes by divine communication. With Weigel, Paracelsus held that the divine illumination reveals both the mysteries of a man's own being and those of the external world. Sebastian Franck, who was followed by Paracelsus, who was himself followed by Weigel, explained the difficulty of the existence of good and evil side by side in this way: God manifests Himself to us by opposites. The peace of the unity of God must develop into the strife of the manifold. Light is known by its contrast with darkness, day with night, yea with nay. Resistance strikes the spark of vitality, and so progress becomes possible. From these writers, then, Boehme gained much of his system. Their doctrines were a mixture of alchemy, astrology, philosophy, and theology, and they influenced his writing far more than he knew.[1]

To Behmen, for so his name was Anglicized, and his followers, the spiritual, starry, and terrestrial worlds are concentric, and man extends through them all. The greater his reception of spiritual truth, the nearer he approaches to the all-circumscribing spiritual world. The highest and inmost in the deepest sense are one. The Divine Nature is an Abyss, the Nothing of unrevealed Godhead. In this there exists from all eternity Desire, a " going forth " on the part of what is called the Father. The object and the realisation of this " going forth " is the Son, while the bond between them, and the result of the reciprocal love of Father and Son is the Spirit.

Every inward presupposes an outward. As there is an Eternal Spirit, so there must be an Eternal Nature, for God is not mere Being. He is Will, and that Will manifests itself in an external Universe. Eternal Nature, the Great Mystery, is the external correlative of the Divine Wisdom. In Eternal Nature

[1] Vaughan, " Hours with the Mystics," II. 72–74.

are seven Forms of Life, or Active Spirits, or Qualities, which may be compared to a system of wheels round a common centre, which is the Son of God, just as the sun is the centre of seven planets. The Father is the dark, fiery principle, the Son the principle of light, the Holy Ghost the creature-preserving principle.

Evil is necessary to make good manifest. God does not create anything for evil, but in everything there is both good and evil, the predominance of one or the other deciding the use and destiny of the thing. Thus, what would be pain and evil in hell would be happiness and goodness in heaven. Behmen elaborated the story of the creation of the universe on lines much resembling those of some of the ancient Gnostics. The method of redemption, as he described it, is similarly reminiscent of them. The mercy of God implanted in fallen man the seed of redemption; in the depth of our nature there is a hidden gift of the Spirit, that inner light that lighteth every man that cometh into the world. All the first movements of desire towards God are the fruit of the working of this indwelling seed, this grace. But man is the arbiter of his own destiny, and of his own free will develops from the depth of his nature his heaven or his hell. Redemption is man's deliverance from the restless isolation of self, and his return to union with God.[1]

Baxter, who thought originally that the Jesuits animated them[2] said of the English Behmenists of his day, " Their opinions go much towards the way of the Quakers for the sufficiency of the light of nature, the inward light, the salvation of the heathen as well as Christians, and a dependence on revelations. But they are fewer in number, and seem to have attained to greater meekness and conquest of passions than any of the rest." [3] Some of the Quakers were undoubtedly attracted by Behmenism. A Quaker prophet named Eccles, writing in 1664 of " the fulfilling of the times," quotes some of the prophecies of Behmen uttered in 1623.[4] But not all the Quakers were thus attracted by the German mystic. John Anderton of Bridgewater wrote in 1661 an eight-page pamphlet called " One Blow at Babel," in which the main grounds of his attack on the Behmenists are, first that their foundation is not upon that of the prophets and apostles, " but upon their own carnal conception, begotten in their own imaginations upon Jacob Behmen's writings," by which he seems to imply that they misunderstood their master, and secondly, that they still made use of the sacraments, or as Anderton expressed it, " mediums of water, bread, and wine." Some of the Behmenists, nevertheless, were ultimately absorbed

---

[1] Vaughan, " Hours with the Mystics," II. 82–94; " Christianity No Enthusiasm," 1678, pp. 86–87.
[2] " Key for Catholics," p. 364.   [3] " Rel. Baxt.," p. 77.
[4] " Christian Information concerning these Last Times," 1664.

into the Quaker movement.[1]   At the time of the Restoration it seems that there was a loose association of individual Behmenists, hardly deserving the name of a distinct sect, and that Behmenism also meant a mystical movement having a much wider influence. Some of the members of this association at a later time, under the influence of Pordage and Jane Lead, bound themselves together more closely in a new society, called the Philadelphians.

In 1661 there was printed a poem, " Mundorum Explicatio, or, the Explanation of an Hieroglyphical Figure, wherein are couched the Mysteries of the External, Internal, and Eternal Worlds, showing the true Progress of a Soul from the Court of Babylon to the City of Jerusalem: from the Adamical fallen State to the Regenerate and Angelical." The title-page gave the authorship as " By S. P., Armiger." The poem consisted of over 12,000 lines, written chiefly in rhyming couplets. An unsigned preface said that the hieroglyphic " came into my hands, another being the author." There is also a prefatory " Enconium on J. B." (Jacob Behmen, of course), and his interpreter and translator, John Sparrow. The verses—for they can hardly be described as poetry—are full of Behmenist mysticism, and extensive theological notes are added. The work is divided into three parts, the first dealing specially with Creation and Hell, the second with Grace and Redemption, and the third with the Glories of Heaven. " S. P." has generally been interpreted as Samuel Pordage, the eldest son of John Pordage. Samuel wrote nothing else like this. He was a violent Protestant in his later years, and was the author of " Azaria and Hushai," published in 1682, and " A Brief History of all the Papists' Bloody Persecutions." " Absalom and Achitophel," Pt. II. referred to him as

> " Lame Mephibosheth, the wizard's son."

" Mundorum Explicatio " was probably written under the influence of his father, and perhaps was his first and last venture into the realms of Behmenist theology.

THE PHILADELPHIANS

John Pordage, M.D., who had studied theology and medicine at Oxford, and became rector of Bradfield, Berks, in 1647, was one of the earliest exponents of Behmenism in England. In 1651 he was brought before the committee for plundered ministers and charged with heresy of a mystical and pantheistic kind,[2] but not particularly connected with the teachings of Behmen. He was acquitted, but in 1654 he was tried again by

---

[1] *Congregational Quarterly*, III. 53.
[2] R. M. Jones, " Spiritual Reformers of the Sixteenth and Seventeenth Centuries," pp. 227–234.

the county commissioners for Berks, and the former charges, nine in number, were renewed. John Tickell, the Presbyterian minister of Abingdon, and Christopher Fowler, of St. Mary's, Reading, were his chief accusers, and before the trial was over fifty-six new accusations were added to the former nine. The new charges included blasphemy, necromancy, and scandalous life, and he was found guilty of heresy and turned out of his living.[1] He returned to Bradfield at the Restoration. As early as 1652 his wife and he began to gather a circle of mystics for the study of the writings of Jacob Behmen. He believed he had occult powers, and professed to hold communion with angels and to be able to distinguish good and bad angels by sight or smell. He tells how he woke from sleep one night and saw at his bedside a giant, horrible and high, with an enormous sword in one hand and an uprooted tree in the other, and how after half an hour he put him to flight. He and his associates frequently saw angels and devils in broad daylight, both with the spiritual and the bodily sight. Even if they shut their eyes they saw them—devils in chariots of black cloud drawn by lesser devils in the form of beasts, spirits of wicked men all deformed, with cloven hoofs, cat's ears, tusks, crooked mouths, and bow legs, passing through walls and closed windows, giving forth a foul smell, and leaving a taste of sulphur in the mouth, and these visions at one time went on for a month.[2]

The most important of the associates of Pordage was Jane Lead or Leade, a widow of a good Norfolk family. Her maiden name was Ward, but in 1644 she married her cousin, William Leade. Pordage became acquainted with her in 1663, and helped her in the study of Behmen's writings. In 1670 her husband died, and her fortune was lost about the same time. Her mystical religious tendencies, and, as she claimed, a divine and special revelation, induced her to join Pordage's circle at Bradfield. There she lived apart from the world, retired into herself, held intercourse with spirits, and received revelations, and it was felt by her friends that she had superseded Jacob Behmen. They treated her as their leader, and it was due to her that there was established " The Philadelphian Society for the Advancement of Piety and Divine Philosophy," the members, as long as they continued to remain at Bradfield, living together in common, and agreeing not to separate from ecclesiastical connection with the churches.[3] Living to God meant more

---

[1] " Truth Appearing, through the Clouds of Undeserved Scandal and Aspersion," by John Pordage, 1654; " Innocency Appearing through the dark Mists of Pretended Guilt," by John Pordage, 1654; " Dæmonum Meridianum: Satan at Noon," in two Parts, by Christopher Fowler, 1655; " Just Narrative of the Proceedings of the Commissioners of Berks," 1655.
[2] R. A. Vaughan, " Hours with the Mystics," I. 109.
[3] Hunt, " Religious Thought in England," I. 239–240.

STUDIES IN ENGLISH PURITANISM

300

than all the sects. " I write not to gain disciples, nor to make
a sect or party, nor to make divisions in the world," wrote
Edward Hooker.[1] So they spoke of the Philadelphian society,
not the Philadelphian church. The true church of Philadelphia
was still in the future; this was a company of persons waiting
for its coming glorious manifestation. Pordage died in 1681.
Jane Leade related that in his later years he had withdrawn
from the public ministry, and lived in retirement.[2] Some of
his writings were published after his death. "A Treatise of
Eternal Nature, with her Seven Essential Forms or Original
Working Properties " is dated 1681, but really is the continuation of another treatise, " Theologica Mystica; or, the Mystic
Divinity of the Eternal Invisibles, viz., the Archetypous Globe,
or the Original Globe, or World of all Globes, Worlds, Essences,
Centres, Elements, Principles, and Creations Whatsoever." This
was published in 1683, the other book bound up with it, and
the whole described as " By a Person of Quality. J.P., M.D."
Dr. Edward Hooker, one of the Philadelphians, and author of
" Divine Breathings " and " A Notion for the Ocean," who had
been entrusted with all Pordage's papers after his death, contributed a quaint preface, humorous and rambling, and full of
quotations in ancient and modern languages, in which he mentioned that the complete work had been published at the expense
of one W. B., a physician living at Wilmington in Kent, evidently
another member of the society. Of revelations by the Holy
Spirit, he said there were four kinds. These were: (1) *Visions*.
These are the lowest kind of revelation. Heavenly shapes or
images are spiritually perceived by the inner sense of man
through the operation of the Holy Spirit. (2) *Illuminations*. By
the same operation a ray of divine light, as it were, falls upon
the soul, and makes some hidden things clear. (3) *Immediate
translations*. In these the spirit is carried up into the *principium*
—that is to say, God—and beholds the mysteries of God. So
St. Paul was carried up into the third heaven, and so Pordage
was carried up amongst the angels, on one occasion for the
space of three weeks. Jane Leade added the further information
that his body lay in a passive stillness all the time. (4) *The
descent of the Holy Spirit into the soul*. This gives it complete
regeneration and illumination, and opens to it the glories of
heaven.

Jane Leade explained that by revelation men may have access
to " the very centre of the Trinity (man's dwelling-place), and
then all shadows and pictures are swallowed up." [3] There is a
centre where the Deity is unveiled, and this is the purest vision,
whereon our spirits can eternally concentrate. St. John had

[1] Introduction to " Theologica Mystica," 1683, p. 109.
[2] Preface to " Theologica Mystica."
[3] Leade, " Wars of David and the Peaceable Reign of Solomon," 1700.

such visions, and Jane Leade claimed to have experienced something of the kind. But those who wish to enter into these
mystical raptures must get away from all bodily sense; they
must " keep low," and cultivate self-annihilation. The will of
the soul, thus yielded wholly to God, becomes a resistless power,
can bind or loose, bless or ban, throughout the universe. If
any considerable number amongst men had a faith strong enough
for this, rebellious human nature would be subdued by their
holy spells and paradise would be restored.[1] By these means
holy men of old were inspired, saw visions, and recorded them
in the Scriptures. So to-day the volumes of Scripture are being
multiplied through new revelations which are made from time
to time.[2]

But there is a sort of vision which comes from the starry
influences and powers of the elements working with the common
spirit and mind of men, who, like Balaam, may have such a
gift without any accompanying spiritual renewal or union with
God, even though the images seen may foretell truly what is to
come to pass. Indeed, there are great dangers for those who
are unspiritual and seek the mystical knowledge, for the serpent
stands ready to effect an entrance whenever possible, for he is a
great magical prince, and the material planetary system operates
with him in the constitution of the mere natural man. But
those who seek such knowledge by yielding themselves wholly
to the will of God ultimately experience all the delight the
angels enjoy.

" Theologia Mystica " expounded the doctrine of the Trinity,
always using the word " number " instead of " person." " The
Eternal World was called the Globe of Eternity at the time
when I was taken up to have a view of it." This Eternal
World, or World of Eternal Nature contains several principles,
globes, or centres:

> The Angelical Heaven, or the Love World.
> The Dark Fire World, Hell, or the Wrath World.
> The Fire Light World, or the Severe World.
> The Light Fire World, or Paradise.
> The Four-Elementary World, or the Outward Visible World.
> The Fireless World, the Visible World.

" The Treatise of Eternal Nature " professed to set forth mysteries
hitherto unrevealed. " The triune Deity has brought forth
Himself into eternal nature, as into a ground whereby He might
be the better manifested to His intellectual creatures, who,
without this Eternal Nature, would not be able to know or
understand anything of His attributes." Eternal Nature is " the

---

[1] Vaughan, " Hours with the Mystics," I. 109–110.
[2] Leade, " Wars of David."

first original and true ground of all created beings, and so of all true knowledge." It is a principle created by God out of the abyssal chaos, containing the seven operative powers for the production of all things. These seven operative powers are the four elements of nature, fire, water, earth, and air, which four are eternal, together with the three eternal *principia*, phosphorus, salt, and mercury. So the efficient cause of Eternal Nature is God, the material cause is the abyssal chaos, the formal cause the seven operative powers, the final cause that it might be the fruitful mother of all things.[1] There are two great mysteries in the Divine Nature. The first is the Trinity in Unity and Unity in Trinity, which refers to the Deity in their single, solitary, and abstracted essence. The second is the Deity in Humanity and Humanity in Deity, which concerns God as being introduced into, and subsisting in, Eternal Nature.[2] The angelic world, which was made out of the seven operative powers, has three divisions, the external court, the inner court, and the Holy of Holies. It has no sun, the light of the Trinity lightens it. Neither has it stars, but instead it has many "powers," which have a certain independent existence. The angels consist of spirit, soul, and love, and a disturbance in the harmony of these three "eternal things" caused the fall of part of the angels. These, having broken the bond of Eternal Nature, fell into a hell which they had really made for themselves, for the element of fire asserted itself and enclosed them. By wisdom (*sophia*) the first man was made. He had both sexes, but of him woman was formed by the "female tincture." The fallen angels have a "tincture" by which they injure the souls of men. In reading the writings of Pordage one seems to hear frequent, though sometimes faint, echoes of Basilides and Valentinus.

Among the circle which gathered at Bradfield was Thomas Bromley, who is said to have held an Oxford fellowship, which he resigned in 1660 because he could not accept the Prayer Book,[3] and so he went to live with Pordage, and remained with him for many years. He seems to have differed in some respects both from Pordage and Jane Leade, as also from Behmen. He rejected all forms of ecclesiastical organisation, and did not believe in marriage, which he considered an inferior condition intolerable to the saints, from whom was required a spotless purity of life. His chief publication was "The Way to the Sabbath of Rest, or, the Soul's Progress in the Work of the New Birth." It appeared first about 1672, but there were several later editions. In it he explained, amongst other things, how man, being an epitome of all the worlds, contains within himself that which corresponds with the four heavens, even the Heaven

---

[1] P. 107.   [2] P. 153.
[3] Calamy does not mention him.

of Heavens itself; thus he is able to enter into them all and receive visions of them all. Bromley's method of scriptural interpretation is shown in his " Divine Explication of the Seven Nations that opposed Israel under Joshua," in which he explained the seven nations as seven evil spirits which encounter the spiritual Israel until they are effectually cast out of the soul by the true Joshua, Jesus Christ.[1] In the British Museum Library is a little pamphlet of twelve pages: " A Catalogue of Mr. T. Bromley's Library, to be sold on August 26th, 1691." This was the year in which he died, and the long list of books in classics and theology, of which the catalogue chiefly consists, shows that he must have been a good scholar. A complete issue of his writings was published in after years at Leipzig and Frankfort; the second edition in two volumes was printed there in 1719 and 1732.

Another of the Philadelphian leaders was Francis Lee, M.D., a zealous student of the Scriptures, who published an edition of the Septuagint in 1707. He was studying medicine at Leyden when he first heard of the movement. On his return to England he sought out Mrs. Leade, who adopted him as a son, and a little later, in accordance with a revelation she received, he married her daughter. It is said to have been he who urged her to put her visions in writing, and he himself edited the *Theosophical Transactions* of the Philadelphian Society, which first began to appear in 1697. He was a very learned man, and was intimate with several great persons, among them Robert Harley, Earl of Oxford. Peter the Great was interested in him, and at that sovereign's request he wrote in 1698 some proposals for a better system of government.[2] He was a very charitable man, who was interested in many charitable works, and he wrote numerous books, but refused to put his name to them.[3]

Mrs. Leade speaks of Pordage as a disciple would speak of a master.[4] Referring to her spiritual experience, she says, " I introverted more and more into my own inward deep; in here I did meet with that which I could not find elsewhere: except it were such as were brought under the same dispensation, such as Dr. Pordage and the Rev. Mr. Thomas Bromley." But she became the great leader of the society. To it she gave what she called the " Laws of Paradise "—the basic principles, that is to say, which they adopted. They were to advance the cause of the Kingdom of God by inculcating holiness, the highest morality, and the doctrine of universal brotherhood. They were not to interfere in politics, and were to give obedience to estab-

---

[1] Leade, " The Wars of David," pp. 42–45.
[2] See " Dissertations Theological, Mathematical, and Physical," by Francis Lee, M.D., 2 vols., 1752.
[3] Leade, " The Wars of David," 1700. Reprinted, 1816.
[4] Preface to Pordage, " Theologia Mystica."

lished governments, unless any of these should act against the
Gospel and the light of Nature.

She believed, and her followers implicitly believed, that she
held intercourse with spirits both good and bad. In mystical
contemplation she obtained a knowledge of things hitherto
unrevealed. She kept a memorandum of her spiritual experiences since 1670, in which year she says the spirit of prophecy
was declared to her. Since then she had tried " to bring back
her soul into eternal and pure Nature's originality again." [1] In
1681 she published her first book, a small pamphlet of forty
pages, called " The Heavenly Cloud now Breaking." It was
followed in 1683 by " The Revelation of Revelations; particularly as an Essay towards the Unsealing, Opening, and
Discovering of the Seven Seals, the Seven Thunders, and the
New Jerusalem State, etc." The title-page announced that it
was printed and sold by Sowle, at the Crooked Billet, in Holloway
Lane in Shoreditch, and " Also by J. Lead at the Carpenter's
in Bartholomew Close." She had evidently moved to London
after the death of Dr. Pordage. The fact that Sowle, the Quaker
bookseller, published her works is interesting, since both Quakers
and Philadelphians, in part at least, traced their spiritual ancestry
to Behmenism. The " Revelation of Revelations " is a mystical
interpretation of the seven seals [2] and the seven thunders [3] from
her own experience and visions, the seven properties of the
Holy Ghost, the five purified and spiritualized senses, which are
the five gates by which we attain the divine wisdom, and after
which there are seven more gates to pass. The work concluded
with the glories of the New Jerusalem state. It was written
very much after the style of the prophetic parts of the Old
Testament, and saturated with the language of the Authorised
Version. Many of her so-called visions can be traced, in fact,
to some scriptural foundation. Some of her books are simply a
record of her visions. Thus, " The Enochian Walks with God.
Found out by a Spiritual Traveller, whose Face towards Zion
was set," [4] published in 1694, gave an account of visions she
had received on May 12th and July 15th of that year, while the
" Tree of Faith," published in 1696, described visions seen in
1691 and at other times, some fully dated, and some dated as to
month and day, but not the year. The preface to the last-
mentioned work announced that an angel had sounded the
trumpet to proclaim that all formal worship set up by man, and
constituted by rational inventions, must now pass away as a
shadow. In the same year she published a supplement to the
last work. This was entitled " The Ark of Faith," and in it
she said that every true Christian ought to pray both for new
divine revelations which might be of the same authority as

[1] Leade, " The Tree of Faith," 1696.
[2] Rev. v. 1.   [3] Rev. x. 4.   [4] Gen. v. 24.

those of Christ and His Apostles, and for miraculous happenings, which might be a declaration of God's sovereignty and kingdom. The visions recorded in this book set forth the laws which were to be observed by those admitted to the " paradisical land."

In the previous year she had published " The Laws of Paradise, given forth by Wisdom to a Translated Spirit." She described how she had seen God's Eternal Virgin Wisdom, who presented her with a golden book sealed with three seals. She explained, and mystically expounded the Ten Commandments as they were to be understood by her initiates. Thus, among the rules for the Sabbath rest she included " a total cessation from the working property of reason, the motion of which must be stopped." The seventh commandment is thus explained : " Thou art not to break the marriage knot betwixt thee and the Lord thine Husband, to whom thou art betrothed through the Eternal Spirit." She described how during and after the delivery of these laws she was much beset with opposition from " the king-crowned beast " and the false prophet,[1] but Wisdom's paradisical inhabitant " rebuked the king-crowned beast." The conclusion of the book was " that there is a mystical paradise as well as a local, chiefly standing in divine visions, revelations, ideas, presentations, manifestations, etc., in sounds, trumpets, voices, inspeaking, etc. . . . Ye that are resolved to taste of these flowing sweets, take heed to the laws of paradise, and be not in the duality, halting between two principles."

1696 was Mrs. Leade's most prolific literary year. She published, as well as the works already mentioned, " A Message to the Philadelphian Society, whithersoever dispersed over the Whole Earth, together with a Call to the several gathered Churches among Protestants in this Nation of England," in which she set forth the chief principles of the society. She also issued the first volume of what was, perhaps, her most important work, " A Fountain of Gardens," a kind of spiritual diary of her revelations and visions. It dealt with the years 1670 to 1676, and began, " The first vision that appeared to me was in the month of April 1670, which was on this wise." The volume contained over 500 pages, nearly 400 being taken up with the visions of 1676 alone. The second volume was published in 1697, and dealt with the revelations which came to her in 1676. The third volume was divided into two parts, Part I was printed in 1700, and dealt with the year 1678, while Part II, published in 1701, described her spiritual experiences from the beginning of 1679 to the middle of 1686.

" The Ascent to the Mount of Vision " (1699) described what she saw on six days in May, June, and July 1698. Thus, on

---

[1] Rev. xiii. 1 ; xix. 20.

May 26th she saw the places of departed souls. There were the wicked, in the tormenting anguishing fire of the dark Luciferian kingdom, where they are to be punished till the decreed ages of ages are expired. Secondly, there were those who have been concerned merely with the worldly principle, and loved temporal things only. These have their places in the lower and grosser parts of the airy region, where they have not much torment, yet, on the other hand, they have but little rest, and sometimes even return to visit their dead corpses. Thirdly, those who led a sober, rational life on earth, but with little care for spiritual things, and without heavenly renovation. They are now in the upper part of the airy region, next to paradise, where " they want not for motives and stirrings up to go on and recover what they omitted and lost while living in the body." Lastly, there was a pleasant flowery and delightful paradise for children. The great saints who are joined with Christ make intercession for the shortcomings of all these people in the regions of the dead, and prophets, pastors, and teachers dwell among them to teach and lead them upwards. She completed her description of eternal things in " The Wonders of God's Creation manifested in the Variety of Eight Worlds: as they were made known Experimentally to the Author." Eight worlds are allotted to human souls, according to their degree of spiritual attainment. These are (1) this mortal, visible world; (2) the astral or aerial world; (3) the waterish, elementary world; (4) the fiery, dark world. In these four all sinful lustings and punishments abide till sin expires. Then follow (5) the paradisical world; (6) the kingdom of Mount Zion, Christ's kingdom; (7) the New Jerusalem, the principal seat of God the Father; and (8) the world called Still Eternity. This is so calm and still that no figures or images are seen, but a wonderful light which flows like a river. From this all beings proceed, and from it must now be expected a new creation, brought forth from the stillness of this light.

In 1699 she published " The Signs of the Times, Forerunning the Kingdom of Christ, and Evidencing when it is to Come." She had been granted visions which showed the immediate coming of the kingdom, and a spirit of discerning analysis was given to her that she might understand. A holy watcher, in the figure of a cherub having many eyes, had appeared. Preparations for the kingdom were going on in the invisible regions, and the mystery of the times was now about to be finished. The gate of paradise was opened, and there was a ministration of fire, called the ministration of Elias and of Sophia, preparatory to the sounding of the seventh trumpet. There would be a sounding of a trumpet to invite the kings and nobles of the earth into the kingdom, and another sounding to invite priests and pastors of the church. She repeated and expanded these prophecies in "The Wars of David, and the Peaceable Reign of Solomon, Symbolizing the Times of Warfare and Refreshment of the Saints of the Most High God. To whom a Priestly Kingdom is shortly to be given after the Order of Melchizedek." It consisted of two treatises, "An Alarm to the Holy Warriors to Fight the Battles of the Lamb," and "The Glory of Sharon in the Renovation of Nature, introducing the Kingdom of Christ." The book was published in 1700, and set forth her experiences during sickness in the preceding year, and told of an age, about to begin, wonderful beyond all human imagining. She was then seventy-seven years of age, and had gone blind in the previous year. She had been very poor since 1670, when she had really been cheated out of her money. Possibly her poverty and disappointments had a good deal to do with her mystical tendencies. All her works had been published at the expense of Dr. Francis Lee. The publisher's " Address to the Reader " prefaced to the last-mentioned work complained of the neglect which her writings had received, but then very few people saw any signs of her prophecies coming true. Dr. Lot Fisher caused all her works to be translated into Dutch, and some were translated into German and published at Amsterdam between 1696 and 1698. Her book " The Wars of David " was reprinted in 1816. A few of her books have been republished at Glasgow in recent years. A modern French writer, M. Seder, writing of the Philadelphians as one of the occult societies, speaks of Jane Leade as *illuminée* and *voyante*, and says, " A part quelques rares personnes, les mystiques de notre époque, qui se rangent sous les symboles des diverses fraternités occultes, sont loin d'avoir acquis la même puissance que leurs aînés des XVII⁰ et XVIII⁰ siècles." [1]

The Philadelphian society in its later years became better known, and several persons of note, including one or two noblemen, joined it. Public meetings were held towards the end of the century at Hungerford House, then at Westmorland House, and later at Hoxton, and a correspondence was maintained with persons in various parts of Europe who were looking for the coming of the Kingdom of Christ. Many ladies joined the society, and it became derisively known as the Taffeta Society. The movement spread from England into Holland and Germany. In 1703 the members drew up a " Confession of Faith," but in that same year the Dutch section formally seceded from the English one. The English Government for some reason or other determined to suppress the English society. But Jane Leade died in the following year, and the movement, as far as this country was concerned, totally collapsed. But it was not entirely without influence. It had made a great contribution to the

---

[1] " Le Messager Celeste de la Paix Universelle," traduit par P. Seder. Paris 1894; " La Mystique Judeo-Chrétienne."

spread of mystical religion in England, and thereby affected
such men as William Law and the founders of Methodism.[1]

THE ROSICRUCIANS

In 1614 there was published at Cassel, in Germany, a little
book, " Fama Fraternitatis," which set forth " the Discovery of
the Brotherhood of the Honourable Order of the Rosy Cross."
This and another pamphlet, " Confessio Fraternitatis," published the next year, revealed to the world how one Christian
Rosenkreutz, a German who was born in 1378 and died towards
the end of the next century, had travelled in Palestine, Egypt,
North Africa, and elsewhere, gathering the occult wisdom of
divers wise men.   The " Fama " described an imaginary gathering of ancient sages to discuss the best methods of reforming the
evil times, and deciding that the best method was a secret
society of wise and philanthropic persons.   Rosenkreutz accordingly erected a mysterious dwelling-place called the Temple of
the Holy Ghost, and gathered to himself eight associates, each
of whom was to provide for a successor to himself after his
death.   The society was to be kept secret for a hundred years,
but now the time had come for a reformation of the world.
The Rosicrucians, for so the fraternity was called, professed a
wisdom and philosophy which were patriarchal, Greek, biblical,
and cabalistic.   They had traditions and MSS. in their possession
which enabled them to make gold for persons who would use it
rightly, especially good kings, and they had also great secrets
of healing, all which great gifts it was their sole desire to use for
the benefit of the human race.   They were all good Protestants,
and they invited all learned and devout men who wished to aid
in the great work to advertise their names, that the brethren
might summon them when necessary.

So far there is reason to believe that the whole thing was a
hoax, and that the two tracts were the work of a Lutheran
pastor, named Valentine Andrea.   But they attracted wide
attention; the story was accepted greedily in many quarters,
and a literary controversy arose as to its credibility.   A number
of enthusiasts adopted the principles set forth in the tracts, and
the name of Rosicrucians became a term for a number of persons
who put forth occult pretensions.[2]   Robert Fludd, M.D., who
lived in England in the early half of the seventeenth century, was
one of these.[3]   He wrote a book called " Mosaical Philosophy,"
first published in England in 1659, in which he elaborated the

---

[1] Schaff-Hertzog, " Encycl. Religious Knowledge," Vol. III., Arts.
Philadelphians, Pordage; Hastings, " Rel. Eth.," Vol. IX., Art. Philadelphians; McClintock and Strong, " Cycl. of Biblical Theol. and Eccles. Lit.,"
Vol. VIII.; Vaughan, " Hours with the Mystics," II. 109–110.
[2] Vaughan, " Hours with the Mystics," II. 108.
[3] " Dict. Rel. and Ethics," Art. Rosicrucians.

argument that the Bible explained the philosophy, or rather theology, of the universe. By the revelation· which God had made of Himself in the Scriptures we can penetrate into the centre and essence of being, and can explain the mysteries of the Creator and creation. The universe is one, and with the universe God is one, though we may speak of them as distinct. So there is one world, but we speak of an aerial world and a temporal world. God has neither beginning nor end, but the temporal world both had a beginning and will have an end. The aerial or angelical world, which is the dwelling of the angels and the blessed spirits, had a beginning, but will have no end. It is the intermediary between the eternal and temporal, and is set forth mystically by Jacob's ladder. These worlds, being one universe in all, may be represented by a wheel within a wheel. The central motive force, or eternal spirit, is in the aerial world, but by it the temporal world is quickened. God, or Christ, who is the wisdom of God, fills all things, virtually and essentially. The mysticism of Fludd's system had great resemblances to that of some of the other sects of the time, such as the Behmenists or Philadelphians, as also his pantheism, which he derived from all the passages of Scripture capable of such an interpretation.[1] Thomas Underhill said of the Rosicrucians that they " set themselves mainly to a mortification of bodily desires and delights, and advancing the intellective part above the sensitive, but the doctrine of Christ crucified is little minded." [2] Robert Fludd was a student of natural magic, " that most occult and secret department of physics, by which the mystical properties of natural substances are abstracted," and venefic magic, which dealt with the properties and preparations of poisons. In modern times he would probably be described as a student of physics and chemistry. In 1616, in his " Tractatus Apologeticus," he denied that the Rosicrucians dabbled in " detestable magic and diabolical superstition." Thomas Vaughan, writing about the middle of the century, declared that the Rosicrucians had gathered their secret knowledge from the east.[3] John Heydon,[4] who was not a Rosicrucian but professed to know all their secrets, wrote several books about them at the time of the Restoration. " The Rosicrucian Infallible Axiomatic: or, General Rules to know all Things Past, Present and To Come," appeared in 1660, and two years later he published " The Holy Guide." This professed to teach " the way to happiness, and to know all, past,

---

[1] Hunt, " Religious Thought in England," I. 240–241.
[2] " Hell Broke Loose: or an History of the Quakers Old and New," 1660, p. 15.
[3] A. E. Waite, " The Brotherhood of the Rosy Cross "; London 1924; pp. 271–309; Wood, " Athenae," I. 610.
[4] A. E. Waite, " Brotherhood of the Rosy Cross," pp. 388–397.

present, and to come, viz.—the way to long life, health, youth, blessedness, wisdom, and virtue: and to cure, change, and remedy the diseases in young or old with Rosicrucian medicines, which are verified by a practical examination of principles in the Great World, and fitted for the use and profit of all people." The title-page said that the book had been long kept from the public owing to the tyranny of the late times, and that it was much desired by the learned men of the Inns of Court and the two universities. Another Rosicrucian tract which was printed in England that same year bore the title "Novum Lumen Medicum." It professed to have been issued out of compassion for the sick, and it explained Van Helmont's theory of "the great mystery of the philosopher's sulphur." [1] Elias Ashmole was a Rosicrucian, and several references to Rosicrucianism are scattered about his diary.[2] One thing seems fairly certain, however: that this loosely connected scientific, theological, philosophical, and occultist sect had no connection with the Rosicrucians of the present day,[3] or even with the degree of that name· in freemasonry, though the writings of Sir Francis Bacon, Ashmole, and Heydon seemed to show some connection between seventeenth-century Rosicrucianism and the craft, at any rate to the extent that some people, like Ashmole, were initiates of both.[4]

THE TRYONITES

The Tryonites were the followers of Thomas Tryon, who was born in Gloucestershire in 1634. He wrote a memoir of his own life as far as his forty-eighth year; after that it is continued by some other persons. The part which he wrote shows his views to be formed of a curious compound of astrology, dreams, teetotalism, and vegetarianism. Thus, he writes, "I submitted and composed my spirits into an harmonious state and went to sleep; where was represented to me the globe of the universe, whereon was only written in capital golden letters, REGENERATION, which to me was a clear manifestation that obedience to God's laws and commandments was the only thing needful to be enquired after: and that there is no other way to obtain the great mystery and knowledge of God, His law and ourselves, but by self-denial, cleanness, temperance and sobriety in words, employments, meats and drinks." [5] He laid great stress on the practice of silence, and on obedience to inward monitions to fast, speak, or write.

[1] Kennet, "Reg.," pp. 595, 734, 736.
[2] Elias Ashmole, "Diary," Oxford, 1926; Waite, "Brotherhood of the Rosy Cross," pp. 365–372.
[3] Webster, "Secret Societies," 1924, pp. 84–98.
[4] Ibid., pp. 119–122.
[5] "Some Memoirs of the Life of Mr. Thomas Tryon, late of London, Merchant, written by himself," 1705, pp. 5–6.

Tryon had not apparently had much schooling. His father, who was a tiler and plasterer, set him to work as a spinner when he was very young, and in his spare time he helped the shepherds for a copper or two. He was taught to read and write by a friend. In 1651 he went to London, and was apprenticed to a hatter. He was one of those boys who could not help getting on. At the age of thirteen he had persuaded his father to buy him a few sheep; now as an apprentice he worked over-time in order to earn money to buy books. It is not surprising, then, to learn that in the end he became a wealthy merchant, who called himself Thomas Tryon, " gent.," and had a coat of arms. For about three years, 1654–1657, he belonged to the Anabaptists. But when he left them he adopted an ascetic life, under the guidance of the voice of wisdom within. For some time he lived on vegetables and fruit, with water as his only drink. An interest in the science of the time—astrology and alchemy—doubtless had its influence in developing his opinions and the manner of life he adopted. To vegetables and fruit the inward voice allowed him, after a time, to add eggs, butter, and cheese. In 1661 he married, but appears to have main-tained his vegetarian and teetotal principles. He travelled in the West Indies and on the continent, and in 1682 his first book appeared. It was called " The Way to Health, Long Life, and Happiness: or, A Discourse of Temperance . . . by Philotheos Physiologus." A second and amended edition came out in 1691. The author's name was then given as " Thomas Tryon, Student in Physic." In the Epistle to the Reader he said, " Whosoever will treat aught, either of divine or natural things and their occult virtues or vices, must make the seven primogenial forms his basis or groundwork, or else he shall never truly display natures and operations." The first chapter dealt with the four grand qualities, bitter, sweet, sour, and astringent or saltish, from which the four complexions, choleric, phlegmatic, sanguine, and melancholy proceed. In the second chapter, which is con-cerned with " the excellency of temperance and the mighty benefits of abstinence and sobriety," he defined temperance as self-knowledge. " If any man will understand any thing truly, he must first turn the eye of his mind inward, not outward, for man is an image and likeness of all things, both spiritual and natural. In him is contained the true nature of all things, and he that doth know and understand himself, and the principles and operations of his own nature, both in body and mind, and what properties in the sevenfold nature of this world are pre-dominant in him, and to what his inclinations are most naturally propensive, both as to virtue and vice, he may thereby not only shun many inconveniences, but also so much as he knows of himself, he also knows of his Creator and of all other things." [1]

[1] " The Way to Health," 1691, p. 33.

He did not approve of smoking. " Tobacco is an herb of Mars
and Saturn : from the first it derives its hot, tart quality; and
owes its strong, fulsome, poisonous nature to the latter. It
makes a most excellent ointment, and is much safer being
applied outwardly than inwardly taken." [1] He spoke with
evident regret of the way in which some reverend divines smoked
" as intemperately as any of the vulgar." [2] He discussed the
reasons why cities and great towns were subject to pestilence
and other diseases, and why a retired country life was so much
more healthful. He saw the harm to health of the smoky air
and bad sanitation of the towns, but he had a more recondite
explanation. Men's actions awaken the like property in the
celestial bodies. When the original poisons in nature and
wrathful spirits are stirred up, they overcome the pure virtues,
they powerfully penetrate all elements and bodies, and when-
soever they find matter capable or disposed to receive them,
they incorporate themselves, and with highest diligence endeavour to destroy the good virtues, and hence arise evil airs
and various diseases. All things in this lower world have their
influence on celestial bodies and elements. Hence men may
stir up the wrath of the celestial bodies, and draw down the
malignant configurations, which may cause epidemics, or wars,
or famines.[3] The book dealt with a great number of miscellaneous matters—the influence of the seasons on health, the
harm done by over-abundance of meats and drinks, of meat
and vegetable foods, of drinks, of medicinal herbs, of diseases
caused by eating food while it is too hot, of the harm done by
eating too much flesh meat and its tendency to arouse the
wrathful nature in man, of cleanliness, and so forth, and it
finishes with the praise of harmony in all things. In short, he
is an advocate of what would be called to-day the simple life.
Dr. Alexander Gordon describes him as a kind of modern
health reformer with a Pythagorean philosophy. He may have
thought that water is best, but one of his twenty odd works
deals with the " new art of brewing beer, ale, etc."

He also wrote a " Treatise of Dreams and Visions," of which
a second edition was published in 1689. Here he showed again
his theosophical bent. Man is the complete image of God and
nature, and contains the principles and properties of all things
corporeal and incorporeal. He is endued with an elemental or
palpable body, actuated, enlivened, or informed by an ethereal
spirit, and so answers to the great body of the world, from
whence the same is taken, and is an abridgment or epitome
thereof. He has the principle of fire and light—that is, soul and
spirit—which gives life and motion to the body of flesh, and
answers to the soul of the great world, or that mighty spirit

[1] " The Way to Hea'th," 1691, p. 124.   [2] Ibid., p. 126.
[3] Ibid., pp. 186–187.

which is the moving, vivifying, and the most wonderful creative and conservative power in this vast system of things which we call the world, and which preserves and sustains it in beauty, splendour, and harmony. The soul or spirit in man sleeps not, as being the breath of God, and eternal. From the soul or spirit in man, which is the image of the divine, eternal spirit, and never stands still, sleeps, or slumbers, all dreams and nocturnal visions arise and proceed.[1] Dreams are caused sometimes by the visits of good or bad spirits, and the departed also communicate with living persons in dreams or apparitions. It is only in dreams and ecstasies, and not by the outward senses, that such communication between man and the spirit world is possible. Communications from good angels by dreams and the like, which were so frequent in former times, have not yet wholly ceased. The best things to promote intellectual communication with such are temperance, regular diet, and a sober and virtuous course of life; which all tend to lead to truly significant and profitable dreams, and so to an honest, useful improvement in our intercourse with good spirits. He followed this work up in 1691 with another on the same subject, " Pythagoras, his Mystic Philosophy Revived; or the Mystery of Dreams Unfolded." Just about the time of his death was published " The Knowledge of a Man's Self the Surest Guide to the True Worship of God . . . or the Second Part of the Way to Long Life, Health, and Happiness." It was a book of over 500 pages, and dealt with a curious medley of subjects—metals, stones, sciences, arts, trades, education, mathematics and many other things. His " Letters on Several Occasions " were published in 1700, and consisted of thirty-seven papers dealing with miscellaneous subjects, such as the senses, the humanity of Christ, the fountain of love and light, coal fires, cotton-planting, corpulence, and predestination.

We know practically nothing, except the titles and dates of his books, of his life after 1682, when the " Memoirs " came to an end. He died on August 21st, 1703, at the age of sixty-eight. He was held in honour by such a person as Aphra Behn, who wrote a poem of fifty-six lines in his praise. He left behind him a number of letters and a MS. collection of rules and laws for his society, which he called " The Society of Clean and Innocent Lives." The world, however, called them Tryonists, or Tryonites. The laws and maxims take up the latter half of his Memoirs, which came out two years after his death.

His society was to be organised under " Governors," who were to hold office for not more than a year, and " Deputies " or " Inspectors." The governors met once a year to choose their successors, the deputies were chosen by ballot. One day in the week was to be kept as a Sabbath, and no work was to be

[1] " A Treatise of Dreams," 1689, pp. 26–31.

done on that day, not even the preparing of food, which had to be performed the day before. On the Sabbath the members were to meet both morning and afternoon for prayer and the reading of the laws, which last was to be done without interpretation, comment, or explanation. Vegetarianism was strictly insisted on. They were not even to cook their food in vessels used by meat-eaters. They were not to use the skins of living creatures for shoes, gloves, or saddles. Fish must not be eaten. The eating of flesh or fish, or anything that had been killed, was contrary to Scripture, the command of God, and the example of Christ. Killing comes from the hellish nature of man. The animals are our fellow-creatures and brethren. Adam was only to eat of herbs and fruit; killing came in after the Fall, and was only permitted after the Flood. The eating of flesh is a doctrine of devils, and qualifies men to be sordid and surly, and so they become soldiers, hunters, pirates, tories, and such as have a bestial nature.[1] A public register was to be kept in every society, wherein all bargains and contracts over £20 were to be registered, and a fixed proportion of each had to be paid to a register-keeper, who, after a settled allowance to himself, should expend the rest on the poor. " Whosoever shall swear, either by the heavens or earth, or anything therein, shall retire alone for forty-one days; he shall not speak one word during the time, nor eat anything but bread." [2] Some rules were given which are as much medical and sanitary as religious. For instance, women expecting to become mothers were told, " Let your houses and rooms be adorned with the pictures of the innocent beauties of young children, especially the rooms where you lie." Another rule for them was not to press the children with tight clothing.[3] Members were not to read plays and romances nor to sing or play love-songs, nor to wear superfluous trimmings or fantastic ornaments. " No girl, maid, or woman shall carry any burdens, do any field labour, sell nor cry anything about the streets, nor do any dirty work. All robustick labour shall be done by man." All women over seven were to go about veiled.[4] It is improbable that this was anything but a very small sect, or that it lasted long after the death of the founder.

THE TRASKITES

The Traskites were the followers of John Traske, a Somersetshire man, who left his native county and went up to London about 1617. He was a schoolmaster, and had some knowledge of Latin and a little knowledge of Hebrew and Greek. He held that none but such as were converted themselves could convert

---

[1] " The Postboy," II. 330.   [2] " Memoirs," p. 107.   [3] *Ibid.*, p. 113.
[4] *Ibid.*, p. 127. See also " A Pythagorean of the Seventeenth Century," by A. Gordon, *Liverpool Lit. and Phil. Soc. Trans.*, 1871.

others, that one child of God might know another's election as
certainly as his own, that repentance was not only begun, but
also finished before justifying faith, that none that were justified
could commit sin. He also taught that it was necessary to keep
all the precepts of Scripture, and that the whole Jewish law
must be observed. For a long time he had many followers, and
under his guidance they observed many Jewish practices.
According to one account, they kept the Lord's Day in the
Jewish manner, and would not even allow fires to be lighted or
cooking to be done.[1] Another account, more probably correct,
is that they kept the Jewish Sabbath and ignored the Christian
Sunday, and that this practice was adopted largely owing to
the influence over Traske of one of his followers who ultimately
became a Jewish proselyte, a proceeding which wrecked the
Christian faith of several members of the sect. Traske believed
himself a second Elias, sent to discover Antichrist. He thought
he could work miracles, and sent a message to King James
offering to cure him of his gout. To extend the number of his
followers he laid hands on four men, thus conferring a sort of
ordination upon them, and sent them forth to preach. He was
brought before the Star Chamber in 1620 [2] for heretical teaching,
was branded on the forehead with a J. for Jew, pilloried and
whipped, and sent to the Fleet prison. His wife and he were
at one time incarcerated together in the prison in Maiden
Lane. His wife remained a prisoner there, and later in the
Gatehouse, for her Judaising doctrines, and died in the latter
place after fifteen or sixteen years' imprisonment, charging the
gaoler to see that she was buried in the fields and not in a
churchyard. Traske himself recanted and was set at liberty.

Among other peculiarities, Traske held that a true minister of
Christ could not teach error, and conversely that no one but a
true minister could convert souls. His followers had peculiar
views concerning prayer, saying that we ought not to offer
general petitions, but should state our requests specifically, *e.g.*
if we say " Give us *this* day our daily *bread* " as a petition to
God, it can only be for *this* day and for *bread* alone. One of his
followers, a man named Rice Boye, wrote a pamphlet entitled
" The Importunate Beggar," in which he defended this position.
This man, it was believed, was the author of a pamphlet which
denied that Traske had ever been punished for Judaizing, in
spite of the records of the Court of Star Chamber.

After his release and recantation, Traske fell into one error
after another. First of all he preached the wildest Antinomianism, and poured scorn on those who said the law of God should
be kept by Christians, and called them legalists, justiciaries,
messengers of Moses, Jews, and worse than Jews. Some of his

[1] E. Norice, " The New Gospel not the True Gospel," 1638.
[2] John Dowell, " The Leviathan Heretical," 1683, pp. 126–127.

opponents accused him of Familism, and various divines wrote in confutation of his errors. He was described as a very dangerous preacher. He would preach ordinary truths in a plain way, with a show of zeal and affection: then in private he would proceed further, and open out his strange tenets. If his hearers accepted these, well and good, if they did not, he denied that they were his own. He contradicted himself, twisted Scripture to suit his arguments, and spoke in such a way that it was difficult to make out what he meant, and there were some who had their doubts about the genuineness of his recantation. His last vagary was to join the Jacobites, or Semi-Separatists, and he died in the house of one of them, somewhere about 1638. There was a scandalous scene at his funeral. Some of his latest co-religionists bore him to his burial in Lambeth churchyard, and lowered him into the grave with his head in the opposite direction to every one else buried there, and lest the minister of the parish should come to bury him, they ran away and left him.[1]

One of Traske's associates was Theophilus Brabourne, who also was punished by the Star Chamber. He is said to have been converted from his errors by Bishop White of Ely, who urged him to write a book on the Sabbath. But White died in 1638, and Brabourne's book on the Sabbath did not appear till 1652. At any rate, he probably did not join the Church of England, for we find him writing pamphlets on behalf of liberty of conscience at the time of the Restoration.[2]

The Traskites—that is to say, the successors of the original flock—continued as a sect into the next century,[3] though they seem to have modified some of their views, for we hear, in 1706, that they held the law of Moses *in part*, *e.g.* not to eat blood or things strangled.[4] They were also known as the Seventh-Day men.[5]

THE CONSIDERERS

The Considerers were chiefly concerned with the study of the Book of Nature. They said that it was enough for all men, and that the study of the prophets lay therein. Consideration was the royal way to the Kingdom of God. They acknowledged

[1] Edward Norice, " A Treatise that Temporal Blessings are to be Sought and Asked with Submission to the Will of God, an Answer both to Rice Boye and Traske " 1636; Edward Norice, " The New Gospel not the True Gospel," 1638.
[2] " God Save the King and Prosper Him in his Parliament," by T. Brabourne, 1660; " The Humble Petition of T. B. to the Honourable Parliament," 1661 ; " Of the Lawfulness of the Oath of Allegiance to the King," by Theophilus Brabourne, 1661.
[3] Ross referred to them in his earlier editions of " Pansebeia," but omitted them from the 1683 edition.
[4] " The Postboy," II. 427.
[5] Pagitt, " Heresiography," pp. 161–214.

the doctrines of the Trinity, the Incarnation, and the Sacraments, and they looked on the Creed as a sufficient instrument of union amongst Christians. They did not believe that the Holy Spirit was confined to any particular sect, and they believed in His immediate inspiration. They did not, however, believe in the Quakers; indeed, their " secretary " prayed to God to preserve him from the spirit of those people. They practised consideration or meditation, and Monck Rogers, one of their leaders, was said to have been so " taken up with God " as not to remember the words a man had just spoken to him. They used the Lord's Prayer, married such as they loved at first sight, were thrifty of their time, and meddled not with State affairs.[1]

THE SOUL SLEEPERS

The Soul Sleepers believed that the soul slept or died with the body, and that both would be raised up again at the last day. The doctrine was derived chiefly from Genesis iii. 19, where Adam is told he must return to the dust. It was maintained in a work by R. Overton, entitled "Man's Mortality: or, a treatise wherein 'tis proved that the whole man (as a rational creature) is a compound wholly mortal, contrary to that common distinction of soul and body, and that the present going of the soul into heaven or hell is a mere fiction . . . also divers other mysteries as of heaven, hell, Christ's human residence, the resurrection, new creation, etc." This little tract of sixty pages was printed by John Canne at Amsterdam in 1643, and caused some excitement. On August 26th, 1644, the House of Commons ordered the author, printers, and publishers to be diligently sought for, and Overton himself was sent to the Tower.[2]

A small sect arose, known as the Soul Sleepers, who accepted Overton's views with some modifications. Pagitt speaks of them as a separate sect, but the doctrine of the sleep of the soul was held by several religious bodies.[3] There were other men who said that soul and body were alike mortal, and that there was no resurrection.[4]

OTHER SECTS

One Thomas Lemar, or Le Mare, appears to have founded a sect called the *Lemarists*, after his name. He had been a Barrowist in London, and his followers claimed that their doctrines were drawn from practically all the religions then known.[5] According

[1] Comber, " Christianity No Enthusiasm, 1678, pp. 97–98, 101.
[2] See also " Man Wholly Mortal," 1655, by the same writer.
[3] Pagitt, " Heresiography," p. 232; " A Relation of Several Heresies," 1646; Ross refers to them in " Pansebeia," 1653, but omits them in the 1683 edition.
[4] Calamy, " Sermon before the Lords on Christmas Day," 1644; Kennet, " Reg.," p. 730.
[5] Burrage, " Early English Dissenters," I. 200–201.

to Pagitt, their chief doctrines, however, were the following:
They denied the doctrine of the Trinity and the doctrine of the
Deity of Christ; they held that Christ would shortly come in
person to reign on earth; they accepted the Lutheran doctrine
of consubstantiation, but denied that Christ took flesh of the
Virgin Mary, and asserted that there was no visible church on
earth.[1] There is no evidence as to how long this sect continued
to exist, or even if it existed at the Restoration period, except so
far as the later editions of Pagitt mention it.

Baxter referred to a sect which he called the *Origenists*, but it
is doubtful whether such a sect really existed; it was more
probably a school of thought. A number of people at the time
were taking an interest in the teachings of Origen, and Burnet
tells us that Vane learnt some of the peculiar doctrines of that
writer. Kennet mentions a tract entitled "A Letter of Resolution concerning Origen and the Chief of his Opinions. Written
to the learned and most ingenious C. L. Esquire, and by him
published. London, 1661." The preface to this says that the
writer, having got from a friend a statement of the opinions of
Origen, sends them to C. L., and advises him to "think no
opinion formidable which does honour to God, renders Him
most amiable to men, and a sure object of our faith and hopes,
which justifies the ways of His providence, and reconciles them
with His most precious attributes, equity and benignity." [2]

At the beginning of the eighteenth century there was a sect of
people who called themselves the *Church of the First Born*. They
were also called Visionaries, Revelation men, and Behmenists,
because they followed the tenets of Jacob Behmen in many
respects. They claimed to be above ordinances, and to be the
heirs of salvation. Their union with Christ was so vital that
He was in them. Consequently the spiritual ties between them
and the fellow-members of their sect were much greater than
the bonds of natural relationship, and so they preferred to
bestow the greater part of their worldly goods on their brethren.
Their doctrines dealt with the most abstruse questions relating
to the Trinity, the nature of God and of angels, and such-like
matters. Their worship took the form of meetings at one
another's houses, where, after a period of silent contemplation,
they broke forth in ejaculations of joy, in the transports which
came from their communion with saints and angels and other
spiritual delights they believed to be granted them.[3]

A very similar sect found in existence at the same time was
that known as *The Children of the New Birth*. They also were
mystics, condemned the ordinary forms of worship, and devoted
themselves to contemplation and meditation, whereby they had
visions of spiritual things, heard the songs and voices of Zion,

---

[1] Pagitt, "Heresiography," p. 89.   [2] Kennet, "Reg.," p. 387.
[3] "The Postboy," pp. 330–331.

enjoyed the odours of paradise, and felt powerful tinctures of Christ's body. All this rather suggests a connection in some way with the Philadelphians, or at least Philadelphian influence.[1]

The title of " *Heavenly Father Men* " is probably a nickname, but the founder of the sect so named is said to have laid great stress on the mercifulness of the Almighty, and taught that there is no penal justice with God, who is willing to forgive all men all their sins, and that whenever a sinner repented he had only to ask for mercy in order to receive it.[2]

The *Anti-Eucharists* said that the Eucharist ought to be administered to the clergy only, because they alone were bound to lay down their lives for the flock as Christ had done. They held that after the Resurrection of Christ the Eucharist was not kept up as a Christian service, unless, indeed, the clergy thought fit to continue it for themselves, but in any case it was a sin to administer communion to a layman unless he should be intending to be ordained.[3]

The *Sabbatarians* said that the Ten Commandments were not abrogated, but were eternal, and that the Sabbath ought to be kept. The Christians in and after the Apostles' days kept both the Sabbath and Sunday, and so they did the same. It was in keeping both that these may be distinguished both from the Seventh-Day Baptists and the Traskites.[4]

The *Anti-Sabbatarians* said that the Law was abrogated, and that there was no longer a duty to observe the seventh day. They kept neither Sabbath nor Sunday, because they believed that every day is a Sabbath to a Christian. This they held in common with several sects, and perhaps they are not to be looked upon as a separate organised body.[5]

A petition was presented to the House of Lords on July 5th, 1661, by some people who called themselves *The Good Christians.* A week later some of them were heard at the bar of the House, and as the Anabaptists were also heard the same day on the subject of taking oaths, it may be that, like the Anabaptists and Quakers, the Good Christians had conscientious objections in this respect. The petition was signed by Dr. Gell and others, and a paper was put in at the same time setting forth Scripture arguments for toleration, written by Dr. Gell.[6]

The Semi-Separatists were also called Jacobites, after their founder, a man named Jacob. They were neither wholly in favour of separation from the Church of England nor wholly against it. Some of them attended the Anglican churches for

---

[1] " The Postboy," p. 230.   [2] *Ibid.*, p. 331.   [3] *Ibid.*, p. 432.
[4] *Ibid.*, II. 427; " A Relation of Several Heresies," 1646. They are mentioned by Chamberlayne, " Present State of England," 1674, and by Tenison, " Discourse concerning a Guide in Matters of Faith," 1683.
[5] Pagitt, " Heresiography," p. 159; " A Relation of Several Heresies," 1646. Ross omits them from his 1683 edition.
[6] Kennet, " Reg.," p. 491; *Lords Journals*, XI. July 12th, 1661; MSS. House Lords. Hist. MSS. Com. VII. i. 148.

the sermon only, " and of these you may see every Sunday in our streets (some) sitting and standing about our doors, who when the prayers are done, rush into our churches to hear our sermons." [1]   But this description would apply to Dissenters of many sects.

The *Anti-Scripturists*, or *Anti-Scripturians* rejected all the Scriptures of the Old and New Testament as of purely human invention, and said that the Scriptures were not the word of God because there is no Word but Christ.   The Bible was insufficient, uncertain, and not an infallible rule of faith; the writers wrote as they thought, moved only by their own spirits.   The Old Testament in particular had no binding force on Christians. Right reason was the rule of faith, and they only believed the Scriptures as far as they considered them agreeable to reason. [2]

The *Apostolicks* said that many Christians in their day had more knowledge than the Apostles, and that a salvation had been revealed which had been unknown to the Apostles.   In a short time God was going to raise up Apostles endued with infallible gifts.   Miracles had not ceased, but were essential to that administration which was given in the commission to baptize. [3]

The *Revealers* appeared as a new sect in Hampshire during the Civil Wars and the Commonwealth.   The name for them is Comber's; he did not know whether they called themselves by any particular appellation.   The founder was a man named Franklin, who claimed visions, revelations, and the gift of prophecy.   His chief proselytes, Spradbury, a minister named Woodward and his wife, and some others, were commanded by visions and voices to join themselves to him, and they were all similarly instructed to go to the land of Ham, which they interpreted as Hampshire.   They had a prophetess, Mary Gadbury, whom the uncharitable declared to be Franklin's mistress. She had voices and revelations and trembling fits, and pronounced him to be God, Christ, and the Lamb that was slain. She spoke slightingly of the Scriptures, though she delivered her revelations in scriptural language, and she called herself the Queen, the Bride, the Lamb's wife, and the Spouse of Christ. [4] This sect, however, had probably come to an end by the Restoration.

The *Virgin Life People* were in existence in 1650. [5]   They were still to be found in 1706, but except that their name seems to imply ascetic principles, no more can be said about them.

---

[1] Pagitt, " Heresiography," p. 94.
[2] " A Relation of Several Heresies," 1646; Edwards, " Gangraena," 1646; Ross, " Pansebeia," 1653, but omitted from 1683 edition; Pagitt, " Heresiography," 1661.   [3] " A Relation of Several Heresies," 1646.
[4] Comber, " Christianity No Enthusiasm," 1678, p. 94.
[5] A. Gordon, " Origin of the Muggletonians," *Trans. Liverpool Lit. and Phil. Soc.,* 1869.

The *Enthusiasts* were said to shun Behmenism, but either believed in, or waited for an infallible prophetic spirit, which would be manifested in an infallible living judge, but not, however, the Pope.[1] Comber referred to them as Seekers,[2] but the title otherwise would fit the Ranters, or several other bodies of sectarians.

During the Commonwealth time one Thomas Moore founded at King's Lynn a sect which was known as the *Manifestarians*, or *Mooreans*, and spread through the neighbouring district. They believed that Christ would shortly manifest Himself upon earth, and that their opponents, the Quakers in particular, were of the spirit of Antichrist. Except that they took their name from a particular founder, they seem to have had few distinguishing features. Edwards speaks of Arminians or Manifestarians,[3] so that they probably inclined to Arminianism.

The rest of the sects mentioned by different writers of the period are mere names. The *Perfects, Perfectists,* or *Perfectionists* suggest their tenets by their appellation.[4] *Mennonists* were the Mennonite Baptists of the Low Countries, and there is no evidence of their existence in England during either the Commonwealth or the Restoration periods. *Pelagianism* was a school of thought, or, still more likely, a term of abuse for the doctrines of those who were not thorough-going Calvinists in respect to the doctrine of total depravity. *Arminians* and *Latitudinarians* represented two schools of thought in the Church of England and among the more orthodox Nonconformist bodies, while *Dippers* in all probability was a nickname for the Baptists; and the *Divorcer*,[5] who held that men might put away their wives for even slight causes, was easily to be found among the Familists and Ranters.

NOTE TO CHAPTER VI.

The following is a list of the translations of Behmen's works published in England during the seventeenth century.

" Two Theosophical Epistles : Wherein the Life of a True Christian is described." London, 1645.

" Forty Questions concerning the Soul." (The Clavis or Key.) Trans. by J. Sparrow. London, 1647.
        (Republished with a Life, 1665.)

" The Way to Christ Discovered," in three Treatises. London, 1648.
        (Reissued in 1656. Reprinted at Canterbury in 1894.)

[1] " The Great Plot for Restoring Popery," 1663.
[2] " Christianity No Enthusiasm," 1678.
[3] " Gangraena," 1646.
[4] Edwards, " Gangraena," 1646; Chamberlayne, " Present State of England," 8th ed., 1674, p. 39.
[5] Ross, " Pansebeia," 1653, omitted from 1683 edition; Pagitt, " Heresiography," 1661.

" Concerning the Three Principles of the Divine Essence, of the Eternal, Dark, Light, and Temporary World." Trans. by J. Sparrow. London, 1648.

" Mercurius Teutonicus, or Christian Information concerning the Last Times . . . gathered out of the Mystical Writings of Jacob Behmen." London, 1649.
    (Reprinted with a new title-page in 1656 and 1664.)

" Epistles." Trans. by John Ellistone. 35 Epistles. 3 Parts, London, 1649.

" Signatura Rerum; or, the Signature of all Things, shewing the Sign and Significance of the Several Forms and Shapes in the Creation." Trans. by John Ellistone. London, 1651.

" Of Christ's Testaments. Baptism and the Supper." Translated by J. Sparrow. London, 1652.

" A Consideration upon the Book of E. Stiefel, of the threefold State of Man and his New Birth. A theosophic Epistle . . . Wherein the Life of a True Christian is described." London, 1653.

" Mysterium Magnum. An Exposition of the Book of Genesis." Translated by Ellistone and Sparrow. 3 Parts. London, 1654.

" The Tree of Christian Faith." London, 1654.

" Four Tables of Divine Revelation." Trans. by H. Blunden. London, 1654.

" A Consolatory Treatise of the Four Complexions." Trans. by C. Hotham. London, 1654.

" Of the Election of Grace." Trans. by J. Sparrow. London, 1655.

" Aurora, that is, the Dayspring or Dawning of the Day in the Orient, or Morning Redness in the Rising of the Sun; that is, the Root or Mother of Philosophy, Astrology, and Theology from the True Ground." London, 1656.

" The Fifth Book of the Author," in 3 Parts. Trans. by J. Sparrow. London, 1659.

" Several Treatises " of J. Behme. (1) A Book of the great Six Points; as also a small Book of other Six Points. (2) The 177 theosophic Questions: the first thirteen answered. (3) Of the Earthly and Heavenly Mystery. (4) The Holy Week, or a Prayer Book. (5) Of Divine Vision. To which are annexed the Exposition of the Table of the Three Principles; also an Epistle of the Knowledge of God and of all Things. Englished by J. Sparrow. 8 Parts. London, 1661.

" The Remainder of the Books written by J. Behme." Englished by J. Sparrow. London, 1662.

" Jacob Behmen's Theosophic Philosophy unfolded; also the Principal Treatises Abridged." By E. Taylor, with a Short Account of his Life. London, 1691.

VII

THE FOREIGN PROTESTANTS IN ENGLAND

THE Protestants of France had been permitted since 1577 to build houses for public worship, though they were not allowed to call them churches, but only " temples." Their chief liberties, however, came from what is usually known as the Edict of Nantes, or, as Henry IV himself expressed it, " Letters of Edict for the establishment of good order and peace between our Catholic subjects and those of the pretended Reformed Religion." The document was issued in April 1598, and consisted of a preamble and ninety-two articles, and was followed next month by fifty-six additional articles. To what extent the Huguenots attempted to set up a Protestant state within the border of the French monarchy, and how far they may have abused the liberties granted to them, it is not necessary for us here to consider. The death of Mazarin in 1661 ushered in a period during which those liberties suffered continual curtailment and many of the " temples " were either destroyed or handed over to the Roman Church; in fact between 1661 and 1673 the Protestants were said to have lost at least half of these buildings on mere pretexts like lack of title-deeds, or an alleged confiscation during the civil wars. Similarly the Protestant colleges and academies were suppressed. The theological colleges at Saumur, Sedan, Montauban, Nismes, Montpellier, and Die were of university rank. Oxford and Cambridge recognised their degrees and admitted their graduates *ad eundem.* Stephen Le Moyne, minister at Rouen, and subsequently Professor of Theology at Leyden, received the D.D. of Oxford in 1676. Samuel de l'Angle, of Rouen and Pau, and afterwards prebendary of Canterbury, was admitted to the D.D. in the same university in 1683, without payment of fees, and the same degree was conferred in 1685 on James Le Prix, formerly Professor of Divinity at Saumur, in 1686 on René Bertheau, formerly of the University of Montpellier, in 1687 on James d'Allemagne, a French minister in England, while in the same year the degree of B.C.L. was granted to Elias Boherel, formerly of Saumur.[1] Henri Justel, a refugee who was created D.C.L. by the University of Oxford, was appointed Keeper of the King's Library at St. James's.[2]

[1] Smiles, " Huguenots," p. 307; Wood, " Athenæ," *passim.*
[2] Evelyn, " Diary," ed. Austin Dobson, III. 122.

The pick of the French Protestant scholars were the equals of any men in the learned world of Europe, and Englishmen like William Penn went to their colleges to be educated, but they were all closed one by one.[1]

For nearly a hundred years Walloon and French Protestants had been flocking to England and establishing congregations in various places. For mutual discussion of matters affecting them all, the Dutch, French, and Protestant churches in England held synods from time to time. The Walloons and French also, for the purpose of settling matters of faith and discipline, held colloques or conferences, at which each congregation was represented by a minister and an elder. Between 1581 and 1660 thirty of these colloques had been held at various places in England, but as various congregations died out or joined the Church of England the colloques diminished in numbers and importance. In the case of disputes between the members and ministers of a congregation, appeal could be made and frequently was made, to the Bishop of London, but in some cases the King was appealed to directly. Amongst the documents of the old Threadneedle Street church there are several under the sign manual of Charles II,[2] dealing with matters that had been submitted to him.

On June 18th, 1660, the ministers and elders of the Dutch, French, and Italian churches waited on the King at Whitehall. M. Stouppe, minister of the French church, made a speech to which the King gave a gracious answer. A letter of Stouppe's dated ten days after this said that he had heard from France that some of the learned Protestants in France, and some of the Professors in Leyden, were writing on behalf of the lawfulness of episcopacy, and that if the King would write to the Assembly in Charenton in July next, there would be no doubt of their approving his purpose to settle episcopacy in England.[3] Some of the French Protestants were certainly not against either the use of the Prayer Book or government by bishops. Kennet quotes a letter written to him just after the Restoration by M. Martel, minister of the church of Montauban, and Divinity Reader in the University, favouring the use of the Prayer Book,[4] and he also refers to a letter to Brevint written by M. Le Moyne, asserting the excellence of the Church of England and the necessity of episcopal government.[5]

Jean Baptiste Stouppe, who made the speech at the presentation of the above-mentioned address to the King, was a native of Grisons, and a pastor of the French church in London. During the Commonwealth he was sent to France by Cromwell to sound the French Huguenot leaders as to the possibility of a

[1] Agnew, " Protestant Exiles from France," I. 25.
[2] Burn, " Hist. For. Prot. Refugees," p. 29.
[3] Rennet, " Reg.," p. 187.   [4] *Ibid.*, p. 190.   [5] *Ibid.*, pp. 463, 466.

Protestant rising if England joined with Spain against that country. Condé, who was living in the Spanish Netherlands, had advocated this alliance, and had assured Cromwell that the Huguenots would rise, but Stouppe, however, soon found that there was no likelihood whatever of their doing so.[1] At the Restoration it soon became clear that he could not stay in England. The Royalists hated him as an agent of Cromwell, and amongst the State Papers of 1661 is a document to the effect that Mr. Stouppe, an intelligencer of the late Government, had gone abroad a second time within the year without licence, and that he was to be dismissed and forbidden to return.[2] A similar notice was sent to the French church at Canterbury, where apparently Stouppe had hoped to serve, ordering them neither to admit nor use him as a minister. He ultimately became a brigadier in the French army.[3] Burnet, who met him in Paris in 1686, said he was then rather no Papist than a good Protestant.[4]

There had been a French church in England for many years. Edward VI had allowed the foreign Protestants to worship in the church of the Augustine Friars, with John à Lasco as Superintendent, and the building became known as the Temple of Jesus. Some time after it was found difficult for the French and Dutch to worship together, and so they were granted by the Dean and canons of Windsor a lease of the old chapel of St. Anthony's hospital in Threadneedle Street. This became the French church, the other remaining with the Dutch, though for a long time they seem to have had some mutual rights in each other's buildings and some joint system of contributions. The first entry in the books of the French church is in 1599. This Threadneedle Street church was attended by French Calvinists, and observed the services and customs of the Calvinist churches in France.

In the September after the King's return the ministers, elders, and deacons of the French congregation in London petitioned Charles for protection, and for confirmation of their privileges. They told the King that when they presented the congratulatory address he had desired them to recall M. Herault, their former minister, who had been obliged to flee the country during the Commonwealth, and although at the time they had three other pastors, they had done so. They took the opportunity of complaining of the existence of a rival French congregation in the chapel of Somerset House. The use of this chapel, however, had now been forbidden them, and the petitioners begged that no other place should be granted. The separatists

[1] Agnew, " Protestant Exiles from France," I. 25.
[2] C.S.P.D., Aug. 23rd, 1661.   [3] Agnew, I. 25.
[4] Foxcroft, " Supplement to Burnet," pp. 229–230.

had not been established by any lawful authority, they had
received persons who were liable to censure, and to allow the
separation to continue would weaken the French congregation
as a whole, and would lessen the available contributions for the
maintenance of the ministry and the poor, thus frustrating the
King's kindness in recalling M. Herault.   They expressed them-
sclves willing, however, to meet the convenience of the separated members by establishing a Sunday lecture for them, if the
French Protestants of the district so desired.[1]

This other French congregation seems to have come into
existence in the following way.   Somewhere about 1640 or
1641 the Duc de Soubise, finding it difficult, because of his age
and infirmities, to go as far as Threadneedle Street to church,
was accustomed to have a French service in his own house every
Sunday.   The French who lived in the Westminster district
found it convenient to attend this service, and after the Duke
was dead they determined to establish a French chapel in the
Strand.   M. Jean d'Espagne, a distinguished French minister,
and author of several important works,[2] had been in the habit
of preaching at Lady Annandale's house [3] and had kept this
French congregation together.   Parliament in 1653 had granted
them the use of the Somerset House chapel, and M. Kerhuel
and M. Hierosme ultimately succeeded d'Espagne as pastors.[4]
But Somerset House was now intended for the Queen-Mother,[5]
so they petitioned the King for a portion of the Savoy hospital
as a place of worship.   When the King granted this, the French
people were able to take their choice of joining this congregation, or uniting with what was called the Walloon congregation
in Threadneedle Street.[6]

On May 10th, 1661, the King wrote to the ministers and
elders of the French congregation in Westminster, giving them
permission to meet in the hospital of the Savoy, provided that
they submitted to the Church of England, used the Book of
Common Prayer in a French translation, which was already in
existence and in use in the Channel Islands, and were ministered
to by pastors approved of by the King and instituted by the
Bishop of London.   He commanded them not to meet without
lawful authority, and promised that he personally would pay
the salary of Durel, who was to be their minister.[7]   A meeting

---

[1] C.S.P.D., Sept. 18th, 1660, 16/82.
[2] " Reformation de quelques passages de la Bible," " An Essay on the
Wonders of God in the Harmony of Times, Generations and Events," a treatise
on the use of numbers in Scripture.
[3] C.S.P.D., Sept. 18th, 1660, 16/82.
[4] Pepys, " Diary," Feb. 24th, 1664.
[5] C.S.P.D., Sept. 28th, 1660, 16/83.
[6] Burn, " Hist. For. Prot. Refugees," pp. 108–110; Durel, " Government
in the Reformed Churches," 1662, pp. 73–74.
[7] C.S.P.D., 32/36.

of the ministers and elders and the heads of the families in the congregation was called to consider this. Two or three refused to submit to the King's wishes, and a few thought that the ministers and elders should communicate with the leading divines of the Reformed churches of France and Geneva, to know whether they might with a good conscience do what was asked of them. Hierosme, one of their two ministers, spoke strongly in favour of accepting the King's offer, and declared that it was an opportunity of clearing the Reformed churches of France from the aspersion that they condemned the principles and practices of the Church of England. It was agreed to submit to the English Church, to send a deputation to express their thanks to the King, and to wait on the Bishop of London and accept him as their pastor.[1]

It was now left free for those who had any doubts to communicate with the consistory of the Reformed church of Paris, with that of Geneva, and with the ministers and elders of Bordeaux, and to inquire whether they approved. The consistory of Paris, as such, made no reply, on the ground that there was no question in the matter, inasmuch as the French churches had always maintained communion and good relationship with the Church of England, but individual ministers acquainted with the facts held that there ought to be no scruple in the matter of uniting with the Church of England. Drelincourt, one of the Paris ministers, wrote to Durel to tell him this. Gaches, another minister at Charenton, wrote to Hierosme expressing his approval. The Princess de Turenne, to whose father, the Duc de la Force, Durel had been till recently chaplain, writing to the latter in general commendation, expressed her pleasure that he was going to translate the Prayer Book into French, and thanked him for a promise of fifty copies. She added " There is not one left of the old edition in our booksellers' shops, and everybody seeks after them. I have promised some to several persons. I gave the last I had to M. Drelincourt." [2] M. Chabret, one of the most distinguished ministers at Geneva, expressed the opinion of his consistory that there could be no objection to the use of the form of liturgy observed in the island of Jersey. He seemed to think, however, that it consisted chiefly of Morning and Evening Prayer, with the Collects, Epistles, and Gospels, and hinted some nervousness as to whether Archbishop Laud's revision were intended.[3] The Protestants of Bordeaux did not directly express their approval, merely because they feared that the establishment of the new place of worship at Westminster might injure the old Walloon congregation, but two of their leaders, M. Goyon and M. Rondelet, wrote privately

[1] Durel, " A View of the Government and Public Worship of God in the Reformed Churches," 1662, pp. 74–75.
[2] Durel, pp. 71–81. [3] Ibid., pp. 81–86.

to express this, and to assure their correspondents that the Anglican system had in no way thereby been condemned.[1] De l'Angle of Rouen and Du Bose of Caen denied the rumour that they were opposed to the scheme,[2] the latter saying, " You shall be as dear to me under the surplice of England as under the robe of France." [3] Durel's own work published a little later in 1662, " A View of the Government and Public Worship of God in the Reformed Churches beyond the Seas," was an attempt to prove the essential unity between the Church of England and the foreign Reformed churches, both in doctrine and ceremonies, and to show from the writings and practice of the continental Protestants that in the matters wherein there were differences, they did not pretend that the English Church ought to conform to their ways, nor did they ever desire the abolition of the Anglican form of church government, or of the Book of Common Prayer, but, on the contrary, they approved of both. Representatives of the foreign Protestant churches in London which did not conform to the Church of England, nevertheless had preached for them at the Savoy. Herault, of the Walloon congregation, Bresmal of the Italian, Escosier of the Piedmontese Church, Gaillard, Reader in Divinity at Mont-auban, were among these, and none had taken any objection to the service.[4] It might be added that on Sunday, January 12th, 1661, M. Morus, minister of the Reformed church in Paris, preached in St. James's Chapel Royal.[5] The French Government thought differently about the Prayer Book. At the end of 1661 or thereabouts an edition was being printed at Paris, but the authorities confiscated the whole impression as prejudicial to the Church of Rome.[6]

With the consent and approval of the King, an agreement was made between the authorities of the hospital of the Savoy and the representatives of the French church in Westminster, by which the dormitory and other portions of the grounds and building were leased to the latter for the practice of the Reformed religion.[7] The Prayer Book was used for the first time by the congregation on July 14th, 1661, and sermons were preached by Durel and Le Couteur, Dean of Jersey. The congregation that day included the Duke and Duchess of Ormonde, the Dowager Countess of Derby, the Countess of Ossory, the Earls of Stafford, Newcastle, and Devonshire, Lord Cavendish, the Vice-Chamberlain and his family, and others.[8] The church became one of the fashionable west end churches, attended both by the English and French nobility and gentry, and noted

---

[1] Durel, pp. 87–91.   [2] *Ibid.*, pp. 70–71, 90–91.
[3] See also Kennet, " Reg.," 447–448, 474–476, 483.   [4] Durel, p. 92.
[5] Kennet, " Reg.," p. 360; Evelyn, " Diary."
[6] Kennet, " Register," p. 637.
[7] Burn, " Hist. For. Prot. Refugees," p. 109.   [8] *Ibid.*, p. 110.

for the excellence of the preaching. Samuel Pepys visited it in 1662. " To the French church in the Savoy, where they have the Common Prayer Book read in French, and what I never saw before, the minister to preach with his hat off, I suppose in further conformity with our church." [1] Usually the ministers of the French church preached with their hats on. The Dutch did not.[2] Durel's sermon on the first day of the use of the Prayer Book was published with Sheldon's approval in the following year, under the title of " The Liturgy of the Church of England Asserted," dedicated to the Marquis of Ormonde, and prefaced by extracts from the letters of five French Protestant ministers abroad.

In 1662 a pamphlet was issued anonymously and with no printer's name, bearing the title " Confessions and Proofs of Protestant Divines of Reformed Churches, that Episcopacy is in the respect of the Office according to the Word of God, and in respect of the Use the Best." It asserted that English episcopacy had been justified by the confession of the most learned Protestants of foreign churches, and especially by the church of Geneva, that episcopal prelacy was acknowledged by the leading divines of those churches to be according to the Word of God and agreeable to primitive antiquity, that episcopacy was the best form of government by the consent of many of the divines of other Reformed churches, and that the most Protestant churches professed and practised a prelacy over presbyters. In a series of twenty-seven theses the writer went over the whole ground of debate with reference to episcopal government in the church, fortifying his argument wherever possible from the writings of foreign Protestant scholars.

In the Act of Uniformity a clause was inserted in favour of the Dutch and French Protestant churches, but some of the congregations felt that this did not sufficiently secure them from possible penalties for Nonconformity. A case for the foreign Protestant churches was therefore drawn up, and presented to Parliament in 1662, praying " that a proviso or clause might be added to the bill then depending, which would free " their members and enable them to continue services in French and Dutch.[3] The Act finally provided " that the penalties in this Act shall not extend to the foreigners or aliens of the foreign Reformed churches, allowed, or to be allowed by the King's Majesty, his heirs and successors." Thomas Woodcock, ejected from St. Andrew's, Undershaft, said the French refugees did not pity, but censured the 2000 ejected, and complained that they used the liturgy, surplice, and ceremonies, " so futile and fickle is the French genius." [4]

[1] " Diary," Sept. 24th, 1662.
[2] Pope, " Life of Bishop Ward," 1697, p. 115.
[3] Moens, " Walloon Church of Norwich," Hug. Soc. London, I. 108.
[4] Calamy, II. 44, III. 62; Camden, " Miscellany," XI. 59.

Evelyn noted in 1670, " A stranger preached at the Savoy French church, the liturgy of the Church of England being now used altogether, as translated into French by Dr. Durel." [1] In the same year M. de Breval, an eloquent ex-Capuchin, was appointed as one of the ministers, but on special terms. He was not to interfere with the salaries of de l'Angle, Dumaresque, and the other ministers, and he was not to share in the royal benevolence which had been granted to them. The present ministers were to maintain their rights of seniority, and in the event of the death of Durel, de l'Angle was to succeed him. [2] In February 1672 Evelyn heard Breval preach in Westminster Abbey. [3]

The French church in the Savoy seems to have suffered financially in the years following the Fire. In June 1675 there was made to the dean and chapter of Westminster a grant of an annuity of £60 to be paid out of the Exchequer, which sum was to be equally divided among the preaching ministers of the Savoy church, in addition to the grant already made them by the King's Order in Council. [4] The fact seems to be that in spite of the immigration some of the foreign Protestant communities suffered a constant drain in numbers. The members and their children, especially those born in England, tended to become absorbed in the ordinary parish congregations. Others married into English families, and became English to all intents and purposes. Those naturalised by the Act of 1673 had to give proof of having received the sacrament according to the rites of the Church of England. James II insisted on the same thing. Sometimes, when trade was depressed, some of them went to other countries such as Holland, evidence of which is seen in the entries referring to certificates of good conduct granted them by the consistories on their departure.

The King seemed to have a great deal of trouble over the appointment of ministers in some of these congregations. In 1680 we find him writing to the ministers and pastors of the Savoy congregation. He had heard that they had appointed the Sieur d'Allemagne as minister on probation for twelve months. He expressed his approval, but gave orders that they should choose no one else as minister during that period, and at the end of that time the appointment should be confirmed unless the probationer should have given good grounds for not doing so. [5] The Savoy congregation has lasted until our day, but the building has been sold within recent years.

The French church in Threadneedle Street was entirely destroyed by the Great Fire, and was rebuilt at a cost of £3300.

---

[1] Evelyn, " Diary," March 20th, 1670.
[2] C.S.P.D., May 11th, 1670, 275/107.   [3] " Diary."
[4] Hist. MSS. Com. Finch. MSS., II. 24.
[5] C.S.P.D., April 5th, 1680, Entry Book 57, p. 17.

The French congregation tried in vain to get the Dutch Protestants in Austin Friars to subscribe, inasmuch as they had some rights connected with the building. The new church was opened for services in August 1669. It remained standing until 1840, when it was purchased by the corporation and pulled down in order to open up the approaches to the Royal Exchange, and a new church was opened in 1843, in St. Martin-le-Grand, near the General Post Office.[1]

Louis Herault, whom the King had insisted on as a pastor of the Threadneedle Street congregation at the Restoration, belonged to a family in Normandy, where he had once been a minister. Coming to England, he became a pastor of the Threadneedle Street church in 1643, but was so zealous for the King when the troubles broke out that he had to flee the country. He returned at the Restoration, and after the Great Fire, in which the church was burnt down, he petitioned Charles for some preferment, because he had grown old, and his flock had become so poor by reason of the fire that they could not give him the necessary salary. He prayed that he might have the next vacant prebend in Windsor or Westminster, and he even sent the King a written declaration of His Majesty's intention to grant him one of these, and prayed that he would add to it " but seven letters, the number of perfection, CHARLES." [2] In 1668 he seems to have received some preferment from the Bishop of St. Asaph.[3]

In 1676 there was a dispute between Herault and the consistory of the French Protestants in London. It began in 1671 with their choice of Marc Michel Michely as one of the ministers in Threadneedle Street. Herault had protested against their disregard of a minister named Bonhomme recommended by the King, and they were very angry with him, turned him out of the consistory, took away his pension, and inhibited him from ministering. Michely was now dead, but the trouble was still going on, and Herault begged the King to refer the matter to the Bishop of London, which was done. The Bishop inquired into the trouble and made a report to the King, in which he said that Herault had been a faithful minister and loyal subject. The King issued an express order to the consistory to fulfil the agreement regarding his pension, and bade them publish this order and a declaration of Herault's innocence of the charges laid against him at the service on the following Sunday, and also to register it in their archives.[4] The proceedings in the consistory seem to have been very heated. M. David Prime-

---

[1] Burn, " Hist. For. Prot. Refugees," p. 26; Kershaw, " For. Prots.," pp. 75–78.
[2] C.S.P.D., December ?, 1666.
[3] C.S.P.D., August 5th, 16/68.
[4] C.S.P.D., May 22nd, 1676; S.P.D. Entry Book 27 f. 84, June 1676, 382/194.

rose, one of the ministers, had advised them to appease Herault before the matter should come to the knowledge of the King, and some of them insolently demanded if he were also one of those who ran after or adored the Beast.[1] Herault died a canon of Canterbury, and was buried in the cathedral there in 1682.[2]

A Walloon church had been established at Canterbury in the reign of Edward VI, and Queen Elizabeth had in 1574 given the members leave to use the crypt of the cathedral as a place of worship. During the Commonwealth a good deal of factiousness displayed itself among them, and in 1657 a number of them, failing to obtain the election of Pierre Jannon as minister of the congregation, had seceded, and held their services in one of the parish churches. In 1661 the mayor and aldermen of Canterbury, acting under instructions from the King, brought about a reconciliation between the two parties, and they joined again, with Jannon as one of the ministers of the reunited congregation. But in a few months there was trouble again, because Jannon had tried to get Jean Stockart[3] appointed as one of the ministers. Philippe Le Queux, who had been pastor of the crypt congregation since 1654, was leader of the opposition to Jannon, and was described by his adversaries as an enemy to the Church and the King, who had called the Prayer Book a book of fables. Jannon and his party, estimated at 500 members, on the other hand, declared their loyalty, professed great readiness to obey the Prayer Book, and petitioned the King that Le Queux and his followers might be deprived of the use of the crypt till they conformed, and that they themselves might have the sole use of it.[4] The King referred the matter to the dean and chapter for investigation, and they procured a royal order to put Jannon and the conformists in possession. Le Queux's party issued a printed sheet. "The Case concerning the Walloons of Canterbury," which was presented to the Privy Council, and in which they declared that their party was four times as large as the other, and contained the ablest and wealthiest men. There is reason to believe that at this time there were only 700 in the two congregations together.[5] In 1665, however, their number was estimated at 1300.[6] The royal order was enforced, and the Jannon party gained the sole right to the use of the crypt.[7] The leaders of the ejected went to London at once to beg Charles to allow them another preaching place in Canterbury, but were followed by a letter from Jannon to the King complaining that they were ill-conducted,

[1] C.S.P.D., 382/195; Burn, " Hist. For. Prot. Refugees," p. 35; Rev. xiii. 1.
[2] Kershaw, " For. Prots.," p. 78.
[3] Rector of St. Alphege, Canterbury, 1663–1709.
[4] C.S.P.D., August 2nd, 1661.
[5] Cross, " Hist. Walloon and Huguenot Churches at Canterbury," p. 136.
[6] Burn, " Hist. For. Prot. Refugees," p. 39.
[7] C.S.P.D., October 12th, 1661.

abused the Prayer Book, and that those of them who were
employers of labour had dismissed poor journeymen from their
service on the sole ground of being conformists.[1]

By the intercession of the French church in London with
Canon Pierre du Moulin and Meric Casaubon, Le Queux was
for a short time permitted by the chapter to preach in the
crypt on Sunday afternoons, but Jannon again appealed to the
King, and the permission had to be withdrawn.[2] The question
of another place being granted to the dissentients for their
meetings was referred to the dean and canons,[3] and to the
mayor and magistrates, in the latter case the ejected being
heard by counsel.[4] The King wrote in September 1662 that
these divisions among the Canterbury Walloons had been going
on for twenty years, and that the chapter had found the differences irreconcilable, and that the Le Queux party were really
Independents, and met like fanatics in private houses, and the
mayor and magistrates were to punish those who would not
conform. He offered that if they should choose a new minister
jointly with the other party, they should be freed from taxes
for the English poor, and be allowed to maintain their own
poor, and their books and communion plate should be restored
to them by the churchwardens.[5] The question of the support
of the poor seems to have been a point in dispute. The Privy
Council next directed the Solicitor-General, Sir Heneage Finch,
to try the case, with the assistance of Sir Thomas Peyton, the
Recorder. They summoned before them the representatives of
each party, and finally terms of agreement were drawn up,
which were embodied in an Order in Council issued on November
14th. They were to unite in one congregation, to elect a new
minister to be approved by the whole body, to conform to the
Church of England, and to maintain their own poor. On these
conditions they were to be allowed the usual place of meeting
near the cathedral. Further, to avoid the penalties of the
Act of Uniformity, they should be declared a part of the foreign
Reformed churches, and they should not be taxed for any poor
but their own.[6] Both the contending pastors then resigned,
and after some time Elie Paul d'Arande was elected. He was
a Fellow of Pembroke College, Oxford, and had held three
curacies in the English church, from the last of which, May-
field, he had been ejected in 1662. He held the pastorate of
the Walloon church from 1664 to 1670.[7] The service was
according to the usages of the Reformed church of France, and
as the worshippers were Calvinist in doctrine, and Presbyterian

---

[1] C.S.P.D., October 18th, October 21st, 1661.   [2] Cross, p. 135.
[3] C.S.P.D., March 20th, 1662.   [4] Cross, p. 135.
[5] C.S.P.D., September 3rd, 1662.   [6] C.S.P.D., November 14th, 1662.
[7] Cross, "Walloon and Huguenot Churches at Canterbury," Hug. Soc.
London, XV. 134-137; Burn, " Hist. For. Prot. Refugees," p. 45.

in their ideas of church government, the Prayer Book was not used till the end of the eighteenth century.[1] About the middle of the Restoration period the prosperity of the Walloon community in Canterbury considerably decreased. Trade had been very bad, and as the number of fresh refugees increased, a great burden was thrown on the funds, so much so that in 1680 the consistory decided it was necessary to reduce the salaries of their pastors.[2] All this time their numbers were increasing. There were 1300 in 1665, 1500 in 1676, and in 1679 it was stated before the judges of assize that the congregation contained 2500 communicants.[3] They occupied themselves in weaving and other trades, and provided work for a great number of poor English people in Canterbury; moreover, they were universally regarded as a sober, industrious people who maintained their own poor without allowing them to become a burden on the city.[4]

In or before 1666 a second pastor had been appointed to the Walloon congregation which met in the crypt of Canterbury. This was M. Vital Delon. In 1676 an attempt was made by the consistorial court of Canterbury to interfere with their privileges. Delon had solemnised in the crypt a marriage between John Six and Mary de Houcq, a son and daughter of refugees, and the vicar-general claimed that as the parties were born in England their banns ought to have been published in the parish church. This question had previously been raised in 1637. They were summoned before the vicar-general's court, and excommunicated on a charge of marrying clandestinely, while Delon himself was suspended. They appealed to the Privy Council, and a Royal order was issued in their favour.[5] The Canterbury Huguenots still meet in the Black Prince chantry in Canterbury cathedral, and to-day have the unique distinction of being the only nonconforming congregation which holds its services in an Anglican building.

At Southampton there was a congregation of Walloons, French, and Channel Islanders as early as the reign of Edward VI. They were put in possession of an old church near the harbour, known as the chapel of St. Julian, or, better still, as God's House of Southampton. It is said that in 1665 a great number of the inhabitants and clergy of the place fled from the town on account of the plague. M. Courand, the French pastor, however, stood in the breach. On July 23rd, by the authority of the mayor, an English child was brought to God's

[1] Burn, "Hist. For. Prot. Refugees," p. 51; C.S.P.D., May 11th, 1676, 381/110; Kershaw, "For. Prots.," p. 132.
[2] Cross, "Walloon and Huguenot Churches at Canterbury," p. 139.
[3] Burn, "Hist. For. Prot. Refugees," p. 39.
[4] C.S.P.D., May 11th, 1676, 381/110.
[5] Agnew, "Protestant Exiles from France," I. 26; Cross, "Walloon and Huguenot Churches at Canterbury," p. 139.

House to be baptised, and several English couples were married there also, and there was besides a second case of baptism. M. Courand himself died of the plague in September of the same year.[1] The French translation of the Prayer Book was not adopted here till 1712, after which the church was known as French Protestant episcopal.

There were two foreign congregations at Norwich, one Dutch and one French. The Dutch congregation was under the spiritual jurisdiction of the Bishop of Norwich, and therefore, it is to be presumed, conformed to the Church of England. The Walloon congregation certainly did not. Jacques Le Franc, the minister of the latter congregation, left them in 1664, and four years later, as James Le Frank, accepted a benefice in the Church of England. In 1669 the French congregation at Norwich was in such difficulties that a meeting of the ministers, elders, and deacons was called to consider what should be done. Even the more well-to-do members were not contributing as they should. It was decided that Onias Philippo should be deputed to petition the King in Council to grant them power to compel their members to pay their due share to the funds.[2] In 1684 or thereabouts Pierre Chauvin became pastor. He was in Anglican orders, and frequently preached in the English churches. In 1686 he complained to the Bishop of Norwich about the congregation, and said there had been trouble among them for the past sixty years. They decreased and withheld his salary, they lived like Independents without law or discipline, they rebelled against his attempts to check their misdemeanours, and they even admitted Quakers to their meetings.[3] The great influx of strangers after the revocation of the Edict of Nantes made little or no difference to the French community in Norwich, for few settled here, and the congregation therefore tended to diminish slowly from natural causes.[4]

Some of the French Protestant ministers who conformed rose to high positions in the Church of England. Peter du Moulin was the eldest son of Pierre du Moulin, pastor at Charenton. He studied at Sedan and Leyden, became tutor to Richard Boyle, took orders in the Church of England, became an ardent royalist, and in 1660 was made a prebendary of Canterbury. He was the author of " Clamor Sanguinis," wrongly attributed to Milton by Alexander Morus. In 1662 he published a folio volume of 852 pages entitled " The Novelty of Popery opposed to the Antiquity of True Christianity," in answer to Cardinal Perron's work in reply to James I. The volume was dedicated to Charles II. and James, Duke of York. He also published

---

[1] Burn, " Hist. For. Prot. Refugees," p. 88; Smiles, " Huguenots," p. 140.
[2] Moens, " Walloon Church of Norwich," Hug. Soc. London, I. 108.
[3] " Publications Hug. Rec. Soc.," I. Pt. II. 237–238.
[4] Moens, " Walloon Church of Norwich," p. 108.

" A Vindication of the Sincerity of the Protestant Religion in the Point of Obedience to Sovereigns," a reply to " Philanax Anglicus." In 1675 he wrote a vindication of the French Protestants in " A Reply to a Person of Honour," who had attacked them on the ground that they suffered the English regicides to be members of their congregations, to which Du Moulin makes the somewhat feeble reply that since the doors of their temples were open to all there was nothing to prevent spies and false brethren from entering.[1]

There was another Peter du Moulin, a grandson of Pierre, who held some minor appointments at the English Court for a time. During the Dutch war of 1672–74 he engaged in intrigues with the Dutch and had to flee from the country. He took service with the Prince of Orange, and remained in Holland, at any rate till 1675, in spite of all the efforts of the English Government to obtain his extradition.[2] John Conant, the son of a Protestant refugee from Normandy, became Vice-Chancellor of the University of Oxford in 1657, archdeacon of Norwich in 1676, and prebendary of Worcester in 1681. John Durel, a Jersey man who had been educated at Merton College, Oxford, at Caen, and Saumur, had been expelled from Jersey for his share in the royalist defence of the island, and had fled to France. In Paris, in the chapel of Sir Richard Browne, the King's resident in France, he had been ordained by the Bishop of Galloway. Later he became a canon of Windsor, and was a frequent preacher at the French church in the Savoy.[3] He was the author of the French version of the English Prayer Book which was issued in 1663. On October 6th, 1662, an order had been made that the new French version of the revised Prayer Book was to be used wherever the French language was used in the King's dominions, as soon as it had been printed and approved by one of the chaplains of the Bishop of London. This approval was given on April 6th, 1663, but the book had actually been used in the Savoy before the end of 1662. A Latin version of the Prayer Book was printed in 1670; it was the work of several divines, but Durel made the final revision with the help of Sancroft.[4] In 1669 Durel published his " Sanctæ Ecclesiæ Anglicanæ adversus iniquas atque inverecundas schismaticorum criminationes vindiciæ." Evelyn noted in his " Diary " in 1679, " Dr. Durel, Dean of Windsor, preached at Whitehall and read the whole sermon out of his notes, which I had never before seen a Frenchman do."[5] Many honours and offices fell to Durel: he was made chaplain to the King,

---

[1] Bastide, " Anglo-French Entente in the Seventeenth Century," pp. 45–48.
[2] *Bulletin Institute Hist. Research*, III. 66.   [3] C.S.P.D., April 10th, 1665.
[4] C. & W. M. Marshall, " Latin Prayer Book of Charles II," Oxford, 1882.
[5] Evelyn, " Diary," February 2nd, 1679.

prebendary of Salisbury 1663, prebendary of Windsor and Durham 1664, Dean of Windsor and Wolverhampton 1677, and Registrar of the Garter. Two other divines who were expelled from Jersey were Brevint and Le Couteur. Brevint, who returned to England after the Restoration, became a prebendary of Durham, and in 1682 Dean of Lincoln. Le Couteur became Dean of Jersey.

Among the distinguished Huguenots who joined the English Church was Pierre Allix, who up to 1685 was pastor at Charenton, where was perhaps the most important of the Protestant " temples " built in France. It was destroyed in that year, and a Benedictine monastery was subsequently built on its site. Allix, after his arrival in England, published a work " Reflections on the Scriptures," dedicated to James II. Clarendon introduced him to the King, to whom he presented his book in person, and met with a very gracious reception from James.[1] He was at first connected with one of the French churches in Spitalfields. He engaged frequently in controversy with Bossuet, and also in controversies with others about the doctrine of the Trinity. He was a great oriental scholar, wrote numerous learned works in defence of Protestantism, several of which were published in England during the reign of William III., and he received the degree of D.D. both from Oxford and Cambridge. He became a canon of Canterbury.[2] M. de Luzancy, an ex-Carmelite monk, abjured the Roman Catholic religion at the Savoy in 1675, and became a minister at Harwich. Another ex-Carmelite, François de la Motte, was sent to Oxford by Secretary Williamson, and afterwards became an Anglican clergyman.[3] He preached a " recantation sermon " in the Savoy church in 1675. It was published in French and in English and dedicated to Sir Joseph Williamson, and to it were added " many curious particulars of the practices of the Papists beyond the seas."[4] Paul Colomies, grandson of a famous preacher of that name in Rochelle, was for a time librarian to Archbishop Sancroft, was ordained in the Church of England, and became vicar of Eynsford in Kent. He wrote several learned works, but in his latter years was suspected of Socinianism.[5] Jacques Abbadie, an able defender of Christianity, came to England with Schomberg in the capacity of the latter's chaplain, and afterwards was a minister in the Savoy church.[6] César Beaulieu, minister of the French congrega-

---

[1] Clarendon Diary, May 18th, 1688.
[2] Kershaw, " For. Prots.," pp. 94-95.
[3] Bastide, " Anglo-French Entente," p. 33.
[4] " The Abominations of the Church of Rome, discovered in a Recantation Sermon," 1675.
[5] Kershaw, " For. Prots.," p. 97; Bastide, " Anglo-French Entente," p. 98.
[6] Smiles, " Huguenots," p. 301.

tion at Greenwich, was recommended to the Crown in 1682 for
his loyalty to the Church of England, and Secretary Jenkins
told him that he had heard of his good report from the Bishop of
London and that he would shortly be promoted, while the
Bishop would choose a suitable person for the congregation
at Greenwich.[1]

The fact that men like these, and Drelincourt and Samuel
de l'Angle, took orders in the Church of England greatly
strengthened what afterwards became known as the Low Church
party. They had no real sympathy with the sacramental
teaching of the Book of Common Prayer, and many of them
were Calvinists, and some distinctly heterodox. They not only
agreed with the Low Churchmen in theology, but also in politics,
for the very reason which had brought them to England confirmed most of them in the Whig principles which that party
held in opposition to the High Churchmen, who were all Tories,
and most of them, at least at heart, Jacobites.

Not all the foreign refugees adopted the principles and practices of the Church of England, or retained their foreign faith
and worship. Two families, the Tyzackes and Tytorys, became
prominent amongst the Quakers at Newcastle. Owing to the
persecution of Protestants, they had left Lorraine and settled
on Tyneside, where a lease for ground, " including the glass-
houses . . . boundering on Ouseburn on the west," was granted
by the town council of Newcastle in 1638 to Sir R. Mansel,
who employed many of these refugees. Some of them became
Quakers, amongst whom were Daniel Tytory, Paul Tyzacke
and Jane, his wife, Peregrine Tyzacke and John and Sarah
Tyzacke. In 1684 John Tyzacke was imprisoned for refusing
to take the oaths. He went to London the same year, and was
tried at the Guildhall for holding a Quaker meeting near Angel
Court. The Ouseburn district in Newcastle was very largely
inhabited by Quakers occupied in the glass-making trade. In
1684 a lease of one of the glass-houses, or glass factories, was
granted by the Newcastle corporation to John Henzell, Peter
Tyzacke, and others as partners.[2]

Among the Baptists there was a foreigner who had had a
very varied career. This was Dr. Carolus Maria du Veil, who
became minister of a Particular Baptist congregation which met
in Gracechurch Street. He was born at Metz, of Jewish parents,
entered the Roman Church, and became a canon regular of
St. Augustine, and later on prior of the monastery of St. Ambrose
at Melun and Professor and Doctor of Divinity in the University
of Angers. He entered into controversy with some of the
Protestant teachers in France, left the Church of Rome, fled to

[1] S.P.D., Entry Book 53, p. 70.
[2] J. W. Steel, " Society of Friends in Newcastle and Gateshead," 1899,
p. 19.

Holland, and in 1677 to England, where he was received into the English Church. He was on terms of friendship with Tillotson, Stillingfleet, and other Anglican leaders, held a chaplaincy for a time in a nobleman's family, and did a good deal of literary work, for though he never mastered the English language sufficiently to speak it fluently, he could write it well. He was not an Anglican long, for in the library of Bishop Compton he read some of the Baptist publications, which set him inquiring again. He made the acquaintance of Hanserd Knollys, Kiffin, Keach, Gosnold, and other Baptists, and about 1680 became one himself. He practised physic for a living, wrote commentaries on some of the books of the Bible (in one of which, his commentary on St. Matthew and St. Mark, he renounced his Roman doctrines), and ministered to the Baptist congregation above mentioned. It is said that his congregation ceased to exist as a separate society soon after his death, or at least before the end of the seventeenth century. He had a brother Louis de Compiègne du Veil, Interpreter of Oriental Languages to the King of France, who also turned Protestant, and fled to England.[1]

Louis du Moulin was a younger brother of Peter du Moulin the canon of Canterbury, but, unlike him, was an Independent. In 1648 he was made Camden Professor of Ancient History at Oxford, but was, of course, ejected at the Restoration.[2] He was the author of several theological works, including " Vindiciæ Ecclesiæ Anglicanæ ad Rev. J. Cosinum," published in 1661. In 1673 he was sent to the Gatehouse for writing and publishing a treasonable and seditious work, " Patronus Bonæ Fidei," and the Attorney-General was ordered to lay all information against him at the King's Bench. He was, however, discharged after about three weeks' imprisonment.[3] In 1680 he published a pamphlet, " The Conformity of the Discipline and Government of the Independents to that of the Primitive Church." In 1657 M. Daille, the eminent French Protestant minister, in his " Vindication of his Apology for two National Synods of France," published at Amsterdam in that year, had spoken very severely of Du Moulin as a man of small judgment, great vanity, rashness, and passion. Now, twenty-three years after, some one took the trouble to republish all that Daille had said. The person who did so said that the people who defended the Reformed cause, " even that great champion of the Protestant cause amongst us, Dr. Stillingfleet," were attacked by the people who should have helped to defend them. Du Moulin in all his books accused the Church of England of leaning towards popery,[4]

[1] Wilson, " Dissenting Churches in London," I. 205–207.
[2] Wood, " Life," I. 326.
[3] C.S.P.D., June 20th, 1673, 326/15; *Bulletin Institute Hist. Research*, III. 66.
[4] *E.g.* " Advances the Church of England hath made towards Rome," 1680.

attacked men like Heylin, Thorndyke, Jeremy Taylor, and
Bramhall, and called Andrew Marvell " that great man,"
though he spoke of the Nicene Creed as " gibberish and cant."
His writings showed that the Dissenters like himself hated the
Church of England as much as the Church of Rome.[1] Du
Moulin during his last illness in October 1680 sent for Burnet
to visit him. Burnet did so, and took the opportunity of rebuking him for his bitter attacks on various Anglican divines such
as Stillingfleet, Durel, and Simon Patrick. The last, who was
now Dean of Peterborough, went to see him, and they discussed
Patrick's book, " The Parable of the Pilgrim," about which
Du Moulin had said some angry things, though he had not read
it all. Patrick told him it was very wrong of him to accuse the
Laudian party of Romanizing, seeing how loyal they were to
the Church of England. He also prayed with him, repeating
the service for the Visitation of the Sick, though without producing a Prayer Book, for which prayers the dying man was
very grateful. He asked Patrick's pardon for things he had
said about him, and a few days later signed three copies of a
retractation of the things of which he had accused some of the
clergy. He died shortly afterwards at the age of seventy-seven,
and the Dean of Peterborough buried him.[2]

Among the refugees there were numbered some distinguished
scientists. Dr. Denis Papin, one of the earlier workers at the
invention of the steam-engine, came to England in 1681, and
three years after was made Curator to the Royal Society. He
ultimately became Professor of Mathematics at the University of
Marburg. De Moivre, the mathematician, came to England in
1667. Between 1681 and 1689 at least nine French physicians
were admitted to membership of the English College of Physicians,
among them Sebastian and Joshua Le Fevre. The latter became
chemist to Charles II.[3]

The Dutch church in Austin Friars was uninjured by the Great
Fire. But the congregation suffered a great deal and the collections consequently diminished, which may account for their
refusal to help their French brethren.[4] The building is still in
the occupation of the Dutch Reformed church. Early in 1668
the Dutch Protestants living in Westminster complained to the
King that they could not without difficulty attend the Dutch
church in London, and begged that some convenient place might
be assigned to them in Westminster, where they might have
service in their own language. The King gave them permission
to find a suitable place in or about Westminster, and to have

[1] " A Lively Picture of Lewis Du Moulin," by M. Daille, 1680.
[2] " The Last Words of L. Du Moulin," 1680; " Autobiog. Simon Patrick,"
1839, pp. 85–87 ; " The Parable of the Pilgrim," Second ed., 1678.
[3] Smiles, " Huguenots," pp. 289–298.
[4] Bell, " Great Fire of London," p. 309.

as many ministers as they should think fit, provided the Book
of Common Prayer in a Dutch translation were used, and that
the names of their proposed ministers should be submitted to
the Bishop of London. The King appointed Nicholas van
Rensalaer to organise the congregation, and to continue his
ministry among them.[1]

Charles II. offered the ruined church of St. Nicholas, Cole
Abbey, to the Swedish Lutherans, if they cared to rebuild it for
themselves, but this was a parish church, and the Court of
Aldermen referred the Swedish Resident back to the King.[2]
In 1669, at the instance of the envoy of the King of Sweden,
the King gave licence to some foreign Lutherans to build a
church on the ruins of Trinity-the-Less, which had been burnt
in the Great Fire. It was intended to hold services there in
German. Having obtained this permission, they bought the
site from the Lord Mayor and Aldermen of London, built the
church and vested it in trustees. But the parishioners claimed
the site as a burial-ground, as there had been a churchyard
attached to the old building, and William Throckmorton, a
parishioner, brought an action against the minister for preventing burials there. The matter was brought before the
Privy Council, and they, after hearing counsel, ordered the suit
to be discontinued. Nevertheless Throckmorton persisted, got
damages by default, and threatened further action. In April
1675 John Leemkuel, and four other London merchants, German
born but naturalised in England, and trustees of this Protestant
Augustan church, as it was called, petitioned the King on the
matter, and they were given permission to tender to the House
of Lords a draft Bill for their relief, if they thought fit.[3] A draft
was accordingly presented, and passed the House of Lords in
an amended form on May 31st, 1675. It provided that the
freehold of the church should be vested in the trustees, but that
the churchyard was the property of the parish, a right of way
over it being granted to the German congregation. But the
Bill got no further.[4] Another draft Bill without the right of
way clause was brought in during the following November,
reached the report stage without amendment, but dropped with
the session after engrossment.[5]

In the early part of the reign of Charles I. Hatfield Chase,
a district of about 70,000 acres, was entirely under water.
Cornelius Vermuyden, a Dutchman of Zeeland, undertook to
drain it, and brought over a great many work-people from
Holland, who afterwards settled down on the reclaimed land,

[1] C.S.P.D., Entry Book 27, f. 5, March 31st, 1668.
[2] Bell, " Great Fire," p. 309.
[3] Hist. MSS. Com. IX. II. 211; Lords Journals, XII. 666.
[4] Lords Journals, XII., May 31st, 1675.
[5] Lords Journals, XIII. November 12th, 13th, 18th, 1675; Hist. MSS.
Com. IX. Pt. II. 231, 305, 320.

as did a number of French Protestants. In 1634 they built a chapel at Sandtoft, in Belton parish on the borders of Lincolnshire, and in it services were held in French and Dutch alternately. But there were many riots amongst the rough people in the district, who disliked the influx of foreigners, and the chapel was badly damaged. Right through the Commonwealth time the disorders continued, to say nothing of quarrels and dissensions among the local landowners. At the Restoration it was even suggested to exempt the people who had damaged the chapel from the benefits of the Act of Indemnity. The troubles still went on, and many of the foreign settlers left the district. In 1681 the chief of those who remained complained to the Court of Servers that they had not had a minister for five years, and that they had reason to believe many of the persecuted Protestants of France would settle in the district if there were one. The original settlers had been promised that a minister should always be provided, and that promise had been kept till a few years past. They had a well-qualified minister ready, M. Le Vaneley, and they asked for a grant of £30 a year for his maintenance. The grant was made in September, and he was appointed, but does not seem to have remained there long, for the register, now lost, ceased in 1681, and before many years the chapel was demolished.[1]

During the Dutch war Charles maintained a faithful and generous protection of the foreign Protestants. When the breach came between England and France he even in his declaration of war specially reserved his promises to them of safety and protection. For this a deputation from the French church in the Savoy waited on him to thank him early in 1666.[2] The Triple Alliance gave hopes to the French Huguenots of making headway against Louis. A Huguenot soldier of distinction, Roux de Marcilly, appeared in London in 1668 and interviewed some of the English ministers. He told them that the Protestant districts of France, Provence, Languedoc, Guienne, and even Normandy, were ready to rise against Louis at the first opportunity, and that it would be possible for the King of England, if he supported them, to get possession of those provinces.[3] But a wild-cat scheme of this kind was not likely to appeal to Charles.

A Bill for the naturalization of all Protestant strangers who might come over to England with their stocks and estates, provided that they took the oaths of allegiance and supremacy and other necessary oaths, with a reference in the preamble to the King's Declaration of June 12th, 1672, was read for the first time in the Lords on February 4th, 1673. It proposed to enact

---

[1] Burn, " Hist. For. Prot. Refugees," pp. 101–108.
[2] January 26th, 1666; Kennet, " Hist. Eng.," III. 281; Eachard, " Hist. Eng.," III. 151.
[3] Ranke, " Hist. Eng.," III. 491.

that any person, being a Christian, though born and bred beyond the seas, under foreign jurisdiction, should have all the rights of a naturalized subject, provided that he took the oaths of allegiance and supremacy, and also subscribed the declaration against transubstantiation before the chief magistrate of any town, or two justices of the peace, and could produce a certificate that he had done so. Such certificates were to be entered in a book by the Clerk of Parliaments or his deputy. But the Bill provided that the clause in the Act 12. Car. II. c. 8, which required that the master and three-fourths of the mariners navigating an English ship must be English, was to be understood of persons born within the King's allegiance and not persons naturalized.[1] The Bill went down to the Commons on February 8th, and though in the Lower House it was read the second time and committed by 108 to 61, it failed to pass the final stages, owing to the prorogation.[2] The merchants and the extreme Protestants were hostile to it.

There were some people who tried to make things difficult for the refugees even after they arrived in England. In 1677 a French Huguenot, Jacob d'Agar, made a sworn deposition before Williamson. He had tried to obtain help from the King for his children, but great efforts had been made in some quarters to prevent his doing so, on the ground that the King was displeased with persons who made charges against the Roman Catholics, and he was advised instead to make his appeal to Barillon. M. Desmaresque, one of the ministers at the Savoy, told him that what he had heard was a scandalous libel on the King and recommended him to tell Williamson. He complained that some Roman Catholics were trying to kidnap his children in order to carry them off to France, so that he had to keep them in hiding, and he pleaded for the King's protection for them.[3]

In February 1678 a petition was presented to the House of Lords from the poor French Protestants of the French church in the Savoy. It stated that the petitioners had fled from persecution by the French King, and had sought refuge in this country, where they had duly conformed to the Church of England. Having served their apprenticeships to their several trades in their own country, they had for a while enjoyed the benefit of King 'Charles's proclamation of February 9th, 1661, and laboured honestly in their callings without let or molestation. Latterly, however, they had been interfered with by the overseers, who, pretending that they had not served their apprenticeship, refused to allow them to pursue their trades

[1] Lords Journals, XII. 522.
[2] House Lords MSS. Hist. MSS. Com. IX. Pt. II. 19; Commons' Journals, IX. 250; C.S.P.D., 333/67.
[3] C.S.P.D., October 19th, 1677, 397/53.

unless they paid great fines, which they were unable to do.
They prayed that they might be allowed to follow their callings
without hindrance. The petition was read in the House on
February 20th,[1] and referred to the Committee for Petitions.
It was then withdrawn, and the Committee was ordered to
prepare a Bill for encouraging Protestant foreigners.[2]

On March 27th, 1678, a Committee on a Bill to prevent the
export of wool reported in the Commons that a Bill was desir-
able to encourage all Protestant strangers, artificers in tapestry,
or other manufactures made of or mixed with wool, to come
and settle in this kingdom, and to be naturalized on the condition of subscribing the declaration contained in the Act for
suppressing the growth of popery. The House referred the
matter to a Committee on a Bill licensing Protestant strangers
to exercise their trades in the places therein mentioned, and
ordered that the Bill should be made general so as to extend to
all Protestant strangers, and not merely those from France.[3]
On March 27th, 1678, part of the Protestant Strangers Bill
was read for the first time in the House of Lords.[4] More fully
it was entitled " An Act for empowering the licensing of Protestant
strangers and foreigners to exercise their trades in the places
mentioned in the Act." Protestant strangers and foreigners
who professed the true Protestant religion as now established
in the Church of England, being householders, and having
exercised their trade seven years after their apprenticeship,
might pursue their craft or occupation in the City of Westminster, the suburbs of the City of London, and the counties
of Middlesex, Surrey, and Essex, without molestation. But to
do so each one must obtain a licence from the justices in Quarter
Sessions, which would be granted on production of a certificate
of membership from the churchwardens of the French church
in the Savoy or the Dutch churches in London and Westminster,
a certificate showing the applicant to be a householder, and a
certificate from a public notary of having been duly apprenticed,
and of having exercised his trade seven years after the apprenticeship was ended. He must also have taken the oaths of allegiance
and supremacy.[5] An amended draft was read for the first time
on May 23rd. It provided for fourteen Commissioners who
should receive gifts of the charitably disposed for the support
of foreign Protestants, especially converts, and for the education
of their children.[6] On May 28th the Bishop of London pro-

---

[1] Lords Journals, XIII. 47.
[2] Hist. MSS. Com. IX. ii., MSS. House Lords No. 342.
[3] Commons Journals, IX.
[4] Lords Journals, XIII. 87, 105; Hist. MSS. Com. IX. ii; MSS. House
Lords, 535.
[5] Hist. MSS. Com. IX. ii.; MSS. House Lords No, 381.
[6] Lords Journals XIII. 224, Hist. MSS. Com. IX. ii ; MSS. House Lords
No. 566.

posed a clause providing for general naturalization, but this was rejected by the Committee. The Bill passed the Lords, was read for the first time in the Commons on July 11th and the second time next day, but it was rejected in the Lower House on the motion to commit it,[1] on account of the opposition of the cities of London and Westminster to it as being likely to hinder their trade.

Henry Savile, brother of Lord Halifax, and British envoy in Paris, did not hesitate to display his Protestantism in France. He attended the services at Charenton, and showed great kindness to the Huguenots. He wrote to Halifax in 1679 that in fear of persecution they would come to England in great numbers if only their naturalization were made easy. In 1681, when their troubles were becoming more severe, he wrote to Lord Halifax and Sir Leoline Jenkins, the Secretary of State, about it, urging upon the latter that hopes of naturalization should be given them, and adding that he had a number of them ready to come to England who would introduce into this country the much-needed manufacture of sailcloth. Jenkins had already urged the matter on the King, and Charles took further steps to receive and protect the refugees, and to raise money for their assistance by a public subscription. The Secretary also encouraged some of the French Protestants in England to draw up a memorial, which was presented to the King on July 21st of that year, on behalf of their persecuted brethren abroad, making some suggestions as to the steps which might be taken by the English Government. The matter was referred to the Committee of the Council for Trade and Plantations, that they should consider and report on it, which they did a week afterwards.[2]

By an Order in Council issued July 28th, 1681, the King declared himself " obliged in honour and conscience to comfort and support all such afflicted Protestants, who by reason of the rigours and severities which are used towards them on account of their religion, shall be forced to quit their native country, and shall desire to shelter themselves under His Majesty's royal protection, for the preservation and free exercise of their religion." He promised them letters of denization under the Great Seal free of expense, together with liberty and the free exercise of their trades or handicrafts. Parliament, when it met next, should be recommended to pass an Act for the general naturalization of all such Protestants. They should pay no greater taxes than the King's own subjects. They should have all the privileges and immunities of subjects for the education of their children in English schools and colleges. The Order in

---

[1] Commons Journals, IX. 459, 462, 513; Hist. MSS. Com. IX. ii. No. 608.
[2] Agnew, " Protestant Exiles from France," II. 11–13; " Savile Correspondence," p. 236.

Council further commanded all civil and military officers to give the Protestant refugees a kind reception at the ports, free passports, and assistance and furtherance on their journeys. The commissioners of customs were to let them pass free with their goods and household stuff, and tools and instruments of their craft and trade. It announced that the King had given orders for a general brief to be issued throughout England and Wales, for collecting charitable contributions on their behalf. Finally, any requests or complaints which they desired to make were to be presented to the Archbishop of Canterbury or the Bishop of London.[1] By this Order in Council making free denizens of the French refugees, 448 persons received letters of denization under Charles II., and 1700 under James II.[2]

About the same time that the Order in Council was issued, the King wrote to the Bishop of London urging that collections should be made in all the churches and chapels for the relief of the hundreds of fugitives who were coming into the country, and this was to be done for them, " not only as distressed strangers, but as persecuted Christians." The clergy should urge their parishioners to give liberally, and the bishop should see to it that relief should be given to as many necessitous persons as possible. The King wrote in a similar strain to the Lord Mayor.[3] In September he issued letters patent for a charitable collection for their relief. But men were saying that all these men were Calvinists, that their principles were inconsistent with monarchy,[4] or that they were really Papists. In October the King in Council ordered that public notice should be given that all care was being taken by the French ministers in London that no refugee should receive relief unless he could produce authentic testimonials that he was a Protestant and had received the sacrament. Furthermore, if any person could discover a Papist among the refugees, he should report it to the Bishop of London or the ministers of the French Protestant congregations.[5] Doubt was being thrown on the reality of the persecution in France, and the Bishop of London gave public testimony to the truth of a little book recently published, " The Present State of the Protestants in France." [6] Sir Leoline Jenkins, Secretary of State, wrote to the justices of Middlesex expressing the King's approbation at their zeal on behalf of the refugees, and suggesting that Clerkenwell workhouse should be used to lodge them till something better could be found. This, however, the

[1] Arber, " Torments of Protestant Slaves," 1907, pp. xxviii–xxx.
[2] State Paper Office, Various, Book No. 964; Lists of Foreign Protestants and Aliens Resident in England, 1618–1688, Camden Society.
[3] C.S.P.D., July 22nd, 28th, 1681.
[4] C.S.P.D., October 15th, 1681, 417/38.
[5] Kennet, " Hist. Eng.," III. 393.
[6] C.S.P.D., 417/275, December 19th, 1681.

justices reported to be inconvenient,[1] and they were urged to
find some other place.[2] The question of finding a dwelling-
place for these people was a serious one. The mayor and four
aldermen of Bristol wrote to the Secretary saying that many of
the new arrivals were in an indigent condition, and they had
so many of their own poor already that their funds were insufficient. They asked therefore if they might use the refugee
funds not merely for the relief of those new arrivals, but also
for the expense of sending them to such places as the King
should appoint.[3] By an Order in Council issued a few days
later, a detailed statement was to be forwarded of the number
of French Protestants in Bristol, the amount of money collected,
the places in the neighbourhood suitable for persons of their
particular handicrafts or trades, and the expense already
incurred by the city of Bristol on their behalf.[4] Writing to the
mayor on December 17th, Jenkins said that though these people
would not be imposed as a burden on any person, parish, or
county, yet the City of London had taken some hundreds in the
building intended for a pest-house, while the justices of Middlesex had assigned the new workhouse in Clerkenwell for others.
If the Bristol authorities would furnish an account of their
expenses, the Archbishop of Canterbury and the Bishop of
London would see to it that they were repaid.[5] Various suggestions were made to meet the difficulty of the sudden influx of
people into the towns. One proposal was that an industrial
colony should be established in the country. The collections
which had been raised would be sufficient to provide the buildings, the looms, and the tools, and also the upkeep for the first
three months, till it became self-supporting.[6]

On November 21st, 1681, Savile wrote to Jenkins recommending to his notice a French linen-draper who desired to
take refuge in England. The man had wound up his business
in Paris and had sent his property in specie to Dunkirk, but,
having reason to fear that it would all be seized and confiscated,
was hurrying to England without it. Savile commended him
to the Secretary, and asked him to do what he could for the
man, who would be useful in this country, inasmuch as he could
give information about introducing the manufacture of sailcloth into England. He further urged that if help were not
given to men of this kind they would betake themselves to
Holland, which would thus get the substantial tradesmen, while
we got only the poor people. The man referred to was M.

[1] C.S.P.D., November 12th, 1681, Entry Book 66, p. 19, December 10th,
417/140.
[2] Luttrell, I. 148; Kennet, " Hist. Eng.," III. 394.
[3] C.S.P.D., December 10th, 1681, 417/142.
[4] C.S.P.D., December 16th, 1681, 417/148.
[5] C.S.P.D., December 17th, 1681, Entry Book 62, p. 372.
[6] C.S.P.D., 417/279.

Bonhomme. A scheme was consequently set on foot to settle some of the refugees at Ipswich and to employ them in the linen manufacture. Money was raised to provide twenty or thirty looms, and Sir Samuel Barnardiston took a warm interest in the scheme. The townspeople, too, welcomed it and, as well as offering the new arrivals the use of one of the parish churches, they undertook to free them from rates and parochial charges.[1] Bonhomme taught the Huguenots how to make sailcloth, which in time became a very flourishing industry in the town.[2] The King wrote personally to the citizens of Ipswich to thank them for their kindness to the poor French linen-weavers.[3]

A deputation from the French church in the Savoy waited on the King in October, and one of their ministers, M. Lambert, made a somewhat fulsome speech in praise of the King's bounty, a speech, however, which gave such satisfaction that it was shortly afterwards translated and published " by His Majesty's special command."[4] Deputations from the other French churches and from the Dutch church were introduced by the Bishop of London on the same day, and after M. Lambert had departed, M. Primerose, on behalf of the others, expressed their thanks for his merciful protection. Charles received them very kindly, and told them they might rest assured of his kindness and favour.[5]

As if it were not enough to have the care of the French refugees on his shoulders, Charles in September received a petition presented by Nicholaus Minwid, who had been recommended to him by the Elector Palatine and the Elector of Brandenburg, on behalf of the distressed Protestants in Lithuania. The King passed it on to the Archbishop of Canterbury and the Bishop of London, and Secretary Jenkins advised that if there was any money in the hands of the elders of the Dutch church, or any which had been collected for the Lithuanian Protestants previously, it should be given to Minwid, if the Archbishop and Bishop approved.[6]

In 1682 the King issued another brief to the clergy for collections for the Huguenots,[7] and Wood noted in his diary that " at the latter end of March and the beginning of this month there was a collection in every college and hall, as also in every parish in Oxford, for succour and relief of poor Protestants that were lately come to England on a persecution from France. People gave liberally."[8] The King also wrote to the East India

[1] C.S.P.D., September 3rd, 1681.
[2] " Savile Correspondence," p. 236.
[3] C.S.P.D., November 18th, 1681, Entry Book 62, p. 21.
[4] " A Speech to the King: made by a Minister of the French Church in the Savoy the 19th of October, 1681."
[5] C.S.P.D., October 20th, 1681 ; Adm. Green Hosp. I. No. 145.
[6] C.S.P.D., September 15th, 1681, Entry Book 53, p. 63.
[7] Stoughton, " Hist. Rel. Eng.," IV. 75.
[8] " Life," Vol. III. 11 ; April 1682.

Company and said that when Parliament met he would assent to any Bill for the naturalization of the French Protestants, and in the meanwhile he wished the Company, in spite of any clause in their charter to the contrary, to allow them to buy stock as though naturalized.[1]

A French Protestant church had existed in the town of Rye since about 1569. In December 1681 the Bishop of London appointed the Sieur Bertrand as minister, with instructions to use the Prayer Book in French. The services had formerly been held in the old chapel of the Augustinian Friars,[2] but now the town offered the Huguenots the use of the parish church out of ordinary service times,[3] and the King expressed his pleasure at the reception which the people of Rye had given to the exiles.[4] In May 1682 the principal inhabitants declared in writing to the Council their willingness that the French Protestants might continue to worship in the parish church from 8 to 10 a.m. and from 12 to 2 p.m. and to have the use of the pulpit.[5]

In reply to the slanders spread by interested persons that the conversions in France to the Church of Rome had been voluntary, and that the people who were crowding to England were doing so for their private ends, and that many of them were Papists or disaffected persons, the vicar and chief officials of the town issued the following testimonial to the character of the refugees dwelling among them: " These are to certify all whom it may concern, that the French Protestants that are settled inhabitants of this town of Rye are a sober, harmless, innocent people, such as serve God constantly and uniformly, according to the usage and custom of the Church of England, and further that we believe them to be falsely aspersed for Papists and disaffected persons, no such thing appearing unto us by the conversation of any of them. This we do freely certify for and of them. In witness whereof we have hereunto set our hands, the 18th day of April, 1682." This was signed by William Williams, the vicar, the town clerk, and others, including the collector of the customs, two jurats, and two searchers.[6]

A rumour spread in 1685 that the French Protestants were sympathisers with Monmouth's rebellion, and probably the more extreme among them were so,[7] for they had reason to be suspicious of a Roman Catholic king. But the ministers and congregation of the French church at Thorpe-le-Soken in Essex, sent a declaration, dated June 21st, 1685, to the magistrates and

[1] S.P.D., Entry Book 66. p. 46, January 4th, 1682.
[2] Kershaw, " For. Prots.," p. 109.
[3] C.S.P.D., December 19th, 1681, 417/275.
[4] C.S.P.D., December 22nd, 1681, Entry Book 62, p. 378.
[5] " Sussex Arch. Collections," XII. 202.
[6] "Prot. Refugees in Sussex," *Sussex Arch. Collections*, XIII, 1861, pp. 180–208.
[7] Bastide, " Anglo-French Entente," pp. 123–126.

the Bishop of London assuring them of their dutifulness to James, and offering him their services, their goods and their lives.[1]

On June 15th, 1685, a Bill was brought into the House of Commons for the naturalization of French Protestant strangers who resided in England, or should come to England within a limited time. Leave to bring in the Bill had been granted by a considerable majority, but there was nevertheless a good deal of opposition, in which Roger North was prominent. He pointed out that the proposed Bill made no distinction of persons; the scum of Europe might come into the country, be naturalized, and become officials and jurymen and what not. If the Bill had proposed the establishment of a court to inquire into the individual cases, and to determine whether the persons to be naturalized would be conformable to the religion and laws of this country, or if it had provided for a record of the persons naturalized, it would have been a different matter, but he opposed this intended indiscriminate naturalization. The Bill was read the second time on July 1st, and an instruction was given to a Committee to prepare an additional clause providing that the persons naturalized should use the Prayer Book in French, and if they attended conventicles they should lose their naturalization. The opposition were anxious for this to be ordered by Parliament because, as Sir Thomas Meres put it, " if you indulge one set of Nonconformists how can you blame the King for indulging the Roman Catholics? " The courtiers like Henry Savile and Lord Antrim saw the point too, and opposed the clause.[2] The Committee was revived on November 19th,[3] but nothing further happened.

The Edict forbidding all public exercise of the " pretended Reformed religion " was issued from Fontainebleau on October 8th, 1685, registered in the Parliament of Paris on October 22nd, and in the other Parliaments soon after. It derived the name by which it was popularly known from the clause which specifically revoked the Edict of Nantes. Protestants who were not prepared to recant were to quit the realm within fifteen days, or else be sent to the galleys. Those who left France might take their wives and such of their children as were under seven years of age. The number of people who went into exile has been variously estimated. Voltaire [4] made it as much as 600,000. This is undoubtedly a great exaggeration. In 1686 it was estimated that 150,000 had fled from the country.[5] The numbers who fled to England were estimated at from 80,000

[1] Agnew, " Prot. Exiles from France," II. 16.
[2] Commons Journals, IX. 738, 755; North, " Lives of the Norths," III. 180–181.
[3] Commons Journals.   [4] " Age of Louis XIV."
[5] " An Account of the Persecutions," 1686.

to a 100,000, but the figure is again probably too large. From the first report of the English relief committee, issued in December 1687, it would appear that 15,500 refugees had been relieved in the course of its first year's work. Of these 140 were persons of quality with their families, 143 were ministers, 144 were lawyers, physicians, or traders. Some 600, for whom no employment could be found, were sent to America.[1]

The English nation had long been stirred by stories of the sufferings of the Protestants abroad, of the terrors of the dragonnades, of the perils of the Frenchmen who had tried to escape. On September 5th, 1680, an open boat arrived at Plymouth with forty or fifty refugees on board from the neighbourhood of Rochelle. Four other boats had left with it, one of which arrived at Dartmouth, but nothing was ever heard of the other three.[2] This was only one case out of many. But now from every port and bay of France men, women, and children were hastening, with what wreck of their fortunes they could carry in a bundle or in their pockets, to seek the hospitable shores of England. Children over seven years of age were being smuggled out at night with whatever secrecy could be managed. Hundreds were arriving with practically nothing but the clothes on their backs, and all had terrible tales to tell of the things they had had to endure. From all parts of England came memorials to the Government urging that active measures should be taken on their behalf.

The brief which Charles II. had issued in 1682 ordering a collection for the French Protestants, had received a hearty response, and the sum raised had been estimated at £14,631 11s. 7½d.[3] Another reckoning makes it £3319 in London and £12,788 in the country,[4] but in either case it was an excellent result when the resources of the nation at that time are taken into consideration.[5] By this time all the money had been spent except £362, and well spent, for the House of Commons, making inquiries into the matter in 1689, came to the conclusion that the funds had been faithfully administered. James had no love for Protestants, French or English: there was no reason why he should have, considering what he had endured at their hands during the days of the Popish Plot and the Exclusion Bill, and the slander with which they had pursued him ever since.[6] He had always been a consistent advocate of toleration. " His aim, partly realised by the two Lords Baltimore, as Roman Catholic Governors of the colony of Maryland from 1632 onwards, was to show that the Catholicism of Rome was compatible with

[1] Smiles, " Huguenots," pp. 313–316.   [2] *Ibid.*, p. 222.
[3] Shaw, *E.H.R.*, IX. 662.
[4] Arber, " Torments of Protestant Slaves," p. xxxi.
[5] Hallam, " Const. Hist.," c. XIV.
[6] See " Revolution Politics," 1733, *passim.*

the widest toleration of other forms of Christianity." [1]   Yet
Louis XIV. had revoked the Edict of Nantes and Pope Innocent
XI. had ordered a Te Deum to be sung in honour of the event.
The Marquis de Bonrepaux told Louis that James looked on the
fugitives as his enemies, but could not resist the national desire
for a collection on their behalf.   Nevertheless, in November
1685 the King not only gave leave for a collection, and ordered
house-to-house collections by the churchwardens of each parish,
but he gave £1500 out of his privy purse. [2]

James was badly served always.   Jeffreys, the Lord Chancellor,
who had to issue the brief for the collection, postponed it as long
as he could, while Barillon obstructed it to the utmost of his
power.   When it was issued on March 5th it was coupled with
an order that no relief should be given to any persons who did
not conform to the Church of England and receive the sacrament according to the Anglican rite. [3]   This was doubtless at
the request of the Anglican authorities, and this is shown by the
fact that when Sancroft brought in a Bill in the House of Lords
to assign them a place of worship in the City of London, the
Bill restricted them to the use of the French translation of the
Prayer Book, and to the ministrations of clergy in Anglican
orders.   Macaulay says this clog to the relief was the design of
the King and Barillon, [4] though why two Roman Catholics
should insist gratuitously on people communicating at Anglican
altars, it is difficult to say.   There was another proviso, that
the clergy should content themselves with reading the brief,
and should not preach on the sufferings of the exiles.   It was
natural that such an order should be made, because the violent
sermons which were being preached in England were making
Anglo-French relations very difficult.   Ken preached at Whitehall on March 14th, a fortnight before the brief was read in the
London churches, and in his sermon he " exhorted to constancy
in the Protestant religion, detestation of the unheard-of cruelties
of the French, and stirring up to a liberal contribution." [5]
The delay in issuing the brief had been partly due to disputes
about the trustees of the fund and the use that was to be made
of the money, and partly due to Barillon, who had done his
best to make matters difficult by objecting to the use of such
words as " persecution." [6]   The order was renewed by proclamation on January 31st, 1687, at which date the King announced
that the money collected had all been spent.   By an Order in
Council of April 15th of that year it was decreed that the sums
raised by charitable contributions for the Protestants should be
paid into the Chamber of London. [7]   Relief was given largely

---

[1] Plumptre, " Life of Thomas Ken," I. 241.
[2] Aylesbury, " Memoirs," I. 103.
[3] Agnew, " Prot. Exiles from France," II. 17.
[4] Macaulay, " Hist. Eng.," I. 434.   [5] Evelyn, " Diary."
[6] Downshire MSS., I. 130.   [7] " Rev. Politics," III. 11.

in the shape of pensions and weekly allowances. Special provision was made for the support of poor French Protestant
ministers, and for churches which had no endowment. In
addition, three French churches were erected in London, and
twelve in the provinces.[1] Of course there were people who
said the money was intended for Papists, but the evidence shows
that it was expended on the people for whose benefit it was
raised.

The total amount collected under James II amounted to
£63,713 2s. 3d. The London parishes gave generously. St.
Matthew's, Friday Street, which contained only 116 houses,
gave £81 9s. 9d. St. Giles' gave £1300.[2] Not all the receipts
are now in existence, but there is documentary proof that the
sum of £56,465 18s. 1d. was paid out; and probably the rest
was spent, though it was remarked that of the collection made
in Cromwell's time for the distressed Piedmontese there was a
balance left at the Restoration.[3] In 1689 a petition was sent
to the House of Commons asking for more relief, and the matter
was referred to a Committee. They reported that the French
refugees had formed three regiments in the King's army, that
20,000 were engaged in trade, but that there remained about
2000 in need of relief, and they estimated that for this purpose
the sum of £17,200 a year would be required. The Government decided to make an annual grant of £15,000, which was
continued somewhat irregularly till the reign of George I.,
when it was reduced by half. As time went on, less was needed,
and in 1885 the last relic, a grant of £250 a year to the French
church in the Savoy, was withdrawn by the Treasury.[4]

There was a great deal of friendliness between the leading
Anglican divines and the French Protestants abroad. Many of
them had got to know the Huguenot leaders well during their
own exile. Cosin had lived at Charenton during the Commonwealth time, and had been on intimate terms with the Protestants
there, and recognised the validity of their orders, and had never
refused to join with them " in all things wherein they joined
with the Church of England." He quoted with approval the
saying of Overall that though we are not to lessen the *jus divinum*
of episcopacy where it is established, yet where it cannot be had
we must not cry down the Reformed churches as though they
had neither orders nor sacraments.[5] Among the papers of
Dennis Granville, archdeacon of Durham, was one in which
he had jotted down his ideas of the French Protestants. He held
that they had retained the essentials of the Christian faith, they

[1] Smiles, " Huguenots," p. 317; Burn, " Hist. For. Prot. Refugees," p. 21.
[2] Downshire MSS. Hist. MSS. Com. I. 160, 184.
[3] Downshire MSS. I. 160.
[4] W. H. Shaw, " The English Government and Relief of the Protestant
Refugees." *E.H.R.*, IX. 662.
[5] Cosin, " Works," 1843-1855, IV. 401-449.

worshipped with some order and decency, and they had a
liturgy. Their book of rules of discipline ordered reverence in
worship, and it was not their fault if services were as irreverent
as in the King's chapel and the cathedrals in England. Their
best ministers approved of the Anglican system, and if, on the
other hand, some spoke against it, so did some of the ministers
of the Church of England. At the time of the Reformation
they were unable to maintain episcopacy, and they could not
get it now if they desired it. As to their lack of what we considered decent ceremonies at the Communion, we ought not to
be unduly influenced by things indifferent. He held that it
was the duty of English churchmen to communicate with them
when travelling abroad.[1]

Bishop Morley, however, said that when he was in France
he did not on any occasion worship with the French Protestants,
either at Charenton or Caen. He gave as his reasons to M.
Bouchart, the eminent French pastor at Caen, that there was
an Anglican congregation available where they not only had
preaching, but a liturgy, and that he was not sufficiently
acquainted with the French language. "And thirdly," he
added, "because if they did not favour and encourage, yet they
did not, at least they had not hitherto, condemned nor reproved
the scandalous and rebellious proceedings of their Presbyterian
brethren in England, against the King and against the Church:
which until they should do by some public act or manifestation
of their judgment to the contrary, I could not choose but think
they approved; or at least did not dislike what our Presbyterians
in England had done, and were still doing. . . . And they were
these reasons of mine which I sent to M. Bouchart in a letter
written in Latin which drew from that learned man the ' Answer '
that he afterwards printed, and wherein he justifies the episcopal
government in England, and condemns the taking up of arms
by subjects against their sovereign in defence of religion, or for
any other cause, or upon any other pretence whatsoever." [2]

Turner, Bishop of Ely, provided for the refugees a chapel at
Thorney Abbey, where they might worship without conforming
to the Church of England. Lloyd, Bishop of St. Asaph, undertook, as long as he held the see, to allow a French Protestant
£20 a year and his board.[3] Archbishop Sancroft, Compton of
London, the Earl of Bedford, and Sir William Coventry, all did
their best to befriend the exiles. The last-named at his death
in 1686 bequeathed £2000 for their benefit.[4] Lady Russell
was a niece of the Marquis de Ruvigny. In January 1686 she
was anxious to find a tutor for her son, and wrote, " I am much

[1] Granville, " Life of Dennis Granville," pp. 199–203.
[2] " Bishop Morley's Several Treatises," preface, London 1682.
[3] Overton, " Life in the English Church, 1660–1714," p. 351.
[4] Downshire MSS., I. 193.

advised, and indeed inclined, if I could be fitted to my mind, to take a Frenchman, so I shall do a charity, and profit the child also, who should learn French. Here are many scholars come over, as are of all kinds, God knows." [1] In 1683 Bishop Barlow of Lincoln took a keen interest in a subscription which was being raised for the exiled ministers, and urged his arch-deacons to busy themselves in the matter. [2] Bishop Ken gave the exiles the greater portion of a fine of £4000 which happened to fall in, and preached on their behalf in the Chapel Royal before King James. [3] Tillotson showed great zeal for the foreign Protestants. When Dr. Beveridge, either from lack of zeal in their cause or from scrupulosity on legal points, complained to him that to read the King's brief on their behalf was contrary to the rubric, Tillotson replied, " Doctor, Doctor, charity is above rubrics." [4] But as time went on the bishops could not fail to see that the Protestant refugees were in large measure increasing the numbers of the Dissenters. [5]

The coming of the Huguenots was a great gain to English com-merce and manufactures, because amongst them were many of the best artisans and workmen of France. They brought im-provements in the manufacture of fabrics known as lustrings, brocades, satins, paduasoys, ducapes, watered tabies, and black and coloured velvets. They were manufacturers of watches, cutlery, clocks, locks, surgical instruments, and toys, and they introduced the art of making crystal, which after this died out in France. [6] Spitalfields was full of them, and there were many of them in Soho and other parts of London. As far as they were able, they brought their money away with them. The French Ambassador wrote to Louis XIV. in 1687 that as much as 960,000 louis d'or had already been sent to the English mint for conversion into English coinage. [7] Louis himself very quickly realised what a blow he had aimed against his own country, and at the end of 1685 the Marquis de Bonrepaux was sent from France as a special envoy to try to entice the tradesmen and artisans and seamen back. James II. gave him a cordial welcome, but his overtures to his fellow-country-men were a failure, for he only succeeded in persuading about 600, [8] although he offered 500 livres to each person who would return. [9]

The poor Protestants, and in particular those of the Savoy,

[1] " Life and Letters," pp. 73–74.
[2] Kershaw, " Prots. from France," p. 50.
[3] Plumtre, " Thomas Ken," II. 270.
[4] Birch, " Life of Tillotson," pp. 121–122.
[5] Overton, " Life in the English Church, 1660–1714," p. 351.
[6] J. S. Burn, " Hist. For. Prot. Refugees," pp. 17–18.
[7] Smiles, " Huguenots," p. 315.
[8] Agnew, " Prot. Exiles from France," II. 17.
[9] Downshire MSS. Hist. MSS., Com. I., 100, 172.

expressed their thanks to James for what he was doing for their compatriots. Some of them were very grateful to the King, but there was a violent party, headed by Jurien, who desired to have no dealings with a Catholic king,[1] and would show him no mercy, as a Catholic king had shown no mercy to them. " He was rewarded ill by them at the Revolution," said Lord Aylesbury of his royal master. " I knew some few worthy persons of the refugees that lamented this as much then as I do now." [2] Even a Whig bishop was moved to write in after years: " Where the benefit is real, 'tis a kind of ingratitude too nicely to enquire into the motive of it." [3] James, in his zeal for toleration, was trying to make his subjects believe that the Church of Rome was as tolerant as himself. But his subjects contrasted the natural kindliness of the Catholic James with the reverse character of his " Most Catholic " brother Louis across the water. The Whigs made great capital out of what was happening in France, for many of the French Protestants had preached passive obedience in France, and this was their reward, and so the English spirit rose more fiercely than ever against popery.

In 1686 there was printed " Les Plaintes des Protestants cruellement opprimés dans le Royaume de France," which was immediately translated into English and printed in Holland [4] under the title " An Account of the Persecutions and Oppressions of the Protestants in France." It was also reprinted in Edinburgh as " An Account of the Persecutions and Oppressions of the French Protestants." It gave an account of all the edicts directed against the Protestants, and their sufferings at the hands of the Catholics, together with a translation of the Revocation edict and of the form of abjuration required from the French Protestants. Barillon, at the order of Louis, formally complained to James about the publication being permitted. He said it contained many false and scandalous accusations against the King of France, and by an Order in Council copies both of the original and of the translation were publicly burnt by the common hangman before the Royal Exchange on May 5th, while both translator and printer were imprisoned. The work seems to have been very thoroughly suppressed. A copy was sent as soon as it was issued by a French merchant in England to his brother in France, but when, some time after this, the brother himself took refuge in England, he was unable after many inquiries to find a single copy.[5] The burning of the work gave great offence. Evelyn wrote, " Thursday was burnt in the Old Exchange, by the common hangman, a translation

---

[1] Bastide, " Anglo-French Entente," pp 123–126.
[2] Aylesbury, " Memoirs," I. 104.   [3] Kennet, " Hist. Eng.," III. 499.
[4] " Revolution Politics," Pt. II. p. 20.
[5] Arber, " Torments of Protestant Slaves "; Kennet, " Hist. Eng.," III. 498-499.

of a book written by the famous Monsieur Claude, relating only matters of fact concerning the horrid massacres and barbarous proceedings of the French King against his Protestant subjects, without any refutation of any facts therein: so mighty a power and ascendant here had the French ambassador, who was doubtless in great indignation at the pious and truly generous charity of all the nation for the relief of those miserable sufferers who came over for shelter. About this time also the Duke of Savoy, instigated by the French King to extirpate the Protestants of Piedmont, slew many thousands of these innocent people, so that there seemed to be a universal design to destroy all that would not go to mass, throughout Europe. Quod avertat D.O.M.! No faith in princes!"[1] Barillon warned Louis XIV. that it was better not to interfere, as feeling had never been so roused since James's accession.[2]

The French refugees in Holland came in contact with the Whig exiles, and strengthened them in their purpose. Men of letters and pamphleteers who had escaped from France wrote violently on the Anti-Catholic side, and their writings were smuggled into England. " Several libels and pamphlets have been lately printed and set about: many of them are come over from Holland," wrote Luttrell.[3] Some of these were scurrilous, violent, and coarse, some in English, some in French. They told stories of intended wholesale massacres of Protestants in France, how the Jesuits had arranged them, and how the Catholics were saying that the throats of the English Protestants ought to be cut likewise. People were almost as credulous as in the Popish Plot days, and all this was greedily accepted. It gave new zeal to the Protestants and spread consternation among the Tories.

While Protestant and Anti-Stuart feelings were rising to fever heat in England, a small body of the Roman Catholics was displaying a singular arrogance, and hotheads at Court were urging rigorous persecution. Louis had found, so it was argued, that the only way to save his crown was to stamp out his Protestant enemies, and if the King of England wished to retain his throne, he must similarly crush out the Puritans.[4] They must have found their position somewhat difficult in the face of the King's constant preaching of toleration. In February 1687 the Jesuits in London bought up a number of houses in the Savoy for the purpose of erecting a college, which was opened in May. They were very anxious to get possession of the French Protestant church, and Father Pulton, the Rector or Principal of the Jesuits, tried to get M. de Dubourdieu to hand it over, promising,

---

[1] " Diary," May 5th, 1686.
[2] Agnew, II. 17; " Sir John Brampston's Autobiography," II. 20.
[3] Luttrell, " State Affairs," I. 654.
[4] " Toleration proved Impracticable," 1685.

on the King's authority, that another church should be built for the Protestants at any convenient place they might choose, and offering them a large sum of money in addition. There is a story that the Jesuits threatened that if they did not get the building they would take it by force, but this seems to have been a suggestion of their enemies. The ministers and wardens of the Savoy sought the advice of Halifax, Danby, and Nottingham, who told them not to trust the Jesuits, and to let themselves be thrust out rather than yield, for if they were thrust out they would " do their own business and the nation's." [1]

When the Declaration of Indulgence came out the refugees were in a difficult position, for they owed a great deal to the King's policy. Wake translated and published " A Letter from Several French Ministers, fled into Germany on Account of the Persecution in France, to such of their Brethren in England as Approved of the King's Declaration, Touching Liberty of Conscience." In this letter the English Dissenters were blamed for their approval of the Declaration, and the French ministers of the episcopal communion who had read the Declaration, and had presented addresses to the King, were also rebuked because they had implicitly condemned thereby the bishops who went to prison. A reply was published entitled " A Letter of Several French Ministers fled into Germany to those that are in England, in answer to a Counterfeited Libel." The writers said they could not understand how persons who had read the Scriptures could speak so boldly against a King who had protected their brethren, granted several collections throughout his kingdom, and given largely to them himself. They said it was not true that addresses had been presented to the King by the French ministers, but that some of them had waited on James to desire him to give them leave to exercise their ministry among their own people according to the faith, liturgy, and discipline as received in France. There was express provision already made for this in the Act of Uniformity, whereby the Dutch, Swedish, Walloon, and French churches exercised their own rites, and not those of the Church of England. The writers of the counterfeit letter had asserted the necessity of episcopal orders, it is to be supposed, in order to get benefices. They should have asked the King's consent to perform their ministry in the manner to which they were already accustomed without taking new orders.

On September 4th, 1688, letters patent were granted to the ministers of the French congregations in London, enrolling them in a body corporate, under the style and title of " The French ministers of the French congregation of Protestant strangers, in or about the City of London, or suburbs thereof, on the foundation of King James II." Two of the chapels built by virtue of the powers conferred on this body commemorated them

[1] Kennet, " Hist. Eng.," III. 499; Ralph, " Hist. Eng.," I. 942.

in their name. One congregation, whose registers begin on August 18th, 1689, first met in Berwick Street, but removed in 1694 to Little Chapel Street in Wardour Street, and called the building in which they met Le Temple de Soho ou La Patente.[1] The other congregation, which had originally held their services in Glovers' Hall, removed to Paternoster Row, Spitalfields, and called their meeting-place La Patente en Spitalfields ou La Nouvelle Patente.[2] So great was the influx of fugitives from France after 1685, that between 1686 and the beginning of the eighteenth century the number of French churches in London and the neighbourhood rose to as many as thirty.

Among the most distinguished of the exiles was the Marquis de Ruvigny, whose niece had married William Lord Russell. At the Revocation his property was not confiscated, and Louis even offered freedom of worship to him and his family. As, however, he was determined to retire to England, he was allowed to take with him whatever he pleased, and to appoint stewards to manage the estates and other property which he had to leave behind. He was well received by James,[3] settled down in a small dwelling at Greenwich, and a French congregation met for worship at his house. Evelyn visited him there, and says of him, "He was the deputy of all the Protestants of that kingdom in the Parlement of Paris, and several times ambassador in this and other Courts, a person of great learning and experience." [4] His son, afterwards created by William, Earl of Galway, did a great deal for the Huguenots. The French congregation soon became too large for the house, and for a time worshipped in the parish church of Greenwich after the Anglican service was ended, but afterwards had a chapel of their own.[5]

Large numbers of Huguenots were in the army of William of Orange, and a great many were enrolled among the troops he brought to England. Three regiments of infantry and a complete squadron of cavalry were composed entirely of French Protestants. Seven hundred and thirty-six French refugees were officers in the army of invasion. Schomberg, once Marshal of France, who had been allowed to retire from France peaceably by Louis,[6] was second in command. Three of the Prince's aides-de-camp, de l'Etang, de la Melonière, and the Marquis d'Arzilliers, and the chiefs of the engineers and artillery, Gambon and Goulon respectively, were all French, and had served in the French armies,[7] and there were numbers of French officers and

[1] Burn, " Foreign Prot. Refugees," pp. 141, 149.
[2] Idem, Ibid., p. 168; Ellis, " Correspondence," II. 157.
[3] Downshire MSS., I. 122, 138.   [4] " Diary," August 8th, 1685.
[5] Burn, " Foreign Prot. Refugees," p. 116.
[6] Downshire MSS., I. 122.
[7] Smiles, " Huguenots," p. 232–233.

gentlemen serving in the ranks of nearly every regiment. It was all this Huguenot influence in military circles which helped to keep William on the throne, and to prevent the Stuarts from returning, and it was the remembrance of his persecutions which stiffened the nation in the long struggle against Louis which was so soon to begin.

THE FOREIGN PROTESTANT CHURCHES IN ENGLAND AND THEIR MINISTERS.

FRENCH.

The French Church in Threadneedle Street.

Founded temp. Queen Elizabeth. First entry in registers 1599. Rebuilt after the Fire. Pulled down in 1840, and a new church opened in 1843 in St. Martin-le-Grand.

Jacques Feller	1660
David Primerose	1660
Louis Herault returned . . .	1660
Marc Michel Michely	1671
Pierre Mussard	1675
Charles Poizet	1683
Aaron Testas	1687
Paul Gravisset	1687
Charles Bertheau	1687

Somerset House Chapel.

Given to the French Protestants in 1653.
Jean l'Espagne.
M. Kerhuel.
M. Hierosme.

The Savoy Church.   Conformist.

Given to the French Protestants in 1661.   In 1737 left the Savoy and merged in the congregation known as " Les Grecs " in Dudley Court, Hog Lane, later known as Crown Street, Soho.   Removed to Bloomsbury Street, where the present building, known as " L'Eglise de St. Jean l'Evangeliste en Savoie," was erected 1845–1846.

Jean Durel	1661
Richard Dumaresque	1675
Thomas Satur	1684

Greenwich.

Begun in 1686. At first in the Marquis de Ruvigny's house, then in the parish church, and finally in a chapel of their own. Dispersed about 1718.

Jacques Severin	1687

Wandsworth.

A congregation here as early as 1573.   The chapel was enlarged in 1685.   The first arrivals were Flemish.   From 1685 to the end of the eighteenth century the services were in French.   The building now belongs to the Congregationalists.   It almost faces the parish church. The French had a special burial-ground here.   The minister in 1688 was Jean de la Sale.

Marylebone Chapel.

Founded in 1656. A small congregation, somewhere in or about Marylebone Lane.

Bernard Perny	1656
Michel Eloy Nollet	1656

Hungerford Chapel.

In Hungerford Market. Opened as a French church in 1687. The Baptismal Register commences in 1688. Moved in 1717 to the chapel in Castle Street.

Spring Gardens Chapel, or the *Little Savoy.* Agnew says the little Savoy chapel in the Strand.

Granted to the French Protestants in 1673. A petition, undated, to the Treasury, praying for a renewed lease, recites that in the reign of Charles II. the petitioners' ancestors obtained a grant of land in Spring Gardens, and erected a chapel at an expense of £2000.

L'Eglise de St. Jean, Swan Fields, Shoreditch.

A congregation was formed about 1687, and was incorporated with the London Walloon church in 1823. The Registers begin on October 2nd, 1687.

M. de Joux	1688
M. Lions	1688

Castle Street Chapel, Leicester Square.

Erected by the Government for the French Protestants in 1672.[1]

Jewin Street, Aldersgate.

A congregation was permitted by letters patent under the Great Seal, July 16th, 1686, to assemble at a chapel situated in Jewin Street, Aldersgate, under the direction of the Archbishop of Canterbury. After several moves they found that the nave and tower of St. Martin Orgar, by Cannon Street, were capable of repair, obtained a lease of the site and ruins, which was confirmed by Act of Parliament, and restored it for worship.

L'Eglise des Grecs.

In the parish of St. Anne, Soho. Built for some Greek refugees from Melos in 1677 by the Duke of York, Bishop Compton, and others. Used after 1685 by a French Protestant congregation. Greek Street was probably named after it.

Canterbury.

Walloons settled here temp. Edward VI. Elizabeth gave them the crypt for a place of worship in 1561.

Philippe le Queux	1654
Elie Paul d'Arande . . .	1664
Vital Delon . . *c.* 1666. *d.* 1686
Arnaud Boucherie . . . 1670 *d.* 1685
Paul Georges 1685–1690
Pierre Trouillart	1687

[1] Agnew.

Norwich.

Begun temp. Elizabeth with refugees from Alva's persecution. The Register says founded about 1590. The Dutch had the choir of the Black Friars' Church. The French, or Walloons, had from 1637 the church of St. Mary-the-Less in Tombland. It was let on lease, but no renewal of the lease is found in the records. The French congregation died out early in the nineteenth century.[1] The ministers of the French congregation were:

Jacques le Franc . 1657–1664. Became Rector of St. Clements, Norwich.
Jacobus Stockmans 1665–1686
Pierre Chovein . 1684. Had Anglican orders and frequently preached in English churches.

About 1680 or 1684 Wilhelmus van Schie was minister of the Dutch Church.

Southampton.

Walloons and others were there temp. Edward VI. The Register bears a certificate that it is the original register book, which has been kept for the formerly Walloon church, but now the Protestant Episcopal French church, congregating in the chapel of God's House at Southampton. The church was founded about the year 1567, and the chapel of St. Julian was granted for its use. The Prayer Book was adopted in 1712.

Gabriel Du Perrier 1660
Jean de la Place Courand . 1665. He died of the plague that year.
Bernert 1665
D'Huissaux 1687

Rye, Sussex.

French emigrants were here about 1569. They first used the chapel of the Augustinian Friars, then the parish church. Nothing is heard of them after 1728.

Thorney.

A French congregation was formed at Thorney in Cambridgeshire in 1652. The first baptism was in February 1654. In 1662 Charles II. issued letters patent giving liberty to the Walloons and other foreigners to exercise their Protestant religion and discipline in the Isle of Ely, using the French tongue as before, with power to choose their own ministers, who must be approved by the Earl of Bedford and the Bishop of Ely. The congregation came to an end in 1727. The last entry in the Registers is dated October of that year.

Ezekiel Danois 1652
Jambelin 1685–1712

Dover.

A congregation was formed in 1646. We hear of it as late as 1719.

[1] Burn, " Hist. For. Prot. Refugees."

Bristol.

Registers commence in 1687. Till the reign of George II. they assembled for worship in the Mayor's chapel, in the hospital of St. Mark, otherwise Gaunt's hospital. After that they built a place of their own. The Register calls it " the chapel called the French Protestant Episcopal chapel, the service of which was first held in what is called the Mayor's chapel, St. Mark the Gaunt."

M. Descairac	.	.	.	.	. 1687
Jeremy Tinel	.	.	.	.	. 1687

Thorpe-le-Soken, Essex.

A congregation was founded in 1683. The church of Thorpe allowed them by Bishop Compton, and M. Severin was permitted to preach in the church. In 1685 Bishop Compton gave them leave to build a chapel of their own. It was opened in 1688. Closed soon after 1732.

Jean Severin	.	.	.	.	. 1683
M. Mestayer	.	.	.	.	. 1687

Sandtoft Chapel, Lincolnshire.

Founded by Dutch and French Protestants. A chapel was built in 1634. Ceased soon after 1681.

Jean Deckeshuel	.	.	.	.	. 1659
M. de la Prix	.	.	.	.	. —
Samuel Lamber	.	.	.	.	. 1664
Jacques la Porte	.	.	.	.	. 1676
M. de Vaneley	.	.	.	.	. 1681

DUTCH CHURCHES.

The Dutch Church in Austin Friars.

Established there by Edward VI. in 1550, under John à Lasco and others.

Jonas Proostius	.	.	.	.	. 1644
Samuel Biscop	.	.	.	.	. 1668
Gerard van den Port	.	.	.	.	. 1680
Johannes van Royen	.	.	.	.	. 1686
Adrianus van Costrum	.	.	.	.	. 1688

Norwich.

Began in Elizabeth's reign. Met in Black Friars' church.

Sandwich.

Began in Elizabeth's reign. Used St. Clement's church.

Colchester.

Began early in Elizabeth's reign. A large chapel and house for the minister in Head Street, built of timber sent from Holland. Burnt down in 1835.

Stamford, Lincolnshire.

Began in Elizabeth's reign. The last minister died in 1711.

Canvey Island, near South Benfleet, Essex. The Dutch came there in Charles I.'s reign to drain the island. A timber chapel was built for them. First notice of the congregation in 1641, when they were represented at a synod in London. The chapel was rebuilt and consecrated in 1712, and a new one again in 1745.

GERMAN LUTHERAN.

Hamburg Lutheran, or High German Lutheran.

In Great Trinity Lane, near Doctors' Commons. The register begins in 1675. The first minister was

Gerharde Martens 1673–1718

VIII

DISSENT was strongest of all in London, but in spite of the Five Mile Act it flourished in the other towns as well. To some places, like Birmingham and Manchester, which were not corporate towns, Dissenting ministers migrated, secure from the provisions of the Act, and this largely accounts for the strength of Dissent there in after years. The corporations were very important bodies. It was necessary, from the Government point of view, that no Dissenters should become members of them, not only because of the protection they would be able to give to their fellow-Dissenters, but also because of the influence they would gain in the choice of Members of Parliament. This was the reason for the Corporation Act. In many places, however, the Corporation Act became a dead letter; the Dissenters took a vigorous share in municipal life, got elected to the governing body and to public offices, and worked to render the other Acts a dead letter also. Examples of the bitterness and strife which all this engendered manifest themselves abundantly in the history of the various municipalities.

Bristol was the second manufacturing and mercantile city in England. According to Macaulay's estimate, the population at the accession of James II, was 29,000. The method by which this total was arrived at was by taking the number of houses and calculating the proportion of inhabitants as five and a half to one. This was found, with regard to London, to be fairly correct, but it is possible that in the smaller towns and districts the ratio should have been rather less. Bristol was one of the strongholds of Puritanism and its opposition to the Crown and Church; consequently the Government looked upon it with a suspicious eye. In the autumn of 1660 a great effort was made to enforce the oaths of allegiance and supremacy upon all persons over sixteen years of age, but the authorities found their effort much obstructed by the Quakers and Anabaptists, of whom there were great numbers in the city. A hundred and ninety conventiclers were charged at one time with refusing the oaths, but were released on the intercession of Margaret Fell.[1] In 1660, the Baptist pastor, Thomas Ewins,[2] had been turned out of

[1] Latimer, " Annals of Bristol in the Seventeenth Century," pp. 300–301.
[2] Palmer, III. 175.

St. Nicholas and Christ Church. At first his followers met at a house within the 'precincts of the Castle, and then they took a hall in the Friars, the old Dominican convent situated at the end of Broadmead. Their first trouble began over the oaths. They proposed alternative forms, which they considered as full as the official ones, but more consonant with Holy Scripture. The mayor, Sir Henry Cresswick, told them that they must take the prescribed form, but were not obliged to bind themselves thereby any further than the Scriptures allowed. So some took it, but others did not.[1] We have a very full account of the affairs of this congregation in " The Records of a Church of Christ meeting in Broadmead, Bristol, A.D. 1640 to A.D. 1688." The principal author, Edward Terrill, became an elder in the Baptist church in 1667, and died in 1685. He appears to have commenced the manuscript in 1672, but his handwriting ceases in 1678. Three years before this two members of the congregation had been requested to keep an exact daily record of the sufferings of their people, which record was kept in what was called the Waste Book. It is now lost, but when Terrill ceased writing his narrative, some unknown person apparently continued it from the Waste Book.

In the general election of April 1661 Bristol returned royalist members, but in that year a writ of *Quo Warranto* was issued, questioning the city charter, and it was reported that though the mayor himself was loyal, yet he kept in office a relative, who was disloyal and an Anabaptist, and a disloyal town clerk. A sectary was deputy-mayor, and a city council in which fanatic aldermen seemed to have been in the majority swayed the mayor in the conduct of his office.[2] During 1662 there was much talk of disaffection to the Government in Bristol and the neighbourhood, and in September orders were sent to put the militia on a good footing in order to prevent the designs of the disaffected, and many arrests were made. In the same month, Secretary Nicholas wrote to the mayor to the effect that the King wished the Corporation Act to be strictly enforced, and that those who refused to take the required oaths were to be reported and proceeded against. The Secretary further promised that if their charter did not empower them to punish those who refused to bear office when elected, it should be amended.[3]

In 1663 there was much turmoil in the city, owing to the widespread plot which had been discovered. It had been arranged that Bristol should be surprised, but Bennet warned the deputy lieutenants to be on their guard. Sir Hugh Smyth and others collected some local military forces, and Sir Thomas Bridges begged the Government to send them a troop of horse to overawe

---

[1] " Broadmead Records," pp. 49–50.
[2] C.S.P.D., 34/39.
[3] C.S.P.D. September 16th, 1662.

the sectaries.[1]   At Michaelmas Sir John Knight became mayor. Little more than a week afterwards he wrote to the Government promising to do his best to execute the law against Dissenters, and affirmed that Ewins had seduced thousands.   The house of Rickard Moon, a bookseller, had been searched, and seditious works like " Annus Mirabilis " had been found there and burnt. Moon dealt with Eliza Calvert, the London publisher, who was frequently in trouble, and a letter was found from Brewster, with whom Moon declared he did not deal, containing suspicious phrases like " the Lord going on."[2]   The Privy Council thanked Knight for his zeal, and told him to continue until he had secured all the fanatic leaders.[3]   On December 27th the mayor ordered the sheriffs to break up a Quaker meeting.   This was done, and three Quakers were arrested; but their counsel insisted that their apprehension was illegal, having been made by militia officers in time of peace.   The jury brought in a verdict of " not guilty of force and arms to the terror of the people " (as stated in common form in the indictment), " but guilty of an unlawful assembly."   The court refused the verdict, and the jury then returned " not guilty according to the indictment."   Some more were brought up on the same charge the next day, but the jury returned their verdict of the previous day; nevertheless, the Quakers were all fined and sent to prison till the fines should be paid.[4]   At this point another John Knight brought himself into prominence.   He was a sugar refiner by trade, and a cousin of the mayor, and to distinguish him from that official was generally known as John Knight the younger.   He persisted in offering himself as security for the Quakers, though they declined his assistance, and he behaved with great violence in court.[5]   It was thought by some that the mayor was over-lenient with his relative, and the deputy-lieutenants and Richard Streamer, one of the sheriffs, consulted Sir Henry Bennet on the subject. The mayor had really intended to prosecute him, but the younger Knight set out for London to get the help of Sir Robert Cann and Sir Robert Yeamans, who were then at Court, though they had formerly been hostile to the King.   Whatever they might or might not have done for him, he was brought before the Privy Council and severely reprimanded.   Sir Robert Cann was described by his relative, Roger North, as a pompous, arrogant, and purse-proud man.   Yeamans and he were members of the Bristol city council, but they were in the habit of stirring up strife therein; Cann absented himself from the council for several months, and the mayor complained that he had refused to attend service in civic robes with the rest of the corporation,

[1] C.S.P.D., October 5th, 1663.   [2] C.S.P.D., October 12th, 1663.
[3] Latimer, " Bristol in Seventeenth Century," p. 324.
[4] Besse, " Sufferings."   For the Quakers in Bristol see Croese, " Gen. Hist. Quakers," II. 97–104.   [5] C.S.P.D., January 2nd, 1664.

on Christmas Day.[1]   The mayor also reported to the Government that the arrested Quakers had refused to take the oaths, even though the word " promise " was substituted for " swear." The Quakers still met boldly.   They had services in a large upstairs room in Broadmead, and on Sunday, February 28th 300 were found there, and fourteen of them sent to Newgate. On the succeeding Sundays other raids were made on the Baptists and Independents.[2]   Cann and Yeamans visited the imprisoned Quakers, and encouraged them in every way.   They had also, in February, caused disturbances in church by quarrelling with the rest of the council over the question of precedence; so much so that the King had to settle the matter.[3]

The persecution raged against the Quakers during the summer and autumn of 1664.   A troop of cavalry had been put at the disposal of the mayor, and the Broadmead meeting-house was harried time after time.   During July and August it was raided nearly every Sunday, and those who were imprisoned suffered great hardships in the crowded and filthy places into which they were thrust.   Fifty-five women sent to Bridewell had five beds between them, and three died from the effects of their loathsome surroundings.   The other Dissenters also suffered; the Baptists in the May of that year had to abstain from meeting in their hall in the Friars, and had to meet secretly in private houses.   Even then they were liable to have their doors broken in with sledge-hammers, and to be invaded by musketeers.   Sir John Knight was able to say that by the end of his year of office he had sent 900 Dissenters to gaol.   After this the persecution died down for a time, for his successor, John Lawford, though he continued to break up the meetings, usually only imprisoned the people in whose house the meeting was held.[4]   In 1665, just before the municipal elections, the King sent a mandate expressing his displeasure at the way in which disaffected persons were disturbing the good government of the city, and ordering that men of fidelity be chosen as officials, and that the mayor should be chosen from the aldermen, and not from the councillors.[5] In 1667 the Bristol Quakers made an agreement with the porter of Newgate covenanting to pay him five shillings quarterly " for his pains and love in opening the gate " of the prison to Friends attending services there, and this payment went on till 1706. In 1669, when a Dissenting minister was imprisoned in this gaol, he preached through a grating to large crowds.[6]

In 1670, as a result of the Conventicle Act, persecution broke

---

[1] C.S.P.D., January 2nd, 13th; February 13th, 1664.
[2] Latimer, " Bristol in Seventeenth Century," p. 325.
[3] C.S.P.D., February 15th, 24th, March 19th, 1664.
[4] " Broadmead Records," p. 54; Latimer, " Bristol in Seventeenth Century," p. 326.
[5] Latimer, " Bristol in Seventeenth Century," p. 335.   [6] Ibid., 346–351.

out once more. Sir Robert Yeamans, who seems to have changed sides, complained that the Nonconformists were so pertinacious that the magistrates were worn out with their obstinacy and their muttered threats. The magistrates who desired to put the Act into force were deserted by their colleagues. Some of the aldermen absented themselves from the magisterial bench, and the first Sunday after the Act was passed all the constables absented themselves from duty.[1] The churchwardens, over-seers, and constables would not execute the warrants issued under the Act till they were ordered to appear at the sessions and explain their conduct. This at last brought about a vigorous prosecution of offenders.[2] The fines levied on the Nonconformists were exacted by distress, but little was gained by this, because no one would buy the goods that were distrained.[3]

The Quakers at this time had three meeting-houses: one at the lower end of Broadmead (this was taken over by the Baptists in the following year), and two which had recently been built, one in Temple Street, near Bristol Bridge, and the second near Broadmead at the Friars. After the passing of the Conventicle Act these were seized by the authorities, but in September 1670 the Quakers broke into one of them, and continued their meetings, and arrangements were made for opening the other two.[4] For this many of them were sent to Newgate.[5] The Baptists were similarly harassed. Their meeting having been broken up, they made a hole through a wall, so that the speaker could stand in the next house, and no one could say that there was a preacher among them. At last the authorities sent the train-bands to keep them out, and nailed up the doors of their meeting-place, and they had to meet for some months in the streets and lanes, until at last they took to meeting at Terrill's house, near Lawford's Gate. However, Alderman John Knight, the sugar refiner, was elected mayor, and they had rest for a time.[6] Sir John Knight was furious at the election, and complained to the Government. The Privy Council ordered a new election, but were disobeyed. Sir John went to London, and laid charges against Sir Robert Yeamans and the mayor, who were both called before the Privy Council and taken into custody. The King, however, dismissed Yeamans, but the mayor was not released for over two months.[7] Ewins, the Baptist pastor, died in 1670. The influence he had had in the place was shown by the fact that hundreds openly attended his funeral. A new pastor being required they asked for a Mr. Hardcastle, who was a member of Henry Jessey's congregation in London. A dispute ensued. The London

[1] C.S.P.D., May 21st, and 31st, 1670, 275/163–164.
[2] C.S.P.D., September 10th, 1670.   [3] C.S.P.D., September 12th, 1570.
[4] Braithwaite, "Second Period," pp. 77–78.
[5] C.S.P.D., September 12th, 1670.   [6] "Broadmead Records," p. 67.
[7] Latimer, "Bristol in Seventeenth Century," pp. 356–367.

congregation accused them of sinful conduct in asking him, as he belonged to them, and it was further discovered that " Lord " Charles Fleetwood and his wife were against his leaving London. Still, in 1671, a " call " was sent to Hardcastle signed by ninety-eight members of the Bristol congregation (twenty-six of these were men and there were two absent members who did not sign), but the London congregation was very angry, and refused to give him letters of commendation or dismissal. Hardcastle went to Bristol, however, and the breach between the two congregations was not healed for years. In the September of this year they took over the meeting-house at the lower end of Broadmead, " where the heretics called Quakers had formerly used to meet." [1]

Their new meeting-place consisted of one great room, 48 by 45 feet, which had been made by knocking four rooms into one. They agreed that the new minister should receive an official stipend of £80 a year, paid quarterly, though any member could make him private gifts if so disposed. It was found that only half the congregation could give anything, so they must have been very poor. Yet we are told that a poor journeyman-shoemaker gave 20s. a year, and a poor woman with two children subscribed 40s.[2] Discipline was strong in this little congregation. A brother was turned out for drunkenness in 1670, and a woman was not admitted because she sold drink and had not paid her husband's debts. Women were not allowed to speak; even at the election of the minister women members had to get a male member of the church to set forth their views for them.[3] In 1678 they refused to readmit an expelled member named Lingwood, who had spoken evil of the bishop and thereby brought the congregation into ill odour, and they refused to visit him in prison. Further, he had promised the bishop to attend the cathedral if let out of prison, and since his release had gone twice.[4] In 1681 an applicant for membership was refused because he was suspected of Arminian error.[5]

In November 1671 Guy Carleton, an old Cavalier officer and a companion of Charles II. on his wanderings, became bishop, and new attempts were made to destroy conventicles. By this time there were three Baptist, one Presbyterian and two Independent meetings in Bristol, and hundreds attended, both members and hearers.[6] These four conventicles were specially attacked, their particular enemy being John Hellier, an attorney by profession, and churchwarden of St. James's parish, in which three of the great meetings, including Hardcastle's, were held. Hellier was described as a man of unclean life, which need not

---

[1] " Broadmead Records," pp. 70–75.   [2] Ibid., p. 79.
[3] Ibid., pp. 90–91.   [4] Ibid., p. 167.   [5] Ibid., p. 212.
[6] Fletcher, " Hist. Independency," IV. c. 3; " Broadmead Records," pp. 92–93.

necessarily mean more than that his behaviour did not satisfy the somewhat narrow requirements of the seventeenth-century Puritans. The four congregations acted together, each appointing two representatives to form a committee for legal matters. The Declaration of Indulgence brought peace for a time, and the usual licences; but after the Declaration was recalled, the bishop cited Dissenting merchants before the consistory court, and prosecuted the ministers.[1] At the Quarter Sessions in 1675 the grand jury delivered a presentment denouncing Dissenting preachers as impostors and firebrands, and their adherents as seditious fanatics, and urging the enforcement of the Conventicle Act. The ministers of these places pleaded their licences under the Declaration of Indulgence, but the bishop told them they were against the law, and he harried the justices into issuing warrants against them.[2] On February 10th the Castle Green Independent chapel was surrounded, and the minister, John Thompson, was arrested. He was sentenced to six months imprisonment, and three other ministers were sent to gaol at the same time. Thompson died of fever on March 4th. The gaoler gave evidence on oath that while in prison he was allowed to walk on the leads as often as he pleased, and had what liberty he liked to see friends, that he had the best chamber in the keeper's house, and not in the common prison. Hardcastle and Weeks, another minister, shared this room with him for some time, till he became very ill. At the inquest it was shown that he had good food and wine provided, and that three physicians attended him, who all said he died of a malignant fever. Stories, however, got about that the four imprisoned ministers had been shamefully treated, thrown into a foul stinking dungeon, denied food, and had to suck what was given them to drink through a tobacco pipe, and all this by order of the bishop. On the contrary, the gaoler declared they had never been without visitors, and had the best lodging that could be provided.[3] Thompson's funeral " was accompanied by a great crowd of all sorts of professors (except Quakers)." [4] Shortly after his burial a paper was found in the mayor's house threatening that if they must be persecuted, there were many eminent and sufficient men, and numbers of apprentices and others of inferior rank who would venture their lives and fortunes for their freedom. The writer who reported this to Secretary Williamson added, " Probably in this city two-thirds are inclined that way." [5] A few days later Hellier broke up

[1] C.S.P.D., 319/131.

[2] C.S.P.D., 319/131; Latimer, " Bristol in Seventeenth Century," p. 369.

[3] " The Bristol Narrative, or a Just Account of the Imprisonment and Death of John Thompson, a Conventicling Preacher there, given on Oath by Thomas Hobson, Keeper of the Gaol in Newgate," London, Licensed June 1st, 1675; " Broadmead Records," pp. 94–95.

[4] " Broadmead Records," p. 100.   [5] C.S.P.D., March 6th, 1675, 368/210.

some meetings, and sent several people to Newgate, where they were thrown into a den with a damp earthen floor and no seats.[1] The shifts to which the Nonconformists were put are well illustrated in the " Broadmead Records." Hardcastle's congregation put a curtain across the room, and the preacher stood behind that, while a crowd of women sat on the stairs to prevent the informers and officers from going up quickly. If the officers came, the preacher sat down, and they all began to sing a psalm. " No one was to read the psalm after the first line, so that they would not find us so much as reading." If the constables tried to drag them away they merely offered passive resistance, the congregation going on singing. Weeks' congregation of Presbyterians had a wooden partition across their room, and the minister could escape from behind it to another part of the house. In Andrew Gifford's Baptist meeting a number of brethren stood round the speaker, and when the informers came they let him down by a trap-door. Thompson's congregation of Independents had two lofts, one above the other, over their meeting-room. The preacher stood in the middle one so that they could all hear him above and below. The door at the foot of the stairs was kept fast against strangers, but if the disturbers broke it down he could escape from the second storey to another house.[2]

In the May of 1675 members of the four chief congregations held a joint prayer-meeting for some of the members undergoing trial. Out of this rose an attempt to arrange united meetings of the congregations, at any rate on week-days. Theological differences, however, proved too strong for this, though the prayer-meetings seem to have been kept up for a time. They even tried this year to carry the war into the enemy's camp by prosecuting Hellier for perjury, but he was acquitted at the Wells Assizes.[3] Hardcastle and Weeks were released early in August, but arrested again a fortnight later. But this autumn Sir Robert Cann was elected mayor. He disliked the persecution, supported the Dissenters and insulted the bishop,[4] but they were still only able to hold their meetings in private houses. Sir Robert Yeamans was still noted as " a great disturber." Weeks' Presbyterians so far gave way to the authorities as to agree to alter the times of their meetings so as not to coincide with the time of the Anglican services. This caused great trouble to the other congregations, who refused to change their hours although asked to do so by Sir Robert Cann, because the suggestion had come from Hellier. The result was that the Presbyterians withdrew from the joint quarterly intercession. In spite of constant harrying, the Broadmead congregation still met regularly, though their meeting was growing " very poor and lean." The

---

[1] Latimer, " Bristol in Seventeenth Century," p. 371.
[2] " Broadmead Records," pp. 101–103.   [3] Ibid., p. 124.
[4] C.S.P.D., 397/86.

other congregations seem to have met less frequently.[1] In 1675 was published a little tract of six pages, entitled " Some Reasons briefly suggested which have Prevailed with the Dissenters in Bristol to continue their open Meetings however Persecuted and Disturbed." However, the persecution died down in 1676.

A little later we find the Broadmead Baptists wrangling once more with Jessey's congregation about Hardcastle, who had not yet been ordained. The Bristol people held that their unanimous choice had appointed him to the office, whereas ordination, by laying on of hands, might be done at convenience. The London congregation asserted that he was a member and elder of their church, and they had need of him, whereas he was neither a member nor a regularly called minister of the church in Bristol. However, towards the end of 1678 Hardcastle died suddenly. He had had a hard life, and had been seven times in prison. The congregation raised £150, a large sum for a small body of poor people, 166 in number, and paid for his funeral and tomb-stone.[2] In September 1678 the Bristol corporation granted to Ichabod Chauncey, a medical practitioner and a Nonconformist, a piece of ground on Castle Green, and a Nonconformist meeting-house was shortly afterwards erected on that site.[3]

Not all the early Nonconformists were averse either to learning or endowments. In 1679 Edward Terrill gave a considerable amount of property in lands and houses to the Broadmead church. £50 per annum of this was to be divided among ten poor persons, the remainder " for the use and subsistence of a holy, learned man, well skilled in the tongues, to wit, Greek and Hebrew . . . as a pastor and teacher for the congregation aforesaid," and for the maintenance of poor students for the Baptist ministry. For the use of the minister and students he also bequeathed some 200 books, English, Latin, Greek and Hebrew.

The greatest persecution of all began in 1681. It had been said in 1679 that two-thirds of the people of the city were now Dissenters, and zealous in their belief in the Popish Plot.[4] Never-theless, another violent attempt was made to suppress Noncon-formity. The chief persecutor was John Knight, who was knighted for his activity and loyalty. This is a third John Knight, to be distinguished from the Sir John Knight who was mayor in 1663–1664, the violent Churchman, and from John Knight the sugar refiner, the violent Dissenter.[5] He was, in fact, the son of the latter, had been a factor in Nevis, and was now sheriff of Bristol, and a more violent opponent of Nonconformity than even old Sir John.[6] In November all the Nonconformist

[1] " Broadmead Records," pp. 147–150.   [2] Ibid., pp. 175–182.
[3] Latimer, " Bristol in Seventeenth Century," p. 388.
[4] Hist. MSS. Com. Finch MSS. II. 57–59.
[5] C.S.P.D., February 12th, 1681, 415/35.
[6] Besse, " Sufferings," I. 59; Latimer, " Bristol in Seventeenth Century," p. 402.

ministers and many of their followers were in Newgate. In December the Presbyterian chapel suffered severe damage, the gallery, furniture and windows being all destroyed. The Broadmead meeting-house was wrecked. The Quakers had their two places of worship taken from them, and damage done to the buildings to the extent of £50. An excuse was found for attacking the house in the Friars because, not having provided a man in arms for the train bands, a fine of £5 had been levied on it, and never paid, though such a demand had never been made before.[1] They did not regain full possession of the Friars meeting-house until July 1686.[2]   Some fifty Quakers were prosecuted as popish recusants. Their meetings were broken up with great brutality; they were knocked down into the mud, street boys were encouraged to pelt them with filth and other missiles, women were beaten and pinched till they were black and blue, and they were all thrust into a filthy, overcrowded gaol, the sanitary condition of which must have been a menace to the city. In 1682, when nearly all the parents were in prison, the children under sixteen actually continued the meetings. For this some of them were put in the stocks and into prison. On several occasions Hellier, who was now town clerk, and others who came with him to break up the meetings, beat the children unmercifully with sticks and whalebone rods. Even children under twelve years of age were imprisoned.[3] The prisoners all suffered from the extortions of the gaolers, to say nothing of the stench from the overcrowding, and the vile characters with whom they were herded. It was said that the Privy Council were angry with the Quakers because in the elections they had voted against the Government and it was rumoured that if Penn and Whitehead would undertake for the Friends that they would not vote at Parliamentary elections, there would be no further persecution.[4] On one occasion the persecutors nailed up eighty-seven men and fourteen women in the meeting-house at Temple Street for five or six hours, while in the afternoon of the same day, at the Friars meeting-house, they kept the Friends in the open court in the rain till about five o'clock. Among the women present on this occasion were two sisters of Sir Robert Cann. Sometimes as many as a hundred at a time were imprisoned in Newgate, " where Sir Robert Cann said he would not put a dog there he loved." [5]

The sufferings of the Friends went on during the next year, and the fines levied on them during that year amounted to £16,440. Richard Lindley, a blind man, ninety years old, was thrust into prison, and was forced to sit upright in a chair for

---

[1] Whiting, " Persecution Exposed," pp. 126–128.
[2] Braithwaite, " Second Period," p. 107; Besse, " Sufferings."
[3] Besse, " Sufferings."   [4] Sewell, " Hist. Quakers," p. 555.
[5] Whiting, " Persecution Exposed," pp. 126–128.

three nights, though others offered to pay for a place where he
might lie down. The prisoners were not allowed to work for
their living, spotted fever broke out in the gaol, and their sufferings were terrible.[1] John Knight, the sheriff, who was soon
afterwards knighted, accused Sir Thomas Earle, the mayor, of
being too lenient with the Dissenters.[2] Earle, in June 1682
wrote to Sir Leoline Jenkins saying that the conventicles were in
a manner wholly suppressed, but though they had dealt in all
tenderness with the Quakers, they were obstinate, and there
were thirty men in Newgate and sixty women in Bridewell,
where they had been sent to allow them more air and to prevent
clamour.[3] The Quakers appealed to the King and Council in
March 1682, and the Council considered their petition favourably
and ordered the mayor and aldermen to visit the prison complained of, and remedy the evil of it as far as the law allowed.
Sir John Knight, the sheriff, however, attended the next Council
meeting with the object of showing that they had no cause of
complaint.[4]

The other Dissenters also suffered severely during this time,
but were unable to make such a firm stand as the Quakers. On
November 19th, 1681, it was reported that over 100 persons had
been indicted for not going to church.[5] The King had already
ordered the Bishop of Bristol to go to his diocese to see that the
law was enforced,[6] and a little later he received the royal thanks
for his services.[7] In 1681 Harford, a member of Andrew
Gifford's Baptist meeting, was arrested for preaching, and the
mayor tendered him the oath required by the Conventicle Act,
and as he refused to take it he was about to be committed, but his
counsel pleaded that, as he was not proved to have been formerly
in holy orders, he could only be convicted for preaching, and
could not be punished under the Conventicle Act until he should
be found preaching within the corporation again. So he was
fined £20 instead.[8] In 1682 and 1683 things were so bad that
the Broadmead Baptists took to worshipping in a cave on Durd-
ham Down, in Kingswood, and in other retired places. Sometimes there were great meetings of 1000 or 1500 in these spots,
and on other occasions they gathered in small parties.[9] Fownes
was prosecuted in 1682, but was discharged owing to a defect in
the *mittimus*, but he had to give recognizances for his appearance
in the following term.[10] Hellier and Sir John Knight tried to
put into operation the Act of Elizabeth under which persons

[1] Besse, " Sufferings."
[2] S.P.D., 418/120, February 26th, 1682, 419/88; Luttrell, I. 166.
[3] S.P.D., June 3rd, 1682, 419/67.
[4] S.P.D., March 21st, 1682, Entry Book 68/47.
[5] C.S.P.D., November 19th, 1681 ; Adm., " Green. Hosp.," I. 151.
[6] C.S.P.D., September 15th, 1681.
[7] C.S.P.D., October 22nd, 1681.   [8] " Broadmead Records," p. 213.
[9] *Ibid.*, pp. 235–236.   [10] S.P.D., 418/98.

refusing to conform and not abjuring the realm were punishable with death. Richard Vickers, one of the leading merchants of Bristol, and a Quaker, was sentenced to death under the Act; but he was removed to London for re-trial, on the ground of errors in the indictment. Penn interested the Duke of York on his behalf, and when the case came before Jeffreys the indictment was quashed.[1] Old Sir John Knight, who had become disgusted with the severities and denounced the outrages, found himself presented by a grand jury as a disaffected person.[2]

The first party of Huguenots arrived in Bristol in December 1681. The mayor and the Tories were angry at this increase of Nonconformists, and suggested that a third of the fines for conventicling might go to the support of the French Protestants.[3] Another body of Huguenots landed in August 1682, and the corporation disbursed £42 10s. for them.[4]

Towards the end of 1682 Thomas Easton, the mayor, and others, including Sir John Knight junior, petitioned for the removal of Sir Robert Atkins, the Recorder, amongst other things for his great encouragement of the factious party and his opposition to the loyal. They complained that the King's government was weakened in the town, and that there would be no peace unless the King interfered.[5] About 100 people in Bristol were mixed up in the Rye House plot. Meetings had been held in various inns, and plans had been made to seize the town. Rumsey had been collector of customs there, Row was the swordbearer, Wade and Holloway were connected with the city, while Ichabod Chauncey, the Nonconformist physician whom Sir Robert Cann called " the bell-wether of the fanatics here," only escaped capital punishment in 1684 by abjuring the realm.[6] Sir Robert Cann had changed his attitude in his old age, and seems to have become a violent supporter of the Government, but his conversion did not make him popular. " Sir Robert Cann died lately, condemned of all," wrote Sir Robert Southwell in 1685.[7] Joseph Tyley, one of Monmouth's captains, came from Bristol. When the Duke of Beaufort entered the city on June 16th he ordered the houses of Nonconformists to be searched for arms and the town prisons were soon filled with suspected persons. The corporation being in debt, money was raised by the trick of electing rich and prosperous Quakers to the city council and other municipal offices, and fining them heavily for refusing to take the necessary oaths. Six men were fined £750 between them.[8]

In 1685 persecution was so severe, as many as 150 being con-

[1] Whiting, " Persecution Exposed," p. 250.
[2] Latimer, " Bristol in Seventeenth Century," p. 408.   [3] S.P.D., 418/3.
[4] Latimer, " Bristol in Seventeenth Century," p. 411.   [5] S.P.D., 421/50.
[6] Whiting, " Persecution Exposed "; Latimer, " Bristol in Seventeenth Century," p. 418.
[7] Hist. MSS. Com. MSS. Earl of Egmont., II. 172.
[8] Latimer, " Bristol in Seventeenth Century," pp. 430–431.

victed in a single week in February, that some conformed.[1]
An Independent minister named Knight and a mercer named
Ford tried to escape when pursued by crossing the Avon. Ford
was drowned and Knight subsequently died of exhaustion. A
coroner's jury found the pursuers guilty of manslaughter, but at
the Gloucester Assizes the judge ordered their acquittal, and
rebuked the coroner.[2] In April the Broadmead Baptists were
gathering together at four in the morning, and in December they
were holding their meetings in the snow in a wood.[3] It was not
till 1687, after five years' absence, that they were able to return
to their meeting-house, and then they had to elect a new pastor,
as Fownes, who had succeeded Hardcastle, had died in Gloucester
gaol nearly two years previously; but henceforth their troubles
were at an end.

In 1682 a grand jury stated that there had only been two
known Roman Catholic families in Bristol during the previous
seven years, but in April 1686 the mayor and sheriffs disturbed
a Roman Catholic congregation and arrested the priest and some
of the worshippers. The King ordered the priest to be discharged. Disgraceful scenes followed. On May 18th and 19th
there was a pageant in which there was indecent mockery of the
Virgin Mary and the Host. Soldiers were sent to put it down,
and there was bloodshed before the affair was ended, and Sir
John Knight the younger was prosecuted, though a jury acquitted
him, and Bishop Trelawney, who was accused of stirring up
Protestant violence by an episcopal charge which he had delivered,
had to make apology to the Government.[4] In the last year of
King James's reign a royal mandate ordered that Thomas
Scrope, the son of the regicide, should be made an alderman, and
Nathaniel Wade, the Rye House plotter, town clerk. Another
mandate ordered a number of Quakers to be admitted freemen
without taking the oaths. But by an Order in Council of
October 17th all the new members of the corporation were put
out, and the old members restored. On December 1st there was
some rabbling of Papists, but some of William's forces entered the
city, and the mayor and corporation gave their allegiance to
William.

The city of Norwich had been extremely Puritan under the
Commonwealth, but there was a great revival of churchmanship
at the Restoration. Indeed, a Norfolk Member of Parliament
stated in the House of Commons that there were 20,000 persons
in the city of Norwich,[5] and not twenty Dissenters.[6] This was

---

[1] " Broadmead Records," p. 247.
[2] Latimer, " Bristol in Seventeenth Century," p. 40; Crosby, " Hist. Eng
Bapts.," III. 155.
[3] " Broadmead Records," p. 268.
[4] Latimer, " Bristol in Seventeenth Century," pp. 438–440.
[5] The population in 1693 was between 28,000 and 29,000.
[6] " Parliamentary History," IV. 418.

manifestly incorrect.   Under Bishop Reynolds, himself formerly
a Presbyterian, the Clarendon Code was enforced with very little
vigour, and Dissent increased considerably.   In the Lambeth
Returns of 1669 was a report from Bishop Reynolds that there
were seven conventicles in the city, and that the Independents
to the number of 300, mostly women, held a conventicle every
Sunday, and once in the week, at the house of John Toft, a grocer,
and also at the houses of Mrs. Morse, a widow, and John Davey,
a merchant.   Efforts were made to suppress them, especially
by a certain Captain Clarke, a warden of one of the parish
churches.   In 1670 the Church Book of the Independents
recorded that while they were obliged to meet in " small parcels,"
baptisms in such small meetings should be registered as public
baptisms.   When they were prevented from meeting in the town,
they assembled in Lovingland and Cobham and other secluded
places.

Among the ministers licensed here in 1672 was Thomas Allen,
who had been ejected from St. George's, ten years previously.
He received permission to preach at a meeting in the house of
John Knight, but he died in the following year.[1]   Another and
more famous name was that of Dr. John Collinges, who had been
one of the Commissioners at the Savoy and had been ejected
from the vicarage of St. Stephen's.   He was licensed to preach
in his old parish, in the house of Jonathan Wilson, and to conduct
Presbyterian services there.   He was a learned man, and a
voluminous writer, and occupied part of his time in taking pupils.
Benjamin Snowden, who had episcopal orders, but had been
ejected in 1662 from St. Giles's,[2] also received a licence.   Collinges and he appear to have been the first pastors of the Presbyterian congregation in Norwich.   Other Dissenting ministers
licensed in the town at this time were John Lucas, ejected from
Statham,[3] Nathaniel Mitchell, Collinges' brother-in-law, ejected
from North Walsham,[4] John Corrie, ejected from Walcot,[5] who
for many years kept a private school in Norwich, Enoch Woodward, who may be the Mr. Woodward ejected from Southwold,[6]
and Martin Finch, a Congregationalist, ejected from Totney,
in Lincolnshire.[7]   All these had been licensed to preach in private
houses, but larger quarters were necessary.   On May 14th the
mayor and corporation granted leases for five years, at a rental
of £12 10s. per annum, of the East and West Granaries, belonging
to the city, to the Presbyterians and Independents respectively.
These granaries were originally the refectory and dormitory of
the Black Friars, and had thus been diverted from their
original purpose.[8]   The licensing authorities in London had
refused a licence for this building, probably thinking, wrongly,

[1] Palmer, III. 11.   [2] Palmer, III. 12.   [3] Palmer, III. 14.
[4] Palmer, III. 16.   [5] Palmer, III. 16.   [6] Palmer, III. 287.
[7] Palmer, II. 434.   [8] Stoughton, " Hist. Rel. Eng.," IV. 200.

that it was a public building. The Presbyterians kept the East Granary as a meeting-place till after the Revolution, when they erected a building of their own.[1] In all, seven places were licensed for the Presbyterians and four for the Independents. But when the Indulgence was withdrawn, persecution broke out again. About 1673 a body of people from Norwich and the neighbourhood emigrated to America, and founded another Norwich there. Interference with the meetings at the Granaries led to a riot at that place in December 1674.[2]

Robert Asty,[3] who had been ejected from Stratford, in Suffolk, and who had been keeping a school at Dedham for about ten years, went to Norwich in 1673 at the invitation of the Independents there, and became one of their pastors. Associated with him was John Cromwell,[4] who had been ejected from Claworth, in Nottinghamshire, and had been ordained by Fisher of Sheffield, assisted by other Independent ministers. He was imprisoned for some years at Newark, under suspicion of complicity in the plot of 1663. After he settled down at Norwich, he was said to have enjoyed but one peaceable Sunday. On his second Sunday he was forced out of his meeting-house, and for nine years was pursued with indictments at the Sessions and Assizes, and citations from the ecclesiastical courts. At last he had to shut himself up in his house, but that was at last broken open, and he had to remove from Norwich altogether. He died in 1685. During his residence in Norwich he was on one occasion invited to dine with the Bishop Reynolds, and found many of the junior clergy present. When he rose to take his leave, the bishop accompanied him to the door, which caused much laughter, for which the bishop rebuked them, and told them that Cromwell had more solid divinity in his little finger than they had in their whole bodies.

In 1678 an anonymous letter threatening to kill Dr. Sparrow, Bishop of Norwich, was thrown into a place near the episcopal throne in Norwich cathedral. Dr. John Collinges was about the same time proceeded against for preaching in conventicles, and the chancellor of the diocese also received a threatening letter, warning him to stay proceedings. Lord Yarmouth, in reporting this to Williamson, referred to Collinges as " a man long famous in this county for ill-affection to the Crown." The Lord Lieutenant and four of the deputy-lieutenants directed the mayor to summon Collinges, Cromwell, Francis Annyson, Robert Scoulden, John Balderstone, and William Nockolls, as persons privy to a design to murder the bishop; and to exact security of £500 from each of them to appear at the next Quarter Sessions.[5]

One had to be careful what one said in public. Thomas

[1] Browne, " Congregationalism in Norfolk and Suffolk," pp. 279–280.
[2] " Victoria Hist. Norfolk," II. 299.   [3] Palmer, III. 288.
[4] Palmer, III. 90.   [5] C.S.P.D., July 22nd, 1678, 405/123.

Firmin, one of the leaders of Unitarianism, happened to be in Norwich in the summer of 1681. Sitting in a coffee-house with a friend, he showed him a copy of Janeway's " Protestant Mercury," in which was an attack on the address recently sent from Norwich to the King. In July Firmin and his friend were both indicted at the Quarter Sessions for dispersing a scandalous and seditious libel, and a true bill was found against them. The coffee-house keeper was at the same time indicted for dispersing the address which had been recently presented to the King by the Lord Mayor and corporation of London.[1]

Martin Finch, whose name has already been mentioned as licensed in Norwich under the Declaration of Indulgence, was chosen as pastor of the Norwich Independents in 1685. At the beginning of his ministry he held services in an old brewhouse in St. Edmund's parish, but after the Toleration Act the " Old Meeting-House " was built, for his congregation.[2]   The Quakers were strong in Norwich, and indeed, in the whole county, but in July 1688, when James II. gave orders for the admission of thirty members of that sect as freemen of the city without taking the oaths, the corporation refused to admit them, thirty-nine voting against the King's proposal, and only eight in favour of it.[3]

Nonconformity was strong in Yarmouth. In October 1663 200 persons were presented at one time for not having received the sacrament.[4]   Some well-known names were connected with Dissent in that town: Thomas Bendish of Gray's Inn, who married Ireton's daughter, Bridget, came from there. His wife was at one time a regular member of Joseph Caryl's congregation in London.[5]   Nathaniel Carter of Yarmouth married another of Ireton's daughters, and there was a tradition that at his house, No. 4, South Quay, the decision was first arrived at to put Charles I to death. Cromwell's friend, Captain Joseph Ames, was another prominent Dissenter here.[6]   During the Commonwealth the Independents held their meetings in the chancel of the parish church, but on November 18th, 1661, they were turned out, the keys taken away, and the vestry door nailed up.[7]   Sir Thomas Meadows had been appointed one of the bailiffs that year, and it was he who was responsible for turning them out. Till 1666 they had no meeting-house, and only gathered by stealth, but about that time the Presbyterians and Independents began to get the civic government in their own hands. Those who had yielded a hollow conformity ceased to attend church, and many who had left the town returned.

[1] C.S.P.D., July 23rd, 1681; Adm. " Green. Hosp.," I., No. 112.
[2] Browne, " Congregationalism in Norfolk and Suffolk," p. 266.
[3] " Victoria Hist. Norfolk," II. 296.
[4] C.S.P.D., October 12th, 1663.   [5] Palmer, I. 146.
[6] Browne, " Congregationalism in Norfolk and Suffolk," pp. 231–232.
[7] Ibid., p. 226.

As early as 1665 Edmund Thaxter, one of the Dissenting leaders, had been chosen bailiff, but the Government had quashed the election, and had appointed two other men bailiffs by *mandamus.* William Watts, the collector of customs, was suspected of being mixed up in the plottings of 1663. He attended church once a month, but never received the sacrament.[1] From 1666 onwards, not half the members of the corporation were Churchmen, and some had not taken the oaths. John Woodruffe, a Presbyterian, had been elected bailiff, and had moved that they should omit from the bailiff's oath the words, " that you shall keep secret the King's counsel," and " you shall govern by law and reason." He also moved that All Saints' Day, Epiphany, and the Coronation Day should cease to be days on which scarlet should be worn by the corporation.[2]

On November 7th, 1667, at a meeting at the house of Isaac Preston, the Independents decided to invite Mr. William Bridge, who had been ejected from the parish church in 1662, to be their minister.[3] He soon gathered a large congregation. His services were held in the early morning, and such numbers attended that it was impossible to find a seat in his meeting-house after seven o'clock. His success emboldened others, and meetings were held at other places in the town, conducted by ministers from the outlying districts.[4]

Four or five hundred persons attended conventicles held in the house of Thomas Raven, who was a common councillor and the chamberlain of the town. The meetings were so full that people could hardly get in.[5] The Independents were the aggressive party, the Presbyterians called themselves moderate episcopalians. In 1662, however, the chief of them had persuaded the then ministers of Yarmouth, Brinsley,[6] and Allen,[7] not to conform, and had pensioned them off, although Allen's pension was not kept up. The Presbyterians were prominent on the town council, and were friendly with the Independents, and the two sects had united to establish house-to-house collections for the relief of the excluded ministers, which were still kept up in 1667. They were so bold that, as they increased in power in the town, they publicly affronted on occasion the leading laymen of the Anglican party.[8] There were complaints, too, against Bridge that he made proselytes among the Church-people, and had baptised some of their children.[9] The local authorities

[1] C.S.P.D., December 13th, 1665.
[2] C.S.P.D., December 14th, 1668.
[3] Palmer, III. 19; Browne, " Congregationalism in Norfolk and Suffolk," p. 233.
[4] C.S.P.D., March 11th, 1668, 236/76.
[5] C.S.P.D., December 16th, 18th, 23rd, 1667.
[6] Palmer, III. 17.   [7] Palmer, III. 11.
[8] C.S.P.D., January 24th, 1668.
[9] C.S.P.D., October 9th, 1668, 247/133.

382   STUDIES IN ENGLISH PURITANISM

now made an attempt to enforce the law. The King's proclamation against conventicles, issued in March 1668, was ignored both
by justices and bailiffs.[1] In October a letter was sent from
Mr. Secretary Morice warning the corporation that the King
had noticed that several of their members had not taken the
required oaths.[2] In December a half-hearted attempt was made
to get two members of the council to conform in this respect,
but without result.[3]

Complaints were made of the aggressiveness of the Yarmouth
Dissenters. Some of them were among the most wealthy
merchants there, and it was said that they tried to keep all the
trade in the hands of themselves and their friends, and that if any
one opposed them, or spoke against them, they would refuse to
trade with him, so that the other merchants and shopkeepers
were afraid of offending them.[4] The Dissenters attended Church
of England funerals, and jeered and laughed, and made such a
noise that the priest could not be heard; and some had even
tried to take his Prayer Book from him. Things were so bad in
this way, that some of the more timid Church-people buried
their dead secretly, to avoid disturbance. The thanksgiving for
the Restoration had been torn out of the Prayer Book in the
parish church, and Bridge had threatened the members of his
congregation with excommunication if they attended the Church
services.[5] There were unseemly scenes when the corporation
attended church.[6] All this was reported to Sir Joseph Williamson
son by one Richard Bower, an excise and customs officer,[7] who
for a long time kept the Government informed of all that was
going on. He was a Yorkshire man, and the son of a schoolmaster, and had come to live there since the Restoration.[8] But
the Dissenters had a friend at Court. Bower suspected Sir
William D'Oyley, who warned Bridge of the information that
was being sent. An order was issued to Lord Townshend, as
Lord-Lieutenant of Norfolk, at the King's command, that
Bridge and two other Dissenting ministers be summoned before
Lord Townshend at Norwich. This gave great offence, and two
Dissenters, James Johnson, formerly an alderman, and Richard
Huntingdon, an old Cromwellian officer and a justice of the
peace, went off at once to interview Townshend on the matter.
Thomas Lucas, one of the local merchants, talked loudly about
persecution, and complained that it should be begun at a time
when the Government was trying to arrange an accommodation

[1] C.S.P.D., March 20th, 1668, 237/22.
[2] C.S.P.D., October 9th, 1668, 247/133.
[3] C.S.P.D., December 9th, 1668, 250/70.
[4] C.S.P.D., February 25th, 1668, 235/86.
[5] C.S.P.D., October 9th, 1668, 247/133.
[6] C.S.P.D., December 21st, 1668, 250/157.
[7] C.S.P.D., February 19th, 1675.
[8] Hist. MSS. Com. VI. i. 380.

with the Dissenters.[1] Further rumours of indulgence came, and alarmed the Church party.[2]

Bridge was called before a meeting of deputy-lieutenants of the county, who were prepared not to prosecute if he would promise to leave the neighbourhood. He refused, and had to appear before the justices at the Sessions at Norwich on January 16th, 1669, and though he was treated with respect and consideration, he was ordered not to appear again within five miles of either Norwich or Yarmouth.[3] He died later on in the year. Less than two months after this the Independents fitted up a large meeting-place in the town, capable of holding 1000 persons, and this shortly proved too small, and they had to erect three galleries in it.[4] Bridge's son-in-law, Captain Thomas Raven, was an alderman, and chamberlain of the town. When, about the time of Bridge's return to Yarmouth, he had been elected a common councillor, he had refused to renounce the Covenant. Thaxter and Huntingdon opposed a motion that he should be made to do so, but he had finally been allowed to make his renunciation at the house of one of them, where he had signed a paper which he afterwards boasted was not a renunciation at all. He attended the Independent services, had had conventicles in his house, and when he attended church with the corporation he behaved with ostentatious contempt.[5]

At the instance of Woodruffe, one of the bailiffs and a Dissenter, the Coronation Day was not observed in 1669. The King's proclamation issued in April of that year against conventicles was posted up at the market cross, but had been pulled down, and though the offender was known, nothing was done. Woodruffe, it is true, advised the Independents to discontinue their meetings, but they refused. So little was the law observed that not half the corporation had received the sacrament.[6]

In 1670 a certain Captain Clark was busy trying to suppress conventicles, which roused open hostility from the opposite party. The bailiffs bound Nathaniel Carter over to appear at the Sessions on a charge of preaching at meetings. Richard Huntingdon, whose wife was one of their supporters, made a pretence of receiving information from three persons who had been reported as present at a conventicle, and there arose a dispute among the justices whether they could act as informers themselves, and divide the third of the fines. Some of the Dissenters met in Cobham Island, which they said was neither in Norfolk nor Suffolk; and also in Lovingland Island, where Alderman Raven had a house and entertained them. There

[1] C.S.P.D., December 9th, 1668, 250/70.
[2] C.S.P.D., December 14th, 1668. [3] C.S.P.D., January 16th, 1669.
[4] C.S.P.D., March 3rd and 22nd, 1669, 257/125, 154.
[5] C.S.P.D., April 14th, 26th, 1669, November 2nd, 1670.
[6] C.S.P.D., August 30th, September 5th, 1669, 264/140, 265/116.

was a meeting-house in Yarmouth belonging to Major Burton, but the justices could not levy the householder's fine, because he was in Holland.[1] The fact was, the justices, or most of them, did not wish to enforce the law, and Captain Clark went to London to lay an information against them. He complained that he had a warrant to suppress a meeting of 400 or 500 persons in Major Burton's house, and on their refusal to disperse he had taken a list of fifty names to the justices, but they refused to interfere. It was also reported to the Government about this time that a motion had been proposed in the corporation to the effect that all members should produce a certificate of having received the sacrament, and that it had been rejected.[2] The King ordered Lord Townshend to institute inquiries, and to draw up a list of fit persons to be justices in the counties of Norfolk and Suffolk.[3] A month later some people were fined for attending a conventicle at a house belonging to Raven at Burgh Castle, but when the constables attempted to distrain, they found that the doors of the house were locked, and that the goods had been removed.[4] Townshend's sympathies were evidently with the Nonconformists. Williamson wrote to him about Clark's information against Huntington and others, and he handed the inquiry over to Sir William D'Oyley and Robert Suckling, the latter's son-in-law. D'Oyley was under personal obligations to Huntingdon and his friends, and was on friendly terms with some of the leading Dissenters. Clark was ordered to attend an inquiry in Norwich on October 5th, but the very day before this Huntingdon was given a captain's commission in the trainbands.[5] Sir Thomas Meadows wrote to Townshend, who had tried to get his support for the captaincy for Huntingdon,[6] and protested against the way in which he was putting Cromwellian rebels into positions of trust. He said, also, that of 12,000 people in the town who ought to be communicants, only 500 had actually received the sacrament.[7] Clark took another journey to London, and his activity seems to have frightened a number of Dissenters into attending church again. On December 23rd there was issued an Order in Council that Clark's petition to the King and an annexed paper, " A True and Perfect Narrative of the Government of the Town of Great Yarmouth," should be forwarded to Lord Townshend for his consideration and report.[8] Huntingdon was made a justice of the peace about the end of 1670.[9]

In the following September Sir Thomas Meadows was chosen head bailiff, which gave great offence to the Dissenters. But

---

[1] C.S.P.D., July 5th, 6th, 1670.
[2] C.S.P.D., August 1st, 1670.
[3] C.S.P.D., August 12th, 1670.
[4] C.S.P.D., October 10th, 1670.
[5] C.S.P.D., October 10th, 1670.
[6] C.S.P.D., January 25th, 1671.
[7] C.S.P.D., November 2nd, 1670.
[8] C.S.P.D., December 19th, 23rd, 1670.
[9] C.S.P.D., January 25th, 1671.

their position was very strong. Clark's efforts against them were in vain. Lord Townshend did nothing, and the Church and King party let things go. When the King visited Yarmouth in October, James Johnson, who had formerly borne arms against the King, and was now major of the city regiment, received Charles at his house. The Churchmen were thrust aside, Sir Thomas Meadows being publicly affronted by Townshend; the Anglican clergy, who wished to pay their respects to the King, were kept back by Townshend's influence, and knighthood was conferred upon the mayor and George England, another Dissenter.[1]

In 1672 William Sheldrake[2] was ordained as pastor of the Independents in Yarmouth. Apparently he had had no ordination before. He had been ejected from Reepham, and had been engaged in the woollen and yarn trade since then. The Declaration of Indulgence, of course, enabled them to hold their meetings without fear of interruption.[3] Their meeting-house had become too small, and they were busy in the following year collecting subscriptions to build a larger one.[4] Bower gave a description of the Nonconformist services. He said that the preacher first went into the pulpit and prayed, then he sat down while the congregation sang a psalm "which is of their own making," whatever that may mean. Then came the sermon. The Scriptures were not read, "not so much as a verse, except it be for proof of their teaching." The meeting-houses, generally about 60 feet long by 50 feet broad, had a gallery running round with six rows of seats, one behind the other.[5] The Declaration of Indulgence had long been withdrawn, and the meetings had been less frequent, but towards the end of 1674 the Nonconformists throughout the country began to meet boldly afresh, especially as it was reported that the King had ordered the justices to grant no warrants against them, and that soon they would have the royal permission again.[6] It was said that Dr. Owen had had an interview with King Charles, and had complained of the Nonconformists being disturbed in various places, Yarmouth being mentioned among them, and the King said he would take speedy measures to redress this.[7] The Dissenters had the support at Court also of Sir John Pettus, who had said that it was known that the laws against Romanists and Nonconformists were not enforced, and so it was probable that the King desired lenience to be shown towards his subjects, whereas the indiscreet endeavours of fiery men to suppress Dissenters would probably lead to an increase in them.[8] The meetings

[1] C.S.P.D., September 1st, October 9th, 1671.   [2] Palmer, III. 13.
[3] Browne, "Congregationalism in Norfolk and Suffolk," p. 239.
[4] C.S.P.D., January 22nd, 1673, 332/177.
[5] C.S.P.D., November 4th, 1674.   [6] C.S.P.D., December 2nd, 9th, 1674.
[7] C.S.P.D., January 15th, 1675.   [8] C.S.P.D., January 27th, 1675.

were continued, but at the beginning of 1675 it was with their doors shut.[1] On the last Sunday in February the bailiffs, requested to do so by Bower, went to the conventicle and urged them to forbear their meeting. It had not begun, and many of the congregation, seeing Bower at the door when they arrived, did not go in. It was decided that some of the members who had been convicted some time before should be proceeded against by distress, but the constables declared they could not get into the houses. Bower threatened them with prosecution for neglecting their duty, so they went to Sheldrake's house. He had been fined £20, but as he would not open to them, they broke in and seized some of his goods, upon which he paid them £10. In retaliation the Dissenters bought Bower's house over his head.[2] At the Sessions at the end of March, one of the Yarmouth Dissenters, who had been fined £5 for conventicling, appealed, but as he had not done this within the statutory time, he had to pay treble costs. This not very vigorous effort at suppression produced little result, for not only were the meetings attended by greater numbers than ever, but the Presbyterians and Independents combined to hold their meetings in the same place.[3] Thaxter was made bailiff again in the autumn, and gave a sumptuous dinner to Lord Yarmouth and the local gentry.[4]

In 1676 a resolution was passed by the Dissenters that in case of trouble about a meeting, the congregation should pay the fines of the minister and of the owner of the house. The members should pay their own fines when they could, but the whole body would be responsible for the fines of the poor members.[5]

When the attempted religious census was made in 1676, there was a fear in Yarmouth, as elsewhere, that if a true return were made the King would be alarmed at their numbers, and would be discouraged from any attempt to protect them. Religion in the town seemed in a bad way. It was estimated that of the professed Anglicans, there were not more than 500 communicants,[6] and though the Nonconformist meeting-house was said to hold 2000 persons, and was sometimes full to the doors,[7] it was believed that not more than 100 men, besides the women, were in full church fellowship with them. But a number of unstable and irreligious persons had joined them, it was said, from the desire to support what would tend to the weakening of authority. Some, doubtless, were of the same opinion as some of the customs officers, who when questioned declared " it was madness to lose an office for a bit of bread and a cup of wine." [8] But when a collection was made in June for the relief of the sufferers by a

---

[1] C.S.P.D., February 22nd, 1675.   [2] C.S.P.D., March 1st, 10th, 1675.
[3] C.S.P.D., April 5th, July 29th, August 27th, 1675.
[4] Hist. MSS. Com. VI. i. 373.
[5] Browne, " Congregationalism in Norfolk and Suffolk," p. 236.
[6] C.S.P.D., February 21st, 1676.   [7] C.S.P.D., June 12th, 1676.
[8] C.S.P.D., July 19th, 1676.

recent fire, it was noted that the church collection was £13, and the chapel collection £24.[1]

Lord Townshend had thrown his influence on the side of the Dissenters, and promoted them to public offices when he could.[2] In 1676 Lord Yarmouth was made Lord Lieutenant of Norfolk, and he, too, seemed inclined to favour them. Robert Doughty wrote to him in March to protest against Sir John Hobart and Sir John Holland being made deputy-lieutenants, and against any of Shaftesbury's party being put into the commission of the peace, " he being as ill thought of here as at Whitehall." [3] Lord Yarmouth was very angry with Sir Thomas Meadows, who refused to serve in any way under him, unless Huntingdon were turned out.[4] Though he had refused to do this, there were nevertheless great outcries at Norwich against the new Lord Lieutenant, who was accused of being a favourer of popery.[5] Sir Thomas Meadows was left to himself, and the Dissenters were appeased by the appointment of Sir George England as colonel of the city regiment, Thaxter as lieutenant-colonel, and Thomas England, one of Sir George England's sons, as a captain. Lord Yarmouth told his wife, " This is a piece of policy amongst ourselves, contrived to disappoint the other party.[6]

In the summer of 1676 the Nonconformists had become much bolder, the military and civil power in the town being in the hands of their friends. They were singing psalms openly at their meetings, a thing they had not done since the withdrawal of the Declaration of Indulgence. Major-General Desborough and Lord Fleetwood were staying in the town during the summer, and apparently attending their services.[7] Three informers, strangers to the place, appeared in Yarmouth in July, and obtained a warrant from Thaxter, who, though himself a Dissenter, took them and the constables to the meeting-house. The constables did not arrest anyone, and said they did not know the people present, though three of them were accustomed to frequent the conventicles themselves. Thaxter told the informers that they had better go round the town to see if they could recognise any who had been present. The following Sunday, however, they succeeded in dispersing a meeting of eighty or ninety Baptists, and these somewhat feeble attempts to enforce the law resulted in a much increased attendance at church that Sunday. The following day the informers left the town on a boat going to Norwich, but they were recognised, and the other passengers refused to travel with them. They were therefore put ashore, where the Dissenters stoned them, and they took refuge in Bower's house.[8] Bower himself, however, was in trouble this year. On

---

[1] C.S.P.D., June 26th, 1676.　　　　[2] C.S.P.D., February 21st, 1676.
[3] Hist. MSS. Com. VI. i. 374.　　　　[4] Ibid., p. 379.
[5] Ibid., p. 375.　　　　[6] Ibid., p. 379.
[7] C.S.P.D., June 12th, September 11th, 1676.
[8] C.S.P.D., July 7th, 10th, 12th, 1676.

July 12th he had sent a letter to Secretary Williamson.   Sir
George England, Thomas England his son, Edmund Thaxter,
one of the bailiffs and Sir George England's son-in-law,[1] and
Richard Huntingdon wrote to Lord Yarmouth complaining that
the letter in question, which Williamson had forwarded to the
Lord Lieutenant, and the latter had passed on to Richard
Huntingdon,[2] was a scandalous libel.   It accused the magistrates
of Yarmouth of conniving at Nonconformist meetings, and said
that the militia officers and justices of the town were such as had
supported the late rebellious government.   It also stated that
Lord Yarmouth was under the influence of Sir William D'Oyley,
an enemy of the Church.   The signatories of the letter to the
Lord Lieutenant asked for Bower's punishment, and made similar
accusations against him of disloyal conduct under the Commonwealth.   Bower kept a coffee-house, and they accused him of
collecting intelligence and making cabals there, and tampering
with the discipline of the militia.[3]   Influence was made with the
Lord Treasurer against him, and it was proposed to send a
petition to the King in Council accusing him, and he was threatened
with actions at law and with ruin thereby.[4]   In September some
of the people of Yarmouth signed a certificate to the effect that
he was a person of sober life amd conversation, obedient to the
King's laws, ecclesiastical and civil, and lived quietly and
peaceably with his neighbours.   On the 20th of that month he
was brought up at the Yarmouth Sessions, confronted with his
letter to Williamson, and bound over until the next Sessions.
Bradford, one of the bailiffs, said that Lord Townshend had
pressed them to take this course, but Lord Townshend told
Thaxter he would have nothing to do with it.[5]   He was summoned for selling coffee without a licence, and though he
promised not to do so any more, he was ordered to pay £5.   He
himself said it was his wife's business, but, however this may have
been, a distress was levied on him on September 28th.   This
method had been taken with him at Lord Yarmouth's advice,
and Lord Paston had said that he would make him leave the town.[6]
A week later he began to sell coffee again, and applied to Huntingdon for a licence, and on the latter's refusal, he threatened to
appeal to the King in Council.   Again his goods were distrained,
and the clique who ruled the town set up a new coffee-house
for one of Sir George England's relatives.   His enemies then
petitioned the King against Bower, and urged Williamson that
the business might be looked into speedily.[7]
    The Nonconformists during September held meetings outside the

---

[1] C.S.P.D., June 12th, 1676.   [2] C.S.P.D., September 20th, 1676.
[3] Hist. MSS. Com. VI. i. 379–380.   [4] C.S.P.D., September 4th, 1676.
[5] C.S.P.D., September 20th, 1676.
[6] C.S.P.D., September 26th, 29th; Hist. MSS. Com. VI. i. 380.
[7] C.S.P.D., October 13th, 23rd, 1676; Hist. MSS. Com. VI. i. 381.

town, but they still carried matters with a high hand. When the constable went to execute a distress on Francis Clifton, who had been fined £5 for conventicling, Clifton snatched the warrant from him, and refused to return it, for which he was sent to gaol.[1] But Huntingdon and one of Sir George England's sons were chosen bailiffs, and the Dissenters returned to their old meeting-house,[2] and in the following February Huntingdon was chosen as one of the Members of Parliament for Yarmouth.[3]

On March 12th, 1677, Bower, who had been in London for six months trying to get protection from the King or the King's Secretary, wrote Williamson an angry letter. For nine months in all, he said, he had been waiting for him to free him from the trouble he had brought upon him. Williamson had told " Mr. Rawlins, Lord Paston's gentleman," that he had not asked for any information from Bower, and that he was a troublesome rascally fellow who loved to busy himself. Bower said angrily in this letter that even if Williamson had not asked for his information, there was the danger to the peace of Church and State to be considered; but he had in his possession Williamson's own letter asking for his information, and for fifteen years he had obeyed his commands and sent it. Then one of his letters had been shown to his adversaries, he had been bound over to the Sessions, his letter had been delivered to them, and he was to be tried in their court, where they would sit as judges in their own cause. Williamson had told him the King had ordered that he should come to London, where his case might be heard. His enemies were trying to ruin him and his wife, and he expected no kindness but words from the Secretary, who had brought all this trouble upon him.[4]

Whether Williamson had asked him to do so or not, Bower continued to send him information for a long time after this. But his enemies still continued their attacks. In Trinity term, 1677, an information was laid against him in the Crown Office for a libel against Lord Paston, Sir William D'Oyley, and other justices of Norfolk.[5] In the beginning of March 1678 he reported to Williamson that he was to be tried at the Assizes at Thetford, before Sir William Scroggs, on the 14th of that month. He was hopeful of the result, unless there should be a factious jury, which, of course, they would try to obtain. He complained to the Secretary that all this might have been avoided if his case had been heard before the King, as Williamson had promised. He begged that Williamson would send a letter to Scroggs to say that he had been his official correspondent, and also Lord Arlington's. His expenses would be great, and even if successful, he would be

[1] C.S.P.D., September 4th, 7th, 1676.
[2] C.S.P.D., September 29th, October 9th, 1676.
[3] Hist. MSS. Com. VI. i. 390.   [4] C.S.P.D., March 12th, 1677, 392/3.
[5] C.S.P.D., February 14th, 1678, 401/102.

unable to recover his costs, and he pleaded that the Secretary would bring his condition before the King, that he might get some relief.[1] For the trial Bower subpœnaed the town clerk to appear, and to produce the Assembly Books. The bailiffs would not permit the books to be removed.[2] Viscount Yarmouth meanwhile had heard, through his wife, that Williamson would prefer the proceedings against Bower to be dropped. He had only heard a few days previously that a prosecution was intended, and he sent to advise the Yarmouth people to put off the trial. The letter reached them just as the witnesses against Bower were about to set off for Thetford, but it was decided there and then that the prosecution should be postponed.[3] In July Sir Thomas Meadows advised Bower to write to Williamson to ask whether he desired him to take his trial at the forthcoming Assizes or not. He did so, but asked Sir Joseph not to put off the trial, for he was prepared to show his adversaries in an even worse light than hitherto. He took the opportunity at the same time to ask for the post of collector of the customs, which had fallen vacant through the death of the last holder.[4] But apparently nothing further was done in the matter, for on August 22nd he wrote to Sir Thomas Meadows boasting that his enemies dared not bring the matter to trial at the Assizes.[5]

The corporation of Yarmouth consisted of twenty-eight aldermen and forty-eight common council men. From among the aldermen two bailiffs were yearly chosen, and they in turn each chose a justice of the peace from the members of the aldermanic bench; the bailiffs for the previous year being also justices for the year following. In 1678 there were thirty members of the corporation who, in defiance of the Corporation Act, had not received the sacrament. Bower estimated that out of 12,000 possible communicants in the town, only 500 were actually so, and many of those were poor people who received a share of the collection at the time of the sacrament. It had been proposed in the council that before the bailiffs were elected the churchwardens should make a return of the names of the persons qualified. Huntingdon and his friends had vigorously opposed, and carried the day. Of how little advantage enforced attendance at church was, may be gathered from the repeated complaints of Huntingdon's irreverent behaviour when he was present.[6] There was a hotly contested election for a vacant seat on the council at the beginning of 1678, and Sir Thomas Meadows and Huntingdon were the rival candidates. There were only 600 freemen, and they only had the right to vote. The Dissenters were accused of all kinds of indirect practices, while

[1] C.S.P.D., March 4th, 1678.   [2] C.S.P.D., March 15th, 1678.
[3] Ibid., 402/80.
[4] C.S.P.D., July 17th, 1678, 405/99.   [5] C.S.P.D., August 23rd, 1678.
[6] C.S.P.D., March 8th, 1678, 402/29.

their opponents threatened to put the Conventicle Act in force against them. Sir William D'Oyley gave great assistance to Huntingdon, but Meadows was elected, to the great jubilation of the Church party and chagrin of the others.[1] The majority in the council agreed that no man should be allowed to purchase the freedom of the town unless he conformed to the Church of England, and in August they decided that the same proviso should attach to the holding of any office in the town.[2] Things then became quieter in Yarmouth than for some years past.

The members of the Independent congregation at Yarmouth expressed their thanks to James II. for his first Declaration of Indulgence, and two representatives presented their address to the King on June 10th, 1687.[3] They had opened a new place of worship on the west side of Gaol, or Middlegate, Street in the April of that year.[4] In 1688 James Hannot, who had been educated at Morton's academy at Newington Green, was appointed their minister.[5]

In South Town there lived Mrs. Bendish, the granddaughter of Oliver. She is said to have been very like her grandfather in character and in personal appearance and once when she heard a man abuse him she challenged him to a duel with pistols. A Calvinist in religion, and a follower of John Owen, she waged perpetual war against the spies and informers who troubled the Nonconforming ministers. She was in the secret of the Rye House plot, and succeeded in freeing from imprisonment a relative who had been arrested on account of it. Before the Revolution she was very active, and made a habit of dropping bundles of Whig revolutionary papers in the Yarmouth shops by way of sowing the seed.[6]

The city of Gloucester afforded a good example of the strife and bitterness caused by religious divisions at this period. In September 1670 the best-qualified candidate for the mayoralty for the ensuing year was Alderman Henry Fowler, a local physician. The Presbyterian party were trying to secure the election of William Bubb, who was not a resident in the city, and who had threatened to crush the royalist interest in the corporation if he were made mayor. All this was reported to the King, who promptly ordered the aldermen and common council to elect Dr. Fowler, or else appear before the Privy Council and give their reasons for not doing so, and Fowler was elected, only five recalcitrant aldermen voting against him.[7] Over the South Gate was a trophy erected in 1643 after Gloucester had been

---

[1] C.S.P.D., December 28th, 1677; January 4th, 7th; March 1st, 1678.
[2] C.S.P.D., August 23rd, 1678.
[3] Browne, " Congregationalism in Norfolk and Suffolk," p. 178.
[4] *Ibid.*, p. 237.   [5] *Ibid.*, p. 239.
[6] Noble, " Memoirs of the Protectorate House of Cromwell," II. 329–346.
[7] C.S.P.D., September 7th, 10th, 22nd, 1670.

delivered by Essex, bearing the words, " A city assaulted by man, but saved by God." Fowler during his year of office had it removed, and the King's arms set up instead, with the inscription :

> Insignia haec regia a nuperis rebellibus cruentis summo scelere demolita, Henricus Fowler, armiger, hujus civitatis, ex speciali mandato Regio, Major, restituenda curavit. 1671

In September 1671 there was a great deal of trouble about the appointment of the next mayor. In August the loyalist party had succeeded in ejecting Dr. Fielding, an ex-mayor, from the offices of alderman and justice of the peace.[1] He was a Dissenter, and disqualified. By the city charter there were bound to be eleven aldermen before they could elect a mayor, while for election in council there had to be thirty present to form a quorum. Dr. Fowler summoned a council meeting to elect an alderman in the place of Fielding. The opposition did not attend, so there was not a quorum, and no alderman could be elected. That meant that no mayor could be chosen either, and Fowler would have to continue for another year. The Nonconformists still wanted Alderman Bubb to be mayor, as they thought they could control him, and they had agreed that if he were elected he could still live on his country farm, while they would bear the expenses of his mayoralty.[2] When the day came for the election, the mayor summoned the council to attend the morning service in the cathedral, and to meet afterwards at one o'clock in the council chamber in the Booth Hall. The opposition, instead of going to the service, met together and chose Bubb as mayor, and two other men, Veysey and Phelps, as sheriffs. It was all over, and the bells of St. Michael's were ringing for the new mayor when the others came out of the cathedral, although John Downey, the town clerk, had told Bubb's friends that they were acting illegally. At the appointed time Fowler and the others arrived for the election. Their adversaries told them it was over, and demanded the sword and mace. For the possession of these some of them came to fisticuffs, but Fowler carried them off in triumph to his own house. After his departure the people who had made the election that morning remained in the council chamber, and swore in their mayor and sheriffs. Next day they summoned the council, which met on October 4th, at which the first thing they did was to break open the treasury and make an order that the sword and mace should be given up to them.[3] All this was reported by Fowler to Whitehall, and he received orders from the Crown that every person concerned should receive notice to appear on October 30th, the day appointed by the King for the matter to be heard. Meanwhile,

---

[1] C.S.P.D., August 7th, 1671.
[2] C.S.P.D., August 30th, 1671.
[3] C.S.P.D., October 4th, 1671.

he was to continue as mayor till the affair was settled.[1] Bubb seems, however, to have had the larger following, and when Fowler summoned the council, as he did twice that month, only a few of his friends appeared.[2] On the 21st a serjeant-at-arms was sent to Gloucester to arrest Alderman Bubb, and to bring him before the Privy Council to answer for his contempt of the King's commands.[3] At the end of November the recalcitrants found, to their surprise, that the charter of the city was forfeited, and that two members of the council had to take it to London to deliver it to the King.[4]

Downey, the town clerk, already mentioned, was a Dissenter at heart, though outwardly he conformed to his parish church. He refused to attend the cathedral, because of the organ there. There was some suggestion of putting a man named John Gise in his place. The latter was a man of good family, and a Churchman, and willing to pay Downey a salary for life. Downey had formerly been out of office for some years because of his fidelity to the Covenant, but he had been persuaded to conform, and Dr. Viner, Dean of Gioucester, thought that in the event of his restitution to the town clerkship, when the charter was restored, he might be persuaded to attend the choir offices.[5]

While the civic affairs of Gloucester were thus in confusion and authority was in abeyance, there was trouble also in the cathedral. Hundreds of people attended the afternoon service daily, and behaved so riotously and profanely that neither the voice of the clergyman nor the sound of the organ could be heard and the hour of service had to be changed from 4 p.m. to 2 p.m. The leader was Anthony Arnold, a Nonconformist attorney, and one of the bitterest opponents of Dr. Fowler. The Dean asked Williamson if the bishop and some other people living within the College might not be made justices of the peace, with authority within the cathedral precincts to punish offenders.[6]

In 1680, James Forbes, the Nonconformist minister, had been prosecuted and imprisoned under the Five Mile Act, much damage had been done to the furniture and fittings of his meeting-house, a copy of his *mittimus* had been repeatedly refused him, and his *habeas corpus* ignored. In the autumn of that year the Earl of Anglesey wrote to the mayor rebuking him for enforcing the laws against Dissenters, especially at a time when such severity was considered an encouragement of popish designs against Protestantism. He reminded him that the liberty given to the London Nonconformists in recent years had shown them to be a quiet, sober people, and said that there was no reason to suppose the Gloucester Dissenters to be in any way different. It was

[1] C.S.P.D., October 13th, 14th, 1671.   [2] C.S.P.D., October 21st, 1671.
[3] C.S.P.D., Entry Book 34, f. 119.   [4] C.S.P.D. November 27th, 1671.
[5] C.S.P.D., December 2nd, 16th, 1671.
[6] C.S.P.D., November 27th, December 9th, 1671.

expected that as soon as Parliament met several of the penal laws would be repealed, and in particular the Five Mile Act, which had fallen almost entirely into disuse. He counselled the mayor and aldermen to set Forbes free the first moment the law allowed, and to tell him that he would experience no more trouble, provided that he and his people did not affront the magistrates and clergy, and were content to wait for the King and Parliament, or the King and Council, to make other provision or give other instructions. Anglesey had written to Forbes, and did not think they would find him vindictive, though he had good ground for action against them, and could claim damages.[1]

For some time after the Restoration, until the Act of Uniformity came out, the Presbyterian preachers in Oxford did their best to keep their flocks together, and by the pains they took in praying and preaching, to show how much superior their way was to the Episcopal way. On the other hand, the Episcopalians did not show up well. They avoided preaching, " which made many think they dared not," and deputed inferior men to do their duty for them. Many people kept their sons from the university, either giving them private tutors, who strengthened them in Presbyterianism, or sending them abroad to be educated; in many cases with bad results for their religion. The organs were restored at Christ Church, Magdalen, New College, and St. John's, and the musical services proved a great attraction. The Presbyterian and Independents in their discourses and pamphlets made fun of the " whining " of the organs, and the prayers and preaching of the Episcopalians, " so formal and superstitious that if one word was displaced, they could not go forward, but begin again." The Cavalier party gave offence to the precisians by their sports, and drinking on Sundays, and by their neglect to rebuke the drunkenness and immorality which were beginning to be rife. The supporters of the late régime were abused in common discourses and even in the speeches at the University Acts. The taking of notes during sermons, the practice of singing psalms after supper on Sundays—things dear to the heart of the Puritan—were abolished and scoffed at. The lecture or sermon on Tuesday mornings, and that at All Hallows, were done away with, " not only that such lectures in the nation had been fomenters of the late rebellion, but that at present they did continue and nourish faction." [2]

Calamy said that there were fifty-five ejections from the university in 1660. Ten of these were Heads of Houses, and seven intruded Fellows were dismissed from Corpus alone.[3] Some of the former holders of office, who had been turned out under the Commonwealth, now came back, but only some. In a contemporary list of the changes at Corpus, drawn up by a Mr.

---

[1] C.S.P.D., 414/109.   [2] Wood, " Life and Times," I. 355–357.
[3] Fowler, " Hist. Corpus Christi Coll.," p. 232.

Joshua Reynolds, the writer said that all the rest of the ejected members were "either dead, married, or preferred, except John Betts, who turned Papist." [1]

Dr. John Conant, Rector of Exeter, Regius Professor of Divinity, and Vice-Chancellor from 1657 to 1660, took to wearing academical costume again, and tried to get the Masters to do the same, and Mr. Edward Bagshawe protested in full Convocation, and was supported by Mr. Charles Pickering, Mr. Henry Bold, and Mr. Henry Thurnam. [2]

Wood said of some of the persons restored to office that they were not learned, and the Presbyterians took great advantage of their ignorance. He painted an unpleasing picture, too, of those who conformed. Some of those who had complied with Presbyterian and Independent ways now changed round and cringed for preferment. Of this he gave several painful examples. " As for the junior scholars, trained up in the Presbyterian discipline, it cannot be imagined what ways they took to express themselves real converts for the prelatical party upon the change." [3] As the iron hand of Puritanism had forced many into hypocrisy, so the swing of the pendulum produced men whose only religion was a loud-mouthed profession of loyalty to the Church, and of hatred of the Puritan and all his works, and this they combined with a disregard for morality, or even outward decency of conduct. Wood said, " Neither wanted there continual tell-tales, and discoverers of conventicles in Oxon, though themselves were drunkards and sneerers." He told of three scholars, two at least of whom were graduates, and one of the two a Student of Christ Church, who, going home late one night in December 1663, and the worse for drink, saw a light in the old Congregation House adjoining St. Mary's, and immediately sent for the Proctor and others to break up a supposed conventicle. Bursting into the building, they found a bookseller named Davis, with his wife and a boy, sorting out books for sale in London. Davis had taken the building a few weeks before to serve as a warehouse. " And so they were frustrated in their design. . . . Before they entered, they, listening under the window, heard Davis say to his wife, ' Oh, the Bible! I had almost forgot the Bible,' which made them verily suspect there had been a conventicle." [4]

In 1663 Clarendon, as Chancellor, summoned John Conant, Christopher Rogers, Henry Cornish and Thomas Gilbert before him, and banished them outside the bounds of the university. [5] John Conant was a Presbyterian, a voluminous writer of sermons, of which thirty manuscript volumes remain in the Bodleian Library, a distinguished oriental scholar, and a Savoy Commissioner. He went out in 1662, but afterwards conformed,

[1] Fowler, "Hist. Corpus Christi Coll.," p. 233.
[2] Wood, " Life and Times," I. 359.   [3] *Idem, ibid.*, I. 355–370.
[4] *Idem, ibid.*, I. 509.   [5] Mallet, " Hist. Univ. Oxford," 1924, II. 240.

was ordained priest in 1670, and died a prebendary of Worcester.[1] Cornish had been ejected from Christ Church, Oxford,[2] Rogers from the Principalship of New Inn Hall and a canonry at Christ Church,[3] and Gilbert from Bridgenorth. The last-named, known in after days as " old Father Gilbert," was an excellent scholar, who, according to Calamy, had all the schoolmen at his finger ends.[4] Dr. Henry Langley, Master of Pembroke, retired at the Restoration to his house at Tubney, where he took pupils, the sons of Nonconformists, and frequently preached in conventicles at Abingdon and Oxford.[5] These were the fathers of Nonconformity in Oxford.

The Baptists had a footing in Oxford before the Restoration, owing to the work of Vavasour Powell. The New Road Baptist Chapel in Oxford claims to go back to the year 1600. In 1672 Laurence King and Richard Tidmarsh were licensed to hold Baptist services in the house of the latter.[6] Langley, Cornish, Gilbert, and John Troughton, an ejected Fellow of St. John's College,[7] set up a meeting in Thames Street, outside the North Gate.[8] An attempt to get a licence for Thomas Gilbert to hold services in St. Peter-le-Bailey was opposed by Dr. Mews the Vice-Chancellor, so he only received a licence as a Congregational teacher, with the right of preaching in any licensed place. However, in 1687 he opened a meeting-house in St. Peter's parish. Robert Pauling received a licence to hold Presbyterian services in the house of Anthony Hall. Robert Rogers, whom Walker described as the son of a miller and " a very dunce," got a licence to be a Congregational minister in his own house and in the house of Michael Mercer in the parish of St. Mary Magdalene. Alderman William Wright and Brome Harwood were elected Members of Parliament in 1679. The former, who was the son of an Oxford goldsmith, was elected for the three last Parliaments of Charles II. He was an influential member of the city council, a Whig in politics, and was later on suspected of complicity in the Rye House plot.[9] The University of Oxford was loyal to the Stuart sovereigns up to the disastrous year 1688, when a great portion at least of the academic body changed right round, and supported William. The town was usually on the opposite side. Thus, in September 1680 Monmouth was made a freeman of the city of Oxford. He was conducted into the city by the mayor and several of the aldermen, one of whom had hired a number of

---

[1] Boase, " Registrum Collegii Exoniensis," p. 111; Palmer, I. 229.
[2] Palmer, I. 215.   [3] Palmer, I. 254.   [4] Palmer, I. 309; III. 145.
[5] Wood, " Life and Times," II. 1.
[6] Summers, " Congregational Churches in South Oxon and South Bucks," pp. 243–244.
[7] Palmer, I. 235.
[8] Wood, " Athenæ," II. 511; " Life," II. 244.
[9] Magrath, " The Flemings in Oxford," I. 298; Wood, " Life and Times," III. 93.

bargemen to march as a guard before him, shouting " God bless
the Protestant Duke! No York! No bishops! No university!"
The following day there was a dinner, at which various toasts
were drunk, such as " To the Protestant Duke and Magna
Charta," " To the confusion of the Bishop of Oxford," " To the
confusion of the Vice-Chancellor," " To the confusion of all
popish dukes, all bishops, and all colleges," " To the next
session of Parliament, when bold Britain would accuse the Duke
of York of high treason." The university kept aloof from the
proceedings. Monmouth was made a freeman of Oxford at the
house of Colonel Crooke, a name hated by all Cavaliers for the
death of Penruddock and his friends, and the chief persons who
attended the ceremony were Lord Lovelace, the two Members of
Parliament for the city, both Dissenters, and the two Members
for the county. Lord Lovelace distinguished himself by riding
about the town bawling with great imprecations that he was for
the Protestant religion and the Protestant Duke. As Monmouth
passed through the streets the mob showed their hope that he
would be King soon. The King wrote to express his approval
of those of the gentry who had given the Duke no encouragement.[1]

As everywhere, the Dissenters tried to seize the municipal
government. Humphrey Prideaux gave John Ellis a description
of the election of a mayor there in 1681. The man who had the
best claim to the office, and the " only person in the corporation
that is for the King's interest," was Taverner Harris, but they
set him aside, and elected F. W. Bailey, who was " old and half-
doted," and who had already had two apoplectic fits. A deputation from the corporation had recently presented a petition to
the King at Newmarket, asking him to make a man named
Prince town clerk, and the King had rejected it. The link-boys
there threw stones and dirt at them, called them Presbyterian
petitioners and Whiggish dogs, and shouted, " God preserve the
King and his whole family and kindred and keep him safe from
the hands of all that are in any ways related to the tribe of
Forty-one." Prideaux complained that everything was in the
hands of Alderman Wright and Pauling, the late mayor.[2] He
had more to say of Pauling. Under the date March 19th, 1682
he wrote that Robert " Pawlin," " the canting, preaching
attorney, as notorious a knave as any in the county," was to be
town clerk. Alderman Wright was responsible for this, and an
arrangement had been made by which Prince was to receive a
sum of money from Pauling, or else was to act for him and receive
a share of the profits. Wood tells how Pauling, when mayor,
had spoken of Dr. Fell, the Bishop of Oxford, as a " grand

[1] C.S.P.D., Entry Book 62, p. 70, September 20th, 1680; Ormonde MSS.,
V. 449.
[2] " Letters of Humphrey Prideaux to John Ellis," pp. 90–93.

398 STUDIES IN ENGLISH PURITANISM

hypocrite," who " though he prayed seven times a day, yet had seven devils in him." [1] In 1685 he was found guilty of high misdemeanour and *scandalum magnatum*. [2]

At Reading the great leader of Nonconformity was Christopher Fowler, [3] who had been deprived of a fellowship at Eton in 1660, and was ejected from St. Mary's, Reading, in 1662. He was the man who had been the great opponent of Dr. Pordage in the Commonwealth days, and he had also been violently hostile to Charles I. It was said that he used to pray in the pulpit, " As for the King, let the blood of England, the blood of Scotland, and the blood of Ireland fly in his face and dog him day and night, and let him never have peace of conscience till he return to Jesus Christ and the Parliament." [4] As soon as he was ejected from St. Mary's, he opened his house for private meetings, and considerably reduced the congregation of his successor thereby. [5] In January 1663 the mayor and constables surprised a meeting there, and sent the people home. [6] Towards the end of the year he was imprisoned in Windsor Castle for seditious practices. [7] Three months later he petitioned the King to release him, pleading that his only fault had been reading sermons in his house, and allowing his neighbours to come and listen. He had a large family and small means, and promised loyalty and obedience in future. The King ordered his release on his undertaking to hold no more meetings. [8] After that, he was quiet for a while; but at the time of the Declaration of Indulgence he asked for a licence. Sir William Armourer, a great enemy of the Dissenters in Reading, opposed. [9] A draft licence allowing him to preach at the house of Griffin Bubby in Reading was made out, but, probably in consequence of this opposition, was never signed. The application had evidently been made by the Reading Dissenters, for Fowler was then living in Kennington, and received a licence to preach in his house there. After Fowler left Reading Thomas Juice, who had been ejected from St. Nicholas, Worcester, kept Nonconformity alive. At one time he and another ejected minister were hidden in a bark rick by a tanner's wife in Mill Lane, and when the coast was clear they crept out and preached, and then retired to their hiding-place again. The mayor told the King's Secretary in 1682 that he had made known the orders about conventicles, and had disturbed them frequently, and tried to capture the preachers, but they had sentries on the watch, the preachers escaped, and when the officers arrived the people had either gone or were sitting in silence. [10] The present Broad Street Congregational chapel

---

[1] Wood, " Life and Times," II. 496. [2] *Idem, ibid.*, III. 155–156.
[3] Palmer, I. 294. [4] C.S.P.D., April 16th, 1672, 305/177.
[5] C.S.P.D., December 12th, 1662. [6] C.S.P.D., January 14th, 19th, 1663.
[7] C.S.P.D., November 23rd, 1663. [8] C.S.P.D., February 17th, 1664.
[9] C.S.P.D., April 16th, 1672, 305/177. [10] S.P.D., 419/19.

claims continuity with the flock of Richard King, who was licensed as a Presbyterian teacher in 1672. It is said that the first meeting-house was built in 1680, but that is doubtful. There was a Baptist conventicle in Pigney Lane in 1669, but the modern King's Road Baptist church claims to go back to 1640. Two other conventicles were noted in 1669, one of them at the house of one Burren, who had been Oliver Cromwell's butler.[1]

In Hull it was said about the time of the second Conventicle Act that the magistrates were disaffected towards the Church, and that most of the aldermen and two-thirds of the people were Presbyterians. Seditious meetings were held there, and Captain Bennett, commanding the garrison, tried to suppress them, but could obtain no assistance from the civil authorities. On May 22nd, 1670, there was a scene in the parish church. The officiating clergyman had gone away, but the mayor and corporation retained their seats. Suddenly a stranger appeared in the pulpit and gave out a psalm. There was no doubt that he was a Nonconformist preacher who was about to deliver a sermon, and that he was doing so with the connivance of the mayor. Mr. Alderman Crowle, a local merchant and justice of the peace, ordered him to come down, and was supported by Captain Bennett. There was a great hubbub, and it seems probable that the intruder was thrust out of the pulpit, only the presence of the soldiers preventing a violent disturbance. Alderman Crowle became the object of great hostility on the part of the Dissenters, especially Alderman Aclam and three or four other members of the corporation.

There was great opposition to the enforcement of the Conventicle Act. The authorities themselves waited to see what was being done in London, and encouraging letters came from thence to some of the Dissenters, saying that the Act would not be enforced there, that the Nonconformists treated the law with contempt and spoke openly against the Government, and that there was no doubt that the King would soon be turned out. But before very long it was discovered that the conventicles in Hull were meeting less frequently, and in September it was reported that such measures had been taken against them that the town was now quiet.[2]

The ejected ministers in Newcastle, for their talents, influential connections and friends, and in some cases for their wealth, were highly respected, and so had a much more peaceful time than their brethren in other towns, where the repressive Acts were more severely enforced. Bishop Cosin, writing to the mayor and corporation in the beginning of 1669, called the town a " nursery

---

[1] Summers, " Congregational Churches in South Oxon and South Bucks," pp. 137–160.
[2] C.S.P.D., May 29th; June 1st, 10th, 12th, 22nd; July 1st; August 6th; September 27th, 1670.

of faction in these northern parts," and threatened them with the King's displeasure if they did not cease to connive at the " scandalous and offensive meetings of those caterpillars," who would not obey the law.[1]   The King had sent a letter through the bishop to the authorities of the town, bidding them put the laws in execution against the conventicles.[2]   Archdeacon Granville wrote to Mr. Secretary Cook in 1674 complaining of the prevalence of these meetings.   He said that many people were being seduced from church, and as archdeacon he could do nothing. Might he not as a justice of the peace put the Conventicle Act into more effective use ?   He desired to know " whether it agrees or not agrees with His Majesty's pleasure if we proceed against schismatics according to the last Act of Parliament."   Cook replied from Whitehall on August 4th, 1674, that he had referred the matter to the King.   " I was told that laws were made to be observed, and that the King's ministers in their respective places knew their duties without having recourse to His Majesty upon every occasion.   It was told also that there is a passage in some play, where a pert, pregnant lad put certain questions to a grave gentleman, who, being unable or unwilling to answer him, and perceiving that he was not very cleanly, diverted the discourse by stroking him on the head and saying ' Wash thy face, my pretty boy, and ask no more questions! '   I have no more to add." [3]

No wonder the ecclesiastical authorities found it difficult to enforce the law.   The Nonconformists of Newcastle were fairly truculent and stubborn.   Thomas Story, the Quaker, tells in his " Journal " how in the reign of Charles II he went to hear a famous Presbyterian preacher there.   " All that he entertained his auditory with was suggestions of jealousy and dislike against the government, and that he delivered in such a way as appeared to me very disagreeable." [4]   There were fairly large conventicles held in the town at times.   In October 1667 one was reported of nearly 200 persons, and on July 22nd, 1669, 100 people had gathered in the house of William Durant, a Congregational minister who had been ejected from All Saints', Newcastle.[5] As a matter of fact, they received a great deal of encouragement from some of the important people of the town.   For instance, soon after the Five Mile Act came out, Richard Gilpin, ejected from Greystoke, Cumberland, who had moved to Newcastle, was fined, and as he did not pay, his goods were distrained. Ambrose Barnes, a wealthy merchant of Newcastle, promptly

---

[1] Mackenzie, " Hist. Newcastle," 1827, II. 370.
[2] " Northumbrian Fragments," Surtees Soc., p. 188; C.S.P.D., December 7th, 1668, Entry Book, 25 f. 78.
[3] " Dean Granville's Letters," II. 13.
[4] " Journal of the Life of Thomas Storey," Newcastle, 1747.
[5] Palmer, III. 77; " Depositions from York Castle," p. 172.

bought them in for him.[1]   This Richard Gilpin was a collateral descendant of the famous Bernard Gilpin.   He had been offered the bishopric of Carlisle at the Restoration, but refused it.   He was a man of means, and while he was rector of Greystoke had purchased for himself the manor of Scaleby Castle, in Cumberland.   Here he had fitted up a chapel, and gathered a Nonconformist congregation.   But a large congregation of Dissenters in Newcastle " who had built a handsome meeting-house," invited him to be their minister, so he migrated thither some time before 1665.   Probably the persecution he received from Sir Philip Musgrave had something to do with it too.   At one of his meetings in the Barber Surgeons' Hall in Newcastle he had a congregation of 500, and the mayor stopped their meeting there.[2]   He had studied medicine, and practised as a physician besides ministering to his flock, and when on one occasion it was proposed to banish him from the town, Ambrose Barnes again saved him by persuading the magistrates that he was very useful to the place by reason of his skill in medicine.[3]   So Gilpin was left undisturbed during the rest of the reign.   He died in Newcastle in 1669.[4]   Barnes had been imprisoned in Tynemouth soon after the Restoration, on suspicion of plotting against the King.   He was cited, excommunicated, distrained, and every possible expedient was tried to force him to conform.   Yet in 1680 we read in the ecclesiastical presentments of St. Nicholas', Newcastle, " Ambrose Barnes and fifty others have not been at church for the last twelve months, or have come when prayers were nearly done."   He was imprisoned during Monmouth's rebellion.   Nevertheless, he was on friendly terms with several of the clergy.   Later on, when James II showed favour to the Dissenters, he could have been mayor of Newcastle if he had liked.   He had been restored to the position of alderman, from which he had been deposed, and James wanted him to be elected Member of Parliament for the town.   His Dissenting friends, however, now turned on him and reviled him as a Papist.

Jeffreys was in Newcastle in 1684 and the following years. Some thirty young men of the town had been in the habit of holding weekly meetings for prayer and religious intercourse. They were brought up before Jeffreys at the Newcastle Assizes in 1685.   One of them was " a mean-looking man called Venner." " Can you read, sirrah ? " said Jeffreys.   When the man said he could, the clerk, at the judge's orders, handed him a Latin New Testament.   He began at the first place on which his eye fell, Matt. vii. 1, " Judge not, that ye be not judged."   " Construe it, sirrah," roared Jeffreys, and when Venner did so, it was

s

---

[1] Collingwood, " Memoirs of Bernard Gilpin," 1884, pp. 243–244.
[2] C.S.P.D., November 23rd, 1668, 249/166.
[3] " Life of Ambrose Barnes," p. 142.
[4] William Gilpin, " Memoirs of Dr. Richard Gilpin."

said that the judge took it so much to heart that at the Assizes of 1686 he dismissed the men with the words, " Go and sin no more, lest a worse thing come unto you." [1]   It is also said, however, that Jeffreys tried to turn the paper containing the rules of the society into treason, but Barnes went up to London and saw the King about it.

Besides Durant and Gilpin, there were two other ejected ministers, Lever and Pringle, who had congregations in Newcastle.   A writer complained in 1669 that if it were not for these four men, the meetings might easily be put down. [2]   They had each collected a considerable band of followers, [3] and were suspected of dangerous correspondence and practices. [4]   Robert Lever, one of the Northumberland ejected, had his home in Brancepeth, but worked chiefly among the Newcastle people, and they were some of his disciples who appeared before Jeffreys in 1684. [5]   John Pringle had been ejected from Eglingham at the Restoration.   He went to Newcastle and assisted Gilpin. [6]   Gilpin's congregation at first met outside Close Gate, then moved to Hanover Square, and then to New Bridge Street, [7] and the Church of the Divine Unity in New Bridge Street is thus the direct descendant of it. [8]   Two Baptist congregations in Newcastle, that in Osborne Road and that in Westgate Road, claim to date back to 1650. [9]   There was a Particular Baptist congregation, which in the days before the Revolution met on the Tuthill Stairs. [10] Durant's congregation met in Pilgrim Street in 1669. [11]

There must have been a strong Dissenting interest in the Newcastle corporation.   They began to capture places on it as early as 1665. [12]   When James II granted toleration the Dissenters held their meetings publicly, and the mayor and corporation went officially " one day to the church, another day to the mass-house, another day to the dissenting meeting-house."   The old pews of the meeting-house on the Tuthill Stairs had two " hands " affixed for holding the mace and sword. [13]

Newcastle Nonconformity seems to have deteriorated.   Barnes found among the Dissenters scepticism, formality, faction, pride, ignorance, conceitedness, covetousness, fraud, and so little of the true spirit of religion " that it was no wonder that men turned Deists rather than Dissenters." [14]   Some of the Scotch refugee

---

[1] Bates, " Hist. of Northumberland," 1895, 254.
[2] C.S.P.D., April 7th, 1669, 258/132.
[3] C.S.P.D., November 23rd, 1668, 249/166.
[4] C.S.P.D., September 25th, 1678; Entry Book 32, p. 52.
[5] Palmer, I. 58.   [6] Palmer, I. 67.
[7] Mackenzie " Hist. Newcastle," II. 371–374.
[8] " Essex Hall Yearbook."   [9] " Bapt. Handbook."
[10] Mackenzie, " Hist. Newcastle," II. 397.
[11] Depositions from York Castle," p. 172.
[12] C.S.P.D., September 2nd, 1665.
[13] " Life of Ambrose Barnes," p. 177.   [14] Ibid., p. 241.

preachers in Newcastle, according to the same authority, did not do their cause any good. Several of them " proved hypocritical, self-seeking, and ungrateful persons, though masked with specious pretences; and others, under show of suffering for their consciences, were knavishly dishonest, and the hotheads among them, who hurried many of them into extravagant actions, and thereby enraged the persecution in that nation," Barnes would have nothing to do with, keeping himself equally at a distance from Neville Pain and Robert Ferguson, from the one because he did not know what he was, from the other because he did.[1]

[1] " Life of Ambrose Barnes," p. 200.

IX

MUCH of the blame for the prevalence of Dissent has been laid at the door of the clergy of the Church of England. Macaulay's account of them [1] was based largely on two works which appeared in the reign of Charles II. The first of these was entitled " Ichabod: or Five Groans of the Church," and was printed at Cambridge in 1663. The first " groan " was a complaint of the laxity of the ecclesiastical authorities in the matter of ordination. Three thousand men had been admitted to holy orders who were unfitted to be leaders of men on account of their youth, and " since the looseness of the late times " there had been admitted to the priesthood men of the meanest of the people. Fifteen hundred debauched men had been ordained, though we are not told who counted them, or what was the exact criterion of a " debauched man " in these cases. Unlearned men had received orders, and among these, within the past four years, 426 trades-men. Thirteen hundred and forty-two " factious ministers " had been admitted to the ministry of the Church; these, of course, being men who previous to the Restoration had held livings without episcopal ordination, and had since shown themselves willing to conform. With many of these the conformity was a mere outward one, and of this the writer complained : " Must I have a sound form of words in the desk, and an extempore effusion in the pulpit? Must I have the same man read episcopally to the walls, and preach factiously to a throng, use the ceremonies and say to his confidants that they are a burthen to him, use the surplice ' yet unwilling to give offence,' use the cross in baptism yet say ' I wish it were forborne ' ? " The other four " groans " put into the Church's mouth were profaneness, simony, non-residence, and pluralities. The author calculated that out of 12,000 benefices or thereabouts, 3000 and more were impropriated, while over 4000 were sinecures, or held by non-residents, and bewailed the poor remainder left for " a painful and honest ministry."

The other work was " The Grounds and Occasions of the Con-tempt of the Clergy and Religion," by John Eachard, Master of St. Catherine's Hall, Cambridge. It appeared in 1670, and seems to have had a good sale, for nine editions appeared within fifteen

---

[1] Macaulay, " Hist. Eng.," ed. Firth, I. 318.

years. The contempt in which the clergy were held was due, he thought, to three main causes: their education, their preaching, and their poverty. Their school education was often bad, and the education given at the universities was also bad. The chief faults of their preaching were ostentation of learning, overdoing of metaphors and similitudes, excessive use of long words, faulty methods of construction, misplaced ingenuity, and the misuse of concordances. But the chief cause of the lack of respect accorded to them was their poverty, and it was largely on this portion of Eachard's work that Macaulay founded his description of them. Because of their poverty they were not free from care, and they could not be given to hospitality. They had to undertake secular work in order to live. They had, consequently, no time for study or preparation of sermons, and if they had, they only possessed a few old books. Their children, too, had to go to low occupations. Hence the Church chiefly attracted low and ignorant persons to its ministry, with the consequence that there was a liability to scandalous behaviour, such as intemperance, among such people. Failures in other professions entered the ministry to get a poor living, and the gentry, if they put any of their children into the clerical profession, put the feeblest of them. A few good livings and rich bishoprics did not make up for the many poor ones; in fact, there were in some places too many churches. Eachard had little that was constructive to offer. He did not suggest a mere redistribution of the funds, but he demanded that in every parish there should be a clergyman who would be respected, and whose advice would be listened to.

Both writers showed a tendency to exaggerate, and Eachard did not go unanswered. "An Answer to a Letter of Enquiry into the Grounds and Occasions of the Contempt of the Clergy" was printed in 1671. The writer admitted that the clergy were held widely in contempt, but did not believe that this was due to their poverty or ignorance. Some of it was the result of the slanders of the emissaries of the Church of Rome, who tried to invalidate Anglican orders and to undermine the influence of the clergy among the common people. There were also people who spread abroad the idea that the conformists were not as good as the men who went out on St. Bartholomew's Day, and said that the latter would have to be received back if the Church was to do any good. As to the young blades and gallants who complained of the preaching of the clergy, the writer said, " It is not always ignorance or poverty of the preacher, it is sometimes the wickedness of the hearer that administers the occasions of this contempt," and he asserted that the clergy had much improved in their preaching, and that, as for learned sermons, it was better to preach for the unlearned majority in the congregation than for the few scholars who might be present. Eachard replied in the same year with " Some Observations upon the Answer to an Enquiry into

the Grounds and Occasions, etc." The title-page said it was by
" T. B.," and so it has been ascribed to Thomas Burnet, Master of
the Charterhouse from 1685 to 1715, but there seems no doubt
that it was by Eachard, and in later editions it was bound up with
his former work. In a racy way he went over much the same
ground as before, but deprecated the idea that he had written
with an intention of making a scurrilous attack on his brethren.
He declared that he had never said that all the clergy were poor
and ignorant, and ridiculed his reviewers for referring to all what
he had written of some. It is possible that Eachard did something himself to increase the contempt of which he spoke. The
frivolous and irreligious are always pleased to hear from a priest
that they are right in despising his brethren, and Eachard seems
to have been one of that not unknown type of clergyman who gets
a spurious reputation for outspokenness by telling them so.

He was answered in 1672 by " A Vindication of the Clergy."
The author of this pamphlet defended them on the grounds that
Eachard's charges were exaggerated, that some of his stories were
old, and that some of his accusations were laid at the wrong door.
Fantastic preaching, for example, should rather be laid to the
account of the intruded ministers of the Commonwealth times.
The Vindicator admitted that after the King's return there had
been a very great number of ordinations, but that was because the
Bishops had to fill so many vacant places. On the whole, he did
not make a very valuable contribution to the dispute.[1]

As for the social position of the clergy, some twenty-eight of the
higher ecclesiastics were scions of noble and knightly families,
and among the lesser clergy there were certainly a number of
men of gentle birth.[2] The names of Compton, Fane, Fielding,
Montague, Annesley, Greville, Berkeley, Finch, Booth, Crewe,
Trelawney, and Fiennes, go to support Jeremy Collier when he
says, " as for the gentry, there are not many good families
in England but either have, or have had, a clergyman in them,"[3]
and in his other statement that " the priesthood is the profession
of a gentleman." The registers of the colleges in the universities
tell the same tale. The higher posts in the Church were naturally
given to men whose rank or wealth already gave them the *entrée*
to the higher circles of society, into which their offices would
naturally throw them.[4] When such men, however, held country
cures in addition, these were often ministered to by a curate, and
the living was thus simply looked upon as a subsidiary source of

[1] See also " The Merit and Honour of the Old English Clergy Asserted,"
1662, on the same subject.
[2] Churchill Babington, " Mr. Macaulay's Character of the Clergy in the
Latter Part of the Seventeenth Century Considered," Cambridge, 1849,
pp. 17-18.
[3] Collier, " View of the Immorality and Profaneness of the Stage," 1698,
p. 136.
[4] Nelson, " Life of Bishop Bull," I. 7-8.

income. Here at any rate was a genuine cause for " groaning."
It is true, as Macaulay said, that the parson sometimes married
the waiting-woman at the great house, though perhaps this did
not happen so often as he thought, and it must not be forgotten
that the position of waiting-woman in great houses was often
held by one who would be described to-day as a lady in reduced
circumstances.[1] The clergy married into all classes, as they do
to-day,[2] and as for their children, there seems insufficient
reason to suppose that as a regular thing they were put to poor
and painful employments.[3] No doubt some of them descended
in life, but so did some of the sons of the country gentlemen.[4]
In every age there have been poor clergy whose children have
been poorer still.

A good deal of Eachard's attack on the education of the clergy
was rather an attack on the methods of the schools and universities. Most of the seminaries in the country taught Greek and
Latin, and seem to have taught them fairly efficiently, if we
may judge by the widespread knowledge of the classics which
seems to have existed in the Restoration period.[5] Eachard, too,
was looking on the worst side of the picture, as he told his critics
in his reply.[6] Thoresby's Diary and Walker's " Sufferings of the
Clergy " give a good deal of information about the books possessed
by many of the clergy during the seventeenth century, as do the
book auction catalogues.[7] The clergy of London, Oxford, and
Cambridge numbered many admittedly learned men; and a
cursory examination of the books and pamphlets produced during
the period will show a great abundance of clerical authors in
every department of literature and learning, and a great part of
this literary work came from the country clergy. There was a
good sprinkling of clergy among the Fellows of the Royal Society.
Eachard admitted that the ordinary clergy of the Church of
England were more learned than those of equivalent standing
in the Church of Rome. Granted that the general requirement
of a university degree in the case of candidates for ordination
did not mean as much in the way of general knowledge as it may
do to-day, yet it meant more than it did a hundred years afterwards. The clergy had in their hands the education of the
upper and middle classes. If the Augustan age soon to follow
was famous for its learning, it was these clerical teachers who
laid the foundation of it. The Caroline clergy were looked on

[1] C. H. Mayo, " The Social Status of the Clergy in the Seventeenth and
Eighteenth Centuries," *E.H.R.* XXXVII. 258–266.
[2] Babington, " Macaulay's Character of the Clergy," p. 49; W. C. Sidney,
" Social Life in England from the Restoration to the Revolution," 1892, p. 172.
[3] Fuller, " Worthies," I. *passim*; Herbert, " Country Parson," ch. x.
[4] Mayo, *E.H.R.*, XXXVII. 258–266.
[5] Burnet, " Own Times," I. 321–322, for learning at Oxford.
[6] " Some Observations," etc.
[7] J. Lawler, " Book Auctions in England," 1898.

with deep respect even abroad for their learning, and it has been suggested that perhaps they would have affected the masses at home more if they had not been so learned. Macaulay directed one of his brilliant passages against the domestic chaplains of the period; yet Ken, Wilson, Sherlock, Bray, Kettlewell, and Hough were all domestic chaplains at one time or another.[1]

Undoubtedly there was a great deal of poverty among the clergy. So there is to-day, but it would be difficult to contend that to-day the clergy have sunk in the public estimation on this account: it might even be said that wealth does more in this respect. Then as now, however, the authorities were trying to alleviate it by finding ways and means to increase clerical stipends;[2] and if the incomes were small then, money was worth a great deal more in purchasing value.

As for the laxity with regard to ordination, Archbishop Sancroft took the matter up in 1678, and wrote to his suffragans concerning the testimonials granted to candidates for orders. He complained that by lapse of time, and the corruption which by insensible degrees creeps into institutions, the granting of testimonials at the universities and elsewhere had become a mere perfunctory matter of civility. Every testimonal, therefore, in future must bear its date and address, and must be signed and sealed. Testimonials from the universities must be under the common seal of the college, attested by the subscriptions of principal persons there, and those from other places were to be under the hands and seals of three priests of known integrity, dwelling in the neighbourhood, and having known the candidate for three years previously.[3]

There was evidence in the seventeenth century, as now, that a clergyman who was a gentleman in any sense was respected as one, but that at any rate his cloth was held in high esteem. The clergy had considerable influence, also, apart from this; some had been in the medical profession, many had served in the army, some were skilled in legal and political affairs, and many had literary talents.[4] The fact that there seems to have been no dearth of candidates for holy orders is against any theory of unpopularity. The things which formed a real basis of complaint against the clergy were pluralities, which tended to deepen the division between those who had one or more livings and those who had no hope of ever being more than assistant curates; non-residence, which staffed many parishes with clergy of the lower grade; and the tendency to subserviency on the part of some of the clergy to those in authority, whether bishop, patron, or squire. Many of the country squires undoubtedly kept

[1] Overton, " Life in the English Church, 1660–1714," 1885, ch. viii.
[2] Cardwell, " Doc. Annals," II. 221–223, 295.
[3] D'Oyly, " Life of Sancroft," I. 182–186.
[4] Overton, " Life in the English Church 1660–1714," ch. viii.

the local clergy under their thumbs.[1] The distinction, however, which Macaulay made between the town and country clergy, taken as classes, was over-stated. There was not, and there never has been, a marked line of distinction between them. Many of those who attained eminence in the town had also been successful parish priests in the country at some time or other during their career.

An anonymous writer in 1674 dealt with the alleged scandalous character of the clergy. As for their lack of preaching power, he pointed to the esteem in which Anglican preaching was held among foreign Protestants. For their learning he pointed to their writings. Their personal characters were often attacked from sheer enmity, because of their zeal for the Church. He admitted the misconduct of a few, but steadily maintained the blamelessness of the majority, and carried the war into his opponents' camp by saying "If impertinent and fantastical talking of religion be religion, if endless scrupulosity and straining at gnats, if censoriousness and rash judging our betters and superiors, if melancholy sighing and complaining be true Christianity, if going from sermon to sermon, without allowing ourselves time to meditate on what we hear, or leisure to instruct our families; if these, and such as these, are the main points of true godliness, then I must confess, the sons of the Church of England are not generally the most holy men, and the Nonconformists are. But if a reverent sense of God, and conscience of keeping all His express laws, if justice, mercy, contentment, humility, patience, peaceableness, and obedience to governors be the principal ingredients of a good life . . . then I do not despair but the churchmen may be good Christians, and of far more holy lives than their accusers notwithstanding all the contempt cast upon them." The writer inquired into " the causes of the present neglect and contempt of the Protestant religion and the Church of England." He admitted, therefore, some failure on the part of the Church, and assigned as the chief reasons for it: the lack of provision in the way of endowment for a sufficient ministry in the large parishes; the unsettling effect of the civil wars; the increase of trade, which brought merchants into contact with many religions and led to indifference with regard to all; the attacks of Papists and atheists, both tending to undermine sound religion by trying to bring the Church into contempt; the Judaizing influence of Nonconformity, with its stress on Old Testament teaching; the rashness, unsteadiness, and prejudice of popular judgment, and the lack of Christian zeal on the part of professing Christians. He declared that many Nonconformists were constantly returning to the Church, while he steadfastly denied the leakage from the Church to Dissent.[2]

[1] Mayo, E.H.R., XXXVII. 258–266.
[2] " Serious and Compassionate Enquiry into the Causes of the Present Neglect and Contempt of the Protestant Religion and the Church of England," 1674.

William Jenkyn,[1] preaching the funeral sermon of Dr. Lazarus Seaman,[2] called the Anglican clergy "a company of uncatechized upstarts," accused them, amongst other things, of Socinianism, and said that some of them preached the sermons of the Puritans as their own, at the same time holding them in contempt. Dr. Robert Grove, afterwards Bishop of Chichester, published " A Vindication of the Conforming Clergy from the Unjust Aspersions of Heresy," a jesting and somewhat contemptuous reply, in which he accused Jenkyn of plagiarism, and showed in parallel columns how, in his " Commentary on St. Jude," he had copied from Adam's Commentary on II. Peter. Jenkyn repeated his charges in Latin, in a tract entitled " Celeuma," and Grove replied in the same language, and in 1681 published " A Short Defence of the Church and Clergy of England." To the accusation of clerical ignorance, he retorted, " It is true that those that are acted by enthusiastical principles are exceedingly prone to despise us for this: when they have raised their fancies with strange dreams of rare discoveries, they are apt to look down upon others with something of contempt. The meanest and most illiterate artisan, that has but a tincture of this conceit, will be ready to pity the blindness of the most learned adversary that opposes his follies, and think himself an over-match for the best studied and most judicious divine. . . . If I am not very much misinformed, there is not a church beyond the seas at this time that can pretend to have a more learned and accomplished ministry than ours is. . . . No unbiassed judge will ever think that the dissenting ministers at the present do generally excel the conforming clergy in any point of useful learning." [3] To the accusation of debauched and scandalous living he replied, " Allowing some exceptions, which I hope, considering our numbers, will not be many, I do not see but that the conforming clergy in the general are of as circumspect, sober, inoffensive a conversation as any of their accusers." [4] They were called proud and ambitious, but perhaps it was " because they are forced to vindicate the honour of their calling in an age that loves to have it despised." [5] The Anglican parson was said to be covetous " because he will not be tamely cheated of what is apparently his due; to the impoverishment of himself and family and all that shall succeed him." [6] As for the accusation that they meddled in state affairs, Groves replied that there were never fewer political questions debated in the pulpit.[7]

Lord Anglesey complained that many of the clergy led easy and pleasant lives, and might be recommended to practise the self-denial they preached. Others he accused of fomenting disorder and " reducing the State to be their executioner." [8]

[1] Palmer, I. 109.   [2] Palmer, I. 80.   [3] P. 59.
[4] P. 64.   [5] P. 68.   [6] P. 71.   [7] P. 83.
[8] The Earl of Anglesey's " State of the Government and Kingdom," published 1694.

This was written in 1682, in which year an Anglican preacher, addressing the Dissenters, said that very few of the clergy were as scandalous as some Nonconformists reported them to be, and that some Dissenters invented lies against them out of prejudice, while others were only too ready to give credit to slander.[1] In an age when drunkenness, loose living, and coarse language were common, no doubt a certain number of the clergy were guilty of these things, and similar accusations were made from tim̃e to time against the Nonconformist ministers, but if we search for actual cases, and then consider the number of clergy and the number of the Dissenting ministers, there is no real proof that open wickedness was common among either. They may have been more common than to-day, but there is no need to exaggerate. It is a gross travesty of the truth to assert, as many of the Nonconformists constantly asserted at the time, that the parish churches at their best only produced formalism, and at their worst irreligion, and that the people, hungering for the Word of Life, turned to the Nonconformist. A great deal has been said against the Anglican bishops of this period, and it would be impossible to answer the accusations fully without a detailed examination of the lives of all of them. They have been accused of worldliness, a vague complaint. Were the bishops who went into exile during the rule of Cromwell particularly worldly, or the nonjuring bishops who gave up everything for their principles? They were also accused of being courtiers, and Crewe, Cartwright, Samuel Parker, and Burnet have been particularised. Crewe's benevolence is remembered in Durham to this day. Parker was a doughty controversialist, who was wrongly accused of joining the Church of Rome to please James II. Cartwright, as his diary shows, was a hard-working bishop. Burnet never had any Church principles, and was a devoted adherent of the Orange cause, but he was at least an industrious man. It is true that Timothy Hall is said to have been a man of bad character, but he never took possession of his see, and it may be admitted that Thomas Barlow was an idle Low Churchman, and that Thomas Wood, a man of the same type, was suspended. On the other hand, Sheldon, of whom Walton and Evelyn spoke in approving terms, rebuked Charles for his adultery, and refused him Holy Communion. Robert Creighton denounced sin with all plainness when preaching before the King; Morley did the same, and Ken̄ would not admit Nell Gwynn to his house. Hardly courtiers these. Brian Duppa was the author of " Holy Rules and Helps to Devotion," a work which could not have been written by a man not spiritually minded. Clarendon said Morley was " the best man alive." Ward, besides being a great preacher, was a founder of the Royal Society. Brian Walton, Pearson, Wilkins, and Sanderson were learned men enough.

[1] Benjamin Bird, " Humble Advice to Protestant Dissenters," 1682.

Morgan was noted as an energetic preacher, and Frampton for his holy life.

A good deal was said on both sides about preaching. The Dissenters spoke scornfully of Anglican preachers; the Churchmen ridiculed Dissenting methods. Sir Joseph Williamson noted in 1671 that the City preachers were not well thought of at the time, " Our men do not preach judiciously, affectionately," said he.[1] On October 14th, 1662, the King wrote to the Archbishop of Canterbury pointing out that abuses and extravagances in the pulpit were increasing, and were heightening the popular distempers and confusions. The bishops were to give orders to the clergy not to meddle in politics, nor to preach on theological and speculative questions which they did not understand, and in dealing with controversial matters they were to avoid bitterness and railing. An anonymous writer issued a commentary on this royal command in a tract published in 1664, bearing the title " Rex Theologus: the Preacher's Guard and Guide in the Didactical Part of his Duty." He complained of the popular preaching of the day, and said that real theological learning was laid aside as superfluous, and as not requisite to the accomplishments of a preacher, and that there was an abundance of preachers, but few divines. Some would preach for half a year upon a single text or a single doctrine, and there was a popular affectation which took the form of using new and strange words and canting language, or, as we should say, catch-words or slang. Another thing complained of was the practice of making a long extemporaneous prayer before the sermon, by which they showed their contempt of the Prayer Book, disseminated false doctrine, and sometimes displayed their ignorance or even blasphemy.[2] The extemporaneous prayer was, of course, the mark of the " Nonconforming Conformist." It was especially common amongst the " lecturers," a class of clergy with whom the bishops found it difficult to deal, because they were appointed by the suffrages of the congregation who maintained them, and were independent of ecclesiastical authority.[3] Burnet said that the King's taste, and the encouragement he gave to good preachers, brought about a reformation of pulpit oratory. Hitherto, preaching had meant long discourses, interlarded with scraps of other languages, either in dull and humdrum style, or else full of bombast; to the King's influence was largely due a more rational style of preaching which in a great measure overcame the prejudices against the Church.[4]

The Churchman looked upon worship as the first thing and preaching the second, while the Nonconformists, perhaps, laid the greatest stress on the ministry of preaching. The latter

---

[1] C.S.P.D., November 23rd, 1671, 294/64.
[2] Pp. 53-54, where he gives examples.   [3] " Rex Theologus," 1664.
[4] Salmon, " Exam. Burnet," I. 544.

published an enormous amount of sermon literature, as the pages of Calamy show, and the learned men among them laboured with meticulous care in the preparation of these discourses, some of which were theological treatises rather than sermons. The study of some of these, and of the learned discourses of the learned Anglicans of the period, arouses the respect of the reader for the intellectual calibre, the unwearied patience, and the interest in theological matters shown by the congregations which listened to them. The lesser Puritan preachers showed a good deal of unctuousness in their discourses, which, together with the frequent repetitions, the heaping up of epithets, and the use of stock phrases and shibboleths, rendered their sermons easy to parody and ridicule.[1]

A sarcastic attack on the Dissenters was licensed in 1673, and bore the title " A Free and Impartial Enquiry into the Causes of that very great Esteem and Honour that the Nonconforming Preachers are generally in with their Followers. By a Lover of the Church of England and Unfeigned Piety." The reasons why they were held in such veneration by " their deluded proselytes " were said to be the following. The common people were always accustomed to be guided by affection rather than by judgment. Some of the Dissenting ministers were not unworthy to be ranked among the learned, but there were others whose abilities would never raise them to distinction in the Church of England, and who found more scope for themselves in preaching to conventicles. People spoke of the benignity of their conversation; that they had the arts of insinuation was true, but no people were really more supercilious than they. They preached up an empty, formal, " notional " kind of religion, and encouraged men to base their hopes of heaven upon very easy and pleasing conditions: the solfidian error had taken great root among them. Their preaching was full of violent abuse of the Church of England, which they called Babylon, " the spiritual Sodom," and other such names. They thought that her liturgy was as bad as the mass, her priests were " priests of Baal," and " dumb dogs," her ceremonies were " rags of Antichrist," her constitution was " a limb of the beast," and the " mystery of iniquity." To flee from her was sufficient to assure saintship and to evince a man to be an undoubted child of God. For one sermon on obedience these ministers preached twenty on faith. Men's sanctity and regeneration were judged by them according to their mode and form of speaking. " I do not mean the dramatist's twang of the nose, though you cannot but have observed how modish that was

Cf. " Vox Lachrymae: A Sermon Newly Held Forth at Weavers' Hall upon the Funeral of the Famous T(itus) O(ates), Doctor of Salamanca. By Elephant Smith, Claspmaker, an unworthy labourer in the Affairs of the Good Old Cause," 1681.

once among the saints," but a peculiar way of wording things, and shibboleths. The writer quoted specimens of their abuse of the Church of England in their public works, described their attitudes and methods in the pulpit, and added, in conclusion, that though they got great veneration for their sufferings in " seeming persecution, they got plenty of flattery for it." [1]

Macaulay threw doubt on the genuineness of the love of the country gentry for the Church of England during the Restoration period. There is no doubt, however, of the dislike of the majority of them for the Puritans, at whose hands they had suffered in what they called " the late times." If only for political reasons—because they felt that Church and King went together, and that the downfall of one meant the downfall of the other—the gentry were, as a rule, on the side of the Church. Generally speaking, they were as anti-papal as they were anti-Puritan, and they believed that the Church of England was as much the bulwark against Smithfield fires and foreign armadas as against the return of the iron-handed rule of the saints. Political reasons, nevertheless, were not the only reasons that had weight with them. Too much stress has been laid on the wickedness of the times; we have an extensive knowledge of the follies and sins of the courtiers, the play-actors, the scandalous verse-writers, and so on; but there were not many of them, after all. Most of the gentry lived quietly on their lands, and only made a journey to London at long intervals; their manners and conversation may have been unrefined, but as a rule they went to church and did their duty, as they saw it, to God and their neighbours. They did not talk much about their religion, only occasionally do we find a reference in letters or diaries, but there seems no doubt that there were many men like Evelyn, of a devout but unassuming piety. Among the ladies of the upper classes there were many pious daughters of the Church, such as Lady Mary Wharton, Margaret Lady Maynard, Anna Lady Halket, Lady Jane Cheyne, and Mary Evelyn. There seems no doubt that the upper classes of the country between the Restoration and the Revolution were, as a rule, loyal to the Church. Among the middle classes there were many Nonconformists, and many who were influenced by Puritanism without actually deserting the Church. Some of the wealthy city merchants were Dissenters, and a fair number of the shop-keeping class. The lower classes were less affected, though of course there were poor Dissenting congregations, like the Baptist congregation at Broadmead, in Bristol; but as time went on the poor were less and less affected by Dissent, down to the time of the Methodists. Apart from the Church, the only people who had any influence among the poor seem to have

---

[1] The writer was probably John Eachard.

been the Quakers.[1] An attempt is here made to inquire how far Nonconformity influenced the upper classes.

Lord Anglesey had great sympathy with the Nonconformists, and usually had one of them living in his house as his chaplain. He was probably not a Nonconformist himself, but the Countess was, and attended John Owen's services; in fact, she had so great an admiration for him that at her death she left instructions that she might be buried in the same vault with him, " that dying as well as living she might testify her regard for him." [2] Humphrey Prideaux, writing in 1681, said that the old Lady Lovelace was " now grown so zealous a Whig that she goes every Sunday to Lady Anglesey's to make one of the holy sisters at her conventicle." [3] Dr. Samuel Annesley, ejected from St. Giles's, Cripplegate, was Anglesey's cousin.[4] Philip Lord Wharton was a Nonconformist, whose house was a regular place of refuge for Dissenting ministers in times of persecution. He was once caught at one of Manton's meetings in White Hart Yard, though the disturbers did not, or pretended not to know him, and he paid all the fines. When he went abroad during the reign of James II., John Howe went with him,[5] and Howe dedicated his " Thoughtfulness for the Future " to the Countess of Wharton, who seems to have been a Dissenter also. The Countess of Exeter, whose house was in Little Britain, was the great patroness of Dr. Thomas Jacomb, and protected him on several occasions, and he died in her house.[6] She seems to have been a Nonconformist herself, and conventicles were held weekly under her roof. On January 26th, 1664, a fast was held at Mr. Jackson's meeting-house in Whitefriars; Matthew Poole, Manton, and Baxter were there, as were also the Countess of Exeter, Lord Wharton, and Sir William Waller.[7] At a fast kept on August 5th of that year, at Mr. Blake's house in Covent Garden, the Countesses of Valentia, Peterborough, and Anglesey, and other persons of quality, 200 in all, were present. George Cockayne, an Independent, who had been ejected from St. Pancras, Soper Lane,[8] and was said to have become a Fifth Monarchy man, was the preacher.[9] Richard Robartes, the son of John Lord Robartes, received Presbyterian ordination in Essex in 1659, and was ejected from Culsden, in Surrey. His mother was a Dissenter.[10] Robert Billio, ejected from Wickham Bishop, was befriended by the Countess of Warwick, who gave

[1] P. H. Ditchfield, " Errors of Lord Macaulay in his Estimation of the Squires and Parsons of the Seventeenth Century," Trans. Royal Hist. Soc., 3rd Series, IX. 77.
[2] Orme, " Life of Owen," p. 287.
[3] " Humphrey Prideaux to John Ellis," September 20th, 1681.
[4] Palmer, I. 124.   [5] Palmer, I. 430.
[6] Calamy, II. 47.   [7] C.S.P.D., February 16th, 1664.
[8] Palmer, I. 175.   [9] C.S.P.D., August 1664.
[10] Davids, " Nonconformity in Essex," p. 427.

him a small pension for many years.[1] She was the patroness of many other Dissenting ministers, and was frequently to be found at their services.[2]

There were others of the nobility who were friendly to the Nonconformists. Lord Sandwich in 1665 had a Nonconformist chaplain.[3] Dr. Thomas Manton had several people of rank among his congregation, either on Sundays or at his Wednesday evening lectures; the Duke and Duchess of Bedford, the Countess of Manchester, the Countess of Clare, Lady Baker, sister of Lord Anglesey, Lady Trevor, and the Dowager Lady Trevor. Some of them had formerly attended St. Paul's, Covent Garden.[4] Some time after St. Bartholomew, Manton had begun to preach in his own house, and had some trouble about it from a certain Justice Ball, who lived close by, and from the churchwardens of his old parish. The Duke of Bedford, who had the right of appointing one of the churchwardens, henceforth always nominated one who would be friendly to Manton; moreover, the Duke's friendship and the kindness of Lord Wharton, who allowed him the use of his house, which adjoined the place where he afterwards held meetings, were a great protection to him. The Earl of Berkshire, a Roman Catholic, who lived next door to him, gave him permission at any time, when he was in danger, to escape over a low wall into his house.[5] Sir John Trevor had married a daughter of John Hampden, which explains, perhaps, why his wife and mother were among Manton's followers. Dr. John Owen probably owed his safety during all the rest of his life to the fact that he had the friendship of Lords Anglesey, Wharton, Orrery, Willoughby of Parham, and Berkeley. The last three had all been on the Parliamentary side, but cannot be considered Nonconformists, though very friendly to some of them. In Owen's congregation were Sir John and Lady Hartopp. The latter was Charles Fleetwood's daughter: her husband became an Independent early in life, and was a great student of the Scriptures. He was three times a Member of Parliament, one of the supporters of the Exclusion Bill, and a great defender of Nonconformists.[6] Other members of Owen's congregation were Mrs. Abney, Lady Tompson, Lady Vere Wilkinson, Sir Thomas Overbury, Mrs. Bendish, "Lord" Charles Fleetwood, Major-General John Desborough, and Major-General Berry. Mrs. Abney, a daughter of Joseph Caryl,[7] had married Thomas Abney, a man of good Derbyshire

[1] Davids, "Nonconformity in Essex," pp. 513–514.
[2] C. F. Smith, "Mary Rich, Countess of Warwick," 1901, p. 198.
[3] Pepys, "Diary," July 16th, 1665.
[4] North, "Lives of the Norths," I. 176; Wilson, "Dissenting Churches," III. 563; Palmer, I. 426–431.
[5] Harris, "Memoirs of Thomas Manton"; Calamy, I. 42.
[6] Orme, "Life of Owen," pp. 280–281.
[7] Palmer, I. 146.

family, and a Dissenter, afterwards knighted by William III. Lady Tompson was the wife of John Tompson, who was made a baronet by Charles II., but was a sturdy opponent of the Government. Fleetwood had refused to have anything to do with the death of Charles I., and it was probably on this account that he was allowed to live privately at Stoke Newington, though he had to endure a good deal for his Nonconformity, and it is said that the fines imposed on him, and on Sir John Hartopp, at one time amounted to £6000 or £7000. Berry had been one of Cromwell's Upper House. After the Restoration, Parliament commanded him to retire to that one of his houses which was farthest from London. John Desborough, another of Cromwell's " lords," had been nominated as one of Charles I.'s judges, but had refused to attend the High Court of Justice. He had been exempted from the Act of Indemnity of 1660, though not as regarded his life.

When Mrs. Baxter bought a chapel for her husband in Oxenden Street, more than a dozen persons of quality contributed to the cost.[1] Sir John Langham was landlord of Crosby Hall, hired as a meeting-house by Thomas Watson, and was a great friend to Nonconformity.[2] So was Sir Harry Ashurst, Bart., who leased some ground to the Independents in Hare Court.[3] Sir Henry Tulse once detained a principal witness against Richard Wavel till the trial was over, but this may have been a matter of mere personal friendship.[4] Thomas Cawton, ejected from a fellowship at Merton College, Oxford,[5] became chaplain to Sir Anthony Irby at Westminster. Lady Irby, the latter's widow, had at one time as her chaplain Samuel Lawrence, who had been ejected from Wem, in Shropshire. Cawton was afterwards chaplain to Lady Armin. Sir William Waller had Edward Veal as his chaplain for a time, and Sir Heneage Featherstone, who lived in Cow Lane, West Smithfield, was said to be a Nonconformist himself. Vincent Alsop had some members of the upper classes in his congregation at Westminster, but the nobility and gentry disappeared from Nonconformist circles after the original ejected ministers died out.

In Northumberland, Sir William Middleton's house at Belsay was licensed in 1672 as a Presbyterian meeting-house. He was made a baronet in 1662, and was sheriff of Northumberland in 1666–1667.[6] John Davis, ejected from Bywell, Northumberland, preached there sometimes,[7] and James Calvert, ejected from Topcliffe, Yorkshire, was for a time his chaplain.[8]

In the county of Durham, Lady Vane of Raby was a supporter of Nonconformity, and Cock, her steward, was a prominent

[1] " Rel. Baxt.," III. 172.   [2] Pyke, " Ancient Meeting-Houses," p. 80.
[3] Wilson, " Dissenting Churches," III. 277.
[4] Palmer, I. 212.   [5] Palmer, I. 252.   [6] Palmer, III. 60.
[7] Calamy, II. 519.   [8] Calamy, II. 831.

Dissenter. Lady Liddell, her daughter, seems to have been a patroness of the Baptists of Muggleswick. At Norton, near Stockton-on-Tees, there lived a Scotchman, locally known as the Laird Swinton. He had been sentenced to death and forfeiture by the Scotch Parliament, and to exile by the Kirk for joining Cromwell against Charles II., but had returned to Scotland and been reinstated owing to Oliver's influence. He had been a member of the Council of State for Scotland, and a member in all Oliver's Parliaments. He became a Quaker in 1657. In 1661 he had been sentenced by the Scotch Parliament to exile for high treason, and seems to have settled down at Norton. In 1669 he was reported as holding a conventicle of 100 persons. These must have been Quakers. He had left the Society of Friends, but had returned to it before 1667.[1] He died in 1679.[2]

Yorkshire was stronger, perhaps, than any other county in the number of its Puritan gentry. Round Rotherham there were many families with leanings in that direction: Mr. Hatfield of Laughton-le-Morthen, Mr. Wadsworth of Swathe Hall near Worsborough, the Westbys of Ravenfield, the Spencers of Attercliffe, the Brights of Cranbrook, the Gills of Carr-House, the Stainforths of Firbeck, the Knights of Langold, and the Taylors of Wallingwell.[3] In Wharfedale there were the Fairfaxes, the Dyneleys of Bramhope, the Rawdons of Rawdon, the Arthingtons of Arthington, the Gunters of Healaugh, and the Huttons of Poppleton.[4] Sir Edward Rhodes of Great Houghton, and after his death, Lady Rhodes, was a great supporter of Nonconformists, and many of the ejected ministers preached in the chapel there. Oliver Heywood noted in his register of burials, " Lady Rhodes, a great upholder of meetings, buried at Darfield, April 22nd, 1681, at twelve o'clock in the night." [5] Her son married a Quaker who was a great friend of William Penn, and her grandson, Sir John Rhodes, became a Quaker.[6] Thomas Lord Fairfax kept Puritan chaplains. The Duke of Buckingham also kept a Nonconformist chaplain, and when Lady Fairfax, his mother-in-law, died, he wanted him to preach her funeral sermon publicly. When the Archbishop of York interfered, the Duke sent him a scornful message by his secretary. On another occasion, when there was a movement on foot to issue sentences of excommunication against non-communicants at Easter, Buckingham went personally to see the Archbishop of York at Bishopthorpe, and induced him to put a stop to it.[7]

---

[1] See Fox's reference to John Swinton in his " Journal " for that year.
[2] Turner, " Original Records," II. 758–759.
[3] Hunter, " Life of Oliver Heywood," p. 184.
[4] *Trans. Cong. Hist. Soc.*, VII. 49–57.   [5] Oliver Heywood, " Diary."
[6] G. C. Williamson, " Lady Anne Clifford," 1922, p. 252.
[7] Hunter, " Life of Oliver Heywood," p. 197.

One of Lord Fairfax's chaplains was Richard Stretton. His
patron settled an annuity upon him as a wedding gift when he
married, and left him numerous legacies in his will.[1] Mrs.
Hutton of Poppleton, sister of Thomas Lord Fairfax, kept a
Nonconformist chaplain, Thomas Burdsall, who had been ejected
from the curacy of Selby.[2] Sir John and Lady Hewley lived at
Bell Hall, between Naburn and Stillingfleet, a house which they
built in 1680. Sir John Hewley had been Member of Parliament for Pontefract, and Recorder of Doncaster during the
Commonwealth, and was knighted by Charles II. in 1662. He
and his wife were enthusiastic Puritans, and friends of Oliver
Heywood, Noah Ward, and Edward Bowles. Sir John was
afterwards Member of Parliament for York. After the Toleration Act he and his wife were among the principal contributors
to the erection of the St. Saviour's Gate chapel, York.[3] Lady
Hewley, who outlived her husband, left large sums of money
for " preaching the pure Gospel," for the training of ministers,
and other educational purposes. Timothy Hodgson, son of
Captain Hodgson, was their chaplain, and spent the greater
part of his life in the family.[4] Various other Dissenting ministers
were chaplains to Yorkshire gentry; Matthew Sylvester to Sir
John Bright,[5] Noah Ward to Sir John Wentworth,[6] James
Calvert, ejected from Topcliffe, to Sir William Strickland,[7] and
Christopher Richardson to Mr. William Cotton of Denby Grange,
Penistone.[8]

The Dyneleys of Bramhope, and Lady Brooke of Ellenthorpe,
had private chapels served by Dissenting ministers, though the
buildings afterwards came to the Church of England. Sir
Henry St. Quintin at Beverley, and Sir John Jackson at Hickleton, were both Nonconformists, the latter being a Presbyterian.[9]
Sir John Jackson sheltered a Nonconformist minister as his
chaplain, and his wife as a housekeeper. Nathaniel Denton,
ejected from Bolton-on-Dearne, found a temporary pulpit in
Hickleton church.[10] In the city of York, Peter Williams delivered
a weekly lecture in the house of Lady Lister, and after her
death, in the house of Lady Watson. This Lady Watson was
the widow of Stephen Watson, who was Lord Mayor in 1646
and 1656; but she had no real right to the title. Lady Hoyle
was another of the " elect ladies " in York. She was the widow
of Alderman Thomas Hoyle of that city, though when Heywood
went to see her in 1668 she was living at Thwaites, near Leeds.
She had suffered from melancholia for several years past, and

[1] Calamy, II. 677. [2] Horsfall Turner, " Northowram Registers."
[3] Walter Lloyd, " Story of Protestant Dissent," 1899, p. 91.
[4] Hunter, " Life of Oliver Heywood," p. 218.
[5] Gordon, " Unity Church, Islington," 1917. [6] Oliver Heywood, " Diary."
[7] Horsfall Turner, " Northowram Registers."
[8] Nightingale, " Lancs. Nonconformity," VI. 84.
[9] Lyon Turner, " Original Records." [10] " Vict. Hist. Yorkshire," III. 68.

died in July of that year.[1] An eminent Puritan layman who lived in York was Thomas Rokeby, who was the chief legal adviser to the Nonconformists in the North. Lady Hewley, the Howards, the Whartons, and the Fairfaxes were all his clients. He became a judge, and was knighted.[2]

In Lancashire Roman Catholicism was stronger than in Yorkshire among the upper classes, but Puritanism was weaker. Lady Stanley of Bickerstaffe Hall was a protector of the Quakers, and a friend of Nonconformity in general. Nathaniel Heywood was a friend of hers, and frequently preached there.[3] Lady Moseley in Manchester was a supporter of Henry Newcome. The Willoughby family, who lived near Rivington, and the Wilsons of Tunley Hall, were patrons of the Nonconformist ministers; Dame Wilson built the Presbyterian chapel at Tunley or Mossy Lee in 1691.[4] When James Wood was ejected from Chowbent chapel he took refuge at Wharton Hall, the property of the Mort family. The owner opened a room in which Wood might hold services for the neighbouring village, and maintained this conventicle in spite of fines and threats.[5] Thomas Risley, of the family of Risley of Risley Hall, was ejected from a fellowship at Pembroke College, Oxford. In November 1662, he received Anglican orders, but later on turned Nonconformist, returned to his estate at Risley, and preached to the Nonconmists there.[6] Josiah Holdsworth became chaplain to Sir Richard Houghton of Houghton Tower.[7] Lady Sarah Houghton, daughter of the Earl of Chesterfield, was a great patroness of the Dissenters. Thomas Cotton was her chaplain some time before the Declaration of Indulgence in 1672.[8] In the Altham and Wymondhouses Church Book there are two interesting entries with reference to her:—

1665. " Lady Houghton kept two days of prayer every month for a long time and pastor was much there."

1670. " Mr. John Bayley was solemnly set apart for the work of the ministry. For admonishing Lady Houghton for leaving her husband he lost a friend." [9]

Samuel Angier's salary as minister of Denton chapel came chiefly from Colonel Holland and Squire Hyde, two of his patrons.[10]

---

[1] Hunter, " Life of Oliver Heywood," pp. 207–208; Heywood, " Diary."
[2] " Memoir of Mr. Justice Rokeby," Surtees Soc. 1865.
[3] " Hist. Soc. Lancs. and Chesh.," 3rd Series, V. 130; Nightingale, " Lancs. Nonconformity," IV. 187–190.
[4] Nightingale, " Lancs. Nonconformity," III. 81–89; IV. 23–26.
[5] *Idem, ibid.*, IV. 94–103.   [6] *Idem, ibid.*, IV. 252–255.
[7] " Northowram Registers."
[8] Wilson, " Dissenting Churches," IV. 377.
[9] In the same volume as " Note-Book of Thomas Jolly," Chetham Soc.
[10] Nightingale, " Lancs. Nonconformity," V. 280–288.

The leading Presbyterian in the county of Cheshire was Sir George Booth, who had raised the revolt on the death of Oliver, and had been one of the twelve Commissioners to negotiate with Charles at Breda. After the Restoration, he was made Baron Delamere of Dunham Massey. He retired from the Court, however, after a time. He had Presbyterian services in his own house, Dunham Hall, and was a good friend to the ejected ministers. His son, who claimed not to be a Presbyterian, and became the second Baron, was one of the first to welcome William III., from whom he received the title of Earl of Warrington. Adam Martindale [1] was for some time chaplain to Lord Delamere at Dunham Park. The terms of his chaplaincy are interesting, as illustrating the life of a " Levite," the contemporary slang term for a domestic chaplain. He had to be in residence from May to October; the rest of the year he could live where he liked. His salary was at the rate of £40 a year, but as he was not in residence for half this period, the most he ever received was £21. Out of that he had to pay fees to servants of the house for waiting on him, to say nothing of the cost of a chaplain's costume. The rest of the year he eked out his salary by taking pupils. [2] The domestic chapel of the Dukinfields, at Dukinfield Old Hall, had been appropriated in the Commonwealth times by Colonel Robert Dukinfield to the Congregationalists, but after the Restoration the chapel was taken from him and handed over to the Church of England. [3] Thomas Brook, ejected from Congleton, continued to preach in the chapel of Old Moreton Hall, the owner of which, Mr. William Moreton, was a patron and admirer of his. But Brook died in 1664. [4] Similarly, James Bradshaw, ejected from Macclesfield, preached for a time in Bradshaw chapel, by connivance of Mr. Bradshaw of Bradshaw Hall. [5]

In Derbyshire Cornelius Clarke of Norton Hall, who was High Sheriff for Derbyshire in 1670, if not a Nonconformist was at least a sympathiser, for in 1694 he gave a site for, and subscribed to, the building and endowment of the meeting house in Elder Yard, Chesterfield. [6]

Lady Bromley, of Sheriff Hales, in Shropshire, was a great patroness of persecuted Nonconformists, and several of them took refuge in her house at different times. [7] Two squires, Thomas Corbet of Stanwardine and Rowland Hunt of Borealton, supported the Nonconforming cause. [8] In Staffordshire Sir Thomas Wilbraham and his wife harboured Nonconformist ministers in

[1] Palmer, I. 341.
[2] Halley, " Lancs. Puritanism," p. 416; Urwick, " Nonconformity in Cheshire," pp. 369-387; " The Life of Adam Martindale."
[3] Urwick, " Nonconformity in Cheshire," pp. 340-347.
[4] *Idem, ibid.*, p. 154.   [5] *Idem, ibid.*, p. 224.
[6] *Trans. Unit. Hist. Soc.*, I. 25.   [7] Orme, " Life of Owen."
[8] Wilson, " Dissenting Churches," II. p. 23.

their house at Weston-under-Lizard;[1] and Philip Foley at Prestwood near Kinver had a succession of silenced ministers as his private chaplains.[2]

George Hammond, ejected from Trinity church, Dorchester, became minister in 1677 to a congregation of Dissenters in Taunton. He was a man of scholarly attainments, and a number of people of rank, including Lady Courtenay and Lady Constantine, sent their sons to board with him.[3] When in 1682 the Surrey Dissenters found the persecution too severe for them to be able to hold their meetings publicly, they held them in private for a short time at Stoughton Place, the home of Sir Nicholas Stoughton.[4]

There were some few Dissenting families among the gentry of Norfolk and Suffolk. Armingland Hall, near Oulton in Norfolk, was the seat of Lieutenant-General Fleetwood, and in the chapel of his house Dissenting services were held.[5] John Collinges published in 1669 " Par Nobile: Two Treatises, the one concerning the Excellent Woman evincing a person fearing the Lord to be the most Excellent Person, discoursed upon Occasion of the Death of the Rt. Hon. the Lady Frances Hobart of Norwich: the other, Light in Darkness, discovered at the Funeral of the Rt. Hon. the Lady Catharine Courten, preached at Blickling, Norfolk." The Brewsters of Wrentham Hall in Suffolk were Puritans,[6] and Mr. Baker, the squire of Wattisfield in the same county, was a person of great influence, zealous for Nonconformity, and a sufferer for it.[7] Charles Morton, after his ejection, went to live for a time with Sir Samuel Barnardiston in Suffolk.[8]

In Essex Sir Gobert Barrington and his wife encouraged John Oakes, ejected from Boreham, to gather a congregation at their house, Little Baddow Hall.[9] Nathaniel Ranew, ejected from Felsted, had a congregation at Billericay. Charles, Earl of Warwick, and the Countess of Warwick allowed him £20 a year.[10] John Benson, ejected from Little Leighs, was much befriended by Lord Fitz-Walter's family.[11] Henry Lukin lived for many years at Matching Hall, the residence of Mrs. Masham, and preached regularly at Matching Green, where a meeting-house was afterwards built.[12] James Small, silenced at Yaxley in Suffolk, became chaplain to Lord Massarene in Ireland, and afterwards to Sir John Barrington at Hatfield Broad-Oak, in Essex.

[1] Palmer, I. 316.
[2] A. G. Matthews. The Congregational Churches of Staffordshire. London, 1924.   [3] Palmer, II. 128.
[4] " Diary of Lawrence Lee of Godalming," Surrey Arch. Collns. XXVII. 1.
[5] Browne, " Congregationalism in Norfolk and Suffolk," p. 328.
[6] Idem, ibid., p. 426.   [7] Idem, ibid., p. 467.   [8] Palmer, I. 347.
[9] Davids, " Nonconformity in Essex," p. 353.
[10] Idem, ibid., p. 390.   [11] Idem, ibid., p. 418.   [12] Idem, Ibid., p. 420.

In Bedfordshire, several members of Lord Anglesey's family upheld the Dissenting interest. Lady Anne Annesley, his fourth daughter, married Sir Francis Wingate. She was second cousin to Susannah Wesley, John Wesley's mother, and all her sympathies were with the Nonconformists. Three of her daughters, Frances, Anna Letitia, and Rachel, became members of Bunyan's old congregation at Bedford, and Frances married one of the deacons there, while Anna Letitia, the fourth daughter, married a Congregational minister.[1]

In Hertfordshire there was Sir Jonathan Keate at the Hoo, who had a Nonconformist chaplain, Joseph Hussey, who preached constantly for him till 1688,[2] while Nathaniel Vincent was chaplain from 1662 to 1665 to Sir Henry Blount of Titten-hanger, " his lady being fanatically inclined." [3] There was a strong Puritan element in Buckinghamshire, especially round Amersham. Charles Fleetwood lived at the Vache, and Russell at Chenies not far off. Oliver Cromwell's widow and her daughters lived at Woodrow High House.[4] Philip, Lord Wharton lived at Upper Winchenden, and was a great friend to the Dissenting ministers, several of whom took refuge in his house, among them John Gunter, ejected from Bedale in Yorkshire, whom he made steward of his Yorkshire estates.[5] Richard Hampden, the son of John Hampden, had a Nonconformist chaplain in the person of George Swinnock,[6] and Baxter often preached for him. Lady Terrill at Castlethorpe was also a supporter of Nonconformity.

At Stanton Harcourt in Oxfordshire lived " the pious Sir Philip Harcourt," who had living with him Henry Cornish, B.D., who had been ejected from Christ Church, Oxford. In Berkshire, Mr. Charles Fettiplace and his wife and daughter were abettors of conventicles. Fettiplace was one of the influ-ential Puritan gentry in West Berkshire.[7] In Wiltshire there were Sir Bulstrode Whitelock at Chilton Foliot, and the Hon. Francis Fiennes at Newton Tony, against both of whom com-plaints were laid at different times as supporters of the Dissenting party. At Cutteridge House, in the parish of North Bradley, near Trowbridge, lived William Trenchard, who was Member for Westbury in 1678 and 1681, and a zealous Dissenter. When James II. wished to find out which of the country gentlemen would oppose his Indulgence policy, he was told that Trenchard was likely to give trouble, and he chose him for one of his Dis-senting deputy-lieutenants. At North Baddesley, in Hamp-

[1] Browne, " Life of Bunyan," p. 145.
[2] Wilson, " Dissenting Churches," IV. p. 411.
[3] Wood," Ath.," II. 1032–1033; Palmer, I. 304.
[4] " Vict. Hist. Bucks," I. 333.
[5] Calamy, I. 820; " Northowram Registers."
[6] Summers, " Congregational Churches of South Oxon and South Bucks," pp. 80–91.
[7] Idem, ibid., pp. 284–285.

shire, lived Samuel Dunch and his wife, described as " the greatest patrons of the ejected ministers in their county," [1] while at Hursley, of course, there was Dorothy Cromwell, wife of the erstwhile Protector.

It does not follow that all these people were active Nonconformists; in fact many of them, like the second Lord Delamere, were probably influenced by the feelings of their class as much as anything to give an outward conformity to the Church of England, without being in any way warmly disposed to the Anglican system. Purely personal influences, too, no doubt sometimes led to the support and protection of individual Nonconformist ministers.

Among the Quakers there were not very many of the upper classes. Lady Conway, the Lady Jane Stewart, William Penn, son of Admiral Penn and godson of James II., and Robert Barclay, who had Stuart blood in his veins, were the most noteworthy. In Wales several of the gentry adopted Quakerism. Charles Lloyd of Dolobran in Montgomeryshire and his brother Thomas, were of the landholding class, and both they and their families suffered much for their faith.[2] William Lewis of Garth, and Richard Davis of Pool, were each described as " gentlemen," and together with their wives endured on several occasions the penalties of the law.[3]

To the Puritan, stage plays were an abomination. The stage was a sink of iniquity, the stage-players were the vilest of the vile. The stage proceeded to give him every ground for his belief, and took revenge on him for the way in which he had suppressed it. Not only was there a great outburst of licentiousness in the Restoration drama, but the Puritan, his manners, his foibles, and his failings were treated with bitter mockery, while the hypocrisy which had disgraced some was ascribed to all. Henry Jessey complained of a play, " The Old Puritan," in which " he that acted the part came with a narrow band, short hair, and broad hat. A boisterous fellow came in after him and tripped up his heels, calling him a Puritan rogue : at which words the old Puritan shook off the dust of his feet against him." [4] " You will hear," wrote Hooke to Davenport, " by the bearer, of the play of ' The Puritan ' before the highest, where were present, as they say, the Earl of Manchester and three bishops, and London one of them. In it were represented Presbyterians under the form of Mr. Baxter and Mr. Calamy, whose habits and actions were set forth. Prayers were made in imitation of the Puritan, with such scripture expressions as

[1] Noble, " Protectoral House of Cromwell," II. 442–443.
[2] T. Mardy Rees, " Hist. Quakers in Wales," pp. 52–56.
[3] " Montgomeryshire Collections of the Powysland Club," XXIV. 201, XXVI. 49, XXVII. 55.
[4] Jessey, " Lord's Loud Call," 1660, 1–2.

I am loath to mention—the matter being such as might have been used by the godly man in the right manner. The case of Zion lying in the dust was spread before the Lord, and God's former deliverance of his people urged in such phrases would amaze you if you heard them, with eyes lifted up to heaven. One representing the Puritan put in the stocks for stealing a pig, and the stocks found by him unlocked, which he admires at as a wonderful providence and fruit of prayer: upon which he consults about his call, whether he should come forth or not: and at last perceived it was his way, and forth he comes, lifting up his eyes to heaven, and falls to prayer and thanks." [1]

In 1661 Ben Jonson's " Bartholomew Fair " was revived. Pepys said it had not been acted for forty years; it was so satirical against the Puritans.[2] He described it as " a most admirable play and well acted, but too much profane and abusive." [3] When he saw it again in 1668 he expressed the opinion that " the business of abusing the Puritans begins to grow stale and of no use, they being the people that at last will be found the wisest." [4] It was the play which contained the character " Zeal-of-the-Land Busy . . . a Banbury man " (i.e. a Puritan). On December 16th, 1661, Pepys went to see Abraham Cowley's " Cutter of Coleman Street," a play " with reflections much upon the late times." [5] Another satire on Puritanism which was acted at the Cockpit in 1661 was Broome's comedy " The Jovial Crew." [6] " The Presbyterian Lash," published in the same year, had a mocking dedication to Zachariah Noctroffe, a minister who had recently been accused of cruelly flogging his maid-servant. He had been for a time a preacher at St. Antholin's, London,[7] but he was not the incumbent, for it was Elias Pledger who was ejected from that parish in 1662.[8] A play called " Ignoramus; or, The Academical Lawyer " was acted with great applause before the King and Queen at Whitehall on November 1st, 1662. It also was played at the Cockpit in Drury Lane. Among the characters were " Ignoramus, an English Lawyer," and " Pyropus, a Phanatick Broker." [9] John Wilson's comedy, " The Cheats," was licensed in 1663, and printed in 1664. One of the characters was called " Scruple Nonconformist," who was represented as a canting hypocrite. Certain passages, which were struck out by the Censor, represented the Puritan minister explaining to a married woman that she might commit adultery provided she had no

[1] " Mather Papers," 4th Series, Vol. VIII. Quoted in Waddington, " Cong. Hist.," I. 569.
[2] " Diary," September 7th, 1661.   [3] Ibid., June 8th, 1661.
[4] Ibid., September 14th, 1668.   [5] Ibid., December 16th, 1661.
[6] Hepworth Dixon, " Life of Penn," p. 31.
[7] Jenkinson, " London Churches," p. 156.
[8] Palmer, I. 92.
[9] Hist. MSS. Com. III. 215.

intention of sinning, and parodied with bitter mockery the worst type of Puritan pulpit oratory.[1] Aphra Behn's play, " The Roundheads: or, The Good Old Cause," had as characters, Fleetwood, Lambert, Warriston, Hewson, Desborough, Dukinfield, Corbet, Whitlock, Lady Lambert, Lady Desborough, and Lady Fleetwood, together with " Ananias Goggle, Lay Elder of St. Clement's parish," and " a Rabble of the Sanctified Mobility." Another play by the same writer was " The Widow Ranter, or, The History of Bacon in Virginia " ; Bacon being " the General of the English in Virginia." One of the characters was " Parson Dunce, formerly a farmer, fled from England and chaplain to the Governor." John Leanerd produced a comedy, " The County Innocent: or, The Chambermaid turned Quaker," at the Theatre Royal in 1677, and the play was licensed for publication in the April of that year.

The verse-mongers were also busy at the Puritan's expense. " The Rump: or, An Exact Collection of the Choicest Poems and Songs relating to the late Times, by the most Eminent Wits, from 1639 to 1661," was edited by Alexander Brome, and published in 1660, an enlarged edition appearing two years later. Here was an arsenal of mockery whereby the Cavalier might hide his fear of the Puritan. Butler's " Hudibras "[2] made the country rock with laughter. It was one of the successes of the age (except for Butler, who died in poverty and disappointment): the King quoted it, and carried it about with him; courtiers prided themselves on their knowledge of it. With its parade of learning, its doggerel rhymes, its mordant satire, its impish mockery, it was a powerful, if not a very Christian, weapon in the hands of the anti-Puritan party. Probably most of the Puritans never read it. They would ban it as an " ungodly " work, which burlesqued everything they held dear. It is noticeable that in the Third Part, as in his other later works, Butler was as fierce as ever against the Dissenters, though he showed his disappointment with his own party. In his " Pindaric Ode upon a Hypocritical Nonconformist " he made fun of the Puritan preaching:—

> " The zealous pangs and agonies,
> The heavenly turnings of the eyes;
> The groans, with which he piously destroys,
> And drowns the nonsense in the noise;
> And grows so loud, as if he meant to force
> And take in Heaven by violence."

Sir John Denham's name was attached, possibly falsely, to some verses published in a broadsheet, and entitled " The

[1] F. S. Boas, " Stage Censorship under Charles II.," *Times Lit. Supp.*, April 15th, 1920.
[2] Pt. I., 1662; Pt. II., 1663; Pt. III., 1678.

THE ENEMIES OF THE CROWN.
From Edward Pettitt's "Visions of the Reformation."

Facing p. 427.

Presbyterian without Disguise: or a Character of a Presbyterian's Ways and Actions." It was a very poor production, and commenced thus:

> " A Presbyter is such a monstrous thing
> That loves democracy and hates a King,
> For royal issue never making prayers,
> Since kingdoms (as he thinks) should have no heirs,
> But stand elective: that the holy crew
> May, when their zeal transports them, choose a new."

A popular ballad of the time was entitled " The Old Cloak," and was aimed at the Presbyterian party:

> " In pulpits it moved
> And was much approved
> For crying out ' Fight the Lord's battles, belov'd.'
> It bob-tailed the Gown,
> Put prelacy down,
> It trod on the mitre to reach at the Crown:
> And unto the field it an army did bring
> To aim at the Council, but shot at the King.
>
> *Refrain:*
> Then let us endeavour to pull the Cloak down
> That cramped all the Kingdom and crippled the Crown." [1]

" The Geneva Ballad " expressed what a great part of the nation felt, and continued to feel, till James II. gave their fears another direction:

> " I would as soon turn back to mass
> Or change my phrase to ' thee ' and ' thou,'
> Let the Pope ride me like an ass,
> And his priests milk me like a cow;
> As buckle to Smectymnian laws
> The bad effects o' the Good Old Cause,
> That have doves' plumes but vultures' claws.
> Yet they all cry they love the King
> And make boast of their innocence:
> There cannot be so vile a thing
> But may be coloured with pretence.
> Yet when all's said, one thing I'll swear,
> No subject like th' old Cavalier,
> No traitor like Jack Presbyter." [2]

Among lesser persons who exercised their wit at the expense of the Puritans was Sir John Birkenhead, Member of Parliament for Wilton and Master of the Court of Requests, who wrote some satirical verses called " The Four-legged Quaker." Most of the writers of this kind of thing, however, veiled themselves in anonymity, and their productions were commonly intended to be sung. " The Lecherous Anabaptist: or, The

---

[1] Wilkinson, " Political Ballads of the Seventeenth and Eighteenth Centuries," p. 172.
[2] *Idem, ibid.*, p. 202.

Dipper Dipped " was printed as a broadside, and contained a scandalous story of Francis Smith, the bookseller. " The Riddle of the Roundhead " was described as " an excellent new ballad to the tune of ' Now at last the Riddle is expounded,' " and was published in 1681. " Presbytery Rough-Drawn: A Satire in Contemplation of the Late Rebellion " was published by Robert Gould in 1683. The name of such productions was Legion.[1] As a last example may be quoted the " Epitaph on Henry Care," the Dissenting printer, who changed sides in the reign of James II.:

> " A true Dissenter here does lie indeed.
> He ne'er with any, or himself agreed:
> But rather than want subjects to his spite
> Would snake-like turn and his own tail would bite.
> Sometimes, 'tis true, he took the faster side,
> But when he came by suffering to be tried
> The craven soon betrayed his fear and pride.
> Thence, Settle-like, he to recanting fell,
> Of all he wrote, or fancied to be well:
> Thus purged from good, and thus prepared by evil,
> He faced to Rome, and marched off to the devil." [2]

On September 29th, 1672, a conventicle was being held in Godalming, when the vicar of the parish came with the constables and tithing men, broke open the doors, seized the ministers, and bore them off to the Town Hall. Many of their followers went with them, and as soon as they were left alone in the charge of the constables they began singing psalms together. Nevertheless, the authorities continued to suppress conventicles with such rigour that the Dissenters had to go to the place appointed for their meeting by devious ways to escape notice.[3] Similar instances of attacks on meetings could be recounted by the thousand, and many of them have been referred to elsewhere in these pages, but the instances of the clergy taking a personal part in these proceedings were much less numerous. They preached against the Dissenters, they reported them to the authorities, and on occasion sued them for their tithes, but it is probably true to say that only a few of them joined in acts of violence. These were mostly the work of justices of the peace, bailiffs, officers, soldiers, and informers, and what these men did was done in the name of the law. The majority of Anglicans stoutly denied that there was anything practised in the nature of persecution. Lord Keeper Finch at the opening of Parliament in 1671 complained that the

---

[1] See " A Collection of One Hundred and Eighty Loyal Songs," 1685; " A New Collection of Poems relating to State Affairs," 1705; W. W. Wilkins, " Political Ballads of the Seventeenth and Eighteenth Centuries," 1860; " Covent Garden Drollery," 1672, ed. by G. Thorn Drury, 1928, p. 29.

[2] " The Muses Farewell to Popery and Slavery," 1690, p. 162.

[3] " Diary of Lawrence Lee," Surrey Arch. Collections, 1914, XXVII. 1.

Nonconformists had " found a way to make even justice itself criminal by giving it a hard name and calling it persecution."

When the Anglican went to church on November 5th he heard the clergyman pray that all in authority might be strengthened " to cut off all such workers of iniquity as turn religion into rebellion and faith into faction." The form of prayer for the day of King Charles the Martyr, January 30th, contained the sentence, " Thou didst suffer Thine anointed, blessed King Charles the First, to fall into the hands of violent and blood-thirsty men, and barbarously to be murdered by them," while another collect recounted how " the sons of Belial were per-mitted to imbrue their hands in the blood of Thine anointed." The Thanksgiving Service for May 29th, the Accession of Charles II., gave thanks for deliverance " from the Great Rebellion and all the miseries and oppressions consequent thereupon," and one of the prayers besought the Almighty, who had overthrown " the wicked designs of those traitorous, heady and high-minded men," to " infatuate and defeat all the secret counsels of deceitful and wicked men against us."

That was the trouble. Almost every Churchman believed that at bottom every Dissenter was a rebel against the Govern-ment, and " rebellion was as the sin of witchcraft." It made no difference what kind of Dissenter he might be. The Presby-terians had led the revolt against the late King. They were looked upon as the origin of all the other sects. They had treated Charles II. with supreme arrogance in Scotland. They were arrogant even towards other Dissenters, like the Independents, between whom and themselves the Churchmen could see little difference. Every time there were whispers of plots and revolts it was found that some of the Presbyterians had been " talking high." But it was not merely the Presbyterians: the more unorthodox men were in religion, the more disloyal they were in politics. Algernon Sidney, that fierce opponent of the Govern-ment who came to an untimely end on the scaffold, was against " everything that looked like a church," and " everything that looked like monarchy." [1] Some writers [2] traced the rebellious principles of the Dissenters to their undisciplined and unguided study of the Bible. Because nothing could lawfully be estab-lished in Church or State which did not find certain warrant in Holy Scripture, they denied the supremacy of the Crown over the Church. Wicked kings might be slain, like the wicked kings in the Old Testament. Some of them believed that amongst themselves was the only Scriptural form of ecclesiastical government, while others believed that this only existed in the Geneva model. Hence, Charles II., who favoured Anglicanism, and James II., who favoured Romanism, were wicked kings,

[1] Burnet, " Own Times," II. 351.
[2] *E.g.* Dryden in " Religio Laici."

and a fierce minority held that they might lawfully be overthrown and put to death.

The Church was wide enough, yet nothing would satisfy these men, or so it was felt. All the troubles in Christendom for a 148 years, said Edward Pettitt, writing in 1683, had arisen from pretences of thorough reformation. They had been the first to ruin the results of the English Reformation, and had continued the same line of action since the King's return.[1] They were the people who

> " Call fire and sword and desolation
> A godly thorough reformation." [2]

Since the Restoration, by pretending great fears of popery, they had levied all their invectives against persons remarkable for their loyalty and conformity, and had kept up a constant habit of clamouring for reformation, petitioning, threatening, and publishing seditious pamphlets.[3] All they did tended to break up the unity of the nation, to overthrow the Church, and to destroy the monarchy. All this was the view not merely of the bishops and clergy, but also of the laity. The Clarendon Code was the work of a lay Parliament, and so were the other Acts of the same kind. The suppression of the Dissenters was made a Government affair. The seventeenth-century authorities took themselves seriously. Dean Inge, speaking somewhere of government during Stuart times, has contrasted it with " the squalid anarchy of democracy, wasteful, inefficient, and generally corrupt, with a Government which quails before every agitation, and pays blackmail to every conspiracy, and in which sooner or later those who pay the taxes are systematically pillaged by those who impose them, until the economic structure of the State is destroyed." Whatever may be said of modern government, there is no doubt that in the seventeenth century, when a law was made, the ruling power generally did its best to enforce it. Whether a particular law was well and wisely made is another matter.

The clergy shared the view of the laity, and on several occasions petitioned, either for the strengthening of the law or its more vigorous enforcement. It is recorded of Bishop Hackett of Lichfield (1661-1671) that he was the enemy of all separation. The Nonconformists accepted the doctrine of the Church, and yet had separated through dislike of its discipline, and " he thought their impudence outwent all preceding histories." He believed that the permission granted to conventicles by the Declaration of Indulgence showed great irresolution and " unsatisfaction with the truth, and administered great temptation to shopkeepers and sedentary people to be tainted with errors

---

[1] Pettitt, " Visions of the Reformation," 1683.   [2] Butler, " Hudibras."
[3] Pettitt, " Visions of the Reformation," p. 191.

and novelties," of which the English temper, he thought, was too receptive. Conventicles, in his opinion, were seminaries of Oliver's warriors. If a man published false divinity to the damnation of souls and the perversion of people from obedience to governors, it was wrong not to regard his action in that light. In the schismatic assemblies people were being taught that the Church of England had made indifferent ceremonies to be sacraments, and in making people kneel at the sacrament, had encouraged them to worship bread. It was only right that people who taught such things, and " depraved Church orders " should be punished, and the authorities ought to do their duty in that respect.[1]

Probably Archbishop Sheldon, Hackett of Lichfield, Gunning of Ely (1675–1684), and the Puritan-minded Seth Ward of Salisbury (1667–1689) were the severest of the bishops towards the Nonconformists. Ward's biographer and friend, Dr. Walter Pope, said of him that he so used his endeavours to suppress conventicles, and so angered the conventicling party, that in the year 1669 they forged a petition against him under the hand of some of the chief clothiers, pretending that they were so molested, and their trade ruined, that the livelihood of 8000 men, women, and children had been destroyed. But the Privy Council discovered that the petition was a notorious libel, that none of those who were said to be persecuted and ruined had ever been summoned in the ecclesiastical court, and that many whose names were subscribed knew nothing about it.[2] Nevertheless, the Conventicle Act was so enforced in the diocese that in Salisbury there was not a conventicle left, and only a few over the borders of Wiltshire in Somerset.[3] When Colonel Blood became a *persona grata* at Court, he brought the bishop a verbal message from the King that he was not to molest the Nonconformists. On this he waited on the King, and told him that there were only two troublesome Nonconformists in his diocese, and he doubted not that, with His Majesty's permission, he should soon bring them to their duty, whereupon the King told him that those were the very men he was not to meddle with.[4] The King was the greatest difficulty in the way of the enforcement of the law. One Anglican, but not the only one, laid all the blame on the Papists. The Parliament, he said, had made good laws, but the Papists, out of a pretended reverence for tender consciences, had hindered the execution of them; and some leading Dissenters, to say no more, had received private encouragement from them to set up a mighty cry of

[1] Plume, " Life of Bishop Hackett," ed. M. E. C. Walcott, 1865, pp. 106–108.
[2] Walter Pope, " Life of Seth, Bishop of Salisbury," 1697, p. 67; Orme, " Life of Baxter," p. 322, mentions the petition, but not the refutation.
[3] Pope, " Life of Seth, Bishop of Salisbury," p. 69.
[4] *Idem, ibid.*, pp. 69–70.

persecution, and to cast all the odium on a " persecuting Church." [1]

The application of the law varied considerably in severity in different places. Archbishop Juxon, Sanderson of Lincoln (1660–1663), and Archbishop Sancroft were much more gentle than some of their companions on the episcopal bench; though there were kindly actions towards Dissenters even on the part of Gunning and Ward. Indeed, there were many instances of personal kindness shown to individual Dissenters by Anglicans. Bishop Frampton of Gloucester (1681–1691) heard of a conventicle on one occasion, and went to it himself. The preacher, a mechanic, hearing this, absented himself, so the bishop preached to them and won many of them over. The place was a converted barn, and some officious persons who attended him began to damage the windows and seats, for which he sternly rebuked them, saying it was no sign of a true religion to affront even a false one. When any of the Nonconformists were cited in his court, if they showed themselves tractable, he would suffer no fees to be exacted from them, and he would bring divines to talk to them, and to try to win them over. Over 900 cases he had discharged from his court without payment of fees, and it was said that such was his influence, that in one part of his diocese there were twenty adjoining parishes which had not nineteen Dissenters among them.[2]

Dr. William Lloyd, Bishop of St. Asaph (1680–1692), was noted for the gentleness and consideration with which he treated Dissenters. He tried patient and temperate argument with them, and, as far as he could, preserved them from the penalties of the law. James Owen, one of the chief Nonconformist ministers in his diocese, had been preaching against episcopacy. This came to the bishop's ears, and he invited him to a public discussion, to be held in the Town Hall of Oswestry on September 27th, 1681, inviting him at the same time to procure what ministers he could to assist him. The Dissenters complained afterwards of the short notice, only four or five days, but though some of them declined, thinking that the discussion would do more harm than good, and might be dangerous to their future liberty, Owen had the assistance of Philip Henry, and also of Jonathan Roberts of Llanvair, in Denbighshire, who was reputed an excellent scholar. Lloyd brought as his assistant Henry Dodwell, chancellor of the diocese. Philip Henry asked the bishop to hold the meeting in private, and that, as he himself lived in another diocese, he might be excused from speaking. This was refused, but Lloyd promised them that nothing they

---

[1] " The Case of Persecution Charged on the Church of England, considered and Discharged, in order to her Justification and a Desired Union of Protestant Dissenters," by Thomas Long of Exon, 1689.
[2] T. S. Evans, " Life of Bishop Frampton," pp. 141–143.

said should be used against them. Many of the clergy, gentry, and magistrates were present, and the place was filled, the debate lasting from two o'clock in the afternoon until eight or nine at night. The discussion was somewhat informal, and was managed with courtesy and good temper on both sides, only tending to become heated at one moment when a local magistrate threatened to root all Dissenters out of the country. However, the mayor of Oswestry took measures for their safety, and all ended peaceably. Of course, neither side convinced the other, but the bishop kept up a correspondence with Henry afterwards, and both of them, we are told, increased the esteem in which they were already held by those who heard them.[1]

Bishop Lloyd behaved in the same way towards the Quakers. He visited Welshpool, and had a long discussion with Charles Lloyd of Dolobran and his brother, Thomas. On another occasion they had a public debate in the Town Hall of Llanfyllin, the discussion extending over two days, during which they debated most of the points at issue between the Church and the Friends before a large gathering of clergy, magistrates, and other people. Dodwell was there, supporting his bishop, and the Dean of Bangor also took a share in the debate, at the conclusion of which the bishop spoke highly of the ability shown by Thomas Lloyd in defending his case. Richard Davies and Thomas Wynne, two Quakers, also held a two days' debate with the bishop at the episcopal palace, on the same lines. Lloyd intervened on behalf of the Quakers in his diocese when they came under the notice of the authorities, and did many kind acts to them, sometimes successfully delivering them from prison.[2] He was one of the Seven Bishops, and it was remarked that when he was in the Tower the Quaker, Richard Davies, was one of his sympathizing visitors.[3]

Baxter tells us the Dissenters lost a good friend when Wilkins of Chester died in 1672.[4] According to Calamy, he brought many back to the Church by his moderation. At his consecration dinner he told Bishop Cosin, who was present, that he thought moderation would serve the Church better than rigour. " For while you, my lord," said he, " are for setting the top on the peaked end downward, you will not be able to keep it up, any longer than you continue whipping and scourging, whereas I am for setting the broad end downwards, and so it will stand of itself." [5] Bishop Lamplugh of Exeter (1676–1689) often stopped proceedings against Dissenters if he could, and

---

[1] Philip Henry, " Diary "; Rees, " Prot. Nonconformity in Wales," pp. 206–209; *Archæologia*, XLIX. 445; Neal, " Puritans," IV. 597.
[2] T. Mardy Rees, " The Quakers in Wales," pp. 67–70.
[3] Noake, " Worcestershire Sects," p. 267.
[4] " Rel. Baxt.," III. 157.
[5] Calamy, " Life of John Howe," Library of Christian Biography, Vol. XI, London, 1839, p. 33.

sometimes dismissed them without costs. He is said to have
tried hard to win them over by persuasion, and to have urged
some of them to study the writings of Hooker.[1] He was a
friend to John Howe and other learned Dissenters. Benjamin
Laney, Bishop of Lincoln (1663–1667), was moderate and conciliatory. In his primary visitation he said to his clergy, " Not
I, but the law." He suffered a worthy Nonconformist to preach
publicly very near him, for some years together.[2] Laney's
successor, Fuller (1667–1675), was more severe. When licences
were issued in 1672 he was much disturbed, and asked for a
return of the preachers in his diocese.[3] Henry Compton,
Bishop of London (1675–1714), made it one of his chief endeavours
to minimise the differences between the Church and the Nonconformists, though he thereby gained the ill-will of the extremists
on both sides. Reynolds of Norwich (1661–1676), who had
been a Presbyterian himself, succeeded in considerably moderat-
ing the harshness of the Clarendon Code in Norfolk and Suffolk.[4]
The learned Dr. Bull, who became Bishop of St. Davids after
the Revolution, married the daughter of Alexander Gregory,
who was ejected from Cirencester, and who after his ejection
was treated with great courtesy by Churchmen as well as Dissenters.[5] Bishop Cosin of Durham (1660–1674) took very great
pains in trying to persuade John Lomax, ejected from Wooler,
to conform. Though he did not succeed, he often spoke of him
with great respect, and on one occasion, when Dr. Cartwright,
a prebendary of Durham, spoke slightingly of Lomax, Cosin
said, " Doctor, hold your tongue, for to my certain knowledge
John Lomax is a learned man." [6] He was known on several
occasions to have rebuked those who laughed at the Dissenters.[7]
Bishop Morley of Worcester (1660–1662) stopped proceedings
against an ejected minister, invited him to dinner, and tried to
win him over by kindness and moderation. He advised a
certain mayor to let the Dissenters alone, and said that he was
satisfied that the fear of God dwelt in many of them, and that
he thought they would not be won over by severe measures.[8]
Bishop Earle, also of Worcester (1662–1663), did his best to
moderate for them the severities of the Five Mile Act.[9]
   It was the same thing with many of the lower clergy. In
the churchwardens' accounts of the parish of Whitkirk, Yorkshire, there are entries which show the existence of a practice
of allowing the ejected clergy to preach in the church, and then

[1] " D.N.B."
[2] " The Conformist's Plea for the Nonconformist," p. 85.
[3] *Trans. Unit. Hist. Soc.*, II. i. 4.
[4] Browne, " Congregationalism in Norfolk and Suffolk," p. 444.
[5] Calamy, I. 505.   [6] " Arch. Ael.," 3rd Series, II. 33.
[7] Stoughton, " Hist. Rel. Eng.," III. 467.
[8] *Idem, ibid.*, III. 466.
[9] " Conformist's Plea for the Nonconformists," 1681, p. 35.

stand in the aisle to receive a collection for their personal use. Thus, there are the following entries in 1670:

April 10th, 1670. Mr. John Rhodes, 12s. 3d.
July 3rd, 1670. Mr. Walker, 9s. 3d.
July 30th, 1670. Mr. Walker, 6s. 3d.[1]

The Bishop of Chichester tried to persuade Richard Stretton to conform, and promised him £100 a year and a future prebend if he would remain at Petworth and do so.[2] When Dr. Thomas Manton died in October 1677, Ralph Thoresby went to Newington to the funeral, which he said was attended by the vastest number of ministers of all persuasions that ever he saw in his life: the ministers walked in pairs, a Conformist and a Nonconformist together.[3] George Hughes, Fellow of Pembroke College, Oxford, was ejected from St. Andrew's, Plymouth. In 1663 Bishop Gauden's visitation at Totnes was forsaken by the whole body of the clergy when they heard that Hughes was in the town, that they might accompany him on horseback to his home.[4] It was not all bitterness between the two parties.

The Dissenters suffered much at the hands of a number of persons who acted voluntarily as common informers, whose pay depended on their energy in reporting conventicles, and who received from £7 to £15 for each conviction. We hear of them especially in the year after the first Conventicle Act. We know the names of some of them. John Poulter, the son of a butcher of Salisbury, "an egregiously wicked fellow," and a man named Lacey, who lived at Risborough, harried the Buckinghamshire Nonconformists for a time, and were nicknamed by the country people "Trepan" and "Informer." After 1670 Poulter had to leave the neighbourhood, having been accused of christening a cat Catherine Catherina in mockery of the Queen, and of feloniously taking goods from a man at Bamford whom he had cheated of money.[5] In Cambridgeshire the chief informers were a man named Audey, who lived at Meldreth, Stephen Perry, Edward Wallis, a cobbler, and Christopher Harris, a labourer. Perry seems to have been originally a servant at St. John's College, though he is also described as a tinker. In 1670 Sir Thomas Slater refused to accept information from him, and the informer himself got into trouble for malicious prosecution, though he went on informing in other quarters.[6] Owen Stockton[7] wrote, in 1675, "A Rebuke to Informers: with a Plea for the Ministers of the

---

[1] Fletcher, "Yorkshiremen of the Restoration," 1921, pp. 173-174.
[2] Calamy, II. 676.
[3] Ralph Thoresby, "Diary," October 22nd, 1677.   [4] Calamy, II. 227.
[5] Crosby, "Eng. Baptists," II. 238.
[6] "News from Cambridge, or a Brief Relation of the Wicked Proceedings of Three Informers," 1675.   [7] Calamy, I. 291.

Gospel called Nonconformists, and their Meetings: with Advice to those to whom the Informers apply for Assistance in their Undertakings." John Bunyan, in his " Life and Death of Mr. Badman," represented Mr. Badman as willing to turn informer for the sake of annoying his Christian wife, and only refraining from doing so because he would lose his trade if he did. In the same book Bunyan told the story of " W. S.," another informer. This was William Swinton, the sexton of St. Cuthbert's, Bedford, " a man of very wicked life," who used to watch at nights, climbing trees and ranging the woods by day, to search for conventicles. Such men were odious to all decent people: the aldermen of London often went out of their way when they heard that they were coming, and Alderman Forth bound over an informer to his good behaviour for breaking into his room without leave. Some of the justices refused to grant them warrants, and risked the penalty of £100 which they thereby brought on themselves.[1] An Order in Council dated December 7th, 1686, forbade any countenance to be given to John Smith, an informer who lived in the neighbourhood of Wymeswold, Northamptonshire, nor was any prosecution of Quakers to be permitted at his instigation.[2] Baxter mentioned an informer, Keating, and another named Marshall, who died in the Compter, where his creditors had put him to keep him from doing any more harm.[3] " The bishops," said Baxter, " appointed two more in their place, who first attacked Mr. Case's meeting and then Mr. Read's," where Baxter was preaching at the time. The congregation locked the two men in, and one of them remained weeping. Another went to Mr. Rosewell's meeting, where his heart was so melted that he retired from the trade. The chief of them all became so friendly to Baxter himself that he rescued him from a half-crazy ruffian in the streets, and declared he would meddle no more.[4]

Naturally, many stories were related of the judgments of heaven on these men. William Swinton was stricken with some kind of paralysis and speechlessness. On one occasion he fell from the bell in the " steeple-house," but escaped with his life, " but after that he also walked about, until God had made a sufficient spectacle of His judgment for sin, and then on a sudden he was stricken and died miserably."[5] An informer near St. Neots died from the bite of a dog, and the wound gangrened, the flesh rotting from his bones. Swinton's colleague

---

[1] Neal, " Puritans," IV. 547.
[2] S. P. Potter, " Hist. of Wymeswold," London, 1915.
[3] " Rel. Baxt," III. 171.
[4] *Ibid.*, III. 166–167. See also for other informers, " The Conformist's Third Plea for the Nonconformists," 1682, pp. 8–10; " The Conformist's Fourth Plea," 1683, which gives examples of several, and in particular John Hunnucks of Braintree; Sewell, " Hist. Quakers," *passim.*
[5] Bunyan, " Life and Death of Mr. Badman."

at Bedford, a man named Feckenham, who had squandered a considerable estate at Turvey, and had fallen in the world, died " the very month after " he had disturbed a conventicle. " He died in pain and anguish, now raving against the fanatics, and now blaming Mr. Foster for setting him in his office." [1] " There was a remarkable blast of Providence upon their persons and substance." [2]

Some feeble rhyming couplets, published in 1682, entitled " The Informer's Lecture to his Sons," give bitter expression to the feeling about these men.[3] Sometimes the feeling against them went further than bitter words. In November 1674 two informers went to the door of a house at Wrentham, about twelve miles from Yarmouth. Those present rose up crying " Thieves," fell on them, knocked them down, dragged them through a foul hogstye, and threw them into a pond. One of them afterwards died of the treatment he had received.[4] In April 1685 an informer, a woman, went with officers to the house of George Whitehead, the Quaker. She declared that there was usually a meeting there, and they threatened to break open the door, but the neighbours came flocking round, and the informer met with such a hostile reception that she was glad to get away.[5] When an informer asked Lord Herbert of Cherbury for a warrant against some Quakers, Lord Herbert asked if it were not sufficient to put peaceable neighbours in prison without giving a warrant to a rogue whereby he could make himself rich by plundering their families.[6]

Nonconformists were strong in Chichester, and were described as being " as factious a sort of people as any in England and . . . ready at an hour's warning to serve the Duke of Monmouth and Lord Grey." [7] In the autumn of 1681 there occurred an incident in this town which increased the feeling between Church and Dissent, and formed an additional cause of strife between Whigs and Tories, and, indeed, had a share in turning the scale in favour of the latter. According to a great mass of sworn evidence, what really happened was this. One Habin of Chichester, formerly a bailiff, had turned informer. Among other grievances against him was the following: on the occasion of a great " Pope burning " in Chichester the mob had broken the windows of a certain Captain Buckley, and Habin, although

---

[1] Brown, " Life of Bunyan," p. 225.
[2] Neal, " Puritans," IV. 556.
[3] See also " The Character of an Informer, wherein his Mischievous Nature and Lewd Practices are Detected," 1675; " The Informer's Answer to the Late Character," 1675; " The Informer's Looking-glass in which he may see himself while he is maliciously persecuting Dissenting Protestants," 1682.
[4] C.S.P.D., November 4th, 1674.
[5] Fox, " Short Journal," ed. by N. Penney, p. 103.
[6] T. Mardy Rees, " Hist. Quakers in Wales," p. 71.
[7] C.S.P.D., September 1681, 416/164.

he was not present, had sworn to the names of the rioters. On Sunday afternoon, August 6th, 1682, he and another informer named Halstead, described as his brother, but more probably his brother-in-law, were returning to the city after a conventicle hunt at Stocksbridge. They were both said to have been the worse for drink, and a crowd of boys shouted after them and stoned them. Halstead drew a sword and slashed at the boys and then got his head broken by a stone. The informers fled for refuge to the nearest house, which happened to belong to Richard Farringdon, or Farrington, a local Whig, with whom Habin was on bad terms. According to one story Habin broke one of Farringdon's windows with his club, saying it should pay for the stoning by the boys, but this was afterwards denied, and it was sworn that the attack was made on him simply because he was an informer. Farringdon ordered his coachman, John Davis, to beat Habin, and this man, who had threatened Habin on a previous occasion, closed with the informer, wrested his club from him, and struck him five or six violent blows on the head. He was so badly injured that he was carried into a stable belonging to the bishop's palace, everyone else having refused to take him in, and died there an hour afterwards. John Davis fled. He was captured a year or so later, and condemned; but at Jeffreys' suggestion his execution was postponed in the hope that some information might be got from him.[1] On Monday, August 7th, Henry Alured and Isaac Butler were brought before the mayor of Chichester on suspicion of having been seen in Farringdon's house when the man was murdered. They were well-known conventiclers.[2] Alured absconded shortly afterwards, and a warrant was issued for his apprehension.[3]

The inquest was held at the Town Hall[4] on August 12th, and an attempt was made to get a verdict of murder against Farringdon. There was a considerable tumult, and it was adjourned till Monday, the 14th. The Nonconformist account of what happened stated that on this day the jury were locked up in the bishop's palace, and were threatened by the bishop that he would have them before the King and Council if they did not find Farringdon guilty. Evidence was brought that Farringdon had rebuked Davis for beating the man too severely. The jury ultimately found Farringdon not guilty,[5] but they found Davis guilty of murder.[6] The jurymen issued a signed statement on September 11th that the coroner had kept the door shut while the inquest was being held, because there was a threatening mob outside, but that the bishop did not come near them all the time.

[1] Kitchin, " Roger L'Estrange," p. 301.   [2] C.S.P.D., 420/12.
[3] C.S.P.D., Entry Book 54/138, August 25th, 1681.
[4] Kitchin, " Roger L'Estrange," p. 301.
[5] Luttrell, " State Affairs," I. 237–238.   [6] " Observator," No. 196.

There was an abundance of contradictory evidence. It was sworn that Habin was not drunk at the time, that the window, if broken at all, was broken from the inside, because the lead was bulging outwards, and therefore could not have been broken by Habin. Witnesses swore that it was broken some time before. The story put forward on behalf of Davis was that Habin first threatened him with his cudgel, and that he acted in self-defence. Some people said that "if the bishop's servants had not used this poor wretch more like a beast than a man," and had put him to bed instead of thrusting him into a stable, he would have lived. To this it was answered that the bishop and his servants were all at church at the time. It was also stated that Habin did not die of neglect, but that everything possible was done for him, and that Farringdon sent a doctor to him. Extraneous matters were dragged in. Habin and Halstead were accused of perjury in having sworn a conventicle at Stocksbridge without having been there. Therefore, of course, his death was a just judgment for his perjury, though why Halstead should go scot-free is not clear, if this were so. The accusation of perjury was, however, disproved. The other side dragged in the fact that two of the bishop's horses had been maliciously maimed, and this was put down to the Dissenters. Great capital was made of the affair in the country, and it undoubtedly did great harm to the Whig and Dissenting cause.[1] Luttrell said that though the jury at the coroner's inquest had acquitted Farringdon, the grand jury at the Assizes brought in a true bill against him for murder.[2] Moreover it was not Farringdon, but Davis who was found guilty.[3] An unpleasant feature of the whole business was the way in which party spirit led to the intimidation of witnesses. A boy was threatened with terrible things unless he contradicted at the adjourned inquest what he had sworn on the previous Saturday, and his mother and he were terrified almost out of their wits. The bishop finally took the boy under his protection until the Assizes.[4] A little later one of the witnesses against Davis was assaulted by a mob, and a man who went to his assistance was severely assaulted too.[5]

Farringdon was tried on November 16th, 1682, and challenged twenty-eight of the jurymen, twenty peremptorily, but in the case of the rest showing cause. The prisoner also prayed that the witnesses might be examined apart, and this was allowed. A boy named Thomas Baines said that between two and three o'clock Habin was coming peaceably out of the South Gate,

[1] " The Chichester Account: or, A Faithful Relation of the Death of Habin the Informer," 1682; "A True Account from Chichester concerning the Death of Habin the Informer," 1682. This last, was answered by L'Estrange, who challenged it as a false, impudent, and seditious libel, in " The Account Cleared. In Answer to a Libel entitled ' A True Account '."
[2] Luttrell, I. 228.   [3] " Observator," Nos. 195, 196, 202, 205, 219.
[4] Ibid., No. 195.   [5] Ibid., No. 205.

and Davis fell upon him with a stick. Farringdon looked out of a window and told Davis to beat him soundly, but witness said that Davis did not strike Habin after this. William Crossingham gave the same evidence, except that Farringdon said "Beat him *stoutly*," and that Davis did strike the man again. Another witness said that a week after the murder the boy Baines made the same statement to him as he had given in evidence.

Farringdon brought about fifty witnesses, of whom only five were examined, three gentlemen who were in the room with him, and two women. The three former positively denied that Farringdon called out anything, or even opened the window, while the women deposed that they heard Habin say that Farringdon's windows should pay for all, and that Crossingham told one of them that he did not see Farringdon nor hear him at the window, and that he would not swear it for the world. The Lord Chief Justice said that enough had been examined; the evidence was first a boy, and then another of as little weight, while the third merely gave hearsay evidence. The jury, without moving from their place, acquitted Farringdon, and the Lord Chief Justice told him that the case had not been brought on by the King's command nor at his charge.[1]

Defoe, in his preface to Delaune's "Plea for the Nonconformists," said that nearly 8000 Protestant Dissenters had perished in prison during the reign of Charles II. This is undoubtedly an exaggeration. Penn said in 1687 that since the Restoration more than 15,000 families had been ruined, and more than 50,000 persons had died for conscience' sake.[2]. In this he is referring to all the Dissenters, and very probably to the Roman Catholics as well. Jeremy White, who had been one of Cromwell's chaplains, collected a list of Nonconformist sufferers between the Restoration and the Revolution, and calculated that in some way or another 60,000 persons had suffered, and 5000 had died in prison. He is also said to have told Lord Dorset that "King James had offered him 1000 guineas for the manuscript, in order to expose the Church, but he had refused all invitations and rewards, and concealed the black record, that it might not appear to the disreputation of the Church of England, for which some of the clergy sent him their thanks, and offered him an acknowledgment, which he generously refused."[3]   A thousand guineas was a great sum to refuse, especially when he might have earned it without injury to his conscience.[4]   The number of deaths is probably a mere conjecture. The Quakers suffered worst of all, and kept the

---

[1] "Newsletter, Admiralty Greenwich Hospital," II. 61.
[2] Penn, "Good Advice to the Church of England," 1687.
[3] Oldmixon, "Reign of Stuarts," p. 715; Neal, "Puritans," V. 22.
[4] Salmon, "Lives of the English Bishops," 1733, p. 183.

most accurate records, and they only claim that 450 died in prison.[1]

Defoe calculated that the Dissenters suffered in their estates, and by loss of trade, at least £2,000,000 in these years. This again is pure guesswork. Neal, after speaking of the flight of many of them to America and Holland, in which latter country there were congregations of them at Amsterdam, Rotterdam, Utrecht, Leyden, and elsewhere, said that if we admit the dissenting families to have been 150,000, and that each family suffered in fines no more than £3 or £4 a year, the total losses of the Dissenters must have amounted to £12,000,000 or £14,000,000.[2] But there is no reason to believe that there were so many families, and it must be remembered that in some years, and in many places, the law was very lightly enforced, if at all.

NOTE TO CHAPTER IX.

Before the Clarendon Code Nonconformity was strictly forbidden by Canon and Statute Law. Even by the Common Law they came under the general rule against breakers of the peace.

The Canon Law inflicted excommunication on those who set up sects and called them churches, and for worship apart from the national Church. No ecclesiastical laws or constitutions were to be set up without royal authority. No minister was allowed to preach without a licence to do so from the bishop of the diocese.

6 Henry VIII. inflicted imprisonment for non-payment of tithes.

27 Henry VIII., c. 20, under which a few suffered, was also concerned with tithes.

32 Henry VIII., c. 7. against non-payment of tithes. Justices of the Peace were obliged to commit the contumacious defendant to prison till he should find sufficient security to give due obedience to the process, decree or sentence of the ecclesiastical court.

2 & 3 Edward VI., commanded under penalties the payment of tithes. The laws about tithes were especially troublesome to the Quakers.

1 Elizabeth, c. 1. The Act of Supremacy, enforcing the oaths of supremacy and allegiance.

1 Elizabeth, c. 2. The Act of Uniformity, enacting a fine of twelve pence, together with ecclesiastical censures for not attending church on Sundays and Holy Days.

5 Elizabeth, c. 1. An Act for the assurance of the Queen's royal power over all estates and subjects within her dominions. Oath required.

5 Elizabeth, c. 23, authorised the writ " *De excommunicato capiendo.*" This writ would issue from the Court of Chancery, on the receipt of a certificate from the bishop of the diocese, stating that forty days had elapsed since the excommunication had been published in the parish church, and specifying the offence for which the excommunication had been issued. (A person might be excommunicated for repeated absence from church, for not having his children baptized, or for many other ecclesiastical offences.)

---

[1] Braithwaite, " Second Period," pp. 114-115.   [2] Neal, " Puritans," V. 22.

23 Elizabeth, c. 1. An Act to retain the Queen's Majesty's subjects in their due obedience. By this Act the penalty for not attending church was raised to £20 a month. An offender who persevered in his offence for twelve months was to be bound over to good behaviour, and to provide two sureties of £200 each until he conformed. A fine of £10 a month was to be inflicted on a person keeping a schoolmaster who did not attend church.

29 Elizabeth, c. 6. An Act for the more speedy and due execution of 23 Elizabeth, c. *1*, which enabled the Crown, by process out of the Exchequer, to seize all the goods and two-thirds of the real property of such habitual offenders, in order to pay the sums due at the rate of £20 a month. The process might be repeated annually. (This Act and the previous one were really directed against the Roman Catholics.)

35 Elizabeth, c. 1. "An Act to retain the Queen's subjects in their due obedience," sometimes called the First Conventicle Act. It had been continued four times, and was made permanent in 1624. A person who absented himself from his parish church for a month might be imprisoned, and could not be bailed out unless he made a public submission in writing in a book which was to be kept by the minister, and such submission was to be certified by the latter to the bishop. If the offender remained in prison three months without making such submission, even after having been warned by the bishop, or by any justice of the peace, he should then be brought up at the next Quarter Sessions. There he should be ordered to abjure the realm, swearing never to return without leave, and then should proceed direct to the port at which he had been ordered to embark. If he refused either to conform or abjure, he should be adjudged guilty of felony without benefit of clergy. (The sentence for this was death.)

3 Jac. I., c. 4. "An Act for the better discovering and repressing popish recusants," imposed the oath of allegiance under pain of incurring the penalties of *præmunire*, which were imprisonment for life, confiscation of goods, and loss of the King's protection. (This Act was really directed against popish recusants.)

3 Jac. I., c. 6. "An Act to prevent and avoid dangers which may grow by Popish recusants."

7 Jac. I., c. 6. Every person above eighteen years of age to take the oath of allegiance in *3 Jac. I., c. 4.*

13 & 14 Car. II., c. 1. An Act against the Quakers.

13 & 14 Car. II., c. 4. Act of Uniformity, 1662.

16 Car. II., c. 4. Conventicle Act, 1664.

17 Car. II., c. 4. Five Mile Act, 1665.

22 Car. II., c. 1. Conventicle Act, 1670.

25 Car. II., c. 2. Test Act, 1673.

30 Car. II., c. 1. "An Act for the more effectual preserving the King's person and Government by disabling Papists from sitting in either House of Parliament," 1678.

The Protestant Dissenters argued that *23 Elizabeth, 29 Elizabeth,* and *3 Jac.* were directed against Roman Catholics and not themselves.[1]

---

[1] See "Tam: Quam," 1683, "A Digest of Legislative Enactments relating to the Society of Friends," by J. Davis, Bristol, 1820; Whitehead, "Christian Progress"; Besse, "Sufferings."

X

THE Puritans founded the whole of their religion on the Bible. Ecclesiastical rules and ecclesiastical traditions were naught, though many of their more learned readers were well acquainted with the Fathers. The Bible was the guide of their actions, especially the Old Testament. The story of Israel, beset by the idolaters, and going forth to the help of the Lord against the mighty, seemed to them their own story. Milton was much more successful with the Old Testament story than with the New. " Paradise Lost " is an infinitely greater work than " Paradise Regained," and " Samson Agonistes " is so great because blind, captive Samson is, in one sense, none other than blind John Milton, who had been so great, and had fallen so low. When the Puritans wrote political tracts, it was to the Bible, especially the Old Testament, they went for argument and illustration. In private life it was the same; quotations from the Scriptures were their constant guide.

One of the most controverted questions between the Puritans and the Anglicans was that of keeping Sunday. The Puritans treated it as the Jewish Sabbath; no work was to be done, no amusements indulged in; it was a day of prayer and worship, and sometimes of fasting too. It is not entirely true to say they made a gloomy day of it. To them it was not gloomy at all. They enjoyed it. It was gloomy to those who had no sympathy with them, who found their services dull and uninspiring, and who suffered from *ennui* during the intervals. The Puritans were zealots, and, like all zealots, severe to the weaker brethren, whose weakness was incomprehensible to them. To the Anglicans, Sunday was not the Jewish holiday, but a Christian festival, the weekly memorial of the Resurrection. In the intervals between the services they thought themselves entitled to indulge in harmless recreation. A saint like George Herbert would not need this. His religion was his recreation as well as his life-work; but the ordinary man, a good Christian he would consider himself, could see no harm in sports and games on the village green on Sundays when service was over. Oliver had, on June 26th, 1658, given his assent to an " Act for the Better Observance of the Lord's Day." Sunday observance occupied the attention of the House of Commons after the Restoration, and in 1663 the Speaker of that House was able to inform the King that they had examined the extant laws on the subject, and where they found them defective, either in rules or penalties, they had amended them.   The Act of Charles II.[1] dealing with Sunday trading still stands in the Statute Book, but, except in a few places, is generally disregarded: passed in 1677, it owed its genesis to the increasing Puritan element in Parliament.   As the Puritans disliked the Churchmen's ways of keeping Sunday, so also they disliked the Church festivals, as heathen in origin, savouring of popery, and tending to superstition.

The extreme Puritans frowned on all amusements as the opportunities of the devil.   Macaulay's jibe, that they hated bear-baiting not because it gave pain to the bear, but because it gave pleasure to the spectators, had enough truth in it to be a jibe, and not merely a joke.   Yet Alsop wrote of the " decent and harmonious bagpipes at a bear-baiting." [2] But, whatever the motive, they did their best to put down brutal pastimes of the kind.   In their zeal the Puritans traced innocent things like maypoles and Christmas wassailing and so forth to a heathenish origin, and therefore they were works of the devil.   Adam Martindale had trouble about a maypole: " The rabble of profane youth and some doting fools that took their part, were encouraged to affront me by setting up a maypole in my way to church, upon a little bank called Bow Hillock, where in times past the Sabbath had been woefully profaned (as tradition goes) by music and dancing, and where in my time there was a *rendez-vous* of rakehells till I took an effectual way to rout them."   After a time Martindale preached to them, " calmly reproved their folly," and told them that " many learned men were of opinion that a maypole was a relic of the shameful worship of the strumpet Flora in Rome; but however that was, it was a thing that never did nor could do good: yea, had occasioned, and might occasion, much harm to people's souls."   Annoyed at this, and " to clear themselves that they were no friends to profaneness, they resolved, upon their own interest, to procure Mr. Brooke of Congleton . . . to bestow his pains upon a Lord's Day with us. . . . When he saw the maypole on his way, and understood by whom and to what end it was set up, he did most smartly reprove their sin and folly, calling them by most opprobrious names, as the scum, rabble, riff-raff (or such-like) of the parish: insomuch as my words were smooth like oil in comparison of his, so full of salt and vinegar."   Not long after this Mrs. Martindale, assisted by three young women, sawed the maypole down, " cutting it breast high, so as the bottom would serve well for a dial post."   The people pieced it together with another pole, but it was such a poor thing that they soon afterwards allowed it to be taken down.   A magistrate sent a warrant to bring the three young women

---

[1] 29 Car. II., c. 7.   [2] ." Melius Inquirendum," p. 23.

before him, but " either there was no proof against them, or no law, and nothing came of it." [1] In 1661 Malachi Duderne was informed against at the Wiltshire Quarter Sessions because he told the people of Downton that it was high time the maypole was cut down and burnt, and that if they did not do it there were those who would. [2]

Cards, of course, were anathema. Ralph Thoresby expressed his sorrow at having played cards one Christmas Day. [3] The theatre was to the Puritans the devil's playhouse, but they did not despise a pageant, say, on November 5th or 17th; on which days they joined in processions, rang bells, lighted bonfires, and burned the Pope's effigy with a right good will. Anti-popery filled their religion. In the case of some of them, indeed, it was their religion, and their ingenuity in detecting popery in the most innocent things was amazing. The Puritans had no objection to alcohol itself, but the ancient English custom of drinking healths was an abominable heathen practice in their sight. The reaction from the narrowness of the Cromwellian régime had been marked by an alarming increase of drunkenness, and the King soon after his return issued a proclamation forbidding his subjects to waste their time in taverns and tippling houses, and in drunken debauches. Prynne had then issued a manifesto of his own against the custom of drinking healths, entitled " Mr. Prynne's Letter of Proposals to our Gracious Lord and Sovereign King Charles and His Majesty's Gracious Resolves to all His Loving Subjects." As early as 1628 Prynne had published " Healths, Sickness; or, A Brief Discourse proving the Drinking and Pledging of Healths to be Sinful and Utterly Unlawful to Christians." Henry Jessey expressed his approval of Prynne's arguments in " The Lord's Loud Call to England." Samuel Ward and Samuel Clarke wrote a " Warning Piece to all Drunkards and Health Drinkers " [4] in which they gave over 120 " sad and dreadful examples of God's severe judgments upon notorious drunkards."

There has been a good deal of exaggeration about the strange names which the Puritans are said to have given their children. They discarded the old English names and those of the saints, and confined themselves to names taken from the Scriptures, especially from the Old Testament. Hence, we find names like Abigail, Bathsheba, Jehoshaphat, and Aphra. The last was the Christian name of Aphra, or, as she always spelt it, Aphara Behn, the woman dramatist, and is taken from Micah i. 10. One of the ejected ministers was called Sabbath Clark. The parochial registers of the Restoration period also show names

[1] " Life of Adam Martindale," pp. 156–158.
[2] Records Wilts. Quarter Sessions, Hist. MSS. Com., MSS. Various Collections, I. 149.
[3] Thoresby, " Diary," 1830, I. 184.   [4] 1682.

like Deliverance, Thankful, Beloved, Accepted, Miracle, Unity, and Preserved. There were, for instance, Accepted Frewen and his brother Thankful. State Papers have preserved for us the name of Handmaid, the wife of Aaron Johnson.[1] But the chief eccentricities of Puritan Christian names are to be found before 1640 rather than after. " There is the most distinct evidence that during the latter portion of Elizabeth's reign, in a district roughly comprising England south of the Trent, and having, say, Banbury for its centre, there prevailed amongst a certain class of English religionists a practice of baptizing children by scriptural phrases, pious ejaculations, or godly admonitions. It was a practice instituted of deliberate purpose, as conducive to vital religion, and as intending to separate the truly godly and renewed portion of the community from the world at large." [2] The familiar name of Praise-God Barebone has led people to believe that such names were characteristic of the Commonwealth period; but, as a matter of fact, the practice of giving such was dying out before that time. Some of the other examples familiar to us are derived from the dramatists. Tribulation Wholesome is a character in Ben Jonson's " Alchemist," Zeal-of-the-land Busy in the same writer's " Bartholomew Fair," while Colonel Fear-the-Lord Barebottle comes from Cowley's " Cutter of Coleman Street." But few such names occur in the parish registers after 1660, and most of them occur in the burial rather than baptismal registers. Faint-not, Hope-still, and Be-thankful are found in the former, Rejoice and Hate-evil in the latter. In a will from the Probate Court of Peterborough, dated June 24th, 1665, is the name of " What-God-will Crosland." Help-on-high Foxe was presented to the living of Lydney, Gloucestershire, in 1660, though the inscription on his tomb calls him Hope-well, and there was the well-known London printer who called himself Livewell Chapman.[3] In Besse's "Sufferings of the Quakers" we find Faith Sturges, Mercy Chase, Provided Southwick, Shunamite Park, and Temperance Higwell. In Palmer's " Nonconformists' Memorial " we find Ichabod Chauncey, Gracious Franklin, Increase Mather, Thankful Owen, Comfort Steer, and Faithful Teate. On the roll of Frankland's students was Godsgift Kerby.[4] The parish registers of North Shields record on June 19th, 1683, the burial of " Mehatophell " Lomax, the daughter of John Lomax, ejected from Wooler, Northumberland. The scribe intended Mehetabel.[5]

The great characteristic of Puritanism, of course, was the abiding fear and hatred of the Roman Church and all its works. All Romanists and the Jesuits in particular were believed capable of

[1] C.S.P.D., June ?, 1660, Petitions VI., No. 191.
[2] C. W. Bardsley, " Puritan Nomenclature," 1897, p. 118.
[3] Bardsley, " Puritan Nomenclature," passim.
[4] Congregational Hist. Soc. Trans., III. 78.   [5] Gen. xxxvi. 39.

acting with the most diabolical cunning and the most fiendish malice. As for the cunning, a pamphlet published in 1674 rebuked the " fanciful dreams which discovered Jesuits in Cromwell's and Vane's coats, and Papists training armies underground." [1] As for the malice, Louis XIV. and other continental sovereigns, by their treatment of Protestants, gave some ground for the accusation. It was sheer fear which led men to accept the lies of Oates and his associates, with all the consequent horrors of the Popish Plot time, and it was the same fear, increased by the tactless behaviour of James II. on behalf of his co-religionists, which brought about that monarch's downfall. The Revolution of 1688 was really a Puritan victory. There were many who honestly believed that no Roman Catholics ever told the truth if they thought their Church would be better served by a lie. That was why, in the heat of the Popish Plot, no Roman Catholic witness received any credence. Some seemed to look upon lying as a habit fostered by the Roman religion. Anne Countess of Balcarres was a cousin of the Duke of Lauderdale, and by a second marriage became Countess of Argyll. She was a great devotee of Baxter, and went about to various places in London to hear him preach. In 1662 her daughter, Lady Ann Lindsay, joined the Roman Church, and Baxter, commenting on the fact, said " Before she turned Papist, her mother said she scarce ever heard a lie from her," but since her conversion she could believe nothing she said. [2] Volumes and volumes were written against Rome, not merely by theologians, but also by scribblers like Henry Care, whose " Weekly Packet of Advice from Rome, or The History of Popery," accompanied by the " Courant," published with it every week from 1678 to 1682, raked up all the abuse and garbage and twisted history that could be found. In the reign of James II. there was naturally an enormous amount of Anti-Roman literature; a single tract, " A Papist Misrepresented and Represented," written by John Gother in 1685, produced within two years over thirty-five replies and rejoinders.

The descriptions left us of Nonconformist services in all the chief sects, show that their worship as performed then was much the same as that offered by the same bodies to-day, except that the services as a rule began much earlier in the morning. There was, of course, a certain amount of variation at the discretion of the minister, but they usually said or sang psalms (though the Baptists were much divided on the lawfulness of singing), the minister prayed extemporaneously once or twice, read a portion or portions of Scripture, of which he gave an exposition, and preached a sermon, which would seldom or never be less than an

---

[1] " The Roman Church Vindicated," p. 70.
[2] " Rel. Baxt.," II. 220; Powicke, " Richard Baxter and the Countess of Balcarres "; " Bulletin John Rylands Library," IX. 585.

hour long. At first these services were generally in private houses. The licences under the Declaration of Indulgence of 1672 specified many of these, but other buildings were named, buildings of a most miscellaneous description—schoolrooms, public buildings, barns, and what not. When the Dissenters braved the law, or at times when the law was slackly enforced, they came out into the open, and used specially erected buildings. Over thirty of these arc known to have been built in London between the Restoration and the Revolution, generally plain, oblong structures, with galleries running round three sides. Sometimes one building was used by several congregations. The Pinners' Hall, near the site of the present Liverpool Street Station, was let by the landlord to the Pinners' Company during five days of the week, to two separate congregations on Sundays, and to a Sabbatarian congregation on Saturdays. The Pinner's Hall lectures were delivered there on Tuesdays.[1]

The members of the congregation were earnest in hearing sermons. Some of them at least took notes, and very commonly groups of members met together in the evenings in a private house, and the sermons which had been delivered were recapitulated from notes or memory. Sometimes the minister did this in his own house. In days when the congregations met in fear of the officers of the law this was a great advantage to those who had been prevented from attendance. Among those sects which retained a belief in the sacraments, the Lord's Supper was celebrated, usually every month, much oftener, indeed, than was the case with their Puritan brethren, who did not leave the Church of England in 1662. One institution of which very frequent mention is made in the diaries of contemporary Nonconformist ministers was the congregational fast. Oliver Heywood kept these fasts frequently at various places.[2] They took the form of devotional exercises lasting from early in the morning till late in the afternoon, those present partaking of no food till the proceedings had concluded. Weekly lectures—that is, sermons on a stated week-day—were common. Many of the ministers, like Oliver Heywood, went on long preaching tours, speaking in whatever building or private dwelling-house was available, and then passing on to the next place; and their indefatigable industry in this respect, in spite of the difficult travelling conditions of the time, was beyond all praise. Many of the ministers, too, were unwearied in the pastoral visitation of their people and the religious training of the children. Some of the congregations, of course, such as some of the London ones, consisted of wealthy people; but all maintained their ministers to the best of their ability, were good to their own poor, and we hear also of collections for charitable objects. One of

[1] W. T. Whitley, " The Baptists of London," p. 14.
[2] See his " Diary," *passim.*

the special characteristics of Puritanism, too, was the institution of family worship. At night, especially on Sunday nights, the members of the family were collected together, the children, servants and apprentices were catechised on the sermons they had heard, psalms were sung, and the head of the family offered prayer, and sometimes, chiefly on Sunday nights, a sermon by some well-known Puritan divine was read.

Many of the Dissenters were excommunicated by the ecclesiastical courts, and the clergy refused to bury them. So they were frequently buried in private grounds, in a garden, orchard, or field. Thus Durant, who was ejected from All Saints', Newcastle, was buried in the garden of his house in Pilgrim Street there.[1] Joshua Kirby, ejected from Wakefield, died excommunicated in 1676, and was buried in his own garden.[2] Mrs. Bavington, the wife of Major Philip Bavington, and daughter of Sir Arthur Haselrigg, died on August 28th, 1670 and was buried in a tomb cut out of the rock under her house, Harnham Hall.[3] In the registers of Over, Cambridgeshire, under the year 1677 we read, " Mary, the wife, and Mary, the daughter, of Edward Rooke, buried in the close without Christian burial." The registers of Bugbrook, Northamptonshire, have an entry under 1669, " Several other sorts of phanaticks who having forsaken the church would not be buried in the churchyard, but in their orchards or backside of their houses." The registers of Hooton Pagnell, Yorkshire, record on September 19th, 1699, " John Burgess the Quaker in his own burial-ground." Frequently when a person was buried in a private ground the same privilege was extended to relatives and friends and so private cemeteries grew up. Later, of course, when the penal laws came to an end, the private grounds fell into disuse and public burial-grounds were opened. In quite a number of cases the earlier grounds ultimately were built over, or put to some other use, and cannot now be identified. The Quakers, however, kept careful and accurate records. The first Quaker Burial Register for London begins on September 8th, 1661. For the establishment of these burial-grounds the Quakers frequently got into trouble; thus in 1677 Richard Ewbank, a Quaker, was cited in the archdeacon's court at Durham for enclosing a burial-place for sectaries at Gateshead. However, he died in the following year, and was buried in the ground in question. The Friends had five burial-grounds in the county of Durham alone.[4] In September 1678 the Quakers were conducting a funeral at their burying-place at Sowerby, Yorkshire, and Dr. Hook, the vicar of Halifax, laid information against them for refusing to bring the deceased Quakeress to be buried in the Anglican churchyard. The funeral passed off without interruption, but as the mourners all

---

[1] " Arch. Ael.," 2nd Series, XIII. 33.   [2] Palmer, III. 455.
[3] *Ibid.*   [4] " Arch. Ael.," 2nd Series, XVI. 189, 274.

went together to a private house after it was over, they were fined
£20 for holding a conventicle there. As they did not pay, a
distress was levied, and some beasts belonging to the owner were
taken away and sold for £18. He afterwards declared that they
were worth £30.[1] The Quaker burial-ground at Barton, in
South Yorkshire, had a curious inscription affixed at the entrance,
said to have been composed by Richard Farnsworth.[2]

These Quaker burial-grounds were frequently gifts to the
society. Thus in 1672 William Wright, clothier, of Bradford,
Yorkshire, gave an acre of land at Goodmansend for that purpose.[3]
In other cases there is evidence of purchase. Quakers' Yard, the
society's place of interment in the parish of Holt, Denbighshire,
was bought by the Friends in February 1682. There is a curious
note in the State Papers of a Quaker burying-ground in " Rad-
cliffe Church," Bristol.[4] This must surely mean somewhere in
the parish of St. Mary, Redcliffe.

The Baptists, too, had their separate burial-places. At Great
Budworth, in Cheshire, the Baptist burial-ground is asserted to
date back to the sixteenth century,[5] but this is very doubtful, for
it can hardly have been Baptist property at so early a time. The
chapel to which it belongs is now known as the chapel at Hill
Cliff and the truer history appears to lie in the statement that in
1663 a little croft at Hill Cliff, Warrington, was given in trust as a
burial-place " for the Anabaptists and such other of the congregational way in Cheshire as wish to bury there." [6] The two
Baptist congregations in Bristol, since the Episcopal clergy refused
to allow excommunicated persons to be buried in the churchyards, united in 1681 to buy a garden in Redcross Lane for a
burying-place. In May 1684 some of them were brought to
trial for burying a child there. The jury refused to find their
conduct a riot, but brought in a verdict of unlawful assembly,
inasmuch as the burial was not in consecrated ground. The
father of the child was fined 40s. and costs, the latter amounting
to £3.[7]

In London the Bunhill Fields, in the parish of St. Giles's,
Cripplegate, formed the Nonconformist Campo Santo, as Southey
called it, though this burial-ground did not belong to them, nor
was it confined to them. Defoe was of opinion that the Great
Plague pit was on, or near, this spot. The land was enclosed by
a brick wall at the sole charge of the City of London in 1665,
and the western gates were finished in 1666. It is stated that it
was set apart and consecrated as a common cemetery for the

---

[1] Heywood, " Diary," September 1678.
[2] *Journal Friends Hist. Soc.*, XII. 181.
[3] Baines, " Yorkshire Past and Present," p. 307.   [4] C.S.P.D., 249/61.
[5] Urwick, " Nonconformity in Cheshire," p. 403.
[6] Whitley, " Baptists of North-west England."
[7] " Broadmead Records," pp. 215, 268.

burial of bodies for which there was no room in the ordinary churchyards in the plague year, though it was never used for that precise purpose; indeed, the keeper was expressly forbidden to dig pits therein. It was leased at first to one Tindal, and after him to others, but the corporation of London took it over again in 1741. The first interment took place in July 1665, and the last in January 1854.[1] Here are still to be seen the monuments of John Bunyan, Thomas Rosewell, John and Thomas Rowe, Theophilus Gale, Richard Wavell, Thomas Goodwin, Thankful Owen, Charles Fleetwood, Edward Bagshawe, Henry Cromwell, and many other Puritan leaders. Though no inscription remains, Thomas Cole, Thomas Doolittle, John Faldo, Henry Jessey, William Kiffin, Hanserd Knollys, Nathaniel Mather, Vavasour Powell, and Nathaniel Vincent lie in unknown graves amongst the 120,000 who from first to last were buried there. Here was also the great Quaker burial-place in London, though in 1677 a vain attempt was made to prevent the Friends from using it, and a presentment was laid against Richard Carter, the gravedigger, in the July of that year.[2] There was another burial-ground at Deadman's Place, crossed to-day by the Southwark Bridge Road. It is believed to have been older than Bunhill Fields, and was used by the Baptists, who, like many other Dissenters, refused the Church service and the Church clergy, and buried their dead in their own way.[3] The great distinction between Anglican and Nonconformist burial-grounds, of course, lay in the fact that no form of consecration was used in setting the latter apart, all Puritans looking upon such rites as superstitious.

The Presbyterians long hoped for reunion, and abstained for some years from perpetuating the schism by ordaining successors, though when they did so, they did not intend a direct act of separation. They had at first hoped for a reconstitution of the Church in the Presbyterian way, and they still looked for ultimate comprehension. Baxter said in 1679 that his brethren " profess to take their own assemblies, but in *chapels*, and not in *distinct*, much less as separate *churches*." They were already members of the Church by baptism, and some of them had been ordained by bishops, were ministers of the Church, and might still conform if they would. The practice of occasional conformity went on for a long time, and up to quite recent years it was a common practice for Nonconformists to come to church for marriages, burials, and such-like. A distinction was frequently made in the seventeenth century between Presbyterians and separatists.[4] The Presbyterians kept on hoping to get back on their own terms

[1] Light, " Bunhill Fields," pp. 1–4; J. S. Burn, " Registrum Ecclesiæ Parochialis," 1829, p. 188.
[2] Besse, " Sufferings."
[3] W. T. Whitley, " Baptists of London," 1929 pp. 18–19.
[4] Evelyn, " Diary," March 29th, 1689.

of a very modified episcopacy; while the other sects, the Independents, Baptists, and Quakers, had no such hope or desire.[1]

The other sects, then, did not hesitate about ordination. Three probationers were ordained in Somersetshire about 1665 or 1666, at the house of Mr. John Mallack, a merchant living about a mile out of Taunton. The candidates read theses, and were examined. Joseph Alleine offered prayer, and then Mr. Ames Short, Mr. Thomas Lye, Mr. William Ball, Mr. Robert Atkins, and Mr. John Kerridge together set the young men apart by the laying on of hands. One of the candidates was an Oxford man named George Trosse.[2] Joseph Alleine is considered a Presbyterian, but it will be observed that he did not take part in the laying on of hands; Ames Short was an Independent, and so this must be considered an Independent ordination. There was an Independent ordination at Lyme Regis in 1687, in which Ames Short again took part. Again, on March 9th, 1670, Obadiah Hughes, B.A., who was ejected from a Studentship at Christ Church, Oxford, in 1662, was solemnly, though privately, ordained to the work of the ministry by Mr. Jasper Hicks and five others of his brethren. This was in Devonshire, and Hughes ministered round about Plymouth for some years.[3] In Montgomeryshire, on August 28th, 1672, Henry Williams was ordained as co-pastor to Hugh Owen, and soon after this Reynold Wilson of Aberhavesp was also ordained.[4] Baptist ordinations are known to have taken place in London in 1668 (Benjamin Keach) and 1669 [5] and there were numerous others in various places during this period.

What is generally considered the first Presbyterian ordination in England after the Restoration took place at the house of Robert Heaton in Deansgate, Manchester, on October 29th, 1672. It was not Presbyterian in the strictest sense, because the Presbyterian organisation was not in existence, and some Independents took part in it. It was a mere association of ministers, without that representative, authoritative, and official character which strict Presbyterianism demanded. The chief ministers who officiated were Henry Newcome and Oliver Heywood. Three men, Joseph Dawson, Samuel Angier, and John Jolly, were ordained, who had all been preachers for several years. Oliver Heywood must have been little troubled at the idea of the continuance of the separation, for he called this ordination service " a hopeful blossoming of Aaron's rod after a sharp

[1] " Ordination, Nonconformity and Separation," *Church Quarterly Review*, XIX. 37.
[2] Stanford, " Joseph Alleine, His Companions and Times," pp. 324–325.
[3] Calamy, II. 235.
[4] Richard Williams, " Hist. Parish of Llanbrynmair," *Powysland Club Trans.* XIX. 336.
[5] Whitley, " British Baptists," p. 146.

winter." [1] His own two sons became ministers of Nonconformist congregations.

There was a Presbyterian ordination in Yorkshire, the first in the county, and claimed as the second in England since the Restoration, at the house of Robert Mitchell, near Winterburn, in Craven, on July 8th, 1678. There were only " three to lay on hands "—Oliver Heywood, Richard Frankland, and Joseph Dawson, and the fact that there were only three was regarded as regrettable. The candidates were John Issot, one of Frankland's students, John Darnton, and a man named Thorpe. John Darnton at the ordination expressed regret for having preached for twenty years without being ordained, though he was able to say that he had never administered baptism. He had been ejected from Bedlington in Northumberland, on the ground that he was a layman, and, according to his statement, had been seeking ordination ever since. [2] Oliver Heywood's manuscripts refer to a number of Presbyterian ordinations during the years 1678—1681, in Mansfield, Warrington, and in various places in Yorkshire. [3] Philip Henry's son, Matthew, was ordained by the presbytery in 1687. [4] In the registers of the High Pavement Presbyterian congregation at Nottingham (now Unitarian) are records of several ordinations in the Presbyterian manner between 1675 and 1703. [5]

Nonconformists were unable to take the oaths required of graduates at the English universities, which were thus practically closed to them. Adam Martindale gave an account of the education of his own son, and the difficulties of the Dissenters in that respect. In 1667 he sent him to Trinity College, Cambridge, but he said, " I am not free to have him engaged in such oaths, subscriptions, or practices as I could not down with myself," so the youth was sent down immediately. Next " I sent him up to Oxford, tabled him in a private house, and my noble friend, Sir Peter Brooke, prevailed with a gentleman of Brazen-nose College to give him his tuition in his chamber. He could not, indeed, be admitted to disputations in the hall, because no member of the college, but he might be present at those in the schools. Here he profited well, but was wearied out with his pragmatical old schoolfellows, that would be for ever asking him when he must be entered, and why he lost his time, to which it was not convenient to give any account." The son next went to Mr. Hickman's academy, near Bromsgrove, Sir Peter Brooke and Mr. Foley of Whitley Court contributing to the expense. Here

---

[1] " Diary "; Hunter, " Life of Oliver Heywood," pp. 244-245; Shaw, " Presbyterianism in Wigan," p. 42.

[2] Miall, " Congregationalism in Yorkshire," gives the date wrongly as 1677. See also " Ordination, Nonconformity and Separation," *Church Quarterly Review*, XIX. 37; *Trans. Cong. Hist. Soc.*, II. 422-229.

[3] Oliver Heywood, " Diaries," II. 21, 24, 25.

[4] Philip Henry, " Diary," p. 358.   [5] *Trans. Unit. Hist. Soc.*, I. 55.

he remained two years.   Then, in April 1670, his father took him
to Glasgow, "where, being examined by the Principal and
Regent for that year's Laureation, he was admitted to the class
of magistrands; that is, such as were to commence Master of
Arts about seventeen weeks after.   In which time he ran through
the whole written body of philosophy," was examined and
admitted M.A.   When he returned home he found his father
had collected a number of pupils for him, whom he was to instruct
in the higher branches of learning.[1]   To meet the difficulty of
obtaining higher education, and also with a view to preparing
candidates for the Nonconformist ministry, some of the Dissenting
ministers opened academies where they "taught university
learning."   These were not entirely theological seminaries, inasmuch as students attended who were not desirous of entering
the ministry.   Undergraduates were much younger in those days
than now, but we hear of some students at the academies who
were too young even for this class, and it is difficult to say where
the school ended and the academy began.   Some ministers
undertook the care of a few divinity students.   Philip Henry was
one of these; John Flavel at Dartmouth was another.   "He
freely taught academical learning to four young men, whom he
bred to the ministry, and one of them he maintained all the
while at his own charge." [2]   William Whittaker, an oriental
scholar, ministered to a Presbyterian congregation in the Long
Walk, Bermondsey, till his death in 1672.   It is said of him that
his house was for many years full of candidates in divinity, and he
had many foreign divines under his care.[3]   Hugh Owen of
Montgomeryshire, Marmaduke Matthews of Swansea, Peregrine
Phillips of Haverfordwest, and John Whitlock and Mr. Hardy,
both of Nottingham, though not regular tutors, occasionally
helped some young men by assisting them in their education for
the dissenting ministry.[4]

The Act of Uniformity ordered all schoolmasters, public and
private, to subscribe the declarations, and take the oaths, and
also to obtain a licence from the ordinary of the diocese.   The
Five Mile Act forbade school teaching on the part of unlicensed
persons, under a penalty of £40.   Prosecution of teachers who did
not hold an ecclesiastical licence went on, though with decreasing
frequency, till 1734, in which year George II. personally intervened to prevent proceedings against Philip Doddridge on this
ground.   One loophole, however, was found in the law.   It was
established by Bate's Case in 1670 that if a founder and pay-
patron of a school nominated a person to be schoolmaster, he
could not be deprived of his post, even if he had no licence.[5]

---

[1] " Life of Adam Martindale," pp. 187-190.
[2] *Trans. Cong. Hist. Soc.*, IV. 252.
[3] Wilson, " Dissenting Churches," IV. 333.
[4] Bogue and Bennet, " Hist. Dissenters," II. 68.
[5] Parker, " Dissenting Academies in England," Cambridge, 1914, p. 50.

Over 100 of the men ejected in 1662 had held university fellowships, tutorships, or other posts. The academic life was closed to them unless they conformed. They were bound by the oath they had already taken not to lecture elsewhere *tamquam in universitate*. In the Middle Ages there had been from time to time secessions from Oxford and Cambridge, and rival but short-lived universities had been set up at Stamford and elsewhere. Hence this oath, which presented a real difficulty to some of the ejected men. Charles Morton, Samuel Cradock, and others held that it prohibited instruction leading to a degree, or the setting up of another university, but not all were satisfied with this explanation.[1]

The purpose of the academies, therefore, was to give higher education equivalent to that given by the universities, and to bridge over the difficulty of training ministers. The name, of course, goes back to Plato, but probably was adopted in imitation of Calvin's academy, founded in 1559 at Geneva, which was really a university, but had not, as the other universities of Europe, been founded under the ægis of the Church, and regularised by papal authority. It was intended that the course at these academies should normally last four years, and that the qualification for entrance should be the same as at the universities, including a sound knowledge of Latin and Greek. These institutions met a real need. At the time of the Restoration the reaction against Puritanism had led to such an outbreak of debauchery and bad manners at the universities that many respectable people refused to send their sons there.[2] Some sent them to the Huguenot academies in France, just as Admiral Penn sent William to Saumur, while other, even Anglicans, patronised the pick of the Dissenting academies in England. Not very many, however, did so, for these academies were small, seldom numbering more than thirty students at the most. In times of persecution money sometimes failed, and the impecunious s·ident had to go home again, or the imprisonment or prosecution of the teachers might close the academy for a time.[1]

Theophilus Gale, Fellow and Tutor of Magdalen College, Oxford, was ejected from Winchester cathedral, and became tutor to the sons of Philip Lord Wharton, who would not allow them to go to an English university, but sent them under Gale's charge to Caen in 1662. Returning to England in 1665, Gale became an assistant pastor of John Rowe's congregation, which had originally met in Westminister Abbey, and after Rowe's death succeeded him in the charge. Theophilus Gale was a voluminous writer, and was the author of " The Court of the Gentiles," written in support of the view, widely popular at the

[1] A. Gordon, " Addresses Biographical and Historical," p. 69; Palmer, III. 178.
[2] Wood, " Life and Times," I. 355-370.

time, that all higher wisdom and speculation were derived originally from the Hebrew Scriptures, and that this connection was confirmatory both of the truth of Scripture and the results of philosophy.[1]   He carried on a theological academy at Newington Green until his death in 1678, and bequeathed his property to the Nonconformists in trust for the education of promising young men, his philosophical books to the academy, and the rest of his library to Harvard College.   Thomas Rowe, the son of John Rowe, succeeded him, but the academy was removed to Clapham, then to Little Britain, then back to Newington Green, and came to an end when Rowe died in 1705.   Among the men educated there were Daniel Neal, the Puritan historian, Josiah Hort, who became Archbishop of Tuam, and Dr. Isaac Watts.[2]

There was another academy at Newington Green, kept by Charles Morton, M.A., of Wadham College, Oxford, a Presbyterian minister who had been ejected from Blisland in Cornwall in 1662.   He opened his academy in 1667, and in 1685, having had to endure much persecution, he accepted a pastorate at Chesterton, in New England, and became Vice-President of Harvard College.   When he departed some of his students went abroad, to Geneva and other places, but those who remained were taken over by Stephen Lobb, pastor of the Independent congregation in Fetter Lane, William Wickens, of Emmanuel College, Cambridge, a great orientalist, and Francis Glasscock, pastor of a congregation which met in Drury Lane, and afterwards in Hanover Street, Long Acre.   Lobb and Wickens died in 1699, and Glasscock in 1706, when the academy came to an end, if it had not done so before.   There were, in the earlier days, about twenty-five or thirty students, and it was their custom on Tuesdays to go to Islington, where they observed a fast and heard sermons. They made themselves prominent in the election of Papillon and Dubois as sheriffs.[3]   Among the students of this academy were Daniel Defoe, Samuel Palmer, and Samuel Wesley.[4]   The last-named·was at Morton's for two years before he went to Oxford in 1683.   He left because Morton had to go into hiding, as a *capias* had been issued against him, and the academy was left in the hands of the senior students.[5]   Wesley said that there was a fine garden with a bowling-green and fishpond, and a laboratory with all kinds of mathematical and scientific apparatus. The tutors had no power, and could exercise very little discipline,

---

[1] Tulloch, " Rational Theology in England," II. 352; " The Court of the Gentiles," I. 1669; II. 1671; III. and IV. 1677.

[2] Wilson, " Dissenting Churches," III. 161–168; Palmer, I. 243; Bogue and Bennet, " Hist. Dissenters," II. 48–51; *Trans. Cong. Hist. Soc.*, III. 274.

[3] S.P.D., September 9th, 1682, 420/53.

[4] Bogue and Bennet, " Hist. Dissenters," II. 44–48; Toulmin, " Historical View," pp. 232–235; " Camb. Hist. Eng. Lit.," X. 385–387; *Trans. Cong. Hist. Soc.*, III. 277–284.

[5] Parker, " Dissenting Academies in England," p. 61.

" we having besides, for what order we had, a sort of democratic government amongst us, every one having power to propose a law, and all laws carried by the ballot as the greater number determined, and pains and pecuniary mulcts inflicted as it seemed best to our own discretion." [1] There were two houses, and the students increased to more than sixty,[2] some of them sons of wealthy parents, and altogether some hundreds were prepared here for the different professions.

Thomas Doolittle, ejected from St. Alphege, London Wall, opened a boarding-school in Moorfields, and built a meeting-house in Mugwell Street, for which he obtained a licence in 1672. Soon after the Indulgence, he opened an academy at Islington, where he was assisted by Thomas Vincent until the latter's death in 1678, and by his own son Samuel. In 1680 he had twenty-eight students, one of whom was Philip Henry's son.[3] Owing to the persecution in 1685, he had to close it for a time, and removed to Wimbledon, thence to Clapham, and thence to Battersea, in which latter place his goods were seized and sold under a distress warrant. During the time of trouble some of his pupils remained faithful, and followed him from place to place, receiving their instruction secretly. After the Revolution the academy was reopened, but it probably came to an end before his death in 1708. Among his pupils were Edmund Calamy the younger, Matthew Henry the commentator, and Thomas Emlyn the Unitarian. Emlyn's son said of Doolittle that though he was a very worthy and diligent divine, yet he was "not eminent for compass of knowledge or depth of thought." Edmund Calamy went to live with Doolittle at the age of eleven years, and was set only to " grammar learning," and when Doolittle was forced to remove to Battersea a few years later did not follow him, though he returned to him for a short time after the academy was reopened. Samuel Wesley said that they boasted at this institution that they could cram up a minister in two years.[4]

Edward Veal, M.A., Christ Church, Oxford, B.D., and Senior Fellow of Trinity College, Dublin, received Presbyterian ordination in Lancashire, and went to Ireland for a time, returning to England in 1661. As the Act of Uniformity prevented him from obtaining preferment in the Church, he became chaplain to Sir William Waller, and afterwards started an academy in Wapping. Among the pupils at his academy were Nathaniel Taylor and John Shower, and others who afterwards became Nonconformist ministers.[5] Samuel Wesley, in March 1678, when

---

[1] *Trans. Cong. Hist. Soc.*, III. 289. [2] S.P.D., 421/94.
[3] Philip Henry, " Diary," pp. 334–335.
[4] *Trans. Cong. Hist. Soc.*, III. 286 Toulmin, " Historical View," pp. 237–238; Bogue and Bennet, " Hist. Dissenters," II. 51–57; Calamy, " Hist. Account of My Own Life," I. 107–108; Wesley, " A Letter from a Country Divine," 1703.
[5] Bogue and Bennet, " Hist. Dissenters," II. 63–64.

he was sixteen years old, went to study under Veal, and said that
Veal closed the academy two years afterwards, an earlier date
than is sometimes given.[1] It is possible, however, because in
1680 Veal became pastor of an Independent congregation in
Old Gravel Lane, Wapping.

Thomas Brand of Merton College, Oxford, and the Middle
Temple, started an academy at Bishop's Hall, Bethnal Green, and
in 1690 there were nine students here. He died in 1691, but Dr.
John Kerr, who had joined him as an assistant, continued it after
his death. Samuel Palmer gave an account of it and of the
books used there. It was in existence in 1708, but how long it
continued after that is not known.[2]

Richard Frankland was a graduate of Christ's College, Cambridge, and received Presbyterian ordination, and had been
appointed to the staff of Cromwell's college at Durham. Bishop
Cosin tried to retain him in the Church, and offered to ordain
him privately and conditionally; but he declined and moved to
Rathmell, in the parish of Giggleswick, Yorkshire, and at the
suggestion of Sir Thomas Liddell of Ravensworth Castle, in the
county of Durham, he set up an academy in 1670, his first pupil
being Sir Thomas Liddell's son, George. He was excommunicated, and much troubled by legal proceedings, and in 1674
decided to move to Natland, near Kendal. While at Rathmell
he had fifteen pupils, of whom six entered the Nonconformist
ministry, and during the nine years he remained at Natland he
had seventy-seven students. The Five Mile Act was put in
force against him in 1683, so he removed to Carlton in Craven,
possibly attracted there by the fact that Mrs. Lambert, the
daughter-in-law of General Lambert, was living there. Then,
in 1684, he moved to Dawsonfield, near Crosthwaite, in Westmorland, and in the following year to Hartbarrow, or Harborough, near the south end of Lake Windermere.[3] During the
greater part of 1685 the academy seems to have been suspended,
but in 1686 it was reopened at Attercliffe, Sheffield, where it
began to flourish again, and during the next three years some fifty
students were enrolled. In 1689 Frankland removed it back to
Rathmell. From this time to his death he suffered a good deal
from prosecutions in the ecclesiastical courts for keeping an
academy and training men for the Dissenting ministry. The
total number of Frankland's pupils was 303, of whom 110 became
Nonconformist ministers, either Congregational or Presbyterian.
He died in 1698, and the academy was discontinued;[4] neverthe-

---

[1] *Trans. Cong. Hist. Soc.*, III. 289.
[2] Palmer, "Defence of the Dissenters' Education," 1703; *Trans. Cong. Hist. Soc.*, VI. 20–24.
[3] "Nonconformity in Cumberland and Westmorland," *Trans. Cong. Hist. Soc.*, III. 212–232.
[4] *Trans. Cong. Hist. Soc.*, II. 422–449; III. 20; Toulmin, "Historical View," pp. 235–237; "Camb. Hist. Eng. Lit.," X. 385.

less, it is claimed that Manchester College, Oxford, founded at Manchester in 1786, " clearly traces its ancestry to the earliest Nonconformist academy opened by Richard Frankland." [1] After Frankland's death, his remaining students completed their course under Mr. Chorlton, who had taken a large house and established an academy at Manchester,[2] and this forms the link between the two.

Timothy Jolly, the son of Thomas Jolly,[3] began in 1691 to rent Attercliffe Hall, and called it Christ's College. He was an old pupil of Frankland, and is sometimes represented as succeeding Frankland at Attercliffe. This is not quite true, for Frankland removed his academy to Rathmell before Jolly started Christ's College,[4] though it is possible that some of the Rathmell students may have migrated to Jolly's institution after Frankland died. Among the men educated at Attercliffe was Archbishop Secker. Jolly died in 1714, and was succeeded by Wadsworth, who died thirty years later, but the academy came to an end long before the latter's death.[5]

Henry Hickman, B.D., an ejected Fellow of Madgalen College, Oxford, opened an academy at Stourbridge, near Bromsgrove, in Worcestershire. Hickman was in Holland in 1664, and returned to Leyden in 1675, so the academy can only have been open between those dates. Four Yorkshire Dissenters, Joshua Kirby of Wakefield, Oliver Heywood, Christopher Richardson, and Mr. Cotton, each sent a son to be trained for the ministry there. They remained there only a short time, for in June 1674 they were sent to Richard Frankland at Natland, so possibly it was in this year that Hickman ceased teaching, according to some accounts through increasing age. Hickman was a learned man, and a celebrated preacher. He wrote the " Apologia pro Ministris " in 1664, a work intended for circulation amongst the continental Protestants. He also wrote the " Historia Quinquarticularis Exarticulata " (1673), in reply to Peter Heylin's " Quinquarticularis " (1660).[6]

Ralph Button, Fellow of Merton College, Oxford, University Orator, and canon of Christ Church, left the University at the Restoration, and started a school for the sons of gentlemen in the neighbourhood of Brentford, his pupils boarding with his next-door neighbour, Thomas Pakenham, who had been ejected from Harrow. For keeping an unlicensed school Button was sent to

[1] " Essex Hall Year Book."
[2] Parker, " Dissenting Academies in England," pp. 68–69.
[3] Palmer, II. 348.
[4] Halley, " Lancs. Puritanism," p. 420.
[5] Bogue and Bennet, " Hist. Dissenters," II. 20–21; " Camb. Hist. Eng. Lit.," X. 385–387.
[6] " Early Nonconformist Academies," *Trans. Cong. Hist. Soc.*, IV. 41–48; Hunter, " Life of Oliver Heywood," p. 253; Nightingale, " Lancs. Nonconformity," VI. 89; Wood, " Athenæ," pp. 893–896.

gaol for six months.   After the Indulgence he opened an academy at Islington, and trained a number of men for the Nonconformist ministry and other walks of life.   Sir Joseph Jekyll, afterwards Master of the Rolls, was one of his pupils.   Button died in 1680, and his scholars were transferred to Morton's academy.[1]

John Woodhouse had been chaplain to Lady Grantham in Nottinghamshire, and after the Restoration had not conformed, but he ought not to be counted as one of the ejected.   He settled down at Sheriff Hales, near Newport, in Shropshire, as a Presbyterian preacher, and opened an academy, and, being a wealthy man, educated some of his students at his own expense.   He trained many men for the Nonconformist ministry, and some distinguished laymen as well;   among them Robert Harley, afterwards Earl of Oxford, Edward Harley, his brother, and Henry St. John, Viscount Bolingbroke.   In 1696 he went to London, and succeeded Annesley as pastor of the congregation in Little St. Helen's, and his academy, which had a considerable reputation while it lasted, came to an end.[2]   At one time there were forty students, and two assistant lecturers, named Southwell and Beresford.[3]

Matthew Warren was born in 1642, kept a few terms at Oxford, and when he was barely twenty years old began to minister in the chapel at Downhead, near Shepton Mallet, in Somerset, but he was ejected soon afterwards.   He founded an academy at Taunton for Nonconformist ministers as early as 1672, and perhaps earlier, and, according to Samuel Wesley, had numerous pupils.   He suffered a good deal of persecution, and frequently had to go into hiding.   In 1687 the Dissenting meeting-house in Taunton, which had been wrecked after Monmouth's rebellion was put down, was repaired and Warren was made pastor.   He died in 1706, and after his death the academy was carried on jointly by Stephen James, who died in 1725, Robert Darch and Henry Grove, the last two dying in 1738.   These three appear to have been local ministers.   Thomas Amory then became Principal.   He went to London in 1759, but the academy had come to an end before that.[4]

John Shuttlewood, B.A., Christ's College, Cambridge, was ejected from Raunston, in Leicestershire, and suffered a good deal of persecution by fines and imprisonment.   He opened an academy at Sulby, in Northamptonshire, about the year 1678,

[1] Bogue and Bennet, " Hist. Dissenters," II. 62–63;   Trans. Cong. Hist. Soc., III. 285 ; S.P.D. 421/94.

[2] Bogue and Bennet, " Hist. Dissenters," II. 59–60; Wilson, " Dissenting Churches," I. 371–373; Toulmin, " Hist. View," pp. 225–230;   Trans. Cong. Hist. Soc., III. 387–398.

[3] Parker, " Dissenting Academies in England," pp. 68–69.

[4] " Camb. Hist. Eng. Lit.," X. 384–385;   Trans. Cong. Hist. Soc., IV. 233–253; Toulmin, " Hist. View," pp. 230–232;   Trans. Bapt. Hist. Soc., IV. 220–227, which latter gives the date of foundation as 1687.

and it is recorded that " six entered in one year." Among his pupils were Dr. Joshua Oldfield, Thomas Emlyn the Unitarian, and John Sheffield. Shuttlewood died in 1688 or 1689, and there is no record of his work being continued.[1]

Samuel Cradock, B.D., Fellow of Emmanuel College, Cambridge, ejected from North Cadbury, Somerset, was a wealthy man who had inherited a considerable estate at Wickhambrook, in the south-west corner of Suffolk. He retired to it about 1670, and established an academy there, and taught not only theology to intending ministers, but the arts and sciences as well. He wrote a number of works: " Knowledge and Practice," a system of Divinity in a folio volume (before his ejection), " The Harmony of the Evangelists," 1672; " The Old Testament History Methodised," 1678; " The Apostolical History," 1683; and " An Exposition of the Apocalypse," 1692. From 1696 to 1706 he preached at Bishop's Stortford, apparently closing his work at the academy. Edmund Calamy the younger was at Wickhambrook for two years. There he learnt logic, natural and moral philosophy, and metaphysics. Cradock " read upon systems that were of his own extracting out of a variety of writers, and all the young gentlemen with him were obliged to copy them out for their own use, which they used to think a great drudgery. But I have sometimes thought that the benefit which this had attending it was beyond the inconvenience and damage."[2] Amongst Cradock's pupils were Sir Francis Bickley of Attleborough, Norfolk, Charles, Lord FitzWilliam of Moulsham Hall, Essex, George Mayo, son of Israel Mayo of Bayford, Hertfordshire, Roger Rant, Esq., of Swaffham, Cambridgeshire, Timothy Goodwin, afterwards Archbishop of Cashel, Joseph Kentish, son of Thomas Kentish, and Robert Billio, Matthew Henry's successor at Hackney.[3] It was said that half the students were the sons of the neighbouring landed gentry.[4] Cradock lived on his estate, kept a good house, was on very friendly terms with the gentry round about, and with the vicar of the parish, and preached in his house every Sunday to his household and neighbours.[5] When Calamy left him he spent some time at Doolittle's academy, who was then living in St. John's Court, near Clerkenwell, and in 1688 he went to study at Utrecht.[6]

Francis Tallents, Fellow and afterwards Vice-President of Magdalene College, Cambridge, after his ejection settled down at Shrewsbury, where he gave instruction to students for the ministry. James Owen, who had been a pupil of Samuel Jones

---

[1] Palmer, II. 398; Toulmin, " Hist. View," pp. 238–239; " Camb. Hist. Eng. Lit.," X. 385–387; *Trans. Cong. Hist. Soc.*, IV. 243.
[2] " Hist. Account of My Own Life," I. 133–136.
[3] Urwick, " Nonconformity in Herts.," pp. 703–704.
[4] Bogue and Bennet, " Hist. Dissenters," II. 61–62.
[5] Calamy, " Hist. Account of My Own Life," I. 135.
[6] *Trans. Cong. Hist. Soc.*, IV. 241; Toulmin, " Hist. View," pp. 239–241.

at Brynllywarch, in Glamorganshire, after acting as pastor for many years in and near Oswestry, moved to Shrewsbury and opened a seminary there in 1699. It is not certain whether there was any connection between Tallents' small group of pupils and Owen's seminary, but as Tallents did not die until 1708, there may have been. Owen was a widely read scholar, and seems to have had a greater number of pupils. He died in 1706, and his work was carried on for a few years by Samuel Benton and John Reynolds.[1]

John Bryan, D.D., in 1663 started an academy at Coventry for candidates for the ministry, but he died in 1675, and Obadiah Grew, who had assisted him, continued it till his own death in 1689. Thomas Shewell, who was ejected from Lenham in Kent,[2] had a school at Leeds, in the same county, but in 1689 he went to Coventry and had an academy there which may have been a direct continuation of the work of Bryan and Grew. He died in 1693.[3] He seems to have worked with Dr. Joshua Oldfield, the friend of Locke. Oldfield and William Tong transferred the academy to Hoxton Square in London in 1702.[4] The whole history of this academy is much confused, but it certainly became extinct after Oldfield's death in 1729.[5]

Thomas Cole, Principal of St. Mary's Hall, Oxford, was ejected at the Restoration, and retired to Nettlebed, four miles from Henley, and there kept an academy, " in which he instructed young men in liberal sciences and theology." [6] One of his pupils, James Bonnell, said that they were taught classics and oratory there, and that Cole preached to them twice every Sunday. He complained that they had no opportunity of receiving the sacrament there, that from his fellow-students he could learn nothing but debauchery, and that Cole, though not personally to be accused of any evil-doing, was remiss in looking after their morals and religion. Bonnell was there during the years 1667 to 1670, but was only seventeen when he left.[7] Samuel Wesley, the father of John Wesley, is said to have been another of his students, but he was only twelve years old when Cole's academy came to an end. In 1672 Cole applied for a licence to use Henley Town Hall for preaching, but it was not granted. Probably the withdrawal of the Indulgence made it more difficult for him at Nettlebed, so in 1674 he closed the academy, and went to London, where he became pastor of the Independent congregation which

---

[1] Bogue and Bennet, " Hist. Dissenters," II. 24–27; " Camb. Hist. Eng. Lit.," X. 385–387; *Trans. Bapt. Hist. Soc.*, IV. 220–227; *Trans. Cong. Hist. Soc.*, IV. 233–253; Parker, " Dissenting Academies in England," pp. 73–74.
[2] Palmer, II. 329.
[3] *Trans. Cong. Hist. Soc.*, IV. 41–43.
[4] " Camb. Hist. Eng. Lit.," X. 385–387.
[5] Bogue and Bennet, " Hist. Dissenters," II. 41–44.
[6] *Idem, ibid.*, II. 58.
[7] " Life of James Bonel, Esq.," 1707, p. 9.

at that time met at Cutlers' Hall, and continued with them till 1697, when he died.[1]

Dr. Henry Langley, who was ejected from the Mastership of Pembroke College, Oxford, retired to Tubney, a hamlet in Berkshire, four miles west of Abingdon, and there took pupils between the years 1668 and 1679.[2] Anthony à Wood said, " Dr. Langley, after he was turned out, took sojourners' (fanatics' sons) into his house at Tubney, taught them logic and philosophy and admitted them to degrees. Thomas Cole did the like at Nettlebed." [3] But there seems no other evidence for the degrees.

Samuel Jones, Fellow and Tutor of Jesus College, Oxford, had Presbyterian ordination, and was vicar of Llangynwyd, in Glamorganshire, from which he was ejected in 1662. He took up his abode on some property of his wife at Brynllywarch, Glamorganshire, which was two miles from the parish church of Llangynwyd, and in 1672 his house was licensed as a Presbyterian meeting-place. He himself was licensed as an Independent teacher for a house at Margam, and as a Presbyterian for a house at Cowbridge. He educated a number of the sons of the nobility and gentry in the neighbourhood, among them Lord Mansel, and also a number of the candidates for the Nonconformist ministry. He died in 1697, and after his death Roger Griffiths had for three or four years an academy at Abergavenny, which may or may not have been a continuation of Jones' or Griffiths' work, but between 1702 and 1704 his venture came to an end, and then the academy was united with a grammar school at Caermarthen, kept by William Evans, who died in 1718. The Brynllywarch academy is " commonly regarded as at least the germ of the Caermarthen Presbyterian College: to which, however, it bears much the same relation as Frankland's academy does to the Yorkshire United College of modern times." [4] One of Jones's pupils was James Owen, who became tutor of the Shrewsbury academy. Somewhere about 1675 there was an academy, apparently short-lived, at Knell, in Radnorshire, of which the tutor was John Weaver,[5] while another Samuel Jones, afterwards tutor at Tewkesbury, was one of the students.

Samuel Wesley, the son of the ejected minister of the same name, and the father of John Wesley, joined the Church of England and published an account of his experiences in the Nonconformist seminaries in which he had been educated. An exhibition of £30 was raised for him in a Dissenting congregation, and he was sent to Veal at Stepney. He remained with him two

[1] Wilson, " Dissenting Churches," III. 79–80; *Trans. Cong. Hist. Soc.*, IV. 233; " Camb. Hist. Eng. Lit.," X. 384.
[2] *Trans. Cong. Hist. Soc.*, IV. 47.
[3] Wood, " Life and Times," II. 1.
[4] *Trans. Cong. Hist. Soc.*, IV. 245–247; VI. 136; " Camb. Hist. Eng. Lit.," X. 386–387.
[5] Palmer, III. 509.

years, and read logic and ethics, but being prosecuted by the justices, Veal broke up his establishment. A further £10 was raised for Wesley, and Dr. Owen advised him " to go to one of the public universities, because they expected times would alter, and that our terms at the private ones would be allowed : so we were directed to enter at a college or hall, as if with intention to tarry, which we might do for some time without matriculation and oaths." If they took the oaths they forfeited the exhibitions (as Wesley did ultimately). However, he went next to Morton, at Newington Green. Morton himself was a quiet man, who would not allow disloyal talk in his presence. But it was very different with the students, who were factious, had a mortal aversion to episcopacy, were mostly against monarchy, defended king-killing, ridiculed the established clergy, and made the Prayer Book the subject of bad jests and sarcasms. One of the students went to the top of a neighbourhing hill and shouted scandalous stories about the vicar of Newington through a speaking trumpet. Milton's " Eikonoclastes " was read there, " though not with the tutor's recommendation," and some of the lads, " without the tutor's knowledge," had some lewd works in their possession.[1] Samuel Palmer replied to Wesley in a small fourteen-page pamphlet, which began with an account of the life and teaching at his own old school, but soon trailed off into the old wrangle of Church and Dissent.[2] Wesley replied, and gave further grounds for his accusation. Palmer next published his " Vindication of Dissenting Academies," and Wesley answered it in a closely printed quarto pamphlet of 160 pages, in which he went over the same ground, and retailed a good deal of gossip.[3] Defoe, writing to Harley on May 21st, 1714, said, with reference to the Dissenters: " As to their academies, if there had never been any, I know not but their interest had been as good, and fewer beggars and drones had bred up for ministers among them." [4]

Toulmin gives an account of the curriculum at John Wood-house's institution at Sheriff Hales. The subjects were Latin Greek, Hebrew, mathematics, history, geography, natural science, logic, rhetoric, ethics, metaphysics, anatomy, law, and divinity. The students were exercised in scholastic disputations in the old syllogistic form. They practised English composition by writing letters and composing speeches. The theological students were set to make analyses of some verses of a psalm or chapter, to draw up skeletons of sermons and

---

[1] S. Wesley, " A Letter from a Country Divine . . . concerning the Education of the Dissenters in their private Academies," 1703.

[2] S. Palmer, " A Defence of the Dissenters' Education in their Private Academies," 1703.

[3] Bogue and Bennet, " Hist. Dissenters," II. 90–91.

[4] Hist. MSS. Com. Welbeck Papers, V. 444.

schemes of prayer, and were called on to pray in the family worship on Sunday evenings, and to set psalms to two or three tunes. Each day an account of the preceding day's lecture had to be given, and Saturdays were devoted to revision of the week's work. Most of the authors studied were read twice. Lay students did practical work, such as land surveying, dissections, and constructing dials.

James Owen used the following as text-books on which to enlarge in his lectures:

Logic: Burgersdicius, Hereboord, Ramus.
Metaphysics: Fromenius, Eustachius, Baronius.
Physics: Le Clerc, Du Hamel.
Geometry: Pardie's " Elements," Euclid.
Astronomy: Gassendius.
Chronology: Strauchius.
Ecclesiastical History: Spanhemius.
Theology: Wollebius, Ryssenius's " Abstract of Turren-
tine."[1]

Palmer said that at Morton's academy they began the morning with logic, for which they read Hereboord as used at Cambridge. " But our tutor always gave us *memoriter* the Harmony or opposites made to him by other logicians: and of these the most diligent took notes, and all were advised to read Smiglecius, Colbert, Ars Cogitandi, and Le Clerc, or whatever books of that nature we occasionally met with. Being initiated in philosophical studies by this art, we made another step of reading Goveani Elenctica, which being done, the next superior class read metaphysics, of which Fromenius's Synopsis was our manual, and by directions of our tutor, we were assisted in our chambers by Baronius, Suarez and Colbert. Ethics was our next study, and our system Hereboord: in reading which our tutor recommended to our meditation Dr. Henry More, Marcus Antonius, Epictetus, with the comments of Arrian and Simplicius, and the morals of Solomon; and under this head, the moral works of the great Puffendorf. The highest class was engaged in natural philosophy, of which Le Clerc was our system, whom we compared with the ancients and other moderns, as Aristotle, Des Cartes, Colbert, Staire, etc. We disputed every other day in Latin upon the several philosophical controversies, and as these lectures were read off, some time was set apart to introduce rhetoric, in which that short piece of John Gerrard Vossius was used in the school, but in our chambers we were assisted by his larger volume, Aristotle, and Tully de Oratore. These exercises were all performed every morning, except that on Mondays we added as a

[1] Bogue and Bennet, " Hist. Dissenters," II. 80.

divine lecture some of Buchanan's Psalms, the finest of the kind, both for purity of language and exact sense of the original: and on Saturdays, all the superior classes declaimed by turns, four and four, on some noble and useful subject, such as De Pace, Logicane magis inserviat caeteris disciplinis an Rhetorica, De connubio virtutis cum doctrina, etc., and I can say that these orations were, for the most part, of uncommon elegance, purity of style, and manly and judicious composure. After dinner our work began in order by reading some one of the Greek or Latin historians, orators or poets, of which first I remember Sallust, Quintus Curtius, Justin, and Paterculus; of the second, Demosthenes, Tully, and Isocrates's select Orations; and of the last, Homer, Virgil, Juvenal, Persius, and Horace. This reading was the finest and most delightful to young gentlemen of all others, because it was not in the pedantic method of common schools; but the delicacy of our tutor's criticisms, his exact descriptions of persons, terms, and places illustrated by referring to Rosin and other antiquarians, and his just application of the morals, made such a lasting impression as made other studies more facile. In geography we read Dionysius Periegesis compared with Cluverius, *ed.* Bunonis, which at this lecture always lay upon the table. . . .

"Mondays and Fridays we read divinity, of which the first lecture was always in the Greek Testament, and it was our custom to go through it once a year; we seldom read less than six or seven chapters, and this was done with the greatest accuracy. We were obliged to give the most curious etymons, and were assisted with the Synopsis Criticorum, Martinius, Faverinus, and Hesychius's Lexicons, and it was expected that the sacred geography and chronology should be particularly observed, and answered too, at demand, of which I never knew my tutor sparing. The other divinity lecture was on Synopsis Purioris Theologiæ, as very accurate and short: we were advised to read by ourselves the more large pieces of Turretine, Theses Salmuriensis, Baxter's Methodus Theologiæ, and Archbishop Usher's, and on particular controversies many excellent authors, as on original sin, Placaeus, and Barlow de Natura Mali; on grace and free-will, Rutherford, Strangius, and Amyraldus; on the popish controversy, Amesius, Bellarminus Enervatus, and the modern disputes during the reign of King James; on episcopacy, Altare Damascenum, Bishop Hall, and Mr. Baxter; Bishop Stillingfleet's Irenicum, Dr. Owen, and Rutherford; and for practical divinity, Baxter, Tillotson, Charnock; and in a word, the best books, both of the Episcopalian, Presbyterian, and Independent divines, were in their order recommended and constantly used by those of us most able to procure them, and all, or most of them, I can affirm were the study of all the pupils."

He goes on to say that the tutor was never heard to make one unhandsome reflection on the Church of England, and that " on all controversial points he never offered to impose on the judgment of his pupils." The social conversation of the house was unexceptionable. School began in the morning with prayer in English or Latin. At theological lectures the eldest students prayed. Family prayer was never omitted. Every student had to be indoors by 9 p.m. " Obscene or profane discourse, if known, would have procured expulsion, and the smallest vanities reproof, which my tutor knew how to give with a just and austere resentment."[1]

Henry Fleming, an undergraduate at Queen's College, Oxford, in 1678 was reading practically the same books as were being read in the academies.[2] Latin was the chief medium of instruction; the students had not merely to read and write Latin, but to speak it. In addition to the classical languages, modern languages, such as French and Italian, were taught. Defoe, who was at Morton's academy at Newington Green, afterwards boasted that he was " a master " of five languages.[3] He tells us that he entered at the age of fourteen, his father sending him there at the advice of Dr. Annesley, for whom the family had a great respect and affection, which Daniel expressed in 1697 in some verses on " The Character of the Late Dr. Samuel Annesley, by way of Elegy." Defoe always retained affectionate memories of Morton, but he realised that the academies could never be really successful training-places for the ministry. Poor lads were sent there, supported by Nonconformist funds, but they had no access to large libraries, and they consorted chiefly with other lads of the same class as themselves.[4] Defoe said that " at Newington the master or tutor read all his lectures, gave all his systems, whether of philosophy or divinity, in English, and had all his declaimings and dissertations in the same tongue. And although the scholars from that place were not destitute in the languages, yet it is observed of them, they were by this made masters of the English tongue, and more of them excelled in that particular line than of any school at that time." [5]

About 150 of the ejected ministers are described by Calamy as keeping schools.[6] This may mean in some cases nothing more than taking a few private pupils. Thus David Noble, a Nonconformist minister at Morley, in Yorkshire, had the care of the early education of Oliver Heywood's two sons.[7] Henry Newcome is credited with having commenced a school at Manchester, but at most he only took a few pupils, and the school did not

---

[1] Palmer, " Defence of Dissenting Education," pp. 4–7; Bogue and Bennet, " Hist. Dissenters," II. 80–83.
[2] " The Flemings in Oxford," Oxford Hist. Soc., I. 250–255, 321.
[3] Parker, " Dissenting Academies in England," p. 60.
[4] H. Morley, " Earlier Life and Works of Daniel Defoe," p. 16.
[5] Defoe, " Present State of Parties in Great Britain," 1712.
[6] *Trans. Unit. Hist. Soc.*, II. iii. 60.
[7] Hunter, " Life of Oliver Heywood," p. 234.

begin till some years after his death.[1]   Thomas Waterhouse, who was silenced at Ash, in Suffolk, had some experience in teaching, and kept a school at Ipswich for some years.[2]   Adam Martindale kept a school at Warrington, and obtained sufficient pupils to bring him in 20s. to 25s. a week.   When the Five Mile Act came out he removed to Manchester, and there took pupils.

Samuel Shaw, a Presbyterian, ejected from Long Whatton, in Leicestershire, became master of a decayed free school at Ashby-de-la-Zouch in 1668, and had 160 boys in his charge, who came from all parts of the country.   When the Indulgence was granted, he got his school licensed, and in connection with it he afterwards built a chapel.   He wrote " Emmanuel," and some interludes for performance by his scholars at Christmas time, one of which, entitled " Poikilophronesis: or the Different Humours of Men," was performed at the school in 1691.   Shaw obtained from the Archbishop of Canterbury a licence to teach school anywhere in the province, and he got another licence from Bishop Fuller of Lincoln, in neither case making the requisite subscriptions.   He built a gallery in the parish church for the use of his scholars, so that his Nonconformity can hardly have been very definite.[3]

Edmund Calamy the younger in his early youth went to a school at Epsom kept by a Mr. Yewel.   He described him as no great scholar, a sort of Fifth Monarchy man, but harmless and inoffensive.   " This good man had a considerable number of boys under his care, but they fared so well, and the rates he had with them were so low, and he was at the same time at so great an expense to keep up a meeting on the Lord's Day in his school-house, to which ministers came down every week from London, that he got very little for his pains, and he was often in trouble. And it was observed that he proved at last but unhappy in some of his own children, who discredited their strict religious educa-tion.   My being there increased and confirmed my health, though it did not much advance me in learning." [4]   Calamy next went to Mr. Tatnall's academy in Winchester Street, near Pinners' Hall.   The master was a good scholar, who had been a pupil of Busby at Westminister and a Fellow of Trinity College, Cam-bridge.   He took pains with the boys, and turned out some good scholars.   Calamy was for a time "his uppermost scholar, and I have sometimes said by heart a satire in Juvenal for my part in a morning." [5]

Hanserd Knollys kept a school for some time in Bishopsgate Street, London.   Here he is said to have prospered so greatly that he was able to portion off his sons and a daughter hand-

---

[1] *Trans. Bapt. Hist. Soc.*, IV. 220–227.
[2] Palmer, III. 248.
[3] M'Crie, " Annals of Presbytery," p. 253; Calamy, II. 428; IV. 592–593.
[4] Calamy, " Hist. Account of My Own Life," I. 75–76.
[5] *Idem, ibid.*, p. 77; Calamy, II. 29.

somely.   One son assisted him at a salary of £60 per annum;
another, on setting up on his own account, received from him
fifty scholars and £250 in money; another had a like amount;
and his daughter on her wedding morning received £300.[1]

Richard Kennet, Fellow of Corpus Christi College, Cambridge,
ejected from East Hatley, Cambridgeshire, was enabled, by the
assistance of Stillingfleet, to take a capacious house at Sutton,
in Bedfordshire, where he set up a school, at first keeping a conformist to teach it.   Many of the gentry and Church-people sent
their sons to him, and when the schoolmaster left he taught the
school himself, a proceeding which the neighbouring gentry
connived at, having a great esteem for him.   His stepson, however, had a licence, and acted as his usher.   Apparently he did
not attempt to preach, and went to church twice every Sunday,
so that, though ejected, he can hardly be described as a Dissenter.
He died in 1670.[2]

At least three of the ejected ministers in Sussex started schools.
William Wilson of Billingshurst, Edmund Thorpe of Sedlescombe,
who had amongst his pupils Titus Oates, and Joseph Bennett of
Brightling, who was so faithful during the Plague time that no
one would put the Five Mile Act in execution against him.[3]

Joseph Hallet opened a school at Exeter, and when he died in
1689, his son, Joseph, continued it; but, as he was unorthodox,
with Arian tendencies, it dwindled away.[4]   John Moore became
pastor to a large congregation of Dissenters at Bridgewater in
1676, and kept a school which shared the same fate as the last,
because he also left it to a son who turned Arian.[5]   There was
another John Moore who had a school at Tiverton.[6]   Matthew
Toogood, ejected from Semly, in Wiltshire, had been a schoolmaster before he became a minister, and he opened a school at
Semly after his ejection.   It is related that a local justice of the
peace who had formerly harried him afterwards sent his son to be
educated by him.[7]   Ames Short is said to have kept a school at
Lyme, in Dorsetshire.[8]   His son, John, certainly had one at
Colyton, in Devonshire, until 1698, when he removed to London,
and the school was taken over by Matthew Toogood.[9]   Walton,
ejected from West Ham, had a very flourishing school first at
Bishop's Hall, and then at Bethnal Green.[10]   Edmund Calamy
spent a few months with him at the latter place, and said that he

[1] Culross, " Hanserd Knollys," p. 92 ; Trans. Hist. Bapt. Soc., IV. 220–227.
[2] Kennet, " Reg.," p. 780; Calamy, II. 118.
[3] " Victoria County Hist. Sussex," II. 39.
[4] " Camb. Hist. Eng. Lit.," X. 385; Palmer, III. 383.
[5] Palmer, II. 130; " Camb. Hist. Eng. Lit.," 386.
[6] Bogue and Bennet, " Hist. Dissenters," II. 37.
[7] Palmer, III. 374.
[8] " Camb. Hist. Eng. Lit.," X. 385.
[9] Bogue and Bennet, " Hist. Dissenters," II. 37.
[10] Palmer, II. 223.

formerly had a school, but then only a few boarders.[1]   Theophilus Brittain, ejected from Brocklesby, in Lincolnshire, took a small house at Swinderby, about seven miles from Lincoln, where he kept a small school for a livelihood.   For this he was prosecuted and imprisoned.   Later on he took a small farm at Roxham, near Sleaford, and taught a few scholars.[2]   Christopher Nesse had a house of his own at Hunslet, Leeds, and had a school there between 1666 and 1672.[3]   Edward Rayner, formerly minister of St. Peter's, Lincoln, is mentioned as an early Nonconformist schoolmaster, but most of his schoolmastering seems to have been done in early life, and he died somewhere about the time at which he is said to have been ejected.[4]   His son, John Rayner, who was ejected from a fellowship at Emmanuel College, Cambridge, took up medicine as a profession, and practised in Nottingham.   He was urged to take pupils, and did so, but died of the smallpox a very short time afterwards.[5]   John Malden kept an academy, or perhaps a school, at Alkington, in the parish of Whitechurch, in Shropshire, from 1668 to 1680.[6]   Ambrose Rigg kept a small school at Gatton, in Surrey.   Samuel Jones kept a school or academy at Gloucester, which he afterwards removed to Tewkesbury.[7]   Other Nonconformists who kept private schools were William Angel at Houndsditch,[8] Matthew Clarke at Market Harborough,[9] Joseph Porter at Alcester, in Warwickshire,[10] Charles Segar at Blackburn,[11] Edward Terrill at Bristol,[12] Robert Whittaker at Fordingbridge,[13] Julius Saunders at Bedworth, in Warwickshire,[14] and there were many others.[15]

The schools so far mentioned were private schools, opened to provide a means of livelihood to the people who kept them.   In Zoar Street, Gravel Lane, Southwark, a charity school, known as the Gravel Lane Charity School, was founded in 1687, by the joint efforts of Arthur Shallet, Samuel Warburton, and Ferdinando Holland, and was attached to the Presbyterian meeting-house of which John Chester was the minister.   It was the first of its kind set up by the Dissenters, and began with forty children. The minister of the meeting-house for the time being was to superintend the concerns of the school, and to make collections

[1] Calamy, " Hist. Account of My Own Life," I. 130.
[2] Palmer, II. 413.   [3] Palmer, II. 441.
[4] Bogue and Bennet, " Hist. Dissenters," II. 68; Palmer, II. 421.
[5] Trans. Cong. Hist. Soc., IV. 251; Palmer, I. 263.
[6] Idem, ibid., III. 149.
[7] Bogue and Bennet, " Hist. Dissenters," II. 137.
[8] Wilson, " Dissenting Churches in London," III. 337.   [9] Ibid., I. 474.
[10] Bogue and Bennet, " Hist. Dissenters," II. 37.
[11] Nightingale, " Lancs. Nonconformity," II. 249.
[12] " Broadmead Records."
[13] Wilson, " Dissenting Churches in London," IV. 411.
[14] Bogue and Bennet, " Hist. Dissenters," II. 67.
[15] For further lists and names see " Camb. Hist. Eng. Lit.," X. 387; Trans. Bapt. Hist. Soc., IV. 220–227; Bapt. Quarterly, IV. 283.

for its support.[1] A Nonconformist school, though not apparently
a charity school, was built and endowed at St. Helen's, in
Lancashire.[2]

The Quakers did a great deal for the education of their own
people. While the Friary prison at Ilchester was filled with
Quakers in 1662, they even kept a school there for the children of
the neighbourhood. In 1671 there were over fifteen boarding-
schools kept by the Friends. A school was established by Fox
at Waltham Abbey in 1668, and Christopher Taylor, who had
hitherto kept a school for Quaker children in Hertfordshire,
became the first master. He was brought before the Chelmsford
Quarter Sessions in 1670 for keeping a school without a licence.[3]
John Matern, a German Quaker from Silesia, came to England
in 1674 and was made assistant. Fox disapproved of the school-
books of the period,[4] and with the help of Ellis Hooke, he produced in 1673 " An Instruction for Right Spelling, Reading, and
Writing." Taylor enlarged this book, and translated it into
Latin, under the title of " Institutiones Pietatis," which was
published in 1676. In 1679 Taylor, Matern, and Hilarius
Prache, Matern's father-in-law, published " Compendium Trium
Linguarum," a compendious grammar of Latin, Greek, and
Hebrew, the Hebrew part being chiefly the work of Prache. The
book claimed to lay aside all heathenish methods, and to illustrate
the languages from Scripture. In 1679 the school was transferred
to Edmonton.[5]

In 1674 the Quakers decided to establish a school in one of
the rooms attached to their meeting-place in Devonshire House.
Richard Richardson was appointed master, and was to receive
a guaranteed £20 a year, and in addition what fees the children
might pay, but he was to receive for nothing any poor Quaker
child committed to his charge by the Monthly Meetings. In the
following year Thomas Rudyard and Christopher Taylor were
instructed to prepare a text-book of court hand and law Latin,
so that the pupils might be taught how to read a legal writ and
to know something of legal processes.[6] Richardson went to
America in 1682. There were other schools in London belonging
to the Friends. There was one at the " Bull and Mouth "
meeting-house, conducted for a time by John Field, and there
was a girls' school at Hackney, known as the Shacklewell
School. It is known that in 1677 the name of the mistress of the
latter was Jane Bullock, and that the school was not prospering,
but that is all.

Various estimates are extant of the number of the population
in later Stuart times, but on the whole it seems safe to conclude

[1] Wilson, " Dissenting Churches in London," IV. 188.
[2] Nightingale," Lancs. Nonconformity," IV. 131.
[3] Besse, " Sufferings," I. 204.   [4] See his " Battledoor," 1660.
[5] *Journ. Friends Hist. Soc.*, X. 149–152.
[6] M. Sefton Jones, " Old Devonshire House," 1923, p. 144.

with Lecky that during the reign of Charles II. the population numbered between 5,000,000 and 5,250,000. In 1669 Archbishop Sheldon asked his suffragans in the province of Canterbury to send in a return of the number of conventicles in their respective dioceses and the number of persons attending them. Some of these returns are still to be found in the Lambeth Palace Library, but they are very incomplete. Twelve hundred and thirty-four conventicles were reported, and the total number of persons attending them works out at 70,875. For a great number. of conventicles, however, the number of persons is not given, and the reports from some dioceses do not exist. Working on a basis of an average of ninety persons to a conventicle, a somewhat generous allowance, Professor Lyon Turner came to the final conclusion that the number of Dissenters in 1669 was 120,000 or 123,000.[1] At the most the result can only be a rough estimate; many of the reports themselves only give round numbers, and accuracy in statistics was not a marked feature of the seventeenth century. But Professor Turner thought the number an understatement, if anything, and seeing that under persecution the Nonconformists concealed themselves as much as possible, the episcopal returns really represented the irreducible minimum.[2]

Under Charles II.'s Declaration of Indulgence in 1672, though the most careful attempts to make an accurate reckoning, either of the number of preachers licensed or the number of meeting places, have produced very diverse results, we may with a fair amount of safety assume that between 1500 and 1600 persons applied for preachers' licences. If we take the average congregation of each teacher as seventy persons—a high estimate when we remember how many small private houses were licensed —the number of Nonconformists in 1672 ranged from 105,000 to 112,000. Taking an average of fifty persons to each teacher, we should get from 75,000 to 80,000. In either case the Quakers are not included. They did not apply for licences, nor did the minor sects, unless they applied under the name of Presbyterians or Independents. In 1676, at the instigation of the Archbishop of Canterbury, another religious census was taken.[3] The result showed the number of Dissenters in the country as 108,476, but some of the returns were far from complete, and some addition should be made for the places omitted. It might be safe to say that there were 120,000 Dissenters. Sherlock in after years said that the returns showed that the Dissenters were only a twentieth of the population.[4]

It was believed that the Quakers were about half the Nonconformists, that is, in number equal to the Presbyterians,

[1] Turner, " Original Records," III. 116.   [2] Idem, ibid., III. 28.
[3] The returns are in the Salt Library, Stafford.
[4] " Test Act Vindicated," 1718, Salt Archæological Society, 1915; Turner " Original Records," III. 59; Whitley, " British Baptists," p. 127.

Independents, Baptists, and Roman Catholics together.[1] It is stated that between 1689 and 1700, by virtue of the Toleration Act, 2418 Dissenting places of worship were licensed in England.[2] It was calculated that in 1715 there were 1107 Dissenting congregations in England and Wales, of whom 247 were Baptist, the rest Presbyterian or Independent; the Presbyterians being as numerous as the Independents and Baptists together.[3] This computation does not include the Quakers.   How great an omission this was is shown by a single example.   At the Quaker Sessions at Thirsk, on October 8th, 1689, licences were granted for eighty Quaker meeting-places in the North Riding alone.[4] At a rough estimate there were between 30,000 and 40,000 Quakers in England at the time of the Restoration.[5] According to the episcopal returns of 1669 there would be about 25,000, but this is certainly an under-statement.   The totals of births, marriages, and deaths recorded in the Monthly Meeting Books between 1670 and 1689 are 18,964, 5418, and 21,387 respectively.   The marriage rate was perhaps higher than the present yearly rate of fifteen persons per thousand, and so the number of marriages given above may imply over 37,000 Quakers.   Even then allowance must be made for persons whose marriages may not have been recorded, or who were married before entering the Society of Friends.   It may be safe, therefore, to presume that the number of the Quakers was between 40,000 and 50,000.[6] Charles Leslie's statement, made in 1696, that there were 100,000 Quakers in England,[7] was undoubtedly a wild exaggeration, intended to alarm Church-people.   To say that there were 60,000 at that date would be a very generous conclusion indeed.

[1] Turner, " The Quakers," p. 245.
[2] " The Baptists of Yorkshire," Centenary Memorial Volume, Bradford, 1912.
[3] Bogue and Bennet, " Hist. Dissenters," II. 98–99.
[4] " Quarter Sessions Records," North Riding Record Society, VII. 102–103.
[5] Braithwaite, " Beginnings of Quakerism," p. 512.
[6] *Idem*, " Second Period," pp. 458–459.
[7] Charles Leslie, " The Snake in the Grass," 1696, p. 245.

XI

TOLERATION had been tried by the Kings of France, but the
Huguenot places of worship had been attended by armed
fanatics, and there had followed iconoclasm, outrage, and civil
war, St. Bartholomew, and more civil war. Henry IV. had
put an end to much of the trouble by the Edict of Nantes, but
Louis XIV. had undone his work. In Geneva Servetus had
been burnt by Calvin. In 1526 the Council of Zurich decreed
that any Anabaptist who should thereafter baptize another
should be drowned without mercy.[1] Presbyterianism in Scotland rivalled the Papacy at its highest exaltation in its domination over the civil power and its interference with the private
lives of individuals.[2] In England Presbyterianism overthrew
the Church, and was itself overthrown by the Independents.
Samuel Fisher, the Quaker, complained of the way in which
Dr. John Owen had stirred up the Rump Parliament " to more
persecution than they were free for." [3] Massachusetts decreed
the cutting off of ears and the boring of tongues with red-hot irons
as a suitable punishment for Quakers, and when this failed,
banishment on pain of death was ordered for them. " Bonds and
imprisonment awaited all Baptists in New England." [4] Before
the Restoration religious toleration was only to be found in
Maryland, where neither Romanist nor Puritan could persecute
or be persecuted. In July 1663, however, Charles II. signed
the charter of the colony of Rhode Island, where religious
liberty was recognised for all. This charter had been drawn
up on lines indicated by Roger Williams, who had been turned
out of intolerant Massachusetts.

In England the laity were more bitter in their intolerance
than the clergy. The laymen of Parliament passed by large
majorities the statutes of the Clarendon Code. It was the
House of Commons which protested against the King's action
in delivering Edmund Calamy from gaol, where he had been
sent for, as it seemed to them, impudently entering a pulpit

[1] Kidd, " Documents of the Continental Reformation," 1911, p. 455.
[2] Figgis, " Divine Right of Kings," 1914, pp. 197–198.
[3] S. Fisher, " Rusticus ad Academicos," 1660.
[4] Cramp, " Baptist Hist.," p. 409.

THE ENEMIES OF THE CHURCH.
From Timothy Puller's "Moderation of the Church of England."

Facing p. 474.

where he had no right to be, and seizing the opportunity to preach a seditious sermon.

The Presbyterian divines in Scotland tried to dominate the State. The Anglican divines in England, after the Restoration, showed too much dependence on, and subservience to, the State. Preaching in season and out of season the doctrine of the divine right of kings, the English clergy tended to give the King, as representing the State, an absolute supremacy over the Church. Church and King stood or fell together. Sober laymen, and not only eccentrics like Arise Evans who believed that Charles II.'s return was prophesied by Merlin, were constantly saying that ever since the days of Queen Elizabeth there had always been a party which had opposed the sovereigns, had tried to abolish the Christian festivals, had preached down and destroyed the Church, and finally had killed the King.[1] Nevertheless, in spite of the exuberance of royalist eulogies, the Anglicans did not really mean that the State or the King could arbitrarily prescribe forms of faith or worship. Their insistence on passive obedience showed the reaction in their minds from theories of clerical domination over the Government; but their theory of passive obedience had its limitations. There might at any time arise a persecuting heretical sovereign, whom they must disobey if he tried to make them alter their religion; but in such a case they were quite clear as to their course of action: they would embrace martyrdom, but they would never enter upon armed rebellion.

The nation by its rulers and representatives and clergy had accepted a certain definite system of religion, which in practice met with the favour of the great majority of Englishmen. How could there be any unity if unlearned and self-willed men divided the nation on the all-important question of religion? " The meanest of you," said Simon Patrick, " takes upon himself to be wiser than the best of us, than any of our bishops and priests, nay, the whole clergy put together. And if we will not have such a man in the same esteem that he hath himself, presently we are looked upon as enemies of the power of godliness, formal fellows, or mere moralists." [2] The argument for the necessity of national unity was strengthened as time went on by the discovery that the Papists looked to France and its despot for help, while the irreconcilable Nonconformists found refuge with the Dutch. The majority of Churchmen still maintained the theory that the only sound basis of government was religion. They drew parallels from the union of religion and monarchy in the kingdoms of Israel and Judah, and they clung to the mediæval parallel between Church and State and soul and body; separation in each case resulting in death. Unity was prevented, so

---

[1] Arise Evans, " An Epistle," 1660.
[2] " Continuation of the Friendly Debate," 1669.

it seemed to the Churchman, by the wilful obstinacy of the
Dissenter. Sir Leoline Jenkins, addressing the clergy of the
diocese of Canterbury, said, " There is a sort of men, whose
tenderness of conscience (as they say) will not allow them to
own our ecclesiastical constitutions, because they find them
not in Holy Scripture, but I fear the true and only cause is
because they are not of their own making." He looked upon
Dissenters as "ungovernable and ambitious men whom no
concessions would satisfy." [1] Yet men, Christian men at any
rate, could not be satisfied with all this disunion and bitterness.
At first the talk was all of comprehension; but how could so
many and varying sects be comprehended in one church?
Tenison, writing about reunion in 1683, said the Church might
be able to unite with the Presbyterians, and possibly some of the
Independents, but as for " Arians, Socinians, Anabaptists, Fifth
Monarchy men, sensual Millennarians, Behmenists, Familists,
Seekers, Antinomians, Sabbatarians, Quakers, Muggletonians—
they may associate in a caravan, but cannot join in the communion of a church." [2] Some of the Presbyterians continued
to desire comprehension, but the numbers of such decreased,
and the only alternative was toleration, and the movement in
that direction swelled greatly as time went on. The Quaker
preached it, and Charles and James were in favour of it; Charles
from his innate kindliness and general scepticism, and perhaps
from what he had seen and learnt in France, and James from
the desire to benefit the men of his own religion. If James had
had the sense to content himself with freeing Roman Catholics
from the persecuting laws, and had not tried to improve their
civil status by thrusting some of them into positions to which
they had no legal right, the subsequent religious history of
England and Ireland might have been very different.

Various factors were combining to produce a new spirit. As
the memory of the Commonwealth faded, and a new generation
arose which knew not Oliver, feeling became less harsh, and it
could not be forgotten, at any rate by the Dissenters, that the
sects at least had enjoyed religious freedom in his time. Moreover, what was done during the year of Charles II.'s Indulgence
was never quite undone. As the fear of Rome revived between
1678 and 1688, many Churchmen began to look to Dissenters
as allies and friends in the cause of Protestantism. The Independents and Baptists urged that religious liberty for all Protestants was a guarantee for civil liberty. The Quakers, with their
doctrine of the " inner light," looked upon religion as a purely
personal matter between the soul and God, and therefore out
of the jurisdiction of the State or any secular authority, and so
some of them were found arguing in favour of toleration even

[1] W. Wynne, " Life of Sir Leoline Jenkins," 1724, I. lxxiii.
[2] Tenison, " A Discourse concerning a Guide in Matters of Faith," 1683.

for Romanists. There had always been a number of Anglican divines who were opposed to violent methods, and the growth of the Latitudinarian school, concerned with moral life rather than doctrinal distinctions, and influenced by the Cartesian doctrines of the authority of reason and the necessity of a rational basis for religion, helped to spread the milder tendency. Joseph Glanville's " Vanity of Dogmatising," revised and reprinted in 1665 under the title " Scepsis Scientifica," illustrated the doubts and uncertainties of this school, and though in his " Zealous and Impartial Protestant," published in 1681, he attacked toleration as destructive to government, yet he himself, with Fowler, Tillotson, Burnet, and the other leaders of the school, had a great influence in producing a more gentle and tolerant spirit. Theories of natural religion and the Law of Nature caused men like Milton to consider whether religious freedom might not be one of the natural rights of mankind. Milton thought that the only solution of the religious problem lay in the complete separation of the functions of Church and State.[1] Unorthodox himself, and constantly becoming more so, he advocated toleration for all forms of Protestantism, though not for Catholicism.[2] The growth of the scientific spirit, exhibited in the foundation of the Royal Society, tended in the direction of tolerance, if not actual indifference to religious questions. Shaftesbury, Buckingham, Halifax, and Temple, deistic and indifferent in religion, showed the new spirit in high places among the politicians. They were Hobbists, to this extent at any rate, that they held that religion, any religion, is only recognised by the State so far as it tends to peace, order, and obedience, while scepticism and indifference to the relative values of rival religions tended, if nothing else, to tone down harshness.

A new conception of Government arose: that Government exists for the security of liberty and property, for the extension of trade, for the material well-being of the people, and has nothing to do with religion. This fell in with the attitude of mind of many Dissenters, who held that certain forms of worship and ceremonies might be lawful, but became unlawful if ordered by the State. The traders' side of the question began to loom large; in England trade was declining; in Holland, where there was a large measure of toleration, trade was prosperous. The inference appeared obvious. The foreign Protestants fleeing from intolerance found a welcome and favour in England, because they brought new industries with them, and were also a standing lesson on the evils of intolerance. Persecution crippled business, undermined the rights of property, and especially injured the middle class trader.

[1] J. Milton, " Civil Power in Ecclesiastical Causes," 1659.
[2] *Idem*, " True Religion, Heresy, Schism, Toleration, and the Growth of Popery," 1673.

The sects which in time past had taken the sword felt themselves now perishing by the sword, and pleaded earnestly for the right to worship in their own way.   On the other hand, the attempt to restrain by force turned out a failure: in the hottest times of persecution Dissent was in part driven underground, but in times of reaction it appeared as strong as ever.   It became commonly argued that compulsory uniformity only covered a hidden discontent, and led to hypocrisy, and often to war.   The Whigs, fighting, as they claimed, for political liberty, found in their ranks the Dissenters fighting for religious liberty, as they claimed; but only a partial religious liberty, in which the Roman Catholic was to have no share.   But how could it be given to one and not the other?   No formula or principle could be found except that Papists were dangerous and Dissenters were not.   Hence the one-sided and partial nature of the toleration provided by the Revolution of 1689.   The State washed its hands of religious affairs, unless any particular form of religion should be thought dangerous to the Government. The idea of comprehension or reunion disappeared.   The Dissenters, who in the mass had refused toleration from the King, accepted it from Parliament.   They did not at once obtain the same civil status as the Churchmen, for the Corporation Act and the Test Act remained unaltered, and there were Unitarians and free-thinkers who received no concessions.   The Dissenters were still barred from the universities, and their ministers were hampered by lack of education, and came to be looked upon as socially inferior.   Their congregations were largely confined to the lower middle class.   Arianism and Unitarianism spread rapidly among them, and on the whole their numbers and influence declined for a long time to come.   Nevertheless, the Revolution was in essence a Nonconformist triumph.

James II. had tried, by his Declaration of Indulgence, to unite the Nonconformists and the Romanists against the Church of England, and had failed because the fear of Rome was too deep in the hearts of Englishmen.   The Roman Catholics therefore gained nothing by the Revolution; toleration was not for them.   It would have been impossible in 1689 to repeal the Acts against popery, and so they remained as blots upon the Statute Book for nearly a century and a half.

• Between 1660 and 1688 the Press poured forth " prodigious swarms of dull books of fanatic and bombast divinity."   So Samuel Parker described the controversial output of the Dissenters, and he said of their controversial methods, " What in them is sanctified wit is in us profaneness and scurrility; and what in them is tenderness of conscience is in us superstition. When they are peevish and censorious, they are only offended and scandalised; and when they are cruel and unmerciful to dissenting brethren, they are then zealous for God and His

Truth. But do we expose the follies of their divinity with any briskness of reason? That is arrogance. Do we upbraid the impostures of their superstition with any sharpness of wit? That is profaneness. Do we demonstrate any of their notions of practical godliness to be giddy and unwarrantable-conceits? That is to blaspheme the influences of the Divine Spirit. Do we but press people to an imitation of the life of Christ? That is enough to brand us for Socinians. Do we urge the absolute necessity of good works, or a holy life? . . . What can we be but Papists? And do we assert the practice of morality to be the great and most essential design of religion? We . . . preach Plato and Şeneca and ourselves, but not Jesus Christ. . . . What think they of themselves, who, when they are demanded to give a rational account of their outrage against the government and discipline of our Church, only inveigh against it in rude unmannerly phrases, and manage the quarrel by calling names, and instead of propounding modest exceptions, stuff their pamphlets with boisterous words and unclean invectives, and familiarly salute us with the cleanly titles of Locusts of the Bottomless Pit, the Limbs of Antichrist, Baal's Priests, Romish Wolves and Foxes, Beelzebub of Canterbury, Antichristian Beasts, Bishops of the Devil, with innumerable others of the same generous strain? " [1]

When the King came back the most pressing problem was to find some way of restoring religious peace and unity. Immediately there arose a great clamour of debate about bishops and liturgies and the Solemn League and Covenant. There were not wanting men of goodwill who strove in the cause of unity to reduce the matters in dispute to their lowest terms. Such was Edward Stillingfleet, then Rector of Sutton, in Bedfordshire, who shortly after the Restoration published a work entitled " Irenicum: or, A Weapon Salve for the Church's Wounds." [2] " My main design," he said, " throughout the whole treatise, is to show that there can be no argument drawn from any pretence of a divine right that may hinder men from consenting and yielding to such a form of government in the Church as may bear the greatest correspondency to the primitive Church, and the most advantageously conducible to the peace, unity, and settlement of our divided Church." The necessary form of the government of the Church has not been clearly revealed, as is manifest from all the controversies about it, and evidently, therefore, Christ never intended any one form as necessary to the peace of the Church. Nothing can bind Christians as a

[1] S. Parker, " Defence and Continuation of the Ecclesiastical Policy," 1671, pp. 82–83.
[2] There is some doubt about the date, which is frequently given as 1659. The copies of the first edition are dated 1661, but one of the British Museum copies has a MS. note that it was published on Nov. 21st, 1660, which is probably correct.

positive law but what may certainly be known to have come from God, either as a law of nature or some positive law of God. Things undetermined both by the natural law and the positive law of God may be lawfully determined by the authority of the Church, and whatever is determined by lawful authority binds the consciences of those subject to that authority, which authority may, however, revoke, limit, or change such laws. There must be some form of ecclesiastical government over a nation as a Church, as well as of civil government over it as a society governed by the same laws. " There must be a standing perpetual ministry . . . and this is of divine and perpetual right." There is no form of Church government so determined by divine law as to be unalterably binding; Christ gave no such law to His Church as Moses did to the Jewish Church: we have nothing but general rules which are applicable to several forms of government. Stillingfleet acknowledged episcopacy as a human institution, and argued that even if it were proved apostolic it does not follow that an apostolic practice might always bind succeeding times. The most eminent divines of the Reformation period never asserted that any one form of church government was necessary. Yet this is not to say that episcopacy is unlawful. His general conclusion was that for the peace of the Church it was most prudent to approach as nearly as possible to primitive practice. That meant a system of presidency for life over an ecclesiastical senate, a combination of episcopal and presbyterian systems. By way of immediate reform, dioceses should be lessened in size, and provincial synods should be held twice a year, an easy and reasonable method of accommodation between the contending parties.

Stillingfleet leaned more or less to Latitudinarian views. The Laudian school of High Churchmen, on the other hand, held strongly that the Church of England had never separated from the organization of the Catholic Church as it had existed from the beginning. Rent by schisms, that Catholic Church, divided now into Roman, Anglican, and Greek, had a faith which was a divine revelation, and an episcopal and apostolic organization which was of divine appointment. Without losing her essential Catholicity, the Church of England had merely thrown off mediæval corruptions, and had made her appeal to the primitive centuries of the undivided Church. Therefore, the Catholic faith and order were a trust which the Church could not yield up for the sake of sects of man's invention within recent times. In " The Due Way of Composing the Differences on Foot, Preserving the Church," published in 1660, Herbert Thorndyke declared that unity with the whole Church was not to be sacrificed for the sake of uniting the English sects. On the contrary, where, as in the case of the Anabaptists, Fifth Monarchy men, Quakers, and Independents, heretical positions were held, and congregations founded to uphold them, before there could be any union with the Church these opinions must be expressly renounced, either by individuals or by congregations. If toleration were to be granted to sectaries it should be only to the extent of allowing them the private exercise of their religion, and if this were done, the same privilege should be granted to Papists. But this raised a difficulty. Papists who believed in the right of the Pope to depose kings should be treated as the enemies of their country. Not all Papists, however, believed this, and it was easier to secure the allegiance of Roman Catholics, in spite of the possibility of a papal dispensation, than to secure that of sectaries, who dispensed themselves when they pleased under " the pretence of God's spirit." Thorndyke, like Stillingfleet, thought it would not be difficult to compose the differences between the Anglicans and Presbyterians, and made similar proposals about decreasing the size of the dioceses, and allowing presbyters to act with bishops in ordination. He thought, too, that there would be no difficulty in the revision of the Prayer Book, which he admitted capable of amendment; but the Directory must be abolished, for it was as bad in one way as the Roman service books were in another.[1] In a later work Thorndyke laid down that it is not for men to make reformation at their own will; it is for the Church to make it. Dissenters asked for forbearance, but it was more than forbearance " to allow their orders, or to change the laws for the sake of the weak. The true forbearance was the method adopted by the Church of England in holding conferences to try to satisfy their demands." [2]

Jeremy Taylor preached a sermon on these questions before the University of Dublin, and published it in 1662, under the title " Via Intelligentiæ." Assuming that government by kings and bishops is of divine ordinance, he maintained that those who held another doctrine did so through evil affections and unrighteous lives, and were morally incapable of doing the will of God. Some men tried to find a common body of truth in which all believed, and would make this a basis of union between the contending sects. Others thought that if each sect would only exercise moderation, the differences between them might be reconciled; each sect discarding something, and all coming together to hammer out terms and phrases in which they might all agree. That could only result in " a fantastic peace," for the common toleration of all opinions might be a way of peace, but it is not the way of truth. His destructive criticism was sound enough, but he had little that was constructive to offer. He suggested that men ought not to be punished for mere

[1] Thorndyke, " Works," V. 25–66.
[2] *Idem.*, " A Discourse of the Forbearance of the Penalties which a Due Reformation Requires," 1670; " Works," V. 381–488.

opinions unless those opinions were such as would lead to violence in the State. " If any man do His Will he shall know of the doctrine." That was the only real solution. Good men can see what is good, and will follow it, and thus at last a state of mind will be produced which is conducive both to truth and peace.

At the Restoration the Hon. Robert Boyle, desirous of doing something towards putting an end to persecution, asked Dr. Thomas Barlow and Sir Peter Pett to publish something on behalf of liberty of conscience; Barlow to write on the theological side of the question, and Pett to write on the political side. Boyle also asked John Drury, who had lived many years on the Continent, and had taken a great interest and an active part in schemes to reconcile the Lutherans and Calvinists, to publish some account on the position of the question abroad. Barlow's tract was not published till long afterwards, partly because it was felt that nothing would stay the vigorous measures intended against Dissenters, partly because he was himself under suspicion for some views he had expressed on the subject of infant baptism.[1] Pett and Drury both published tracts in 1660. Drury's was entitled " The Plain Way of Peace and Unity in Matters of Religion," and made the following suggestions: Let all Protestants have equally a well-regulated liberty, so that they would neither fear the Government nor desire to make tumults. Consider what matters are fundamental. Abolish party names. Discourage controversial writings by individuals. Instead of synods and conferences, which are useless, let treaties be made between the contending parties. For this the writer suggested a somewhat complicated method, beginning with all the parties to the proposed treaty sending in to the King a written statement of their opinions. In view of the state of contemporary feeling, some of Drury's suggestions were counsels of perfection, while his proposals for ending theological strife by a system of treaties were too cumbrous to have any possibility of success.

John Corbet, a Presbyterian, subsequently ejected from Bramshot, in Hampshire, wrote " The Interest of England in the Matter of Religion." It was published in London in October 1660, and a second part appeared early in the following year. He pleaded that the Presbyterian party should be protected and encouraged, and urged that this could be done without disobliging the Episcopalians, and that to maintain a just balance between the two was fairer than the exaltation of one to the subversion of the other. Union between the Churchmen and the Presbyterians would be a great safeguard against the sectaries and the papists, and would promote the general good of Protestantism as a whole. It would also be better for

[1] " The Works of the Hon. Robert Boyle, with a Life by Thomas Birch," 1744, I. 89.

the country, for to force men's consciences led to dissoluteness and indifference in the case of the pliable, while it made martyrs of others, which would prove a great hindrance to the Government. While Corbet thus argued for the toleration of Presbyterianism, he was not prepared to grant it to Roman Catholics. Roger L'Estrange replied to him in " Interest Mistaken, or the Holy Cheat," 1661, in which he roundly affirmed that the Presbyterians designed to enslave both King and people. They professed great scruples about the Church, they declared that the late war against the King was lawful. Swarms of petitions were presented to the King by them as soon as he came back. Douglas's coronation sermon of 1651 had been reprinted, " Smectymnuus " had also reappeared in the press with a recommendation by Manton, and hundreds of other similar pamphlets had been published. They justified the Solemn League and Covenant, and by defending the last war made room for another. " They " (the Presbyterians) " did me once the honour to condemn me almost at midnight, by a packed committee and without a hearing : well-nigh four years they kept me in Newgate upon that account." The tract went on to deal with their doings under the Commonwealth, their doctrines about the kingship, and their claims to alter the Church, their theological system, and their history, and the story of " Presbyterian practices towards their sovereign."

The attempt to enforce conformity produced, of course, many outcries. " A Fanatic's Address," published in 1661, which from the title may have been written by Henry Adis, pleaded for toleration for all to worship God without constraint or restraint. The writer said that he and his religious associates recognised the authority of the Government, but as they had " no warrant to alter or abrogate the laws of God in heaven," they should go on worshipping in their own way, and should endure without resistance whatever persecution resulted. He concluded with an appeal to consider how Episcopalians and Romanists cried out against persecution in Cromwell's days. The General Baptists would have done so also if his rule had lasted much longer, and " if this Rome-bred persecuting spirit " were to continue, the Presbyterians would next be roused to protest. The Baptist production, " Sion's Groans for the Distressed," urged that the power to impose anything in the worship and service of God belonged neither to the magistrate as a magistrate nor as a Christian.[1] John Sturgeon, a Baptist, wrote in the same year " A Plea for Toleration of Opinions and Persuasions in matters of Religion differing from the Church of England."

One of the great obstacles in the way of reunion between the Church and the Presbyterians was the Solemn League and

[1] Crosby, " Hist. Baptists," II. 97–144.

Covenant, which the Presbyterian ministers had taken themselves and forced others to take. Still more difficult became their case when renunciation was demanded of them. The King himself had taken it three times, though it is true he had very little choice in the matter, but in the Presbyterian view to renounce it was to commit perjury. Indeed, the authorities would probably have been wiser if they had allowed it to sink into oblivion; that is, of course, if they had been permitted to do so. In August 1660 there had appeared "A Declaration of the Presbyterians concerning His Majesty's Royal Person and the Government of the Church of England, with several Propositions touching the Solemn League and Covenant and the setting up of Bishops." The writers argued that the Covenant, though not directed to the absolute extirpation of prelacy, was clearly against "the unjust and anti-Christian" prelacy, and pleaded for episcopacy in the form set forth by the late Primate of Armagh, at the same time pleading earnestly for the maintenance of the Covenant. Against the Covenant two former works were reprinted. Daniel Featley, who died in 1645, had written while in prison, "The League Illegal, wherein the late Solemn League and Covenant is Seriously Examined, Scholastically and Solidly Confuted; for the Right Informing of Weak and Tender Consciences and the Undeceiving of the Erroneous." It was now republished (with a gruesome frontispiece representing Dr. Featley as a corpse in a winding-sheet) "by John Faireclough, *vulgo* Featley, Chaplain to the King's most Excellent Majesty." This was in 1660; in the following year "A Review of the Covenant," an attack based on "grounds of Scripture, law, and reason," printed at Bristol in 1644 without an author's name, was reissued as the work of Dr. Gerald Langbaine, late Provost of Queen's College, Oxford. The Covenant was treated by some of the Royalist party with savage mockery. "Manes Presbyterianii," an anonymous pamphlet, "printed for the Reverend Classes" in 1661, had its front page deeply edged with black, and among its contents were "The Groans and Last Breathings of the Covenant to its Dear Parent Presbytery," and "The Speech and Confession of the Covenant at its Burning by the Executioner."

Zachary Crofton, incumbent of St. Botolph's, Aldgate, from which he was ejected in 1662, published a treatise in 1660, "The Fastening of St. Peter's Fetters by Seven Links or Propositions: or, the Efficacy and Extent of the Solemn League and Covenant." His seven propositions were: (1) That it was incumbent on every minister to assert the binding force of the Covenant. (2) That irregularities in the original making of the Covenant did not deprive it of force. (3) That the matter contained in it was just and lawful, and should be maintained. (4) That the form and making of it were good and allowable. (5) The ambiguities and contradictions in it were imaginary and not real. (6) The Covenant in its quality, and for its obligations, was public and national as well as private and personal. (7) It was permanently binding, and could neither be dissolved nor discharged. While defending the Covenant, the book attacked the Church of England, the Prayer Book, and the prelacy. The title was due to a metaphor used by Dr. Gauden, who had spoken of the Covenant as binding the Church like St. Peter's chains.

Dr. Gauden replied the same year with "Analusis. The Loosing of St. Peter's Bands, setting forth the True Sense and Solution of the Covenant in Point of Conscience so far as it Relates to the Government of the Church by Episcopacy." The Covenant was one of the great stumbling-blocks in the way of the restoration of the Church from the ruins of the last twenty years, because those who had taken it thought episcopacy was thereby barred. It was defective in authority and law, was the result of the violence of the times, was of foreign origin, forcibly thrust on the English Church and State, and had had sad and tragic consequences in the Civil War and the destruction of the Church. Moreover, it was complicated or annulled by counter engagements, it was contrary to the oaths of allegiance and supremacy and to the binding force of canonical obedience, it was designed to overthrow the episcopal government of the Church, and consequently it threatened the Church with schism. Though it derived its pretended authority from examples in the Old Testament, it was a thing hitherto unknown in the Christian Church, and the only way in which it could be lawfully taken would be if it were imposed by lawful authority, and if it were directed, not against episcopacy in general, but against excesses or defects in that form of Church government. How could the Covenant bind the nation, when not a quarter of the people ever took it? No covenant could bind men to the injury of others, nor to extirpate the use of what was good because of abuses which might have crept in. It had done infinite harm in this country, and the Boanerges who thundered against Covenant-breaking might far better thunder against such Covenant-taking.

Crofton, in July 1660, returned to the subject in a tract entitled "Analepsis: or, St. Peter's Bonds Abide." It was written in the form of a letter to Sir Lawrence Bromfield, who had been concerned with the question of the consistency of episcopal church government with the Solemn League and Covenant. Crofton said that Gauden's answer to himself was characterised by uncertainty of object, inadvertency of expression, and imbecility of argument, and so it would leave St. Peter fast fettered, as it found him, that true episcopacy made the bishop the same as a presbyter, and was quite consistent with the

Covenant, but the vulgar and late acceptation of episcopacy was not. He hotly denied that the Covenanters were responsible for the late King's death. The chief part of the argument of this work, however, dealt with the question whether oaths are always binding. Gauden, in an " Epistle " prefixed to an anonymous work called " Doubts and Scruples," repeated more or less his former arguments.

Crofton therefore followed his last work up with " Analepsis Analephthe." In the preface he said that he had been loyal to the King during his exile, and nevertheless the Covenant was binding on his conscience. He had been told both by his enemies and his friends that he was indiscreet, but some one must speak out. Those who had first promoted the Covenant seemed now to have cooled down, but as he himself spoke up for the King under the Commonwealth, so now he would dare to speak up for the Covenant. The " Reasons of the Present Judgment of the University of Oxford, concerning the Solemn League and Covenant, approved by general consent, in a full Convocation," on June 1st, 1647, in which the Oxford Convocation set forth why its members could not take the Covenant, had recently been reprinted, and Crofton replied to this in the present pamphlet. But he could not leave Gauden alone. " I pursue Dr. John Gauden's metaphor, that the solemn and sacred oaths should be deemed St. Peter's bonds, and that Protestant divines should not by Popish arguments attempt his release to the establishment of the *Papatum alterius mundi* of episcopacy in lawn sleeves." " I did send out my Analepsis after the Doctor's Analysis, and made bold to withstand St. Peter to his face. I love St. Peter in bonds better than in the Pope's chair."

Gauden in reply wrote " Anti-Baal Berith." The title sufficiently explains its contents. The Covenant was a Covenant with Baal. Crofton replied with " Berith Anti-Baal: or Zachary Crofton's Appearance before the Prelate Justice of the Peace." The prefatory letter was dated March 14th, 1661. He called Gauden, amongst other things, a fool and a heretic, and accused him of talking blasphemy and nonsense. He asked if Gauden were a justice of the peace, that he presumed to bind people to good behaviour. The bishop had said that some of the Covenanters were beginning to see that the Covenant was not opposed to the true episcopacy, to which Crofton replied that at a general meeting of the Presbyterian Covenanters in London the cause of the Covenant was debated, and its opposition to episcopacy owned. At this meeting a petition to the King was drawn up in which the signatories asked " that the things of God and religion, which have been so solemnly convenanted for, may be owned and confirmed by your royal authority; which, notwithstanding, we do sincerely profess our readiness to accommodate with our godly and orthodox brethren dissenting from us, so far as may consist with our consciences and covenant." He went on to say, however, that the petition, " by some State stratagem, and cowardice of some who, contrary to the due order of all assemblies, would never let it be reported," was prevented from being presented to the King.

Zachary Crofton's work evoked pamphlets from a number of combatants. The Rev. John Rowland wrote " A Reply to the Anonymous Answer to the Doctor," John Russell of Chingford wrote " The Solemn League and Covenant Discharged," while anonymously there appeared " Aliquis Nemo," " Doubts and Scruples against Taking the Solemn League and Covenant," and others. One of the most stinging appeared in 1660, and bore the title, " The Anatomy of Dr. Gauden's Idolised Nonsense and Blasphemy. (Gauden replied to this in his " Anti-Baal Berith.") The Anatomist, as Crofton called him, made fun of Gauden's title, and wanted to know what St. Peter had to do with the Covenant. This writer was evidently acquainted with Martin Marprelate, whom he somewhat feebly imitated. Confusing the deliverance of St. Peter with that of Paul and Silas, he said that it was the gaol-birds in the prison, and not the two saints, whose bonds were loosed, and that if any such had taken the Solemn League and Covenant, no doubt " Dr. John " would take them out of it. He accused the bishop of pretending to give the sober sense of the Covenant while really trying to make it odious. " In spite of him, the Covenant (even as to the point of extirpating that hierarchical prelacy lately laid aside) is to be kept by those who wish to avoid destruction here and damnation hereafter." Those who had signed it had agreed to the extirpation of popery and prelacy, that is, " Church government by archbishops, bishops, their chancellors and commissaries, deans, deans and chapters, archdeacons, and all other ecclesiastical offices depending on that hierarchy."

Thomas Tompkins, a Fellow of All Souls, in some " Strictures " [1] which he wrote on Crofton's arguments, accused his adversary of treason and rebellion: treason in saying that the Parliament had jurisdiction over Church and Crown, rebellion in his defence of the Covenant. Roger L'Estrange, too, found treason in his assertion that the Parliament which accepted the Covenant and overthrew the King was a lawful authority. Crofton replied to these and others in 1661 in " Mr. Crofton's Case." He defended the statements that his two opponents had found treasonable, and went on once more to defend the Covenant and abuse episcopacy. In this and all his pamphlets there was much railing, and very little understanding of the question at issue, a great parade of learning, but very little real

[1] " Short Strictures, or Animadversions on so much of Mr. Zach. Crofton's ' Fastening of St. Peter's Bonds ' as concern the Reasons of the University of Oxon. concerning the Covenant," 1661.

knowledge of theology. In contrast to his later violence against episcopacy was his earlier work, "A Serious View of Presbyters' Reordination by Bishops," in which he had maintained the validity of Presbyterian orders, but allowed that Presbyterian ministers might be reordained, provided they received the new ordination as merely accumulative, and did not in any way renounce their former orders.[1]

In March 1661 Crofton was preaching every Sunday night to crowded congregations that episcopacy was a Roman institution, and tended to papacy,[2] that the work of the Covenant should be carried on by force, that Parliament had the right to impose an oath which should bind both King and people, and that the power of the people was above that of the King.[3] On March 23rd he found himself in the Tower, whence he sent a petition to the King protesting his loyalty, and affirming that his "late inconsiderate expressions on things out of his sphere" were not intended to disturb the peace of the kingdom. He defended himself, too, in a pamphlet already referred to, "Mr. Crofton's Case." He admitted that he had held the positions which had been charged against him as treasonable, but this had been before June 24th, 1661, when an order had been issued making it unlawful to defend the Covenant, before which date, indeed, it had been the duty of subjects to do so. Claiming that a casuistical debate was not a crime, he pleaded that the controversy had been provoked by Dr. Gauden. While a prisoner in the Tower, Crofton attended the Anglican services in the chapel there, and got into trouble for it with his fellow-Dissenters. He defended himself in a pamphlet, "Reformation not Separation: or Mr. Crofton's Plea for Communion with the Church, under those Corruptions, and by that Disorderly Ministration, to which he cannot Conform." In this he protested against separation from the Church, for though the Prayer Book was defective and disorderly, he found nothing in it to which a sober Christian might not say Amen. This set another controversy going. "T. P." replied to Crofton in 1662, with "Jerubbaal, or the Pleader Impleaded." Crofton, or a friend of his, wrote "Jerubbaal Justified" (1663), at the end of which was a paper which set forth "Mr. Crofton's Creed touching Church Communion," which desired the Anglican clergy to resolve Mr. Crofton's great difficulty about conformity, viz., "that a minister of the Gospel could not without sin receive a liturgy which was generally and exclusively imposed." He could accept any such work as the Directory, but not such an one as the Prayer Book, which gave the very words to be used. "T. P." published a rejoinder entitled "Jerubbaal Redivivus," but a more doughty opponent had entered the fray, in the shape of Dr. Lawrence Womack, archdeacon of Suffolk, and afterwards Bishop of St. Davids.

[1] Kennet, "Reg.," p. 384.   [2] C.S.P.D., 32/108.   [3] C.S.P.D., 32/21.

When Edmund Calamy was imprisoned at the beginning of 1663 for preaching his sermon (afterwards published) on " Eli Trembling for Fear of the Ark," Womack wrote, and dedicated to the House of Commons, " Aaron-bimnucha: or, an Antidote to Cure the Calamites of their Trembling for Fear of the Ark." It was a discourse on I. Chron. xvi. 1, and had nothing flippant about it except the title. He drew a parallel between England under the Commonwealth and Israel at the time when Oreb and Zeb, Zebah and Zalmanah said, " Let us take to ourselves the houses of God in possession," and God made the enemies of the Church " like stubble before the wind." He warned his opponents not to profane the Ark, and turned Calamy's interpretation against himself and his party. Next he dealt with " Jerubbaal Justified," and Crofton's difficulty with regard to the use of the Prayer Book. He answered it with a syllogism: " To do whatsoever is morally possible for uniformity and peace' sake is your duty. But to submit to the use of a prescribed liturgy is morally possible. Therefore to submit to the use of a prescribed liturgy is your duty." To receive such a liturgy upon the authority of one's superiors did not reduce people to the dilemma of obeying God or man, as Crofton pretended, for God and man were not here in opposition. " Whether the Church of God be not more secure in her freedom from corruptions and disorders by fixed stated forms than by such as are undigested, transient, and extemporary, I appeal to the reason and common sense of all the world." This tract was followed in the same year by " A Word to Dr. Womack: or, a Short Reply to his pretended Resolution of Mr. Crofton's Position." This was by " R. S.," the publisher of " Reformation not Separation," who responded in the same pages to " Jerubbaal Justified." Womack, in " Pulpit Conceptions, Popular Deceptions " (1663), discussed more fully the relative merits of a prescribed liturgy and extemporary prayer. In the preface he laid stress on the differences of the Dissenters among themselves, and quoted a saying of Mr. Thomas Case, the Savoy Commissioner, who had been ejected from St. Mary Magdalene's, Milk Street,[1] " If either saints may make opinions, or opinions may make saints, we shall quickly have more opinions than saints in the land." Womack did not hear of the tract by " R. S." for a long time after it was published, but in 1664 he replied to it in " Conformity Reasserted," which commenced with a quip that the letters " R. S." might stand for Rebellion and Schism. He described his adversary as " very waspish," but when he allowed himself to write, " I shall not suffer my pen to rake into the filthy ulcers of this feeble Lazar," or " This proud Philistine doth strut and advance himself with crest erect, as if he designed to defy the armies of the living God," the " waspish " character of the controversy was not all on one

[1] Palmer, I, 153.

side. The dispute was largely over Crofton's statement that no minister of the Gospel could receive an imposed liturgy without sin, and Womack argued that the plea to be guided by one's own judgment against the judgment of authority was simply self-will and vanity.

Crofton was released from prison in 1662, and after trying to make a living as a grocer, and then as a farmer, he opened a school in his old parish of St. Botolph's, and continued there till his death.[1] In 1671 he published " The Saints' Care for Church Communion," in which he expressed his satisfaction that, owing to the good offices of Sir Samuel Starling, the Lord Mayor of London, he had been able to preach in an Anglican church, St. James's, Duke Street.

The Dissenters objected to the Anglican system in its doctrine, its worship, and its government. They would have nothing of episcopacy except what they called Usher's Model, which was not episcopacy as the Catholic Church understood it at all. Prynne was against bishops, and in 1636 had written an essay entitled " The Unbishoping of Timothy and Titus and of the Angel of the Church of Ephesus," and this he reprinted in 1660. In an appendix he complained of the proposals which had been made in the Commons on August 15th and 17th of that year, that persons having only Presbyterian ordination should be turned out unless they received episcopal ordination within a month. Robert Brooke, in " A Discourse opening the Nature of that Episcopacy which is Exercised in England " (1661), laid stress on the distinction between episcopacy and prelacy, though he soon forgot it as he proceeded with his work. In his view, bishops were proud prelates, men of little learning, taken from the lowest of the people, raised to high place, and meddlers in State affairs, who spent their time in critical, cabalistical, sceptical, scholastic learning, which fills the head with empty notions. They ruled without their clergy, issued orders about indifferent things, what the clergy should wear, when the people should stand or sit, and had forced unlawful things, like the Book of Sports and bowing to the altar. They carried themselves as lords, had great estates and revenues, and excommunicated whom they would. Since the Reformation the churches of Christ had done without bishops. Episcopacy stood near to popery, was consonant neither with antiquity nor Scripture, and had been the source of schism, sects, and heresies. " A Reverend and Godly Divine " accused the bishops of a design to enervate and alter English Protestantism and so reduce the people to popery. He said that a Jesuit had recommended the following methods for that purpose. They should begin by suspending all the orthodox powerful preachers and

[1] Palmer, I. 103–104; Neal, " Puritans," IV. 312; Smith, " Obituary," Camden Soc., p. 97.

by putting down the lecturers. (The Puritans felt keenly the attempts to suppress the lecturers, who, exempt from episcopal control, could use Anglican pulpits to undermine Anglican doctrines.) The old ceremonies should be revived, the validity of Presbyterian ordination denied, and Arminian theology inculcated. The Protestant religion should be held up to the people as an odious thing, and quarrels should be fomented among Protestants. Conventicles should be forbidden, and severe laws made against them. All this was being done. Anglicans were stealthily introducing Romanism. Had not Hammond, Bramhall, and Jeremy Taylor all admitted that the Pope was not Antichrist, and that the Church of Rome was a Christian church? The unnamed Jesuit had recommended that the rulers should lead good lives, but this part of his advice had not been taken, for the episcopalians were profane, atheistical, and debauched, and the great leaders of the party made pretence to a piety which consisted in nothing but outward observance.[1] Henry Hickman, Fellow of Magdalen College, in a more dignified and moderate manner than the last writer, had in 1660 attacked the doctrines of the " High Church clergy " in his " Laudensium Apostasia," in which he set forth the view that the clergy who followed Laud had fallen from the true doctrine of the Church of England. But the great danger which some of their more moderate and scholarly opponents saw in the Laudian divines was not so much their ceremonialism as their Arminianism.

Of course the great trouble with regard to episcopacy was that the Anglican Church, clinging to Catholic order, refused to recognise Presbyterian ordination. The bishops were willing to meet scruples by ordaining conditionally with the words, " If thou art not already ordained," or some such expression. This a very great number refused. Zachary Crofton wrote on the subject with a great display of learning but very little real knowledge, and asserted that Presbyterian ordination was surer than episcopal. How little he understood the Catholic system may be seen in the following quotation: " Who do you mean by a deacon? I take it for granted not a Scripture deacon, for he is a stranger to our Church, unless under the name of an overseer to the poor; and if she knew him I find not that he was ever entrusted with the power, or had a hand in ordination of ministers; nor can I suppose you mean a deacon *in sensu ecclesiastico*, who is at most but half a minister (though I know no warrant for it), and is not admitted to consecrate wine (though water), much less to ordain ministers. I must therefore conclude you intend a deacon *in sensu cathedrali*, who is a presbyter in office, but archdeacon in hierarchical order, and

[1] " The English Prelates practising the Methods and Rules of the Jesuits," 1661.

presenteth to the bishop (too commonly with a lie in his mouth) the persons to be ordained, and accompanyeth the bishop in imposition of hands." [1] " Josiah Webb, Gent.," who described himself as " a Detester of the Dregs of the Anti-Christian Hierarchy," was the author of " Erastus Junior, or a Fatal Blow to the Clergy's Pretensions of Divine Right," in which he took the position that the episcopal and Presbyterian ministers alike derived what authority they had from Parliament only. [2] Another writer, in " Prelatic Preachers none of Christ's Teachers " (1663), dissuaded the " people of God " from attending the " so-called ministry " of those who preached by virtue of an " apocryphal ordination " by Lord Bishops. The other side was not unheard. Dr. Thomas Bayley wrote a short treatise in defence of *jure divino* episcopacy, [3] and Bishop Sanderson wrote " Episcopacy as Established by Law in England not Prejudicial to Regal Power " (1661).

The various sects differed in doctrine from the Anglican Church on different points, but they all agreed in differing. They all disliked the " liturgy," by which they meant the Prayer Book, and they objected to a vast number of details: the too general confessions of sin, the shortness of the collects, the " vain repetitions," the " disorderly " responses by the congregation, the prayers from ancient service-books, the use of the Apocrypha, the practice of giving the sacrament into the hands of the communicants, the sign of the cross, godparents, surplices, and many other things. [4] " Several Treatises of Worship and Ceremonies," by William Bradshaw, originally published in 1604, were reprinted in 1660. One of the treatises was specially concerned with proving that the use of the ceremonies enjoined by the Prayer Book was unlawful, as being against the law of God. The book spoke of " the unconsecrated attire of a filthy mass-priest, the most abominable idolater in the earth," and said, " We cannot but account that priestly attire that is enjoined unto us by our prelates an apparel more unbeseeming the minister of the Gospel than a cloak with a thousand patches, or a coat with torn elbows, for beggary and folly being judgments and not sins, the notes of beggary and folly cannot be so odious in a spiritual eye as the notes of idolatry." All this is about the surplice.

William Prynne was one of the most ardent loyalists at the Restoration, and so unrestrained in his expression of it that he had to be warned by General Monk that he was doing more

---

[1] Zachary Crofton, " A Serious Review of Presbyter's Reordination by Bishops," 1661.

[2] Parts I. and II. 1660. "Webb " was really a Roman Catholic priest. Wood calls him Lewgar. Gillow. Bibliog. Dict. ; Church Hist. Soc. Tracts. xxxi.

[3] T. Bayley, " The Royal Charter Granted unto Kings," 1660.

[4] W. Clagett, " An Answer to the Dissenters' Objections against the Common Prayer," 1684.

harm than good.[1] However zealous he was for the King, he was not equally zealous for the Prayer Book, and in 1661, in " A Short Sober Pacific Examination of some Exuberances in and Ceremonial Appurtenances to the Book of Common Prayer," he suggested that several set forms of prayer might be allowed, and not simply one imposed on everybody. He complained of the bad translation of the Scripture portions of the Prayer Book, objected to the repetition of the Lord's Prayer, Gloria Patri, and responses in the Litany; but chiefly he found fault with the ceremonies and vestments; in fact the greater part of the pamphlet was about vestments. He showed a wide knowledge of the Scriptures and of ancient and mediæval writers, but indulged in a great deal of quibbling and cavilling.

" The Old Nonconformist Touching the Book of Common Prayer and Ceremonies," was an anonymous publication which appeared in the summer of 1660. It offered as an expedient for the happy settlement of ecclesiastical affairs that every eleven parishes should be united in a diocese or classis, of which one of the pastors was to be bishop or president: that every Sabbath morning, before preaching, a general prayer should be " devised in good style," without any repetitions, one in which the minister should be " alone the mouth of the people ": that there should be toleration for everything except blasphemy; and that unnecessary ceremonies, vestments, and times, except the Lord's Day, should never be imposed.

The Puritan objected very strongly to the practice of bowing at the Holy Name. Henry Burton, who had his ears cut off, wrote " Jesus Worship Confuted, or Certain Arguments against Bowing at the Name Jesus. Proving it to be Idolatrous and Superstitious and so utterly Unlawful." [2] Edward Bagshawe, who claimed to be a Churchman and to believe in episcopacy, and who had been ordained by a bishop, offered a novel solution to the problem of the ceremonies. " Instead of declaiming against, or too rigid enforcing our old rites, fitted only for the infancy of the Church, he doth heartily wish that all parties would agree to refer the whole cause of ceremonies to His Majesty's single decision." The imposition of things, indifferent in themselves, which by abuse had become occasions of superstition, such as the sign of the cross and the surplice, was contrary to Christian liberty, tended to give undue weight to the ceremonies themselves, and gave rise to disorder and confusion.[3] Other writers objected to liturgies altogether, as not primitive and not appointed by God. Some carried their dislike of set forms so

[1] Muddiman, " The King's Journalist," p. 82.
[2] See also " Several Arguments against Bowing at the Name of Jesus," 1660; W. Wickins, " The Warrant for Bowing at the Name of Jesus Produced and Examined," 1660.
[3] E. Bagshawe, " The Great Question concerning Things Indifferent in Religious Worship," 1660.

far as to object to the use of the Lord's Prayer.[1]   Amongst other
attacks on the Prayer Book, Philip Nye wrote " Beams of Former
Light; Discovering how Evil it is to Impose Doubtful and
Disputable Forms or Practices upon Ministers " (1660).   R.
Bayley published a " Parallel of the Liturgy with the Mass
Book and other Romish Rituals " (1661), while the title of a
tract by Vavasour Powell in 1661 roundly declared " The
Common Prayer Book no Divine Service."   Richard Lyttler,
a London citizen, maintained from the Scriptures and the
writings of Protestant divines that there was nothing demanded
by the Act of Uniformity that was forbidden by the law of
God.[2]   Roger L'Estrange's " Toleration Discussed " (1663), a
dialogue between Conformity (a Churchman), Zeal (a Presbyterian), and Scruple (an Independent), in which, of course,
the Churchman got the best of the argument, denied that the
Act of Uniformity restrained conscience.   Another writer urged
Dissenters to beware of the temptation and glory of the world,
and said, " If propenseness to suffer makes the martyr, the
Anabaptist, the Quaker, yea, the Jesuit and the heathen, the
lunatic and the madman, even such as have neither grace nor
reason are far before you."   It was generally said that the
Dissenters would have conformed but for the declaration required,
but the Act of Uniformity merely required them to affirm their
assent and consent to the *use* of the Prayer Book, and that in
conforming they did nothing against their consciences.   As for
the Covenant, they were simply asked to declare that it did
not bind them to attempt alterations in Church and State.
The present ecclesiastical system was established in England
before the Covenant, which was a document directed against
the liberty of the subject, a defiance of Parliament, and a breaking of previous obligations.   As for ordination, the Act did not
judge foreign Protestants; but it merely said that Nonconformist ordination could not pass for legal ordination in this
Church and State, or entitle those who had received it to hold
legally the profits of their places.[3]   Henry Hammond published
in 1660 a " Vindication of the Ancient Liturgy of the Church
of England," replying to the reasons alleged for altering or
abolishing the Prayer Book.   Someone else issued a statement
of " The Judgment of Foreign Divines " touching the discipline,
liturgy, and ceremonies of the English Church (1660).   John
Gauden wrote " Considerations touching the Liturgy " (1661),
and John Barron, vicar of Dallington, near Northampton, produced in 1663 a learned defence of the Prayer Book, entitled
" Liturgy a Most Divine Service," in reply to Vavasour Powell.
Sir Charles Wolseley, who had been one of Oliver's lords,

[1] " A Discourse concerning Liturgies and their Imposition," 1662.
[2] Richard Lyttler, " The Reformed Presbyterian," 1662.
[3] " The Grand Case of the Present Ministry," 1662.

wrote in 1668 two vigorous pamphlets in favour of toleration. In one he pointed out that men vary in understanding, education, and spiritual illumination, and so there were necessary differences of mind and outlook.   If the Church had to appeal to the magistrate for assistance, it betokened insufficient spiritual power.   This, however, was not to say that the magistrate had nothing to do with religion: on the contrary, his duty was to see that the Gospel was preached, to preserve peace, to encourage the zealous, and as far as in him lay to see Christ's will done upon earth.   Force and compulsion were against the spirit of the Gospel and the example of Christ, had always been ineffectual, and postulated infallibility in the sovereign power.   Since every man had to judge for himself in all matters of the Christian religion, he ought not to be forced to believe or practice anything of which he was not convinced.[1]   In the other pamphlet he argued that persecution fomented faction, while liberty won men to obedience.   In punishing for religion on the ground of faction, some would be punished who did not deserve it; many persons would pity them, and so they would get hearers; moreover, punishment always fell on the best of the party, whilst those of lax principles escaped.   The Nonconformists were too numerous to be put down.   Liberty of conscience was the glory of Protestant States, though there must be no liberty for Papists, and persecution of Dissenters meant a great injury to trade.[2] The argument about trade was frequently brought up in this connection.   Sir William Petty, writing in 1671, said that the Nonconformists were increasing, and that they were for the most part " such as believe that labour and industry is their duty towards God . . . how erroneous soever their opinions be."   Trade being most vigorously carried on " by the heterodox part," he pleaded for religious freedom, only, as in Holland, " restraining licentious actings." [3]   John Corbet said that " by relations and commerce they were so woven into the nation's interests that it was not easy to sever them without unravelling the skein," and he feared the harm which would be done if they were driven out of the country.[4]   Sir William Temple, too, held up the example of the Dutch Republic.   On the establishment of the United Provinces it was agreed that every man should be free in the matter of religion.   In 1583 Protestantism was made the State religion, and the property of the Church of Rome became the property of the State.   The Roman Catholics alone were excepted from the protection of the laws, because they believed in a foreign and superior jurisdiction.

[1] C. Wolseley, " Liberty of Conscience, upon its True and Proper Grounds, Asserted and Vindicated," 1668.
[2] C. Wolseley, " Liberty of Conscience the Magistrate's Interest," 1668.
[3] Petty, " Political Arithmetic," 1671, preface.
[4] Corbet, " Discourse of the Religion of England," 1667.

But on payment of a certain sum they were permitted to exercise their religion, though they were not admitted to public offices. Any sect whose doctrines were not subversive of civil society was tolerated on condition that its meetings were open to the public commissioners appointed to see that no traitorous doctrines were preached. Temple's own view on toleration is given in these words: " Nor could I ever understand how those who call themselves religious men . . . come to put such weight upon those points of belief which men never have agreed in, and so little upon those of virtue and morality, in which they have hardly ever disagreed. Nor why a State should venture the subversion of their peace and their order, which are certain goods and so universally esteemed, for the propagation of uncertain and contested opinions." [1]

The controversialists went far afield for their arguments. A paper was published in 1668 entitled " A Speech Touching Toleration in Matters of Religion, delivered a hundred years since by a Privy Councillor to King James V. of Scotland." This person had argued that two religions could subsist side by side in one country, " because a little time will bring persons of opposite religion into custom and familiarity together," and that the interest of the common weal ought to be consulted rather than the interest of the clergy. " So soon as a prince beginneth to spoil, banish, kill, burn his people, for matters abstract from sense and altogether spiritual, he becometh as it were a plague unto them."

Subsist side by side they might: agree they never would. A Dissenter urged that the Scriptures teach us to avoid the ordinances of men, that God rejects all worship not commanded by Himself, and that the Church has no power to decree rites and ceremonies. This was a challenge to the Anglican Articles, but the writer went further, and said it was unlawful to join with the Church of England in its public worship, because that worship was not performed by officers of the churches of Christ, the clergy of the Church of England being antichristian idolaters. [2] In 1668 Dr. Roland Perrinchief, prebendary of Westminster, in " A Discourse of Toleration," replied to Corbet's " Discourse of the Religion of England." He pointed out that there were other causes of division than conscience: divisions were also due to aversion to sound doctrine, affectation of novelty, too much liberty, envy, and laziness in searching the truth. The separatists swallowed perjury and rebellion, and strained at a ceremony. Toleration did not remove dissensions, it increased them. It was now being urged as a necessity on the ground that Nonconformists would not conform, but they did not talk

[1] Temple, " Observations upon the United Provinces of the Netherlands," 1673, ch. V.
[2] " Vindiciæ Cultus Evangelici," 1668.

that way in Oliver's day.   To the argument that the Clarendon
Code had proved a failure, Perrinchief replied that that was
due to the slackness of those who had to enforce it.   As to the
complaint that the decline of trade was due to persecution, he
answered that the Plague, the Fire, and the Dutch war were
to be blamed for that, and not the bishops; but it was the
custom of these men to blame the bishops for everything.   Corbet
had pleaded that the Dissenters were peaceful people, who
intended no war, but Perrinchief told him " there be sullen
mutinies that make no noise, but may loosen all the joints and
ligaments of policy."   The Dissenters admitted that some of
the things ordered by the Prayer Book were matters indifferent,
but that some of them had long been disputed.   Well, then, if
they were indifferent they might lawfully be ordered by the
magistrates.   As for their being disputed, there was scarcely
any truth which had not its heretic, but was it not better to
keep unity and peace than to cause schisms and factions?
Corbet urged that the Church did not claim infallibility, and
therefore could not dominate consciences which were opposed
to the ceremonies.   His opponent replied that that argument
would destroy all government: the commandment to be subject
to the higher powers enforced obedience to all human laws
which were not in themselves unlawful.   Corbet thought that
men would be more likely to agree to the use of these little
things if subscription to them were not demanded.   Perrinchief
said that experience showed just the opposite.   After all, the
Presbyterians only claimed toleration for themselves, and it
was no use their saying how much there was in which Churchmen and they agreed: the trouble was where they differed.
Corbet had said that the present standing of episcopacy in
England was weak.   That might well be so after twenty years'
proscription, and as for the clergy, the bishops had not the
powers of the Triers, and if patrons presented unworthy persons
who had the legal qualifications, the bishops could not reject
them, nor could they arbitrarily turn men out of their livings
as the Committee had formerly done.   Corbet had urged the
bishops to promote an increase in holiness, but they were hindered
in doing so by the dissensions caused by the Dissenters.

Corbet replied with " A Second Discourse of the Religion
of England " (1668).   He went over much the same ground,
but he made it clear that what he wanted for his own party was
comprehension.   The best remedy against dissensions and dissenters was comprehensiveness on the part of the Establishment
and a great latitude for differences of opinion.   Pointing to the
already existing diversities of opinion and practice in the Church
of England, he urged that the bishops would gain more by
moderation than by severity, and that it was to the interest
of Nonconformists to prefer comprehension to toleration where

conscience permitted. For Dissenters of narrower principles, however, toleration was the only way to peace.

This, and another book called " A Peace-Offering: or, Plea for Indulgence," the joint production of several Nonconformists, led to a reply from Perrinchief entitled " Indulgence not Justi-fied " (1668). He first defended the laws for uniformity. No man was forced to profess anything contrary to his beliefs, nor was he denied liberty of worship in his own family. The law desired to secure truth and peace by forbidding any to be admitted as ministers except those persons who would perform the prescribed worship and refrain from preaching error. Such laws had been the practice of all rulers, well-known instances being the Kirk of Scotland and the Independents in New England. The writers of the " Peace-Offering " had argued that men's apprehensions of spiritual things were not absolutely in their own power, and therefore could not be the subject of the civil laws. But the laws did not interfere with their apprehensions, but only with their practices arising from those apprehensions. All the laws of England did was to coerce those who did things contrary to the peace of the Church and would not obey the just commands of their superiors. The Dissenters in England did not rest in a bare dissent; they endeavoured to abrogate the established order and repeal the laws. Their maxim that an indifferent thing became unlawful by being commanded gave little hope for stability on their part. They would not say what would satisfy them, they only offered generalities about " sufficient latitude." It was necessary not only to enjoin, but also to continue the ceremonies. Corbet had said that such as liked the ceremonies might have them, but he did not wish them enforced. Perrinchief replied that this was an impossible position. Suppose that in a parish the minister was against the ceremonies, and some of the people wanted them, should those who wanted them have another minister? This frequently happened under the Commonwealth, and resulted in multiplied divisions, in war to abolish ceremonies, and in the murder of the King. To comprehend the Nonconformists in the Church meant admitting men of contradictory views and practices, to make confusion in every office of religion, and men who would not be content with liberty, but would endeavour to gain domination. Necessity only could justify such a tolera-tion, and a standing army would be required to make it safe, to make one party leave the other party alone, and to suppress tumults and quarrels.

In 1668 appeared Simon Patrick's " Friendly Debate between a Conformist and a Nonconformist," an attack on the Dissenters, with illustrations from their own teachings. The matter of the book was not well arranged, but Patrick managed at times to treat a well-worn theme in an illuminating way. The Nonconformists laid stress on what they called " spiritual " preaching, and accused the Anglican clergy of being legalistic. It was the old controversy about faith and good works, so he devoted a section to the subject of the necessity of good works. He accused some of the Dissenters of a foolish application of the Scriptures, of pretending to have a special divine seal upon their ministry, " though all are not Christian ministers who pretend to the office," of time-serving and men-pleasing—all faults which they were apt to lay at the Church's door. He told them that by their pretence of praying in the Spirit some of them had brought religion into contempt. Not all the godly, nor even the generality of the godly, as they claimed, were Nonconformists, neither were the Dissenters, as they claimed, the strictest people, the most serious people, nor the most tender-conscienced. In common worship some things must be done which God has not expressly commanded, and the enjoining of things indifferent did not make them unlawful. There were none more superstitious than those who were most afraid of superstition, but, as a matter of fact, those who spoke most against the forms of prayer used by the Church did not always really think them unlawful. He urged Nonconformists to be reconciled to the Church, and said that if the Presbyterian ministers themselves, who had formerly preached against separation and had enjoined ceremonies of their own making, were to use their influence with their people in the right direction, the schism would be ended.

The work had a considerable influence, and ran through six editions. It " strengthened men's spirits against the Nonconformists," [1] and " it was greedily read by all that desired matter of contempt and scorn against both Nonconformity and piety." [2] Patrick himself said that he had written the book to invite the Dissenters to join the Church, or " at least not to have us in contempt, as if they were the only godly people, and we at the best but moral men, as they called us, who had not the grace of God in us." [3] In " A Continuation of the Friendly Debate," published in 1669, Patrick again attacked the way in which the Dissenters arrogated to themselves the title of " the godly." They applied all the blessings on Israel to themselves, and all the Old Testament curses on the surrounding nations to their neighbours. In the confusion they had made they had driven many to Rome as the only religion of unity and order. Patrick gave quotations from their writings, showing their violence against the Church and their quibbling and fault-finding objections against the Prayer Book. They thought they kept the laws, not by doing what those laws commanded, but by suffering what they inflicted. They argued that the non-enforcement of the penal laws showed the King's desire that they should not

[1] Salmon, " Exam. Burnet," I. 598.   [2] " Rel. Baxt.," III. 40.
[3] S. Patrick, " Autobiog.," 1839, p. 59.

be observed, yet when it suited them, they said the law was the King's superior. The " Continuation " also attacked their false interpretations of Scripture, their revelations, their spiritual pride, their self-will, their love of phrases and shibboleths. Everything in the way of decency of worship they called popish. When they were in power they did not teach the youth of the country, and they put difficulties in the way of people receiving the sacrament. They excused schism by saying that they withdrew from men of the world. They proved little, and accused stoutly. They could not agree among themselves, and were divided and subdivided. They called the Prayer Book a popish mass-book, and those who used it were, according to them, ignorant, profane, superstitious, and immoral. But even if that book had been composed by angels, the imposing of it would still have been called " imperious blasphemy," and the use of it base and wretched idolatry.

" A Further Continuation and Defence : or, A Third Part of the Friendly Debate," appeared the same year, and in 1670 there was published an Appendix to the Third Part. Baxter said of the Second and Third Parts, " Having met with the weak passages of some ministers (especially Mr. Bridge and some of their Independent party, who in excessive opposition to the Arminians spake something unwisely, if not unfoundedly, under the pretence of extolling free grace), he scrapes these together for matter of reproach. And having heard the crude and unmeet expressions of many well-meaning women and unlearned private men, especially those given to conceit and singularity, he gathers them all up in a debate, and makes the Nonconformists speak as foolishly as he has a mind, the idea being to show them the errors and weaknesses among themselves." [1]

" A Sober Answer to the Friendly Debate " appeared in 1669, and replied both to the " Debate " and to the " Continuation." The author, who called himself " Philagathus," was Samuel Rolls, sometime Fellow of Trinity College, Cambridge. His name appears in Calamy's list of the ejected, but he does not seem to have taken up any definite work as a Nonconformist preacher.[2] In the " Answer " he complained that the persons especially singled out by Patrick for attack were not representative Nonconformists. He said that he hoped others would have answered, but they were probably afraid that Patrick had public authority behind him. The two " Debates " he stigmatised as a plan for the extirpation of all practical holiness and true religion, and he accused the writer of a desire to blast good men with the name of hypocrites, and of contemptuous treatment of his opponents. Rolls denied that Dissenters thought the King a tyrant; on the contrary, they loved him for his indulgent disposition, and they looked to him for

[1] " Rel. Baxt.," III. 39.   [2] Palmer, I. 298; D.N.B.

succour. He admitted that the Clarendon Acts were not severely enforced, especially the Five Mile Act, and suggested that this was because their opponents realised that many Nonconformist ministers could not leave the towns, owing to the difficulty of getting a living in the smaller places. Patrick had asked why, if they must preach, they could not wait till the Church services were over. He replied that there were so few churches in London since the Fire that if someone did not preach to the people the Quakers would get hold of them. He spoke strongly of the sufferings of the ministers, and urged that if Nonconformists were the " weak brethren," it was the duty of Churchmen to bear with them, and not to put stumbling-blocks of ceremonial in their way. He defended the Dissenters against the accusation of believing in faith without works, and instanced Baxter and Burgess as doughty opponents of Antinomianism. He admitted that such faults as flippancy and irreverence in prayer existed amongst his brethren, but deprecated the accusation that they were all alike. He wrote in a colloquial style, with some humour, but with much wrangling over small matters, and too much of the *tu quoque* style of argument, and he accused Patrick of flouting, scoffing, and jeering. Patrick described the " Sober Answer " as " full of frivolous things and foul mistakes," and said that in consequence of it he wrote the " Further Continuation," " a little too jocular, my friends thought," but never answered by his opponent.[1]

William Assheton, Fellow of Brasenose College, Oxford, vicar of Beckenham, in Kent, and prebendary of York, published in 1670 the second edition of a work, " Toleration Disapproved and Condemned." He began by discussing the definition of persecution. Persecution was the infliction of temporal evils for the exercise of true religion. If a man was punished for believing the truth, or doing the duties, which were taught and commanded by Scripture, or if he was punished for not believing, or not doing, things contrary to the Scripture, that was persecution. Nonconformists complained that they were punished for preaching and praying. These were necessary duties which could not be performed without certain circumstances, such as forms, posture, dress, and so forth. These circumstances were not determined in Scripture, nor must they be left undetermined, and therefore were decided by the supreme magistrate, and set forth in laws enforced by penalties. The infliction of these penalties was the execution of justice, and the duty of the magistrate, but not persecution. The Dissenters therefore were not persecuted, but punished, for not observing what authority required, or for not performing the duty of preaching and praying in the manner prescribed. Magistrates were not permitted to tyrannise over men's consciences, but it was the duty

[1] S. Patrick, " Autobiog.," pp. 59–63.

of magistrates to keep men from infecting their subjects with soul-destroying error. The Dissenters said they were neither heretical nor turbulent, but the men who refused to give the magistrate, by oath and subscriptions, an assurance that they were orthodox and peaceable, must be assumed the opposite. If they said that they only differed in minor matters, why did they secede and make divisions? Such men were not innocent sufferers, but injurious aggressors. But, after all, their demands for toleration were vague and contrary to their own principles. In support of this statement Assheton gave the testimony of twenty Dissenting divines against toleration and in favour of enforced uniformity, during the time of the Civil War. He concluded, " Unless there be something which is sinful required as the condition of our communion, it appears to me to be schism to withdraw ourselves. Is it religion or policy to tolerate those who hate and detest, and desire to extirpate the government of the Church? "

It was in 1670 that Edward Fowler wrote the book so savagely attacked by Bunyan. This was " The Principles and Practices of certain Moderate Divines of the Church of England." Writing as a Latitudinarian, he urged that charity would solve the problems at stake, and that the power of the magistrate should not be used to impose rules and conditions on Christians. He said that the Nonconformists held a middle position in respect to Church government and ceremonies, and pleaded for mercy for them. His own position was shown in his argument that though episcopacy was the best form of government, it was not indispensable; and that though rites and forms of prayer might be imposed by authority, they should always be indifferent, and must always be consonant with the teachings of Scripture.

In 1669 there came from the pen of Samuel Parker, Sheldon's chaplain, " A Discourse of Ecclesiastical Polity, wherein the Authority of the Civil Magistrate over the Consciences of Subjects in matters of External Religion is Asserted, the Mischiefs and Inconveniences of Toleration are Represented, and all Pretences pleaded in behalf of Liberty of Conscience are fully Answered." The book, which was published at Sheldon's request, contained a preface in which the author described himself as a person of " a tame and softly humour," but talked about " the pride and insolence of a few peevish, ignorant, and malapert preachers," " proud, ignorant, and supercilious hypocrites," " morose and childish zealots." He bade the author of the " Friendly Debate " be careful how he laid aside his vizor, or, if discovered, he would be pelted with slander. He then turned to attack the unbelievers and Hobbists and wits, who talked loudly about credulity and the impostures of priests, and those who mocked at religion as hypocrisy and superstition.

Parker set forth the necessity of an ecclesiastical sovereignty over conscience in matters of religion. Religion was so far from being exempted from the restraints of law and penalties that nothing required them more. The remiss government of consciences had ever been the most fatal miscarriage in all commonwealths. Endless mischiefs ensued from allowing liberty of conscience. In the first ages of the world the kingly power and priestly function were always vested in the same person, and when they were separated in the Jewish State, the supremacy was annexed to the civil power. There was no need for our Saviour to give princes any new commission to exercise the power antecedently vested in them. The power of the Church was purely spiritual. When the Emperors became Christian, the ecclesiastical jurisdiction was reannexed to the civil power, and so continued till the usurpation of the Bishops of Rome, though since the Reformation the ecclesiastical power of princes had been invaded by some pragmatical divines. Moral virtues were the most material part of religion. As the civil magistrate might enjoin anything in morality that contradicted not the ends of morality, so he might in religious worship, if what he enjoined did not debauch men's practices or their conceptions of the Deity. Men had a liberty of conscience over all their actions, whether moral or strictly religious, as far as it concerned their judgments, but not their practices. The substantial part of religious worship was eternal, and out of the reach of the civil magistrate. Under the Christian dispensation God had left the disposal of outward worship to the power and discretion of the Church.

Religion was useful or dangerous in a State as the temper of mind it bred was peaceful or turbulent. The dread of invisible powers was not of itself sufficient to awe people into subjection, but tended more probably to tumults and seditions, as shown by the ungovernableness and tempers of some of the sects. The fanatics of all nations and religions agreed in the same principles of sedition, and to permit different religious sects in a Commonwealth was to allow occasions of constant public disturbance. The corrupt passions and humours of men made toleration infinitely unsafe. Toleration was praised by oppressed parties because it gave them opportunity to overthrow the settled state of things. Every man who desired indulgence was engaged by his principles to strive for alterations, while a bare indulgence only exasperated them against the State. Puritanism asserted that nothing ought to be established in the worship of God but what is expressly commanded in the Bible. This was a wild, novel, and unreasonable principle, taking away all possibility of settlement in Church and State, and was the main pretence of all pious villainies. The argument of the Puritans would prove that God ought to have determined all the circumstances of worship. They refused to obey the magistrate, with the result that the magistrate's only hope of obtaining obedience lay in forbidding what he wished to be done. They objected that he might impose things sinful or superstitious, an argument against all government. Ecclesiastical jurisdiction might be abused, yet it was less mischievous than liberty of conscience, as tyranny was less mischievous than rebellion or anarchy.

A great deal was being made of the argument of scandal—that is, anything which occasions sin in others. But the proper obligations of scandal extended only to indifferent things. The Dissenters made a pretence of scandal to excuse their refusal to conform, but was not their separation a worse thing? They scrupled to renounce the Covenant, but that was no excuse for their conventicles. It would be sinful to comply with their groundless scruples. They themselves were a cause of scandal in their resistance to the command of authority and their denial of the obligation to obedience. The apostolic maxim about obeying God rather than men referred to a great and obvious duty, and not to doubtful and disputable cases. Of two conflicting obligations the greater cancelled the less. In public affairs men were governed not by private, but by public judgment. The Puritans' tenderness of consciences was really one of the rankest heresies.

Owen asked Baxter to answer " The Ecclesiastical Polity." " But," said Baxter, " I had contended so often and with little thanks from the Independents that I would not." Moreover, Parker had spoken kindly of Baxter in his book. So Owen answered it himself in " Truth and Innocency Vindicated; in a Survey of a Discourse of Ecclesiastical Polity " (1669). He took the line that the determination of what is true or false in religion binds the consciences of men antecedently to any commands of the magistrate. The right to control morals does not give the right to control worship. There could be no mistake about morals, but there are great differences of opinion about worship. In cases of conflict of authority that of God is superior, and this recognition will guide men with regard to the things of God. He maintained that if liberty of conscience were granted, men who had a sense of duty would use it peacefully, and therefore it should be allowed to all but wilful disturbers of the peace.

The anonymous author of " A Case of Conscience " (1669) dealt with the question whether a Nonconformist who had not taken the Oxford oath might live in London and yet be a good Christian. He replied generally to the " Friendly Debate," the " Ecclesiastical Polity " and the two tracts of Sir Charles Wolseley already mentioned. The author of the " Case of Conscience " dealt with his three opponents separately, but his main thesis was the same throughout: the absolute supremacy of conscience. Patrick had asked, " How can a minister of

Christ disobey his sovereign in matters where Christ and His laws are not concerned?" Thus, the law that a Nonconformist minister should not reside within five miles of London was in no way repugnant to the law of God. The answer was ingenious. Not every transgression of a statute is a deadly sin, for a command which is not for the people's weal has no authority over conscience. The magistrate must judge as to the making of the law, but we must judge as to our obedience to it. Some laws, too, like the law ordering people to be buried in woollen, had fallen into desuetude, and could make no claim to obedience. Turning to Parker, this writer said that the circumstances of worship must either be necessary or not necessary. If not necessary, what authority had the Church to impose them? Nay, rather it was an ill thing to impose them. Either the ceremonies edified or they did not: if they did not, men could not be expected to observe them. As for scandal, to wound weak consciences was to sin against Christ.

Another reply to Parker may be noticed for its title. It appeared in 1670, and was called " Insolence and Impudence Triumphant: Envy and Fury Enthroned. The Mirror of Malice and Madness in a late Treatise entitled ' A Discourse of Ecclesiastical Polity, etc.': or, the lively Portraiture of Mr. S. P., limned and drawn by his own Hand: and a brief View of his tame and softly, *alias* wild and savage Humour. As also an account of his cold and frigid, *i.e.* fiery complexion. Being (in short) a Collection of some of his Intemperate Railings and profane Satires: wherein he hath abused Religion and the Power of Godliness, drolled on Piety, and all that is sacred. Together with a Complication of notorious Errors, repugnant to the Doctrine of the Church of England."

In 1671 Parker replied to his critics with " A Defence and Continuation of the Ecclesiastical Polity." It was chiefly directed against Owen, against whom he quoted that divine's own intolerant speeches and sermons in the days when Puritanism was in the ascendant. " And this man, this tender man, that will not endure any of his disciples to be so much as present at our antichristian way of worship, is no doubt a fit agent to treat with us for indulgence and mutual toleration." [1] " The tenderness of vulgar conscience is nothing else but the stubbornness of popular folly. They have been abused into absurd principles and seditious practices, and then to be at all adventure tenacious of their casual prejudices, against the convictions of reason and the commands of authority, shall be gloried in as the pure result of a nicer integrity and more precise godliness." [2]

But now a much abler controversialist appeared on the scene in the person of Andrew Marvell, whose first contribution to the debate was " The Rehearsal Transprosed: or Animadversions

[1] " Continuation," p. 500.   [2] *Ibid.*, p. 539.

upon a late book entitled A Preface, showing what Grounds there are of Fears and Jealousies of Popery." The title-page said it was printed by J. D. for the Assigns of John Calvin and Theodore Beza at the Sign of the King's Indulgence on the South Side of the Lake Lemane." In the summer of 1672 had been published "Bishop Bramhall's Vindication of himself and the Episcopal Clergy from the Presbyterian Charge of Popery." To this Samuel Parker had contributed the preface mentioned in the title of Marvell's book. It was a violent production, in which he accused the Dissenters of preaching rebellion and joining with atheists to mock at the Anglican clergy. Their champions were statesmen who were aiming to bring in popery under the pretence of giving toleration, and "the great bell-wether of disturbance and sedition" was Dr. John Owen. The title of Marvell's book, of course, had reference to the Duke of Buckingham's play, "The Rehearsal," which appeared in the previous year. In that play, Bayes (who is Dryden satirized) tells Johnson that his rule of transversion is that if a book is in prose, he turns it into verse, but if it be in verse, he turns it into prose. Johnson replies that "putting verse into prose should be called transprosing." [1] Throughout Marvell's book " Mr. Bayes " stands for Parker, " I. O." for John Owen, and " Mr. B." for Baxter. There is, perhaps, more of boisterous railing and mockery than solid argument. Wit, vulgarity, scurrility, and learning are all there. Marvell poured ridicule on Parker, jeered at incidents in his past history, and altogether handled him very roughly. This is what Parker thought of him: " Among these lewd revilers the lewdest was one whose name was Marvell. As he had lived in all manner of wicked-ness from his youth, so, being of a singular impudence and petulancy by nature, he exercised the province of a satirist for the use of the faction, being not so much a satirist through quickness of wit as sourness of temper: of but indifferent parts, except it were in the talent of railing and malignity." [2] But this was not published till long after, and Marvell never knew it. What he did know was that Parker, now an archdeacon, produced in 1673 " A Reproof to the Rehearsal Transprosed in a Discourse to its Author." It was a work of over 500 pages, and was an attempt to answer both Marvell and Owen. Marvell had called him a mad priest, a buffoon, a *pestis ecclesiæ*, and had told some vulgar stories. So Parker called Marvell an awkward dunce, a poor rat, a smutty lubber, a buffoon, a despicable scribbler, and other choice things, and spoke of Dr. John Owen as an old cob nut in controversy. He repeated his old arguments, reviled the Dissenters as rebels, with their Puritan army, their Good Old Cause, and their Martin Mar-prelates, and pointedly referred to Charing Cross and Lincoln's

---

[1] Act I. sc. i.   [2] S. Parker, " History of His Own Time," p. 332.

Inn Fields, where rebels had been executed in times past. " The rudest book that ever was published " was Marvell's description of it.[1]

There were other replies; " Rosemary and Bayes," " A Common-place Book out of the ' Rehearsal Transprosed,' Digested under these several Heads, viz. his Logic, Chronology, Wit, Geography, Anatomy, History, Loyalty, with Useful Notes "; " S'too him Bayes: or Some Observations upon the Humour of Writing Rehearsals Transprosed "; the last, " writ by one Hodges." [2] Edmund Hickeringill published " Gregory, Father Grey-beard, with his Vizard Off," described as " printed by Robin Hood, at the sign of the He-Cow I.O., if it be not a Bull, on the South-West and by West end of Lake Lemane." It was intended as an answer to Marvell, but was a furious attack on the Nonconformists, particularly Calamy, Owen, and Baxter. Hickeringill was an Anglican clergyman, who had the leading characteristics of the tribe of Ishmael, and in this, as well as in all his writings, he showed a wild humour, a tendency to coarseness, and a facility in the production of ribald rhymes. Richard Leigh, of Queen's College, Oxford, then an actor in London, wrote " The Transproser Rehearsed; or, the Fifth Act of Mr. Bayes's Play." Marvell was under the impression that Parker had written it. Other people thought that Milton had helped Marvell in the first part of the " Rehearsal Transprosed," and so several of these writers, including Leigh, and Parker himself in his " Reproof," attacked Milton, it would seem undeservedly. Robert Ferguson, the plotter, dedicated to Sir Charles Wolseley in 1673 " A Sober Enquiry into the Nature, Measure, and Principle of Moral Virtue," which contained " reflections " on three late books: the " Ecclesiastical Polity," the " Defence and Continuation," and the " Reproof." Marvell finally replied to all his opponents in " The Rehearsal Transprosed. The Second Part. Occasioned by Two Letters: the first Printed by a nameless Author, entitled ' A Reproof etc.' The Second Letter left for me at a Friend's House, Dated Nov. 3rd, 1673, Subscribed J. G. and concluding with these words: ' If thou darest to Print or Publish any Lie or 'Libel against Doctor Parker, By the Eternal God I will cut thy Throat.' " This Second Part was published in 1673, and was perhaps a trifle more serious than the first, and still marred by coarseness; but that was a fault of the time rather than the author. Marvell told tales of Parker's Puritan past and his Puritan father and grandfather, referred several times to some scandal about a curate and a girl called Mary Parker, the similarity of name evidently coming in useful, and was generally savage and scurrilous. When he kept to the question at issue

[1] Margoliouth, " Poems and Letters of Andrew Marvell," 1927, II. 312.
[2] *Idem, ibid.*

his general line was that he was against persecution and in favour of toleration except for atheists and Papists.

" The Rehearsal Transprosed " seemed to have caused some trouble in Government circles. Roger L'Estrange, as Licenser of the Press, was examined about it before Secretary Coventry on January 23rd, 1673. He said he had never heard of it till the first impression was on sale. Brome, the bookseller, told him that it was printed for Ponder. When the second impression was preparing, two of the sheets had been seized by one of the Wardens of the Stationers' Company. This was in September 1672, and there was evidently some thought of suppressing it, but Lord Anglesey had told L'Estrange that the King would not have it suppressed, for Parker (one version says " Parliament ") had done him wrong, and this man had done him right, and so he must give Ponder a licence for it. L'Estrange replied that there were some things in the book which ought not to have been licensed, and showed him some of them. Anglesey looked at them, and agreed, and then told him to alter them and let the book pass. At Ponder's request L'Estrange gave him a note of Anglesey's directions from the King. He then read the book, struck out several unbecoming passages, and issued the licence, which was signed by the Warden of the Company, who gave it to a clerk to enter. This the clerk refused to do, though L'Estrange urged him, and said that he had been overruled himself, and so he must also give way. Ponder told L'Estrange that Anglesey had sent for the Warden and clerk and threatened to bring the matter before the King and Council, but, at L'Estrange's personal request, Anglesey directed an inquiry into the matter. L'Estrange told Coventry that the book was not printed according to his emendations. The first licence was accordingly withdrawn, and a second granted to Ponder, who altered the title-page and promised to use the corrected copy. Ponder was brought up and examined two days later. He said he knew nobody who had the proofs in his hands except Dr. Owen. He did not remember saying that Lord Anglesey would have the Warden and clerk before the King and Council, because there was no reason for saying such a thing. He admitted that he had not excised all that L'Estrange had told him to, but said that L'Estrange had waived several of the alterations at his special request.[1]

The King's Declaration of Indulgence led to the printing in 1672 of two pamphlets with much the same title. In " Toleration not to be Abused " the question was put whether the Presbyterians might now cease to attend the services of the Establishment and set up distinct congregations. People were saying they ought to make use of the King's indulgence, or they would seem ungrateful. This writer said that the King had

[1] Hist. MSS. Com. VII. i. 517–518; Finch MSS. II. 9, 10.

permitted, but not ordered, meetings, for reasons of State and to keep the malcontents quiet. Presbyterian writers had declared against schism and toleration. By encouraging separate meetings they would give away their case after all they had said, and would encourage toleration, " with all its frightful consequences, the competition of rival sects, confusion, schism and popery." " A lover of truth and peace," believed to be Francis Fulwood, published at Exeter " Toleration not to be Abused by the Independents." From the writings of Independent divines he argued for the lawfulness of communicating with the Church of England. There were worse disorders in the primitive Church—for example, at Corinth—than those complained of in the Establishment, yet the Apostles discountenanced schism. The English Church had given no ground for separation, as the Roman Church had. The Independents, judged by their conduct in the past, were averse to toleration, and therefore all the more obliged not to abuse the present Indulgence. The bare suspension of the penal laws did not cancel the obligations to avoid causeless division. Let them not so far " idolise a sect or an opinion as to prefer it before the peace and settlement of a Church and nation."

The Rev. William Assheton, chaplain to the Duke of Ormonde, in " The Cases of Scandal and Persecution " (1674), said that the Nonconformists were so hardened with prejudice and blinded with passion that nothing would convince them. To Baxter's argument that to subscribe would cause scandal to the weaker brethren, he replied that it was their not subscribing that was the scandal. Many of them were persuaded of the lawfulness of the liturgy and the rest of the Anglican system, and they were simply disobedient. At the same time he took the opportunity of rebuking the nonconforming conformity of some of the Anglican clergy. Persecution, he said, was " an inflicting of outward temporal evils for the exercise of *true* religion." The Church of England in her *credenda* did not enjoin belief in lies, nor in her *agenda* did she order the commission of sin, but the impossible attitude of the Dissenters was shown in Newcome's sermon in St. Paul's, February 8th, 1646, in which he said, " There is scarce any difference so small and inconsiderable but the divulging and propagating of it may prove dangerous and pernicious, and in the event intolerable." Assheton quoted from Dissenting writings in proof of the doctrine that the supreme magistrate must determine the circumstances to be used in the worship and service of God. Dissenters were not punished for preaching and praying, but for not observing those circumstances about preaching and praying which authority required of them. A man might worship God according to his conscience in his own family, but it was the duty of the magistrate to keep him from infecting his other subjects with soul-destroying error.

Dissenters were really persecutors, for there was another form of persecution. " Bitter taunts, rude sarcasms, unmannerly jeers, scandalous reproaches, are their daily exercise, whereby they vex the righteous souls, weaken the hands, discourage the endeavours of their honest orthodox conforming brethren." The chief reason why so many Nonconformists refused subscription were two: their credit; they were ashamed to confess their error, and their interest; many of them gained more from their party than they would from the Church if they conformed.

Thomas Tomkins, chaplain to the Archbishop of Canterbury, printed in 1675 " The Modern Pleas for Comprehension, Toleration, and the Taking away the Obligations to the Renouncing of the Covenant." The second edition, 1680, bore the title " The New Distemper: or The Dissenters' Usual Pleas for Comprehension, etc." He urged that the man who can submit to no law unless it is perfect can only submit to those made by himself. The terms of communion which the Church of England imposed were not sinful, in the opinion of the most learned Nonconformist leaders. Calamy had said that he could accept all, were it not for causing scandal to others, and Tombes had written a book showing the lawfulness of attending the Anglican services. Those who were against all forms of prayer were but few in number. Yet when the King, after his restoration, issued a declaration inviting them to use only those parts of the Prayer Book of which they approved, many would not even do that. It could not be that they objected to ceremonies as ceremonies; witness the significance they ascribed to sitting at communion and the ceremonies ordered at the taking of the Covenant by the Ordinance of February 2nd, 1643, which enacted that it should be taken with uncovered head, and with right hand outstretched. If they had such " weak brethren " among them as were offended at a simple ceremony, how was it that such persons were chosen as their ministers? If any errors of conscience were sufficient to make void a law, there could be no law. A great deal was said about the declaration of assent and consent, but really the words were made terrible as a trick to rouse men's jealousies; they were nothing like so sweeping as the affirmation of the Covenant. Dissenters were clamouring for liberty of conscience, but they could not agree as to what it meant, or what were its true bounds. Some of them said that if there should be a comprehension which would admit the Presbyterians, the remaining Dissenters would be so few and insignificant that no toleration need be granted them. But if the Presbyterians really wanted comprehension they should show their sincerity by using as much of the Prayer Book as they conscientiously could in their private meetings, and observing as many of the Church's rules as possible. The question had been raised whether force could be used in propagating religion. The very people who raised it were the people who propagated their religion by the sword, and not by the civil power. Force might be used in pulling down Antichrist; there was no question whether Christ or Antichrist should be King. The Old Testament Scriptures witnessed to the magistrate's authority in maintaining religion by force, and if it were said that Christianity gave to the magistrates no powers which they had not before, it might also be said that the magistrates, on becoming Christians, suffered no diminution of power. The severities now used were mild compared with those exercised in enforcing the Covenant. The Presbyterians, pleading for comprehension, were saying that the differences between themselves and the Church were so small that comprehension was only a matter of a few concessions on the Church's part. Yet in the late wars some of their preachers said that the differences were so great that it was worth all the war to get rid of the Church and her authority. How far were these men's demands really genuine? How far did their approval of episcopacy and the liturgy go? Were the bishops merely to be civil officers? Was the Prayer Book to be used or let alone? How much of the " Good Old Cause " did they desire to retain? Churchmen really wanted to know. Having obtained some concessions, would they want more? If so, there would never be any settlement, and what the Church gained by increase of numbers she would lose by instability of principle.

Comprehension, then, being so difficult and uncertain, what could be said for toleration? It would undoubtedly lead to a multiplication of sects and schisms, for everyone who had a freak would demand liberty to propagate it. Men who were dishonest, and men who were weak-minded and liable to be imposed on, would alike plead conscience. Conscience, taken absolutely, can be no safe rule of action or belief. Moreover, these men were not only hostile to the Church, but hostile also to the Crown. They had their New Models in civil as well as in ecclesiastical administration. Their very zeal for the Covenant showed how little they had repented it. What reasons, then, were offered for tolerating these people? First, because they were so few and could do no harm. But were they so few? There were the old army, the purchasers of Church lands, their children brought up in their tenets. In the same breath it was said that there should be toleration, because so many were suffering at the hands of the Church. If there were so many, it were better to hinder them from meeting. If they had no hope of toleration, their numbers would diminish. Their merit was urged. No doubt there were good individuals among them, but as a party they had been of no benefit either to the Church or nation. It was said that they would be a great assistance against popery. The Church of England divines

had been a great bulwark against popery, but the Nonconformists often called popery what was not so, and if they had
made less noise they might have had more weight. Great
threats had been uttered about Nonconformist ministers going
out of the country, but these threats had not alarmed the magistrates. It was said that civil penalties in religious matters only
made hypocrites, but this was an argument effective against all
laws; quite as many hypocrites would be bred by toleration,
which would make it safe for any men to pretend to a grievance
against the Church.

The author of " A Representation of the State of Christianity
in England," published in 1674, blamed the Dissenters for the
low condition of the national religious life, and accused them of
despising the Creed, the Lord's Prayer, and the Ten Commandments as much as the liturgy itself. The Lord's Day was scorned
and neglected by the Anabaptists and Libertines, who made
choice of that day to engage in the most servile works and
drudgeries. The churches in many places were dirty and in
bad repair, because care bestowed on the buildings was called
popery. Not only the Anabaptists, but also the members of
other sects, deferred and denied the rite of baptism, and made
it the object of their scoffs. There was a widespread neglect of
the Holy Communion, even at the three great festivals, and
such was the spirit abroad that churchwardens often refused to
provide the bread and wine for it. Not only was there a common neglect of marriage and a laxity in keeping marriage vows,
but there were people, mostly sectaries, who despised marriage
rites, and for a form of marriage relied on the bare word of the
contracting parties. Even the decent rites of burial were disregarded. Excommunication used to be a terrible penalty, but
now few were excommunicated who had not already excommunicated themselves. Many of the clergy, for fear of their
people, and some of the gentry at that, dared not use the whole
Church service without omission and mangling. Because of
those who refused to pay their tithes, many of the clergy were
deprived of part of their livelihood, and had to put up with it
if they wished to live in peace. The clergy were not to be
blamed for this state of affairs, for though it was true there were
ignorant and immoral clergy, and there were those who pretended to conform for the sake of their livings, and acted in
such a way as to make their people despise the Prayer Book,
yet never, perhaps, had a higher standard been set than was
set by the generality of them. On the other hand, the dregs of
the people gathered " churches," and expounded the Scriptures
with ignorance, nonsense, rudeness, and impudence. It seemed
that to be fanatic and seditious rendered men incapable of
rational argument or instruction. The sectaries preached the
vilest errors, and claimed the same infallibility as the Pope.

The Papists might withhold the chalice, but the sectaries withheld communion altogether from those who could not give what their teachers considered proofs of conversion.   The Latin service was just as intelligible as their mystical nonsense and bold blasphemy; the idolatry of the Papist was just as excusable as the superstitious sourness and irreverence of the Dissenters. The Declaration of Indulgence had given the widest liberty ever granted by a sovereign, yet the greater part of the Independents and Baptists, as well as all the Quakers, just went on in their own way, without leave or licence.   They had no respect for authority, and aimed at popular government; in fact, the sticklers for liberty of conscience were the fighters for the Good Old Cause.

Complaints of the turbulent and rebellious character of the Dissenters were common enough.   Marchamont Nedham,[1] in his " Character of a Rigid Presbyter " (1661), blamed the Presbyterians for the ruin of the King and kingdom; Thomas Bellamy, in his " Philanax Anglicus " (1663), showed from history and from Protestant writings that they had always been the seditious and rebellious enemies of princes, and Edward Pettitt, in 1683, argued the same way in his " Visions of the Reformation."   Henry Foulis published in 1662, and republished in 1674, at Oxford, " The History of the Wicked Plots and Conspiracies of our Pretended Saints."   He said they were now boasting that they had brought the King back, though they did nothing for him until 1660.   On the other hand, they had made many laws against him and his friends.   When the Rump was restored by Monk, they had promptly ordered the Solemn League and Covenant to be read in every church every year,[2] and had passed another order that no man could hold office till he had declared that the war against the King was just and lawful.[3]   The Covenant, which they were still anxious to retain, allowed only a conditional obedience to the King. Their attitude to the Church had not changed.   They had refused any toleration to Churchmen, they had tried to beggar the clergy, and they now said that conformity " would strip these nations of the glory in which they had excelled all the rest of the world, even a learned, able, holy ministry, and a people sincere and serious and understanding in matters of religion."   Crofton said episcopacy must be extirpated if the King and kingdom were to be preserved from God's anger. It was the same with the Prayer Book.   Kneeling at the sacrament was a stumbling-block; the man who knelt was a thief. If people would only refuse to communicate with those who introduced such practices, they would have to desist.   Though

---

[1] Wood, " Athenæ," II. 625–631.   [2] March 5th, 1660.
[3] March 12th, 1660.

men might receive good comfort from the Prayer Book, yet they sinned if they went where it was used.

The same attack was continued in " The Countermine: or, a Short but True Discovery of the Dangerous Principles and Secret Practices of the Dissenting Party, especially the Presbyterians." It was published in 1677, by Dr. John Nalson, who was not a clergyman, but a justice of the peace for the Isle of Ely. His main thesis was that under the cloak of religion the Dissenters were always scheming rebellion, and were now busy with their old stratagem of rousing fears of popery, and thereby ingratiating themselves with the common people. The Dissenters pleaded great regard for the Scriptures, though they did not obey the authorities set over them in Church and State. They evaded plain commands by saying they were unlawful. No doubt many of them were honest, but ignorant, men, who were led astray by the ringleaders of faction. To gain esteem they made a pretence of exemplary piety in their actions, words, looks, gestures, and garments, and they were violent in denouncing the sins of other people. They were maintained by free-will offerings, a system which suited their followers, who could withdraw their gifts at will. They took advantage of punishment to call it persecution and render the Government odious to the people. They endeavoured to insinuate themselves into the favour of persons of quality, and yet were great enemies to the nobility and gentry. They endeared themselves to the people by poisoning their opinion of the clergy. Their doctrine was the Calvinist view that God only chose a few to eternal life, their followers being the select few; a pleasing doctrine which filled them with a boundless confidence in themselves and a proud contempt for others. No people were so addicted to debates, envyings, strife, slander, and condemnation of others. They propagated uncharitableness, separated friends, beguiled silly women, divided husbands and wives, and set whole towns by the ears. Thus they became the cause of widespread unbelief.

Holding that all people, princes, and magistrates were bound to pull down Antichrist, which with them was episcopacy, they said that if princes would not do it, the people must get the power in their hands and do it themselves; hence they were continually grasping at dominion. They exalted preaching because they gained people by it, but their preaching was largely self-advertisement, and they taught, untruly, that the Church was against preaching. They had turned the Lord's Day into a Jewish Sabbath. They tired out the inferior magistrates with their obstinacy; then, when the laws were suspended, they persuaded their followers that this was the peculiar blessing of God on their cause. All expedients to reclaim them were useless, and it would be better to banish them all.

In " The Common Interest of King and People," published

in the following year, Nalson continued the same line of argument, with special reference to the Presbyterians. He said it was a common saying that " the Presbyterians brought the late King to the scaffold, and held him by the hair while the Independents cut off his royal head." Presbytery was, nevertheless, just as great an enemy to democracy and parliaments as to monarchy, for Presbyterians really ruled by a tyrannical consistorial government over magistrates, clergy, and laity, in a way destructive of the people's liberty and property. There was but small difference between a Jesuit and a Geneva presbyter, for both aimed at supremacy.

In " The Project of Peace," also published in 1678, Nalson complained that the Nonconformists, following their own traditions, strained at gnats of ceremonial and swallowed the camel of disobedience. " It is you," he said to them, " who are popish, while you endeavour to obtrude upon us your infallibility." The great obstacles to reunion were their education which hardened men in their habits and customs, their self-interest, their pride, and their ambition; and the decay of Christian piety lay at their door. The Anglican Church did not deny a single article of the Christian faith, or order a single unlawful custom. Without unity, happiness was impossible. Government was appointed by God to promote unity; therefore, disobedience was a damnable sin. The Dissenters now objected to the dignity and honour of the higher clergy, but they were glad enough to accept both their power and their revenues under the usurpers. The Papists were making common cause with the Dissenters: " I have heard from authentic hands of one Father Brown, a Jesuit, who boasted on his death at Ingeston Briggs in Scotland that he had preached as downright popery in the field conventicles as ever he had preached at Rome itself." [1]

Amidst the strife and contention one Anglican had been making a well-meant, if ill-received, effort at peacemaking. In 1675 there was printed a little work entitled " The Naked Truth," advocating the policy of comprehension. It was published without an author's name, but it leaked out that it was the work of Dr. Herbert Croft, Bishop of Hereford. He began by urging that Churchmen and Dissenters had a common ground in the Scriptures, in which both sides expressed their belief. He would not contend for ceremonies if they gave offence. Personally, he had no objection to a surplice, if it were a clean one, and he saw no reason for forcing men with conscientious scruples to kneel at Holy Communion. He was willing that the Prayer Book should be revised to meet the wishes of the greatest number, but once revised it should be conformed to without exception. He did not despise a university educa-

[1] " Project of Peace," p. 246.

tion, but he would not insist on a degree in admitting candidates to ordination; piety should be the great criterion, learning when it could be got. He did not insist absolutely on episcopal ordination in the case of the clergy, and he would not even limit the administration of confirmation to the Bishops only. He sympathised with Dissenters in their dislike of lay officials. He disliked them himself and their procedure in the ecclesiastical courts, and he disliked lay ministers. He wound up by appealing to Nonconformists to drop their attitude of mere opposition, and urged them to remember that Protestant disunion was Rome's opportunity.

This work caused great excitement, and incurred much abuse. On February 20th, 1676, Gunning, Bishop of Ely, preached before the King from John xx. 21–23, and controverted Croft's pamphlet. Three days later an *imprimatur* was granted to a tract, " Animadversions on a Pamphlet entitled ' The Naked Truth.' " This was by Dr. Francis Turner, Master of St. John's College, Cambridge. He suggested that Croft should have called his work " The Truth Flayed," for why not skin it as well as strip it? He defended the Creeds, General Councils, and the bishops, and said that Croft had admitted that the New Testament condemned the Nonconformists for breaking a plain commandment, and then blamed the Church for enforcing it. The Nonconformists in some dioceses did not number one in twenty, yet for these he wished to abolish all the ceremonies, and make not only a naked truth, but a naked Church as well. Everyone could see what patience and gentleness the Church had shown towards the Dissenters in the matter of ceremonies To Croft's complaint that the surplices in the cathedrals were often dirty, he replied that the cathedrals were dirty too. Did he propose to abolish them? He told a story which threw an unpleasant light on the way conformity was observed by some of the Anglican clergy. " I have heard of one that wore his surplice over his heel. . . . When he came into the reading pew, where he must put on his whites, he used to hold up one of his legs behind him (like a goose), and resting it upon his mat, he would hang his surplice upon his foot, that he might be able to swear he both wore the surplice, and bowed the knee at the Name of Jesus."

Another reply was " Lex Talionis: or, the Author of ' Naked Truth ' Stripped Naked." This also came out in 1676, and has been ascribed variously to Dr. Gunning, to Dr. Philip Fell, Fellow of Eton, and Dr. William Lloyd, Dean of Bangor. It referred to the " Animadversions " as well as " Naked Truth." The writer argued that ceremonies did matter, and that causing scandal to the conformists was a greater mischief than causing scandal to Dissenters. He maintained the excellence of Anglican preaching, and controverted what the Bishop of Hereford had said about bishops and priests; he had acknowledged the apostolic dignity and antiquity of the episcopate, and then went about to destroy it. To the statement that separation had caused some persons to despise the Church and turn to popery, this pamphlet replied that giving way to separatists would not bring them back again. " A Modest Survey of the most considerable things in a Discourse lately published, entitled ' Naked Truth,' " was licensed on May 23rd, 1676. The authorship is uncertain; Burnet has been suggested, but the arguments do not seem to be his. The writer said that the author of " Naked Truth " meant well, but his suggestions would only make the divisions worse. He should have first consulted his ordinary and the bishops. Evidently the writer had no suspicion of the real author of the work he was attacking. He accused him of irrelevancy, saying that there was really no trouble about the Thirty-nine Articles, so he need not have spent fifteen pages on them; the Church was so far from being attacked by the Nonconformists for dogmatizing that they thought the Articles too wide and vague. The Dissenters dogmatized about much smaller matters, and any relaxation in that respect would drive them further from the Church. Bowing to the altar had never been ordered, and so his discussion of that point was also needless. But as for ceremonies in general, it was unreasonable to make changes without very great cause. This writer also spoke highly of Anglican preaching, and said that the separatists had nothing to boast of in that respect. He controverted Croft's statements about the episcopate, both from the point of view of history and theology, but admitted that the Church of England did not unchurch the foreign Protestants, who had no bishops through no fault of their own. Finally, he accused his opponent of having made all the enemies of peace to triumph, and of putting arguments into the mouths of the Church's adversaries.

Andrew Marvell also took part in the controversy, not against Croft, but against Turner's " Animadversions." His contribution was entitled " Mr. Smirke: or, The Divine in Mode." The name of Mr. Smirke was taken from Sir George Etherege's comedy, " The Man of Mode." Speaking of Croft's work, Marvell said, " It is a book of that kind, that no Christian scarce can peruse it without wishing himself had been the author, and almost imagining that he is so: the conceptions therein being of so eternal an idea, that every man finds it to be but the copy of an original in his own mind, and though he never read it till now, wonders it could be so long before he remembered it." [1] In an appended essay on General Councils he endeavoured to set forth the absurdity of imposing new articles of faith, as shown by the controversies at and after the early councils. Bishop Croft wrote personally to Marvell to

[1] Marvell, " Works," III. 9.

thank him for his " humane civility and Christian charity shown
to the author of ' Naked Truth,' so bespotted with the dirty
language of foul-mouthed beasts," and for setting forth " Mr.
Smirke in so trim and proper a dress." Marvell replied, on
July 15th, 1676, " As long as God shall lend you life and health
I reckon our Church is indestructible." [1] On March 29th,
1676, an order was issued from the Council to Roger L'Estrange
to search for certain unlicensed books, together with their
authors, printers, and publishers. Among the books in question
was " The Naked Truth." [2]

In 1676 there came out " The Catholic Naked Truth," by a
Papist. Some people, Dr. William Bates among them, thought
Marvell was the author. Marvell was amused, and noted
gravely that the divines of the Church of England thought it
was not so good as the merry parts of " The Rehearsal Transprosed," and that though well written it had been written
with an ill purpose. The Bishop of London several times called
the attention of the Council to it, but no one took any notice.[3]

There was a controversy in 1679 about the right of bishops
to sit in judgment in capital cases. It soon drifted into an
attack on episcopacy in general. In a revised reprint of a tract
published at the time of the Rebellion, and bearing the curious
title " Omnia Comesta a Bello," the author charged the poverty
of the nation on the pride, luxury, and oppression of the prelates, declared that all the reformed churches had cast off
episcopacy except the Church of England, inquired why there
should be this waste of money which might be given to the
poor, and whether other nations had not got on much better
without bishops. A Churchman promptly replied with " Ananias
and Sapphira Discovered." Ananias and Sapphira kept back
part: this man would take all. The question about waste
was first asked by Judas. England was not poor, it had never
been so wealthy. England kept bishops because episcopacy
was part of the universal system of the Church, and because
episcopacy was the greatest hindrance to the Papacy, as was
shown by the way the Pope treated the bishops at Trent. The
State had its officials, the Church had to have hers, and whether
other countries were better off without bishops let the world
judge. The complaint about the bishops' wealth really came
from those who had had to give up Church lands of which
they had taken unlawful possession.

Another attack on the bishops bore the title " A Disputation:
Proving that it is not convenient to grant unto Ministers Secular
Jurisdiction and to make them Lords and Statesmen in Parliament " (1679). The writer argued that if the clergy did their
proper work they would have no time to hold State offices.

---

[1] Marvell, " Works," I. xxxii.   [2] C.S.P.D., March 29th, 1676.
[3] " Poems and Letters of Andrew Marvell," ed. Margoliouth, 1927, II. 323.

If the Government wished to consult the clergy, let it consult all the most experienced and prudent divines in the nation. The clergy pleaded prescriptive right to these State offices and functions; no matter, let the Sovereign and Parliament correct this abuse. An archbishop was but an eminent presbyter, as was Peter among the Apostles, or as the foreman of the jury, the rest of the Apostles had equal commission and authority with him. He objected to the title " Lord Bishop," and to the princely state some of the bishops kept, and he said, quite incorrectly, that archbishops were ordained presbyters, ordained bishops and ordained archbishops, the last two " ordinations " being null and void. Like all the Puritans, he objected to lay chancellors. He complained, too, that excommunications were bought and sold (this is probably a reference to the fees), and that while the worst men were spared and countenanced, the best men were harassed and anathematised.

Dr. Henry Dodwell, formerly Fellow of Trinity College, Dublin, published in 1679 a ponderous and learned treatise of over 600 pages, entitled " Separation of Churches from Episcopal Government, as practised by the present Nonconformists, proved Schismatical." It was a general defence of the divine and supreme authority of the episcopate in the Church, and a demonstration that the action of the Nonconformists tended to destroy all discipline. An address was presented to Parliament that year entitled " A Proposal of Union among Protestants," which said that the Nonconformists would do anything for peace, only they dared not forsake holiness, nor neglect their duty, nor wound their consciences by offending God. An Anglican writer, in " The Late Proposal of Union among Protestants Reviewed and Rectified," commented on this: " If there be not some foul tincture of malice in these insinuations, yet are they no less unjust and scandalous than extravagant. . . . Whether it be more reasonable that the Church should run into their conventicles, which can never be united, or their conventicles into the bosom of the Church, let wise men judge." The squeamish refusal of things indifferent was superstition, for a vain and scrupulous abstinence from such things as God had not forbidden was superstition. " Does not every particular Church and party adhere to its own rites and forms . . . and must we of the Church of England be the only changelings of the Reformation? " For which of all the numerous sects must concessions be made, for it would be impossible to please them all? Dr. John Collinges, who had been ejected from St. Stephen's, Norwich,[1] put forth " A Reasonable Account why some Pious Nonconforming Ministers in England Judge it Sinful for them to Perform their Ministerial Acts in Public Solemn Prayer by the Prescribed Forms of Others." [2] He said the question was

[1] Palmer, III. 9.   [2] 1679.

not about the lawfulness of forms in general, nor the forms of
a man's composition for his own use, nor about any good use
of forms, nor about the lawfulness of the use of Scriptural forms,
but only concerning the lawfulness of forms of prayer composed by fallible men and prescribed by others to be ordinarily
used in stated solemn prayer by those whom God had fitted
for the ministry by giving them the gift of prayer. Collinges in
the following year added a " Supplement " to this work, in
which he replied to two Anglican books, Falconer's " Libertas
Ecclesiastica " and Pelling's " The Good Old Way," and asserted
that there was no general use or imposition of forms of prayer
in any considerable part of the Church till the time of Gregory
the Great (which was not true), nor in any church since the
Reformation, except that of England, and perhaps in Saxony.
Of course, the Roman and Eastern Churches did not come
within his consideration.

Dr. Timothy Puller tried to set forth the moderation of the
doctrine and discipline of the Church of England, together
with the wide latitude allowed in her communion.[1]   Richard
Stretton wrote " The Protestant Conformist: or, a Plea for
Moderation, contained in a Letter from one Conforming Minister
to another, and his Answer to it." [2]   The Rev. John Goodman,
Rector of Hadham, wrote " A Serious and Compassionate
Enquiry," and was answered by Vincent Alsop in " Melius
Inquirendum: or, A Sober Enquiry into the Reasonings of the
Serious Enquiry." This was in 1679. Goodman said that
there had been a good and moderate reformation of the Church
of England, but the Nonconformists complained that the Thirty-
nine Articles did not agree sufficiently with the five Calvinist
Articles and the Synod of Dort. The faith was once for all
delivered to the saints, and Calvinist doctrines dated no further
back than St. Augustine, whose piety was better than his reason.
Alsop replied that the Church of England had not been sufficiently reformed, that there were unscriptural statements in
the Anglican Articles, and that it was a crude notion to think
that the older a doctrine was the better it was. Goodman had
said that the Dissenters complained that the Church of England
was not sufficiently purged of Roman superstitions, but their
real quarrel with the Church was that she was not continually
reforming. As for the charge of Romanism, there was no need
to depart further from Rome than she had departed from the
truth. Alsop said that popery and Arminianism always went
hand-in-hand, and that the real difficulty in the way of reform
in the Church was the covetousness and pride of Churchmen,
though he admitted the learning and piety of many of the
clergy. As for separating from Rome, he asked why men should
be " so tender of departing from an abominable strumpet."

[1] " The Moderation of the Church of England Considered," 1679.
[2] 1679; Palmer, III. 326; Publications of Thoresby Society, XI. 321.

Alsop was against universal toleration, but said that he would not oppose a reasonable comprehension. He denied the charge of schism and the accusation that Dissenters considered themselves discharged from all obedience to the laws. Goodman said there was no reason to perpetuate the divisions, unless it was a point of honour to perpetuate what they had begun, and for which some people had praised them. Alsop showed a great deal of learning, was witty, mocking, and clever; but he hardly made a real answer to his opponent.

Slingsby Bethel, in his " Interest of the Princes and States of Europe," 1680, pointed out that the Church of Rome allowed Greeks, Armenians, and others, who agreed with her in faith, but differed in ceremonies, to have their own churches in Rome itself, whereas the Church of England, which made no pretence to infallibility, imposed rules, with penal sanctions, not merely in fundamental matters, but also in all material points of faith, worship, and obedience. " I cannot conceive the reason," he said scornfully, " except without ceremonies to administer matter of employment in punishing tender consciences, they think they should be without work of any kind adequate to their great revenues, and that they dread the consequences of uselessness." He thought that care should be taken that the clergy should be able to preach, and nothing should be imposed which was unnecessary. Among the things to which he objected, he specified the communion tables set altar-wise and the practice of people sitting with their hats off during sermon time, contrary to the practice of all Christian nations, and a custom conducive to catching cold. Acts of Parliament should be passed against popery, e.g. to prevent a popish mother having the care of her children after the death of a Protestant husband. Popery should be suppressed in all places where the Church of England was in control, as at Ripon, where there were said to be 2000 Papists. The argument that it was necessary to tolerate Catholics in this country to prevent the persecution of Protestants abroad was absurd, because neither the King of Spain nor the Pope had any Protestant subjects; they had driven them out. The Emperor had nearly ruined himself by persecuting them, while the King of France persecuted in spite of the Edict of Nantes; moreover, it would be a lessening of the King of England's sovereignty if he had to have respect to the doings of other kings. It was to England's advantage to breed a race of seamen, who, going to foreign countries, would see with their own eyes the follies of popery abroad. Liberty of conscience should be given to all Nonconformists, in order to raise the value of land and advance trade and wealth by encouraging the settlement of sober and industrious foreigners.

" A Word in Season for Christian Union " was addressed, in 1680, to Dissenters, especially their ministers, by one who claimed to be a well-wisher to both sides. He urged them to strive for unity, and told them that unity could not be attained by toleration, which only " turns the Church, Christ's academy, into the devil's university, where any man may commence schismatic *per saltum*." Another anonymous writer, evidently a Churchman, wrote " A Persuasive to Reformation and Union as the best Security against the Designs of our Popish Enemies " (1680), pleading with Nonconformists to be reasonable. If they would not read the writings of Anglican divines, at least let them read what some of their own preachers had written; such books as Baxter's " Cure of Church Divisions." He urged Dissenters not to administer the sacraments within the bounds of another man's charge, and not to withdraw members from the flocks of others. He granted they were doing good, but asked them to consider whether they would not do much more good in union with the Church.

Mr. John Cheney, or Cheyne, " a public conforming minister," who held Presbyterian views about ordination, wrote " The Conforming Nonconformist and the Nonconforming Conformist." The latter title he gave to himself, and seemed to urge, from the example of his own laxity, that there was nothing to keep Dissenters out of the Church. Baxter, in " The Defence of the Nonconformists' Plea for Peace " (1680) answered this pamphlet and another by the same author, called " Five Undertakings," and asked him what good that kind of conformity would do the Church, and told him that one point would keep a Nonconformist out as much as a hundred, and proceeded to restate all their objections to the Anglican system.

Tillotson preached a sermon before the King at Whitehall on April 2nd, 1680, taking for his text Joshua xxiv. 15. Calamy tells a story that Charles slept through it, and then, hearing it commended, ordered it to be printed. Hicks, who described the sermon as downright Hobbism, related that a witty nobleman standing at the King's elbow while it was being delivered, said, " Sir, Sir, do you hear Mr. Hobbes in the pulpit? " The sermon gave much offence, both to Churchmen and Nonconformists, especially the following passage: " I cannot but think (till I be better informed, which I am always ready to be) that any pretence of conscience warrants any man, that is not extraordinarily commissioned, as the Apostles and first publishers of the Gospel were, and cannot justify that commission by miracles, as they did, to affront the established religion of a nation, though it be false, and openly to draw men off from the profession of it, in contempt of the magistrates and the law. All that persons of a different religion can in such a case reasonably pretend to, is to enjoy the private liberty and exercise of their own conscience and religion, for which they ought to be very thankful, and to forbear the open making of proselytes to their own religion (though they be never so sure that they are in the right) till they have either an extraordinary commission from God to that purpose, or the providence of God make way for it by the permission of the magistrate."

When the sermon was printed Tillotson sent a copy to Howe, who expressed his opinion that in a sermon against popery he had done harm to the Reformation. Howe and Tillotson went on a journey to Sutton together, and discussed the matter by the way; and it was related that Tillotson in the end lamented that he had preached what he could not maintain.[1]

On May 11th, 1680, Stillingfleet, then Dean of St. Paul's, preached a sermon in the Guildhall Chapel before the Lord Mayor and corporation of London, on the text Phil. iii. 16, and published it shortly afterwards, under the title " The Mischief of Separation." In part at least, it was a reply to Baxter's " Nonconformists' Plea for Peace," published in 1679. Stillingfleet argued that " if there be one Catholic Church, consisting of multitudes of particular churches consenting in one faith, then why may there not be one national Church, from the consent in the same Articles of Religion, and the same rules of government and order of worship? " If it were mutual consent and agreement which made a church, then why might not national societies, agreeing together in the same faith, and under the same government and discipline, be as truly and properly a church as any particular congregation? He related that in 1663 some Nonconformist preachers in London met to consider how far it was lawful for them to attend the services and receive the sacrament in their parish churches, and that one of them brought in twenty reasons to prove that it was a duty to join with some parish churches three times a year in the Lord's Supper, and also proved it lawful to use a form of prayer and to join in the other Church services. Baxter himself said that no one of the brethren seemed to dissent from him.[2] After the Plague and Fire they had another meeting,[3] at which they agreed again that communion in this way with the Church of England was in itself lawful and good. Stillingfleet then went on to say that he had only been able to get two things out of them, viz. that though they were separated from the Church, separation was not a sin, and that a state of separation would be a sin, but their practice of meeting by themselves was not a state of separation. Some of them were accustomed to plead that a Christian had no obligation to external communion with a mere congregation. To the Congregationalist, who argued that his system was the primitive one, he asked why they should disturb the peace of the Church we live in to reduce churches

---

[1] Birch, " Life of Tillotson," pp. 63–64; Wilson, " Dissenting Churches," III. 29.

[2] See also " Rel. Baxt.," p. 437.

[3] " The Nonconformists' Plea for Peace," p. 240.

STUDIES IN ENGLISH PURITANISM

to their infant state. No church in this world can be without
blemish, and many things in public institutions and laws must
be allowed a favourable interpretation. He urged them to
consider how separation could be more lawful at that day than
in earlier times, and still further to think of the common danger
to Christianity arising from their divisions.

A number of writers promptly replied to the sermon. Owen
contributed " A Brief Vindication of the Nonconformists from
the Charge of Schism," and Stillingfleet thanked his opponent
for the courtesy of his reply. Baxter, without much courtesy,
published " Richard Baxter's Answer to Dr. Edward Stillingfleet's Charge of Separation," and he also wrote " The Second
Part of the Nonconformists' Plea for Peace." John Howe, in
" A Letter written out of the Country to a Person of Quality
in the City," accused the dean of acrimony and want of serious-
ness, and bade his readers, instead of being angry with Stillingfleet, to pray for him. The latter said that Howe had " discoursed gravely and piously, more like a gentleman than a
divine, without any admixture of rancour or any sharp reflections, and sometimes with a great degree of kindness towards
him, for which, and his prayers for him, he heartily thanked
him." Vincent Alsop published " The Mischief of Impositions,"
which the dean characterised as like " the bird of Athens, for
it seemed to be made of face and feathers." Alsop said that if
the Dissenters' principles were so bad, let them alone, and their
principles would destroy them, and so the Church would be
freed from accusations of persecution. The dean had said that
he recognised the Church of Rome as a true Church. Yet
since the Church of England had nevertheless separated for the
sake of greater purity, why might not the Nonconformist separate for still greater? Alsop twitted Stillingfleet with the " Irenicum " and his present inconsistency with it. Similarly, Mr.
Barrett, a Nonconformist of Nottingham, referred the dean back
to his earlier writings.[1]

A work by John Humphrey and others, "The Peaceable
Design," which had first appeared in 1675, was now reissued in
a revised edition, under the title "An Answer to Dr. Stillingfleet's
Sermon. By the Peaceable Design Renewed." The writers
claimed to be moderate Nonconformists, and acknowledged parish
churches to be true churches. This was their difficulty; it was
their duty to seek unity, but also to preach the Gospel. If they
kept to the parish churches, they could not preach the Gospel; if
they preached the Gospel, they must go to private meetings to
do it. They denied being schismatics, for schism was a *causeless* breach of unity, whereas their people came to hear them

---

[1] " The Rector of Sutton committed with the Dean of St. Paul's." See also
" A Reply to a Pamphlet called ' The Mischief of Impositions ' which pretends
to answer the Dean of St. Paul's Sermon."

because they got greater edification thereby. They could not accept reordination, which was on the level of rebaptism, and they could not give their assent to the Prayer Book, not so much in respect to petty things, as to such things as the order to say Matins and Evensong daily. "We dare not give our consent to the use of anything which we never intend to perform." They pleaded, somewhat naïvely, that if they were allowed by authority to do what they liked there would be no more schism.

Answers to Stillingfleet's critics came from the Anglican side, of course. "An Impartial Vindication of the Clergy of the Church of England" was dated July 25th, 1680, and subscribed "S. R.," possibly Samuel Rolls, now royal chaplain, and replied chiefly to Owen and Baxter. A number of replies came immediately: John Owen wrote "An Answer to the Unreasonableness of Separation, and a Defence of the Vindication of the Nonconformists from the Guilt of Schism." It was published in 1681, along with his "Enquiry into the Order and Communion of Evangelical Churches." John Humphrey published "An Answer to Dr. Stillingfleet's Unreasonableness of Separation, so far as it concerns the Peaceable Design." Arguing that separation was not sinful, he suggested that if the meetings of the Nonconformists were legalised, they would all belong to the National Church, and so the divisions would end. Thomas Wall, in "More Work for the Dean: A Brief Answer to some Scandalous Reports by Dr. Stillingfleet," replied to some of his statements about the Brownists. Barrett appeared in print again with "An Attempt to Vindicate the Principles of the Nonconformists, not only by Scripture, but by Dr. Stillingfleet's Rational Account." Baxter contributed to the discussion "A Second True Defence of the Mere Nonconformists." Stephen Lobb, who asked that if Episcopalians and Presbyterians must argue they should do so less angrily, published "A Modest and Peaceable Enquiry," in which he claimed that the innocency of the Dissenters was "vindicated from the indecent censures of the Doctor." Replying to the accusation that the Nonconformists were advancing Papist designs, he said that the Anglicans were always doing that: all the Anglican doctrines were doctrines of the Jesuits, and so it was useless to blame Dissenters for the divisions. Dissenters would not have things imposed upon them which were not in the Scriptures. The Dissenters would unite but could not; the Anglicans could unite but would not: though they knew that the toleration of peaceable Nonconformists would hinder popery. Stillingfleet had said that the Jesuits were the inventors of extempore prayers, and Lobb replied with the equally rash statement that the Jesuits had always opposed spiritual prayer.

On the Anglican side there were written "A Discourse of

Church Unity " (1681), by a Presbyter of the Church of England, said to be Sherlock, and " Some Additional Remarks on the late Book of the Reverend Dean of St. Paul's " (1681). The " conformable clergyman " who was the author of the last said that separation could not be prevented, and should therefore be put up with, just as drunkards and immoral men, who were worse than schismatics, had to be put up with. Persecution did more harm than good: it might stop a schism at its inception, but not when fully grown. Personal instruction was the only way of warning these people. Till they had thus been won over they must be tolerated, but there should be no toleration for such sectaries as Quakers and Socinians.

John Norris is believed to have been the author of " The Charge of Schism Renewed " (1680), a reply to " The Peaceable Design Renewed." He told the authors of the latter that they were not forbidden to preach—they could preach to their own families, supplemented by five other persons; but there was money to be got from preaching to larger congregations, and besides, there was the delight of keeping up a party. As for the people, they could hear the authorised clergy, and it was their duty to get edification in that way. Nonconformists were not turned out of the Church: they turned themselves out, and became formal schismatics. Until the supreme authority freed them from the obligation of attending their parish churches they were bound to behave as members of the parish. If they did not, then it was a case of unlawful separation—that is, schism.

Meanwhile Stillingfleet had revised and enlarged his sermon into a volume. Under its new form, in which it appeared in 1681, he called it " The Unreasonableness of Separation." In the preface he suggested terms on which the Nonconformists might be comprehended in the Church. They must take the tests against popery and subscribe thirty-six of the Thirty-nine Articles. If they so desired, the sign of the cross in baptism might be omitted, and they might be allowed to receive communion without kneeling. They should pay all legal dues to the parish church, and the statutory shilling a week for absence therefrom. Ministers should give an account of their rule, discipline, and method of worship, together with a list of the names and addresses of the members of their congregation, to the bishops, and a statutory declaration of the existence of their congregations should be made to specially appointed commissioners. Stillingfleet would not oppose a mild revision of the Thirty-nine Articles, together with some alterations in the liturgy. He thought a promise to use the Prayer Book might be substituted for the declaration of assent and consent. In addition, they ought to be made to promise " not to breed up scholars, or to teach gentlemen's sons university learning, because this may be justly looked upon as a design to propagate schism to posterity," and if they preached against the Church they ought to be subject to severe penalties. The work itself falls into three sections. In the first he gave an historical sketch of Nonconformity, and showed how the early Puritans held that schism from the Church could not be defended. In the second he dealt with contemporary Nonconformity, and showed how they differed among themselves as to the degree of conformity that might be permitted. In the third he answered in detail the various defences of Nonconformity which had been made in reply to his sermon. Nye and others, in an " Apologetical Narration," which he quoted, had admitted that the congregations of the Church of England were true churches, and their ministry a true ministry, and he inquired pertinently what then was the ground of separation? If they asked for toleration, why had not Roger Williams in New England an equal liberty of separating from the Independents there? Why had not the Quakers liberty there? The answer was that the Independents had found that they could not maintain unity without civil sanctions.

In an Appendix he gave three letters from three foreign Protestant divines. It was said that Stillingfleet had asked Compton, Bishop of London, to write to these for their opinions of the Church and Nonconformity. The replies were not very enthusiastic for episcopacy, and while they thought their brethren in England might comply, they were against pushing matters to extremes for the sake of a form of government. Le Moyne, Professor of Divinity in the University of Leyden, denied the statement that " a man cannot be saved in the Church of England," expressed his judgment that the ritual and services of the Church must be pure, since they were based on the Thirty-nine Articles, and mentioned that he had heard some Nonconformists preach in 1665 who were not edifying preachers. De l'Angle wrote from Charenton to say that when in England he worshipped in the Established Church, that he accepted Durel's assertion that the episcopal divines at the Savoy Conference were charitably disposed, and that he considered schism as the worst evil of the Church. Claude wrote from Paris and said, " I would not that any one should make episcopacy an occasion of quarrel in those places where it is established," and expressed the view that separate congregations held by those who dissented from the Established Church only on points of church order were schismatic." [1]

" They gave complaisant but wary answers. . . . Claude complained bitterly of this ungenerous treatment, but the letters that contained these complaints were concealed till his death; when they were printed by his son." [2] It would seem

[1] Agnew, " Protestant Exiles from France," II. 11.
[2] Orme, " Life of Owen," pp. 321–322.

that Claude did not intend that his letters should be published. In a letter written from Paris, April 16th, 1681, he " farther explained his sentiments on the subject of his former letter, condemning the excesses of both sides, and wishing they would submit to a just and reasonable accommodation." When he wrote to the Bishop of London he had no idea that his letter would be printed. All he wrote was to justify the French Protestants from the calumny that they believed there was no salvation under episcopacy, and to advance the cause of reunion by urging both sides to moderation.[1] Le Moyne also seems to have complained of the use Durel had made of his letter written at an earlier date.[2] He said that Durel had left out several passages " wherein he did moderate and regulate the episcopal power, which if they were inserted in the letter would not at all have filled his design." Calamy the younger said that Compton wrote at the same time to Dr. Spanheim, but his reply was not sufficiently favourable for Tillotson to publish it.[3]

To some extent connected with the Stillingfleet controversy was a somewhat more académic one on the question of episcopacy. In 1680 Baxter published his " Church History of the Government of Bishops and their Councils Abbreviated." One of Sancroft's chaplains, Morice, replied in 1682 with " A Vindication of the Primitive Church Diocesan Episcopacy," and an anonymous author published " No Evidence for Diocesan Churches." Baxter replied to Morice in " The True History of Councils, Enlarged and Defended," and David Clarkson, who had been ejected from Mortlake,[4] replied to the anonymous writer with a pamphlet, " Diocesan Churches not yet Discovered in Primitive Times." Clarkson also wrote " Primitive Episcopacy," in which he tried to prove that a bishop for the first three centuries was no more than a pastor of a single congregation, but this was not published till 1688.[5] Thomas Long, vicar of St. Lawrence's, Exeter, a very militant Churchman, published in 1682 " No Protestant, but the Dissenters' Plot," in which he attacked most of Stillingfleet's opponents, but especially Baxter. " He that shall read the preface of the ' Vindication of the Primitive Church ' in answer to Mr. Baxter's ' Church History ' will see what cause there is to admire him as a historian. . . . The second part of the ' History of Separation,' by Thomas Long, shows what to think of his piety as a divine." Mr. Baxter " has had his hand against men of all kinds and all persuasions." Long said the Papists refused the

[1] Calamy, I. 358–360; Birch, " Life of Tillotson," p. 85.
[2] Durel, " Government of the Reformed Churches," p. 126.
[3] Calamy, " My Own Life," I. 173.
[4] Palmer, III. 305.
[5] See also " Aaron's Rod Blossoming: or, The Orthodox Government of the Church of England by Bishops, Presbyters, and Deacons Asserted," 1680.

Prayer Book as well as the Dissenters, and therefore had an equal claim to toleration.

In March 1685 Stillingfleet preached a sermon at St. Michael's, Cornhill, in which he referred to the storm raised by his " Unreasonableness of Separation," and also to the " Irenicum," written in his younger days, when, without any desire to encourage faction or schism, he had tried to answer the Presbyterian arguments. For any mistake he made then, his youthfulness must be blamed, and the troubled times in which he was brought up. He said that he now believed that there was more to be said for episcopacy than he had thought then, but declared that he had nothing whatever to recant.[1]

Dr. Nalson made another violent attack on the Dissenters in a work entitled " Foxes and Firebrands," of which a first part was published in London in 1680, and a prefatory note addressed to Baxter and Jenkyn. A second edition with a second part by Robert Ware [2] was published in 1682, and a third in 1689. The story that Dissenters were Papists in disguise probably never went to such absurd lengths as in this work. Part I. gravely accused the Church of Rome of enthusiastic belief in Fifth Monarchy principles. Therefore, of course, the Fifth Monarchy men were Papists. The object of the Roman Church was to divide Protestants by raising sects and schisms. " I have been credibly informed that a St. Omer Jesuit declared that they were twenty years hammering out the sect of the Quakers." The Quakers refused to take oaths, which gave the Jesuits an opportunity to escape taking them. The Quakers despised the Scriptures and scorned the sacraments. So did the Papists. Papists in disguise stirred up Dissenters against the bishops, and Roman recusants made the same excuses for not conforming as the Dissenters did. Papists were the authors of the sect of the Anabaptists. The Second Part said that popish impostors preached heresy among the Dissenters in order to upset the Church of England, and they had papal dispensations for so doing. They even pretended to rail at the Church of Rome in order to avert suspicion. Such emissaries were permitted to marry, because then they would not be suspected, and, in any case, a heretical marriage was to them no marriage. They deluded the Protestant laity by their wilfully false interpretations of Scripture. It was they who brought about the death of the late King. The real gem of this collection of fables is that forty or more priests and Jesuits were present on horseback, as troopers in the Parliamentary army, at Charles I.'s execution. But people who believed Oates, believed any lie about the Church of Rome. Perhaps it was the first part of this work

[1] Stillingfleet, " A Sermon Preached at a Public Ordination at St. Peter's, Cornhill," 1685.
[2] Grey, " Examination of the Fourth Volume of Neal," p. 372.

which made a Presbyterian publish "A Defence of the True Protestants Abused for the Service of Popery" (1680), in which, however, the writer admitted that though Presbyterians and Anglicans disagreed with many of the tenets of the Roman Church, yet there were many so-called Protestants paving the way for Roman Catholicism. Robert Ware returned to the charge in 1683, with "The Hunting of the Romish Fox and the Quenching of Sectarian Firebrands," in which he told more stories of Roman priests among the sects. Anthony Nugent (referred to in "Foxes and Firebrands," Part II.), though a Popish priest, was one of the disciples of James Nayler.[1] Oliver Cromwell was a great succourer of Roman priests.[2] A Jesuit confessed that his brethren were instrumental in sending the first Quakers to Ireland.[3]

A trenchant blow was directed against the Dissenters in April 1681 by Roger L'Estrange, and bore the title "The Dissenters' Sayings." A second part appeared in the August of the same year, with a mocking dedication " to his unknown friends the grand jury of London." The two parts gave a classified catena of extracts from the writings of various Non-conformists, under such headings as "The Dissenters' harmony among themselves," "Their rigour to the episcopal party," "Tumults encouraged by these peaceable ministers," and so on. Chapter and verse were given with each extract. Of course he selected the wildest rantings and the most absurd and heretical statements. The first two chapters, containing the most violent pronouncements against toleration, were thus published at a time when many of them were writing earnest pleas for toleration for themselves. Two years later the work was translated into French.[4] L'Estrange also translated from the French "An Apology for the French Protestants" (1681). In his preface he laid stress on contemporary French approval of Anglicanism, and said he had issued this work really as a defence of the Church of England against Rome and Nonconformity. He made the statement that in France Dissenters were not permitted at all, but apparently in his eyes the French Protestants were not Dissenters because they had State sanction.

Partisan feeling was running high in 1681 and the following year, but there were still some people who were trying to promote kindlier relations. Gilbert Burnet preached a sermon before the Lord Mayor that year, which he published as "An Exhortation to Peace and Unity," in which he attacked persecution, though he was obliged to countenance measures against Roman Catholics for the sake of the preservation of Protestantism. A Latitudinarian production of the same year was a

---

[1] "The Hunting," pp. 229–235.
[2] Ibid., p. 336.   [3] Ibid., pp. 237–241.
[4] G. Kitchin, "Roger L'Estrange," 1913, p. 265.

tract, " Liberty of Conscience, in its order to Universal Peace," in which the writer laid down that as the standard of all human penal laws was set by natural religion, no one should be punished in religious matters unless he had violated the precepts of natural religion. Dr. William Beveridge, in a sermon preached in 1681 at the opening of St. Peter's, Cornhill, which had been destroyed by the Great Fire, and had now been rebuilt, tried to commend the Book of Common Prayer to its opponents in a spirit, on the whole, of sweet reasonableness.[1]

George Hicks, Vicar of All Hallows, Barking, attempted to draw the line between persecution and the just enforcement of the law, in a sermon which he preached on behalf of the French Protestants. The true notion of persecution " consists not in the greatness of any man's sufferings . . . but in the righteousness of the cause for which he suffers. For if he be pursued for doing anything against the law, or government, under which he lives, that God hath not commanded, or for not doing of those things which God hath not forbid, he is not persecuted, but justly prosecuted, for disobeying the powers which God hath bound him to obey." A man could only be persecuted on two accounts: for matters of professed faith (or principles), and for matters of practice. " Men who coin new doctrines, and rules and precepts for Christian practice and communion which God never made, let them suffer never so much from authority in defence of them, yet they are not persecuted, but rightfully punished. . . . Whosoever is truly persecuted must suffer for doctrines and laws which God hath given us, for the common principles of Christianity, and not for private fancies and inventions." He asked for what gospel doctrines or Catholic principles the English Nonconformists suffered. If they were " Gospel " and " Catholic " principles, why was it they had been so long undiscovered ? On the other hand, the French Protestants had been truly persecuted for maintaining primitive Christianity against the corruptions of popery. They were persecuted: the English Nonconformists were not.[2]

The practice of levying distresses on offenders against the Conventicle Act was attacked in 1682 in a pamphlet, " The Case of Present Distresses on Nonconformists Examined." It asserted that the system of levying distresses was contrary " to the original pattern of all government." The method of trial practised under the Act was contrary to the law of nations, in proof of which the writer quoted Acts xxv. 16, contrary to common sense, and contrary to the very purpose of penal laws, which was to inquire into offences for the good of the public

---

[1] " A Sermon Concerning the Excellency and Usefulness of the Common Prayer," 1681. See also the anonymous " Answer to the Dissenters' Objections against the Common Prayer," 1683.

[2] Hicks, " The True Notion of Persecution Stated," 1681.

peace. All security of goods and estates was being taken from many peaceable subjects, and their property was transferred to another person before even the original owner was asked what he had to say against it. Laws ought not to be turned into snares, neither were they to be severely construed to the gain of some other person than the accused. A pamphlet, " Some Sober and Weighty Reasons against Prosecuting Protestant Dissenters," published in 1682, laid stress on the King's anxiety to promote toleration, and his assertion in 1672 that it was evident there was little fruit in forcible courses. God Himself had not imposed religious doctrines by force, and all men were fallible in some divine matters. It was admitted that there was a general agreement between Protestants on fundamental doctrines, and therefore they should be brethren.

The Bishop of Cork had written a treatise called " The Protestant Peacemaker," in which he had advocated some relaxation in the use of the Prayer Book and the ceremonies. A reply entitled " The Harmony between the Old and Present Nonconformist Principles " (1682) spoke approvingly of this as the only possible way, because many Dissenters had conscientious convictions against both. The author of " The Harmony " dated Nonconformity from August 24th, 1662. The clergy were saying that as those " old Nonconformists " continually held communion with the Church of England, they ought to come into full communion; but these men could not give up their ministry, which would be sacrilege, especially as there was a great need of preachers. They did not in reality separate from the Church; they were preaching as lecturers or curates to the parochial ministers. Of the other Nonconformists, some of the Presbyterians and some of the Congregationalists looked on the set forms in the Prayer Book as lawful, but not expedient; though others of the Presbyterians, and most of the Congregationalists and Baptists, considered them unlawful.

In 1681 was published " The Conformist's Plea for the Nonconformists," followed by a Second, Third, and Fourth Plea, the last appearing in 1683, the author being Edward Pearse, a beneficed clergyman in Northamptonshire.[1] He asserted that the Dissenting ministers were well-qualified and worthy men, who had shown a peaceable behaviour in spite of what they had suffered, and had made from time to time just and equitable proposals for union. It was very unlikely that they could be suppressed, and their exclusion was a great injury to the Church of England itself. He poured scorn on the idea of fixing five as the number of a lawful congregation for them. Either their influence was bad or it was not. If it was bad, they ought not to be allowed even five hearers; if not, why were they so re-

[1] A. A. Seaton, " Theory of Toleration under the Later Stuarts," 1911, p. 217.

stricted? In April 1683 the grand jury of Northamptonshire presented " The Conformists' Second Plea " as " a dangerous, seditious, and libellous book, tending to the destruction of the religion of this land . . . and the subverting of the laws and government of this realm." [1]

Among the Anglican opponents of persecution was Samuel Bold, vicar of Shapwick, in Dorset. Preaching on March 26th, 1682, when a brief was read on behalf of the persecuted Protestants of France, he denounced intolerance in religion, and his discourse was published under the title " A Sermon against Persecution." At the next Assizes at Sherborne the grand jury presented him on account of it. Nothing daunted, in the same year he issued " A Plea for Moderation toward Dissenters," in which he replied to the various objections which had been made to the former sermon. The reason why the sermon gave offence was his vigorous attack on the informers, whom he called " the pests of society," " men of a superstitious, blind, and ignorant zeal," " broken in fortune," who " take to informing, swearing, and persecuting as a trade," and whom he described as " profligate and scandalous in their lives." " All the Dissenters in the nation," said he, " cannot prejudice the Church half so much as your drunken, swearing, profane informers and persecutors."

William Saywell, Master of Jesus College, Cambridge, published in 1682 " Evangelical and Catholic Unity maintained in the Church of England." While advising moderate penalties for Nonconformity, he advocated sober and serious conferences between the two parties, for the claims of the Church required long arguments in order to be proved, and many persons became Dissenters out of intellectual sloth, and followed their teachers blindly. Such persons should be compelled to listen to instruction.

The wording of the oath imposed by the Five Mile Act was a real difficulty to many of the Nonconformist ministers, and a real stumbling-block to any *rapprochement* between Nonconformity and the Church. John Corbet, therefore, in " An Enquiry into the Oath required of Nonconformists by an Act made at Oxford," which was published posthumously in 1682, endeavoured to set forth a new and acceptable form of the oath, and one which would make the meaning intended by the Churchmen more clear. He suggested that it should run : " I do swear, that I do believe that it is not lawful, upon any pretence whatever, *for any of the King's Majesty's subjects* to take arms *against his person or authority, or any of his rights and dignities,* and that I abhor the traitorous position of taking arms by his authority against his person, or against those that are *legally* commissioned by him, in *the legal* pursuance of such commissions. And that I will not at any time endeavour any alteration of government

<hr />

[1] " Observator," No. 328.

either in Church or State, *by rebellion, sedition or any other means forbidden or not warranted by law.*" The italics show Corbet's additions. In this sense, as a renunciation of the principles of schism and rebellion, Corbet thought there would be no difficulty· in taking the oath.

John Corbet wrote another work, " An Account of the Principles and Practices of Several Nonconformists," which was not published till after his death, and was seen through the press by Baxter. His widow said that several eminent Nonconformist divines had read it through and approved of it.[1] In it Corbet said, " We desire the clergy of England to take notice that we have no mind to promote the popish design of nullifying and treading down the parish churches and ministers. . . . It is a palpable injury to burden us with the various parties with which we are now herded by our ejection, in the general state of Dissenters, and to make us responsible for them all." [2] In " A Defence of my Endeavours for the Work of the Ministry," he declared that, as he had received from Christ the office of a pastor, he was bound in his present state to fulfil it. Next he asserted, " I am not obliged either by the nature of my office, or by any oath or promise, or by being under the regulation of authority, to exercise my ministry no otherwise than in subordination to, and as authorised and regulated by, the bishop of the diocese." Yet he allowed that he ought not to invade the bishop's rights by exercising his ministry where the bishop claimed the right of being pastor. He did not realise, apparently, that the bishop claimed to be pastor of the whole diocese. He admitted that he was bound not to violate any true bonds of church unity, that he must not in any respect cause divisions and offences, and that he must not oppose the authority of the civil magistrate.[3]

In a paper, " A Consideration of the Present State of Conformity in the Church of England," Corbet displayed the tendency of his party to put a strained interpretation on the words " assent and consent." A single example will suffice. Referring to the Christmas Collect, he pointed out that it was by no means certain that the Nativity of our Saviour took place on December 25th, and asked how a man could give his assent and consent to the words, " And as at this time to be born." [4] In another paper, " Of Divine Worship," he showed that he had no objection to bowing at the Holy Name, to wearing a surplice, to kneeling at communion, to the marriage ring, or the sign of the cross; but he deprecated compulsion in such matters.[5] In another paper, published posthumously (he died in 1680), he made the following statements: " I own parish

---

[1] *Church Quart. Rev.*, XXXI. 382.   [2] " An Account," pp. 26, 27.
[3] " Remains of the Reverend and Learned Mr. John Corbet," 1684.
[4] *Ibid.*, p. 148.   [5] *Ibid.*, pp. 218–221.

churches, having a competent minister and number of credible professors of Christianity, for true churches, and the worship there performed, as well in the liturgy or common prayer, as in the preaching of the Word, and prayer before and after sermon, to be in the main sound and good for the substance or matter thereof." " Though I judge their form of worship to be in many respects less perfect than is to be desired, yet I have found my heart spiritually affected, and raised towards God therein, and more especially in the receiving of the Lord's Supper. . . . I am desirous of joining, as far as I may, with all congregations worshipping God in Christ, out of my high regard to all Christian worship." " Though I am constrained by force of conscience to be among those that dissent from the enjoined conformity; yet my design and business is not to advance a severed party as such." [1] A similar statement was made by James Jones, a London Dissenter, who said that Non-conformists acknowledged that the Holy Communion as adminis-tered in the Church of England was right in matter, in manner of administration, and in design, but " notwithstanding all this, it may be unsafe and dangerous for the Dissenters to come to it at such times, and in such places, and with such administrators and communicants as their tender conscience is not satisfied with." [2]

" A Catholic Catechism," written by a Nonconformist in 1683, set forth the Dissenting conception of Christianity as opposed to the Romanist or Anglican. The Catholic religion could not, without the loss of truth, be varied to the degree of a thought from the pattern left sealed by the Apostles; there-fore, popery or anything else not strictly founded on Scripture, could not be Catholic. Bishops in the true sense were only persons of eminent holiness, and only had the authority con-ferred on them by such holiness, not by any setting apart or succession from the Apostles. The ministers of the church were pastors, elders, and evangelists. The State, in its religious aspect, only existed to maintain morality and the principles of natural religion, and must therefore allow the widest liberty, in which alone could unity be found.

In 1683 Daniel Whitby, precentor of Salisbury cathedral, published anonymously " The Protestant Reconciler," in which he pleaded for " condescension " to dissenting brethren in matters indifferent and unnecessary. He quoted a sermon preached by Tillotson at York, on December 3rd, 1678, in which the preacher said, " It is not for private persons to undertake in matters of public concernment, but I think we have no cause to doubt but the governors of our Church (notwithstanding

---

[1] " The Nonconformists' Plea for Lay Communion," 1683.
[2] James Jones, " Mercy and Faithfulness in Opposition to Envy and Rash-ness," 1683.

all the advantages of authority, and we think of reason too, on our side) are persons of that piety and prudence, that for peace sake, and in order to a firm union among Protestants, they would be content, if that would do it, not to insist upon little things, but to yield them up, whether to the infirmity, or importunity, or perhaps, in some very few things, to the plausible exceptions of those who differ from us." The book roused great indignation, provoked many replies, was condemned by the University of Oxford on July 21st, 1683, and publicly burnt by the university marshal in the schools quadrangle. Whitby was chaplain to Bishop Ward of Salisbury, and when he was discovered to be the author the bishop made him publicly retract, which he did on October 9th.[1]

Dr. Benjamin Calamy, a conformist, preached a sermon at St. Mary, Aldermanbury, the church from which his father had been ejected, and published it in 1683 under the title " A Discourse about a Scrupulous Conscience." The sermon itself was a general challenge to Dissenters, though there was no direct challenge to anyone in particular to reply. Nevertheless, Thomas Delaune did so, and shortly afterwards was thrown into prison, where he died, for all which the Dissenters blamed Dr. Calamy.[2]   The printed sermon was accompanied by an " Epistle Dedicatory " to Jeffreys, in which the writer said that he knew the sentiments of the sermon would cause anger and displeasure to the enemies of the Church and Government, " but when men are scrupulous only on one side about the things commanded by lawful authority, and make no scruple of disobedience, schism, faction, and division; when men set up their private humour, fancy, or opinion, in opposition to established laws; when they become peevish, pragmatical, and ungovernable; nay, when men's consciences prove so generally tender and scrupulous as to doubt and suspect the rights of the Crown, for that conscience that is so tender against the Church is also usually as tender against the King, such wayward, skittish consciences ought to be well-bridled and restrained."

" In the midst of these violent proceedings," said Neal, referring to the storm of persecution in 1683, " the divines of the Church of England published the London cases against the Nonconformists; they were twenty-three in number. . . . Their champions of the Church were very secure from being answered after Mr. Delaune had so lately lost his life for writing against one of them." [3]   As a matter of fact, Delaune was still alive and at liberty while most of them appeared. " Several most useful

---

[1] See " Three Sermons Preached at Salisbury," 1685; Birch, " Life of Tillotson," pp. 97–105; Neal, " Puritans," IV. 607.

[2] Delaune, " Plea for Nonconformists," 1684; " Narrative of the Trial and Sufferings of Thomas Delaune," 1684.

[3] Neal, " Puritans," 1738 ed., IV. 523.

tracts against Dissenters, Papists and fanatics, and resolutions
of cases, were now published by the London divines," said
Evelyn.[1] These tracts were written by Dr. John Scott, Dr.
Clagett, Dr. Fowler, Dr. Hascard, Dr. Tillotson, Dr. Tenison,
Simon Patrick, and others. They dealt with " cases of conscience," and these were some of the subjects: " Whether the
Church of England's symbolizing so far as it doth with the
Church of Rome makes it unlawful to hold communion with
the Church of England." " Whether it is lawful for any man
to forsake the communion of the Church of England and go to
separate meetings because he can better edify there." " Whether
it is lawful to communicate with two churches which are in a
state of separation from each other." " The difference in the
case between the separation of Protestants from the Church of
Rome and the separation of Dissenters from the Church of
England." " The case of indifferent things in the worship
of God." " The case of kneeling at the Holy Sacrament."
" Concerning the lawfulness of joining with forms of prayer
in public worship." All these came out in 1683. " The case
of compelling men to the Holy Sacrament " was one of those
published in the following year, and it was really a discourse on
the text " Compel them to come in." Twenty years previously,
the writer said, the Dissenters who had taken the Covenant
pleaded that if they were not compelled to renounce it, they
would have no difficulty in conforming, but now that excuse
had gone they had invented new ones. The Dissenters complained of excommunications, but what could excommunication
mean to men who had already excommunicated themselves?
This writer dealt in particular with church censures and their
enforcement, the cause of the greatest complaints on the part
of the Dissenters. The various pamphlets in this series, at first
published separately, were afterwards collected and issued in
two volumes.

In 1684 Baxter published a work, " Catholic Communion
Defended against both Extremes." It was in two parts, the
first giving his reasons for making his communion at the altars
of the Church of England, a proceeding for which he had incurred censure from his fellow-Nonconformists. Dr. John Owen
had drawn up twelve reasons against it, and Baxter replied to
these twelve reasons in his Second Part.

Many important people were coming round to the idea that
the only possible solution of the trouble was a greater or less
amount of toleration. Sir William Petty wrote a Latin and
English catechism such as he hoped might meet with pretty
general agreement.[2] He thought that religious liberty might

---

[1] " Diary," February 22nd, 1685.
[2] " The Petty–Southwell Correspondence, ed. by Marquis of Lansdowne,"
1928, p. 171.

be given to people who made a declaration of the exact points on which they differed from the State religion, giving at the same time their promise to obey the laws.[1] He held that people should not be punished because their beliefs were contrary to the Scriptures, but only when they were dangerous to the peace of the realm, and he deprecated weakening the solemnity of oaths by making people swear what they did not believe, or what they did not know.[2]

The Duke of Buckingham wrote in August 1685 a " Short Discourse upon the Reasonableness of Men's having a Religion or Worship of God." Arguing in it for liberty of conscience, he said that he had long been convinced that there was nothing more antichristian, nor more contrary to reason, than to molest our fellow-Christians because they could not be of the same mind as ourselves in all things relating to the worship of God. Every man must choose for himself; he only being answerable to God Almighty for his own soul. It was ridiculous and barbarous to attempt to convince a man's judgment by anything but reason. Persecution had always been destructive to the country where it was practised, and he urged men to cease quarrelling and cutting one another's throats about those things which they all agreed were not necessary to salvation.

There quickly appeared " A Short Answer to his Grace the Duke of Buckingham's Paper concerning Religion, Toleration, and Liberty of Conscience." The author, after laying down that toleration would bring ruin to King, Church, and State, said that the consequences of the Duke's argument were that reason was the safe guide of every man's religion, and that Divine revelation was not necessary to salvation. The punishment of offenders whose religion was false or feigned, and who only made a show of it in order to carry on other designs, was not only lawful, but just and necessary. No man in England was persecuted purely for his religion; he was allowed to exercise it in his family, but disturbers of the peace and order of the realm were rightly punished. He twitted Buckingham with having had a share in the making of the laws to which he now objected. There was but one God, one faith, and one truth. Was it charity to give men liberty to go headlong to the devil? The wars and plots of the Nonconformists had shown how religious feuds weakened the State, encouraged usurpers, and reduced the country to misery. For one republic which allowed toleration, with restrictions, there were a hundred happy countries which had no toleration at all. This provoked a brief reply by the Duke to " my nameless, angry, harmless, humble servant," in which he said that his anonymous opponent had not even understood what he, Buckingham, had written, nor what King

---

[1] " The Petty Papers, ed. by the Marquis of Lansdowne," 1927, I. No. 42.
[2] *Ibid.*, No. 43.

James had meant when he promised not to let anyone injure the Church of England, which did not mean that he would allow the Church to persecute everybody else. He concluded by signing himself "your grateful friend, Buckingham." [1]

Henry Payne, who is said to have had the distinction of being the last person to suffer by the boot and thumbscrew in Scotland, wrote "The Persecutor Exposed: in Reflections, by way of Reply to the Ill-bred Answer to the Duke of Buckingham's Paper." He said that the argument of the Duke's opponent was in substance that "the vicar of Bray will be vicar of Bray still," and "Great is Diana of the Ephesians." "A Reply to the Answer of the Man of No Name to the Duke of Buckingham's 'Liberty of Conscience'" was subscribed "G. C.,[2] an affectionate friend and true servant of his Grace." Referring to the work of the "Man of no name," he asked, "Could a man fetch anything more savage out of the Highlands of Scotland, or from the lakes of Canada?" Did he think it was better to be a hypocrite than a Dissenter? Opinions would not bring danger to the Government which tolerated them. Those who would plot to gain liberty would never plot to lose it; and, in any case, there were plenty of laws to punish disorder. Care asked whether a man could believe without conviction. If not, could a man give himself conviction? If not, did this put an end to coercion? A tract, "Considerations moving to a Toleration and Liberty of Conscience . . . Occasioned by an Excellent Discourse published by the Duke of Buckingham," is said to have been written by William Penn.[3] Penn also wrote "A Defence of the Duke of Buckingham's Book of Religion and Worship from the Exceptions of a Nameless Author." Other papers written in connection with this controversy were, "The Antithelemite: or, An Answer to Certain Queries by the Duke of Buckingham, and to the Considerations of an Unknown Author," by Henry Maurice, rector of Chevening, in Kent; "Toleration and Liberty of Conscience Considered, and proved Impracticable, Impossible and even in the Opinion of Dissenters Sinful and Unlawful," an answer to Penn; "The Vanity of all Pretences for Toleration"; and "A Defence of the Duke against the Answer to his Book and the Reply to his Letter." All these were published in 1685.

"The fanatics growing very troublesome for a toleration, and uniting with the Papists in their clamours against the Church of England, I wrote also and printed a small 'Apology for the Church of England against the men of no conscience,' which was published that very day this loyal parliament first met (May 22nd, 1685)." [4] The "men of no conscience" were

---

[1] "The Duke of Buckingham his Grace's Letter to the Unknown Author."
[2] *I.e.* George Care.   [3] Smith, "Catalogue of Friends' Books," I. 42.
[4] "Autobiog. of Edmund Bohun," p. 69.

" the Duke of Buckingham's seconds," and Edmund Bohun, the writer of the above, scornfully said that liberty of conscience had fed the press and maintained many of its patrons ever since 1660, yet these men who clamoured for it were the people who had refused to let Charles I. have a chaplain of his own persuasion. When liberty of conscience was given them in 1672 they called it a trick to bring in popery and arbitrary government, and they had since shown their zeal for liberty of conscience by clamouring for the Exclusion Bill.

Another aristocratic defender of the Nonconformists was Lord Delamere, who wrote a paper, " Some Reasons against Prosecuting the Dissenters upon the Penal Laws." It was written some time after 1680, but apparently not made public till 1694, when his " Works " were published posthumously. In this paper he told the Dissenters that as there was a suspicion that sedition was preached at their meetings, though he personally knew no instance of it, they would be wise not to hold their meetings, or at least to be so moderate in their numbers that they would not appear to glory in multitudes. The people who exercised severity, if severity were necessary, should take care to lead a good life, or their zeal would appear only a pretended one. He asked what encouragement it could be to the French Protestants to flee from persecution in one country and find it raging in another. It had never been publicly decided that the Dissenters cut off the King's head; far more people believed the Papists had done it, and it was known that the Papists rejoiced at it in England and Rome, and said their worst enemy was dead. But even if the Dissenters had done this thing, the Act of Oblivion had been passed since then. Laws ceased when they failed in their purpose, and the laws against Nonconformists had failed, because so many people pitied them; and, in any case, they ought not to be touched till the Papists had been put down.[1]

In " A Persuasive to an Ingenuous Trial of Opinions in Religion," published in 1685, the writer asked, " If every man hath a just liberty and right to examine for himself, is not this a good reason for Toleration? " But this would be no good reason for toleration unless it were also apparent that every man used that right with industry, deliberation, and impartiality. The law would, however, deal with those who, from wantonness or conceit, or faction, or interest, or such-like cause, were prejudiced against reason and truth. Force, then, would sometimes be necessary. It was not true that force in religious matters only made hypocrites; sometimes it cured hypocrisy, ignorance, or partiality, and that was a good step in the direction of conversion. The moderation of the English laws for uniformity in religion was visible to all disinterested persons,

[1] Delamere, " Works," 1694, pp. 411–416.

yet many had left the Church, and when asked the reason, could only reply that they got better preaching or praying elsewhere. They abused the Prayer Book, and called it " porridge," without having read it, and called Churchmen antichristian, superstitious, or idolatrous, without knowing what the words meant.

In a short tract, " The Protestant Resolution of Faith," published in 1686, Sherlock referred to the abundance of books which Anglicans at that time were writing against popery, and said that these treatises, like their similar works against Dissent, were too learned for popular consumption. People were saying that the clergy were now writing against popery in order to gain the Nonconformists, whose favour they had lost by the former bitter attacks on them, but the favour of Dissenters was only of value in proportion as it gave opportunities for doing them good. If writing against popery would win Dissenters back to the Church, so much the better; the clergy had to fight both popery and fanaticism, and had been so far successful that they had gained over some of the Nonconformists.

During the reign of James II. the controversies took a new form; the question was now not so much the toleration of Dissenters, as the complete freedom of the Romanists from the repressive laws. The fact that James was himself a " Dissenter " as far as the Church of England was concerned, complicated the problem for everybody. James's Quaker friend, William Penn, in 1686 dealt with the new aspect of the religious problem in " A Persuasive to Moderation to Church Dissenters." It was being said that as the Church of Rome and the Church of England were united in loyalty to the monarchy, therefore the Church of Rome should have indulgence. But was this possible? They differed in doctrine, as could be seen by a comparison of the Thirty-nine Articles with the decrees of the Council of Trent; and in interest, for one had the property which the other claimed. Indulgence to Roman Catholics not only offended a great number of Nonconformists, but also gave the Church of England the lie. On the other hand, if the Church claimed the King's promise of protection, the Nonconformists could not forget the offer of his clemency. They believed in it, for who should give them ease more than a prince who had himself suffered? Moreover, the King had given an illustrious example of his integrity and constancy in hazarding the loss of three crowns for conscience' sake. Therefore, let the Nonconformists' constancy be respected and treated as worthy of some toleration. Other countries had practised toleration without any evil results. If it were objected that English Dissent had led to the Civil War, it might be replied that the war made the Dissenters rather than the Dissenters made the war; that the Dissenters at the outbreak of the war had not been tolerated but persecuted, and that they did not lead the party hostile to the King, but followed great numbers of churchgoers. In the first Dutch war of Charles II. the insistence on conformity robbed the King of many able officers, like Vice-Admiral Goodson, Captain Hill, and Captain Potter. Was the King ever better served than by the old Roundhead seamen like the Earl of Sandwich, Sir William Penn, Sir John Lawson, Sir George Ayscue, Sir Christopher Minns, and others? If it were said that most of these were conformists at that time, it must be admitted that they served the King none the better for that. Toleration made men loyal to the sovereign, but if the Crown embarked on a policy of persecution, it drove men to turn to Parliament. The Church of England herself was persecuted under the Commonwealth; all the more reason, then, that she should not be a persecuting Church now. Surely, she should not be less tender of men's consciences than the Common Law was of men's lives. Finally, Penn proposed a general toleration on condition that the names of all Nonconformists, and their meeting-places, should be registered, that meetings should be held with open doors, that coming armed to a meeting should be an offence punishable with a *præmunire*, that each sect should appoint officials to report on any misbehaviour of their members, and that all nicknames and terms of reproach should be punishable.

James II.'s two Declarations of Indulgence gave fresh life to the toleration controversy, and the Roman Catholics joined in. A great number of pamphlets came forth from the press, and it is difficult at times to be certain whether they have an Anglican, a Roman, or a Puritan origin. There was no question now of suppressing the Dissenters with a strong hand, it was whether full toleration should be extended to the Romanist, and on that point the Dissenters were divided. Among the pamphlets which appeared in 1687 was "A Discourse for Taking Off the Tests and Penal Laws about Religion." It took the line that ecclesiastical and temporal power should be separate, and the curious view was expressed that the union of the State and religion was based on the Wycliffite doctrine that "dominion is founded in grace." The writer further urged that the fear of Romanist domination was ungrounded, since liberty of conscience was as important to the Papist as to the Dissenter. A "Minister of the Church of England" wrote "Indulgence to Tender Consciences shown to be most Reasonable and Christian." "The Plea of the Harmless Oppressed against the Cruel Oppressor" was apparently by a Dissenter, and defended King James against the bishops and their deeds. "The Good Old Test Revived and Recommended to all Sincere Christians" was a short tract whose main theme was "let us have no other test but loyalty and love." "A Letter concerning the Test and Persecution for Conscience. To an Honourable Member of the House of Lords " was, according to a MS. note in the British Museum copy, written " by W. H., a Papist." It was not calculated to do the cause of toleration much good, inasmuch as he flaunted before the Protestants at a critical time one of the doctrines they most disliked—that of the invocation of saints. One of the chief arguments was that if invocation of saints be idolatry, then when His Sacred Majesty invokes saints he is an idolater. " That Shaftesbury-men should revile His Sacred Majesty 'tis no wonder; but that a truly loyal Parliament, such as by the good providence of God this present is, of which you are a worthy member, should tell His Sacred Majesty in his royal presence that he is the blackest of criminals, an idolater . . . this, methinks, is so amazing and so astonishing, as nothing can be more." It was not a very helpful contribution to the discussion. A great many of His Sacred Majesty's subjects did believe him an idolater, and feared that he intended to dragoon them into idolatry, as his other Sacred Majesty across the Channel was dragooning his loving subjects.

" A Letter from a Gentleman in the City to a Gentleman in the Country about the Odiousness of Persecution " [1] pointed out the weak point of all religious persecution—that it was usually laxly carried out, and caused the rise of that universally hated race, the informers. " Some Free Reflections upon Occasion of the Public Discourse about Liberty of Conscience " showed the failure of persecution to bring peace, and argued that liberty was a fundamental law of nature. William Penn, of course, must have his share of the discussion. In " Good Advice to the Church of England, Roman Catholics, and Protestant Dissenters " he argued against any religion being put in a pre-eminent position in the State, and urged toleration for the Romanists. If they were seditious, there were laws against sedition, and nothing else need be done against them. " A Letter from a Dissenter to the Divines of the Church of England in order to a Union " called attention to the change of spirit which had come over the Church of England preachers. Some time previously nothing had been heard but thunder against Dissenters, their obstinacy, disobedience, schism, and rebellion, " which is as the sin of witchcraft." On the other hand, Dissenters were suspicious of Anglican leanings towards popery and doctrines resembling popery. *Now* Dissenters were being invited to unite with the Church, but let the Church set forth some reasonable scheme of agreement. [2]

The stand which many of the clergy of the Church of England made against the Indulgence was ascribed by both Romanists and Dissenters to a persecuting spirit. Hence there appeared several pamphlets defending the Church against this charge.

---

[1] Signed " A. N." ? A Nonconformist.
[2] See also " Liberty of Conscience Asserted: or a Looking Glass for Persecutors," 1687.

Such were " A Plain Account of the Persecution now laid to the Charge of the Church of England," and the " Apology for the Church of England with Relation to the Spirit of Persecution for which she is Accused " (1688). Amongst the crop of pamphlets on the toleration question in 1688 was one entitled " Two Plain Words to the Clergy: or, An Admonition to Peace and Concord at this Juncture." Another was " An Important Query for Protestants, viz. Can Good come out of Galilee?: or, Can a Popish Ruler propagate the Reformed Religion? " The general argument of the latter tract was that a popish ruler promoted the Protestant religion by granting liberty, while a Protestant Church or ruler denying liberty was a hindrance to Protestantism. Another was " Old Popery as Good as New." It bore the motto " *Magnam Chartam dedit Henricus, Majorem dabit Chartam Jacobus.*" It was described as written by a private gentleman in the country to his friend, a clergyman in the city, accused the Established Church of unreasonableness in some of its doctrines and practices, and defended the reasonableness of liberty of conscience. Yet another work was " An Expedient for Peace." It repeated the usual arguments about the unreasonableness of persecution and the justice of toleration. Religious differences were not due entirely to wilfulness, but depended on a man's education, environment, and many other things, and the best thing that Christian people could do would be to agree that they could never agree. The Dissenters themselves were much divided on the question of the King's proceedings, but in " An Answer by an Anabaptist to the Three Considerations proposed to Mr. William Penn by a pretended Baptist concerning a Magna Charta for Liberty of Conscience," which appeared in September, the writer, who defended Penn and the King's dispensing power, told his brethren that their best policy was to take the opportunities offered, and be thankful. John Locke, a very nominal adherent of the Church of England,[1] had as early as 1667 written a long article in favour of toleration in his commonplace book.[2] In 1683 he took refuge in Holland, and during the winter of 1685–1686 he wrote at Amsterdam his " *Epistola de Tolerantia* " in the form of a letter to his friend Limborch. In it he gathered up all his thoughts and reading and the results of the discussions of many years. He had not intended to publish it, but it was printed in an English translation, without his knowledge or consent, in 1689. It was not generally known that he was the author until after his death, when an acknowledgment of the authorship was found in a codicil to his will. When it appeared the Toleration Act had already been passed, but his thoughts on the subject had no doubt had their place in the growing volume of opinion in favour of religious liberty.

[1] Lord King, " Life of Locke," 1829, pp. 272-273.   [2] *Ibid.*, p. 156.

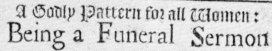

A Godly Pattern for all Women:
Being a Funeral Sermon
On the Deceaſe of that Worthy Gentlewoman

Mrs. *Margaret Baxter*,

The Wife of that reverend Miniſter of the Goſpel, Mr. *Richard Baxter* ; by that Godly Divine Mr. *John How*, Preacher of the Goſpel
of Jeſus Chriſt ; upon this Text,

2 *Cor.* 5. 8. *We are confident, I ſay, and willing
rather to be abſent from the Body, and to be pre-
ſent with the Lord.*

With her *Character* and *Chriſtian Deportment* in her Sickneſs,
and ſerious ejaculations on her Death-bed, left as a pattern to her Sex, She dy'd the 28th of *June*, 1681.

With Two Prayers, one before and another after Sermon.

Be faithful unto Death, and I will give thee a Crown of Life

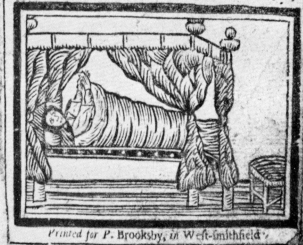

Printed for P. Brooksby, in Weſt-ſmithfield.

A CHAP-BOOK.

Facing p. 545.

XII

FROM the point of view of purely literary excellence, with a very few exceptions, the Puritan party had no great contribution to make to English literature between 1660 and 1689. Milton was, of course, at the zenith of his greatness. " Paradise Lost," " Paradise Regained," and " Samson Agonistes " were the glories of the Restoration period. Marvell was the only Puritan of the period, besides Milton, who acquired distinction in the field of poetry. He claimed not to be a Nonconformist, however, and said he merely wrote " what I think befits all men in humanity, Christianity and prudence towards Dissenters." [1] Apart from his poetry, his work was concerned with controversy, either in religious or political matters. George Wither also made excursions into politics. In 1660 he wrote " Fides Anglicana: or, a Plea for the Public Faith of these Nations," an attack on the restoration of the ecclesiastical lands to the Church, by which he himself suffered severely in pocket, and ended by finding himself in Newgate, and later on in the Tower.[2] He became a violent opponent of the Government. " This man was a dangerous incendiary, and able to do a great deal of mischief." [3] In prose there was the great master, John Bunyan, whose immortal " Pilgrim " [4] was translated into Dutch, French, and German before the century was out. Apart from these, the Puritan literature of the time was as a rule theological and controversial. The biographies and narratives produced by the Quakers, some of which have a literary flavour, were produced in order to spread their cause. Diaries like those of George Fox, Thomas Ellwood, Henry Newcome, and others were not written for publication, readable though some of them are. Robert Wilde was the only man with a turn for verse.

The Puritans had to endure constant ridicule, which hurt none the less because one of the characteristics of Puritanism in its severest forms was the lack of a sense of humour. Consequently there was none among them who could reply to the rhyming

---

[1] Camb. Hist. Eng. Lit., VII. 179.
[2] Harris, " Life of Charles II.," I. 380–388; Wood, " Athenæ," II. 392.
[3] Eachard, " Hist. Eng.," III. 208.
[4] Bunyan occasionally read Anglican writings, and he may have been influenced by Simon Patrick's " Parable of the Pilgrim."

satires of Samuel Butler or John Dryden. Some of them tried to answer " Absalom and Achitophel." " Towser the Second " was probably written by Henry Care, and " A Whip for the Fool's Back " was by an anonymous Nonconformist; but as literary productions they were hopelessly outclassed by Dryden's work. Slingsby Bethel, Ferguson, Forbes, Johnson, and the rest had none of them the ability to answer in Dryden's vein. Edmund Hickcringill, who held a living in the English Church without the slightest belief in the Anglican creed or practice, replied to " The Medal " in 1682 with " The Mushroom: or, A Satire against Libelling Tories and Prelatical Tantivies." In a postscript he said it was written in a day, and the title-page asserted that it was published the day after Dryden's verses, but it was a poor performance. Samuel Pordage, the author of a long, dull poem, " Mundorum Explicatio," in which he set forth the theology of the Behmenists, wrote " Azaria and Hushai " in reply to " Absalom and Achitophel," but with no more success than the rest of Dryden's adversaries.

Many of the Nonconformists were quiet people enough, but there was a comparatively small party of them distinguished by the violence with which they assailed both the Government and the Church. Many of them were Baptists and Fifth Monarchy men, and were of the party which kept the country in constant turmoil with their plotting. Much of their writing exceeded all bounds of theological controversy, and from the point of view of the Government was seditious.

The purpose of one group of these writings was to warn men of the severe judgments of God sent in anger upon the nation for the late changes. The first work of the kind was published in August 1660, and bore the title " The Lord's Loud Call to England. Being a True Relation of some late Various and Wonderful Judgments or Handiworks of God, Earthquakes, Lightning, Whirlwind, great Multitudes of Toads and Flies; and also the Striking of Divers Persons with Sudden Death, in several Places: for what Causes let the Man of Wisdom judge, upon his Serious Perusal of the Book Itself. Also of the Strange Changes, and Late Alterations made in these Three Nations. As also of the Odious Sin of Drinking Healths, with a Brief of Mr. Prynne's Solid Arguments against it, and his Epistle to the late King Charles to Redress it. Published by H. J., a servant of Jesus Christ, and a lover of Peace and Holiness." The writer was Henry Jessey, a graduate of St. John's College, Cambridge, who had been successively an Episcopalian, an Independent, and a Baptist, and had been ejected from St. George's, Southwark, in 1660.[1] He held Fifth Monarchist views, and on occasion preached at Venner's meeting-place in Swan Alley.[2] The printers were Livewell Chapman and Francis Smith. Jessey

---

[1] Palmer, I. 129.　　　[2] J. Muddiman, " The King's Journalist," p. 34.

and Chapman were both sent to prison. The book told of " the Lord's strange hand at Oxford," where several actors who had performed a play there were cut off by sudden death. The play was " The Guardian," and among the actors " cut off " were Mr. John Glendall and Mr. John Ball: the former, according to Jessey, broke a vein and died suddenly. Anthony Wood relates what really happened: " Mr. Glendall acted a part therein with much applause " but he did not break a vein. It was known in Brasenose College, of which he was a Fellow, that he had an infirmity of his lungs, but he was not taken ill till a week after the play was acted. After that he recovered, but went out too soon, caught a fresh cold, and died two months later than Jessey says he did. As for Mr. John Ball of Wadham, another of the actors " cut off," he did not act at all. He was ill before the play was given, had no taste at all for acting, and his death was due to a cold caught in riding to see Bishop Skinner, who was to have ordained him.[1] Another story was told about the terrible fate which befell the first man who used the Prayer Book in the university after the Restoration. He was also the last person who used the Prayer Book in the Civil War time, and now " the Lord had cut him off." A clerk's daughter at Brookington,[2] in Gloucestershire, had reviled some Puritan preachers, and on June 3rd, 1660, she fell down dead. The book also contained " a relation of the imprisonings, plunderings, and barbarous inhumanity and cruelty that hath lately been practised towards several ministers of the Gospel, and other peaceable people in Wales, Lincolnshire, Gloucestershire, and other places, especially since the late remnant of the Long Parliament, " by their outing of many, prepared a coffin for themselves and others."

Robert Clarke contradicted some of these stories in " The Lying Wonders, or the Wonderful Lies," published the same year. John Gadbury, who published in 1661 " A Brief Examination of that Nest of Sedition and Fanatic Forgeries published by Mr. H. Jessey," gave a categorical denial to most of them, while in addition he defended the Prayer Book, and answered Jessey's arguments against stage plays and health drinking.

In 1661 appeared a work entitled " Ἐνιαυτὸς Τεράστιος, Mirabilis Annus: or the Year of Prodigies and Wonders." It was a pamphlet of eighty-eight pages, and bore no printer's name or place of publication. It gave an account of eighty-seven alleged prodigies seen in the sky or on earth, and twenty-seven terrible judgments of God falling upon various evildoers. These prodigies had happened between August 1st, 1660, and the end of May 1661, and therefore, as the writer observed, at the rate of two a week. The preface said, " We have not feigned any one

[1] Wood, " Life and Times," I. 322–323; Wood, " Hist. Univ. Oxf., ed. Gutch," II. 704–708.
[2] Brokingham, Muddiman, " King's Journalist," p. 132.

of the particulars here inserted, nor so much as a circumstance relating to any of them, but have faithfully and impartially published them as they were communicated to us from credible persons, whose proofs also we scanned and weighed to the uttermost, and received ample satisfaction in the validity thereof before we made them public." Such signs, it went on to say, usually signify some remarkable changes and revolutions, which bring with them very sad calamities and distresses to the generality of the people amongst whom they happen. They bode misery and calamity to the profane and wicked, but good to the sober and religious. Let, therefore, " the hellish rout of profane and ungodly men," and " especially the oppressors and persecutors of the true Church," look to themselves.

Among the prodigies recounted were the following: two suns seen at one time at Hertford, a blood-red rainbow in Huntingdonshire, fire in the sky at Hull, a ball of fire out of the heavens, a rainbow over the moon, blazing stars, wells dried up, and strange tides. At Shenley, in Hertfordshire, on October 17th, the day Scrope and Jones, the regicides, were executed, five naked men, exceeding bright and glorious, were seen moving very swiftly in the sky. On November 5th two stars, each as big as the moon, were seen contending with each other at Avery Hatch, near Ilford, and one of them poured down blood and fire. Armies were seen fighting in the sky at Horsham, in Sussex, and on other occasions at London Bridge. Six sober, discreet persons in Yorkshire saw a fiery apparition in the air, wherein they discerned two or three steeples and several cathedrals, some burning, others rent and torn irreparably, others subverted with the pinnacles downwards, and by one of the pinnacles stood an angel with a flaming sword. Terrible hailstones, such as appeared in the days of King John and Queen Mary, " at what time the people suffered greatly," are recorded. A rain of frogs was noted at Beverley, of spiders at Bury, in Suffolk, and another of flies at the same place. The devil appeared in the likeness of a bishop to a scholar of Magdalen College, Oxford. A monster was born of human parents in the county of Buchanan in Scotland. It was like a hairy man, and had two heads, one above the other, the upper one like a lion. As soon as it was born it ran up and down the house, crying " Woe, woe to the world." The father knocked it on the head and killed it. The writer adds gravely, " This is a certain truth."

The judgments all fell on those who conformed, or even intended to conform, to the use of the Prayer Book. Mr. White, minister of Rougham, in Suffolk, was struck, apparently with paralysis, while reading the Prayer Book for the first time. Persons who interfered with those who refused to conform either died, or were struck with palsy, or were drowned, or suffered some other sad fate. A minister who used the sign of the cross in baptism fell from his horse dead. One who rejoiced at the death of Hugh Peters was bitten by a great dog, and his life was despaired of. While the Bishop of Oxford was ordaining some persons, a ledge of wainscot fell on the communion table.

In 1662 appeared " Mirabilis Annus Secundus, or the Second Year of Prodigies," relating those which were alleged to have appeared since the issue of the first part. The preface compared them to the plagues of Egypt, God's judgments on Pharaoh because he would not let His people go to serve Him. Accusations had been made against the former work that the statements were all false. The parhelia, blazing stars, meteors, storms, whirlwinds, double tides, and several, if not the greater part, of the accidents and judgments mentioned were all confirmed by public testimony. As far as the writer could inquire, most of the rest were true in substance, but he now acknowledged that some were doubtful. In the former work he had inserted historical parallels from sacred and profane history. " Great exception was made that some of the parallels, in the ears of the many, trumpet out nothing but sedition and rebellion." But he said " we openly testify our abhorrence of such practices."

More monstrous births were related. We have the story gravely recounted how a magpie disturbed an episcopal parson while preaching, and still worse, a bishop while giving the blessing. After that we are not so distressed at hearing of a mere prebendary's sermon being disturbed by a bat. Among the judgments, we read how a young man who abused the Solemn League and Covenant was smitten by the hand of the Lord. An episcopal clergyman who had been active in indicting a godly Nonconformist minister was murdered by a distracted man of his own family. One Colonel Carnaby, who lived in or about the city of Durham, did affirm to divers sober persons in Durham that Hugh Peters was drunk on the scaffold. Carnaby, after dining at Colonel Stewart's house, two miles from Durham, and being the worse for drink, lost his way and was found drowned in a pool. " This is notoriously known at Durham, and it is observed by the people there, that he who falsely and maliciously accused another for dying in his drunkenness, was himself really overtaken with that sin, and by the righteous hand of the Lord cut off from it."

Names, dates, and places are given with great detail in this work. It was widely read and accepted. Philip Henry noted in his diary, "I read a book called ' Annus Mirabilis,' containing a narrative of several strange appearances of the great God this last year in all the elements, chiefly witnessing against profaneness and persecution," [1] and quoted the work from time to time. " The Kingdom's Intelligencer " [2] had tested some of the stories, and found that nobody in the places mentioned knew

[1] " Diary," December 1st, 1661.   [2] October 14th, 21st, 1661.

anything about the matter alleged to have happened there. Kennet mentions a certificate, produced in May 1661, from the people of Wincanton, in Somerset, declaring that the story in the book about their minister, Mr. Sacheverell, was a horrible falsehood.[1]   " Mercurius Publicus " [2] ·gave similar evidence. Baxter said that while some of the stories, *e.g.* the unexplained drying up of the river Derwent in Derbyshire in winter time, were true, yet others were proved false.   Since this was the case, men were moved to say that the fanatics, in order to cheat the people into a seditious humour, were ready to belie God Himself.   He ascribed the authorship to the Fifth Monarchy men.[3]

The work was at first believed to have been printed by Francis Smith.   He was later understood to be in partnership with Brewster, Chapman, and Calvert in a second printing.[4] and they were all sent to prison for it.   On September 20th we find Smith appealing from the Gatehouse, where he was a prisoner charged with a share in compiling and printing the book.[5]   He said in 1673 that when he was imprisoned he did not know who printed it.[6]   On October 4th, 1661, Elizabeth, the wife of Giles Calvert, was sent to prison for being concerned in the publication of the work with an intent to promote disaffection to the King.[7] Francis Smith was examined on December 19th, 1661,[8] and declared he knew nothing about it, and had nothing to do with its compilation.   On June 24th, 1663, Creake, the printer, was examined, and said that Calvert, Chapman, and Brewster were the compilers, and divided among themselves an impression of 2000 copies." [9]

The history of the book is very complicated.   It would seem that originally Calvert was responsible for, perhaps compiled, with the help of Henry Jessey, " Several Prodigies and Apparitions seen in the Heavens from August 1st, 1660, to the end of May 1661."   This was seized by L'Estrange in June 1661. Calvert went to prison for that and the " Phœnix," and while he was in prison Elizabeth gave Smith the order to print it as the " Mirabilis Annus or the Year of Prodigies," and for this she was sent to prison.[10]   Kennet said there were three parts, published respectively in August 1661, August 1662, and December 1662.[11] The explanation is this: " The Second Year of Wonders " was issued in two books, one dealing with events from April 1661 to June 1662, and the other continuing to November 1662.   Henry Jessey was thought to be the author.   Examined on December

---

[1] Kennet, " Reg.," p. 454.   [2] July 2nd–9th, 1663.
[3] " Rel. Baxt.," p. 433.   [4] C.S.P.D., September 11th, 1661.
[5] Kennet, " Reg.," p. 537.
[6] Smith, " Symptoms of Growth and Decay of Godliness," 2nd ed., 1673.
[7] C.S.P.D., October 4th, 1661.
[8] C.S.P.D.   [9] C.S.P.D., June 24th, 1663.
[10] Kitchin, " L'Estrange," pp. 112–113.   [11] Kennet, " Reg.," p. 538.

8th, 1661, he admitted that he had long been in the habit of collecting notes of remarkable events. He had given one sheet of such to a Mr. Stanbridge in November 1660, and another had been found in his house when it was searched by the Government officials in the December of that year. His last sheet contained an account of the death of Major Orde in the bishopric of Durham which was in Annus Mirabilis. He admitted that he had talked to Francis Smith about strange events, and he had seen a copy of the book since it was printed,[1] but he denied that he had written it. Mr. Muddiman points out that the first volume showed signs of being edited by a man of learning. No doubt he did not invent the stories, but he probably wrote the preface.[2] He was set free after a month's imprisonment, but on August 30th, 1662, he was imprisoned again, apparently on suspicion of knowing more than he would tell about the plotting that was going on, and remained in the custody of a messenger for six months. He died in September 1663. Four or five thousand people were said to have attended his funeral, and it was reported that on his deathbed he prophesied that the Lord would destroy the powers that then ruled, and he urged his hearers to help in that good work.[3] His friends published " A Pillar Erected to the Memory of that Holy, Humble, and Faithful Servant of Jesus Christ, Mr. H. Jessey." It is not known where his meeting-house was, but as he was buried from Woodmongers' Hall, in Duke's Place, he may have used that as his preaching place. He is said to have been a great oriental scholar.[4] The Annus Mirabilis gave a great deal of trouble to the authorities, and there are many references to it in the State Papers.

A similar work was "The Panther-prophecy: or, a Premonition to all People of the Sad Calamities and Miseries like to Befall these Islands. To which is added an astrological discourse concerning that strange apparition of an army of horse seen in Wales, .near Montgomery, December 20th, 1661." It was printed by Simon Dover in 1662, and it predicted the rising which was arranged for October 1663.[5] The author was Owen Lloyd, and he prophesied the destruction of the King, lawyers, clergy, and citizens of London, and urged the wholesale slaughter of the ruling classes and the burning of the city.[6] Lloyd had communicated his visions to John Rogers in the year 1653 or 1654, and the work was printed, evidently in a revised form, in 1662. A Dutch translation was issued in 1688.

[1] C.S.P.D., December 8th, 1661.
[2] Muddiman, " King's Journalist," pp. 153–159; C.S.P.D., 45/33; Wood, " Life," I. 322–323 and notes.
[3] C.S.P.D., September 22nd, 1663. Palmer, who mentions some of his dying words, does not say this.
[4] Cramp, " Bapt. Hist.," pp. 356–360.
[5] C.S.P.D., 1661–1662, p. 543; 1663–1664, p. 162; " Trial of John Twyn," 1664. [6] N. and Q., 11th Ser., VIII. 324.

In 1662 Edward Bagshawe published a sermon entitled " Signs of the Times: or, Prognostics of Future Judgments, with the Way to Prevent Them." It was an argument in defence of the belief that the Almighty vouchsafes to grant signs of His approaching judgments on a wicked nation; such manifestations of His coming wrath as earthquakes, eclipses, strange portents in the elements. Another sure sign is when God's preachers are led to speak against the abominations of a land, and meet with no success, but are rather scorned, imprisoned, and put to silence. When the iniquities of a nation have reached their height; when a people, newly escaped out of a great affliction, have relapsed into the same sins for which they were afflicted; when there is a general corruption among the preachers, and they preach vainly, or live viciously, or both; when the commandments of God are generally broken by such sins as idolatry (he means the Prayer Book); when preachers preach for doctrines the commandments of men (he means episcopacy and the ceremonies); when forswearing, vain swearing, and perjury are rife; then the wise in heart can see sudden destruction coming from God upon that nation.

In the following year a general answer to this kind of literature came from the pen of John Spencer, a Bachelor of Divinity and Fellow of Corpus Christi College, Cambridge. It bore the title " A Discourse concerning Prodigies," and the writer referred particularly to a lost treatise of a certain Dr. Jackson, " Prodigies; or, Divine Forewarnings betokening Blood." Spencer complained that in recent years if any distempers incident to humanity had befallen persons who attended the services of the Church of England, they had been rashly urged " as caveats from heaven against their prayers." Referring to the " strange relations which of late have been pressed upon the faith of the nation," he animadverted on the credulity of the narrators, who, on quite insufficient testimony, related stories which were easier to assert than disprove. Spencer did not attempt to criticise these stories in detail, but argued the general question.

Among the books which were specially obnoxious to the Government was one called " A Phoenix; or, The Solemn League and Covenant." It gave an account of Charles II.'s coronation in Scotland, his " Declaration to all his loving subjects " in 1650, laying stress on the fact that the King himself had taken and promulgated the Covenant, and added a summary of a sermon by Edmund Calamy in 1645, entitled " The Great Dangers of Covenant-breaking." The title-page stated that the " Phoenix " was printed in Edinburgh " in the year of Covenant-breaking." The preface gave as the object of the publication: " For that things of such public concernment have been acted by the Heads of these nations, and in so solemn a manner, in the presence of Almighty God, it cannot soon be forgotten, but ɔught to be weighed and laid to heart." The real place of its publication was London. Giles Calvert, Livewell Chapman, and Thomas Brewster were responsible for its compilation and sale. Thomas Creake, of Little Britain, to whom it had been handed over in May 1661, did most of the printing.[1] Simon Dover, another printer, finished the impression, and Thresher did the binding. Creake and Thresher were imprisoned, and so was Calvert, but Chapman and Brewster escaped for a time. The discovery of the persons responsible for the work was made by Roger L'Estrange.[2]

Another work of a similar nature in some respects was " The Old Parliament Revived," [3] in which the author, Thomas Phillips, tried to prove that the Long Parliament had never been lawfully dissolved. His book was voted seditious by Parliament, and an impeachment was drawn up against him.[4]

Some of the Puritans, assuming the mantle of the Old Testament prophet, sternly rebuked the nation for what seemed to them apostasy. " Yet one Warning More to Thee, O England," by " D. B.," was published in December 1660. " D. B." was Daniel Baker, and he wrote from Worcester prison, fulminating prophecies from the Old and New Testaments against a country which had apostatised, in spite of the blessings granted her under her late rulers. " O nation, O England, who hast been so sweetly, so tenderly and terribly and wonderfully visited by the eternal word of power," he cried: but there were many who doubted the origin of the visitation, and also failed to see that the rule of the saints had been sweet and tender. He addressed London as " Thou impudent harlot, thou whorish, bloodthirsty mistress of abomination," and in fact kept up such a continual screech, all on the top note, that he failed to be impressive.

Another work which caused a great deal of trouble to the authorities was " Mene Tekel: or, the Downfall of Tyranny. A Treatise wherein Liberty and Equity are Vindicated, and Tyranny condemned, by the Law of God and Right Reason: and the People's Power and Duty to Execute Justice, without, and upon Wicked Governors, asserted by Laophilus Mysotyrannus." It was published in 1663; Nathan Strange printed 1000 copies, and others were printed in Holland, from whence copies were sent to Scotland and Ireland. Mrs. Calvert was suspected of knowing something about it.[5] One informer reported that Jones, one of the Council of Six conspirators in London, was the writer, but this seems a mistake; Mene Tekel was a nickname by which he was known. Another informer said that John Goodwin was the author.[6] Anthony à Wood attributed

[1] C.S.P.D., June 29th, 1661.
[2] " Truth and Loyalty Vindicated," 1662, p. 56.   [3] 1661.
[4] Hist. MSS. Com. V. i. 158, 200.   [5] C.S.P.D., February, June 2nd, 1664.
[6] C.S.P.D., September 9th, 1664, March 1665, and March 18th, 1665.

it to John Owen, but the style is against this.[1]   The printer was ordered to be hung, drawn and quartered.[2]

An anonymous writer, in " The Voice of a Cry at Midnight; or, An Alarm to Churches and Professors Speedily to Revive their Temple-Work, or Open Worship, Before the Present Prohibition be Reversed," published in 1664, urged the Dissenters to conduct their meetings openly, and not to betray civil and religious liberty by complying with the law, and above all things to be steadfast in spite of persecution.   Another tract, published about the same time, was called " Antipharmacum Saluberrimum : or, A Serious and Seasonable Caveat to all the Saints in this Hour of Temptation.   Wherein their Present Dangers are Detected and their Present Duties Vigorously Urged."   The writer said that, like Christ, seeing the faithful without shepherds, and that the pretended shepherds had taken to themselves the instruments of a foolish shepherd, he had come to their aid, and, like David's worthies, brought them water through the hosts of the Philistines.   He advised them to stand fast to their profession, and not to touch idolatry and superstition under whatever name or notion presented.   The worship of the Church of England was will-worship—that is, such worship as had no ground or warrant but in the will of men; it was idolatry, and its origin was in the proud heart of men; it was superstitious—that is to say, it was excess in religion.   They were to beware of such persons as were factors and agents of Antichrist, and to keep off from such a ministry as that of the Established Church, the scope of which was only to draw men into idolatry.   The writer admitted, however, that some of the Anglican clergy, though deriving their orders from bishops, a thing of naught and sinful, were true ministers of Christ.   He pressed upon his readers to give their utmost diligence to promote religion and godliness in their families and neighbourhoods, especially as the ordinary and public means of edification had been cut off, and they were to prepare for a day of great trouble approaching.

Another attempt to throw odium upon the Government was the forged " Speeches and Prayers of the Regicides."   It was printed by Dover and Creake at the instigation of Calvert, Brewster, and Chapman.   There were several editions of this work, with slight variations in the title.   At the trial of John Twyn and other printers it was admitted that these speeches and prayers were an imposture, invented by the enemies of the Government.[3]

Various volumes purporting to be the farewell sermons of some of the ejected London ministers came forth from the Press.   Dr. William Bates, the retiring incumbent of St. Dunstan's-in-the West, published an official copy of his two sermons, to prevent the

[1] Orme, " Life of Owen," p. 387.   [2] " Tanner MSS.," XLVII. 70.
[3] " The Exact Narrative of the Trial of John Twyn," 1664.

harm done by imperfect copies, " which we hear are coming forth." There was very little reference in these to the troubles, but the second sermon concluded with these words, " I know you expect I should say something as to my nonconformity. I shall only say this much. It is neither fear, faction, nor humour that makes me not to comply, but merely for fear of offending God. And if after the best means used for my illumination, as prayer to God, discourse, study, I am not able to be satisfied concerning the lawfulness of what is required; if it be my unhappiness to be in error, surely men will have no reason to be angry with me in this world, and I hope God will pardon me in the next.[1] Matthew Newcomen ejected from Dedham, in Essex, also published his sermons.[2]

" A Complete Collection of Farewell Sermons . . . to which is added their several prayers," contained what purported to be the sermons of thirty-one of the ejected ministers, and claimed to be more perfect than any other collection. It was published in 1662, and a second edition was issued in the following year. There was another collection in two volumes. In these sermons there were but few references to the actual occasion, merely exhortations to stand fast in the day of trial, and to beware of popery; but the general attitude taken up was that England and the Church were being punished for their sins. Another volume, " England's Remembrancer, or a Collection of Farewell Sermons preached by Divers Nonconformists in the Country," printed in 1663, contained seventeen sermons, but the preachers' names were not given, nor, for that matter, was the printer's. It was remarked at the time that the sermons of the country ministers were better than those of the town ministers, and the reason assigned was that their volume was from their own notes, while the others were " for the most part but some mangled scraps from ignorant scribblers." [3] Altogether ten or twelve impressions of these " Farewell Sermons " came out by 1663, and did much harm to the Government.[4] They contained a varying number of sermons, but they all seem to have been forgeries. Dr. Thomas Manton, in the *News* on September 24th, 1663, disclaimed what was ascribed to him, and other ejected ministers did the same.[5] In July 1663 Peter Lillicrap the printer petitioned the Government for release from prison, at the same time loudly proclaiming his loyalty. He petitioned again in September, saying that he had been ten weeks in prison, although he had done more to suppress sedition than all the printers in England. This time his prayer was successful, and he was released.[6]

[1] Bates, " The Peacemaker," 1662.
[2] " Ultimum Vale: or, the Last Farewell of a Minister of the Gospel to a Beloved People," 1663.
[3] Kennet, " Reg.," p. 750.   [4] Kitchin, " L'Estrange," p. 109.
[5] Kennet, " Reg.," p. 779; *N. and Q.*, 11th Ser., VIII. 284.
[6] C.S.P.D., July 23rd, September 5th, 1663.

"The Dying Father's Legacy," ascribed untruthfully to Hugh Peters, published in 1660, and republished in 1683, had a preface which was initialled "G.F., N.B.," a clumsy attempt to make George Fox and Broad, the Quaker who concealed Peters, responsible for the work, and to let the odium fall on them. The fanatics were very bitter against the Quakers, and loved throwing mud at them. A pamphlet came from the printers entitled "The Speech and Confession of Humphrey Stone, a Quaker," which stated that Humphrey Stone was tried in October 1661 before the Lord Mayor of Dublin on a charge of murdering one William Frith by stabbing him, that he was guilty of blasphemy at his trial, and was finally sentenced to death. "Mercurius Politicus," January 23rd–30th, 1662, published a certificate that no such trial had taken place.[1]

Among the most ribald of the Nonconformist writers was one Ralph Wallis, who called himself "the Cobbler of Gloucester." He was a married man with four children, and said that he had many calls to the pulpit, ranging from £8 to £30, with "my diet and the use of a study of books." He wrote "Rome for Good News, or Good News from Rome: In a Dialogue between a Seminary Priest and a Supposed Protestant, at large. An Exhortation to Bishops. Whereunto is also Annexed a Discourse between a Poor Man and his Wife." It was printed in London without date.[2] Another tract was called "Good News from Rome," while the title of a third was "More News from Rome: or Magna Charta, Discoursed between a Poor Man and his Wife. As also a new Font erected in the Cathedral Church of Gloucester in October 63 and consecrated by the reverend and moderate Bishop Dr. William Nicholson, Angel of the said Church, according to the account of that infamously famous man, Dr. Lee. As also an Assertion of Dr. William Warmestry, Dean of Worcester, where he affirmeth that it is a lesser sin for a man to kill his Father than to refrain from coming to the Divine Service established in the Church of England. The one was the Killing of a Particular Person, The other made a breach in the Mystical Body of Christ. The Members of the Mystical Body distinctly discoursed on by the said Poor Man and his Wife." The Epistle Dedicatory to his wife spoke of "that *ridiculus mus* the Church Catechism, which teacheth to tell three lies in one breath, viz.: 'Wherein I was made, etc.'". "My father and mother," said Wallis, "were both Church papists," who lived in a country village where there was only a reading priest: they commonly went to the service "or evensong, as it was called." His mother taught him popish prayers, his father left him books with fine red letters, images, beads, and a crucifix, though he never taught him to use any of them. "It were better that all Rome's remnants, relics, rites, etc., now in use in the Church of England

---

[1] *N. and Q.*, 11th Ser., VIII. 284.   [2] *Ibid.*, 1–3.

were sent to hell, whence they came, rather than that one godly honest preacher should have his mouth stopped." It was a vulgar production, full of abuse and of tales of the drunkenness and immorality of the clergy, their livings, pluralities, exchanges, and conformity for the sake of a living. A specimen of the humour is a story that St. Francis, looking out of a window, saw a friar kiss a nun, and was very thankful that there was so much charity in the world. There was a fourth pamphlet called " The Honour of a Hangman."

In January 1664 Wallis was known to be lurking in London, and the Government got hold of a letter to his wife, in which he said he had some more books and papers to dispose of, and more books ready for the press, and that James Forbes, a Scotsman, one of Oliver's old preachers, now a shoemaker in Clapham, was collecting money for the cost of the printing.[1] Another of his letters was intercepted in June, and in it he boasted that Bishop Nicholson of Gloucester and Dean Warmestry had done their worst; but a friend had told him all that passed between them and L'Estrange.[2] However, Ralph Wallis, *alias* Gardiner, was seized on September 28th,[3] and was brought up for examination on October 1st. Thomas Rawson, a journeyman shoemaker, living in Little Britain, said that Wallis lodged in his house, and brought in many books which he had written, including the four already mentioned. James Forbes, who had from 1654 to 1660 preached to a " gathered " congregation in Gloucester cathedral,[4] had been arrested, and his house searched by Roger L'Estrange, who found there a number of Wallis's books, and another called " The Sufferer's Catechism." Forbes was now examined, professed to know nothing about them, and said he had not read them and could not tell how they came into his possession.[5] The truth was that he had helped Wallis to distribute literature of this kind all over England by means of carriers.[6] Wallis himself admitted that he had formerly lived at Gloucester, and was the author of the books.

Wallis, before the year was out, petitioned Secretary Bennet not to crush a worm, nor to starve a poor family because their father had scribbled a little drollery and published stories for bread. He had only attacked the priests that they might learn better manners, and promised to scribble as much against the fanatics " when the worm gets into his poor cracked pate, as it did when he wrote these books." [7] He seems to have got his freedom before long, for in April of the next year the Bishop of Gloucester wrote to the Archbishop of Canterbury complaining about him, and saying that Wallis denied the King's supremacy,

[1] C.S.P.D., January 18th, 1664.   [2] C.S.P.D., June 16th, 1664.
[3] C.S.P.D.   [4] Palmer, II. 249–250.
[5] C.S.P.D., October 1st, 1664.   [6] Kitchin, " L'Estrange," p. 171.
[7] C.S.P.D., 1664.

scoffed at the liturgy, and by his scurrilous wit gained much applause among the people. In spite of the kindness shown to him, he was still selling his books in the town, and glorying in the fact.[1] In 1668 we hear of him again. L'Estrange wrote to Williamson describing some books he had seized. One of them, " Felo de Se," he thought to be undoubtedly by Wallis. Another he described as " the damnedest thing has come out yet." This was " Room for the Cobbler of Gloucester and his Wife, with several Cartloads of Abominable, Irregular, Pitiful, Stinking Priests: as also a Demonstration of their Calling after the Manner of the Church of Rome: but not According to Magna Charta, the Rule of the Gospel. Whereunto is added, a Parallel between the Honour of a Lord Bishop and the Honour of a Cobbler; the Cobbler being Proved the more Honourable Person." This work had just been published. The title is sufficient to show its scope, its scurrility, its Anti-Romanism, and its accusations of popery hurled against the clergy and bishops, giving names and places, but no shadow of proof. Wallis, how-ever, had escaped in disguise, for the time being, out of L'Estrange's clutches,[2] and must have died within a year or two, for in 1670 there appeared " The Life and Death of Ralph Wallis," which has been ascribed to L'Estrange.

Though Wallis was dead, there were others who could write in the same vein. In 1673 appeared " Room for News, or News from Rome. Being a Dialogue between the Pope and the Devil at a late Conference." It was a tract of eight pages, " published by Martin Marpope," and was followed in the same year by " Room for Miracles: or Miracles from Rome. A Cart-Load for a Penny. Pleasantly yet truly exposing the Wonderful Foppery imposed by the Popish Church, to be Believed by her Catholic Children. To which is added a Lump of Holy Relics, worth nobody knows what, as a Cast into the Bargain. London. Printed by Stout D." The preface stated that the late " Dia-logue between His Holiness and his Cloven-footed Tutor " was bought up as fast as Gazettes after a sea-fight, and encouraged the writer " to play the fool once more." If this publication proved successful, there was an intention of publishing weekly " some fresh piece of popish fopperies " at a penny. The pamphlet scoffed at the mass, at St. Francis, and at various mediæval legends and relics.

The one humorous verse-writer who appeared on the Puritan side was Dr. Robert Wilde, who had been minister of Aynho, in Northamptonshire, till the Restoration. After that he retired to Oundle, where he died at the age of seventy, in 1679. Wood described him as " a fat, jolly, and boon Presbyterian." He wrote a number of poems which were collected into one volume in 1670, and were very popular with all classes. Dryden called

---

[1] C.S.P.D., April 15th, 1665.   [2] C.S.P.D., 238/202.

Wilde " the Wither of the City," and told how he had seen men reading his verses even on 'Change. After his death various pieces which were not his were published in his name. By his will he left a curious charity to the parish church of St. Ives. Every Whit-Tuesday at 9 a.m. twelve persons, six male and six female were, after prayer by the minister, to cast lots with dice on the altar of the church. and the six who got the highest throws were each to receive a Bible, the value of which was not to exceed seven shillings. A sermon was then to be preached on the divine authority of the Scriptures. The preacher was to receive ten shillings, and the clerk one shilling, and if any surplus remained from the funds the minister, churchwardens, " and such other grave persons as they think good to invite " were to spend it on a friendly meal.

Just before the Restoration appeared "Iter Boreale: attempting something upon the Successful and Matchless March of the Lord General George Monk," in which Wilde says:—

> " I that enraged at the times and Rump,
> Had gnawed my goosequill to the very stump
> And flung that in the fire, no more to write
> But to sit down, poor Britain's Heraclite,
> Now sing the triumphs of the men of war,
> The glorious rays of the bright Northern Star,
> Created for the nonce by Heaven to bring
> The wise men of three nations to their King."

There is a spark of the real thing in the last lines. He had it sometimes, as in his epitaph " For a Godly Man's Tomb ":—

> " Here lies a piece of Christ, a star in dust,
> A vein of gold, a china dish that must
> Be used in heaven, when God shall feast the just."

Only it is somewhat marred here by a straining after quaint conceits. What he can sink to is seen in the " Epitaph for a Wicked Man's Tomb," which runs:—

> " Here lies the carcase of a cursed sinner,
> Doomed to be roasted for the devil's dinner."

The lines on " The Norfolk and Wisbeach Cockfight " were not written by one who had never been to such an entertainment, nor were those " Upon some Bottles of Sack and Claret laid in Sand and Covered with a Sheet " by a total abstainer. In the volume of the complete " Works " there follows " An Essay upon the late Victory obtained by H.R.H. the Duke of York against the Dutch upon June 3rd, 1665." It begins:

> " Gout! I conjure thee by the powerful names
> Of *Charles* and *James*, and their victorious fames,
> On this great day set all thy prisoners free,
> Triumph demands a gaol delivery."

But he was not a mere *bon vivant*. He could be grateful for small mercies and be merry over his misfortunes. Sir J. B. Knight sent him a present of ten crowns in the year 1665. He replied with " The Grateful Nonconformist," in which he described himself as

> " A limping Levite, who scarce in his prime
> Could woo an Abigail, or say grace in rhyme."

and thus addressed his benefactor :—

> " What, now to help a Nonconformist ! Now
> When ministers are broke who will not bow !
> When 'tis to be unblest to be ungirt !
> To wear no surplice doth deserve no shirt;
> No broth, no meat; no service, no protection;
> No cross, no coin; no collect, no collection.
> You are a daring knight thus to be kind.
> If trusted Roger [1] gets it in the wind,
> He'll smell a plot, a Presbyerian plot."

There are no fat and comfortable ministers among the Non-conformists now :—

> " One Lazarus amongst us was too much,
> But ere it be long we all shall look like such;
> And when that come to pass, the world shall see
> Who are the Ghostly Fathers, they or we."

When Edmund Calamy was imprisoned in 1663, Wilde congratulated him in this wise :—

> " Hundreds of us turn out of house and home;
> To a safe habitation you are come.
> What though it be a gaol? Shame and disgrace
> Rise only from the crime, not from the place.
>
> Indeed the place did for your presence call:
> Prisons do want perfuming most of all.
> Thanks to the Bishop and his good Lord Mayor,
> Who turned the den of thieves into a house of prayer."

Even if his metre is not always all it might be, and if he did rhyme " mittimus " with " dealt with thus," he had a pretty wit. He expounded his own hard lot to Dr. Calamy :—

> " For if in suffering we both agree,
> Sir, I may challenge you to pity me:
> I am the older gaol-bird: my hard fate
> Hath kept me twenty years in Cripplegate:
> Old Bishop Gout, that lordly proud disease,
> Took my fat body for his diocese,
> Where he keeps court, there visits every limb,
> And makes them, Levite-like, conform to him.
> Severely he doth article each joint,
> And makes enquiry into every point:

---

[1] Roger L'Estrange.

> A bitter enemy to preaching, he
> Hath half a year sometimes suspended me;
> And if he find me painful in my station,
> Down I am sure to go next visitation:
> He binds up, looseth, sets up and pulls down;
> Pretends he draws all humours from the crown.

> " He hath me now in hand, and ere he goes,
> I fear for heretics he'll burn my toes.
> Oh, I would give all I am worth, a fee
> That from his jurisdiction I were free."

Even the Anglican bishops must have laughed at that. In 1666 appeared " The Loyal Nonconformist: or, An Account of what he Dare Swear, and he Dare Not Swear."

> " I'll pray that all his subject may agree,
> And never more be crumbled into parts;
> I will endeavour, that his Majesty
> May not be King of Clubs, but King of Hearts."

But some of his friends must have shuddered at this card-playing, cockfighting, gouty, jovial soul!

> " I dare not swear Church government is right
> As it should be; but this I dare to swear,
> (If thou should'st put me to't) the bishops might
> Do better, and be better than they are.

> For holy vestments I'll not take an oath
> Which linen most canonical may be:
> Some are for lawn, some holland, some Scots'-cloth,
> And hemp, for some, is fitter than all three."

In "The Recantation of a Penitent Proteus " he poured scorn on the men who had changed their religion with the times during the previous twenty-five years. In " The Poring Doctor " he jeered at a divine, probably Prebendary John Lake of St. Paul's, who was accused of having bowed at the name of Judas during the service on November 5th, 1663. The practice of bowing at the name of our Lord was hateful to the Puritan; but the piece is in hopelessly bad taste—and this verse is quite unworthy of the writer:—

> " Some say that his sight,
> Poor man! is not right.
> I wish that it be no worse,
> But others think he
> To Judas bowed the knee
> For love he bears to the purse."

Perhaps the gout made him irritable. Usually he was a lovable, witty man, a good man, and a genial, broad-minded soul. To " The Fair Quarrel," a dialogue in verse purporting to be between himself and a Mr. Wanley, a Churchman, he spoke thus to his episcopalian friend:—

" May thy rich parts with saving grace be joined,
As diamonds in rings of gold enshrined.
May He that made the stars create a sphere
Of heavenly frame of life, and fix them here;
May that blessed life credit conformity,
And make e'en Puritans to honour thee.
May'st thou to Christ such store of converts bring,
That he whose place thou fill'st for joy may sing.
May God love you, and you love God again;
And may these prayers of mine not be in vain."

Wilde also wrote a comedy called " The Benefice." Henry
Newcome's " Diary " has several references to it, tending to
show that Newcome either corrected or annotated a copy.[1] If
both Puritan and Anglican had possessed Wilde's sense of humour,
his tolerant, genial outlook, and his Christian charity, a different
ecclesiastical history would have been written.[2]

John Bunyan wrote some verses. Among his early works in
metre were " Serious Meditations," " Ebal and Gerizim," and
" Prison Meditations." Besides these, we have the verse scattered about his prose works. The most popular of the Nonconformist verse writers, however, was Benjamin Keach. His
verses, for they can hardly be called poetry, went through many
editions, and had a great sale in chapbook form. In 1673 he
produced " War with the Devil: or, The Young Man's Conflict
with the Powers of Darkness." This was followed by " The
Glorious Lover: a Divine Poem upon the Adorable Mystery
of Sinners' Redemption," which appeared in 1679. An advertisement at the end of the first edition said, " There will be
suddenly published another treatise of this author's, entitled
' Sion in Distress: or, The Groans of the True Protestant
Church.' " The first edition of this was published in 1681, but
the Address to the Reader says, " You are here presented with a
revived poem with such additions and enlargements as makes it
very different from the first impression. Nothing, however,
seems to be known of this first impression. Still, what is known as
the second edition, dated 1682, described itself as corrected and
amended, though no alterations appear to have been made.
The poem bewailed the hard lot of the Dissenters, but the strain
changed with the Revolution, for in 1689 appeared " Distressed
Sion Relieved: or, The Garment of Praise for the Spirit of
Heaviness," from the pen of the same writer.

Keach was a stout advocate of the singing of hymns in church
worship, about which there was much controversy among the
Nonconformists, and in 1693 he issued a collection of hymns and
psalms from the Old and New Testaments, entitled " Spiritual
Melody, containing near three hundred Sacred Hymns." An

---

[1] Halley, " Lancs. Puritanism," p. 401.
[2] Calamy, II. 486; IV. 633; Palmer, III. 26; Wilde's Poems, ed. J. Hunt,
1870.

ardent Baptist, he attacked the Quakers in 1675 in " The Grand Impostor Discovered : or, The Quakers' Doctrine Weighed in the Balance and Found Wanting." This was a poem in dialogue form, in which he argued against the chief Quaker tenets one by one, and refuted them to his own satisfaction from Holy Scripture.

Keach's piety was better than his poetry. He wrote some dreadful doggerel at times. Perhaps a single example will suffice :—

> " Let grace and knowledge now abound,
> And the blest Gospel shine so clear,
> That it Rome's harlot may confound
> And popish darkness quite cashier :
> Oh! let Thy fire on Sion shine,
> But plague these cursed foes of Thine.
> Nay, precious God, let light extend
> To China and East India.
> To Thee let all the people bend,
> Who live in wild America!
> Oh! let Thy blessed Gospel shine
> That the blind heathen may be Thine.
> Send forth Thy light like to the morn,
> Most swiftly, Lord, Oh! let it fly
> From Cancer unto Capricorn!
> That all dark nations may espy
> Thy glorious Face on them to shine,
> And they in Christ for to be Thine."

An anonymous publication, " Vox et Lacrimae Anglorum : or, The True Englishmen's Complaints to their Representatives in Parliament, humbly tendered to their serious Considerations at their next Sitting," complained of the persecution of the Nonconformists and of the predominance of popery; and said that religion was being made a stalking horse to idolatry. The writer asked for the restitution of the faithful ministers who had been ousted; and since he demanded justice against " perfidious Clarendon," these sixteen pages of bad verse must have been issued before the Chancellor's fall.[1]

Thomas Grantham, the Baptist, wrote a collection of verses in 1661 or 1662, " The Prisoner against the Prelate : or, a Dialogue between the Common Gaol and Cathedral of Lincoln; wherein the True Faith and Church of Christ are Briefly Discovered and Vindicated, by the Authority of Scripture, Suffrages of Antiquity, Concessions and Confessions of the Chief Opposers of the same Church and Faith. Written by a Prisoner of the Baptized Churches in Lincolnshire." It was an attack on the Church for its State establishments, its pomp, carnality, and errors, and the pride, cruelty, avarice, and immorality of the clergy. The book began with " The Author's Expostulations with himself, and his Appeal to God about the Publication of the ensuing Poems." This was followed by " The Conference," a dialogue between

---

[1] C.S.P.D., 234/85.

Lincoln gaol and Lincoln cathedral, written chiefly in six-lined stanzas, and dealing with the whole argument between Church and Dissent. Also included in the volume was " A Lamentation for the Reigning Abomination of Pride in the Congregations."

" England's Faithful Monitor, being the Works of that Suffering Protestant, Mr. Stephen Husnance, when under Exile and Confinement, in the years 1685 and 1686," was a volume (not published, however, till 1689) containing 236 pages of very poor verse against popery; while the verses of Joseph Stennett, in 1687, had some influence in keeping Dissenters from siding with James II.'s toleration schemes.

The Quakers were not much given to poetry, but Benjamin Antrobus, a linen-draper by trade and a Quaker by religion, who lived at the sign of the Plough and Harrow in Cheapside, made some excursions into verse. A volume entitled " Buds and Blossoms of Piety," which was published in 1684, was a collection of verses on different subjects written by him, some in his early days, when he was an apprentice, some during imprisonment, and at other times. There was little in them which would specially mark the writer as a Quaker, and it would hardly be unjust to say that they showed more godliness than poetry.

One other Quaker verse-writer may be mentioned. This was Thomas Ellwood, the friend of Milton and the author of the better-known autobiography. In 1712 he published his " Davideis. The Life of David King of Israel: A Sacred Poem in Five Books." His association with Milton did not at any rate fill him with poetic fire. The biblical story is related in rhyming decasyllabic couplets, without a spark of poetic genius. He had a sense of metre, but occasionally produced some very feeble rhymes. One wonders whether " Absalom and Achitophel " had anything to do with the choice of subject. The first three books were written, he tells us, in 1688, and he found opportunity to make his subject a peg on which to hang his political views. When he came to the story of how Saul ordered the slaughter of Ahimelech the priest and all his family, he made this digression:—

> " How miserable is the state of those,
>   Whose frame of government doth them expose
>   To arbitrary power! Where law's not known!
>   Nor any man can call his life his own!
>   Where innocency is of little force!
>   Because impartial justice hath no course,
>   Where one man's rage keeps all the rest in awe;
>   Whose will and pleasure are his only law.
>
> Oh, how much better is their case, who live
>   Under a constitution, which doth give
>   To every man, in government, a share:
>   And binds the whole to have of each a care.

> Where even-handed justice freely flows:
> And each the laws, he must be tried by, knows.
> Where none, by power, can be oppressed: because
> Both Prince and people subject are to laws.
> None there an arbitrary sentence fears,
> Since none can be condemned but by his peers;
> Where common interest doth them wary make,
> How they their fellow's life away do take.
> For the same sentence, wherewith they condemn
> Another, may be shortly turned on them.
> These too the accused party may reject
> If their indifferency he suspect:
> And, ne'er so mean, may for his birthright stand
> Fair trial, and full hearing may demand."

Whatever we may say of the poetry, the sentiments are surprising. The Quakers had suffered as much as anyone in the English courts. In despite of much that had happened, this Quaker leader evidently was satisfied with the general fairness of the English legal and judicial system, for the words can have been written of no other system. Of course, however, matters improved considerably with the Revolution. He goes on:—

> " Prize your good fortune, ye whose lot is fell
> Under so good a government to dwell.
> Where no dispensing power can make a breach
> Upon your freedoms: nor your persons reach.
> But all ye have, life, liberty, estate,
> Is safe by law: which none can abrogate
> Without your own consents—Be therefore wise:
> And learn, so great a benefit to prize.
> Look to't—Be watchful, none, by any wile
> You of so rich a jewel e'er beguile."   (Book II. 11. 1–36.)

It is due to Ellwood to say that when he published his poem he had not seen Cowley's work on the same subject. He also wrote " A Collection of Poems on Various Subjects," but his great work, apart from his own " Life," by which he is best known, was the transcription and preparation for the press of George Fox's Journal. The literary problems connected with this work are manifold; Fox kept a number of different journals, known to us as the " Great Journal," the " Short Journal," the " Itinerary Journal," and so on. In 1683 he appointed a committee, of which Ellwood was a member, to prepare these for printing. In 1691, the year after his death, the Journal was published in a folio edition, with a life of Fox prefixed. Ellwood was certainly responsible for the publication and for the biography, but he hardly took his editorial duties in the same light as a modern editor would do, and it is often difficult to say what parts of the finished product are pure Fox and what parts have practically been rewritten by Ellwood.[1]

[1] For the whole question see Dr. Norman Penney's edition of the " Short Journal." Cambridge, 1925.

Over twenty works were published in the Welsh language by Nonconformists between 1660 and 1688. It was a very difficult thing to do, because there were no printing offices in Wales, and probably no Welsh compositor at the English presses. It was therefore necessary, when a Welsh book was to be printed in London or Oxford, for a Welsh scholar to be on the spot to correct the proofs. Of the works mentioned above, two were editions of the Bible, the rest were either devotional or didactic. Between 1641 and 1690, out of five editions of the whole Bible, and five of the New Testament, it was stated that only one folio edition was the work of a Churchman. Thomas Gouge, Fellow of King's College, Cambridge, and ejected from St. Sepulchre's, distributed the Bible, and procured the translation of several works into Welsh; the Church Catechism, " The Practice of Piety," " The Whole Duty of Man," etc. He was responsible for a new impression of the Bible, and of the Prayer Book, in Welsh. On the strength of his ejection, he is frequently counted as a Nonconformist, but Tillotson, in the sermon which he preached at Gouge's funeral in 1681, said, " For several of the last years of his life he continued in the communion of our Church, and, as he himself told me, thought himself in conscience bound so to do." Powell, in his " History of Wales," published with additions by W. Wynne in 1697, said, " It is notoriously evident that since the Reformation was settled in that country, and the Bible with the Book of Common Prayer translated into the Welsh tongue, no place has been more exact in keeping to the strict rubric and constitution of the Church of England, both as to substance and form of worship. But what may more truly be attributed to Mr. Gouge is that since his travels in Wales, and the propagating of his doctrine among the ignorant of the country, presbytery, which before had scarce taken root, has daily increased and grown to a head." Gouge began work in Wales in 1670. He set up an organization, which, however, did not last long after his death, for sending children to school to learn English, and for distributing Bibles and works of instruction and devotion. He was excommunicated, apparently for preaching without a licence.[1] Many of the writings of the Puritans of this period were translated into foreign languages, but Richard Baxter had the honour of having his " Call to the Unconverted " translated into one of the North American Indian languages. Only one copy of it is known to exist at the present day. It was in the library of the Royal Society, but was sold a few years ago.

The books for children written by Puritan writers in the time of Charles II. give the feeling that their readers must have been very solemn and serious little mortals. The seventeenth century child knew no beautiful volumes like those issued to-day, yet he was probably just as happy with his little brown books, with

[1] Rees, " Protestant Nonconformity in Wales," pp. 195–206.

their queer woodcuts, and as he was drilled in the elements of religion and knew what discipline meant, he had some advantages over his descendants. Nevertheless, one would hardly wish children to be quite so precocious as those mentioned in Henry Jessey's "Looking-glass for Children," published in 1673, with such success that three or four editions appeared within a year. This was a narrative of "God's gracious dealings with some little children," two of them, as a matter of fact. One was Mary Warner, aged six, who wept because she was afraid that her fine clothes would send her to hell. In her eighth year, when bonfires and drinking of healths and much shouting were going on in London, she wept and said, "Here is a deal of wicked joy. They know not but they may be dead before the morning. Methinks I see our sins fly up to heaven as fast as the sparks fly upwards." On her deathbed, at the age of ten, asked if she were willing to die, she replied, "Aye, very willing, for then I shall sin no more, for I know that Christ's blood hath made satisfaction for my sins." She then gave her family parting advice, and talked to them like a middle-aged woman; but one cannot help feeling that what the child said must have been rewritten in grown-up language. A similar story, however, was told of the deathbed of Mary Sam, the grand-daughter of William Dewsbury.[1] Next we have the story of Mr. Edward Scarfield's daughter, who was eleven years of age, and experienced a great difficulty in believing, but faith was given to her on the 24th day of the sixth month of 1661, while her father was conducting family prayers. By far the greater part of the book is taken up with the poems of Abraham Cheare, written whilst he was a prisoner. As poetry, they are rather worse than the poems of Isaac Watts, and the religious lessons they convey are frequently of a depressing kind :—

> " Few tender-hearted youths, as was
>   Josiah, Judah's King.
> Hosannah in the high'st (alas!)
>   How seldom children sing.
> Youths rarely ask for Zion's ways,
>   They'd rather pleasure find.
> But oh! in these your youthful days
>   Your Great Creator mind.
>
> What children pulse and water choose
>   Continually to eat,
> Rather than conscience should accuse
>   For tasting royal meat?
> Would you not bow, a King to please
>   Though tortures were behind?
> Oh, then in these your youthful days
>   Your Great Creator mind."

Another poem is written to a young girl. After some verses

[1] " The Faithful Testimony of William Dewsbury," pp. 348–352.

addressed to her, Cheare provides her with a song to sing, which begins :—

> " When by spectators I am told
> What beauty doth adorn me
> Or, in a glass, when I behold
> How sweetly God did form me.
> Hath God such comeliness displayed
> And on me made to dwell?
> Tis pity such a pretty maid
> As I should go to hell."

A letter sent to the child of a friend counsels him to sing :—

> " Lord, what a worm am I!
> What could'st Thou here espy?
> What kind of love is this?
>
> What reason can it have?
> Shall God through grace Himself abase
> So vile a wretch to save? "

This, of course, is the doctrine of the total corruption of human nature held by many of those who were later called Evangelicals. Some of the poems in the book are addressed to relatives, others to children friends of the writer. For their instruction he takes Vavasour Powell's description of an elect person as given at the close of his " Catechism," and translates it into simple verse for children's better remembrance. There are also one or two pious meditations in verse, and a couple of elegies on departed friends. Perhaps the most touching thing in the book is a set of " Verses affixed to the wall of the prison at the Guildhall in Plymouth : where A. C. was detained a month, and thence sent to the Island, Sept. 27th, 1665." In halting rhymes he tells the story of his imprisonment, and finishes up :—

> " But since my lines the Lord assigns
> In such a lot to be,
> I kiss the rod, confess my God
> Deals faithfully with me.
> My charged crime, in His due time
> He fully will decide,
> And until then, forgiving men,
> In peace with Him I bide."

It was the doctrine of total corruption and Divine vengeance on sin which gave this book a somewhat gloomy tinge. There is a good deal of fear of hell in it. But, after all, the fear of hell, like the fear of punishment from a father, did teach children that wrong-doing was a thing that mattered. It was an age that did not spare the rod and spoil the child, and it was an age that believed that God was just as well as merciful.

Abraham Cheare was the son of John Cheare, the lessee of two of the fulling mills built by Sir Francis Drake at Plymouth.

After the Restoration he soon got into trouble. At Easter 1661 he was sent to Exeter gaol for three months for encouraging unlawful religious assemblies. In August of that year the oath of allegiance was tendered to him under the Act of 1610, and, as he refused to take it, he was committed to Exeter gaol again. He was given two or three opportunities of reconsidering his decision about the oath, and at last, at the Midsummer Sessions of 1665, he was sentenced to the penalties of *præmunire*, i.e. outlawry, forfeiture of all his goods, and imprisonment during the King's pleasure. Shortly afterwards he got leave from his gaolers to visit his relatives, but being discovered at large, was imprisoned in Plymouth Guildhall until September 27th, when he was sent to the island of St. Nicholas in Plymouth Harbour, where he remained till his death in 1668.[1]

A slightly more cheerful book for children than those of Jessey and Cheare was John Bunyan's " A Book for Boys and Girls: or, Country Rhymes for Children," [2] published in 1686. It had a practical purpose as a primer, and it began with the letters of the alphabet, lists of the names of boys and girls " to learn children to spell aright their names," and the numerals both in Arabic and Roman symbols. Then followed various instructions in jingling rhymes. Thus, the Ten Commandments begin :—

> " Thou shalt not have another God than me.
> Thou shalt not to an image bow the knee.
> Thou shalt not take the name of God in vain.
> See that the Sabbath thou do not profane."

There is " The Awakened Child's Lamentation," commencing :—

> " When Adam was deceived,
> I was of life breaved.
> Of late, too, I perceived
> I was in sin conceived."

This goes on for twenty-nine verses. All the poems in this book have " morals." We have meditations upon an egg, the swallow, the bee, a candle, the cuckoo, the mole in the ground, the spider, the postboy, etc. The " moral " is usually called " the companion." Thus, take the verses " Upon the Whipping of a Top " :—

> " 'Tis with the whip the boy sets up the top,
> The whip makes it run round upon its toe,
> The whip makes it hither and thither hop.
> 'Tis with the whip the top is made to go.

---

[1] " Early Bapt. Writers of Verse," *Bapt. Hist. Soc. Trans.*, III. 94–110.
[2] Only two copies of the first edition are known; one in the British Museum; the other, from the library of the late Mr. Walter Herries Pollock, was sold by Messrs. Hodgson in December, 1926, for £2100.

Companion.

Our legalist is like unto this top
Without a whip he doth not duty do,
Let Moses whip him, he will skip and hop,
Forbear to whip, he'll neither stand nor go."

We cannot but hope that the child theologians understood this last. We have also verses drawing the moral from " The Cackling of a Hen," and on an elegant subject, " A Stinking Breath." The lines entitled " Upon Death " begin: " Death's a cold comforter to girls and boys." This is Bunyan's trenchantly expressed opinion " Of Man by Nature " :—

" From God he's a backslider.
Of ways, he loves the wider.
With wickedness a sider,
More venom than a spider.
In sin he's a confider,
A make-bate, a divider.
Blind reason is his guider,
The devil is his rider."

For two pieces the air is given. This kind of thing did not necessarily turn children into little prigs. There is an infant piety, coupled with a saving grace of humour, which most children possess, quite free from priggishness. And there is at times a pleasant lilt in Bunyan's work which would make the book far more acceptable to children than others of its kind published in the latter half of the seventeenth century. " The Child's Instructor: or a New and Easy Primer," was the book for which Benjamin Keach, the author, suffered at Aylesbury in 1664. It contained the alphabet, lessons in spelling and composition, verses and hymns, and theological instruction of a very controversial kind. Hanserd Knollys wrote a preface, and the price of the work was fivepence. Later editions bore the title " Instructions for Children: or, the Child and Youth's Delight." One of the " delights " was a long poem called " A Short Dialogue, showing the Woeful State of an Ungodly Youth." [1]

Benajmin Harris, the Dissenting bookseller, published in 1679 " The Protestant Tutor, Instructing Children to Spell and Read English, and Grounding them in the True Protestant Religion, and Discovering the Errors and Deceits of the Papists." A second edition in 1681 was dedicated to the Earl of Doncaster, eldest son of the Duke of Monmouth. It contained " proper lessons for children divided into distinct syllables," and was illustrated by crude woodcuts of " A Massacre," " the burning of London by the Papists," " Popish tyranny and cruelty," and " the burning of the Pope at Temple Bar on November 17th." Among the subjects treated of in the letter-press were the follow-

---

[1] " Early Bapt. Writers of Verse," *Trans. Bapt. Hist. Soc.*, III. 94–110.

ing: the exhortation of Mr. Rogers, the martyr, to his children before his burning, A prospect of popery containing the treasons and massacres committed by the papists since the reign of Queen Mary, an account of the martyrs in Queen Mary's day, the Armada, the Gunpowder Plot, massacres in Ireland, France, Piedmont, Poland, and Lithuania, the burning of London in 1666, Oates' plot, illustrated, a Scripture dialogue between Dives and Lazarus (in verse), an account of the various Popish tortures practised on Protestants, the wicked lives of several Popes, and a compendium of the Book of Martyrs (in verse). The price of a bound copy was sixpence. The book resulted in his trial for sedition.[1]

Edward Clarke was responsible for "The Protestant School-Master," the third edition of which appeared about 1680. It contained plain and easy directions for spelling and reading English . . . together with a "Brief and True Account of the Bloody Persecutions, Massacres, Plots, Treasons, and most Inhumane Tortures committed by the Papists upon Protestants for near six hundred Years past to this very time in Piedmont, Bohemia, Germany, Poland, Lithuania, France, Italy, Spain, Portugal, the Low Countries, Scotland, Ireland, and England." It was a small octavo, illustrated by plates, showing the torture of Protestants.

[1] Whitley, " Brit. Baptists," p. 144.

INDEX

Nailsea, John Whiting's house, 204
Nalson, Dr. John, 514, 529
Naturalisation Bill, 342, 350
Nayler, James, Quaker, 123, 140, 153, 275
Naylor, James, Presbyterian, 35
Nedham, Marchamont, 513
Nelson, Richard, 96
Nesse, Christopher, 56, 467
New Conformists, 14
Newcastle, 399
Newcome, Henry, 2, 10, 19, 54, 71, 192, 420, 461
Newcomen, Matthew, 21, 555
Newton Heath chapel, 35
Newton, Sir Isaac, 265
—— Samuel, 34
Nicholas, Henry, 285
Nicolaitanes, 273
Nightingale, Dr. B., 13
Noble, David, 467
Noctroffe, Zachariah, 425
Nonconformists in the towns, 365
Norbury chapel, 34
Norman, John, 56
Norris, John, 527
North Meols, 38
Northowram, 66, 67
North Shields, 63
Norwich, 377
—— Dutch congregation, 335
—— French congregation, 335
—— Independents, 380
—— Quakers, 178, 209, 380
Nugent, Anthony, 530
Number of the Dissenters, 472
Nye, Philip, 73, 494
Nye, Stephen, 72, 265

Oakes, John, 422
Oates, Titus, 191
Occasional Conformity, 19, 80
Oddy, Joseph, 123
Old Mill Yard Baptists, 84
Orders in Council, 156, 163, 345, 436
Ordination, 451-453
Origen, 294
Origenists, 318
Ormskirk, 38, 64
Osborne, John, 280
Osborne Road Baptists, Newcastle, 402
Osgood, John, 166
Overbury, Sir Thomas, 78, 416
Overton, R., 317
Owen, James, 461, 463
—— John, 73, 74, 76-78, 119, 262, 266, 416, 504, 524, 525
Oxford, 394
Oxford, Robert Harley, Earl of, 303

Palmer, Samuel, 8
Papin, Dennis, 340
Paracelsians, 295
Park, James, 173
Parker, Alexander, 152, 179
—— Samuel, 120, 150, 502, 506
Parrott, Thomas, 110
Parton, Colonel John, 98
Pastors, 93
Patient, Thomas, 235
Patrick, Simon, 37, 60, 98, 498
Paul, Thomas, 181
Pauling, Robert, 396, 397
Paul's Alley, Baptist congregation, 95
Payne, Henry, 539
Pearse, Edward, 532
Pearson, Bishop, 33, 36
Peat, John, 257
Pelagianism, 321
Penistone, 65
Penn, Admiral, 154
—— Guilielma, 228
—— William, 80, 137, 139, 154, 158, 161, 163, 164, 166, 167, 170, 175, 176, 177, 180, 181, 185, 187, 196, 229, 247, 259, 539, 541, 543
Pennington, Isaac, 152, 153, 205, 247
Pennsylvania, 139, 177
Pennyman, John, 193, 199
Pepys, Samuel, 17, 329, 425
Perfects, Perfectists, or Perfectionists, 321
Perrin, Matthew, 200
Perrinchief, Dr., 496, 498
Perrot, John, 153, 196
Persecution in France, 351, 356
Peterborough, Countess of, 415
Peters, Hugh, 73, 556
Petitions, 11, 99, 102-4, 110, 144, 146, 319, 325, 343
Pett, Sir Peter, 266, 482
Pettitt, Edward, 513
Petty, Sir William, 495, 537
Philadelphians, 298
Philippo, Onias, 335
Piers, Bishop, 18
Pilgrim, Richard, 110
Pinners' Hall, 75, 131, 269
Plant, Thomas, 130, 167, 168
Plantations, 187
Player, Sir Thomas, 111
Polhill, Edward, 79
Polonian Arians, 258
Poole, 33
Poole, Matthew, 415
Pooley, Christopher, 113
Popish plot, 95, 175
Pordage, Dr. John, 298, 398
—— Samuel, 298, 546
Poulter, John, 156, 435